Medici Women

Portraits of Power, Love, and Betrayal
from the Court of Duke Cosimo I

The ducal court of Cosimo I de' Medici in sixteenth-century Florence was one of absolutist rule and rigid protocol, but also a flourishing centre for the arts. Portraiture especially served the dynastic pretensions of its ambitious ruler, the Duke, and his Spanish consort, Eleonora di Toledo, and was part of a Herculean program of propaganda to establish legitimacy and prestige for the parvenu dynasty in the European arena.

In this engaging and original study, Gabrielle Langdon analyses selected portraits of women by Jacopo Pontormo, Agnolo Bronzino, Alessandro Allori, and other masters. She defines their function as works of art, as dynastic declarations, and as encoded documents of court culture and propaganda, illuminating Cosimo's conscious fashioning of his court portraiture in imitation of the great courts of Europe. Langdon explores the use of portraiture as a vehicle to express Medici political policy, such as with Cosimo's Hapsburg and Papal alliances in his bid to be made Grand Duke with hegemony over rival Italian princes.

Stories from archives, letters, diaries, chronicles, and secret ambassadorial briefs open up a world of fascinating personalities, personal triumphs, human frailty, rumour, intrigue, and appalling tragedies. Lavishly illustrated, *Medici Women: Portraits of Power, Love, and Betrayal from the Court of Duke Cosimo I* is an indispensable work for anyone with a passion for Italian renaissance history, art, and court culture.

GABRIELLE LANGDON, a former museum educator, is adjunct professor for the Department of Visual Arts at the University of Western Ontario. She has taught Renaissance art history in Europe, the United States, and Canada.

Medici Women

Portraits of Power, Love, and Betrayal from the Court of Duke Cosimo I

GABRIELLE LANGDON

UNIVERSITY OF TORONTO PRESS
Toronto Buffalo London

© University of Toronto Press 2006
Toronto Buffalo London
Printed in the U.S.A.

Reprinted in paperback 2007
Reprinted 2008, 2013

ISBN 978-0-8020-3825-8 (cloth)
ISBN 978-0-8020-9526-8 (paper)

Printed on acid-free paper

Library and Archives Canada Cataloguing in Publication

Langdon, Gabrielle
Medici women: portraits of power, love and betrayal from the
court of Duke Cosimo I / Gabrielle Langdon.

Includes bibliographical references and index.
ISBN 978-0-8020-3825-8 (bound) – ISBN 978-0-8020-9526-8 (pbk.)

1. Women – Italy – Florence – Portraits.   2. Medici, House of – Portraits.
3. Cosimo I, Grand-Duke of Tuscany, 1519–1574 – Art patronage.   4. Medici,
House of – Art patronage.   5. Portraits, Italian – 16th century.   6. Portrait
painting, Italian – 16th century.   7. Women – Italy – Florence – Biography.
8. Women – Italy – Florence – History – 16th century.   I. Title.

ND1318.2.L35 2006   757′.409455109031   C2005-906418-8

University of Toronto Press acknowledges the financial assistance to its publishing
program of the Canada Council for the Arts and the Ontario Arts Council.

This book has been published with the help of a grant from the Humanities and Social
Sciences Federation of Canada, using funds provided by the Social Sciences and
Humanities Research Council of Canada.

University of Toronto Press acknowledges the financial support for its publishing
activities of the Government of Canada through the Book Publishing Industry
Development Program (BPIDP).

To Abe, our daughters,
and to the future, con amore:
Marcus and Claire Alexander,
and
Rachel and Aoife Nolan

Contents

Illustrations

Plates

Figures

Acknowledgments

Many people have contributed to the evolution of this book, but I must first pay tribute to Karla Langedijk's magnum opus, *Portraits of the Medici* (1981–7), the landmark catalogue on which all who work in this field must rely. Two scholars who deserve heartfelt thanks for many refinements to this study, Ann Davis and Paola Tinagli, bravely read earlier versions of my manuscript; their expertise, friendship, and encouragement were an ever-present spur to my work. Others who have contributed by reading drafts of individual chapters include Donna Cardamone, Konrad Eisenbichler, Corinne Mandel, Sheryl Reiss, and David Wilkins. Many scholars gave special support or advice, and I thank Lorne Campbell, Janet Cox-Rearick, Elizabeth Cropper, Bruce Edelstein, and especially Edward Goldberg, director of the invaluable Medici Archive Project Database, Florence, for his kindness in alerting me to elusive documents, and for many transcriptions. His role as host created memorable diversions from my labours in Florentine archives. Konrad Eisenbichler's collegial, informal seminars at the University of Toronto's Centre for Reformation and Renaissance Studies and his scholarly support over many years have been significant. He is to be thanked also among those who offered some refinements to trickier translations; they include Maire McHugh Barisone, Donna Cardamone, Susan Scott-Cesaritti, Paola Tinagli, and Robert Rodini. Any shortcomings are, of course, my own.

Among many, there are museum and gallery staff whose responses have been especially warm. Silvia Meloni gave generously of her time in the Uffizi's miniature collections; invaluable help was provided by Carole Haensler and Mar Borobia to keep me informed of the status and locations of portraits in the holdings of the Fundación Colección Thyssen-Bornemisza at Lugano and Madrid; Erich Schleier of the State Museums in Berlin kept up a vivacious correspondence with me; former Keeper of Western Art at the Ashmolean Museum, Oxford, Dr Nicholas Penny's detailed, annotated sketches were invaluable; and I thank Dr Catherine Whistler, the Museum's Senior Assistant Keeper, for her enthusiasm and practical help during visits there. Julien and Simon Stock of Sotheby's, London and Rome, were generous in relaying documentation on portraits and alerting me to other portraits, as were Robert Simon and Deborah Gage. I am indebted to His Lordship, the Earl of Wemyss, who shared information and sketches on portraits in his collections. The hospitality given to me in Florence by Andrea Daninos to share his knowledge is warmly remembered. Marchese Fabrizio Barbolani di Montauto's sharing of his expertise in Florentine genealogies was enhanced by the memorable hospitality of his family. Robin Crum and Ippolita Morghese acted as lifelines during my absences from Florence; I thank them both. Catherine Voorsanger of the Metropolitan Museum, New York, whose *sprezzatura* made my visits there so memorable, is sadly missed.

Staff at the Archivio di Stato, the Biblioteca Nazionale, the Kunsthistorisches Institute, and the Uffizi's Gabinetto dei Disegni e delle Stampe in Florence were a mainstay to my research, as were those at the Library of Congress in Washington and the Robarts Library at the University of Toronto. Philip Oldfield, of the Fisher Rare Book Collection at the University of Toronto has been unfailingly responsive to many queries, as have Katherine Kuehn and Barbara Peacock at the Library of the History of Art Department of the University of Michigan. Librarians at the University of Western Ontario, notably David Murphy and his staff, deserve my special gratitude, as does my colleague Brenda McEachern and her staff at its Department of Visual Arts.

Fellow faculty in several countries whose collegiality delighted and informed my labours are numerous, but Madeline Lennon, Marian Jackson, Michael McCarthy, Illustrissima Doña Rosemarie Mulcahy, Lynne di Stefano, Charles Bright, Susan Crowell, Roger Crum, and Mignonette Cheng especially come to mind. Over almost two decades of teaching at the University of Michigan's Center for International Programs in Sesto Fiorentino, collegiality, outstanding cuisine, and significant creature comforts in magnificent surroundings lightened my labours. I warmly thank its directors, faculty, and staff. Students in my Renaissance portrait seminars there, in Canada, in the United States and in Dublin brought fresh, often fruitful insights to bear. I thank them for their enthusiasm.

Scholars who share their research and insights are a special breed. Those who deserve particular mention include John Bury, Lorne Campbell, Janet Cox-Rearick, Elizabeth Cropper, Konrad Eisenbichler, Robert Gaston, Philip Gavitt, Robert Hariman, Diane Owen Hughes, Marvin Lunenfeld, Sheryl Reiss, Mary Rogers, Patricia Rubin, Robert Simon, Rick Scorza, Carolyn Valone and Hank van Veen; Donna Cardamone's expertise in sixteenth-century Italian musicology, and Paul Kaplan and John Brackett's on race in Renaissance portraiture, is deeply appreciated. Paola Tinagli's alertness to current Renaissance scholarship in Florence and Italy, and her vivacity in sharing her expertise have especially warmed my labours. I thank Maria Ausilia Pisani, whose expertise in Latin texts in sixteenth-century contexts has been so important in this study. The last but not least of those who shared work came from the extended fellowship of scores of members of scholarly listserves such as H-ITALY, ITER, and most notably the University of Toronto's website, FICINO, through which I have made some valued scholarly contacts, and some lasting friendships.

Generous funding made to me over several years by the Social Sciences and Humanities Research Council of Canada (SSHRC), the University of Western Ontario, Brescia College, the University of Michigan, Wayne State University, and University College Dublin spurred my research, and I owe them all much gratitude for sustaining my efforts.

Friends who have given me unstinting hospitality while I was researching far afield include Anita Burck, John and Veronica Carter, Susan Scott-Cesaritti, Columba Hoban-Brumby, Jane MacHugh, Joe and Lynne di Stefano, Maureen O'Neill, Mignonette and Dick Cheng, Elida Giles, Bridget Cameron Neumayr, Sylvia and Peter Sellwood, and Tina and Ward Bissell, all of whose friendship and support continued over many years. Graham Smith's scholarship and succinct wit as mentor, colleague, and friend have been an inspiration, as has the friendship and mentoring of Marvin Eisenberg, whose effervesence in all things scholarly and universal belie his deep commitment to excellence. Lastly, for his patience and invaluable work as proofreader, I thank my husband, who, with my family, has tolerated the intrusion of the ghosts of Medici women in our lives for many years.

Portions of chapters 1, 2, 4, and 7 have appeared elsewhere, as noted; I thank my former editors for their help with earlier versions. John St James's valiant copy-editing and Barb Porter's finely tuned organizational skills were especially reassuring. Finally, I express particular gratitude to Suzanne Rancourt, my editor, who was a tower of strength and good humour in guiding this study to fruition.

London, Ontario, Canada
July 2005

Medici Women

Portraits of Power, Love, and Betrayal
from the Court of Duke Cosimo I

Introduction

We paint not with our hands, but with our brains.

Michelangelo[1]

One of the signal events in the ill-starred life of Maria de' Medici (1573–1642), Queen of France, is enshrined in Rubens's monumental panel *The Presentation of the Portrait*, in which her portrait is ardently received by her future husband, Henry IV, in 1600 (fig. 1).[2] The portrait was one of several Marias sent to familiarize the reluctant Henry with his future queen. Now lost, it was painted in Florence at the court of her uncle, Grand Duke Ferdinando I. Luckily, when they were finally united, Henry professed that Maria 'surpassed in beauty all the portraits that had been sent to him.'[3] Whether we choose to believe Maria's account of Henry's enrapturement or not, her perspective on the event confirms that the painted portrait was regarded as a surrogate presence with intrinsic power to captivate and to nurture love in the beholder.[4] Her inclusion of the scene in the series celebrating the high points of her life also expresses the important function served by panel portraits in cementing alliances between powerful ruling houses.

Maria was probably aware that portrayal of eligible Medici princesses had been initiated from 1551 as a new genre of Medici portraiture by her grandparents, Duke Cosimo de' Medici and Duchess Eleonora di Toledo, who almost certainly intended that such portraits should function as part of a greater plan to establish alliances for their new dynasty on the European stage. More public expressions of Cosimo's grandiose ambitions had transformed the fabric and face of Florence during his reign, from 1537 to 1574. Eulogizing him in 1582 as one of the most illustrious and erudite men of the sixteenth century, Francesco Sansovino recalled that Cosimo had embellished the city with sumptuous buildings, enriched its spaces with antique statuary, and decorated it with paintings to appeal to every taste.[5] Additionally, as a result of a tremendous surge of interest in art generated by the mid-sixteenth-century ducal court, modern scholars have made us familiar with the ubiquitous frescoes, lavish tapestry cycles, statue-filled urban spaces, gardens, and even lost, ephemeral art for the stupendous ceremonial processions that paraded before Florentines the great moments of Medici advancement in the European arena through carefully managed marriage alliances.[6] This civic transformation served to legitimize Medici rule and promoted Florence as the locus of a fast-rising power in sixteenth-century Italy. Cosimo's 'mania' for portraiture was part of this vigorous promotion of Medici interests in which visual imagery asserted the parvenu court's claims to dynasty, the duke's absolute rule in Tuscany, and his bid for hegemony over more illustrious Italian courts.[7]

Where, exactly, did women's portraiture fit in the wider scheme of Medici ambitions and what forms did it take? It is agreed that Cosimo's official portraits express his role as founder of a dynasty and as captain of his people.[8] It might be assumed that Medici women's portraits were commissioned out of love to be surrogate 'presences' that gave rise to fond reveries or consoled the living in the absence of those they loved.[9] This alone, however, would not explain the unusual number of portraits of Medici women and girls commissioned by the new court. Cumulatively, these commissions greatly exceeded earlier Medici patronage for this branch of art, and several genres of court portraiture were to become evident with many of them. Exquisite portraits by Jacopo Pontormo (1494–1556), Agnolo Bronzino (1503–72), and Alessandro Allori (1535–1607) of the eight women of Cosimo's close family survive: his mother, Maria Salviati; his wife, Eleonora di Toledo; his daughters, Bia, Maria, Lucrezia, and Isabella; and his two wards, Giulia d'Alessandro de' Medici and Eleonora 'Dianora' di Toledo, both raised from infancy at court and intimately associated with it into their maturity. From an art-historical perspective, the most famous is Bronzino's state portrait of Duchess Eleonora (pl. 4) of 1545, which as a multi-layered symbol of power and dynastic pretension rivals later, sixteenth-century state portraits of Elizabeth I of England as a vehicle of intensive propaganda. Other genres, too, emerged: the amorous, private portrait; the 'pre-nuptial' panel; portraits of young brides and of widows; posthumous tributes; and, lastly, the miniature, whose distinctive Italian forms were probably invented in this court. Many portraits were painted in the course of these women's lives, often illuminating rites of passage. Cumulatively, the expansion in this branch of art suggests efforts by Cosimo and Eleonora to create a body of court portraiture in imitation of that typical of the great courts of Europe.

The intention in this study for the portraits selected (all painted on panel except the miniatures) has been to explore this phenomenon as it evolved over Cosimo's reign, in contexts of patronage and rites of passage, and for the place they hold in the development of court portraiture in political, religious, and socio-cultural contexts and in the history of art. This includes a search for an understanding of their place and meaning in the conscious fashioning of the court's image, of their particular functions, and of their patrons' intentions for them, and an effort to illuminate the responses expected of the spectators for whom they were intended. A parallel concern was to investigate the demands and complexities of court portraiture from the viewpoint of the artist's apprehension of his role, one that for Pontormo was new, and for Bronzino was only briefly explored by him before 1537.[10] In the course of this enquiry, portraits were discovered that had had their identities confused or even deliberately obliterated in the distant past; others had been believed 'lost.' New questions arose in the course of restoring them to the body of women's portraits generated at the court. Not least, the lives of some of these women had been shrouded in myth, made notorious by rumour or dramatic stereotyping, or sometimes barely acknowledged or damned to oblivion. Conversely, interpretations of their portraits have served as spurious 'testaments' to their characters and personalities. It is hoped that these errors may be untangled so as to place their portraits within the wider context of the overwhelmingly propagandistic art engendered in the court, as well as to provide a better historic perspective on their lives.

Although their biographies and the setting and circumstances of their lives are woven through chapters devoted to each woman, a brief summary of the establishment of the court by its Medici rulers and a sketch of the environment they created follows to assist in understanding the extraordinary, rapid rise of this Italian dynasty in the European forum.

The Court and Its Rulers, Cosimo and Eleonora

Cosimo de' Medici was born in Florence in 1519 to Maria Salviati (1499–1543), a direct descendant of the main Medici line, and Giovanni 'delle Bande Nere' (1498–1526), her cousin from a cadet branch. (See the genealogical table, appendix A.) On both sides of his family tree Cosimo could trace his roots to the fourteenth-century founder of the Medici fortune and line, Giovanni di Bicci (1360-1429). In spite of occasional anti-Medicean plots, expulsion, and exile, the Medici had developed a talent for survival and had dominated Florence's fortunes and civic affairs for almost two centuries. Recent promotion to the papacy, and interference in its affairs from Rome by two Medici popes – Leo X (1513–21) and Clement VII (1523–34) – had further whittled away the city's long-vaunted republican status. Weakened by plague, Florence bore the brunt of Clement's fall from grace during the brutal sack of Rome in 1527, the climax of a papal-imperial struggle. On the subsequent siege in October 1529, the city became a Hapsburg fiefdom of the Holy Roman Emperor, Charles V (1500–58), who installed Cosimo's cousin Alessandro – Clement's natural son – as ruler in 1530. The duchy was formally established in 1532.[11]

Cosimo's father, the legendary *condottiere* Giovanni 'delle Bande Nere,' died heroically in action in 1526. From the age of seven, the boy's life had been directed by his mother, who, as his guardian and cognizant of his role as the sole legitimate Medici scion, steered him through these tumultuous years. Towards the end of what was to be the last republican period for Florentines, the newly widowed Maria was forced to flee the city, in November 1526, to avoid marauding foreign armies. Accompanied by Cosimo, she used their peripatetic existence to advance his cause by paying their respects in high places until peace was restored in 1530 by imperial decree, and the duchy instituted. Following the dissolute Alessandro's assassination on the Feast of the Epiphany, 6 January 1537, Maria's tenacity and resolve were severely tested when a cadre of oligarchs sought to effect a puppet regime by installing Alessandro's illegitimate four-year-old son Giulio.[12] In the face of formidable opposition, Maria's obdurate stand to secure seventeen-year-old Cosimo's succession to the new dukedom in 1537 was crucial in convincing Florentines to elect him. On his election, Cosimo routed dissenters and quickly showed his essential character: single-minded, decisive, implacable, stoical, intensely ambitious, and determined to advance peace and to ease his duchy away from imperial control. Any intended factional control over the young prince was ably deflected through his precocious acumen as ruler.

For marriage, the stakes were high from the outset. In 1539, after Charles V had refused him a Hapsburg union with his illegitimate daughter, Alessandro's young widow Margaret of Austria, Cosimo married Eleonora di Toledo. He refused to have her father, the imperial viceroy in Naples, 'palm off' an older daughter on him, complaining that this was 'outrageous and disagreeable' to him.[13] Instead, the young duke stubbornly held out for Eleonora, to whom he had been attracted when he saw her in 1536 in Naples.[14] Her credentials were impressive. Toledo, Christendom's wealthiest benefice, had royal cachet: it housed the Spanish court until its relocation to Madrid by Philip II in 1560. Eleonora's upbringing at the powerful viceregal court in Naples had the great advantage that she could be relied upon to confidently take her place as Duchess of Florence. It was a union that stood to enhance Cosimo's financial and political standing and, because this genuinely was a love match, Cosimo would portray Eleonora as his personal 'prize.'[15] Theirs was an enduring love story, and Eleonora's position as regent was to serve as linchpin to Cosimo's assiduous climb to power. Her wealth and blood ties to the powerful family of Spanish grandees, Alba, were crucial to Medici advancement in the first decade of their marriage, enabling the couple to ransom lands in Tuscany under imperial garrison and to develop lucrative tracts of territory by draining Pisan marshlands. Peace, prosperity, and territorial expansion moved in tandem with Cosimo's resolute bid for precedence over all other Italian principalities.

Throughout the 1540s and beyond, Fortune showered the young Medici with her favours. Dynastic ambitions were grandly fulfilled: Eleonora produced a child almost annually, with four sons to guarantee the succession; another, Giovanni – considered *papabile* from infancy – was clearly the couple's hope for a third Medici papacy.[16] Three daughters were important to promote alliances with the more illustrious Italian nobility and to bind mutual political interests toward strengthening the Italian peninsula against foreign interests. In an age that had just witnessed the extravagant efforts of Henry VIII to secure an heir, Eleonora's fecundity was considered by Florentines to be a particular blessing.

In 1565 Francesco married the Hapsburg princess Giovanna of Austria, daughter of the Holy Roman Emperor, Ferdinand II (successor to Charles V), and in 1569 Cosimo finally grasped his highest political prize, becoming Grand Duke of Tuscany. His alliance with the Albas had continued apace; in the Hapsburg court of Philip II they wielded control throughout the 1550s and 1560s.[17] Eleonora's brother Garzia's reliance on Cosimo's military input proved crucial at the Battle of Lepanto in 1571, a victory marked by the marriage of 'Dianora' – Garzia's daughter, raised from infancy in the Florentine court by Eleonora – to the youngest Medici, Pietro.

In spite of recurring, scurrilous rumours manufactured by Florentine exiles and enemies of poisonings, incest, murder, and treachery surrounding the court and its ruler from the outset, documentary evidence proves Cosimo to have been an ardent husband and deeply affectionate father. His devastation in 1557 on the sudden death of the couple's eldest daughter, Maria, is recorded by courtiers; in 1560–1, poignant, mutual exchanges with the Este court lament Lucrezia's decline and death. There would be no Medici papacy – the dreadful loss of two sons and Eleonora within three weeks of each other in 1562 is recorded in a stoical, strained letter filled with love and concern as Cosimo conveyed this devastating news to his absent heir, Francesco.[18] (Observers opined that his resolve and even his integrity ebbed after Eleonora's death.)[19] To Isabella, his remaining daughter, who tacitly assumed Eleonora's role as consort, he was indulgent to a fault, and Eleonora ('Dianora'), Eleonora's niece, appears to have been an abiding source of delight to him.[20]

Duchess Eleonora's upbringing in the viceregal court was instrumental in the institution of what was to become an enduring feature of Florentine rule: a complex ordering of rank around the centrality of the ruler, and a high degree of ostentation and display.[21] Giovanni della Casa (1503–56) disdainfully noted in his *Galateo* a growth of meticulousness in etiquette and rank, imported, he charged, from Spain. Eleonora must surely have come to mind.[22] Her imperiousness is recorded, and in public festivals the two consorts appeared as demigods in the eyes of their subjects.[23] An ideology of absolutism was persistently promoted by court iconographers using biblical and classical identities from which rulers typically drew reflected glory. Cosimo's metaphorical associations with Augustus, Apollo, Hercules, Jupiter, Moses, or Joseph are just a few.[24] Eleonora's association with Juno, Diana, Petrarch's 'Laura,' and even with the Madonna is evident in her state portrait (chap. 2). Such strategies served to support absolutism and deflect their subjects' awareness of their rulers as being merely human figureheads. Ducal deification made Medici power appear to be part of a natural, eternal law of things, successful precisely to the extent that its maxims were shared by those who had to submit to absolutist control.[25]

If Cosimo's *gravitas* and Eleonora's pride presented an exclusive public front, it is probably because of rigid courtly protocol instituted by her rather than any public display of affection.[26] This promotion of exclusiveness and elevation has a bearing on the approaches taken to portraiture by court artists and on its patrons' expected response to it by spectators. Not surprisingly, the portraits of women of the court are found to carry much overt and subliminal propaganda. Their intricacy, preciousness, and beauty is also generally expressive of a wider European court culture in which *maniera*, the associated courtly, artificial style, was a central characteristic.[27] Exquisite portraits of women, of which Eleonora's are notable examples (pls. 4 and 5), reflect prevalent canons of style and beauty current in the court's intensively cultured environment. An aesthetic and decorous symbolic framework was worked into its portraiture, a branch of art in which 'sense became sensibility and desire, longing and love were sanctioned responses,' even as it subtly conveyed its absolutist and dynastic messages to spectators.[28]

One of Cosimo's most enduring characteristics was his personal control over the ever-increasing barrage of propaganda coined to glorify him. (In the new age of print, his direct control over material disseminated through ducal presses extended even to his choice of fonts used in classical texts.)[29] For the 1565 decorations for Giovanna of Austria's *entrata* into Florence for her marriage to Francesco, copious deferential references to Cosimo's meticulous direction were made by his iconographer Vincenzo Borghini and by Giorgio Vasari, his chief court artist.

Elaborate programs for street decorations and a grandiose Sala Grande renovation flowed from Cosimo's own mind and will; Borghini, Vasari, and others were *directly* answerable to the duke as they coined extravagant Medici tributes.[30] His intellectual interests as humanist and connoisseur were served by his promotion of Florence as a centre of culture through his institution of the Accademia Fiorentina in 1541. It put Florence firmly at the centre of the *questione della lingua* – the codification of the Italian language – and gathered intellectuals safely into the ducal purview. Cosimo's Accademia del Disegno, founded in 1563, was the first to promote the fine arts. Nothing of any importance touching on imagery generated by the court escaped his notice, and portraiture demanded his particular attention. The biographer Paolo Giovio (1483–1552), famed for his portrait collection of illustrious exemplars, became adviser, mentor, and critic in the commissioning of Medici portraiture. This association would contribute to the significant expansion of this branch of art from the late 1540s.[31] Eleonora's interactive role as patron to Bronzino in his role as portraitist is well documented.[32]

If a court is by definition a 'precise spatial, social, political and cultural entity,' it is only with Duke Cosimo's that it is possible to affirm such an establishment in Florence.[33] A court may exist where a prince 'holds court,' but Cosimo's very liberal predecessor Alessandro's was an untidy business if considered within a framework of distinct administrative institutions accompanied by legal norms and ceremonial practices.[34] A court is also defined by precise rules regulating courtly behaviour and as a social milieu with its own culture – not just in arts and literature, but as a whole way of life with its own values. In the early modern period these concepts became increasingly connected with the ideology of sovereign power of the ruler.[35] The phenomonen may be observed as Cosimo, with strong Hapsburg support from Emperor Charles V and eventually his son, Philip II, steadily appropriated the trappings of royalty – essentially combining governance of the realm of Tuscany, a princely household with its inner circle and outer ceremonial, and active cultivation of a cult of majesty.[36] His court was promoted from the outset in 1537 as dynastic. The dynasty founded by Cosimo and Eleonora was to last almost two centuries, from their union in 1539 to its extinction on Grand Duke Gian Gastone's death in 1737.[37]

In historical terms, the Medici fortunes until 1530 had often been precarious. The dilemma of this able prince lay in choosing to bridge the chasm between the traditional power of an Italian lord and the role of tyrant conferred by the emperor (Alessandro's, for example), or of tyrant by popular acclaim with imperial approval (Cosimo's initial role). Soon, his claim to seniority over more illustrious Italian principalities impelled him to overcome an abyss that extended between the power of a duke and the charisma and *sacralità* of a king. His chosen model of rulership was symbolically realized in the ducal couple's triumphal entry into vanquished Siena in 1560, a display resplendent with all the equipage to suggest an anointed *rex divinitas* – which Cosimo borrowed from the *entrata* of Emperor Charles V into Florence a generation before.[38]

It was a court striving to be royal, and women were essential players in expressing the regal power structures it espoused. Recognizing Eleonora as Cosimo's regent in 1549 and implying her status as an exemplary woman, Lodovico Domenichi commented in his *Nobilità delle donne* of 1549: 'Tuscany may indeed be called blessed today, governed by two such exceptionally just and humane rulers.' The Treaty of Cateau-Cambrésis in 1559 shifted the balance of the greater European powers in Cosimo's favour, recovered the north forever from the French, and brought Savoy into alliance with Florence. His elevation to Grand Duke of Tuscany in 1569 made him undisputably the most powerful ruler in Italy. By the time of his death in 1574, the new Medici dynasty had consolidated itself in Europe through Francesco's marriage alliance in 1565 with the imperial house of Austria and, within a few years, with the crown of France.[39]

The efforts of the iconographers Benedetto Varchi, Paolo Giovio, and Vincenzo Borghini to symbolically invest the duke and his family with an aura reserved for anointed rulers were carefully orchestrated.[40] As Janet Cox-Rearick's landmark study showed, Bronzino strove intensively to express this ethos even in so private a space as Eleonora's tiny chapel. The portrayal of women was no exception. Genres new to Italian portraiture emerge in this study that reveal a search for models and an inventiveness that pays tribute to artistic erudition and a deep awareness of wider issues within and without the court.

The Portraits

Inscrutable to his subjects but prone to sometimes 'duke' and 'unduke' himself at whim with courtiers, Cosimo, behind the calculated pomp, was a warmly loving husband and *paterfamiglia*.[41] Expressions of his affection and protection are expressed in some portraits of women in his family, but close examination of their images at pivotal moments of their lives typically reveals dynastic claims and the pursuit of a steady ascent of Medici power. Idealized, and overlaid with absolutist symbolism familiar to us in much other ducal court art, women's portraits were ideal vehicles to promote notions of semi-deification or absolutism in validation of the Medici rule. Complex jockeying for power, frenetic efforts to make Florence a hub of culture and religious counter-reform, webs of international and peninsular alliances, and presentation of a superior ruling caste find expression in them. Although absent, Cosimo is implicitly hailed as childhood scion in his mother Maria's portrait (pl. 1), and subtly alluded to as ruler in others. Even private love tokens – Dianora's miniature (pls. 14 and 15), for example – could be freighted with such messages of hegemony, increasingly so as Cosimo's reign progressed.

The women's images also display a wide range of dress and adornment, fine nuances in expression, pose, gesture, and settings, and great artifice in the choice of accessories such as fans, books, dogs, rosaries, and music, all effecting a variety of different levels of approved decorum. Distinct genres emerge: they mark rites of passage for women that frequently serve Medici promotion of near-royal birthright and dynastic claims pushed to extremes by a parvenu court. Nubile girls symbolically guarantee unsullied bloodlines to prospective princely suitors; the duchess is simultaneously Madonna, poetic ideal, and fecund guarantor of dynasty; sexuality and crucial fertility are promoted for newly married women; widows are paradigms of chaste abnegation to dead Medici husbands; and symbolic near-canonization of dead Medici women and children reflects the intense 'image magic' that underlies a deep cultural engagement with death, love, and remembrance foreign to us today. Reflections of the Medicean literary revival, musical tastes, territorial pride, lineage, religious reform, political alliances, and even enmities between courts find subtle reference in the hands of the successive Medici portraitists Pontormo, Bronzino, and Allori. Each artist's legacy of training, influence, and particular style responded to the duke's overarching presence as the implicit, fixed, central point of patronage, and to the intensive propaganda coined under his aegis.

It became impossible in this study to ignore how much the actual existence of these women had been subsumed in myth, been misunderstood, or simply become obscure. Their lives are illuminated in this study as foil to the conventional masks invented for them, and are woven through the chapters devoted to each. A trove of fascinating, varied personalities belies their idealized images; personal triumphs and some appalling human tragedies are revealed. They include the redoubtable, courageous Maria Salviati, Cosimo's mother, guardian against great odds of his legitimate claim to Medici succession; Eleonora, his ardent, temperamental, astute, and immensely wealthy Spanish regent; his love-child Bia (1536/7–42), illegitimate delight of the court; Eleonora's first-born, the regal Maria (1540–57), dead only months before she could fulfil her destiny as Duchess of Ferrara; Lucrezia (1545–61), the tragic, consumptive child-bride who briefly inherited that title; brilliant, charismatic, notorious Isabella (1542–76), murdered by her husband with her brothers' connivance to save Medici 'honour'; Eleonora ('Dianora') (1553–76), Eleonora's niece and Cosimo's beloved, vivacious daughter-in-law, whose beauty garnered admirers and led her psychotic Medici husband to kill her; and finally Cosimo's ward, Giulia (ca. 1535–after 1600), Alessandro's natural daughter (granddaughter of Pope Clement through a liaison with a slave or Moorish servant), whose portraits force into focus issues of legitimacy and race in late Renaissance Italy.

Portraits are documents, but they can subtly or inadvertently deceive, as do biased chroniclers, ambitious courtiers such as the renowned art historian Giorgio Vasari (1511–74), ingratiating biographers, embittered exiles, or careless scribes taking inventory. The deliberate suppression or loss of portraits inevitably skews our understanding of the intentional scope of portraiture at the court. Several have unresolved identities, attributions, or dating; the status of others has been obscured due to successful attempts to obliterate the memory of women who had 'sinned' or been rejected as unpalatable to Medici myth-makers. It has been necessary to untangle these anomalies and come to reasoned conclusions about their import.

Above all, the portraits are beautiful and complex. They cover a range of decorum for individual women from engaging to severely formal, marked even in a range of portrayals of one individual. But decorum seems a modern notion, one rooted in our understanding that the conventions bound up in it can evolve and shift rapidly even in the span of a few years. If a true 'period eye' is to inform any study of the art of a culture, then decorum has to be framed in that period's terms. The nature of decorum in sixteenth-century contexts is a leitmotif from which questions arise about private reverie and the covert viewing of portraits, the purpose of some near-hallucinatory 'presences' of subjects in this cultural context, or the reception by subjects of the iconic Medici representation of their rulers. Validation – persuasiveness – is a declared end of sixteenth-century apprehensions of decorum that has to be taken into account.

Decorum and the Codes and Canons of Court Portraiture
in the Sixteenth Century

No precise theoretical framework has been proposed for comprehensive investigation of the complexities of the late Renaissance portrait.[42] The art-historical ranking of Florentine portraiture, however, opens avenues of approach, in which Leonardo's (1452–1519) enormous stature in this branch of art is widely recognized. His *Ginevra de' Benci* (1474–8) and *Mona Lisa* (about 1505) had signalled a pivotal new impetus for Renaissance portraiture, transforming the roles of both sitter and beholder through the three-quarters view he favoured over the typical profile format. Eyes could now connect, implicitly allowing a beholder to engage in mutual exchange and reverie. This was an enthralment that Leonardo held to be peculiar to the painted portrait – one that would outdo poetry in its power to captivate the spectator:

> If the poet says that he can inflame men with love ... the painter has the power to do the same, and to an even greater degree, in that he can place in front of the lover the true likeness of one who is beloved, often making him kiss and speak to it. This would never happen with the same beauties set before him by the writer. So much greater is the power of a painting over a man's mind that he may be enchanted and enraptured by a painting that does not [even] represent a living woman.[43]

This power of 'captivation' is a recurring theme in this study.

Jotted down in the span between 1489 and 1518, Leonardo's commentaries continued to influence artistic development because, until his death in 1570, his disciple Francesco Melzi made Leonardo's manuscripts readily available to artists. (They were not published until 1651.)[44] As a result, scores of handwritten excerpts were in circulation, and several found their way to Florence by mid-century.[45] Of some interest is Leonardo's aide-memoire to artists on decorum ('Dell' osservanza del decoro') for the creation of *personae* in believable world contexts for narrative art, 'istoria':

> Observe Decorum, that is to say the suitability of action, dress, setting and circumstances to the dignity or lowliness of the things which you wish to present. Let a king be dignified in his beard; let a place be rich, and let the attendants stand with reverence and admiration, in clothes worthy of and appropriate to the dignity of a royal court. Common people should be shown unadorned, disarrayed and abject ... Let the movements of an old man not be like those of a youth, nor those of a woman like those of a man, nor those of a man like those of a child.[46]

Alberti's 'decorum' had appeared in his *Della pittura* of 1435, broadly implying repudiation of the unseemly or incongruous.[47] Nevertheless, Leonardo's writings span the years 1489 to 1518, when Horace's witty *Ars poetica* stood as *the* guiding text in poetics and drama.[48] Possibly Leonardo drew on this popular parody of the norms of appropriateness, but other classical references on the topic were also known.[49]

This spirit of fittingness, comprehensiveness, and overall congruence implied by Leonardo's aide-memoire for decorum appeared to hold some promise for an examination of portraiture in this study, but the approach to figures in historical, classical, biblical, or New Testament scenes could not simply be aligned with that for individual portraits of the living. Portrait treatises written in the sixteenth century, however, revealed parallel elements of decorum: individuals were to be portrayed according to social rank, sex, dress, and age; attention to 'setting and circumstances' could articulate their existence in a web of specific and interrelated social contexts. Second, early-sixteenth-century commentaries on the *Ars Poetica*, the wellspring of widespread interest in the precept of decorum, had all emphasized the maxim *convenientia* ('fittingness' or congruence), used interchangeably with '*decoro*' by Leonardo, as central to it. Third, Leonardo's older contemporary, the Florentine, Cristoforo Landino (1424–92) declared also that Horace's *decoro* is rooted in nature.[50] Cristoforo's audience is held to be custodian of a particular conception of what is 'natural,' which it uses as its touchstone of credibility. The critical issue was not nature itself, but what an audience *believed* it to be.[51] Cristoforo emphasized, too, that if *decoro/convenientia* is observed, the audience will be given pleasure or moved as the poet intends. As that maxim remained fundamental in all Horatian commentaries, it must be seen as implicit in Leonardo's version of decorum: the spectator will be transformed more or less by the result of the poet's or painter's efforts.[52] Finally, it was clear that, from the outset of the Cinquecento and beyond, decorum had been seen as desirable for poet and painter alike; Horace had declared that 'Poets and painters ... have ever had equal authority' and '[A]s is painting, so is poetry.' Pomponius Gauricus's Horatian commentary of around 1541 reiterated this equation, 'ut pictura poesis,' and reaffirmed Horace's concern with 'nature': 'As for what is said about poets and painters, that they may do what they please, this is valid [only] to the extent that they do not depart from nature.'[53] We hear its insistent ring again in Lodovico Dolce's linguistic treatise of 1550: '[V]erses and words are the brush and the paints of the poet with which he shades and colours the canvas of his invention to make so marvellous a portrait of nature that the minds of men are ravished by it ... with words so beautiful and so appropriate to the matter of which he treats.'[54] Dolce knew Horace intimately, having produced his own Italian translation of the *Ars poetica* in 1535.[55] In his art treatise of 1557, the rhetorical end he posited for the 'marvellous portrait of nature' that will 'ravish' his audience is consistent with the Horatian outcome, to move or profit his audience, and Dolce's extended metaphor for the poet's words as paint, brush, and canvas makes the painter at least the equal of the poet.[56]

Decorum is axiomatic in Baldassare Castiglione's landmark *Book of the Courtier* (1528), which enjoyed pan-European popularity by mid-century; his ideology of decorum and appropriateness was to permeate many areas of life and the arts.[57] Castiglione's intention was twofold: to create 'a portrait' of the court of Urbino and to evince a behavioural ideal of nobility. The spirit of his *dialogo* consistently informs art treatises that began to appear just after Cosimo's accession, including Paolo Pino's *Dialogo di pittura* of 1548 and Dolce's *L'Aretino* in 1557.[58] Throughout Cosimo's reign, decorum was invariably coupled with an outcome for the spectator: to delight, inform, or edify. How these features might resonate for the spectator of women's portraits engendered in the court was an underlying quest in the examination of their images.[59]

For the interpretation of Medici women's portraits in this study, Leonardo's implicit exhortations to the artist to pay attention to setting and circumstances were especially instructive. If his insistence on congruence of rank, sex, dress, age, and gesture was to take in several decades of political, social, religious, and cultural change in the court from 1537 to 1574, 'setting' would have its own contexts; 'circumstances' would imply temporal, evolving dimensions in those contexts bearing on what the spectator would accept as 'natural.' A brief sketch of what was understood as 'natural' for portrayal in Medicean Florence, and specifically in the ambit of the new court, makes it clear that it was not a concept that could be confused with literal depiction or simple verisimilitude in recording a subject. We may turn to Giorgio Vasari (1511–74), famed for his *Vite* or *Lives of the Artists*, artist, art historian, theorist, iconographer, and self-styled familiar of Cosimo's court, and to others in the court's purview, to apprehend specific ideologies related to portrayal.

Medici Theorists and Portraiture: Vasari and Danti

In his *Vite*, Vasari claimed that to list his portraits would be 'tedioso,' and was not an enthusiast in this field. ('To tell the truth, I have avoided painting them whenever possible.')[60] He was, nevertheless, constrained to place great emphasis on this branch of art, and was privately a dogged collector of portraits.[61] He advances beyond maxims such as Leonardo's to state that, in portraiture, the artist must observe the greatest possible truth to nature.[62] Leonardo's *Mona Lisa* – which Vasari had never seen – is praised for its amazing truth to nature, but Vasari's cataloguing of the subtleties of rendering of her features, her brow, her nose, neck – the skin 'not painted but flesh itself' – comes closer to a lover's lyric and echoes the eulogistic, poetic Petrarchan mode admired almost obsessively by the court.[63] (His eulogy to the portrait, then in France, testifies to the influence it already enjoyed in Vasari's time.) Theoretically speaking, however, Vasari believes that art must surpass nature: 'When portraits are like [*somigliano*, i.e., a good likeness] and beautiful, then they may be called rare works, and their authors truly excellent craftsmen.'[64] But Titian (1487/90–1576) is found lacking, as he does not 'improve the things which he copies from life [by] giving them the grace and perfection which in art goes beyond the scope of nature.'[65] In his description of Raphael's *Leo X with Cardinals Giulio de' Medici and Luigi de' Rossi* of about 1518 – held in Cosimo's *guardaroba* and familiar to Vasari – he briefly comments on how much the figures stand out in relief, but describes at length how Raphael's artistic artifice gives remarkable realism to the surfaces of things. The Medici pope borrows splendour from the beauty of accessories, surfaces, lavish surroundings, and artistic perfection of finish. The sitter's station in life and his world may be suggested in cunning ways by the painter:

> In this the figures appear not to be painted but in full relief; the pile of the velvet, with the damask of the Pope's vestments shining and rustling, the fur of the linings soft and natural, and the gold and silk so counterfeited that they do not seem to be in colour, but real gold and silk. There is an illuminated book of parchment, which appears more real than reality; and a tiny bell of wrought silver, more beautiful than words can describe. Among other things, too, is a ball of burnished gold on the Pope's chair, wherein are reflected as if in a mirror (such is its brightness), the light from the windows, the shoulders of the Pope, and the walls around the room. And all these things are executed with such diligence that one may believe without any manner of doubt that no master is able, nor is ever likely to be able, to do better.[66]

Contemporary observers would read in these details a world of meaning and significance: the burnished sphere on the chair that mirrors both papal environment and greater world purview is simultaneously the abiding Medici symbol, the golden *palla* or sphere; Leo's exquisitely embellished Gospel implies erudition, connoisseurship, and above all his role as Vicar of Christ at the historic moment of Luther's challenge to papal power; his damask robes denote princely rank.[67] Vasari also describes his own *Portrait of Duke Alessandro de' Medici in Armour* of 1534, where his heroic efforts to excel in portraying the mirror-like armour are vividly and proudly recalled. In 1553, Rouillé described the human face as 'a bright mirror of the soul' (*un chiaro specchio dell'animo*).[68] Mirror-like effects in portraits held resonance for notions of a ranking noble as a 'mirror of princes,' and references in the portrait treatises of Francisco de Hollanda (1517–84) of 1549 or Gabriele Paleotti's of 1582 that an exemplary role for the sitter was an inherent function in portraiture probably underlie Vasari's 'mirror' references.

Unlike his literal account for the *Leo X*, Vasari's account of his own *Portrait of Duke Alessandro* expounds on the involved symbolism of Medici power and control. It was a referential body of visual language that had expanded and become entrenched by the time he wrote his *Vite* and took a leading position as painter to the Florentine court of Cosimo and Eleonora. For Vasari, successful portrayal – one in which the subject 'only lacks life,' 'only lacks breath,' or lacks 'nothing but the soul' – results from the contribution of all elements in the composition to the *virtù* or praise of the sitter.[69] This includes signifiers of rank, power, setting, and current circumstances, created in his own and Raphael's portraits through accessories made vividly present through *trompe l'oeil* effects.[70]

More abstract qualities discussed by Vasari particularly apply to portraits of women in the court. *Grazia*, the supreme decorum for ranking women in Castiglione's *Courtier* (1528) and Firenzuola's Florentine treatise *On the Beauty of Women*, dedicated to Duchess Eleonora (1541), has special resonance for Vasari and his circle.[71] *Grazia* should not be confused with an artistic facility to merely improve on nature.[72] A deeply moral overtone for physical *grazia* is implied by Vasari's colleague, Vincenzo Danti (1530–76), consul of Cosimo's Accademia del Disegno, in a brief treatise, *Il primo libro del trattato delle perfette proporzioni* of 1567, which he dedicated to the duke.[73] Vincenzo, sculptor, art theorist, and Neopetrarchan poet, cautions the artist: 'If one has to shape a man either in painting or in sculpture there is no doubt that in addition to perfect proportions this quality of grace is also required of him. It is of the greatest importance ... [S]uch grace gives us sign and splendour of the beauty of the mind.'[74] Vincenzo, like Vasari, locates grace in the psyche of the individual and is the first art theorist to define the term *ritratto* as incorporating portrayal of metaphysical grace, beyond aesthetic concerns, likeness, mood, or expression.[75] Their definitions acknowledge a spiritual dimension of the persona as a point of departure in portrayal.[76] It has been proposed that Vasari's sources were Ficino and Castiglione, who described *sprezzatura* as having its 'true source' in grace and also implied both moral and courtly qualities for the term.[77] Outer grace had its spiritual counterpart, 'without which all other properties and good qualities would be of little worth ... [because] one who has grace finds grace.'[78] Vasari's other source, Ficino's Neoplatonism, was the focus of a revivalist poetic current in the ducal court and adhered to by its artists in the 1540s and 1550s. Denizens of the court, Bronzino, Varchi, Benvenuto Cellini, and Danti all exchanged Neopetrarchan poetry, replete with Neoplatonic underpinnings.[79] If both Vasari and Danti were in agreement on the metaphysical quality of grace, it is to be understood that their philosophy belonged in the wider context of the cultural interests of the court itself.[80] Apprehension of this in any assessment of the idealization of the faces in Bronzino's portraits, or in the exquisite optical perfection of his technique, is crucial.[81] Visual beauty inherent in notions of *grazia* had deep spiritual implication at this court and for art generated in its ambit.[82]

Benedetto Varchi (1503–65), Vasari's contemporary, a brilliant scholar around whom intellectual concerns revolved in Cosimo and Eleonora's early court, differentiated between physical beauty and grace too, specifically in relation to women, in his *Discourse on Beauty and Grace* of the early 1540s.[83] In his *Due Lezzioni* of 1547 he also expounds: 'We must then know that beauty exists in two ways ... one following Aristotle which consists of the proportions of the limbs, and this is known as corporal beauty ... [T]he other beauty consists in virtue and manners of the soul, whence is born the grace from which we reason, called spiritual beauty.'[84] Varchi's agreement with his friend Firenzuola on the implicit spirituality of *grazia* is evident.[85] An immeasurable quality, *grazia's* mysteriousness made it elusive to overt description, but that spiritual grace should be cultivated and its expression made visible. In the first decades of Cosimo's reign, when Petrarchism and Neoplatonism were actively promoted, efforts to infuse *grazia* into portraits of women of the ducal family were probably imperative.

This is a logical expectation for Bronzino's portraiture. The artist was a founding member of the Florentine Academy and was shortly joined in 1543 by Varchi, who came, forgiven and enticed from exile, on Cosimo's invitation to steer the duke's new literary institution, one founded to gather any dissident voices under ducal control and to formalize the codification of the Tuscan vernacular. Varchi and Bronzino were friends in the late 1530s when Bronzino was already established as a Neopetrarchan poet and wit in Florentine circles.[86] Their philosophy of beauty is expressive of the court's revival of Ficino and Neoplatonism.[87] Even apart from emblematic references, metaphysical notions of beauty could be conveyed, for example, in the perfection in rendering accessories in the composition, which could stand as abstract metaphors for inner beauty.

Vasari's holistic ideal of portrayal as expressed in Raphael's *Leo X* was a widespread notion in the European courts. Its importance for official portraiture resides in the record that, in 1552, the Italian artist Niccolò da Modena had presented the boy-king Edward VI of England with 'a fayre picture paynted of the French King his hoole personage.'[88]

Lastly, in the preface to his *Vite* in 1550, Vasari provides insight into a philosophy for the artist vis-à-vis a notional spectator: the viewer's appreciation of art will occasion a spiritual transformation. Moral qualities were invoked to qualify the artist for his task:

> I am persuaded that this work of mine will please those who do not participate in these occupations ... [T]hey will see their modes of working and in the *Lives* of these artists ... perceive how much praise and honour is deserved by one who accompanies the virtues of such noble arts with honourable morals and a good life, illuminated by the praises which result from these acts, [and] will elevate themselves still higher to true glory.[89]

It was a responsibility staunchly defended by Gabriele Paleotti in his portrait treatise of 1582.

The Portrait Treatises of Francisco de Hollanda and Gabriele Paleotti

Leonardo had recorded nothing to presage Varchi's, Vasari's, or Danti's concerns regarding the metaphysical dimension in portraiture and a didactic outcome for the spectator. His exhortation that artists attend to rank, gender, age, gesture (or pose), and place are, however, leitmotifs of the two sole treatises to codify Italian practices for portraiture, Francisco de Hollanda's *Concerning the Portrayal from Life* (*Do tirar polo natural*), written in 1549 after his sojourn in Rome from (1538–40), and Cardinal Gabriele Paleotti's *Discourse around Sacred and Profane Images* (*Discorso intorno alle imagini sacre e profane*) of 1582.[90] The Italophile Francisco's *Four Dialogues on Painting*, 1548, had cast Michelangelo, Vittoria Colonna, and their circle as interlocutors.[91] There, Francisco has Michelangelo declare that decorum was a commonplace in art theory.[92]

Francisco's dialogue *Do tirar polo natural* was never given a final 'polish' and proceeds stolidly in the manner of a catechism.[93] Although unseen in sixteenth-century Italy, the treatise – the first devoted to portraiture – is especially useful because Francisco had royal sponsorship from João III for his Roman immersion, and his declared aim was to introduce Italian perspectives in this branch of art to the Lisbon court, where his father had been court portraitist. Francisco affirms the exemplary purpose of portraiture and asserts that only the high-born should be portrayed.[94] He rules on the practicalities of approved perspective and set poses designed to emphasize noble rank and virtue, and does not neglect to include queens and female consorts.[95] Not to be outdone in his role as court portraitist, he promotes himself as a new Apelles.[96] He also advances a 'modern' decorum for artist-courtiers by placing them in the company of sympathetic royalty and enthralled courtiers as they paint.[97]

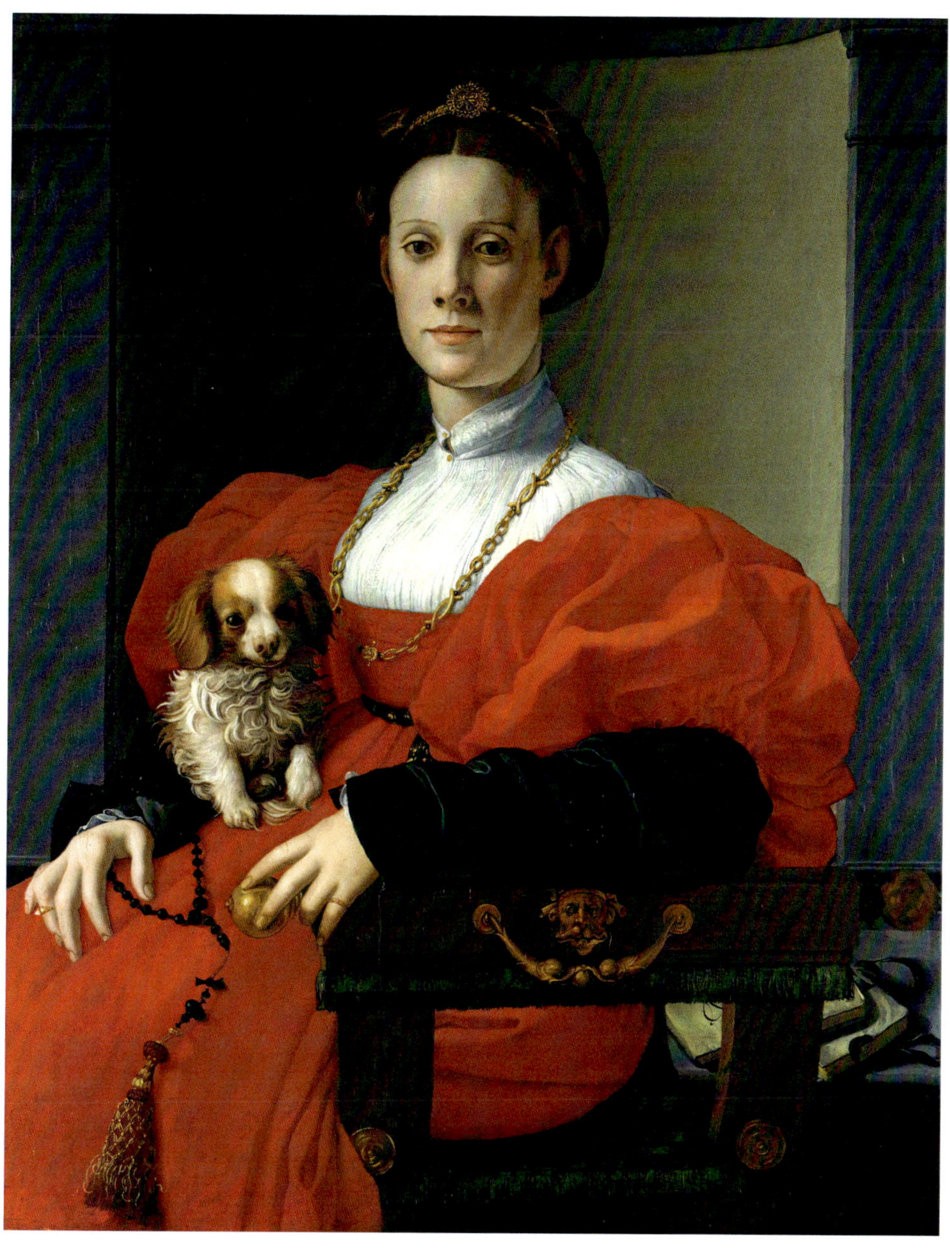

Plate 1 Agnolo Bronzino, *Lady in Red/Lady with a Lapdog* (here identified as Maria Salviati), circa 1526. Oil on panel, 90 × 78 cm. Frankfurt am Main, Städelsches Kunstinstitut.

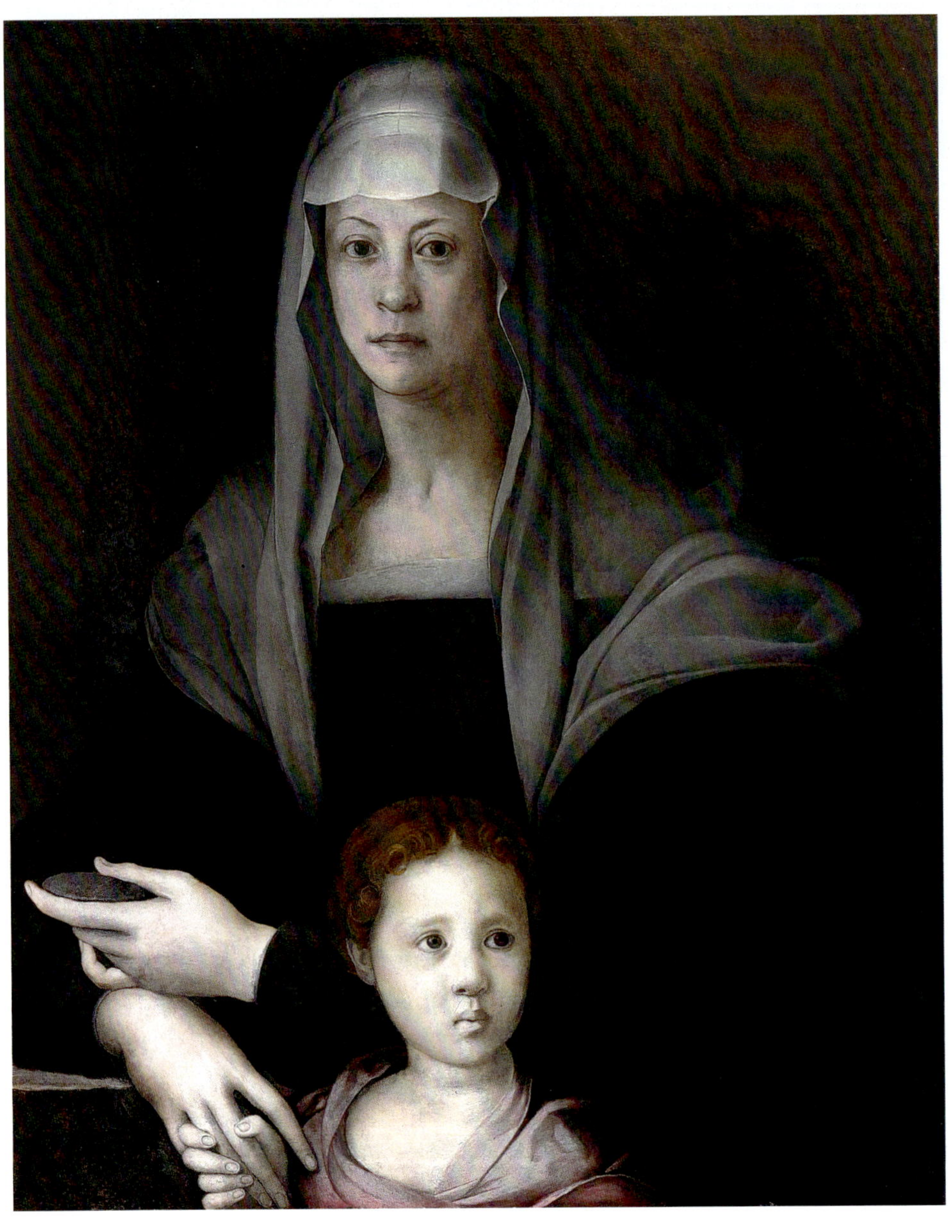

Plate 2 Pontormo (Jacopo da Carucci), *Maria Salviati with Giulia de' Medici*, circa 1540. Oil on panel, 88 × 71.3 cm. Baltimore, Walters Art Museum.

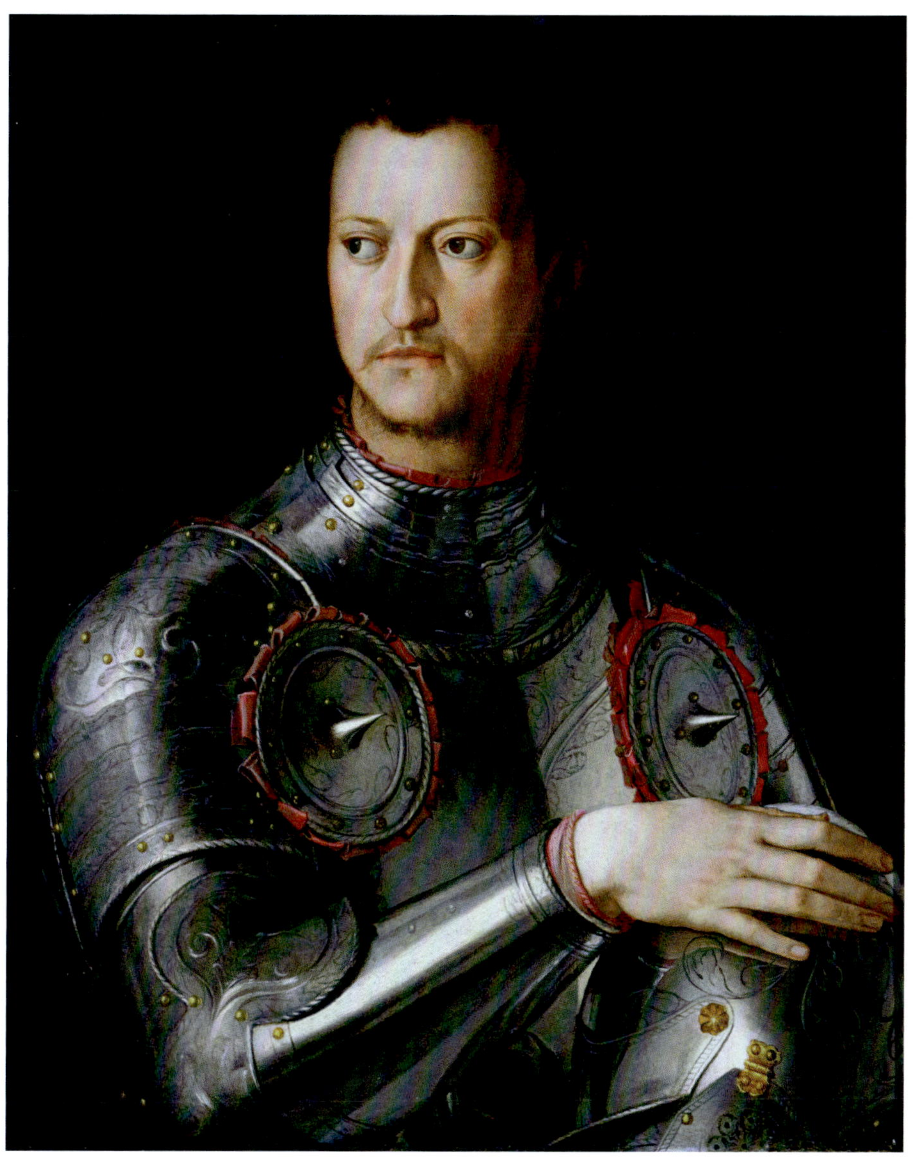

Plate 3 Agnolo Bronzino, *Cosimo I in Armour*, 1543–44. Tempera on panel, 74 × 58 cm. Florence, Galleria degli Uffizi.

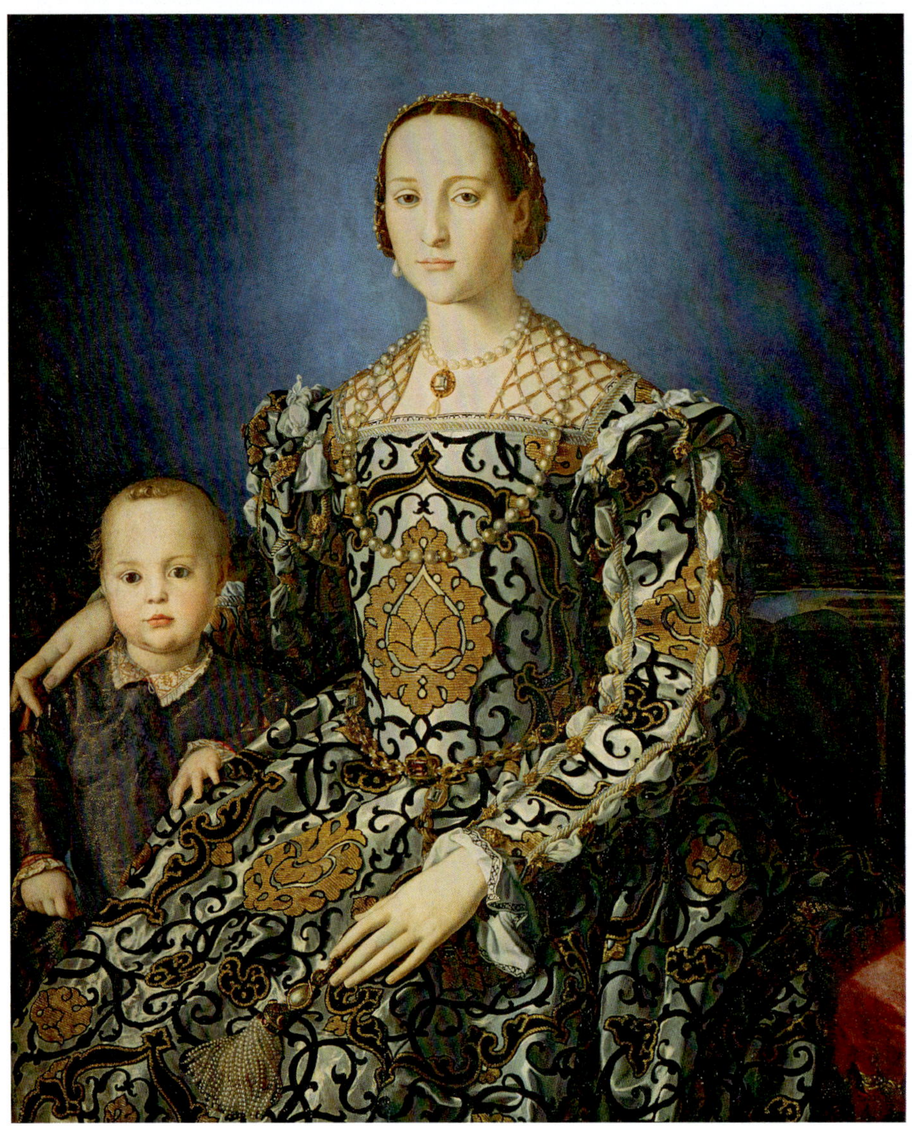

Plate 4 Agnolo Bronzino, *Eleonora di Toledo with Her Son Giovanni*, 1545. Oil on panel, 115 × 95 cm. Florence, Galleria degli Uffizi.

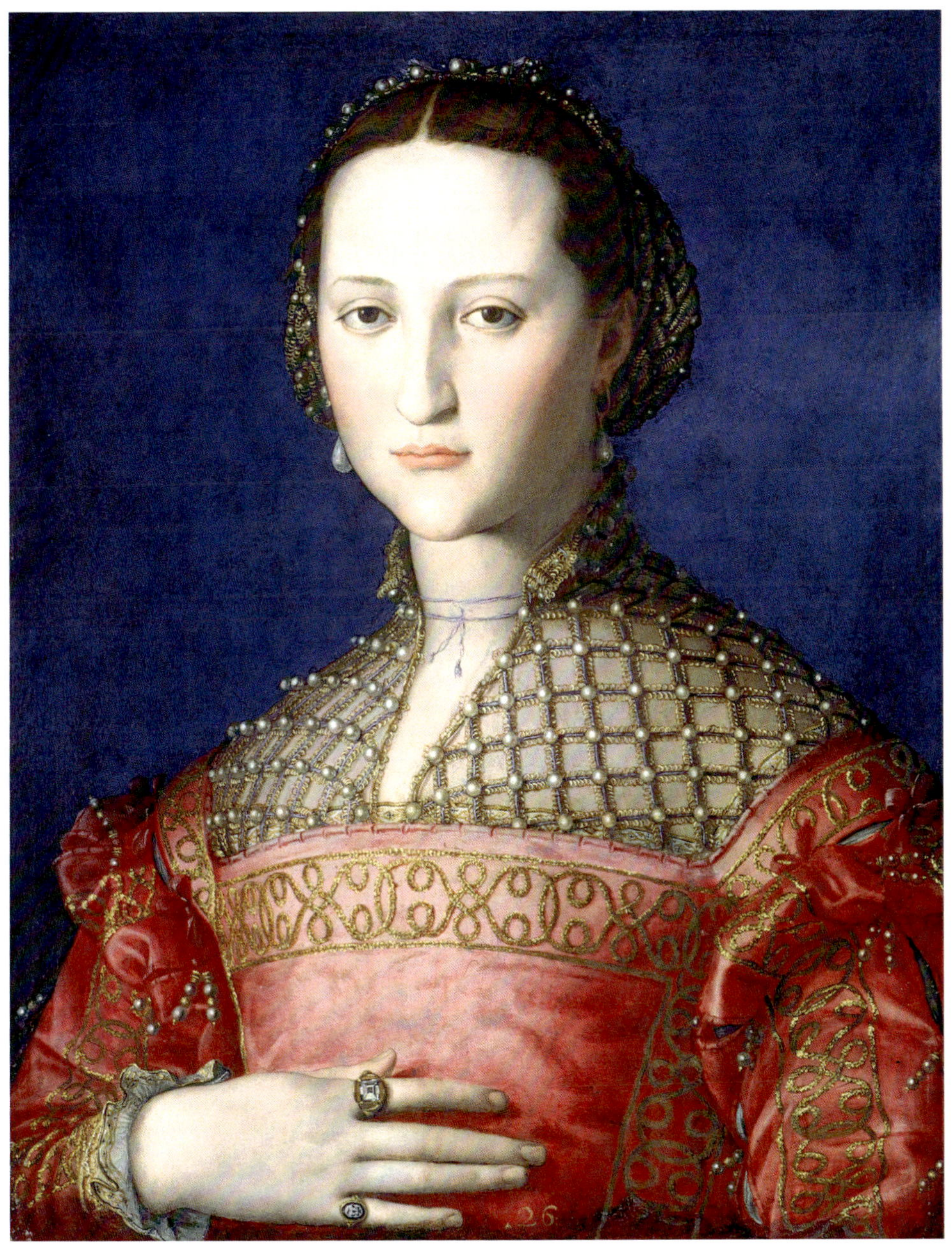

Plate 5 Agnolo Bronzino, *Eleonora di Toledo*, 1543. Oil on panel, 59 × 46 cm.
Prague, Národní Galerie.

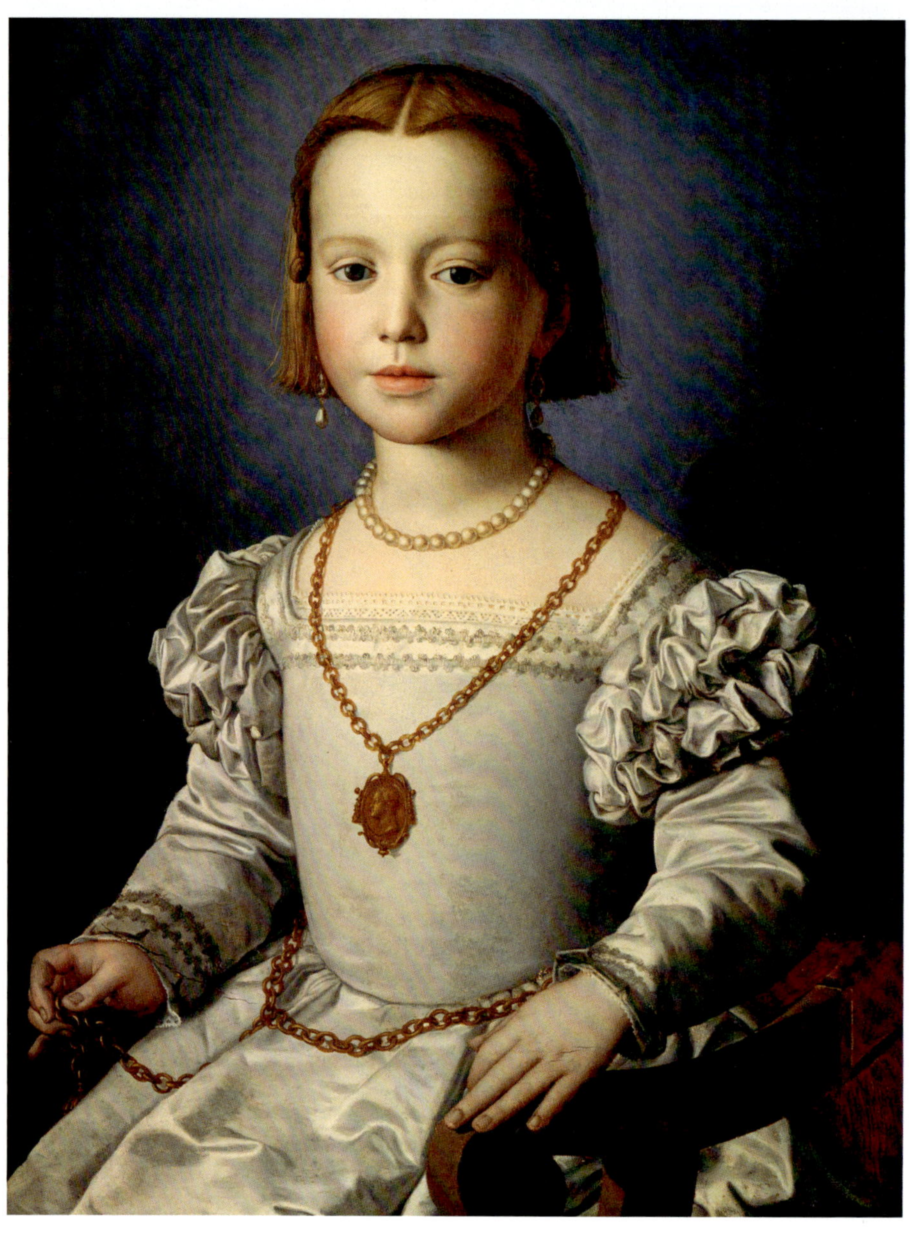

Plate 6 Agnolo Bronzino, *Bia de' Medici*, circa 1542. Tempera on panel, 63 × 48 cm. Florence, Galleria degli Uffizi.

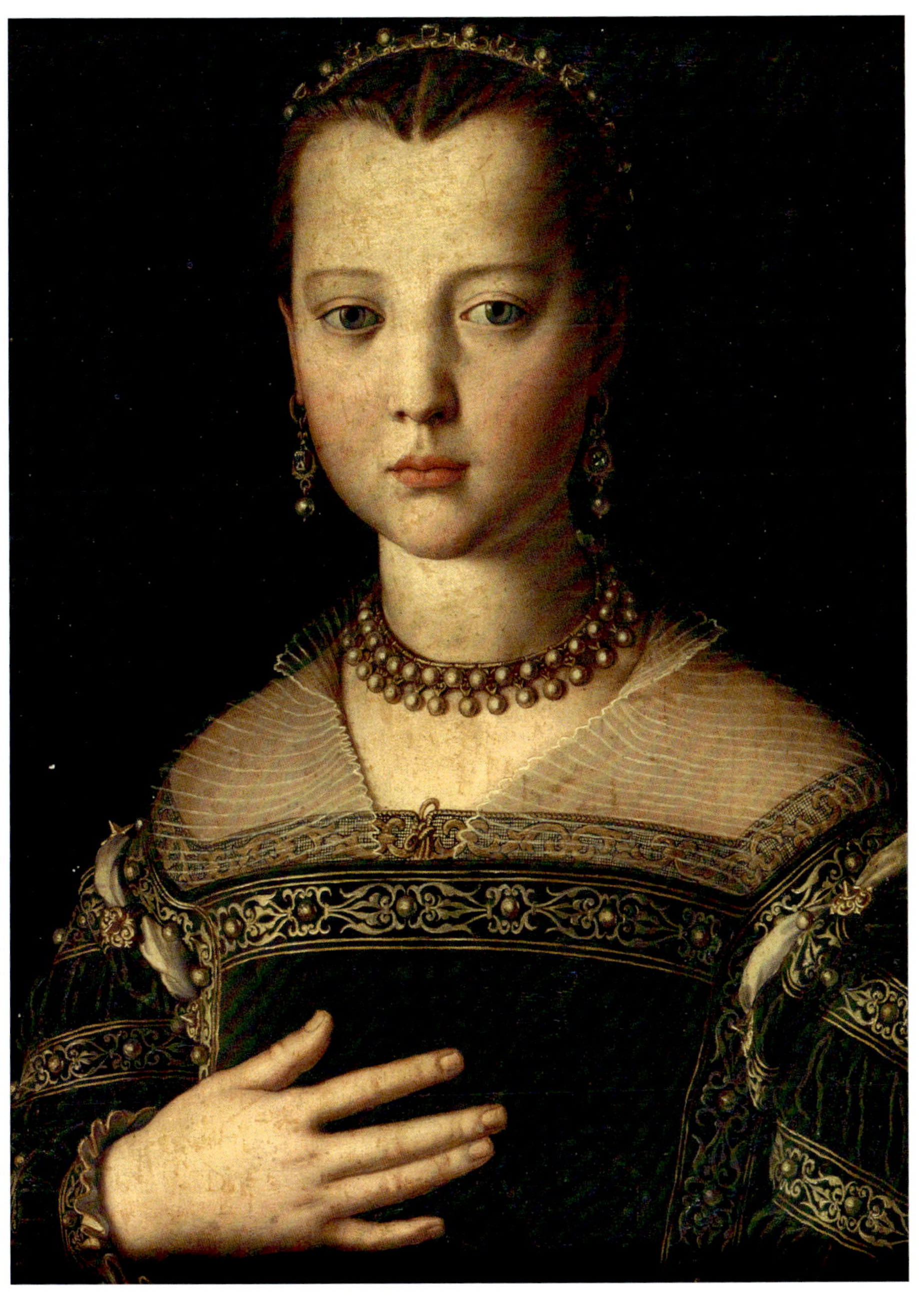

Plate 7 Agnolo Bronzino, *Maria de' Medici as a Girl*, 1551. Tempera on panel, 52 × 38 cm. Florence, Galleria degli Uffizi.

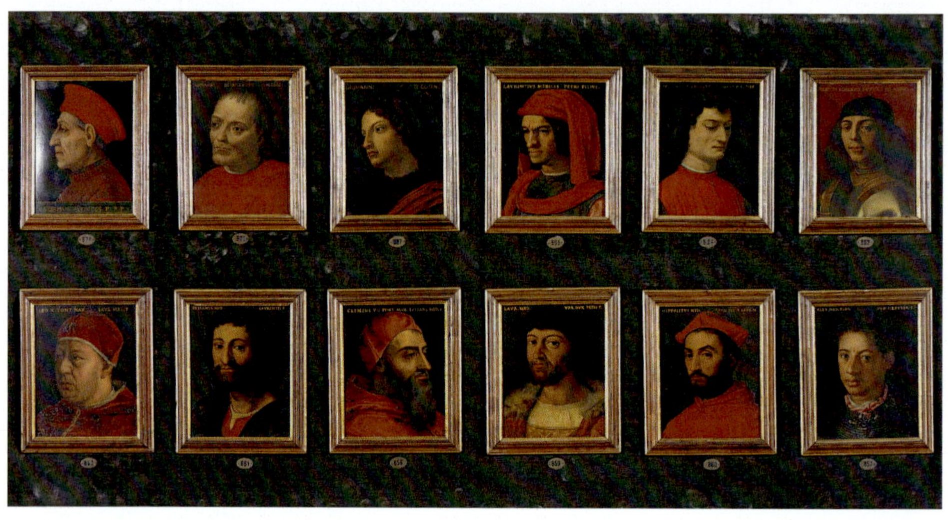

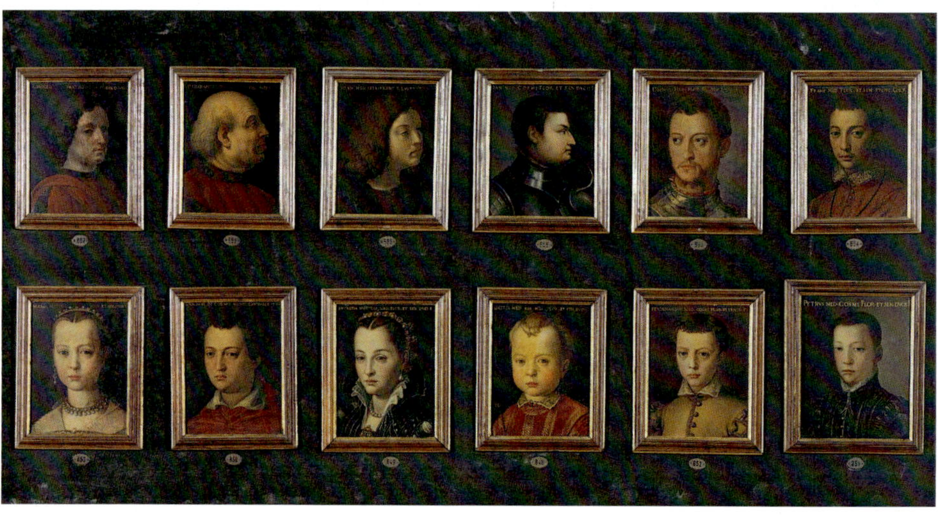

Plate 8 Bronzino workshop. Miniatures, Medici family portrait set, after 1553. Each oil on tin, 17 × 12 cm. Florence, Galleria degli Uffizi.

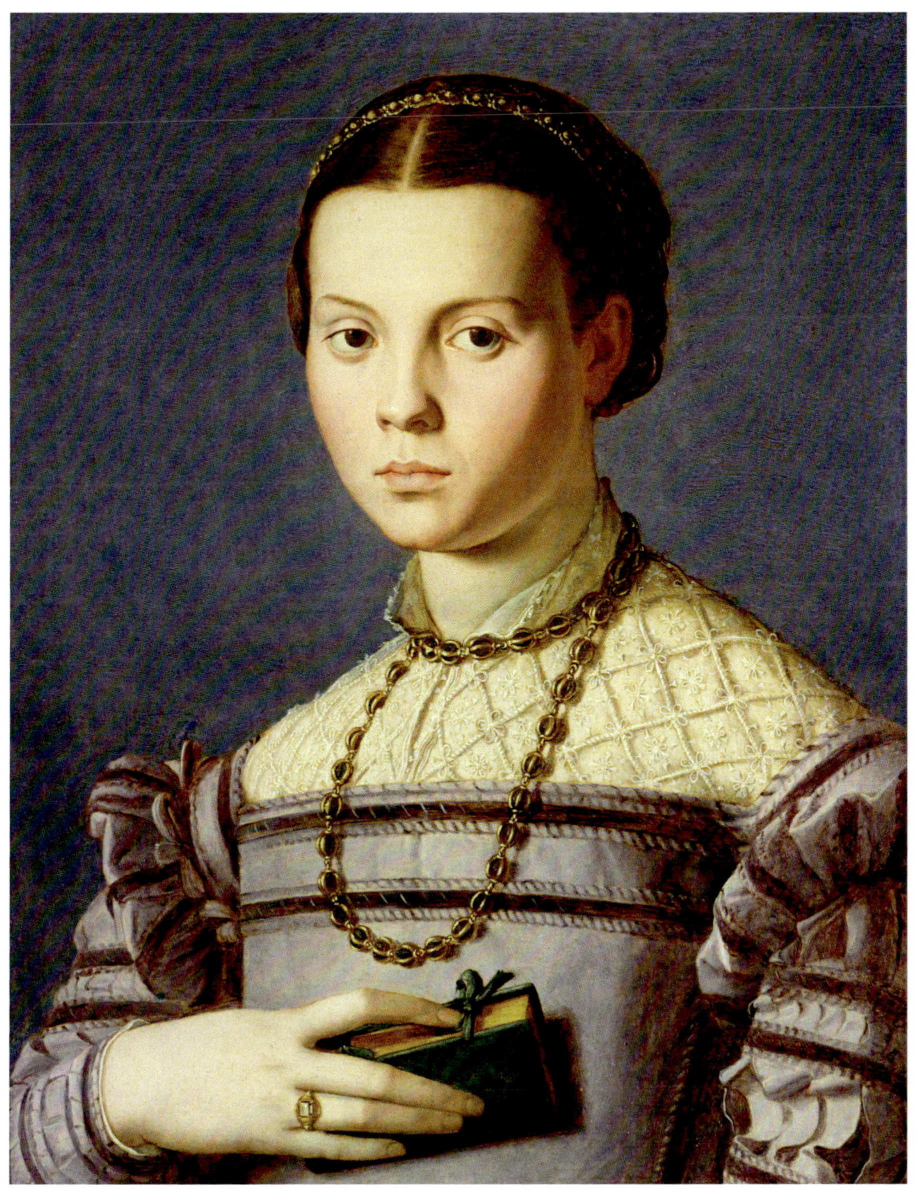

Plate 9 Agnolo Bronzino, *Girl with a Book*, 1541–5. Tempera on panel, 58 × 46 cm. Florence, Galleria degli Uffizi.

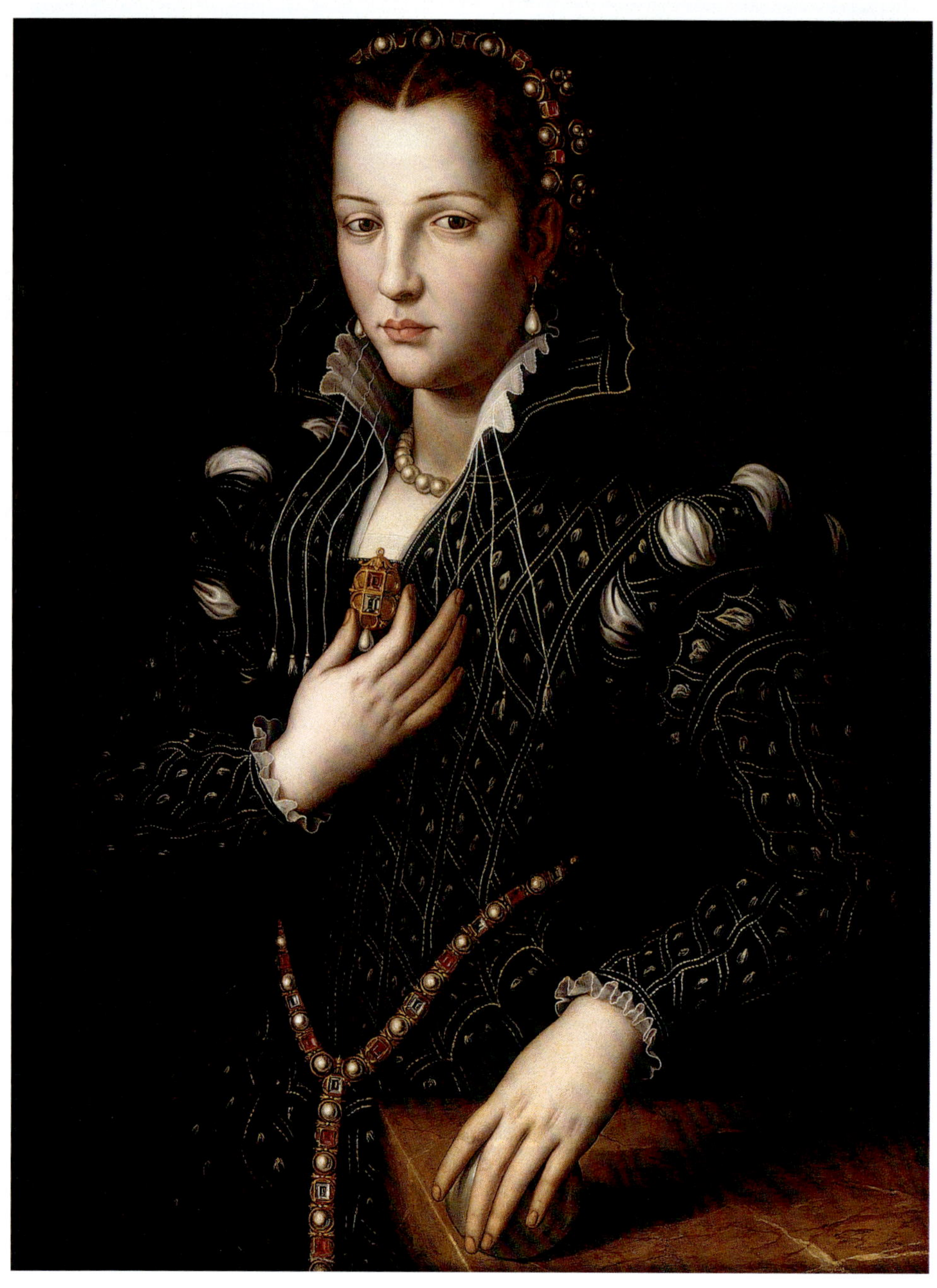

Plate 10 Alessandro Allori, *Lucrezia de' Medici d'Este*, circa 1560. Oil on panel, 75.5 × 62.5 cm. Raleigh, North Carolina Museum of Art.

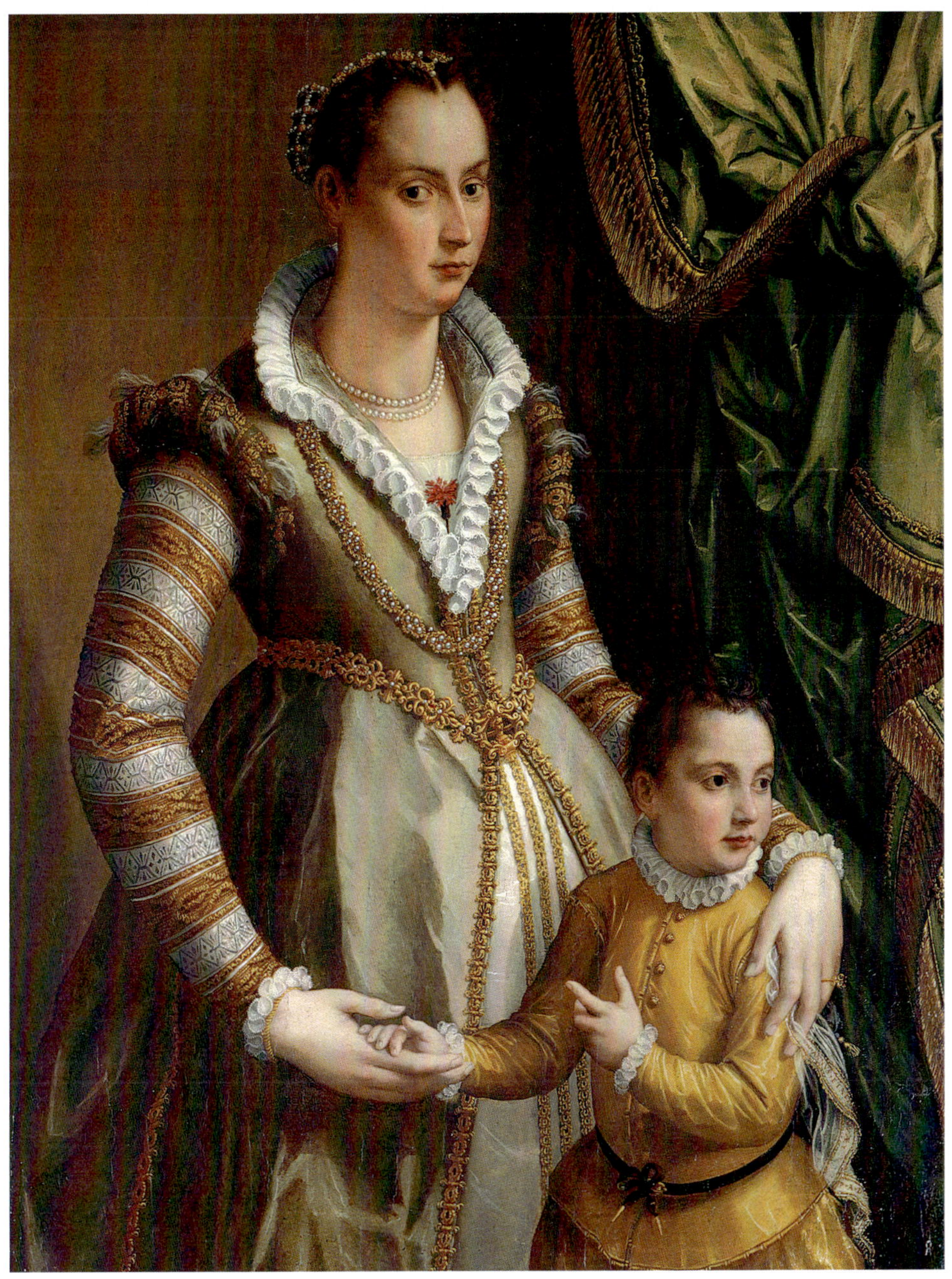

Plate 11 Alessandro Allori, *Isabella de' Medici Orsini with Her Son Virginio*, 1574. Oil on panel, 108.75 × 86.25 cm. Wadsworth Atheneum Museum of Art, Hartford, CT. The Ella Gallup Sumner and Mary Catlin Sumner Collection Fund.

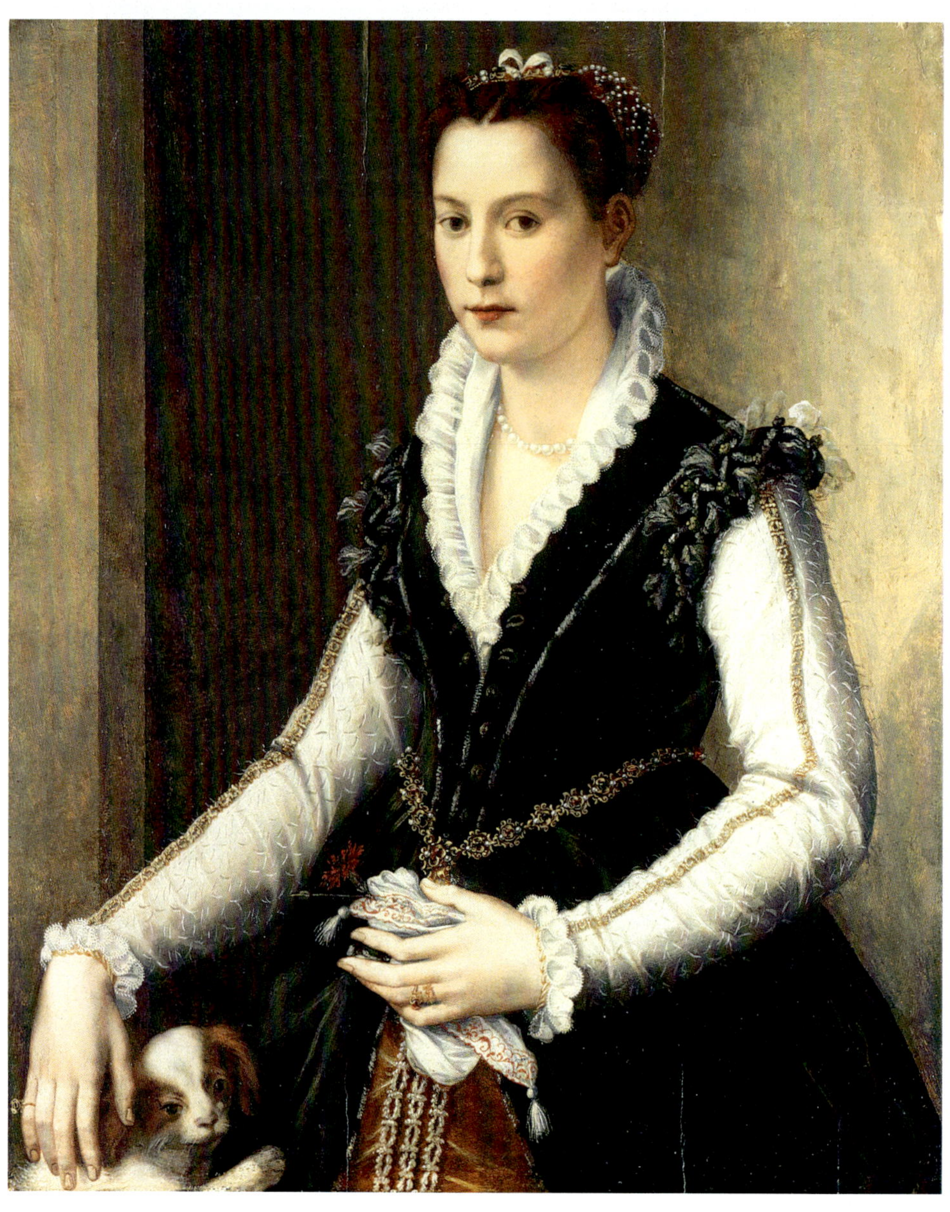

Plate 12 Alessandro Allori, *Isabella de' Medici Orsini with a Dog*, early 1560s. Oil on panel, 88 × 71 cm. Private collection, England.

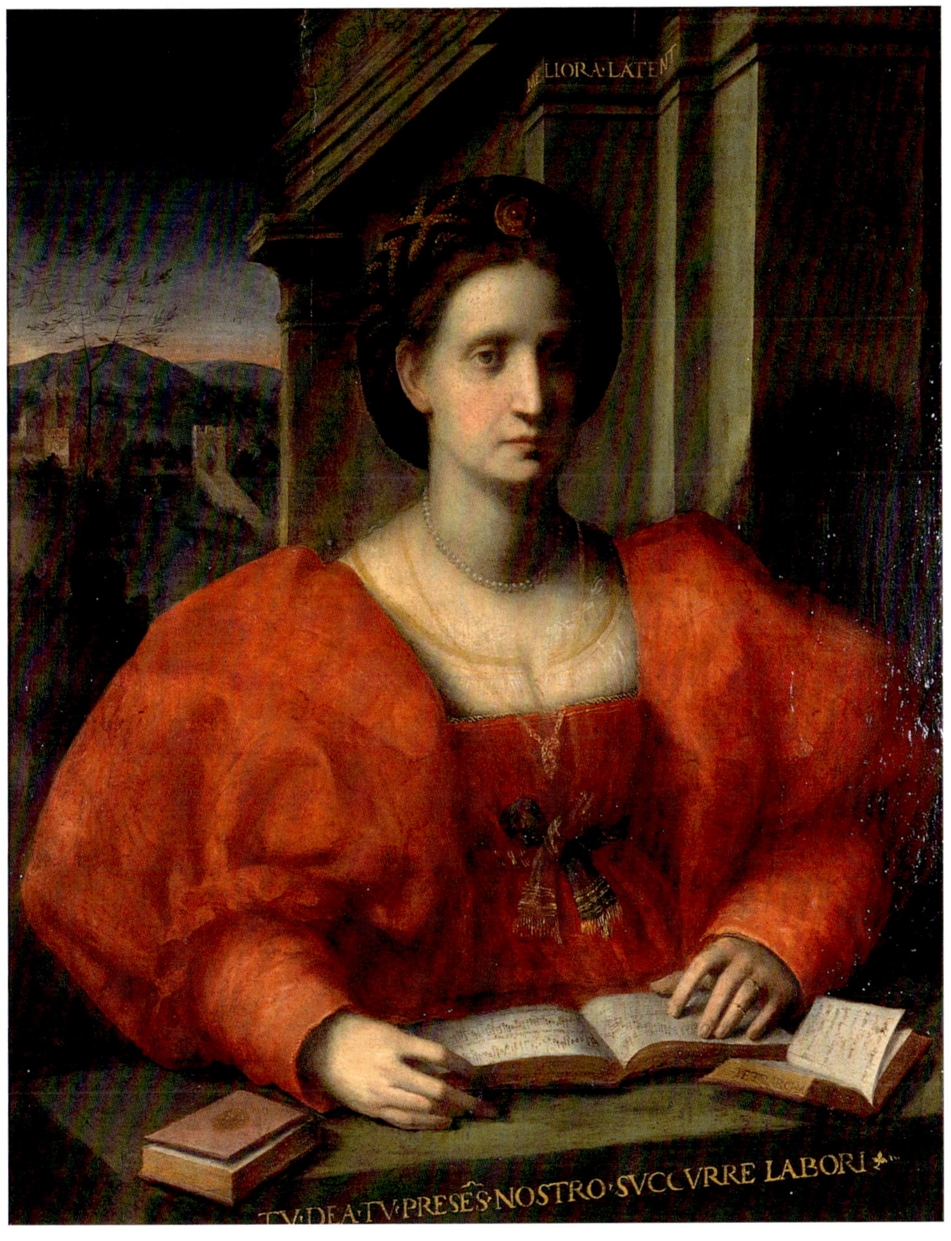

Plate 13 Domenico Puligo, *Barbara Salutati*, circa 1525. Oil on panel, 96 × 78.8 cm. Private collection, England.

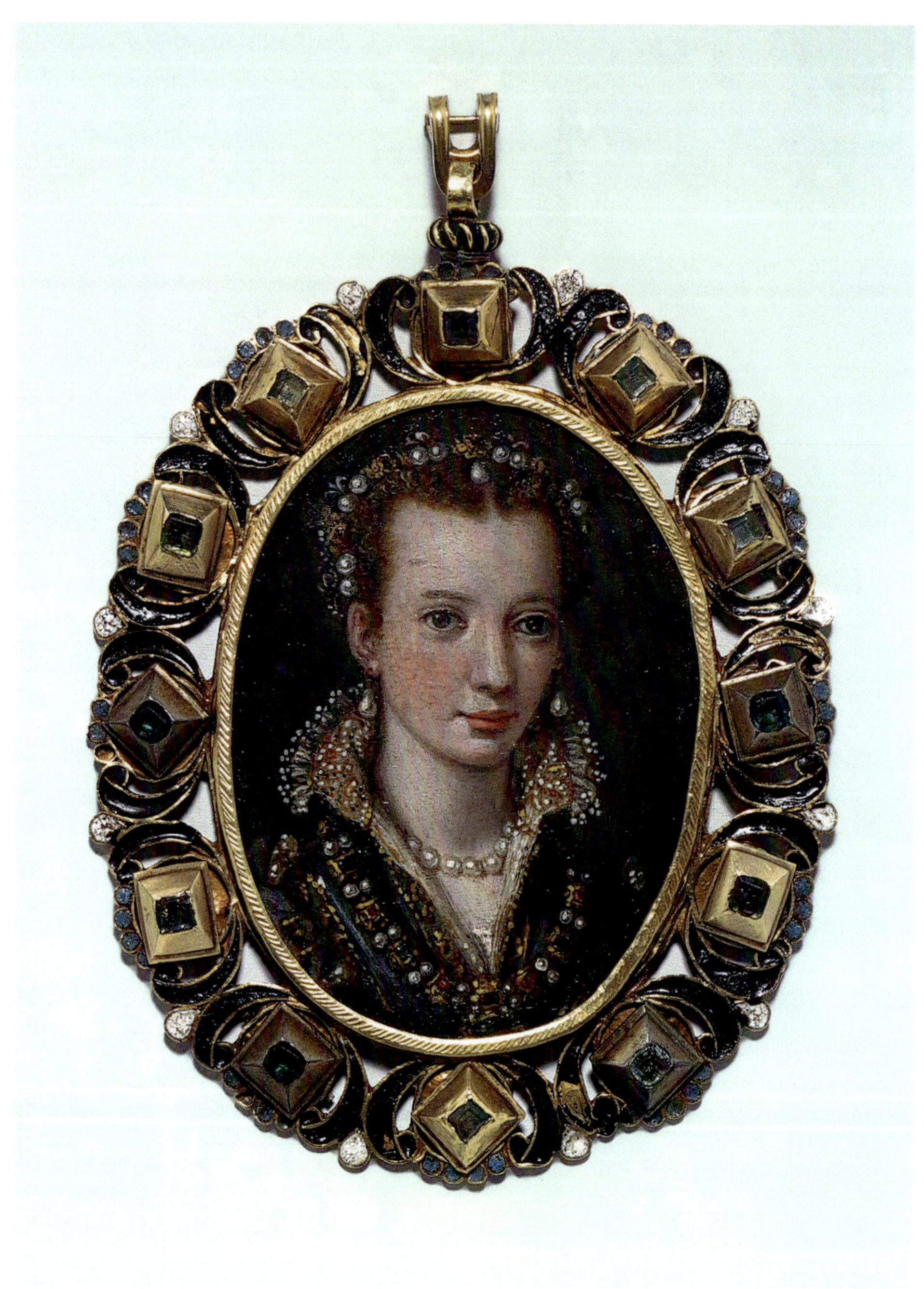

Plate 14 Alessandro Allori. *Eleonora ('Dianora') di Don Garzia di Toledo di Pietro de' Medici*, 1571. Portrait miniature. Oil on silver, 5.5 × 4 cm. Thyssen-Bornemisza Collections.

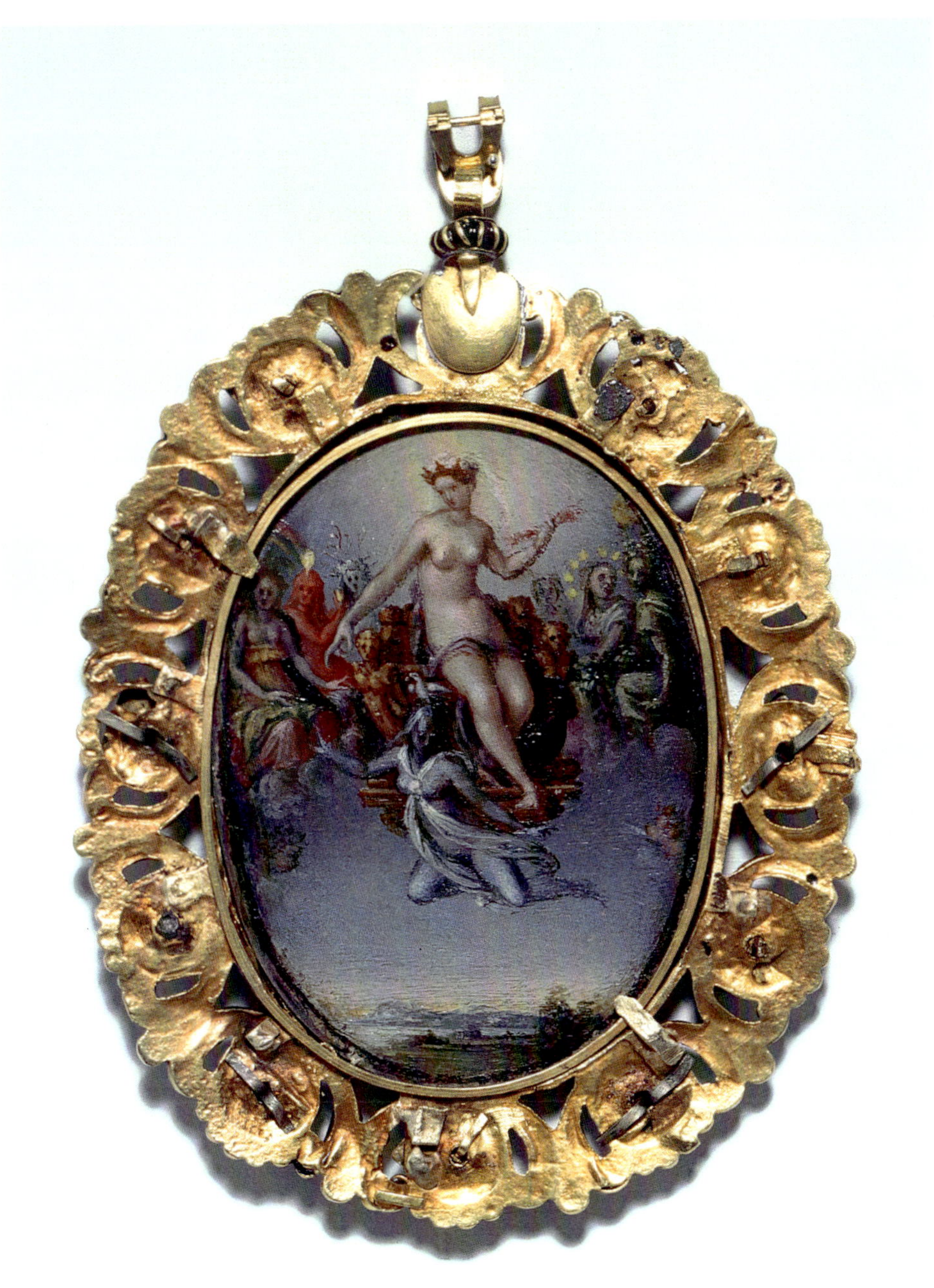

Plate 15 Alessandro Allori. *Eleonora ('Dianora') di Don Garzia di Toledo di Pietro de' Medici,* reverse of plate 14: *Juno, with Nymphs of the Air.* Portrait miniature.

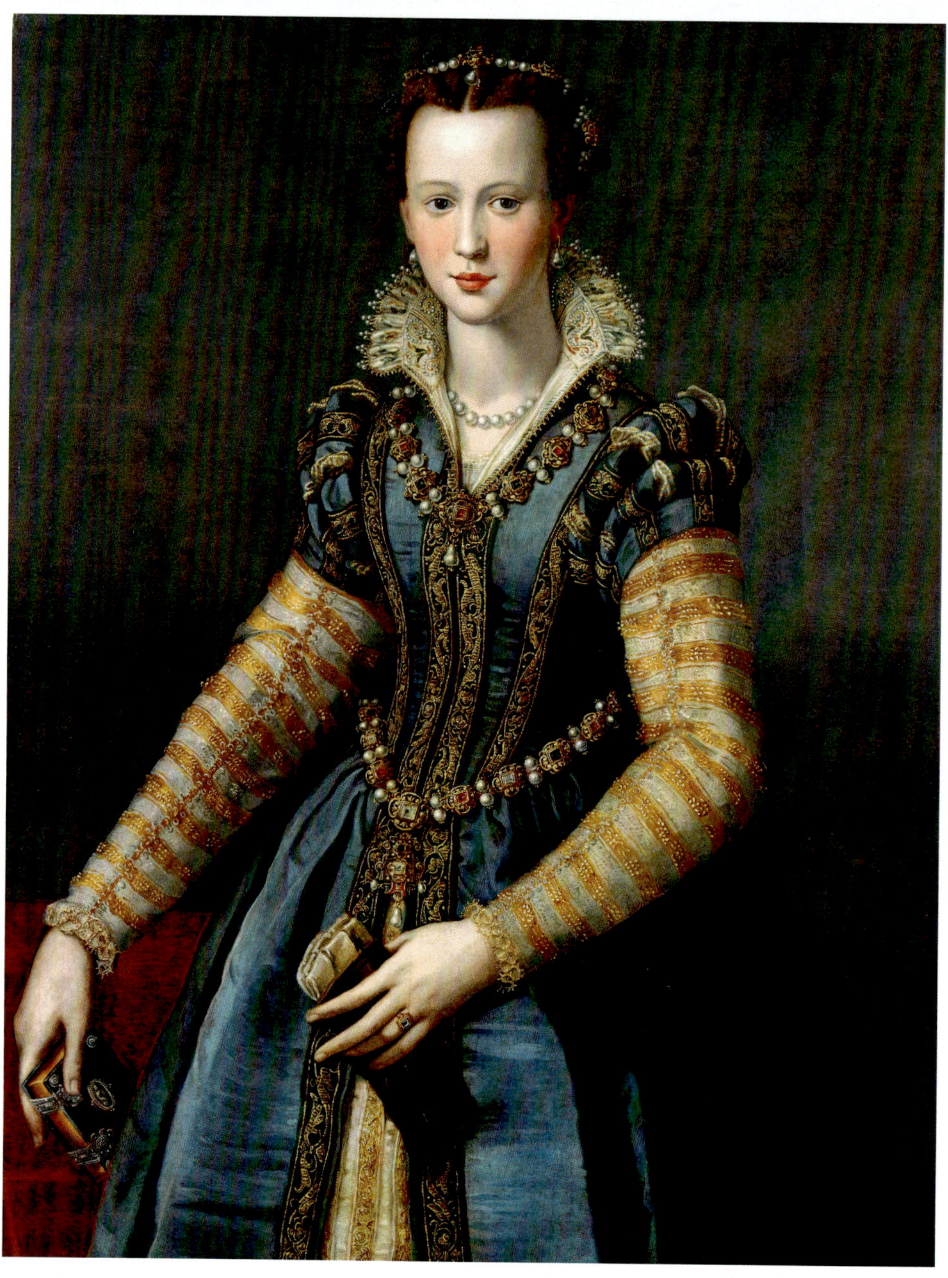

Plate 16 Alessandro Allori, *Eleonora ('Dianora') di Don Garzia di Toledo di Pietro de' Medici*, circa 1571. Oil on panel, 114.5 × 89.5. Vienna, Kunsthistorisches Museum.

It was forty years before the topic of individual portrayal received undivided attention in Italy. This came couched in denunciatory tones from Cardinal Gabriele Paleotti, writing officially in 1582 from the see of Bologna. His reactionary vision on portraiture allows a retrospective eye to be cast over the status quo of portrayal towards the end of Cosimo's reign. Censuring what the Church felt were unacceptable developments in the genre, he cuts to the very quick of the responsibility of patron, artist, subject, and viewer to plumb the moral implications surrounding an individual's portrait for *all* concerned. Paleotti's call for a curb on the growth in the volume and genres of portraiture allows wider insight into who was traditionally thought worthy of portrayal (mainly the nobility). He, too, stresses its didactic role.[98]

In 1564, the duke had been quick to implement the promulgations of the Council of Trent, when departures from decorum in religious art were censured by churchmen.[99] While private art had not been a stated target, the Tridentine reforms reflected and gave impetus to a stringent moral climate that could not but influence the presentation of subjects in portrayal – especially those destined for public consumption. Paleotti left no doubt that portraits must fulfil the Tridentine definitions of decorum.[100] Although he abrogated any claim to be either an artist or theorist, the echo in his writing of elements detailed in Leonardo's precept implies that their application to individual portraits was long entrenched and believed to be expressly implicit to the genre. Decorum related directly to the dignity of a person in *any* portrayal and it was sinful not to fulfil its precepts: 'But we leave contention to others – being less wise – and assign decorum appropriate to the dignity of the person, and on the contrary we call unsuitable that which sins [by] attributing to him actions, manners, expressions or others that are not decorous to his or her age, sex, dress, or rank.'[101] Specifically addressing himself to individual portraiture, Paleotti would not judge its merits as likeness, or – here he coyly plays the Philistine – for that matter, as art, but he is concerned with the decorum expressed and its potential effect on the viewer:

> In the first place, we can only say that a portrait in itself, as an image, is neither good nor bad, rather [that it is] indifferent, since it may be applied to good or bad use. Nevertheless, those things we call indifferent, when they are reduced to particular circumstances by the intelligent deliberation of man, do not belong to the large category of 'indifferent' anymore, and *are necessarily circumscribed and defined by the circumstances of people, place, time, and other such things.* It then follows that, from these particulars, they lose their undefined nature, and begin to acquire a new degree of praise or culpability.[102]

The passage expresses the elements set out in Leonardo's precept on decorum as entrenched norms for portrayal. Moreover, in Paleotti's mind portraits had significant power to edify or corrupt a spectator. This hints at the psychological impact the portrait could exert in an era that experienced images of the powerful very rarely.[103] An intense 'image magic' associated with portraits as surrogate 'presences' is documented at many points throughout this study, as are yearnings for possession of portraits of absent loved ones or instances of insults to images and cases of *damnatio memoriae* that conversely express just how dangerously 'present' a portrayed subject was perceived to be.[104] An enhanced sense of Renaissance portraiture has evolved today that views it as an art of 'purposeful manipulation.'[105]

Paleotti was friendly with one of the most powerful prelates of the Tridentine era, Cardinal Carlo Borromeo, nephew of the pope and a Medici intimate famously sensitive to imagery. His censorious tone expresses the dogmatic position that court portraitists must have been expected to follow in spirit after the Church's strictures on religious art were promulgated in 1564. Counter-Reformation winds of change permeated society and art, and a Counter-Reformation ethos was infused into Medici portraiture by Alessandro Allori as early as 1559 due to his six-year immersion in Rome before the reconvening of the Council of Trent in 1562.[106]

It is no small tribute to Leonardo that his precept seems to echo strongly through de Hollanda's and Paleotti's writings, and the ideology of decorum serves as an important touchstone for an assessment of portrayal.[107] A careful reading of Leonardo's precept reveals that it is not a dogmatic, closed strategy to which an artist would be bound; rather, its elements, especially 'setting and circumstances,' were intended as an aide-memoire to inspire the artist to account for the contexts of an individual's existence. The precept's flexible framework is formulated to shape itself readily to any newly evolved 'setting and circumstance' – including, as Paleotti showed, the Tridentine climate – because its intent is to respond to circumstances intelligible to a notional audience and what that audience would hold to be 'natural' in its own world order. The focus of approach to an analysis of Medici portraits in this study is to clarify the sixteenth-century perception of what would be received as 'natural' for patron and audience in the intellectual and temporal world of the court, as well as pursuit of an apprehension of 'settings and circumstances' related to each individual Medici woman portrayed.

One circumstance bearing directly on the ideology of what could be 'natural' was the growth in popularity, from the mid-sixteenth century, of Aristotle's writings, which in essence rejected the metaphysical perspectives of Plato and Petrarch for an objective, secular, and analytical eye. Vincenzo Borghini, Cosimo's learned iconographer and Varchi's successor, was an adherent of Aristotle's philosophy, which probably has a bearing on the dramatic change of style between, for example, Bronzino's exquisitely idealized, abstracted, poetic *Eleonora di Toledo with Her Son Giovanni* (pl. 4) and his successor Allori's rather pragmatic potrait of Eleonora's daughter, *Isabella de' Medici Orsini with Her Son Virginio* (pl. 11), a generation later.[108] Idealism is not, however, excluded. Aristotle proposed, like Plato, that beauty reflected goodness, and called on the poet to imitate 'good' portrait painters, who, 'while rendering likenesses of their sitters by reproducing their individual appearance, also make them better looking.'[109] In tandem with Counter-Reformation demands for directness and clarity in religious art, Aristotle's impact on the art of the court from about 1560 was considerable.

As Vasari and de Hollanda suggested, the artist's commitment to decorum was important. Paleotti implies a high moral tone for the portrayal of noble subjects: 'Moreover, in portraits of people of rank and dignity, patrons must make sure that they are represented with the gravity and decorum that is appropriate to their condition.'[110] Such demands were not taken to extremes, but there can be no doubt that the principal court-portraitists in this study, Pontormo, Bronzino, and Allori, were steeped in the Medici court environment, its philosophies, and its propagandistic concerns.[111] Their portraits assuredly reflect the precise wishes of their ducal patrons concerning how, for whom, and to what ends they presented their individual Medici female sitters to a specific viewer or audience, how they presented their courtly world, and the extent to which the response intended for a viewer would be effected as they wished. In deference to the spirit of the sixteenth-century ideology of decorum and to its implications, the interpretation of each portrait in this study is understood to be that intended for the sixteenth-century spectator.[112]

There is a deepening awareness today of the coercive potential of representation over an early-modern spectator. Who that spectator might be and understanding just how a distinct context – physical or intellectual – might exist for viewing a subject must inevitably be an important quest. As it has also emerged in the course of this study that the Medici court had devised a range of genres of court portraiture for women, the notional viewer for any one genre must be assessed in his or her own right.[113]

Other concerns arise. The notion of the portrait's implicit 'mask' is well accepted now – the cover for Bugiardini's 'La Monaca,' ca. 1510–20, decorated with a mask and grotesques and inscribed 'SUA CUIQUE PERSONA' ('To each his own mask'), attests to the Renaissance beholder's implicit acceptance of this notion.[114] The artist typically created an expanded *persona*, or body of information, around the likeness of an individual – it was expected of him. More or less subliminal messages could inhere in a portrait; in the mid-sixteenth-century court this practice became an art of complex symbolic referencing. Apart from the inscribed miniatures copied from original portraits to form ancestral sets destined for other courts, the Florentine court apparently saw no reason to inscribe Medici names on their portraits. But identification must generally have been held to be crucial in view of the portrait's traditional ancestral role: to celebrate the sitter's fame, beauty, or virtue for posterity.[115] The identities, rank, and status of Medici women were to be recognized by contemporary viewers through many prompts devised by the artist or patron. Commonplace among these were armorial colours used to clothe the subject, mottoes cleverly worked into furniture decoration, a subject's jewellery, or significant accessories. Circumstances too could be implied. Just as Pontormo's *Francesco Guardi* is posed to actually guard his city's walls, Maria Salviati's name is allegorized in her pose as *salvatrice*, or 'saviour' as she shelters young Giulia (pl. 2).[116] *Maniera* – a modern term describing the period's courtly 'artifice that conceals art' – was a style that called for sophistication in the viewer's response. Layered references to conjure a personal *impresa* or motto served to define a subject's moral code, as symbolized in the earrings in portraits of Cosimo and Eleonora's daughters Maria (pl. 7 and fig. 31) and Isabella (figs. 32 and 33). 'Dianora' di Toledo, their niece and ward (pl. 14 and 16), wears the Toledan armorial dark blue that links her to her aunt, the first Eleonora di Toledo, who shared her name and *stemma*. Such cues were coined to challenge, delight, and entertain a spectator who, during this process of recognition would be compelled to engage more deeply with a portrait. Connoisseurship, and implicit admission to the court's witty, intellectual coterie inevitably became a flattering part of this extended exchange.

Levels of preciousness, beauty, and extraordinary technical virtuosity in portraiture that evinced astonishment – *stupore* – promoted an exclusiveness native to the court and its artists. The optically beautiful surface of Duchess Eleonora's gown in her state portrait (pl. 4 and fig. 15), or the microscopic detail of a figured allegory and landscape backing the miniature portrait of Dianora, on a surface of 5.5 by 4 cm ($2^1/_8 \times 1^5/_8''$ approx.) (pls. 14 and 15), come to mind. This intentional enthralment of the viewer coexisted with wider displays of magnificence fostered, for example, in courtly pageantry, tapestry, and fresco. It served to evoke awe for the regime and to erase memory of the Medicis' bourgeois origins.[117]

Contexts for the art of the court are expressed most importantly in writings generated by ducal academies, copious court archives, contemporary chronicles, Medici biographies and histories (some scurrilous), diaries and reports by citizens and ambassadors, and eulogies, madrigals and poetry addressed to individual women. Emblem books that circulated in this new age of print engaged iconographers and artists in the court's ambit. The customary eulogizing language of the court was not antithetical to understanding symbolism and expression in its portraiture. Attempts are made in this study to resolve persistent incongruities or uncertainties related to a subject's identity, sex, dress, setting, circumstances, or other contexts – and to address the motives behind the deliberate defacement of some images.[118]

Our grasp of the 'script' for portrayal from life or posthumously of a particular woman lies in codes of conduct for Renaissance women that sought to fashion them as paradigms of their sex, and in treatises on portraiture that upheld the notion that only the good should be portrayed and, ipso facto, that the ends for portrayal were implicitly didactic. Renaissance portraits had traditionally been viewed as enshrining exemplars for the edification of their descendents. For women it was understood, too, that idealization was to be expected – outer beauty expressed inner goodness, beauty in portraiture was 'natural,' and such inherent expressions of goodness fulfilled the exemplary function.[119] An informed Renaissance viewer of a portrait knew that even if resemblance was the starting point, extra dimensions of identity, traits of character, essential clues to fealty, rank, locale, and circumstances, and expressions of love and allure could all be conjured through the many referential ploys known to the informed painter. What was essential to a portrait's successful reception was the world view held in common by patron, artist, viewer, and, usually – but not always – the sitter.

The world of the Medici ducal court, its vocabulary of symbolism and propaganda, its cultural interests, its public spectacles, its philosophy of rule, and its assiduous rise to power have engaged scholars in recent decades. Cosimo's striving ambition, the expansion of Tuscan territory, his tight control over all branches of the arts, the contributions made by his stable of iconographers, his academies and presses, archival gleanings that illuminate both the lives of members of the Ducal family, the fledgling court's internal organization, its pageantry, and even the daily life or attitudes of some of the least ranking of his subjects have recently been examined.[120] Eleonora's role as regent and patron has enjoyed enormously expanded interest; this, in turn, has prompted new perspectives on her cultural milieu, tastes, imaging, and impact on the evolution of the new court.[121]

Lavish artistic patronage by Cosimo and Eleonora ensured that this court left a legacy of evidence of its intentions, not least in portraits. Scholars who have plumbed the environments and responsibilities of court artists to illuminate ideations of power have concluded that the genre was one of the most important mediums of cultural policy.[122] General studies of Renaissance portraiture express fresh attempts to refine or redefine women's portraits, and recent exhibitions have strengthened them.[123] Petrarchan notions of beauty are now well understood to have saturated sixteenth-century approaches to women's portrayal and its reception, and knowledge of contemporary conduct books for women is seen as vital to our apprehension of codes of beauty and decorum for women of the time.[124] The 1990s marked a watershed of interest in these pioneering topics.[125] Bronzino's portraits of women are now recognized as a distinct category of his oeuvre.[126] Medici women's portraiture was, above all, a distinctive expression of the court's cultivated ethos of exclusiveness and supremacy.

The Twenty-first Century Viewer Before the Late Renaissance Portrait

At a distant remove of almost half a millennium, meaning in portraits is inherently problematical for the modern viewer. Even a cursory viewing of Bronzino's art prompts an awareness that its beauty conceals complexities and subtleties that demand considerable effort from us to appreciate it more fully. The 'artifice that conceals art' in his London *Allegory of Venus*, 1545, for example, is of a high order and may even be perceived as extreme abstruseness from our modern world view.[127] Layers of cultural referencing in portraits are challenging, but they exist to anchor the subject appropriately as a persona in a sixteenth-century theatre of life.[128] If we assume a rapidly evolving, complex milieu for women in Cosimo and Eleonora's court, and the court's role in changing history and being changed by it, the task is made even greater. Historicity is crucial to a search for truth and if, like Baxandall, we find ourselves 'marooned' in a world of 'stranded objects' that demand full recognition, an attempt may be made to read them from a temporal vantage point that transcends our own. His emphasis on the 'cognitive style' of a period and his concept of the 'period eye' of the Renaissance viewer has been assessed by many scholars.[129] Paola Tinagli's apologia of 1997 refutes crude application of strategies driven by modern philosophies as ahistoric and anachronistic.[130] This same plea has been voiced by many scholars over recent decades.[131] Approaches to solving issues around the nuances of presentation of the portraits of Medici women cannot be framed in present attitudes arising from gender-based indignation or from new theories of the 'self' or the 'gaze,' or from current notions of 'otherness,' to name a few.

In order to make sense of the art of the past, we need to be aware of the ways in which artists interpreted that vision of their world for consumption by an intended spectator. Gombrich has defined their approaches as 'schemata,' a term that carries resonance for elements of Leonardo's decorum (*decoro/convenientia*) and its usefulness today as an aide memoire for unlocking the meaning and contexts of women's portraits from the Medici ducal court.[132] We must also take account of what Gombrich allotted to the spectator, 'the beholder's share'[133] – a different kind of subjectivity for a Renaissance beholder of beauty, one that will deeply engage the affections, with its origins in the spectator's cultural conditioning and world view.[134] These scholars' perceptions suggested that in order to assess a genre of art commissioned in the Medici ducal court setting, this study should take account of the often densely woven, overlapping abstract signs, allegories, and similes promoted in its environment. The mission here must be to approach the portraits as documents of a specific court culture and to explore them in as many ways as their artistic and cultural contexts demand. If Castiglione claimed that his book presented 'a portrait of the Court of Urbino,' Medici women may also have been portrayed as ideal expressions of the new ruling order in the Florentine court. Cosimo and Eleonora's court may have been perceived as a parvenu phenomenon, but the contributions of its patrons to language and art alone were of a high order. Of the many other genres of art generated under the patronage of the duke and duchess already studied, the court's portraiture of women deserves a similar kind of comprehensive approach.

The status of portraiture in the sixteenth century, how it was viewed, and how it mirrors shifts in the philosophy and theory of the portrayal of women and the ruling castes are recurring themes in this study. Each chapter is devoted to a Medici woman, with chapter 3 devoted to girls. In the course of this exploration, the actual lives of Medici women were often revealed to be remarkable – courageous, tragic, vain, tempestuous, pious, intellectually brilliant, reckless, discontented, and charismatic, some even unenviable and depressing – as seen by those who recorded them. Their biographies are woven through these pages to commemorate them, but they stand, too, as a sharp foil to the distinct court conventions and canons developed for their portrayal. The concluding epilogue examines the peculiar fate of some portraits, of *damnatio memoriae* or the mythology created around some women, the persistence of the traditional imagery coined for rulers in the light of modern examples, and how race may be contentious even after almost half a millennium.

1

Bloodlines: Portraits of Maria Salviati de' Medici by Bronzino and Pontormo

In his *Vite*, Vasari indicated that the first Medici woman to have been portrayed by ducal commission was Maria Salviati, Cosimo's mother.[1] Maria, grandaughter of Lorenzo the Magnificent through Lucrezia de' Medici and Jacopo Salviati, was born in 1499. In November 1516 she married Giovanni delle Bande Nere, son of Giovanni il Popolano and Caterina Sforza. This union joined the two branches of the Medici line in their only child, Cosimo, born in 1519 (see appendix A). Giovanni, a legendary *condottiere* and close companion of the raffish man of letters, notorious wit, and 'scourge of princes' Pietro Aretino, died of wounds received in combat in 1526, leaving Maria widowed at twenty-seven.[2] With great prescience, she then devoted herself to young Cosimo, aware in a period of oscillating fortunes for the Medici in Florence, papal Rome, and the European forum that he should be groomed for the role of scion of the Medici house. Her letter to a 'Giovanni' in Rome, 3 May 1531 confirms her resolve:

> As soon as the blessed soul of my lord husband had departed, in that instant I decided to live forever with my son for many reasons that would be too long to relate by letter; and for a very special consideration that my son, having been born above all of those fortunate ancestors, was not to be abandoned by me, since it will be much more useful to him to remain with him rather than leave him, the self-same purpose I held until this time and principally hold [now].[3]

Cosimo's father's reputation for stoic heroism and his mother's strict devotion to duty seem to have made a lifelong impression on him.

On Cosimo's accession in 1537 at seventeen, Maria, then thirty-eight, became responsible for his wards, the two illegitimate children of his predecessor, Duke Alessandro de' Medici. They joined Cosimo's own illegitimate daughter, Bia (1536–42), who was already in Maria's care. After Cosimo's marriage to Eleonora di Toledo in 1539, Maria continued as caretaker to Eleonora and Cosimo's children until her death on 12 December 1543.[4] She was then forty-four and Cosimo was in the sixth year of his reign.[5]

Although she died only six years after Cosimo's accession, the importance of Maria's rank as mother of the duke is suggested by the number of portraits recorded for her in Medici and Riccardi inventories, as well as those mentioned by

Vasari. She is also included in the monumental propagandistic frescoes painted by Vasari for Cosimo in the Palazzo Vecchio, and is commemorated in posthumous panels. These official tributes all serve to document her contemporaries' consistent declaration of her faithful adherence in dress and demeanour to conventions that define her as a paradigm of decorous widowhood.

Three panel portraits of Maria will be examined, not all of which reflect this emphasis on a ponderous freight of perpetual grief. They encompass portrayals of her, first, as a vivacious young wife and mother; second, in her official role as widowed mother to Duke Cosimo; and third, posthumously, as elevated to near-celestial standing. Although these portraits have not been chosen merely for their complex art-historical status – attributions, identifications, and dating are to some degree problematical for each of them – the challenges they offer go to the very heart of issues surrounding the sixteenth-century subject's decorum and its demands on the painter. For these reasons, an examination of each *Maria* panel has had to be flexible, and has depended on which or how many of the concerns related to decorum were still at issue. What emerged in the exercise of seeking the coherence of decorum in Maria's individual portraits were some surprising revelations of her stature in early Medicean affairs, and a humbling awareness that, for the sixteenth-century viewer, great portraiture far exceeded the sum of an artist's ability to record a mimetic likeness for posterity. Fortunately, two artists of consummate skill, Pontormo and Bronzino, rose to the challenge in portraying Maria at signal moments in her life. These portraits also initiate the consistent pattern that would characterize all genres of portraiture for women of Cosimo's court: a strong element of propaganda informs every one.

Bronzino's *Maria Salviati with a Lapdog*

Vasari recorded that both Pontormo and Bronzino portrayed Maria. He related that, when the newly elected, seventeen-year-old duke had routed disaffected challengers to his election after the Battle of Montemurlo on 1 August 1537 and consolidated his position in Florence, he promptly commissioned fresco decoration for Maria's villa at Castello from Pontormo. The commission included portraits of mother and son, but Vasari does not state explicitly whether the portrait of Maria was in fresco or on panel. The existence of either or both is possible. As the Castello frescoes deteriorated within decades and are now lost, it is impossible to know.[6] Although several portraits of her exist, we have no secure record of Maria's likeness during this period of Medici triumph.[7] Vasari's account of a Bronzino portrait is even less helpful, as he merely lists it with others of the ducal family: '[Bronzino] portrayed ... the Lord Giovanni, Lord Garzia, and Lord Ferdinando in more panels, which are all in His Excellency's wardrobe, along with portraits of Don Francesco di Toledo, Signora Maria, mother of the Duke, and Ercole II of Ferrara, with many others.'[8] Some further help may be sought in Medici inventories. A portrait of Maria is mentioned in the 1560 Medici *guardaroba* inventory and repeated in the 1562 version: 'Un ritratto della Illma Signora Maria di man' del Bronzino, a'ornamento di noce intagliato tocca d'oro.' ('A portrait of the Illustrious Lady Maria by the hand of Bronzino, with a carved walnut frame decorated with gold.') The entry precedes one for a portrait of 'Signor Giovanni' (delle Bande

Nere), her husband, attributed there to Titian, and is also preceded by a record of a portrait of Maria Salviati's ancestor, Lorenzo the Magnificent. This entry likely does record a portrait of Cosimo's mother, but there is some ambiguity in the case of the second entry, a 'ritratto della Signora Maria,' as Cosimo's unmarried, deceased daughter, Maria, is also referred to as 'S^{ra}' in the inventory. The entry probably does record a portrait of Maria Salviati, as it is located separately from those for Cosimo's other children.[9] In any event, the Bronzino portrait of Maria Salviati to which Vasari alluded is probably accounted for in the 1562 inventory, and a second portrait of her by the artist may have existed.[10]

Among portraits by Bronzino identified today as being of Maria, there are two possible contenders for correspondence with these portraits of her recorded in Medici inventories. The first, only rarely identified as Maria Salviati, is the youthful, arresting *Portrait of Lady with a Lapdog* in Frankfurt (pl. 1 and fig. 2), now overwhelmingly attributed to Bronzino.[11] The second, Bronzino's *Portrait of an Elderly Lady* in San Francisco (fig. 3), has also been identified as Maria.[12] But Maria did not live to old age, and the intense gaze of this vigorous, elderly sitter does not resemble Maria's heavy-lidded, slightly drowsy appearance in her later years (pl 2), making it an unlikely candidate for either of the two Bronzino *Marias* listed in the inventories.[13] Maria's facial characteristics are common to the securely identified Baltimore panel, painted by Pontormo shortly before her death at age forty-four (pl. 2), in Vasari's identical *Maria* in the Palazzo Vecchio tondo of 1556 (fig. 4), and the posthumous image in Naldini's double portrait with her late husband (fig. 5).[14]

A growing possibility exists, however, for reconsidering her portrayal from life in Bronzino's early portraiture. Scholarly consensus is now almost unanimous in attributing the riveting, vivacious *Lady with a Lapdog* (pl. 1 and fig. 2) to him. Robert Simon saw a close resemblance between the Frankfurt *Lady* and the secure Baltimore *Portrait of Maria Salviati with a Child* [*Giulia de' Medici*] (pls. 1 and 2) discussed below.[15] When compared also to the drawing believed to be of Maria as a young woman (fig. 6), his observation is persuasive and deserves rigorous examination. Scholarly datings for the Frankfurt panel range from around 1527 to nearly two decades later, which again demands more stringent attention. Craig Hugh Smyth confidently gave the work to Bronzino five decades ago after exhaustive examination of its style and brushwork. He also linked the *Lady with a Lapdog* stylistically to heads such as those of Mary and Joseph in Bronzino's Washington *Holy Family* (1525) and of the Magdalene in the Uffizi *Pietà* (1528). He especially saw correlations of style in the mid-1520s Washington panel, and was certain that the *Lady with a Lapdog* predates the artist's Pesaro immersion from 1530. In order 'to give it all possible leeway,' he dated the portrait to 1527–9, and proposed it as a harbinger of Bronzino's later court style. He is supported by McCorquodale, and Cropper implies this too.[16] Its 'strong and audacious' colour has also been noted.[17] This is a characteristic of Bronzino's early painting; that trait, with the incisive outlines and strong illumination in the faces of the Saints Mark and Luke tondi of 1525 in the vault of the Capponi Chapel, Santa Felicita, have also been included in this assessment of the Frankfurt panel's earlier dating.[18] Other proposals range from around 1530 to 1545, a twenty-year span in all.[19]

Smyth's assessment of the *Lady*'s stylistic contexts and assignment to circa 1525–9 demands some attempt to date her dress, which, in the case of a young woman, is likely to be modish. This style of dress does correspond to women's costume in portraits of that decade. The high-waisted bodice, billowing upper oversleeves, and exaggerated, halo-like coiffure for the *Lady with a Lapdog* may be compared to similar trends in dress in Pontormo's *Woman with a Basket of Spindles*, of around 1525; in Andrea del Sarto's *Portrait of a Girl with a Volume of Petrarch*, circa 1525, and *Portrait of a Woman in Yellow* (Windsor), circa 1526–9; and especially in Domenico Puligo's *Barbara Salutati*, painted before he died in 1527 (pl. 13). Even if less sumptuous, these – especially Puligo's *Barbara* – follow the same fashion.[20] The Frankfurt woman's dress contrasts with trends of the late 1530s to mid-1540s, as witness the longer bodice in Bronzino's portraits of that time, the *Young Woman with her Little Boy*, *Lucrezia Panciatichi*, Eleonora di Toledo's Tribuna portrait, and the *Bia de' Medici* (see fig. 27 [Lucrezia] and pls. 4 [Eleonora] and 6 [Bia]), where a shift to the natural waistline is evident for young women.[21] The very short bodice and enormous upper sleeve of the *Lady with a Lapdog* belong to an earlier era than any of Bronzino's other Tribuna portraits. Fashionable in the mid 1520s, the style would be *outré* in the 1530s.

Can this be Maria, as Robert Simon proposed? On the basis of dress, accessories, and personal decorum in this portrayal, November 1526, when her husband died in battle, is the latest date that can be proposed if she is indeed the subject of this panel. The entrenched veiled decorum, drab colours, and prescribed lack of adornment that was *de rigueur* for widows would not have been ignored by her, and never was.[22] This sitter's head is uncovered, and she wears a brilliant red dress with several items of jewellery. Widowhood would have determined the wearing of a heavy veil, dark clothing in prescribed colours of dull green, brown, grey, or black, and no jewellery. Even for manifestly festive occasions, Maria diligently observed this practice after 1526.[23] A lapdog, commonly understood to signify faithfulness and conjugal love, would be an unsuitable accessory for a widow.[24] (It could even carry overtones of erotic love.)[25] Churchmen and commentators on manners expressly promoted chaste abstinence for all widows, and contemporary references support the widowed Maria's faithfulness to her dead husband – her motto was 'JAMAIS AUTRE' ('Never another').[26] In sum, the sitter's dress and accessories in this portrait would testify to contemporaries that Maria could *not* be widowed when it was executed. If this is Maria, a *terminus ante quem* for it of November 1526 is certain, when widowhood initiated her lifelong adherence to mourning.

Circumstances in Bronzino's own artistic career suggest, too, that the portrait was probably painted in 1526. On his return from a two-year sojourn with Pontormo at the monastery of the Certosa at Galuzzo on the outskirts of Florence, they worked together in Florence, notably in the Capponi Chapel, Santa Felicita, in the mid-1520s. The forceful, brilliant colour scheme in the Frankfurt portrait suggests a confidence going beyond the Santa Felicita tondi of 1525: on Maria's face we find no trace of the slightly plaintive, hollow-eyed legacy from Pontormo that persists in Bronzino's Santa Felicita figures.[27]

Bronzino (1503–72) would have been about twenty-three in the mid-1520s when he painted this memorable portrait, a period that marks his emergence as master from his status as Pontormo's assistant. The incisive contour, brilliant colour, sparkling quality of the sitter's expression, and the winsome but not over-sentimental charm of the little lapdog all convey a youthful verve in execution coupled with an elegance of finish that will mark Bronzino's career for more than three decades to come. The complex organization of the composition, its meticulous rendering of detail, and its subtle but sophisticated visual playfulness are traits native to Bronzino's poetry and to such works as his *Pygmalion and Galatea* or the later London *Allegory*. Lively counterpoints abound here: the gold-and-black lattice of her hair cover are echoed in the gold-latticed tassel in her lap; the little dog's shaggy hair is a lively contrast to the precisely trimmed, silken fringes on the chair, and its wide-set brown eyes glint with similar lively catch-lights as the sitter's own; above all, the extraordinary equilibrium of her square, composed face is delightfully contrasted with the slightly quizzical tilt of the puppy's cocked head and its uplifted paw. Her familiar, the puppy, becomes in effect an extension of the sitter herself – hardly a mere accessory – and extends a similar, warm glance to the viewer outside the frame. Finally, the sitter's *grandezza* and serenity are contrasted with the grimacing mask on the chair's armrest – slyly echoed by a laughing mascaron in her gold pendant. They make, perhaps, a succinct, witty commentary on the sitter's personal constancy and grace in the tragi-comic arena of life.

The Frankfurt *Lady with a Lapdog* appears to be among the earliest of Bronzino's female portraits to come down to us. It opens a window on a moment in his career when his struggle to conform to his master's style could be abandoned for his own meticulous artistic urges in an independent commission. It also presages his departure for Pesaro, where he painted the equally arresting *Portrait of Guidobaldo della Rovere* in 1532.[28] Indeed, no earlier work of Bronzino's is so assiduously optical in capturing glittering, enamelled, surface detail as do these two, and Bronzino's court style is forged in this dramatic show of virtuosity. It has recently been observed that Bronzino's enamelled finish, the new study of light, acute attention to details of clothing, jewellery, accessories, and even the grotesque decoration on the chair all combine to express what at that time must have been a highly modern idiom.[29] This early portrait by Bronzino is evidence of a compelling personal style that presages his approach as portraitist to the future Medici court.

Vasari stated that Bronzino had 'painted many portraits [before the Siege of Florence, 24 October 1529], which gained him a great reputation,' so that a date for this portrait around 1526 should not cause surprise.[30] Bronzino did not spring Athena-like to the attention of the della Rovere circle at Pesaro in 1529; rather, the arresting qualities of the *Lady with a Lapdog* defined him as a new, artistic force for portraiture.[31] His talent in conveying the riveting quality of manifestly high rank that the Frankfurt and Pesaro portraits have in common would have been recognized *before* he left for Pesaro in 1530 on commission to portray Guidobaldo della Rovere, scion to one of the most illustrious houses in Italy.

There are compelling artistic reasons for accepting Robert Simon's careful consideration for identification of the *Lady in Red* as Maria Salviati. First, the features and turn of the sitter's head in the Frankfurt portrait closely resemble those in a drawing almost always identified as Maria, one made when she was young (fig. 6), which exhibits all the tautness and near-fanatical precision of Bronzino's hand.[32] There her head is conceived, as for the sitter's in his *Lady with a Lapdog*, as a solid, rhomboidal, geometric sphere mounted on an elongated cylinder, and the finely defined contour, underlit modelling for the face, and precision of detail are common to both drawing and panel. The pattern of lighting in each is identical, as is the cylindrical form of the long neck. (All this stands in marked contrast to the evanescent, chiaroscuro effects of Pontormo's study for a portrait of Ippolito de' Medici with a dog made around the same time, 1524–5.)[33] Comparison of the Frankfurt woman's features with Pontormo's securely identified *Portrait of Maria Salviati with a Child* [*Giulia de' Medici*] (pl. 2), which dates to about 1540, when Maria was around forty (discussed below), leaves little doubt about the identification. In the earlier image, vitality and robust health define her youthfulness, characteristics missing from the later portrait, but Maria's abiding physical appearance – a long neck, square face, broad features, widely set, heavy-lidded brown eyes, sweeping, arched brows, a broad nose with wide nostrils, and the wide, smooth forehead seen in the Frankfurt panel – are common to all her portraits. These, and particularly the shape of her lips, are identical in Bronzino's youthful drawing, in the Frankfurt panel, and in Pontormo's *Maria Salviati with a Child* [*Giulia*] meticulously calibrated comparisons reveal that the features of the *Lady with a Lapdog* correlate at all critical points with the securely identified *Maria with a Child* (pl. 2) and the youthful *Maria* drawing (fig. 6).[34]

If this compelling portrait is of Maria, it can be dated fairly precisely. Apart from the crucial matter of her widowhood from 1527, historic circumstances surrounding her suggest that she probably would have posed for the Frankfurt portrait between 1525 and 1527, and not later. We know that she took Cosimo to Rome in 1524, and was back in Florence from 1525 to 1526. Bronzino, who was then at work with Pontormo on the Capponi Chapel in Santa Felicita, could easily have visited Castello to portray Maria, her home there being a few miles from the city walls. Her movements during the turmoil of the late 1520s make it unlikely that she would have been been available for any sittings between 1527 and 1529. She hastily left for Venice soon after her widowhood in November 1526 to avoid the terrifying possibility of an encounter with marauding German *landsknechts*.[35] Following the sack of Rome, the early months of 1527 in Florence were troubled by shortages of food and continuing panic in expectation of the approaching army; by May, Maria's kinsman Pope Clement VII became a prisoner in Castel Sant' Angelo, where he remained until September. Florence was now in turmoil and Medici fortunes at their lowest ebb, forcing Maria to remain in exile through 1528 and 1529. This ended with the siege of Florence by imperial troops in October, followed by an outbreak of plague in September 1530. The city's population of 110,000 was now depleted by almost half.[36]

It was at this moment that Bronzino finally left Florence for his two-year absence in Pesaro. At the end of hostilities, Charles V was crowned Holy Roman Emperor by Pope Clement in Bologna on 24 February 1530; Maria and Cosimo, still in exile, were witness to this event. Clement in turn was allowed to install his illegitimate son, Alessandro, as ruler of Florence in 1530 – effectively ending the Republic and making the city an imperial fiefdom. Given Maria's years of exile from Florence from 1527, and Bronzino's own absence in Pesaro from 1530 to 1532, the *Lady with a Lapdog* must have been painted before 1527. Surviving panels suggest, too, that Pontormo alone served as portraitist to the Medici from the installation of Alessandro in 1531 (duke from 1532) until Duke Cosimo's accession in 1537 and even to about 1540.[37] The sumptuous costume style and accessorizing in this portrayal of her as a young, unwidowed, patrician wife would restrict the portrait to the early or mid-1520s, when both artist and sitter were in Florence.

Iconography in the Frankfurt panel is especially telling of Medici links and association with Maria herself as a young, married woman of high rank. Her devoutness is proclaimed by the rosary draped across her lap, but she epitomizes, too, the young wife as Venus, who grasps a golden apple – emblematic of her patronage of love – in Bronzino's *Allegory of Venus* (1545). Here, Maria's left hand is posed to enclose the golden sphere of the chair's finial. Her faithfulness and conjugal love are appropriately expressed here by the inclusion of the little dog. Alciati described the lapdog as emblematic of faithfulness and fecundity in his *Emblemata*, 1531; the illustrated 1550 edition has a description that implies physical love and resulting fertility to support the illustration of a loving couple:

> Here the lady gives her hand to her husband
> and plays with a puppy at her feet
> which is perceived as the examplar of true faithfulness.
> The tree, which is seen between them
> is the fruit, which sincere love produces.[38]

The 'tree,' of course is the genealogical tree produced by 'sincere,' that is, licit, love.

Implicit too is a statement of rank and familial pride. Maria is dressed in red, white, and dark green, the Medici colours, and the Florentine lily is a repeat motif on the collar of her chemise. This combined use of armorial colours for costume with iconographical references for identity was commonplace in the sixteenth century. Maria wears on her right hand the traditional pyramidal *diamante* associated with Medici lineage since Cosimo the Elder, with Leo X, and eventually with her son. It was adopted by Maria herself as her personal *impresa*, and a triple, interlocking version appears on Allegrini's engraved portrait of her of 1761 (fig. 8).[39] Her left hand rests on a golden sphere – one of two Medici *palle* used as finials on the armrests of the chair in which she sits. If further consideration is given to these, it is clear that six *palle* may be accounted for: two more as finials at each end of the farther armrest (invisible to view); the paired dolphins that form the handle on the armrest with a *palla* grasped in their mouths have a hidden counterpart, too, on the far side of the chair, making six in all. Six *palle* form the armorial decoration of the Medici *stemma*. The use of the symbolic *palla* may even have been inspired by Raphael's portrait of Maria's uncle, Pope Leo X, where a similar golden *palla* appears as a finial on the upright of his chair. The obliquely placed armchair functions to organize the compositional structure here in the same way as in Raphael's portrait, and its use for the first time as a compositional device by Bronzino for the Frankfurt *Maria* probably reinforced the association. Maria was said to resemble her famous uncle, so that this visual reference could not have been lost on Florentines familiar with Raphael's portrait and with the pride with which it was exhibited by the Medici from the moment it arrived in Florence in 1518.[40]

The fortunes of the Raphael's famous portrait also bear on the date this portrait was executed, that is, before Maria's widowhood in November 1526. Bronzino would not have seen it after March 1527, when it was stored with Medici panels for safekeeping by Ottaviano de' Medici. During those years, anti-Medicean feeling raged because of Clement's invitation to Charles to lay siege to Florence on his behalf, which culminated in Clement's son, Alessandro's installation as duke in 1531. Bronzino did not return from Pesaro until 1532. If the *Leo X* did inspire Bronzino's *Lady with a Lapdog*, it probably did so before 1527.[41]

Further Medici references are copiously scattered throughout the panel. The paired dolphins on the armrest of the chair appear in an engraved version of the Medici *diamante* with three feathers, as the *impresa* of Lorenzo the Magnificent, Maria's grandfather.[42] (Their wider iconographical significance will be discussed below.) Books seen to the right of the panel probably refer to her documented literacy and humanism.[43] Finally, Maria's husband, Giovanni delle Bande Nere may be alluded to where black satin ribbon-bindings – *bande nere* – hang loosely from one partly visible book; the other exhibits green highlights, the Medici armorial colour, on its reflective satin fastenings. (The folios bear no resemblance to the usual books of prayer found in women's portraits such as the *Lucrezia Panciatichi*, and one exhibits a tantalizing, half-concealed monogram. Its significance is mysterious.) If these *bande nere* refer to the valiant Giovanni and his troops, the 'Bande Nere' (Black Bands), they necessarily narrow the date of the painting to between 1522 and 1526: the insignia was adopted by Giovanni's troops after the death of Leo X in December 1521. After Giovanni's death in November 1526, Maria's customary dress was widow's 'weeds.' The panel was begun in his lifetime: in the mid-1520s a dog, emblem of faithfulness and conjugal love that signalled potential growth of the family tree, would be apt for her married state. Perhaps its closeness to Maria, and its alert, winsome expression is intended to evoke Cosimo, too.

Cosimo – born June 1519 – would still have been a little boy at the time of the panel's execution. His role as legitimate Medici scion had been celebrated by his great-uncle Leo X – who named him and who, on his birth, charged Maria with upholding his claim to Medici succession. One very important symbolic reference to this charge is alluded to in the portrait by the intertwined, budding twiglet motifs that form the principal elements of the sitter's weighty golden necklace (pl. 1 and detail, fig. 2, where the nubbed surfaces of the twigs are best seen). The *broncone* emblem, a sprouting twig on a lopped laurel branch, had been in use to symbolize regeneration of the Medici line. It was introduced to celebrate Cosimo's birth and legitimate right to Medici succession in 1519, when Leo X commissioned the celebratory *Vertumnus and Pomona* fresco for the *salone* lunette at the Medici villa of Poggio a Caiano. It was painted by Pontormo between 1520 and 1521. The unique intertwined arrangement of the *broncone* in the portrait is readily explained: Maria and her husband, Giovanni 'delle Bande Nere,' were descended from the two branches of the Medici line and, as mentioned above, Cosimo's birth united both branches in their son.[44]

The dolphin was important to Leo, who had the Medici emblem inlaid in the Vatican. It almost certainly had sentimental associations for Maria and Cosimo – it had squirmed playfully in the arms of Verrocchio's bronze *Boy with a Dolphin* since 1470 in the garden fountain of the Medici Villa at Careggi, close to Maria's villa at Castello.[45] Alciati shortly recorded in his *Emblemata* for *Princeps* ('The Ruler') that the protectiveness of the dolphin is related to princely responsibility. Twined around an anchor to curb its own exhuberance, the dolphin, he asserted, was an appropriate symbol for a ruler to be circumspect and ever mindful of his role in protecting his people.[46] The dolphin's lively nature may symbolize a boy who would grasp Medici power and whose mother would prove to be his exemplary anchor and guide.[47] Both the emblem and its associated motto, *festina lente*, were featured in multiple Medici iconographical schemes, from the time of Lorenzo the Magnificent until Vasari copiously used them to promote Cosimo's prudence as ruler in the Palazzo Vecchio fresco program of 1555–65.[48] The emblem became Cosimo's chosen *impresa* on his accession in 1537 as legitimate Medici heir and ruler of Florence, when the dolphin, entwined with an anchor and the rudder of Fortuna, was paired with his motto 'FESTINA LENTE' ('Make haste slowly').[49] For the wedding of his heir, Francesco, in 1555 he moved Verrocchio's *Putto with a Dolphin* from Careggi to adorn the entrance courtyard of the Palazzo Vecchio. Possibly, the implications of this *impresa* had been consciously imparted to him in early childhood, about the time when Bronzino painted the *Lady with a Lapdog*. The *putto*'s struggle with the anchorless, antic dolphin would have been a delightful vehicle for cautionary tales of restraint, prudence, ancestral *virtù*, and character-building nostrums for a little boy. And there was a need even at a tender age to encourage Cosimo to maintain his resolve in the face of possible turns in Medici political fortunes: in the mid-1520s, claims to legitimacy by two older Medici boys, Ippolito and Alessandro, resurfaced. With his father Clement VII installed as pope, Alessandro's claims stood in 1526 at the closest they could ever be to realization.[50] The panel asserts Cosimo's legitimacy and Medicean dynastic hopes.

In sum, the Frankfurt portrait is identifiable from other portrayals in drawings, panel, and fresco of Maria. It declares Maria Salviati de' Medici's armorial and marital links, her married state, her faithfulness and fecundity, and alludes to her famous husband's identity and, most especially, to her importance as perpetuator of the Medici line. An 'Olympian security, produced by the subject's luminous face,' together with rich apparel and jewellery that proclaim her rank, are totally in keeping with Maria's status, a woman lauded by two popes – Leo X, her uncle, and Clement VII, her cousin – for her guardianship of this destiny. It portrays Maria at about twenty-six as a young wife and proud mother: its subtle, aristocratic declarations are wonderfully lightened by her steady, gentle gaze, the winsome puppy, the brilliant expanse of scarlet in her dress, and the lively contour of its sleeves. The panel also enshrines Bronzino's portrait style in the mid-1520s before he was patronized by the Medici court. His *Guidobaldo della Rovere* shows that he absorbed Titian's influence in Pesaro after 1530, of which there is no trace here. The extraordinary aloofness, enigmatic tone, and marmoreal abstraction of his years as portraitist to Duke Cosimo and Eleonora from the 1540s are yet to come. The 'shocking' red expanse of the dress has recently been remarked upon, and in the sixteenth century would have had implications for its owner's rank, but also for her strength of character. The pigment that contributes to the arresting quality of the entire composition is vermilion, a colour derived from red mercury sulfide. It produces a blazing, fiery hue. It was one of the most opaque – and expensive – of pigments and, in artistic and literary circles, it had particular connotations. In Aretino's ekphrastic description of Titian's *Francesco Maria della Rovere* (1536–8), the fiery reflections on Francesco's armour are ascribed by Aretino to a red screen in the composition, painted with what Aretino wrongly supposed to be vermilion. Vermilion deserved special praise in Dolce's *Dialogo della Pittura ... intitolato l'Aretino* (1557). Dolce connected vermilion, and only vermilion red, to 'sanguis ruber' – blood red – and emphasized that, in the della Rovere portrait, Titian had used colours not to demonstrate the firmness of the flesh, but to discover '*la virilità d'anima*,' that is, strength of character. As we shall see, this spiritual strength and courage was the code by which Maria lived, a code that was to be decisive in ensuring the succession of her son.[51]

Contemporary descriptions of Maria's unaffected lifestyle, her fortitude and stoic courage, and her energetic devotion to her son are uncannily reflected in Smyth's perceptive analysis of the sitter's decorum in the Frankfurt *Lady with a Lapdog*. He did not identify her, but observed that, while the portrait presages Bronzino's inherently lavish courtly portrait style well before the Medici ducal court was established in 1537, what defines it as a record of Bronzino's earlier portrait *oeuvre* is its sincerity of expression:

> the freshness, in the lady's want of withdrawn sophistication, in her look, on the contrary, of self-conscious but resolute equilibrium (the counterpart of the picture's calculated stability and simplicity of form) and in the animation of her personality, with which we are still in touch in spite of its reserve. The conventions and stylising principles of later mannerism are not at all in evidence.[52]

The portrait was begun in 1526 or sooner, before Maria acquired the dreary attributes of widowhood. It is one of many portraits Bronzino is recorded to have painted before the siege of 1530, and probably one of the two of Maria by his hand mentioned in the Medici inventories of 1560 and 1562. Working alone now, he was not obliged to synthesize his style with Pontormo's. It was portraiture at this time that offered him the most scope for his native style and expression. The Frankfurt portrait made manifest Bronzino's potential as court portraitist. Indeed, his summons to the Montefeltro court in 1530 confirms that this was known in Italian court circles a full decade before Cosimo's reign began.

Maria as Exemplar of Widowhood, and
Pontormo's *Maria Salviati with Giulia de' Medici*

Maria's decorum in portraits after 1526, when she became forever a paradigm of decorous widowhood, is a startling foil to the seigniorial splendour of the vivacious young wife and progenitor of rank in the *Maria Salviati with a Lapdog*. It sharply contrasts with Pontormo's matronly portrait of her in middle age now in the Walters Art Museum, Baltimore, which was recorded in the Riccardi inventory in 1612 as showing her in the company of *'una puttina'* – a little girl. The two *Maria* panels were then linked – both were displayed with other Medici portraits in the courtyard lunettes of the casino of Riccardo Riccardi's Florentine estate, Valfonda.[53]

In spite of Maria's undisputed identity in it, the Baltimore double portrait is a contentious one today. The quest for clarification of the identity of the child has raised complex issues of sex, race, rank, setting, and circumstances – including the portrait's date. Its examination here leads to revelations about Cosimo's struggle for control of Florence and his dependence on Maria's image for full credibility in the political arena.

Maria, white-faced and large-eyed in all her portraits, was seen increasingly to resemble her uncle, Pope Leo X.[54] The resemblance is confirmed in Vasari's matching tondo portrait of her in short-bust format on the ceiling of the Sala di Giovanni delle Bande Nere in the Palazzo Vecchio (fig. 4).[55] Because the tondo was commissioned by Cosimo and painted in 1556 in a room that commemorates his father, Maria's identity there is not disputed.[56] Furthermore, Vasari features it in his *Ragionamenti*, begun in 1558, in his account of Francesco de' Medici's 'tour' of the decorative cycle in the room, where he has the prince 'recognize' his grandmother on sight.[57]

In his *Zibaldone*, Vasari also listed portraits in the room and the locations of paintings that had been their source, including one of 'La Sig[no]ra Maria ... in guardaroba.'[58] The ceiling tondo was painted about fourteen years after Maria's death in 1543, but there was evidently a reliable likeness of her in Cosimo's collections, and Vasari did not have to depend on her death mask.[59] In the tondo, her demeanour is consistent with a contemporary courtier's displeasure in the widowed Maria's disinterest in appearances amid the sumptuous trappings of Cosimo and Eleonora's new Medici court in 1541: 'The Signora Maria has her rooms adorned with fair blue leather hangings with only a touch of gold, and a bed of black taffeta. She usually wears bombazine with coarse black silk, and often of plain camlet without a pattern, and it is heavy, as if of wool, and by no means contents me.'[60] It is clear that even for a widow in middle age, and in failing health at this time, her dowdiness and lack of grandeur were considered by some to be unusual, even unseemly, for her rank and position as the duke's mother. Her sumptuous apartments in the Palazzo Vecchio were unoccupied for most of the year, as she preferred to reside at her old home, the country villa at Castello.[61]

Other securely identified posthumous portraits, not all on panel, are important to this study in assessing Maria's decorum. She appears in Vasari's *Marriage of Catherine de' Medici to Henry of Valois* in a ceiling cove in the Sala di Clemente VII (1556–9), a scene commemorating her official role as witness at the marriage in Marseilles in 1533 with Pope Clement VII, her kinsman, officiating, when she was thirty-four. She is opaquely veiled to the waist in white, an austere figure in contrast to the sumptuous finery around her. (Jacopo da Empoli repeated the scene in 1600, showing Maria heavily veiled in black, to the bride's right.)[62] In a double portrait, *Maria Salviati with Giovanni delle Bande Nere* (fig. 5), Maria is posed three-quarter face, copiously veiled and ravaged by illness and age.[63] It was painted by Battista Naldini in 1585–6 as part of the Serie Aulica.[64] From her appearance, this portrait is probably based on her death mask.

The tiny shoulder-length portrait in the Ambras series in Vienna (fig. 7), inscribed 'MARIA SALLVIATTI' (*sic*), was painted in 1587.[65] It is similar to the insert in Naldini's double portrait, but Maria's face is tilted downwards. As in all of these portrayals made after 1526, she is invariably heavily veiled and completely unadorned.

In 1761 Francesco Allegrini made one hundred engraved portraits of the Medici in chronological order, among them a *Maria Salviati* (fig. 8), identified by the inscription 'MARIA IACOBI SALVIATI ET LUCRETIAE MEDICES FILIA IONNIS MED. COGNOMEN. INVICTI. UXOR I.S[occhi] del F.A[llegrini]. sc. Ex. Mus. Ducis. Salviati.' Evidently based on the *Maria* in the Baltimore portrait discussed below, but showing her older, and dressed in religious habit, it excluded the child, and includes the motto 'JAMAIS AUTRE' on a scroll beneath her image.[66] It is the last of the posthumous portraits of Maria, and is especially valuable in this study for reference to its inscriptions and *imprese*.[67]

This short survey of Maria's portraits confirms that her decorum as a widow is consistent with codes set forth in books of manners, and is made evident in Pontormo's securely identified *Maria Salviati with a Child* [*Giulia de' Medici*] (pl. 2). But two notable problems concern the sex and identification of the child. In spite of the child being recorded as a girl ('una puttina') in the 1612 Riccardi inventory entry for the panel, scholars have persistently identified it as 'Cosimo' since 1940; to add to this complication, the child's image had mysteriously been painted out at some moment between the 1612 Riccardi record and 1902, when the panel was purchased by the Walters Art Museum, Baltimore.[68] At this juncture, it is useful to discuss art-historical contexts proposed for known portraits of Maria in order to clarify the Baltimore panel's relation to Florentine history and its place within those contexts.

Maria had been widowed for just over ten years when Cosimo was elected Duke of Florence in 1537. As noted, the seventeen-year-old duke was no amateur propagandist when he promoted the legitimacy of his sudden succession: according to Vasari, he routed dissenters at the Battle of Montemurlo on 1 August 1537 and, peace established, promptly commissioned Pontormo's frescoes at Castello. There Niccolò Tribolo's garden program promoted him in sculpture both as a new Augustus and as Apollo.[69] Whether the *Maria* portrait mentioned by Vasari in association with the now-lost Castello frescoes was on panel or simply frescoed has never been established.[70] Some scholars do believe that the *Maria Salviati with a Child* is tied to that commission.[71] As the subjects' decorum in this portrait is explored – notably the sex of the child and contexts for its pairing with Maria – other Pontormo Medicean portraits made in the decade before and after Cosimo's accession are reassessed. New dates and identities, and one re-attribution, will be proposed for some of these.

The Baltimore portrait shows Maria pale, serious, unadorned, and heavily veiled – a paradigm of decorous mourning.[72] She shelters a young child and holds in her right hand a now undecipherable medallion. Her pose, the overall dark scheme with touches of pink and soft violet, the clasp of their hands, and a slight air of tremulousness in the child's expression make this an affective grouping. Attribution to Pontormo has been almost universally accepted, and Maria's identity has been secure since 1940.[73] But which Pontormo panel is this? If it is, as a few scholars have proposed, the 1537 Castello work referred to by Vasari, it would be the first recorded, official portrait of Maria as mother of the new duke.[74] Maria's appearance in the portrait is not wholly incongruous with this assumption: she was thirty-eight at the time of Cosimo's accession. (She died in 1543 at the age of forty-four.)[75] Other scholars take the child's tender age – believing it to be Cosimo, in spite of the inventory reference to a girl – and Maria's evident widowhood into account to arrive at a date very late in 1526, the earliest moment of her widowhood.[76] The child seems much younger than almost eight, however, the age when Cosimo was orphaned, leading a few scholars to maintain that this must be Cosimo in a retrospective commission, executed after his accession in 1537 or after Maria's death in 1543 to commemorate her guiding role in his life.[77]

The portrait has a remarkable art-historical status. Previously in the Riccardi collection, it was acquired by the Walters Art Museum, Baltimore, in 1902. Maria's identity was secured by Edward King in 1940, when he matched her image to Vasari's ceiling roundel of Maria (fig. 4) in the Sala Giovanni delle Bande Nere of the Palazzo Vecchio, painted in 1556, where Vasari's program extols Cosimo's genealogy. King believed that the panel had been the source for the Palazzo Vecchio tondo. When the panel was X-rayed in 1937, the unsuspected presence of the child was revealed under an overlayer of dark paint in the lower section. It was restored to disclose the child. King proposed its identity as Cosimo, Maria's only child, in 1940.[78] Privately, however, the famed connoisseur Bernard Berenson caustically commented in 1941 that 'the prodigiously learned gentleman who wrote on the Pontormo portrait makes a serious mistake in the sex of the child. This is certainly a girl and therefore not the *boy* destined to become Cosimo I.'[79] Carlo Gamba, too, noticed the child's girlish appearance but settled on its identity as Cosimo.[80]

Berenson's comment was prophetic. Almost two decades later, in 1959, Keutner announced his discovery of the 1612 Riccardi inventory record of Pontormo's portrait with its unequivocal entry for the child as a little girl, or a baby girl ('una puttina').[81] This reference to a little girl was largely ignored in favour of Cosimo. Freedberg also believed the child to be a girl, but reluctantly followed suit.[82] Luciano Berti allowed for two decades that the child may be a girl, lately opted for 'Cosimo,' but summarized scholarly unease that the sex and identity of the child might still be unresolved.[83] With the exception of Pontormo scholars Berti and Cropper, many scholars had resigned themselves to believe that the inventory record was an error and that portrayal of any child with Maria other than her only child, Cosimo, was 'inconceivable.'[84]

The panel itself, however, has internal evidence of demonstrable inconsistencies in this assumption. As noted, a matronly Maria is in widow's weeds, but the child looks too young to be nearly eight, Cosimo's age on his father's death. Artistic convention in Vasari's Florence was to idealize, not to prematurely age a female sitter.[85] It is all the more extraordinary that Pontormo would not have portrayed Maria in her twenties, as she would have been then, when a direct source for her appearance as a young woman was available to him. Bronzino's preparatory drawing for a portrait (Uffizi 6680F), almost universally identified as Maria, shows her hardly past her mid-twenties (fig. 6). Its probable outcome was the Frankfurt portrait (pl. 1).[86] To help assess Maria's age in the Baltimore portrait, it is logical to take into account, too, a very late Pontormo drawing of her in the Uffizi (fig. 9), and posthumous portraits derived from the death mask made by Santi Buglioni on the day she died, 12 December 1543.[87] In sum, the Baltimore *Maria* looks far older than the youthful Bronzino drawing (fig. 6), but somewhat younger than in Pontormo's very late drawing (fig. 9), probably a posthumous portrayal derived from the death mask. From this comparison, it seems that a date in the late-1530s – before her decline in health after 1540 – would be appropriate for the *Portrait of Maria Salviati with a Child* in Baltimore.

Vasari leads us to believe that his identical tondo portrait in the Sala di Giovanni delle Bande Nere in the Palazzo Vecchio (fig. 4), which depends on the Baltimore *Maria* or an identical prototype, does depict Maria as she appeared in life and in her rank as mother of the duke, that is, between Cosimo's accession, 1537, and her death in 1543. Casting himself in his *Ragionamenti* dialogue with Cosimo's heir, Francesco, he instructs the boy on his Medici ancestry as they tour Vasari's complex fresco cycles in the Palazzo Vecchio. Francesco, born in 1541, unhesitatingly 'recognizes' his grandmother on sight:

P.[Prince Francesco]   The division of this vault is likewise magnificent, as much as those we have just seen, and in particular you have placed very well these arms of the Medici and Salviati; why have you placed the arms of the house of Sforza facing these?

G.[Giorgio Vasari]   Because Giovanni, [the] father of Lord Giovanni had for his wife Caterina Sforza, as you know, and I have painted these trophies to beautify and greatly embellish this room.

P.   Well done; tell me about these *tondi* supported by putti in low relief under these stories, where there are those portraits, and amongst others in this one I think I see Giovanni di Pierfrancesco de' Medici, father of Lord Giovanni.

G.   Your Excellency has recognized him very well, and this other one facing here is the Lord Giovanni.

P.   I recognize him myself, as in the other I can recognize the Lady Maria, daughter of Jacopo Salviati, mother of the duke my lord: but in this last I cannot recognize that youth.

G.   That is Lord Cosimo, Your Excellency's father and son of Lord Giovanni, portrayed in fact six years before he became Duke.[88]

This last portrait is a copy of Ridolfo Ghirlandaio's *Cosimo de' Medici at Age Twelve*, 1531 (fig. 10). Pontormo's profile portrait of 1537 is the source for another portrait of Cosimo as a youth in this setting.[89] Oddly, the Baltimore child is nowhere to be found in this cycle, nor does it appear in any of the multiple sets of Medici family portraits, commissioned by Cosimo, which include Medici children from babyhood to adolescence.[90]

The omission is telling. From the outset of his accession, Cosimo never missed an opportunity to glorify his status. Bearing this in mind, the child's timorous demeanour is of great interest. It is hard to imagine this child serving as a model for a putative prince and ruler in a room designed to eulogize Cosimo's childhood and genealogy. Furthermore, the Baltimore child is too puny to have been almost eight. Its nondescript costume is at odds, too, with the mythology surrounding Cosimo, whose biographer, Mannucci, describes him as a boy persistently 'clad like a cavalier and seeming such in his actions.'[91] Valour was prophesied for him by his godfather and great-uncle, Pope Leo X, on his birth, and honours reflecting his father's bravery and military prowess were showered on the boy on his father's death in expectation that he had inherited Giovanni's greatness.[92] By 1532, at twelve, he was so dedicated to wearing military costume that Clement VII, irritated by his martial dress and demeanour, ordered him to abandon it during a boyhood visit to Rome. (Clement was then grooming his own illegitimate son, Alessandro, as future leader of Florence.) In 1534, the fifteen-year-old Cosimo defiantly marked Clement's death by a return to his military dress and, one assumes, overt evocation of his heroic father.[93] In Bronzino's state portrait circa 1543–4 (pl. 3), Cosimo wears armour similar to Giovanni's and embodies his image, as remarked on by Paolo Giovio.[94]

Artistic promotion of Cosimo's single-mindedness and *virtù* in childhood is expressed in his portrait by Ridolfo Ghirlandaio of 1531 (fig. 10), painted in the year when Alessandro became duke and was likely to produce heirs, but Ghirlandaio's unabashed gaze for the lofty boy indicates that Cosimo is a force to be reckoned with.[95] He is sumptuously dressed in velvet embroidered with an overlapping scallop pattern reminiscent of plate armour, suggesting a man of action. The luxurious red velvet and white-fur lining would be appropriate for a potential ruler. Balancing the soldierly symbolism, his book documents his humanist education.[96] Cosimo leans easily against a pilaster, symbol of fortitude, fulfilling an ideal Castiglionesque decorum, a *sprezzatura* that augments the courage of a potential man of arms. The pilaster may also be a veiled reference to the new Medici *principato* under Charles V's protection, one of whose *imprese* showed the eagle between two pillars.[97]

Cosimo's face in the Ghirlandaio panel, as later described by Benedetto Varchi, is inscrutable – 'né lieto, né mesto' (neither happy nor sad).[98] This reflects a stoicism patterned, according to his contemporaries, on that of his father.[99] In contrast, the face of the child in the Baltimore panel is 'indecorously' anxious in expression.[100] Such lack of mettle is difficult to justify in any retrospective portrayal of Cosimo after his succession, but especially so in a double portrait with his mother. Contemporaries applaud Maria's role in forming his stoic, brave, and urbane character. Also, Mannucci, Cosimo's official biographer, refutes any notion of his seclusion, crediting Maria for his exposure in influential places, and for directing her son's education in Latin and Greek.[101] Mannucci also records her insistence that he be widely read in the Tuscan language and its history, which the boy did 'con ardore a gli studi delle lettere.' Maria moved him to Venice soon after her widowhood – the earliest date that can be proposed for the Baltimore portrait – exposing him for two years to powerful European interests. Fêted as Giovanni's son, the boy was officially received by the doge, the papal legate and the Venetian council, and presented to the French and English ambassadors.[102] In Bologna he witnessed Clement's historic coronation of the Hapsburg emperor, Charles V, in 1530.[103] When the frugal Maria hesitated to attend Caterina de' Medici's marriage to the dauphin in Marseilles in 1533 because of her reluctance to make inroads into Cosimo's patrimony to dress herself for the occasion, her father, Jacopo Salviati, adamantly urged her not to forego the opportunity to keep Cosimo at the forefront of European interests.[104]

This boy's childhood was not sheltered. Records of martial mythology surrounding him are evident in Ghirlandaio's 1531 portrait of the young Medici scion, confirming the pose, dress, decorum and expression of the Baltimore child to be incongruous with the historic facts. If the Baltimore portrait's conflicting late age for Maria and too-childish appearance for 'Cosimo' are to be explained by retrospective ducal commission, about 1537–43, it is illogical to assume that a propagandistic duke would have himself portrayed in childhood as undersized, timid, sheltered, poorly dressed, or anxious.

The relationship of mother to child is at odds, too, with contemporary pedagogy. Cosimo was diligently groomed for greatness by his mother, to whom he wrote about a year before Ghirlandaio portrayed him, 'Your words are my precept and law.'[105] The sheltering relationship between Maria and the anxious, dependent child conflicts with Vives's directives to widows with young sons, that they be raised stoically.[106] On Cosimo's birth, Leo X, and on his father's death, Clement VII, each promoted this staunch temperament for Giovanni and Maria's child.[107] Varchi lauded his stoicism, as did historians. Charles V implicitly expressed the expectation that Cosimo would follow his father's brave course.[108]

Maria's own resoluteness was extraordinary. She declared herself unflinching in the face of any dangers to which he would be exposed, even if it were a matter of life or death for him. (Indomitable Medici widowhood was already mythologized: the heroic challenge of her redoubtable mother-in-law Caterina Sforza [1462–1509] to Alexander VI Borgia's troops is recorded.)[109] Finally, the stoic calibre of the boy and his mother, and reflections of her diligent response to contemporary urgings on the strict upbringing of noble, orphaned sons are enshrined in Diego di Sandoval's elegy for Maria's obsequies in 1543.[110]

In sum, these consistent references to Cosimo's destiny and his valour occur from his birth until Maria's death, and include descriptions of his earliest years. *Any* official portrayal of Maria with Cosimo as a child, whether painted circa 1526, 1537, or after Maria's death, should presage or emulate Ghirlandaio's staunch boy, confirm Cosimo's role as legitimate scion and guardian of his father's fame, and applaud Maria's formative influence on him.

Precedents for dynastic portraits in this tradition existed in Italy. In portraits of Prince Guidobaldo da Montefeltro with his father executed in the 1470s in Urbino, the tiny child is given regal bearing.[111] In one, Guidobaldo's jewel-encrusted costume is in effect a robe of state. He holds a sceptre, symbol of rule, and is tellingly positioned beneath the tiara of Urbino and at the knee of his armoured father, knight and humanist, surrounded by the accoutrements of war. The second portrait places them with scholars, orators, and courtiers. These, and other scion portraits, supply contexts for the physical and intellectual commitment of a prince to his destiny.[112] Guidobaldo's portrayal and decorum emphasize his resemblance to his father, his conscious modelling on him, his princely responsibility to rule, and his integration into humanist affairs of the court in progress around him.[113]

Apparently anxious to offset any suggestion that the death of Giovanni delle Bande Nere left Cosimo bereft of such an exemplar, contemporary chroniclers cast Maria as her husband's surrogate. Giovanbattista Adriani eulogized her as both father and mother to Cosimo ('a cui ella era stata invece di padre, di madre' – 'to whom she had indeed been a father and a mother'):

> inasmuch as the Lady Maria mother of the Duke ... passed to a better place, leaving the name of a good and valorous woman, who being left a widow of Lord Giovanni de' Medici in the flower of her youth with one very small son, toiled through much trouble, maintained the good reputation of the house [of Medici] and her rank with dignity, and raised her son in such a way that much hope was placed in him and, the City being without a Prince, those citizens who had to decide [what to do] resorted to him. Very sad was the Duke on her death, since she had been for him both father and mother and every other beloved person, he not having known anyone else who had benefited him or taken care of him. All the people grieved because she was very humane and used to help all the needy and afflicted.[114]

On Maria's death, Sandoval recalled her nurturing of stoic virtues in Cosimo. Severance of their deep bond was now a potential threat to his fortitude, one that he must overcome:

> And you, great Cosimo, to whom virtue and fortune
> Gave reign over the City that restraint
> Over magnanimous Tuscans let slip and tighten,
> You could never weep to the full [for]
> Such a great Mother, as none was ever to be seen
> Under the moon. I will not say to what extent
> Your grief pushes you to be so sad.
> She being happy imparts eternal bliss in her,
> I will not say that this should make you happy,
> But it may appease in part
> The despondency that the weak flesh
> Shares with the aching heart.[115]

Maria did instil in Cosimo independence and good governance, a pedagogy implicit in scion portraits, and his fortitude and stoicism are traced to Maria in these elegies. Why then is her decorum so relaxed, sheltering, and merely affectionate in the Baltimore panel? Why is the child seemingly anxious and inattentive? Above all, why does this child not resemble Ghirlandaio's Cosimo or his demeanour? Observing convention, Adriani had especially lauded Maria's *youthful* courage in raising him with such dignity when a young widow, and beauty in a widow was not at odds with the widowly decorum and pedagogy described.[116] Pontormo had no reason to depict her aged by at least ten years past the time when

Cosimo was just past infancy, as the Baltimore child appears to be. It must be concluded that doubts raised about the child's documented sex as a girl and anomalies of decorum for it as a prince deserve better than tacit acceptance of King's proposal in 1940 that Maria could only be portrayed with Cosimo.[117]

Mistaken identities are to be expected for portraits at such a great divide in time. A Riccardi entry for Pontormo's *Halberdier* mistakenly identified the subject as Cosimo, but he has been convincingly identified as Francesco Guardi.[118] Still, the decorum in Guardi's case nicely expresses the martial mythology ascribed to Cosimo, and there was no confusion about sex or significant inconsistencies of age. Logic suggests that the 1612 Riccardi description of the child in the Baltimore portrait is hardly spurious, however. When the Baltimore panel was recorded in the Riccardi inventory, Cosimo's son, Grand Duke Ferdinando, was recently deceased and Medici power at its height.[119] A portrait of the first Grand Duke of Tuscany as a child would have been of great consequence, but the Riccardi entry recorded unequivocally that Maria is shown with 'una puttina.' Further, at some time before the panel's acquisition by the Walters Art Museum, the child was completely painted out, leaving only Maria visible. Possibly the Riccardi, knowing the child was *not* Cosimo, obliterated her image to concentrate attention on the mother of the duke. Another possibility is that the Riccardi did know the child's identity and that she had become historically unimportant, or even a *persona non grata* – an obliteration that would be a classic case of *damnatio memoriae*. Or, perhaps the defacement was later effected to make the panel more saleable – on its acqusition in 1902 the single figure was identified as the famed, childless poet Vittoria Colonna (1492–1547).[120] The child's identity may supply the answer.

First, the pictorial evidence supports the inventory record that this is a girl. Her hair is coiffed exactly as Maria's, the outlines of which show beneath her veil. Tightly curled at the forehead and parted in the middle, the little girl's reddish curls are gathered into a smooth, halo-like *rouleau* around the back of her skull and possibly held in a net to keep them in place. It is a coiffure that can only be dressed with hair several inches long, and contemporary portraits of young boys by Titian and Parmigianino show them all close-cropped. Cosimo's dark hair is cropped in Ghirlandaio's portrait of him at age twelve (fig. 10).[121] The Baltimore child's hairstyle was popular during the 1530s, 1540s, and later for Florentine women. It imitates that of Bronzino's *Lucrezia Panciatichi* of about 1540. Further, his *Laura Battiferri* of around 1560 shows such a coiffure in profile.[122]

Above all, Ghirlandaio's *Cosimo* at age twelve bears no resemblance to the red-haired Baltimore child, with its round, full, almost pouting lips and a markedly round nose. That Cosimo is dark-haired, has a long nose, a short upper lip, and lips especially thin and drawn out by comparison. These characteristics are still marked in Bronzino's *Portrait of Cosimo in Armour*. The Baltimore child cannot be the boy Cosimo as he was a few years before Ghirlandaio portrayed him. It appears to be a girl, just as the Riccardi inventory recorded.

Who is the child? Several girls in Maria's circle had been entertained as possible contenders, but were usually dismissed as unlikely partners for the duke's mother: Giulia, the late Duke Alessandro's illegitimate daughter, or any of her Salviati nieces, who were frequent visitors to Maria's villa: Cassandra, Francesca, and their unidentified sister. Other illegitimate daughters of Alessandro were associated with her, too.[123] Cosimo's daughters may readily be eliminated by age and by comparing Bronzino's portraits of them. Bia, illegitimate, was born before Cosimo's marriage in 1539 and died in 1542; she had very straight, reddish-blond hair (pl. 6).[124] Maria, born in 1540, had light, grey-blue eyes (pl. 7).[125] Isabella, blond with dark eyes, born 1542, was in early infancy when Maria Salviati died. The child is not dark-haired, dark-eyed Lucrezia (pl. 10), born after Maria's death.

If the Baltimore portrait was commissioned around 1537, then this child, who appears to be about four years old, would have been born about 1533 to 1534 and fathered when Cosimo was around fourteen. But contemporary sources mention only the blonde Bia in this context, who is recorded as being in the ducal nursery and under Maria's care in 1541.[126]

There was, as already noted, another Medici girl in Maria's direct charge – Cosimo's ward, Giulia. Giulia's father was the recently murdered Duke Alessandro, and her brother Giulio was also Cosimo's ward.[127] These namesakes of Alessandro's father, Pope Clement VII – formerly Giulio de' Medici – had been promoted by Clement as potential Medici heirs.[128] For a brief moment of history, they were extremely significant in Cosimo's life, and until well into their maturity they were intimately linked to the ducal court and Cosimo's good offices. Their story has been almost forgotten over four centuries.

Benedetto Varchi records that in 1537, Cardinal Innocenzo Cibo, the late Pope Clement's powerful apostolic legate to Florence, proposed four-year-old Giulio as successor to the child's murdered father, Alessandro. When Cosimo was the unanimous choice of Florentine senators, Cibo insisted that the new duke agree to avenge Alessandro's death and also 'see that Signor Giulio and the Signora Giulia were well treated.'[129] Contemporaries chronicle that Cosimo responded to this demand in good faith. Referring to Cibo's efforts in 1539 to discredit Cosimo's guardianship of the child, Adriani commented in 1583: '[T]he Duke had always loved the Lord Giulio and had in spirit kept him honoured according to his rank, as he subsequently ever would do; of this Giulio himself may testify.'[130] Court documents and Maria's letters report on Giulia's progress from this time until Maria's death in 1543.[131] A private letter dated 1541 from Cibo's sister Caterina to her sister Eleonora Gonzaga, Duchess of Urbino, details the luxury of the Florentine court and the full integration there of Cosimo's and Alessandro's children, natural and legitimate: 'They all live in great pomp ... The children have their rooms hung with gold-stamped leather and all, both legitimate and bastards are in the care of Signora Maria ... Firenze, July 8th, 1541.'[132] The recent move in 1540 from the Palazzo Medici to the former Republican centre of government, the Palazzo della Signoria (the Palazzo 'Vecchio,' or 'old' palace), has been recognized as the defining moment of the birth of the *Principato*, and Caterina Cibo's comment implicitly expresses the demand to conform to the princely ideals of magnificence.[133] Evidently, the luxury in which the children lived was balanced by Maria's dedication and tenderness, as recorded by major-domo Pierfrancesco Riccio on 4 February 1542: 'The Lady Maria with these young gentlefolk (God's gift) are very well, Bia has a fever, and Giulia is in good health.' ('La Sig.na Maria con questi Sig.ni Figli [grazia di Dio] e di bonissimo essere, la Bia ha la sua febretta, et la Julia sta bene.')

Tragically, Bia, about seven, died shortly thereafter. She was buried in San Lorenzo on 1 March 1542.[134]

After Maria's death in 1543, Cosimo and Eleonora continued as guardians to Alessandro's children into their adulthood, and court rolls confirm that from the early years of their marriage, Giulia was integrated with their children as part of the ducal family. She and Giulio appear to have been well loved.[135] In 1550 Cosimo ennobled her by arranging her marriage to Francesco Cantelmo, Lord of Abruzzi, and provided her with a generous dowry of twenty-five thousand *scudi* – almost nine million U.S. dollars in equivalent value today.[136] If her age at marriage was typical – about fifteen or sixteen – she was younger than Giulio (born 1533), and was born probably around 1534–5. Perhaps not coincidentally, two Florentine Baptistery entries found by Sabine Eiche appear to support the linkage of the two children, and their dates of birth: a 'Giulio Giovanbattista Romolo' is recorded for 5 December 1533; a 'Giulia Romola,' father unknown, was baptized on 5 November 1535. The name 'Romolo/Romola' may be significant: Romulus, mythical founder of Rome, carried connotations of dynastic continuity in the Medici orbit; the name was given also to Cosimo and Eleonora's second daughter, Isabella, in 1542.[137]

Giulio's rank as pretender to the Medici ducal succession did not end with Cosimo's election. Until Francesco's birth on 25 March 1541, he was the only male other than Cosimo who had any claim to the succession. (His illegitimacy in this respect will be discussed later.) No securely identified portrait of Giulio has come to light, and my 1992 proposal that the long-debated *Alessandro as a Boy / Portrait of a Medici Youth / Giuliano de' Medici / Portrait of a Youth in a Pink Cloak* in Lucca might be Giulio must be abandoned.[138]

Taking Giulia's probable birthdate, 1535, and her age in the Baltimore portrait, about four or five years, 1539–40 would be an appropriate date for the panel. Maria would have been close to forty then, and still in good health. Giulia was at that time in her charge.

Giulia was described in a detailed Medici history covering the years up to Francesco's death in 1587 as 'the living image of her father,' which is borne out in figs. 11, 12, and 13.[139] The roundness and set of his eyes, his round, full lips, tightly curled hair, and even the fold in the skin around his neck are poignantly replicated on the Baltimore *puttina*. Alessandro was believed to have been born in 1511 to Giulio de' Medici (later Pope Clement) and a servant or Moorish slave, 'Simunetta,' in Alfonsina Medici's house in Rome. A letter addressing him in 1529 as 'Alessandro Figliuolo carissimo,' begging his help because of her destitution testifies to his maternity. Overtones of implicit racism in Ceccherelli and Ammirato's comments may lend support to records citing Simunetta's ancestry as Moorish, but Alessandro's nickname, 'il Moro' may not prove this. Slavery had existed for some time in Italy, but descriptions of any unique personal appearance could in any event usefully identify his children's inherited physiognomy.[140]

Familial resemblance of Giulia (fig. 13) to her father – a canon promoting ancestry in portraiture of the period – is evident from several portraits, notably Pontormo's *Alessandro de' Medici* in Philadelphia (fig. 11), a bust-length version in Chicago, and a related Uffizi miniature (fig. 12 and pl. 8).[141] The Philadelphia version may even provide a context for the artist's *Maria Salviati with Giulia* (pl. 2).

Giulio and his sister were apparently named for Alessandro's father, Giulio, who died on 15 September 1534. Given the linkage of the children's names, it may be assumed that Giulio's mother, often recorded as a member of the powerful Malaspina family, was Giulia's mother too.[142] Giulia was probably born around 1534–5, precisely the period when, according to Vasari, Pontormo's Philadelphia portrait was commissioned as a gift to Taddea Malaspina, 'sorella della marquesa di Massa.' Alessandro, if dressed in mourning for his late father, Pope Clement, was portrayed soon after September 1534. He is shown drawing a female profile *all'antica* in silverpoint – epitomizing him as the essential Castiglionesque courtier. Evidently, the female head is linked to Taddea.[143] The duke frequented the extremely wealthy and emancipated Malaspina-Cibo household, then installed in the Palazzo Pazzi, according to the contemporary historian Bernardo Segni. His attentions were directed at the young widow from the early 1530s until his murder in 1537, and the Palazzo served as an unofficial court. Pontormo was a member of this circle.[144] Significantly, Taddea's *Alessandro* has been seen as 'dongiovannesco' in expression and detail.[145]

Later circumstances, too, tend to confirm that Taddea was the mother of Giulio, aged four when Alessandro died, and Giulia, then about one. As adults, Alessandro's children seem to have had considerable emotional attachment to the Philadelphia *Alessandro*. Decades after its execution, in 1568, Cosimo initiated a search for it and offered a reward for its recovery. According to Alessandro's former courtier, Constantino Ansoldo, it was through 'Julia, daughter of Taddea Malaspina' that the painting was finally found in the possession of the late Taddea's nephew and heir, Alberico Cibo. Ansoldo, Giulio's former tutor, then sought Giulio's help to recover it. A trusted dependent of Cosimo's, Giulio procrastinated and eventually passed a poor copy to Ansoldo in 1571, presumably to ensure that the original portrait of his father remained in his mother's family.[146] His risky subterfuge and Giulia's silence on Alberico's ownership of the painting when the duke sought its whereabouts strongly suggest their mutual interest in keeping the panel given to Taddea by Alessandro with their maternal relatives. Besides, Giulio's association with his Malaspina-Cibo relatives began at birth: until the time of Alessandro's murder, the boy had been under the guardianship of Taddea's brother-in-law, Cardinal Innocenzo Cibo, in Massa.[147] All of these circumstances tend to confirm that Taddea, Cibo's relative, was Giulio's mother.

The Malaspina-Cibo family had ties to the Emperor Charles V and to Clement's papacy, and Cibo's promotion of Giulio in 1537 arose from ambition and from strong ties of ancestry that he held with the two children. Innocenzo (1491–1550) was a direct descendant of Cosimo the Elder; his mother, Maddalena, was daughter of Lorenzo the Magnificent. Ties of kinship reinforced his determination: his brother Lorenzo was married to Ricciarda, Taddea's sister.[148] Elected cardinal in 1513 by Leo X – his cousin – Cibo's influence in Medici affairs and in Florentine governance was considerable. As Clement's papal legate he had ruled as regent for Alessandro, and continued to wield power after his accession.[149]

Predictably, Clement had intended that Giulio be Alessandro's successor.[150] He entrusted this task to his apostolic legate, Cibo, to whom the business of state had been largely left by the lax Alessandro.[151] As a seasoned survivor in Medicean political fortunes, Cibo was a formidable opponent to Cosimo. Committed to perpetuating Cosimo the Elder's line, the principal Medici branch to which he, Clement, Alessandro, and now Giulio and Giulia belonged, Cibo was as antagonistic as Clement had been to Cosimo, sole legitimate descendant of the cadet Pierfrancesco branch. As ally to Charles V, Clement had been in a powerful position to eventually legitimize his infant grandson Giulio to succeed Alessandro, but the closeness of Clement and Alessandro's deaths forced Cibo's hand. Giulio, four, and Giulia, then an infant, were thus important pawns in a struggle for power between representatives of each branch of the Medici line at the time when the unmarried Cosimo unexpectedly succeeded their father. Until Cosimo produced heirs – which was not until his son Francesco was born in 1541 – these two children with powerful political connections represented Medici continuity. Cosimo's agreement to keep them by him on achieving his accession was a shrewd political move. It prevented any further split in Florentine political loyalties and promoted his image as conciliator of his family and head of a revitalized, united Medici dynasty.[152] Ironically, as he was unmarried and as yet without legitimate issue, the prospect of legitimising Alessandro's son Giulio – and thus Giulia – to maintain Medici hegemony must have loomed in Cosimo's own mind. It seems that bastards were often considered to be a 'blood bank' in the absence of a legitimate heir. It was a two-edged sword: Giulio might be legitimized, for example, by Emperor Charles V – father-in-law of the late Alessandro, to whom Cosimo now owed allegiance – who was deeply sympathetic to the Malaspina-Cibo family.[153] In these contexts the portrayal of Maria with Giulia carries the moral force of a document proving that Alessandro's children were under Cosimo's benevolent guardianship, in accordance with his promise to Cibo and the Florentine senate.

Let us now return to Pontormo's lovely portrait, which Giulia's age dates to within two or three years of Cosimo's accession, about 1539–40. This dating would explain Maria's appearance as a widowed matron of about forty in the role of caretaker of Alessandro's bereaved orphan. The focal point of the composition, the grouping of Maria's and the little child's hands, expresses a deep mutual bond, but here there is a curious tension expressed by the little girl's tremulous, wandering glance. Perhaps this was meant to evoke some trauma resulting from her fractured existence through her infancy. Initially, at about eighteen months, she must have been taken from her mother into Maria's care when Cosimo became her legal ward in 1537. As will shortly be described, she was exiled to seclusion in Naples soon thereafter. Now about four, and returned to Maria's care in Florence, this tiny child had much to dwell on. Her pathetic expression is also particularly appropriate to her status as an orphan in need of protection and, as Cropper's further appraisal of the portrait suggests, her simply swathed, bare shoulders provide a shared femininity with Maria but also accentuate her vulnerability.[154] Indeed, her hand, reaching to Maria's, accords with Juan Vives's pedagogical directive to supply the guidance of an older matron for a newly orphaned child.[155] (Vives's pedagogy on the raising of a Christian woman had achieved pan-European popularity after its appearance in 1523.)

The oddness of the child's costume is a departure from contemporary sixteenth-century clothing for little girls. Her swathed shoulders evoke the classical, Roman portrait bust and, unlike Cosimo's illegitimate daughter Bia (pl. 6), Giulia is portrayed without any jewellery.[156] This could betoken mourning – the lilac hue, as a version of purple, was a colour associated with mourning and with Passiontide. In classical contexts, however, purple had associations with exalted rank, which may be hinted at in Giulia's case. She symbolizes the eponymous 'Giulia' who, as daughter of Caesar Augustus, had become an exemplar in the sixteenth century for little girls because of her legendary virtue and long-held filial obedience in adhering to simplicity of dress and decorum:

> As Isaac did in the sacrifice that his father was obliged to make of him, and as shown also by Giulia, the daughter of Caesar Augustus ... [who, even when] no longer in his jurisdiction but married, having understood that her sumptuous clothes would not have pleased her father, dressed herself in ordinary, modest clothing in order to seem so.[157]

Giulia's own father, Alessandro, was implicitly understood to have died as did Julius Caesar, at the tyrannicidal hand of a friend – a 'Brutus' – for political gain. Typically used for rulers, the honorific 'Caesar' for Alessandro would appear in Paolo Giovio's *Elogia virorum bellica virtute illustrium* under the title of 'ALEXANDER MEDICES FLO. / rentiae princeps.' He is hailed on Tobias Stimmer's engraved portrait in armour as 'Capta ubi Romano Florentia Caesare victus/ ...'[158]

Fusco's *La vedova*, a handbook for widows published in Rome in 1570, proposes laudable responsibilities for them – notably the upbringing of orphaned girls – and its codes of behaviour are full of import for the entire composition of this panel.[159] Maria, tenderly grasping the child's hand and holding a plaque perhaps inscribed with her father, Alessandro's impresa or reference to Cosimo, shelters her. As in Vasari's tondo, she is portrayed here in her official rank as ducal matriarch. Her pose and expression evoke her protectiveness, and perhaps not coincidentally, the portrait of older woman and female child has overtones of contemporary portrayals of St Anne's sympathetic pose with the Virgin as a child.[160] Also, Maria's gesture and the child's tremulous gaze may be an implicit play on Maria's name, Salviati, which resonates with associations of *salvare*, to deliver or rescue.[161]

The direct quotation of this *Maria* in the posthumous tondo in a state room of the Palazzo Vecchio (fig. 4) suggests that an official prototype for Maria was the common source for it and the Baltimore portrait. The commission of such a prototype in the early years of Cosimo's reign, when Maria was his closest adviser and confidant, seems very likely. The import of the Baltimore panel would have carried most weight if an established, official image of Maria, linked to Cosimo's accession and triumph at Montemurlo, was used for the double portrait showing her with Giulia. The lost Pontormo *Maria* recorded by Vasari at Castello would have been a logical model. Painted around 1540, the portrait with Giulia was probably the last portrait of Maria from life, before progressive illness incapacitated her in the early 1540s.[162] The two Uffizi drawings, one youthful and made before 1527 (fig. 6), the other showing her prematurely aged, circa 1543, and probably drawn from her death mask (fig. 9), must be ranked chronologically on either side of the Baltimore panel.[163]

The portrait appears to have no art-historical precedent, but peculiarly pertinent circumstances may have provoked its commission. From 1538, the welfare of

Alessandro's children was the focus of a series of diplomatic crises for Cosimo from which he emerged in triumph. First, he successfully sought imperial help to prevent Margaret of Austria, Alessandro's fifteen-year-old widow and natural daughter of Charles V, from taking Giulio with her to Rome on her marriage to Ottavio Farnese in 1538:

> The Signora Duchessa, it is reported to me, designs to take to Rome the Signor Julio (son of Duke Alessandro of happy memory), as one who has ever had, and has, a singular affection for the boy, due both to the memory of her husband, and to his own gracious disposition. Thus carried away by this affection, she unfortunately does not consider of how great import it is that she should now take him from her house to lodge him in the house of the Farnese, nor what blame and prejudice to my honour and my house would follow on such a decision. Whence it seemed good to say a word concerning this to your Excellency, begging you to consider the importance of the event.[164]

Soon he was incensed by a rumour circulated by papal legate Cibo's cohort that he was plotting to poison the six-year-old. Because of Cibo's ready access to Charles V, Cosimo was compelled to exonerate himself.[165] Cibo's ruse was exposed and, having arranged for Giulio to join his household under Maria's care, the duke then shrewdly 'allowed' Cibo to care for him for a time in Florence to deflect any further rumours of plots to kill him. Finally brought to heel, Cibo retreated to the Malaspina seat at Massa Maritima.[166]

By 1540 new arrangements were also set in motion for Giulia. In January 1540, before Eleonora produced an heir, Giulia was being kept secretly in Naples, Eleonora's former home, the Spanish viceregal base in Italy. Coded messages from the duke's agent in Naples, Pyrro Musipsilo, give account of how the little girl was to be housed and cared for, also confirming that she had been reassured about her temporary removal from Salviati's care. It appears that she was to remain sequestered there, but returned by the end of the year.[167] Possibly Cosimo shortly hoped to settle the question of succession and kept both children out of Florence in the interim. Eleonora presently brought an end to Giulio's status as pretender, giving birth to Francesco on 25 March 1541, less than a year after her daughter, Maria's birth. She produced at least seven more children in the next dozen years.

In these circumstances, this portrait of the duke's mother as protector of Giulia would carry a strong political charge. Maria's appearance and especially Giulia's age both indicate a date around 1540, consonant with a period when Cosimo was consolidating his strength in diplomacy and in dealing with his enemies.[168] The portrayal of Cibo's young kinswoman, Giulia, safely under the protection of his mother documents fulfilment of the young duke's legal obligation as guardian of Alessandro's children. Its dynastic import is inescapable: the new duke controls, nurtures, and represents both branches of the Medici family. The theme echoes Cosimo's personal adoption of the *broncone*, the lopped but revivified laurel bough, to symbolize his claim as sole legitimate Medici successor.[169] As already described, Pontormo had long been acquainted with this imagery: his *salone* fresco at Poggio a Caiano was the first instance where the *broncone* alluded specifically to Cosimo's legitimate right to succeed.[170]

In conclusion, the *Portrait of Maria Salviati with a Child*, here identified as Giulia d'Alessandro de' Medici, is commemorative, not retrospective. The impact of the Baltimore portrait on Cibo and the Malaspina – his sister Caterina, as mentioned, was a strong presence at the Florentine court – must remain in the realm of speculation.[171] The painting also documents Maria's political stature early in Cosimo's reign, when he 'greatly used the counsel of Lady Maria, his mother, who administered his many affairs with authority.'[172] Having acted as his champion in his hour of danger, Maria is portrayed as visible symbol to Florentines of her son's authority and benevolence.[173] The Baltimore *Maria Salviati with Giulia* is a timely document of dynastic, political, and moral suasion.[174] The identity, rank, sex, and age of each are historically accounted for, as is the linkage of widowed Medici exemplar and female orphan.

Alessandro's children were politically eclipsed once Cosimo produced heirs. This child's image would have had no import in the Sala di Giovanni delle Bande Nere or elsewhere in Vasari's later Palazzo Vecchio cycles. There are those who believe, too, that Giulia alienated herself from the duke in the 1560s.[175] This may explain why this portrait of Maria had been passed to the Riccardi by 1612.[176] It is also possible that obliteration of Giulia's image by the Riccardi sometime after 1612 directly responded to a Medici-instituted *damnatio memoriae* of her as a *persona non grata*, or indirectly did so because her identity *had* faded from memory. No one then confused her sex and opted for 'Cosimo.' Even in the twentieth century, her femininity prompted questioning of the notion that only a 'Cosimo' would do. But this always was, and still is, a girl.

The *Portrait of Maria Salviati with a Book*

The majestic decorum, compelling presence and otherworldly aura of the sitter in the Uffizi *Portrait of Maria Salviati with a Book* (fig. 14) has been remarked upon.[177] This identity is widely accepted, but its attribution had been contentious, Berenson's to Pontormo in 1933 being a long-standing topic of debate.[178] With regard to its decorum, this *Maria* is of great interest. Her arresting demeanour contrasts strongly with the Baltimore *Maria*, but dates for the two panels must be close. Scholars never date the Uffizi portrait earlier than 1537, and Maria died in 1543. The Baltimore *Maria with Giulia* has been dated here to 1540, and if the Uffizi *Maria Salviati with a Book* is not posthumous, there would be only two or three years between the two works. Problems with that assumption will be addressed here. What is starkly evident is that this commission commanded a strikingly different artistic response to Maria's decorum in the politically charged Baltimore *Maria with Giulia*.

Of the many scholars who have studied the Uffizi *Maria Salviati with a Book*, only Gamba (1956) and Keutner (1959) disagree on the sitter's identity. Some overpainting, scouring, and damage to the panel then may have contributed to this earlier reticence to name the sitter, but two Uffizi drawings already touched on, each unquestionably a source for the portrait and both almost invariably attributed to Pontormo, are associated with it by most scholars.[179] These were the two drawings chronologically ranked here on either side of the Baltimore *Maria*

Salviati with Giulia. The first, circa 1527, shows a woman not past her twenties (fig. 6). It has been proposed here as an unused preparatory sketch by Bronzino of Maria as a young wife, possibly even 'worked up' for the Frankfurt *Lady in Red / Maria Salviati with a Lapdog* (pl. 1). The other drawing, by Pontormo, shows the same woman at the age of at least forty (fig. 9). Oddly, this last drawing depicts a separate head and torso on one sheet.[180]

There is no reason to doubt the broad scholarly consensus that the Uffizi panel depicts Maria Salviati. Medici historians were confident that this was so, as it was used as a partial source for the Allegrini engraving of 1761 (fig. 8), on which her name is inscribed. Allegrini's *Maria* appears to be a hybrid evolved from selections made from both the Baltimore and Uffizi portraits, or from prototypes of each.[181] Like the Baltimore portrait, the format in Allegrini's engraving is half-length. Whereas Maria's right hand is posed to allow young Giulia to clasp her fingers, in the engraving it is tipped into the foreground with the fingers rather awkwardly severed at the knuckles by the engraved oval 'frame.' Maria's engraved features are also fairly close to the Baltimore version, as are her right arm and the folds of the veil over her right shoulder and arm. The Uffizi *Maria* has, however, supplied the left arm and hand, which in the engraved version holds an open prayer book with trailing fastenings. The pose was altered only slightly to adapt the arm to the oval frame. Allegrini's selections for his Medici series usually have their sources in existing paintings, and it may be concluded that, at least in the eighteenth century, these two portraits were seen as legitimate sources to allow Allegrini to embody Maria's rank and reputation.[182]

The aloofness of the Uffizi *Maria Salviati with a Book* contrasts with the empathy Pontormo created between Maria and the viewer in the *Maria Salviati with Giulia*. Her looming pose, the elongation of her neck, and strong lighting combine to emphasize physical attributes given her by contemporary writers, 'alta di statura, bianca di volto, occhi grossetti' (tall in stature, pale faced, [with] large eyes).[183] Her remote gaze, monumental pose, and erect carriage make for a compelling but distant presence. The tightening of contour, and the abstraction of the forms to a rhomboidal sphere for the head and massive pyramid for her body contribute to this monumentality. Drapery supplies the only background. Here Maria's features have been abstracted, idealized, and shorn of vivacity and reference to age. Contoured beneath her widow's veil, the *balzo* headdress acts as a halo around her head, reinforcing a strong suggestion of sanctification. Her veil emphasizes her eminence as a widow, her demeanour suggests her stalwart nature, and the open book affirms her piety.

Perspective contributes significantly to Maria's dramatic presence here. She looms above the viewer by virtue of the *di sotto in sù* viewpoint and is further distanced by the iconic near-frontality of the pose. In his dialogue on portraiture of 1549, written to expound on Italian principles of portraiture, de Hollanda declares the frontal pose to be rarely used, except when it is deemed advantageous to certain persons.[184] He then describes the particular challenge to the artist of upward perspective. Foreshortened features will be seen from below, making the nostrils, chin, and neck 'very difficult, but noble': [T]here are other modes of painting from life besides the frontal, profile, and three-quarter views, modes known as *recursa-*

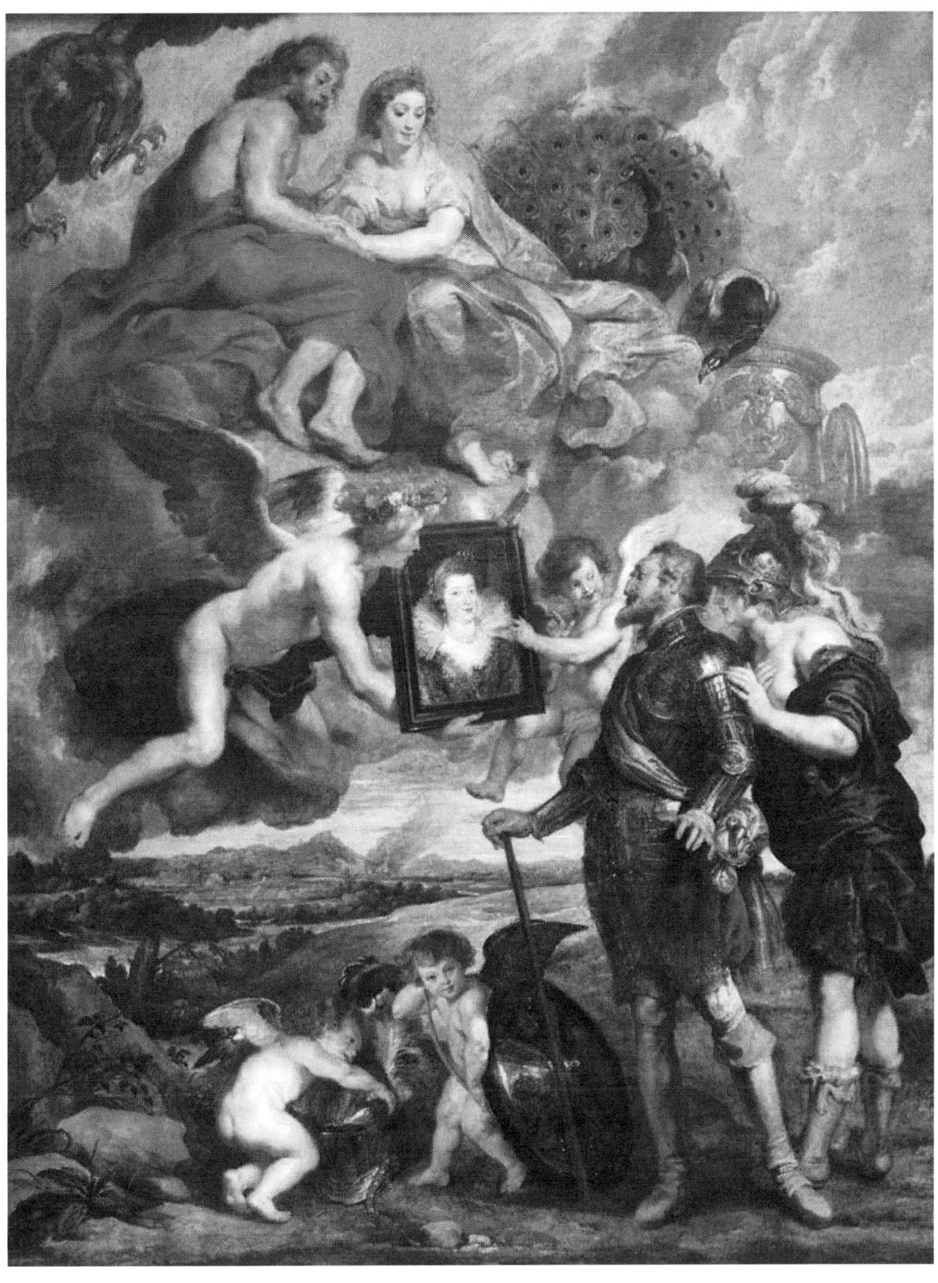

Figure 1 Peter Paul Rubens, *The Presentation of the Portrait of Maria de' Medici to Henry IV*, circa 1623. Oil on canvas, 394 × 295 cm. Paris, Musée du Louvre.

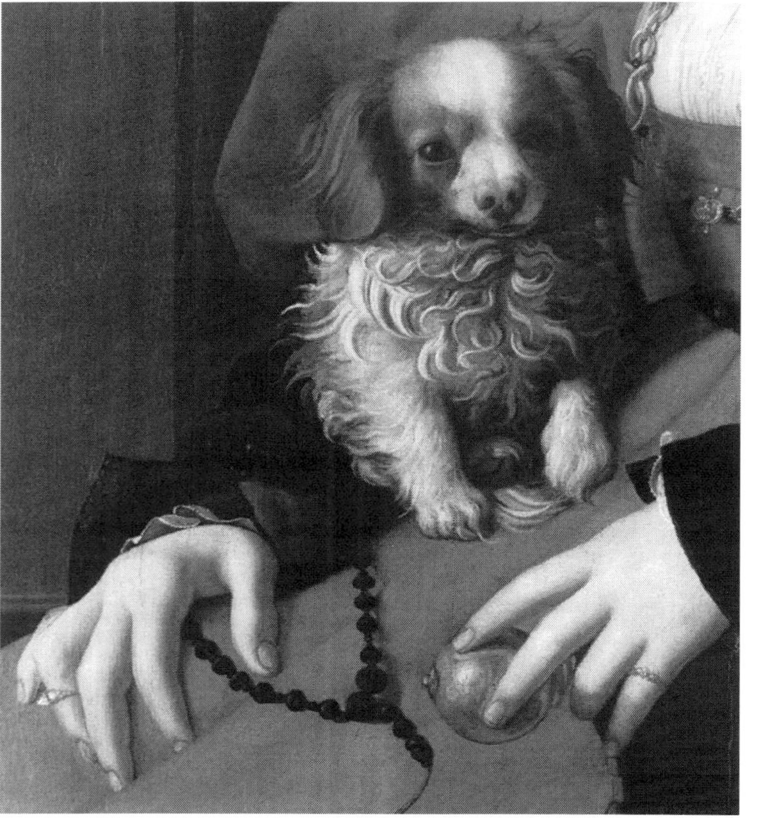

Figure 2 Agnolo Bronzino, *Lady in Red/Lady with a Lapdog* (here identified as Maria Salviati), detail of plate 1.

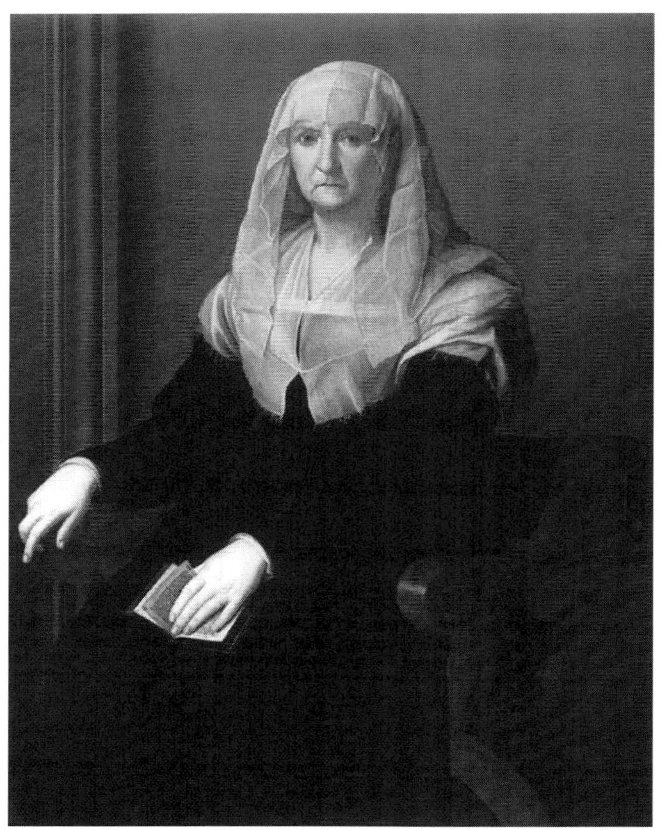

Figure 3 Agnolo Bronzino, *Elderly Lady*, circa 1540. Oil on panel, 127 × 100 cm. Fine Arts Museums of San Francisco. Gift of Mr Samuel H. Kress.

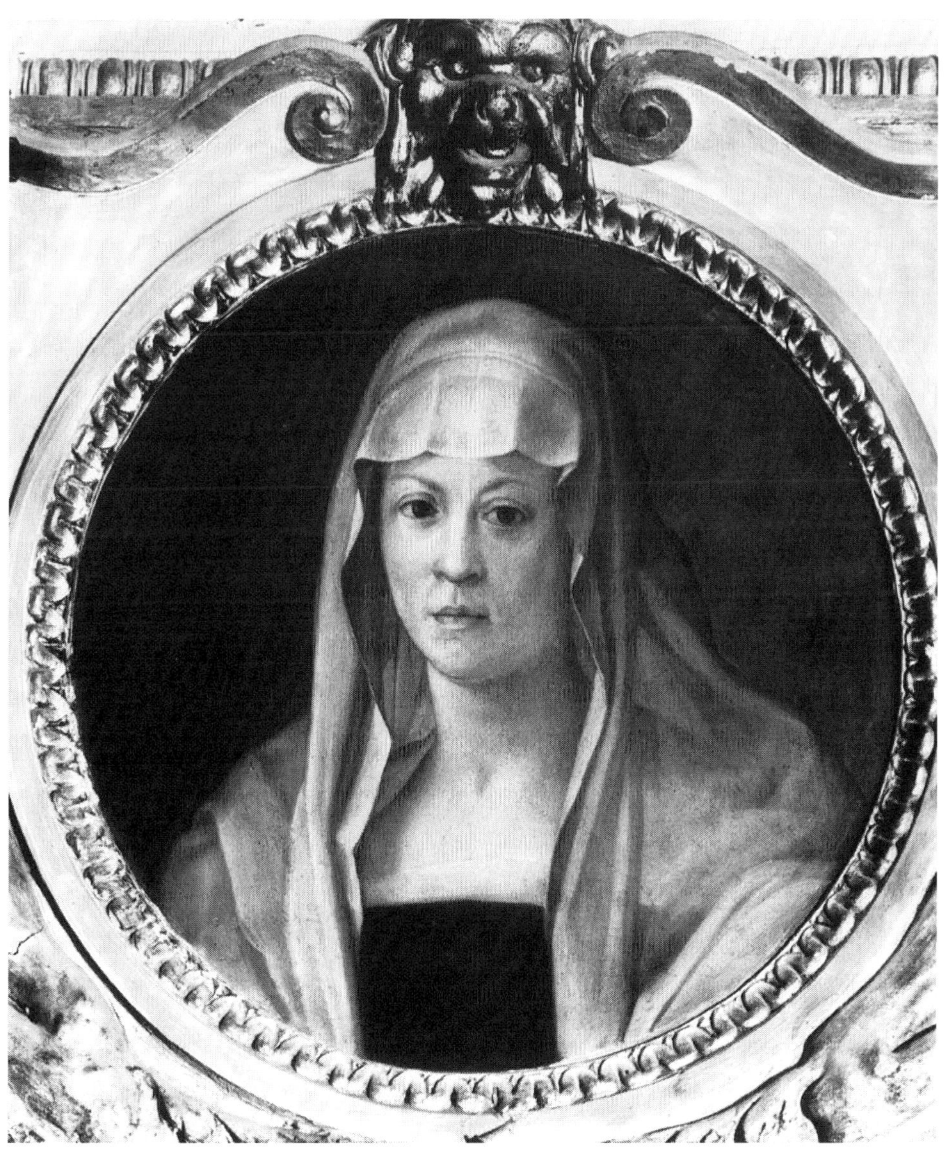

Figure 4 Giorgio Vasari, *Maria Salviati de' Medici*, 1556–9. Ceiling tondo, Sala Giovanni delle Bande Nere. Florence, Palazzo Vecchio.

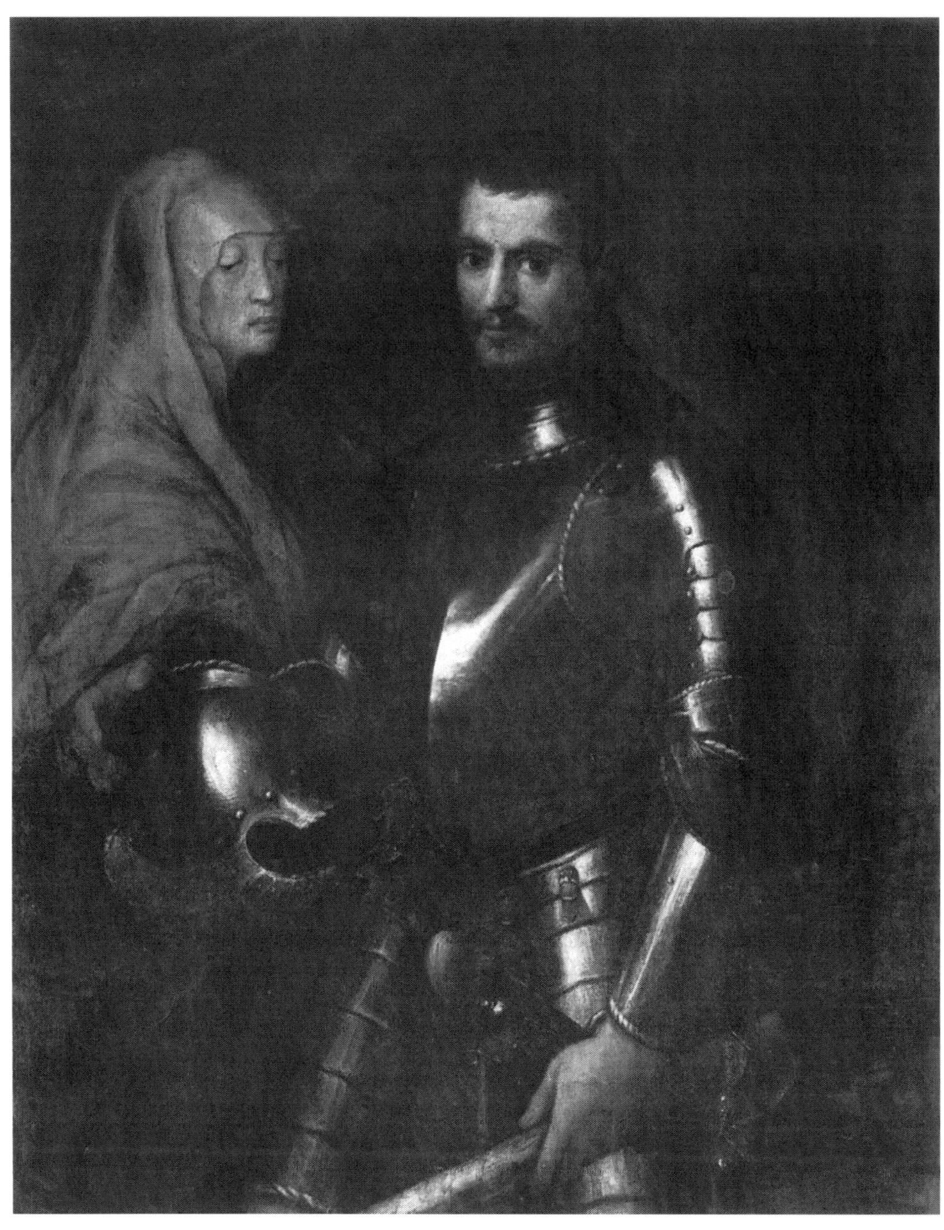

Figure 5 Battista Naldini, *Maria Salviati with Giovanni delle Bande Nere*, 1585–6 (Serie Aulica). Oil on panel, 140 × 116 cm. Florence, Galleria degli Uffizi.

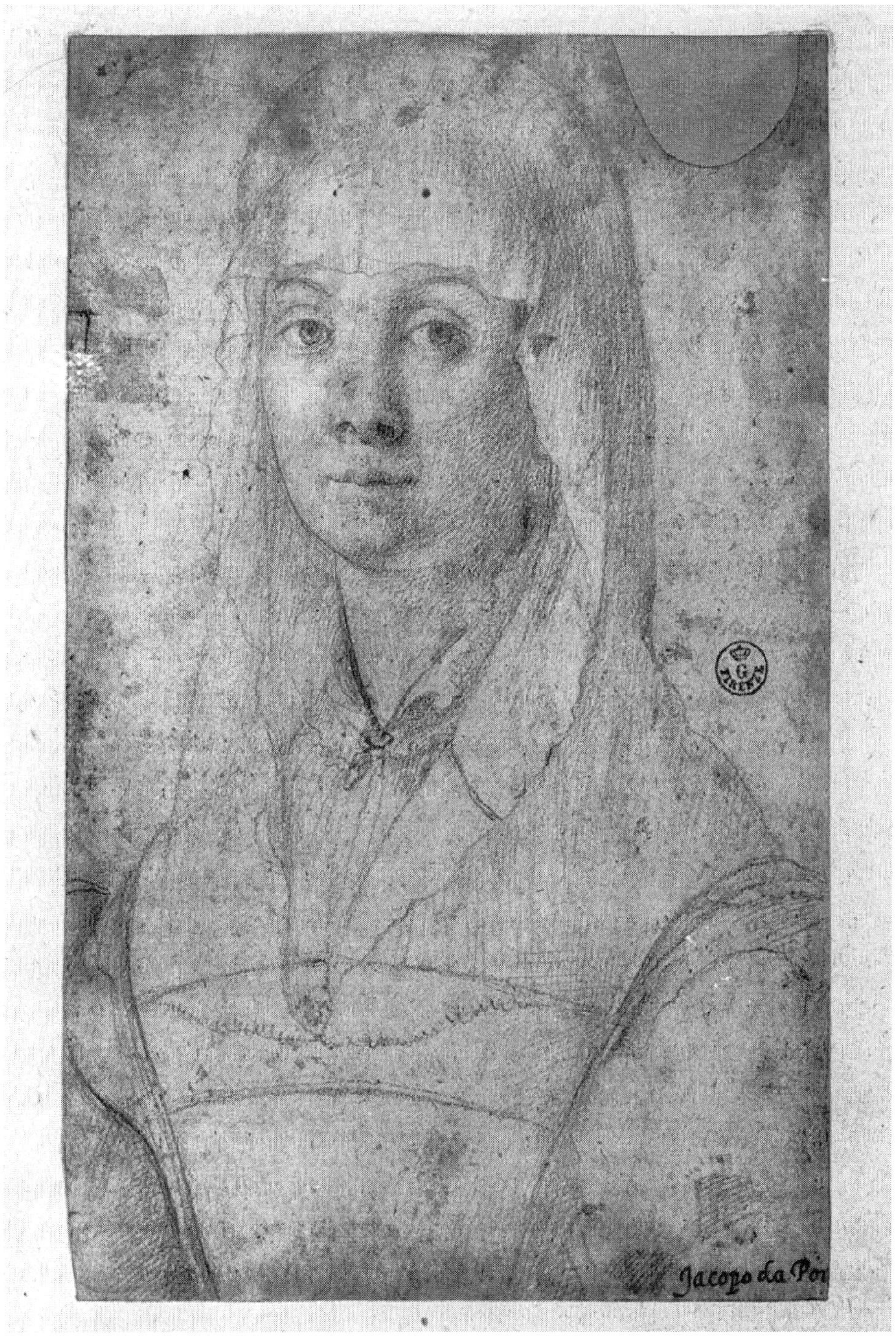

Figure 6 Agnolo Bronzino, *Maria Salviati*, drawing, circa 1526. Black chalk, 20.2 × 12.3 cm. Florence, Gabinetto Disegni e Stampe degli Uffizi, no. 6680F.

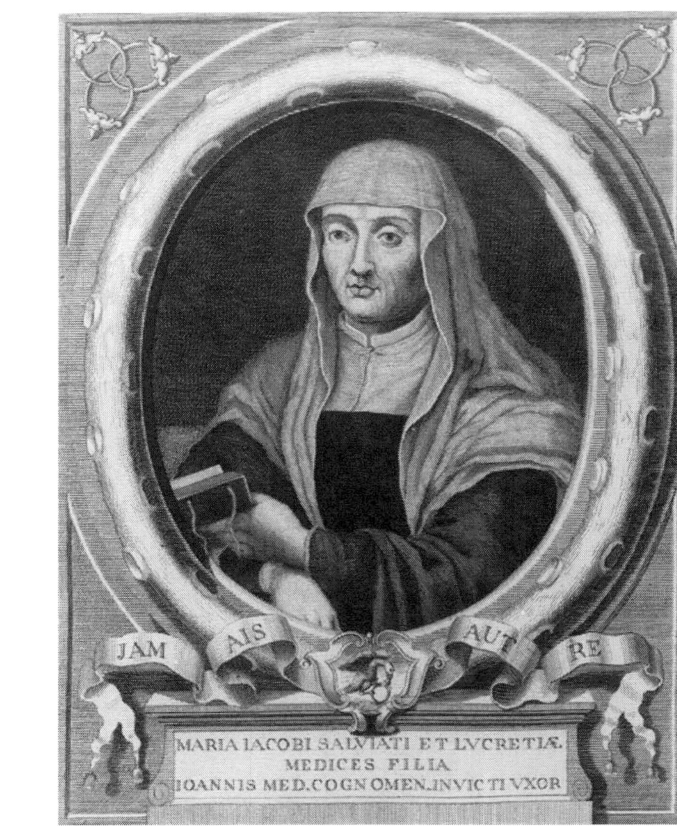

Figure 7 Anonymous, *Maria Salviati*, 1587. Paper on panel, 13.5 × 10.5 cm (Ambras Series). Vienna, Kunsthistorisches Museum.

Figure 8 Francesco Allegrini, *Maria Salviati*. Engraving. Giuseppe Zocchi, *Chronologica series simulacrorum regiae familiae Medicea*, Florence, 1761.

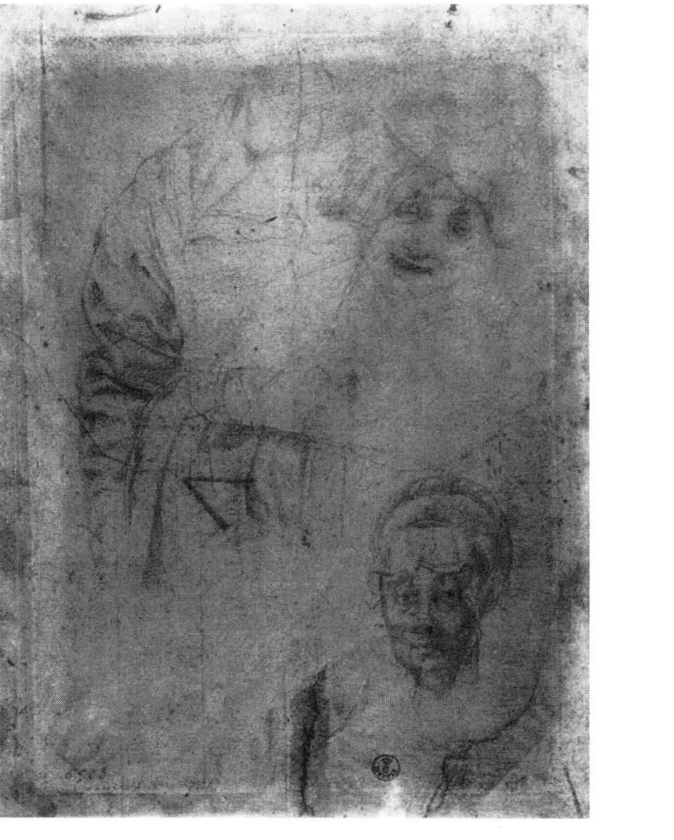

Figure 9 Pontormo (Jacopo da Carucci). *Maria Salviati*, circa 1544. Drawing. Red chalk, 26.5 × 18.8 cm. Florence, Gabinetto Disegni e Stampe degli Uffizi, no. 6303F.

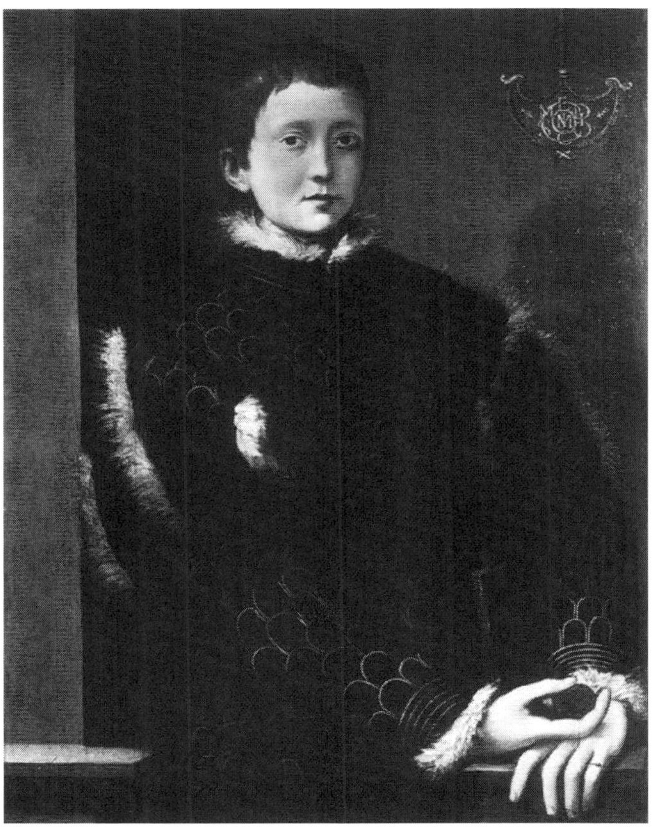

Figure 10 Ridolfo del Ghirlandaio, *Cosimo de' Medici at Age Twelve*, 1531. Oil on panel, 86.5 × 66.5 cm. Florence, Galleria degli Uffizi.

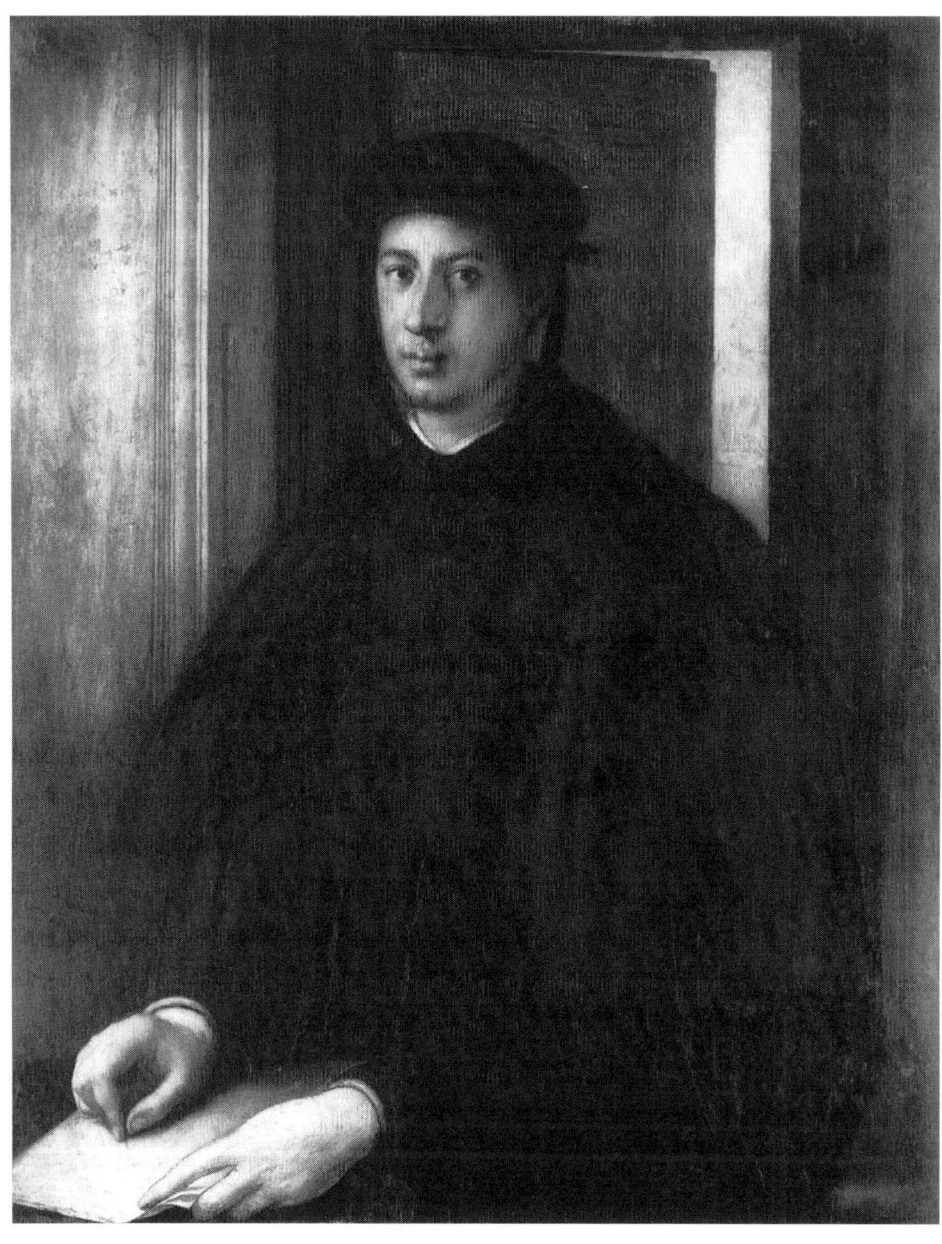

Figure 11 Pontormo (Jacopo da Carucci), *Alessandro de' Medici*, 1534–5. Oil on panel, 101.2 × 81.9 cm. Philadelphia Museum of Art, John G. Johnson Collection, 1917.

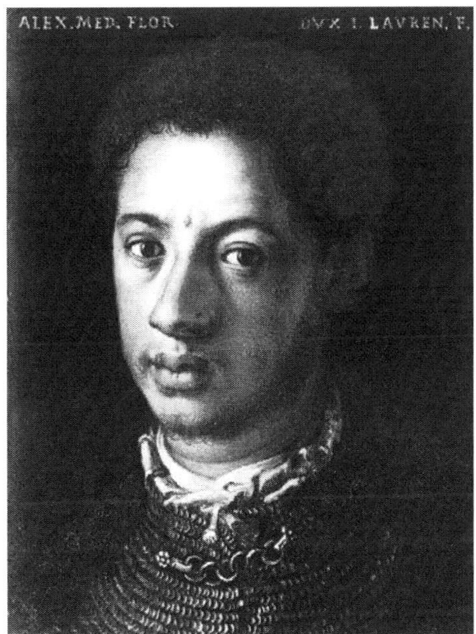

Figure 12 Agnolo Bronzino workshop, after Pontormo, *Alessandro de' Medici*, after 1553. Oil on tin, 16 × 12.5 cm. Florence, Galleria degli Uffizi.

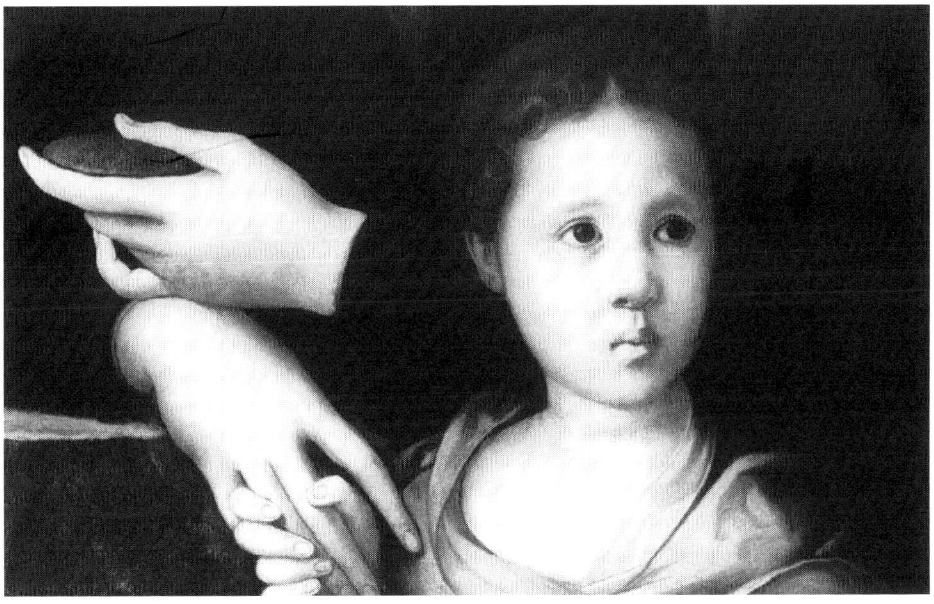

Figure 13 Pontormo (Jacopo da Carucci), *Maria Salviati with Giulia de' Medici*, detail of plate 2: lower area.

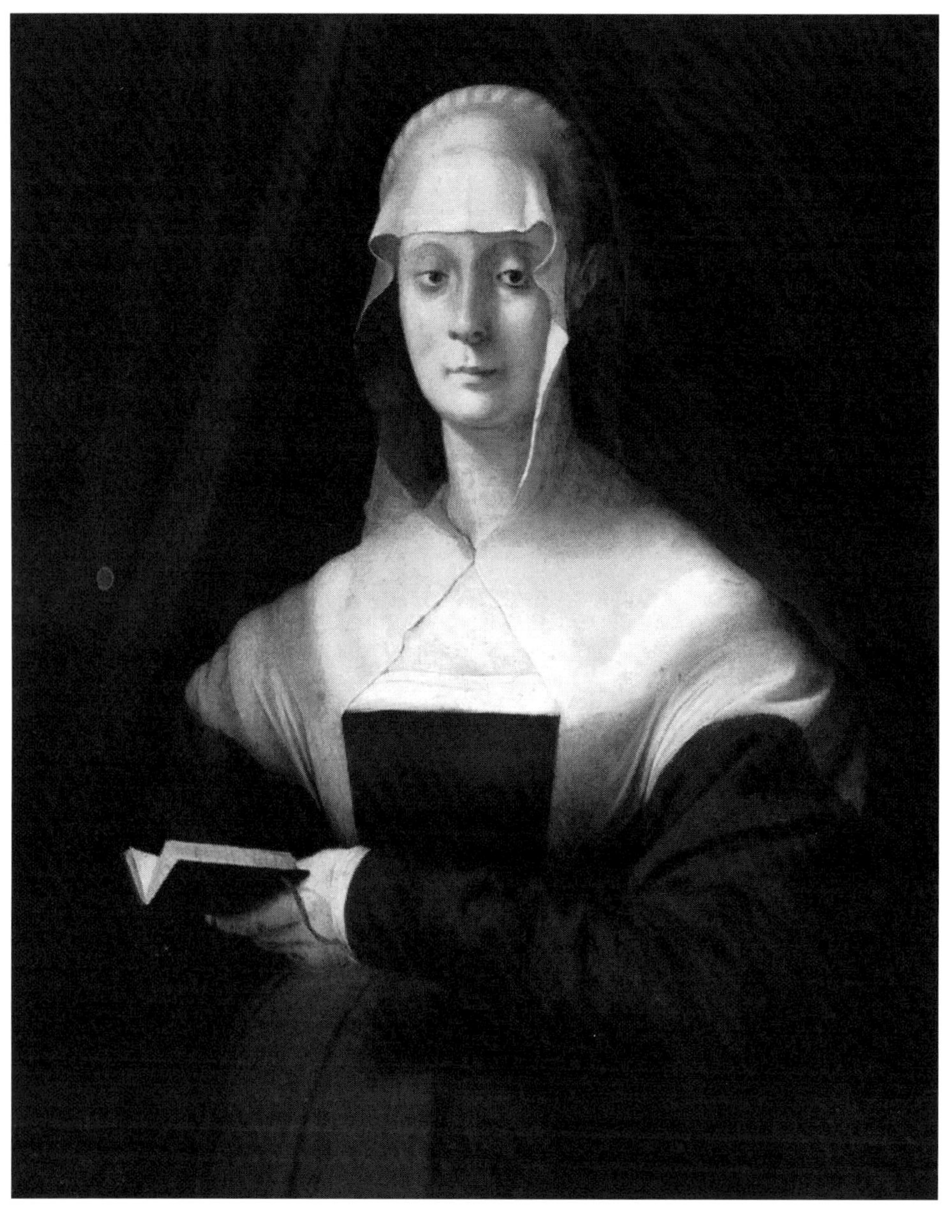

Figure 14 Pontormo (Jacopo da Carucci), *Maria Salviati with a Book*, circa 1544–5. Oil on panel, 87 × 71 cm. Florence, Galleria degli Uffizi.

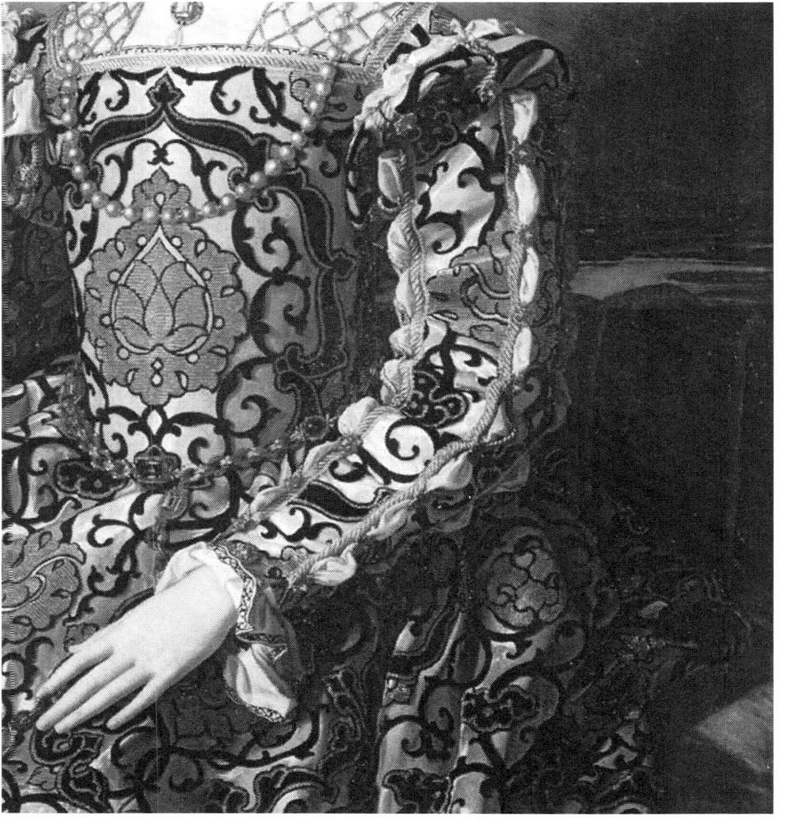

Figure 15 Agnolo Bronzino, *Eleonora di Toledo with Her Son Giovanni*, circa 1545, detail of plate 4: dress and landscape.

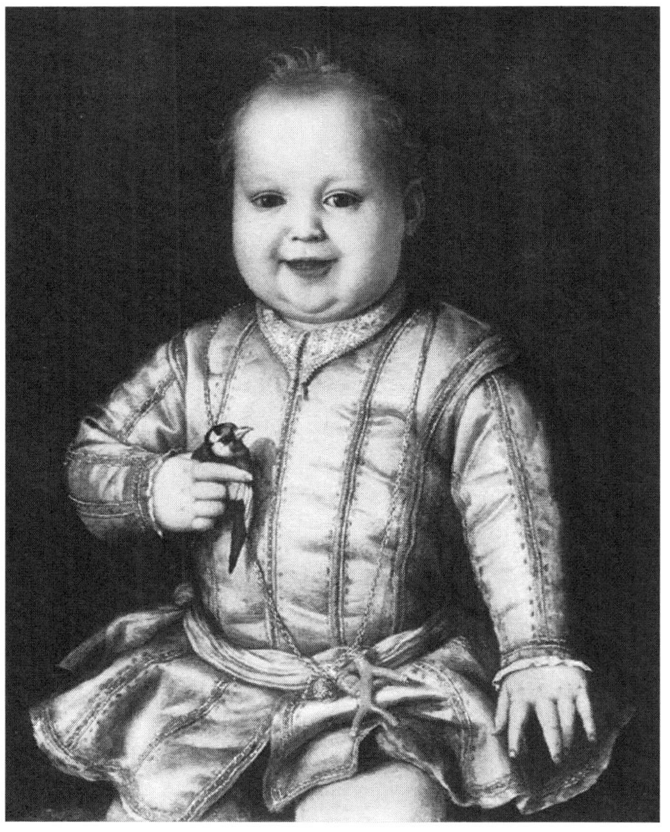

Figure 16 Agnolo Bronzino, *Giovanni de' Medici with a Goldfinch*, 1545. Tempera on panel, 58 × 45 cm. Florence, Galleria degli Uffizi.

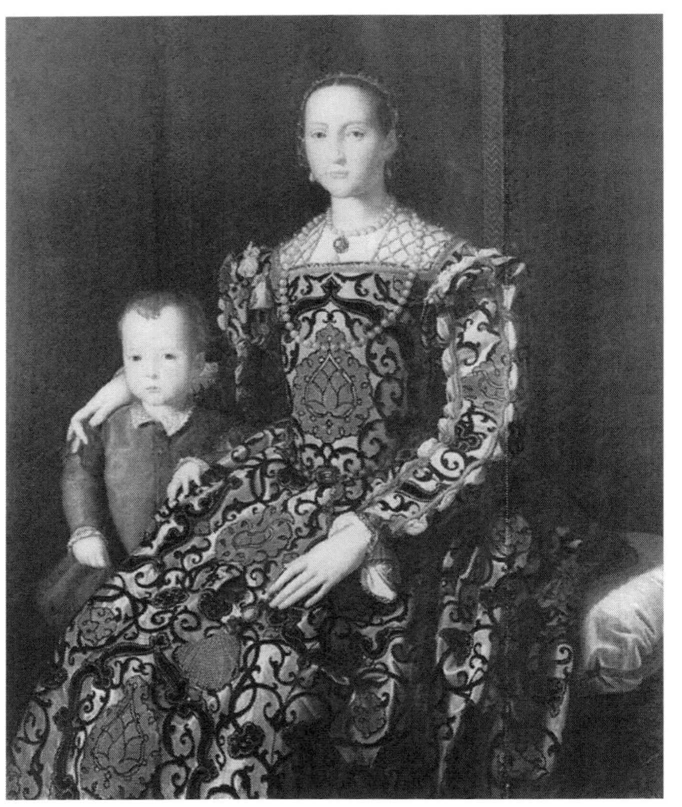

Figure 17 Agnolo Bronzino and workshop, *Eleonora di Toledo with Her Son Giovanni*, circa 1545. Oil on panel, 121.8 × 100 cm. Detroit Institute of Arts, Gift of Mrs Ralph Harman Booth in memory of her husband, Ralph Harman Booth.

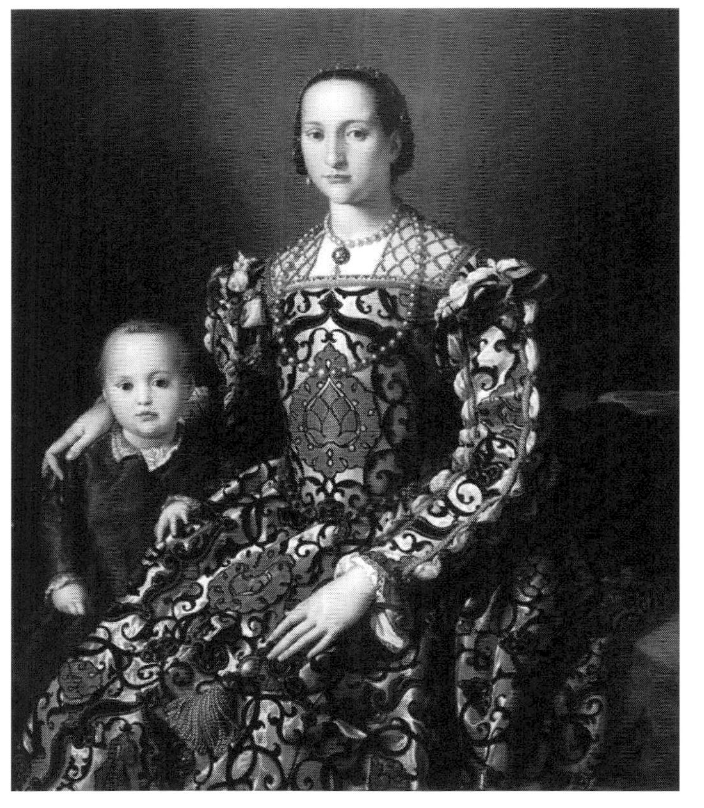

Figure 18 Lorenzo della Sciorina, *Eleonora di Toledo with Her Son Garzia*, 1584 (Serie Aulica). Oil on panel, 140 × 116 cm. Florence, Galleria degli Uffizi.

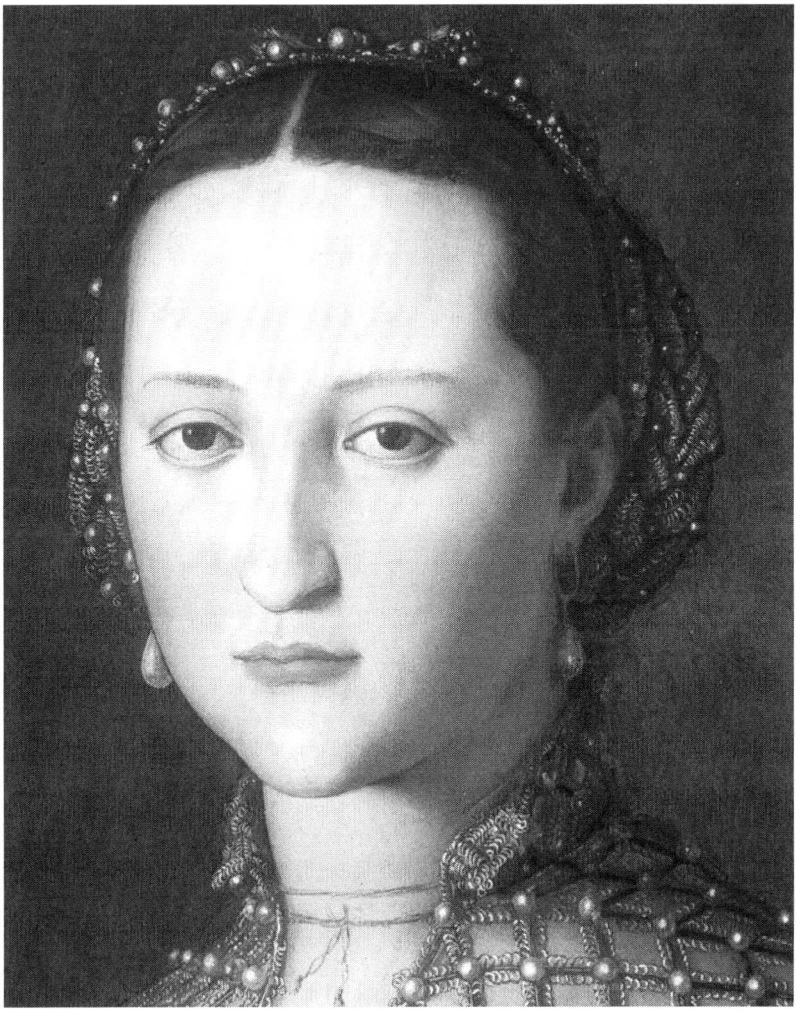

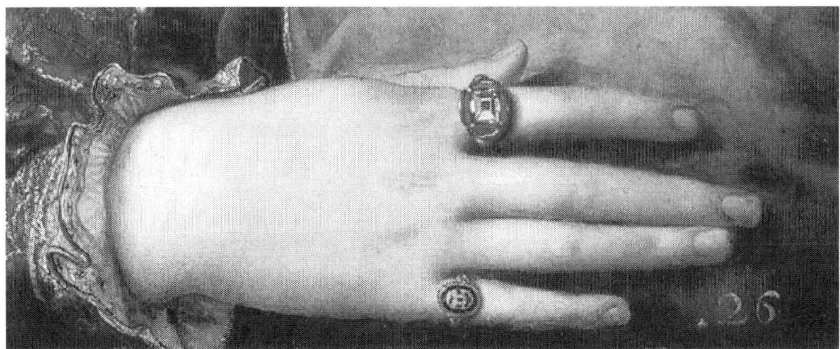

Figure 19 Agnolo Bronzino, *Eleonora di Toledo*, 1543, detail of plate 5: face.

Figure 20 Agnolo Bronzino, *Eleonora di Toledo*, 1543, detail of plate 5: hand.

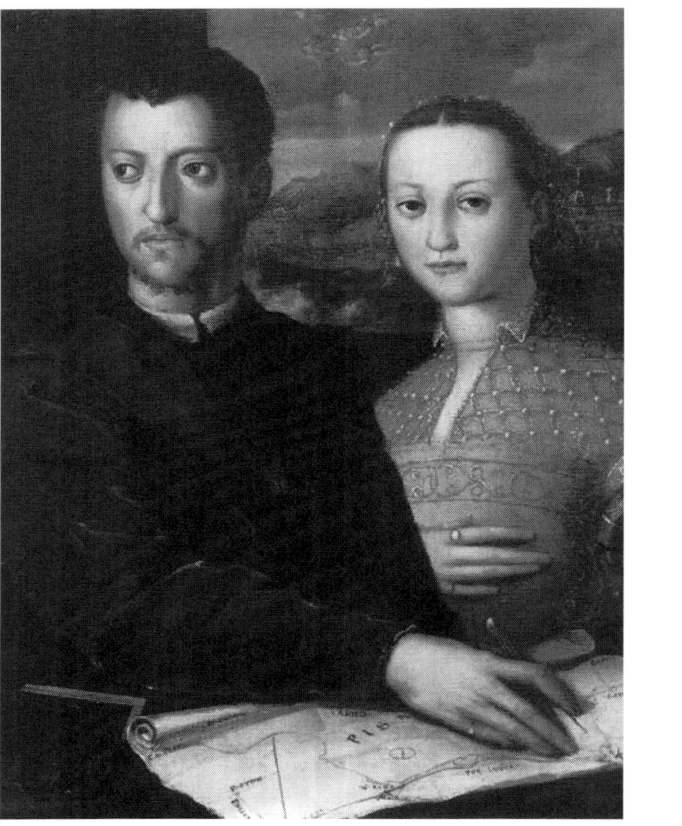

Figure 21 Anonymous, *Cosimo de' Medici and Eleonora di Toledo with Maps*, 1546. Oil on panel, 30.5 × 24 cm. Connecticut, Collection Mrs Arthur Erlanger.

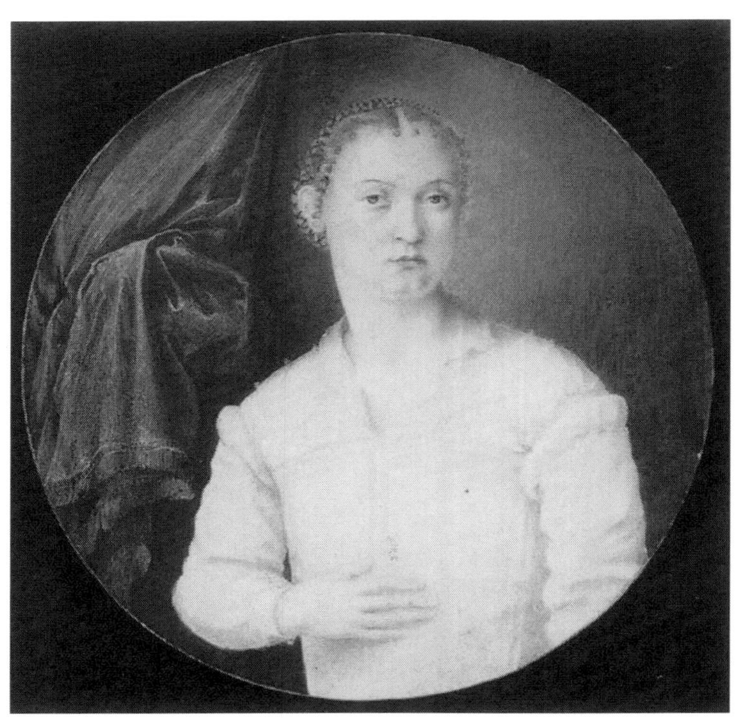

Figure 22 Giulio Clovio, *Eleonora di Toledo*, 1551–3. Portrait miniature. Tempera on vellum, 8.4 cm diameter. Private collection, England.

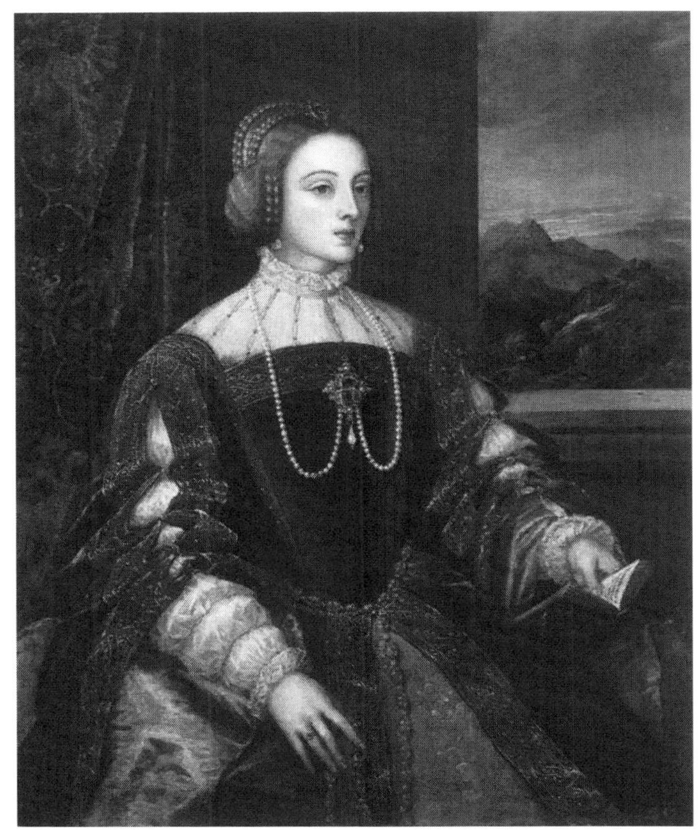

Figure 23 Anonymous copy of Titian, *Isabella of Portugal in Black*, 1543–4. Oil on panel, 110 × 98 cm. Private collection, location unknown.

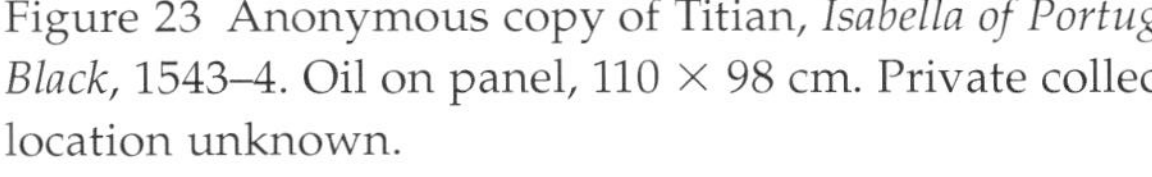

Figure 24 Titian (Tiziano Vecellio), *Isabella of Portugal in Red*, 1545–8. Oil on panel, 117 × 98 cm. Madrid, Museo Nacional del Prado.

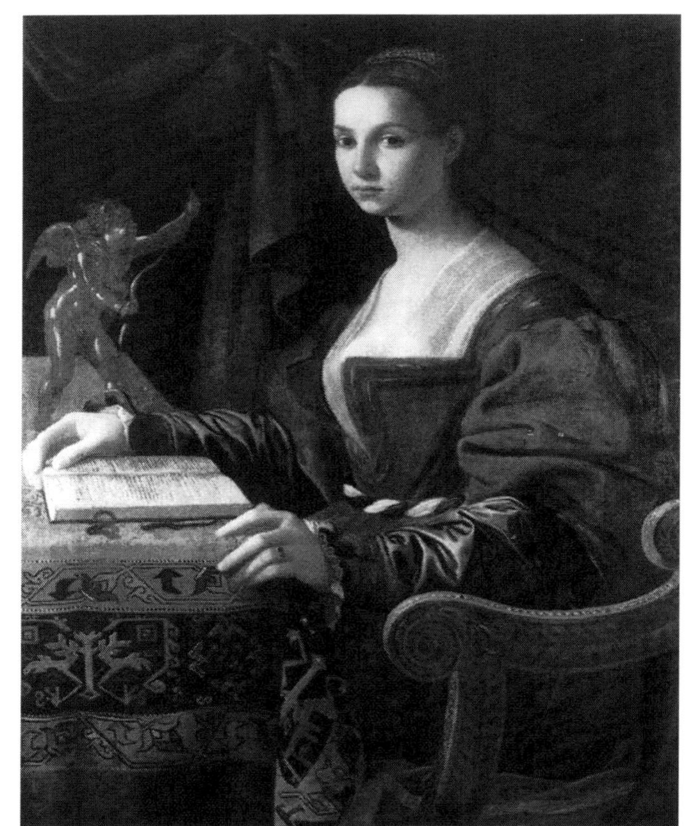

Figure 25 Baccio Bandinelli, *Eleonora di Toledo*, portrait bust, 1544. Bronze, 40 cm high; 28 cm high without pedestal. Florence, Museo Nazionale del Bargello.

Figure 26 Francesco Salviati? *Woman with a Statue of Eros*, early 1530s. Oil on panel, 105 × 80 cm. Collection of the Earl of Wemyss and March KT, Scotland.

dos: some are, having the face uplifted, looking skywards with the eyes raised, the features [being] seen from beneath, [including] the nostrils, mouth, beard and the entire neck, and this perspective is very difficult and noble.'[185] De Hollanda confirms that the 'upward,' skyward pose imparts spirituality and nobility to the sitter. Maria's pose here is contrived to place her in a noble, elevated category, one perhaps analagous to Badius's 'sublime' or 'altisonum' category for a ranking persona in poetics.[186]

The perspective of Maria's figure also emphasizes her recorded tallness, a physical trait that Agnolo Firenzuola's courtier, Celso, links to queenly decorum. In the Uffizi *Maria*, her towering height and her remove correspond to his prescription for *maestà*:

> About majesty, ... it is a commonplace made in daily speech that, when a woman is tall, well-formed, carries herself well, sits with a certain grandeur, speaks with gravity, smiles modestly, and finally, recalls the aura of a queen; then, we say: This woman seems majestic; she has majesty; [all of] which derives from the regal throne, where every gesture, each act, comes to be admired and revered. On this account, majesty becomes nothing but the movement and deportment of a woman as a certain royal display; of [this type of] woman, it is said that she is as a person a little haughty and restrained.[187]

Although his *Dialogo* was published posthumously in 1548, Firenzuola wrote the preface in 1541, having circulated the manuscript to his friends 'and enemies' – presumably fellow Florentine *letterati* – 'regnante lo Illustrissimo ed Eccellentissimo Signor Cosmo Duca meritissimo di Fiorenza.'[188] Significantly, Agnolo had already dedicated a discourse on Love to Caterina Cibo, Duchess of Camerino, the courtier who, as we saw, disparaged Maria's lack of grandeur at about this time. Contemporaries seem to have deferred to the liberated Cibo's formidable role as literary figure and arbiter of taste, and to her powerful political and social connections – not the least of which was her close association with the rising Florentine court.

It was a court to watch. The dynastic and political implications of the 1540 move to the former seat of republican government were momentous. Cosimo had disingenuously described the enormous building to his father-in-law, Don Pedro of Toledo, simply as 'un palazzo maggiore dove sono stanze regali' ('a larger palace where there are regal rooms').[189] Its true import was soon promoted through extensive renovations. Propagandistic cycles emphasized Cosimo's absolutist role as semi-divine saviour of his people and as second founder of his family – Cosimo il Vecchio (1389–1464) being the original Medici *capo*.[190] There would have been intense interest in the conduct of the ducal family – and its Spanish retainers – in this elevated setting. The beautiful young duchess's stateliness and rigid adherence to protocol – mastered in her father's viceregal court in Naples – was unprecedented for Florence.[191] Caterina, a recognized arbiter of protocol, seemingly felt qualified to comment on how the ducal family was adapting to the new appointments.[192] The *grandezza* of the *Maria Salviati with a Book* may reflect this great surge of formality in the court between the 1540 and Maria's death, one that promoted the parvenu Medici as the leading aristocracy in the Italian sphere.

Luisa Becherucci has described formal aspects, especially lighting, that contribute to an otherworldly, mysterious magnetism in the portrait, which recent restoration has enhanced:

> It has the magical fascination of an apparition, with that sudden white light bathing her face and veil, contrasting with the sombre harmony of the black background and the steel-grey of her gown. Within the nimbus of the lighting, the face stiffens in marmoreal haughty fixity. That pure sublime lighting brings back a lyrical atmosphere [to this example] ... of Pontormo's art.[193]

This suffused, metaphysical quality works in tandem with its iconic frontality, extreme abridgment of detail, and the shadowy, dark drapery filling the background. The indistinctness of setting emphasizes Maria's remove. The idealization and 'otherworldy' effects in this portrait may be contrived to represent Maria in death or, more precisely, after life. Her body, exhumed in 1857, was dressed in a nun's habit distinguished by a frontal black panel.[194] As a member of the tertiary Order of St Dominic she would have been privileged to be shrouded and entombed in the habit of the Order.[195] She is fully robed in the habit in the later, official Allegrini engraving (fig. 8); here her veil is decorously drawn across her throat. Careful study of the preparatory drawing (fig. 9) for the *Maria Salviati with a Book*, in which she is similarly dressed, confirms that the portrait is posthumous.[196] As noted, the drawing depicts a separated head and torso, which, when combined, match the facial features and pose of the Uffizi panel. The late drawing will be discussed here in tandem with the drawing of Maria as a young woman (fig. 6), both proposed as associated sources of reference for the Uffizi portrait.

The two drawings are separated by at least fifteen years. Maria's pose in the portrait is closest to the later drawing, the direct source for the torso, the pose of the head, and the lines of the veil. As de Hollanda would shortly advise in his treatise, difficulties arose with such upward poses as chosen by Pontormo for this portrait. Maria's nose is made longer in the panel to modify any 'graceless' foreshortening, and the very wide-open nostrils seen in the drawing have been narrowed and modified to make them less obtrusive. The set and gaze of the eyes are derived from the late drawing, too, but Maria's mouth appears to be quoted directly from the earlier drawing of her (fig. 6) and, reflecting de Hollanda's advice, it is 'lifted' slightly, imparting a more confident air.[197] The youthful drawing inspired, too, the smooth planes of Maria's face and the sweeping curve of her brows in the posthumous Uffizi portrait. This composite approach must have served to distil Maria's most memorable traits and to idealize her. Comparison of her face in the Uffizi panel with both the earlier and later drawings, and with the Baltimore panel (pl. 2), reveals a greater tautness of skin over the bony structure and the elimination of all wrinkles to provide a flawless surface. In the later drawing (fig. 9), the eye sockets are sharply defined concave forms. In the panel their shutter-like lids are firmly convex and smoothed of the heavy folds below them that appear in the drawing.

This later drawing was almost certainly derived from Buglioni's death mask of Maria. She was ill during the last years of her life and it is unlikely that she would have been exposed to arduous posing through several sittings. In fact, it would seem extraordinary if the death mask had *not* been used as a direct source for a posthumous portrait, as 'the right to have an image for preserving the memory' and to provoke 'emulation and imitation' was a key source for the Renaissance adherence to this classical tradition of casting the subject in death. Also, a portrait, possibly this one, was exhibited at her memorial ceremony.[198] Residual evidence of post-mortem morbidity in the drawing is suggested by a peculiar flattening of the nose and very wide open nares. Flattening of forms (due to the weight of plaster on the face), loss of muscle tone, drooping lips, and sunken cheeks and eye sockets are diagnostic of death-casts.[199] Pontormo has adjusted and refined the visible evidence of death, but has not disguised it completely. Naldini's posthumous portrayal of her alongside her husband in 1585–6 (fig. 5), forty years after her death, left overt evidence of morbidity.[200] It is greatly modified in the contemporary Ambras version (1587) of the same pose, possibly also by Naldini (fig. 7), where Maria has been made youthful.[201]

Schuyler has documented such signs of posthumous portrayal in her study of Renaissance busts.[202] Maria's portrayal may be compared with Francesco Laurana's *Battista Sforza*, circa 1473, also 'worked up' from a recent death mask.[203] The backward and upward tilt of the head, the impassive face, the strong convex forms of the eyes in the deeply concave sockets – carved to appear open in Battista's case – are all telling points. In particular, posthumous casts usually showed considerable elongation of the neck.[204] Morbid distortions on the extant original casting were evidently eliminated as far as possible on the marble *Battista*; Laurana streamlined and refined forms, softened transitions between them to eliminate post-mortem rigidity in expression, and eliminated surface detail to provide an idealized face. Laurana's lovely marble 'released' a girlish, exquisitely graceful *Battista* and provided her with a queenly deportment by which she would be remembered for posterity. A certain blandness of expression in the *Battista* bust, not entirely eliminated in the austere *Maria Salviati with a Book*, is characteristic of such modifications.[205] All adjustments could readily and more extensively be worked in paint – Maria's neck and head are not tilted unnaturally in the Uffizi portrait, but her face is blandly idealized, her deportment made queenly, and her entire persona monumentalized.

In conclusion, reference to the later drawing and traces of formal corrections made to Maria's image in the Uffizi portrait confirm that it is posthumous, and indeed the character of its realization in paint suggests that Pontormo intended contemporaries to recognize this status for the panel. In no other portrayal of her in life, or in any retrospective portrayal, does she appear with the black panel on the front of her dress. Her contemporaries would be reminded of the religious habit that would honour her in death. It was intended to be viewed as a posthumous tribute, and its function is eulogistic and didactic. From comparisons between drawings and the panel portrait, it clearly emerges that this work is a composite that strives to convey a particular persona rather than an accurate record of appearance. Pontormo implicitly fulfilled what Domenico Ghirlandaio called on art to achieve in his posthumous *Giovanna degli Albizzi*, inscribed to invoke manifestation of the *virtù* and soul of the subject. ('O art, wert thou able to depict the conduct and the soul, no lovelier painting would exist on earth.') Giovanna died in 1488.[206] The Uffizi *Maria*, too, is elevated to a kind of sainthood and commemorates a persona passed from our mundane sphere.

Removal of indications of mortality, temperament, foibles, or neuroses in the Uffizi *Maria with a Book* recalls the approach associated with late Renaissance, Florentine portrait busts. Then the tradition was linked to revival of the classical *imagines* or death masks of family members.[207] In the Uffizi panel, the bust format is recalled by the solidly pyramidal form, upward perspective, frontal presentation, and marmoreal finish. The effect is of petrified immutability. The unusual perspective suggests high placement, a setting typical for the traditional *imagines*, a grey stone niche of *pietra serena*. In most cases busts were displayed against a wall in niches or gables, placed to be seen from below and frontally.[208] Tombs, too, utilized such montages for busts of the deceased, and one woman's elevated wall tomb proves to be a sixteenth-century parallel for Maria's pose of actively reading a book and pausing to face the viewer.[209] The typical viewing positions for *imagines* may be reflected in the Uffizi *Maria* and would contribute to its iconic effect.

The origins of preserving the memory of a deceased stems from classical traditions. Cicero's concept, *ius imaginis ad memoriam posteritatemque prodendam* (the right to have an image for preserving the memory), had been a key impulse for this Renaissance custom.[210] The Medici had been dedicated to commemorative *imagines* from at least the second half of the fifteenth century. Marble busts of Piero di Cosimo ('il Gottoso') and his wife Lucrezia Tornabuoni by Mino da Fiesole had been mounted over doorways in the Palazzo Medici on the Via Larga; Lucrezia's remained there for generations.[211] Andrea Verrocchio's Medici busts were placed above eye level in the old Palazzo Medici cortile.[212] Vasari noted – without surprise – that sculptured versions of frank death-masks were widely displayed, for example, above fireplaces, doorways, windows, and cornices in many Florentine houses.[213] However ghoulish this seems to modern sensibilities, Florentines were neither repulsed nor unnerved by death masks. Vasari records a bust of Eleonora di Toledo in Cosimo's *guardaroba* (which served as a family portrait gallery), possibly from life, but Contessina dei Bardi, the long-dead wife of Cosimo il Vecchio was represented *en buste* there too.[214]

In addition, Florentines had a tradition of drawing or casting the deceased in anticipation of the execution of painted commemorative panels. Domenico Ghirlandaio's *Portrait of an Old Man with a Child*, circa 1480, in the Louvre is based on a drawing of an elderly deceased on his bier, once in Vasari's collection.[215] Bronzino probably used her death-cast for his portrait of Maria's young charge, Bia (pl. 6), who died in March 1542 and whose death mask is recorded in the *guardaroba* inventory of 1553.[216] Vasari's oval portrait of Maria's mother-in-law Caterina Sforza (1462–1509), painted for the Sala di Giovanni delle Bande Nere in 1556, was certainly based on a cast, presumably the one recorded in the same *guardaroba* inventory.[217] Caterina, in profile, is given similar proud bearing and height as the Uffizi *Maria*; her neck is stretched to double the length that appears on a medal of her made during her life.[218]

It would seem that Pontormo's portrait of Maria holding a book follows a venerable Medici tradition in commemorative portraiture. Pontormo's composite portrayal from drawings of Maria before and after death allowed him to create a posthumous *Maria* that recalled her youthful perfection even as it stressed her mature dignity as mother of the new Duke of Florence. The *Maria Salviati with a Book*, in contrast to the Baltimore portrait, has as its proper setting an eternal, atemporal, spiritual environment, and evocative overtones of sculpted *imagines* in it are integral to its commemorative canons.

Pontormo particularly emphasized the painter's ability to conjure both the effects of sculpture and its qualities of endurance in his response to Varchi's invitation in 1547 to defend painting over sculpture. (Artists' responses were published in Varchi's *Due Lezzioni* of 1550 under the stamp of Cosimo's printer, Lorenzo Torrentino.)[219] Endurance was, of course, an essential end in the promotion of love, *virtù*, and commemoration, one that, along with its traditional associations with oratory in the fifteenth century, had given sculpture the edge in portrayal.[220] Pontormo, at pains to defend painting as equal to sculpture, described it as equally arduous.[221] He comments: 'But what I said to be very daring is the importance of surpassing nature by infusing [a semblance of spirit] in a figure and making it seem alive, while painting on a flat surface.'[222] The painted illusion of relief ('farla in piano') in Michelangelo's painting, he argues, contributes to the great artist's esteem. As to endurance, it is already inherent in the stone of the Carrara caves before it is worked; the great artist's *invenzione* does not depend on his material.[223] From this we infer that Pontormo's marmoreal rendering of Maria subsumes sculpture's endurance and imparts the *virtù* long associated with commemorative busts.

Pontormo also understood how art could impart the occult essence of the persona that surrounded the *imagines* in the sixteenth century. The infusion of this element is not merely dependent on his use of the death mask, but informed by the Neoplatonic beliefs of his cohort, the satellites of Cosimo's new Accademia Fiorentina. It will be recalled that its leader, Varchi, who was referred to by Michelangelo as 'the light and splendour of the Florentine Academy' ('luce e splendore dell' Accademia Fiorentina'), had arrived to steer the Academy only months before Maria's death.[224] There was widespread agreement among Florentine *letterati* that the imitation of nature by the painter included perfection of nature's highest forms. It must rise above the commonplace and visible.[225] Pontormo's creation of an elevated persona for Maria is informed by such sentiments, and Varchi's language when he speaks of art reflects this philosophical climate. He affirms Pontormo's power to create the illusion of sculpture's 'divine and miraculous powers,' and to portray miraculously, for posterity, and with 'stupefying' effect. The ends of decorum in poetics were stated in similar language by Dolce in 1550.[226] As the iconic quality of the sculpted work depends partially on its allusions to the antique, the translation of a relief form into a two-dimensional illusion of it in paint constitutes a magical act, responsible for the overwhelming effect on the viewer. Starkness of portrayal contributes to this end, too, according to Vasari. It evokes awe because it conjures sculpture's 'essence.'[227] Hence, the Uffizi *Maria*'s sparse externals and undefined setting are indicative of its links to the *imagines* and the veneration they elicited from those bereaved, 'aflame to be bound to emulation and imitation' of the subject.[228]

The quality of 'apparizione' so aptly described by Becherucci and evidently familiar to Varchi and Vasari informs elegiac poetry and Florentine funeral oratory of the period. The passage of Diego di Sandoval's elegy addressed to Cosimo on the occasion of Maria's death is an important key to understanding the Uffizi *Maria Salviati with a Book*. A Spanish humanist at the ducal court, Sandoval was well informed on appropriate decorum for state occasions, and he probably knew Pontormo and Bronzino, who were both at work in the Florentine court at the time of Maria's death.[229] The poet addresses Maria's spirit, now removed to another plane. She is assigned the role of a new saint with powers of mediation:

> Lady, who now among the other blessed spirits
> Who live up in Heaven, along with more superior and more perfect
> Spirits, with whom you compare
> In the presence of this Lord who to so many honours
> Wished to raise you in the middle of your epoch,
> Look again on earth and with merciful affection
> Gaze on Florence and your beloved children.[230]

Sandoval's panegyric may be seen as the equivalent of a funeral oration in verse.[231] The visual elevation and transcendental effects of lighting in the Uffizi panel, together with the suggested 'interruption' to Maria's meditations, are explained by him for us. Maria has been elevated to a venerable Medici pantheon. Her new spiritual state is depicted, and her relationship to the viewer is that of sanctified intercessor.

The Neoplatonic mode is woven through Sandoval's elegy, explaining the image's flawless finish and the irradiating light Becherucci observed in the portrait:

> You, sitting on high at the side of the Creator
> Gazing on Him only, and He, resplendent
> On you ... [232]

The lines evoke Dante's *Paradiso*:

> Beatrice was fixing her eyes on the eternal spheres [of Heaven]
> And I, diverting my eyes from them,
> Gazed at her ...[233]

The exultant expression on Maria's face is not one we find promoted in Firenzuola's or Luigini's treatises on decorum for women or widows. Sandoval's opening words are invaluable in explaining its context:

> Since cruel, untimely Death
> Triumphed on the face of the great Lady
> Who now triumphs over it, nor does she fear
> That her true joys will ever be stolen from her;
> She happily departed with her cruel retinue all [left] behind her.

In these, Pratesi recalls Petrarch's *Trionfo della Fama*, 1: 1–2, 'After Death had triumphed over that face / which used to triumph over me,' where, ultimately, Fame comes to vanquish Death.' ('Da poi che Morte trionfò nel volto / Che di me stesso trionfar solea.')[234] Sandoval's lines explain the worldly remove, triumphal elevation, and majestic expression infused by Pontormo into the *Maria with a Book*. It is possible, too, that he was aware of Poliziano's lines, inscribed beneath a death mask of Lorenzo the Magnificent:

> Cruel death, which in this body arrived
> That after death the world was turned upside-down,
> Whereas when you lived all were maintained in peace.[235]

Sandoval's inspiration stems from the Florentine tradition of the *laudatio funebre* of Lorenzo's time, one that seems to have implicitly influenced Maria's decorum in this portrait. It is a posthumous, elegiac tribute with associated Medici traditions. Indeed, Sandoval's sentiments are echoed verbatim in Varchi's funeral oration for Maria:

> [And] to her, who now reigns from the highest empyreal heaven, sees, I am certain, and perhaps compassionately hears our weeping, I humbly and devotedly beg forgiveness and pray to her with all my heart, so, as she already deigned to lend me her benign ear sometimes here on earth, so may she now grant to me, and may this not be painful to her up there in Heaven, that I may speak of her as becomes her greatness, at least in so far as my humble state permits.[236]

This cross-semination from rhetorical traditions did not flow only in one direction. Funeral orators had not hesitated to describe themselves as painters. In 1472, Niccolò Capranica aligned good oratory with the painter's ability to condense a mass of data into a coherent representation on a small canvas, an analogy that implied the orator's duty to compose and colour his oration carefully. He also emphasizes the humanist orator's fundamental task: to 'conjure' a verbal image of the deceased that would impel the audience to imitate the subject's excellence. Commemorative sculpture was traditionally perceived to have a close relationship to the exercise of funeral oratory.[237] Maria's depiction as a painted version of the sculpted bust enshrines this and many elegiac associations.

Renaissance oratory had also habitually mined the topic of ancestry to demonstrate the power of moral exemplars. The more visible the exemplar, the more powerful it was. In his eulogy for Doge Leonardo Loredan in 1521, Andrea Navagero declared that ancestors were like torches that illuminated descendants' souls, inflaming them to perform deeds worthy of their parentage.[238] His 'irradiated' simile is an apt description of Pontormo's lighting effects for the Uffizi *Maria Salviati with a Book*. Predictably, Sandoval, too, stresses this exemplary sentiment, reminds Cosimo of his moral debt to Maria, and enjoins Eleonora to produce more descendants.[239] She should, he concludes:

> ... honour your great, proud Mother

> And say: 'He [Cosimo] who sends me to you, hopes in time
> To sing so highly of your great, illustrious deeds
> Which will live forever after a thousand eons.[240]

This philosophy supplies us with the rationale for Maria's decorum in the Uffizi portrait. Unlike the Baltimore portrait, it is not overlaid with political implications, but serves as an ancestral exemplar for descendants. Francisco de Hollanda expounded upon this serious function, echoing Navagero's defence for portraiture as an exemplary genre:

> [As] an imitation of God's work of creation [portraiture] was the highest of the arts. Only famous princes deserved to be portrayed and in so doing [be] remembered, or famous men distinguished in war, art or letters or in liberality and virtue. It was right for children to keep portraits of their parents and ancestors so that they were always present for the emulation of their virtues and the honour of the family.[241]

Castiglione's Count Ludovico seems to have believed that virtue was an inherent quality in the 'wellborn.' 'Noble birth … is always honoured by everyone, because it stands to reason that good should beget good.'[242] We may view this elevated portrayal of Maria as having particular significance in the scheme of Medici dynastic pretensions at this time. She has joined a venerable Medici pantheon. Her portrayal is an essay in *virtù*, intended as a vehicle of emulation for the edification of her descendants. No copies of the portrait are known. It may have been intended for a restricted audience, probably in the spirit of placement of eminent Medici women's *imagines* positioned over doors and in niches in the old Via Larga palace. Maria's was probably kept in Cosimo's *guardaroba* in the Palazzo Vecchio, which functioned as a gallery and depository for surviving earlier busts of Cosimo's ancestors.[243]

The majestic demeanour of the *Maria Salviati with a Book* is one Cosimo consciously sought to perpetuate Maria's memory, and to provide her with a noble decorum suitable to her recent elevation in rank (a demeanour seen by Caterina Cibò as appropriate and desirable – if wanting in life – for the mother of the young duke). The Uffizi panel was painted no earlier than January 1544 – Maria died in December 1543 – but its date is close to Pontormo's *Monsignor Giovanni della Casa, circa* 1541–4, which it imitates by a strong downward slope of the shoulders, the half-length pose, and a broad triangular expansion of the body to fill the frame.[244] They share the dignity, composure, stateliness, and monumentality one might expect for the individual rank of each.[245]

Pontormo's commission for the *Maria Salviati with a Book* appears to have followed on Bronzino's for state portraits of Cosimo and Eleonora in 1543.[246] Maria was chronically ill and weak from 1540 and would not have been able to withstand the rigours of posing during her final years. Prompted by her death, Cosimo commissioned a commemorative portrait from Pontormo using an earlier drawing and one recording her death mask (figs. 6 and 9). It was not the only Medici commission for a posthumous portrait. Two portraits of Giovanni delle Bande Nere, one now in Florence, another in Turin, were also executed in Florence between 1543 and

1545.[247] Evidently, Cosimo's commissions in the mid-1540s from Bronzino, Pontormo, and others were designed to set in motion a comprehensive ancestral record of his family.

Becherucci's observation of unusual luminosity and elevation in this portrait was reflected in Sandoval's poetic references to apotheosis, and by Pontormo's and Bronzino's association with the Florentine Academy, which in 1543 had revived the Platonism of the earlier, Medici court of Lorenzo the Magnificent through the translation of Ficino.[248] Bronzino's familiarity with Dante and authorship of Petrarchan and Neoplatonic poetry testifies to his intellectual loyalty.[249] This, and the duke's recognition of his brilliance as a portraitist in 1543, may explain why Pontormo exhibits some traces of Bronzino's portrait style: sharply defined volumes, marmoreal finish, rarified lighting, and extreme grandeur. A new court style in portraiture was being formulated in the fledgling court. The Uffizi *Maria Salviati with a Book* exhibits a growth in formality of Medici expression, one that presages the splendour of Bronzino's state portrait of the duchess, the subject of the next chapter.

Pontormo as Court Portraitist

Jacopo Pontormo enjoyed Medici patronage before Pope Leo X's death in 1521, and was well informed of Medici propagandistic symbolism. He was in demand as a portraitist by eminent Florentine patrons, yet his career as ducal portraitist appears to have waned after Cosimo's accession in 1537.[250] Vasari's bias is revealed in his aspersions on Pontormo (or when he deigned to faintly praise him), but does enlighten us on factors that might determine success or failure for an aspiring court portraitist.[251] Pontormo's self-effacement when Alessandro wished to pay him for the superb Philadelphia portrait (fig. 11), his choosiness about clients, or a deeply sensitive nature may have been incompatible with prolonged personal contact during sittings with his punctilious ducal clients.[252] Lack of an organized workshop, essential for generating copies of official Medici portraits to other centres, may have been a drawback.[253] If we are to believe Vasari, dilatoriness in executing larger commissions dogged him.[254] Tardiness would be unacceptable because of close personal involvement with sitters, changes in a subject's appearance over time, and rigid court schedules.

Bronzino, whose reputation in portraiture was established by 1540, also secured a reputation for reliability with his decoration of Eleonora's chapel.[255] It was after this that he became portraitist to the court – most likely because of Eleonora's satisfaction with him.[256] Probably the biggest strike against Pontormo was his role as unofficial Medici portraitist during Alessandro's lax reign. Cosimo, punctilious to a fault and married to a notoriously demanding duchess, was determined to bring acclaim to his name and city; Eleonora perhaps disdained Pontormo's links to Alessandro's libertinous Malaspina-Cibo circle. Vasari managed to create a whiff of unorthodoxy around Pontormo's religious works, but this and his humanism have been defended.[257] Deeper reasons for the lukewarm response to his talent by the new regime may reside elsewhere.

Portraiture demands much mutual accommodation between artist and sitter. It may have made the shy Pontormo extremely guarded in his choice of patron and location. His reluctance to accept Alessandro's payment for the Philadelphia panel suggests that he jealously protected his creative independence. De Hollanda's dialogue allows 'Michelangelo' to expound on this: distracted by the insistent enquiries of Paul III, the great artist makes the point that 'the vain conversation of idle persons … degrades [artists'] thoughts from the intense and lofty imaginings in which they are continually rapt.'[258] Echoes resound here of Vasari's spiteful description of Pontormo's 'caprices and daydreamings' ('ghiribizzi e considerazioni'). Michelangelo avoided portraiture, and Vasari declared an aversion to it, either to stress imitation of his champion or to defend his own lack of patronage in portraiture.[259]

It was Bronzino – urbane, literate, and of singularly affable disposition – who would fulfil the role of court painter. His credentials included the stately portrayal of Cosimo's mother, *Maria Salviati with a Lapdog*, and a two-year immersion in the della Rovere court, the most sophisticated in Italy, to paint the grandly impressive *Guidobaldo della Rovere in Armour*. Emotionally 'unglimpseable' in his art, Bronzino could rarify and abstract the essentials of a face to an immutable mask, one that acted as psychological armour to conceal any human weaknesses in his patrons.[260] In this respect, Pontormo's swirling, atmospheric envelope is inappropriately charged with an emanation from his sitter that flows outwards, breaking the frame's boundary to bind a viewer to the sitter's psyche. Alessandro and his daughter's portraits are typical (pl. 2, and figs. 11 and 13). Giulia's apparent apprehension and Alessandro's melting expression are simply not in keeping with the aloofness of the court-portrait genre. Poignancy and wistfulness could find no place there. Vulnerability is an unthinkable decorum for state portraiture, a genre designed to elevate the sitter and induce awe in the viewer. Pontormo's evanescence was antithetical to Cosimo's official court portraiture, which came to prefer Bronzino's sculptural, chilled, optical effects.[261]

Bronzino's strictly delineated figure is unreachable in its chilly light, 'through an air so thin it seems unbreathable.'[262] This expression of exclusion and elevation is fine tuned to the demands of propaganda. In 1546, Paolo Giovio asserted that Cosimo's 'marvellous' official portrait (pl. 3) demonstrated the 'blessed' hand of Bronzino and his ascendancy over Pontormo in this genre.[263] Bronzino's equally impressive pendant portrait of Eleonora, the subject of chapter 2, marks Bronzino as a new breed of court painter to the Medici.

2

Declarations of Dynasty: The State Portrait of Eleonora di Toledo[1]

When Eleonora became Regent of State in 1541, it was not a position the young Spanish duchess could assume lightly. On Cosimo's departure for Genoa, her donation for prayers of 27 August 1541 to S. Pietro in Pistoia recorded her hope that 'she could obtain that wisdom and inspiration necessary so as not to fall into errors.' Two days later, Major-domo Pierfrancesco Riccio reported to Cosimo's secretary, Grifoni, on her progress: 'The City (thank God) is calm ... The Duchess ... passes time with business ... and during this morning with four bishops and other prelates with her, she said, "I feel like a Pope," may God bless her.'[2] Her political empowerment during Cosimo's absences included her direction of military affairs, recorded in August and September 1541, and again in 1543.[3] It was inevitable that this heavy burden of responsibility would fall on Eleonora. Wary of threats to his power following treacherous challenges by political foes on his accession and the hard-won acquisition of his ducal title soon after, Cosimo's approach to rule was independent and Machiavellian.[4] Soon, the young couple's triumphal consolidation of Medici power in the early 1540s was expressed in a continuation of the propagandistic imagery that had been initiated in 1537 with the now-lost frescoes for Maria's villa at Castello. On his audacious move in 1540 to the old seat of republican government, the Palazzo della Signoria, the duke made it the locus of increasingly grander statements of dynasty and power in which Eleonora's role as his consort is a recurring theme. In Bronzino's exquisite frescoes for Eleonora's chapel, begun between 1540 and 1541 and completed in 1545, the duke is symbolically acclaimed as a vanquishing Moses and dynastic figure. Eleonora is represented dynastically, too, in the *Crossing of the Red Sea*, stately in advanced pregnancy and wearing the Medici green and red armorial colours.[5] The sumptuous *Story of Joseph* tapestries were next to assert biblical legitimacy for Medici autocracy and for Cosimo as leader of his people. A new Medici 'Golden Age' was proclaimed to initiate a vigorous cultural programme far-reaching in its scope.[6]

The large-scale allegorical cycles were soon supplemented by official portraits, the proliferation of which is highly significant. Only in courts such as those of François I or Henry VIII had the commission of court portraiture been so comprehensive. Choice of a suitable artist was not at issue – Bronzino's potential as a court portraitist must have been evident before his sojourn at the Este court at Pesaro, certainly by the end of the 1520s. Vasari, however, recorded that it was during the execution of the chapel that his outstanding gifts as a portraitist claimed Cosimo's attention. A burst of ducal portrait commissions followed, including the official portrait of Cosimo armoured in steel and posed with his hand resting on his helmet ('armato tutto d'arme bianche e con una mano sopra l'elmo') (pl. 3).[7] Vasari lists further portraits of Cosimo's family by Bronzino:

> [I]n another panel [Bronzino portrayed] the Lady Duchess his consort; and in another the Lord Francesco their son, Prince of Florence. And not much later he portrayed another of the Duchess, one that pleased her especially, in different manner to the first, with Lord Giovanni her son beside her.[8]

This last portrait, Bronzino's *Eleonora di Toledo with Her Son Giovanni* (pl. 4 and fig. 15), today in the Tribuna of the Uffizi, is the focus of this chapter.[9] Its widely acknowledged beauty and complexity suggest that it is rich in potential for exploration in contemporary contexts of decorum and in its long-recognized official status as state portrait of a regent.[10] Other aspects of Eleonora's decorum in it are explored here, the most important being the dignity appropriate to her rank as Regent of State at a pivotal moment in Cosimo's reign.

Contemporary observers document the complex personality of the young duchess. Passionate, imperious, and volatile, she could rebuke and reprove without restraint, to the distress of courtiers and retainers. Deeply in love with Cosimo, she was often fractious during his absences. The amusements of the young couple included hunting above all, prelate baiting, practical jokes, and energetic equestrian sports, despite Eleonora's annual pregnancies. Her taste was notoriously luxurious – and readily indulged, thanks to her enormous personal wealth. The duchess was an incorrigible gambler, known for her success in bidding for high stakes, but known, too, to bet on the sex of her courtiers' unborn children. She was also an astute mercantile investor and reclaimer of vast tracts of Tuscan marshes. Diligent especially in supervising her children's upbringing, she was devout to a fault.[11]

The duchess's state portrait should not, however, be interpreted as a reflection either of her actual appearance or of her documented personality. Her containment in the portrait has been offered as 'evidence' of the real Eleonora's proud Hispanic upbringing, of seigneurial arrogance, and of a glacial personality – she has even been vilified as a cold and remote mother.[12] Such assumptions are misguided.

Instead, as pendant to the duke's state portrait, Bronzino's *Cosimo in Armour*, Eleonora's state portrait will be examined here in its cultural contexts and revealed as a vehicle of Medici propaganda in its own right. The portrait, which we instinctively view as layered in meaning, rings with the observation that the sixteenth-century artist's subject is not simply the visible particulars he depicts, but is shaped by a hierarchy of mediating abstractions.[13] Forensic study of Bronzino's *Allegory of Venus and Cupid* of 1545 recently manifested the truth of this observation – its underlayers unveiled a complex tissue of pentimenti that evidence the artist's teeming intellect and a willingness to push the spectator's engagement with his subject to unsuspected depths.[14] The *Eleonora with Giovanni* has stood the test of time, holding us in thrall even as it suggests a complexity not fully within our modern comprehension. We instinctively yearn to have its underlying power exposed, perhaps to better understand the artist's construction of the decorum of power itself that it so patently promotes. This exploration of Bronzino's *Eleonora di Toledo with Her Son Giovanni* suggests that his portraiture was as allusive, inventive, urbane, and meticulous as his *Allegory*.

Paolo Giovio's glowing response to the duke's gift of a copy of Bronzino's *Cosimo in Armour* in 1546 proves that, from its completion in 1543, the impact of Cosimo's own official portrait was strongly felt.[15] It seems that Cosimo eagerly awaited completion of a contemporary *Eleonora*.[16] Clearly, portraiture was now of the utmost importance at the court, and Bronzino must have felt his creative and technical powers especially challenged by the commission.[17] As discussed in the Introduction, decorum was a conscious construct for the sixteenth-century artist. Its end was always understood to be persuasion of the audience to a writer or artist's point of view. Indeed, truth could be manipulated by the artist in the interest of persuasion,[18] as patently would be in Cosimo's official portraits: he had never fought in battle, but his official portrait shows him in armour, and there are countless manifestations of him in the guise of classical heroes, borrowed to symbolically eulogize his virtues.[19] In effect, the portrait depicts a persona, emblematic of the office he holds. The challenge in approaching Eleonora's state portrait is to respect its sixteenth-century origins in order to reveal its evolution and its import in the Medici court milieu. In its comprehensiveness and historicity, Leonardo's precept suggests avenues into examination of the portrait's evident complexities.

The State Portrait of Eleonora and Her Son

Bronzino's compositional structure for his *Portrait of Eleonora di Toledo with Her Son* (pl. 4) is unique in Florentine portraiture for the period. The duchess is presented in three-quarter-length pose and turned slightly to her right, seated on a red velvet cushion on a bench against the low balustrade of an open loggia. Her right arm is posed around the shoulder of a small boy aged about two years, and her left arm is placed to allow her hand to lightly rest on her gown. She is lavishly dressed in white satin brocade, woven in elaborate figures of black velvet and gold motifs. Twisted gilt-braid trim decorates her bodice and sleeves, the latter fastened along their length with gold clasps. A *camicia* of white linen, its borders embroidered in blackwork, is visible at the wrists and across the top of the bodice of her gown.[20] The gown itself is made the riveting focus of the composition, and tends to restrain the viewer from too-immediate scrutiny of the young duchess's impassive face. The braided, pearl-studded, gold snood that closely covers the sitter's hair is echoed by a gold, reticulated fichu that frames her shoulders. The duchess's jewels complement the sumptuousness of her costume. At her throat she wears a short necklace of pearls, mounted with a large diamond hung with a pendant pearl. A rope of pearls falls to her breast, and a weighty gold girdle set with an enormous topaz, together with large rubies, diamonds, pearls, and other stones encircles her waist.[21] It terminates in a swirled tassel constructed of hundreds of 'seed' pearls that lies prominently displayed in her lap.[22]

Eleonora's bearing is noticeably erect. Although her glance is direct, her expression discourages any empathy. Giovanni, dressed in shimmering ultramarine taffeta shot with gold, looks engagingly out to the viewer. He is slightly older and more composed in expression compared to Bronzino's ebullient portrait of him completed in April 1545 (fig. 16), where he is dressed in crimson and holds a gold-finch ('cardellino') – a visual pun marking his predestination for the Church and hopes for a third Medici papacy.[23] Behind Eleonora, and occupying a large area of the panel, is a low-lying landscape showing a river or estuary under a night sky, painted in expensive ultramarine pigment. Around her head the intense blue lightens. Oddly, from the front, the child and his mother are fully lit by bright daylight, which picks out every warp and weft of the Duchess's elaborately brocaded gown with mesmerizing precision (pl. 4 and fig. 15).

The Date of the Portrait and the Identity of the Child

No dispute has ever arisen with regard to Eleonora's identity, but disagreement exists concerning the child's. It is most often accepted as Giovanni, which can be easily verified. We know that Bronzino requested a further quantity of precious *azzurro* – ground lapis lazuli – from his patron on 9 August 1545, 'because the background is extensive.'[24] Bronzino's original *Deposition* for Eleonora's chapel has a large expanse of ultramarine, but it was ready for framing by the end of July.[25] The bust-length *Eleonora* in Prague (pl. 5 and figs. 19 and 20) also includes a lapis background, but that panel is small.[26] As Robert Simon proposed, the painting for which an extra quantity of *azzurro* was needed was most likely the *Eleonora with Her Son Giovanni*, which was therefore not completed until the late summer of 1545.[27] A date in early August 1545 for its completion would have had particular political significance. Cosimo's sought-after imperial decoration, the Order of the Golden Fleece, was officially conferred on him on 11 August 1545, in a solemn ceremony in the Cathedral of Santa Maria del Fiore.[28] It was just days before the event that Bronzino had requested further ultramarine for the background of the panel. As the precious *azzurro* would only be applied on completion of a composition, this confirms that the portrait was then nearing completion.[29] As Cosimo was notified of the award on 30 November 1544, it is likely that his anticipated investiture in August 1545 prompted the commission of a state portrait of his regent as a pendant to his own.[30] If so, this hope was thwarted – completion of the chapel's contemporary *Lamentation*, now needed as a diplomatic gift, took precedence.[31]

The date of Eleonora's portrait may be secured by addressing the identity of the child and his probable age. Vasari's record of Bronzino's first portrait commissions of Cosimo's family, quoted above, describes a portrait of Eleonora, a portrait of the ducal heir, Francesco, and one of Eleonora with her second son, Giovanni. But by the time Vasari's second edition of the *Vite* was written, several more sons had been born to the ducal couple.[32] Since portraits do exist of Eleonora posed with other sons, it has not been universally accepted that the round-faced, blond, brown-eyed boy portrayed with her in the Tribuna is her second son, Giovanni, born in 1543. Francesco, Giovanni, Garzia, and Ferdinando have all been proposed as contenders. (Pietro, born 1554, has never been proposed.)[33] Eleonora's first son, Francesco, was born in March 1541. To judge from the boy's age in the 1545 portrait, around two, this would exclude him – Francesco was then four. As heir apparent he has, nevertheless, often been identified in this portrait.

A conclusive identification may be made by comparing records of eye colour and physical characteristics from secure portraits of Eleonora's sons. We may eliminate Francesco, who had very dark eyes, black hair, and who was rather sharp-featured even as a child, as his portrait in the Uffizi Tribuna shows.[34] Garzia, born in 1547, whose portrait as an infant is also identified by inscription in the miniature series (pl. 8, third from the left, bottom row) painted in the late 1560s, had a round face but his eyes were greyish-blue.[35] Ferdinando, born in 1549, appears in many later portraits as grand duke always with very light grey-blue eyes, consistent with his portrait beside Garzia in the miniature series. Pietro had dark eyes but a sharp, triangular face, as his miniature shows, and his presence would move the date for the portrait to about 1556.[36] Eleonora would have been thirty-five by then, rather late for a portrait that emphasizes her fecundity and role for dynastic potential. Moreover, when Vasari wrote his revised *Vite* in 1568, Giovanni was dead. Vasari would hardly have confused his patron's adolescent son Pietro with the deceased and much-admired Giovanni in the revised *Vite*.

The child can only be Eleonora's second son, Giovanni, born September 1543, who as an infant was dark-eyed and blond, with a very full, round face. These characteristics are confirmed in his other portraits.[37] Moreover, Bronzino's documented *Giovanni with a Goldfinch*, painted in April 1545 (fig. 16), is unmistakably the same boy as the child in Eleonora's state portrait.[38] Consequently, it is safe to identify the Tribuna portrait with Vasari's description of a portrait of Eleonora with Giovanni, the panel that gave her such particular pleasure. It was still in progress in August, and he was then close to his second birthday, 28 September 1545. Eleonora would then have been twenty-three, consistent with Bronzino's portrayal of her as a young mother in her prime.

Other portraits of Eleonora support a date of August 1545 for the *Eleonora with Her Son Giovanni*, and they provide support, too, for Vasari's sequence of Bronzino's portrait commisions of the duke and duchess. There are no portraits of Eleonora recorded before or during the first year of her marriage. For Cosimo, apart from the Ridolfo Ghirlandaio version of him as a child, there is only the erotic *Cosimo as Orpheus*, in Philadelphia, possibly painted as a private wedding gift to Eleonora around 1539, when Cosimo was just twenty. No pendant *Eleonora* exists for this.[39] After the decorations for the *entrata* of Eleonora into Florence on Sunday, 29 June 1539, and for the wedding of the couple on 6 July the most immediate claims on court artists were for the decoration of living quarters in the Palazzo Vecchio of 1540, including the chapel, sets for comedies, more *apparati* for court festivals, and the elaborate *Joseph* tapestry designs.[40] Vasari refers first to the duke's state portrait, *Cosimo I in Armour* (pl. 3), commissioned before 1545.[41] He then lists a single portrait of Eleonora, a portrait of Cosimo's heir, Francesco, and lastly the portrayal of Eleonora with Giovanni. He stipulated that the latter, painted not much later than her single portrait, was in a different manner.[42] It is not clear how soon after he finished Eleonora's chapel in 1543 Bronzino commenced work on the portraits listed by Vasari before the *Eleonora with Giovanni*, but the prototype for all ducal state portraits – the Uffizi *Cosimo in Armour*, portraying him without the insignia of the Golden Fleece – was surely made before November 1544, when he was notified of the imperial decoration.[43] It certainly was made before August 1545, when Cosimo was invested with the Order.

Although Vasari makes no reference to a portrait of the duchess before the *Cosimo in Armour*, receipt of a portrait of Eleonora at Poggio a Caiano is acknowledged in a letter by Pietro Camaiani, dated 23 October 1543.[44] This may correspond to the single portrait of Eleonora that followed on the *Cosimo in Armour* in Vasari's description, suggesting that the original portrait of the duke in armour may, in fact, have been made as early as 1543.[45] It is widely accepted that the bust-length *Portrait of Eleonora di Toledo* in Prague inscribed '.26' (pl. 5) corresponds to the 1543 portrait referred to in Camaiani's letter.[46] It is certainly the precise source for the *Eleonora* in an anonymous double portrait in the Erlanger Collection (fig. 21), which shows the young duke posed in civilian dress, with a faithful version of the Prague *Eleonora* inserted beside him. Dated 1546, the couple appears with an unfurled map of Pisa and its environs prominently displayed in the foreground.[47] The Prague and Erlanger *Eleonora*s are close contemporaries to the *Eleonora with Giovanni* (pls. 4 and 5, and fig. 21). The clothing varies in the Prague and Uffizi panels, but the fashion of dress is identical; her age and the pose of Eleonora's face and shoulders are similar in all three.[48]

In the Prague panel Eleonora is dressed in a crimson satin gown embroidered with a gold scroll pattern and posed against a plain ultramarine background. The panel's small size, and an intaglio on her little finger (fig. 20) figured with *palle*-filled cornucopias and a caduceus – signifying good fortune with virtue – flanking a bird, perhaps Alciati's wifely turtledove, suggest a commission made for Cosimo's personal enjoyment.[49] (The ring, and another cast in gold in the form of clasped hands, were recovered from her tomb.)[50] The panel's diminutive size suggests that it was intended for close-range viewing, and Eleonora may even have intended it to accompany the duke on his absences. Its sentimental appeal is suggested by her relaxed, hand-over-heart gesture and the brilliant red-and-ultramarine colour scheme, which recalls the gold-embroidered crimson dress she wore for her wedding *entrata* six years before, paired with the peacock blue livery ('pavonazzo') of the Toledan armorial colours used for that occasion.[51]

The Prague panel is evidently close in date to the *Eleonora with Giovanni*, but is more relaxed in expression and shows a less abstracted rendering of her features. It was probably painted from life, and its youthful freshness and mutability of expression, unsurpassed by all later panels of the duchess, has not escaped attention.[52] It is almost certainly the single portrait of her painted by Bronzino after his state portrait of the duke, as Vasari recorded. If he felt constrained to note that the *Eleonora with Giovanni* showed her in a dress different to that in her single portrait, perhaps it was because the second *was* an official portrait, which would show her in robes of state instead of less remarkable attire.[53]

Portrait sittings were notoriously tedious and exhausting. Isabella d'Este particularly hated them, as did her brother Ippolito, and Vasari famously claimed that Leonardo engaged singers, players, and jesters to keep Mona Lisa amused at sittings 'to remove that melancholy which painting usually gives to portraits.'[54] Eleonora's annual pregnancies and her impatient nature suggest that she would have been unwilling to endure protracted sittings. Probably preparatory sketches for the Prague panel provided a direct source for the formal, abstracted, and monumentalized official *Eleonora with Giovanni*. A 'fresher' rendering in the Prague panel, the subtlety of modulation of her facial planes and greater mutability of expression all convey a vivacity missing in the state portrait. Given an existing facial record, it was not necessary for the subject to wear Medici regalia and trappings of state; these were loaned to the artist's workshop and recorded from the model.[55]

In sum, the Prague *Eleonora*, probably painted by October 1543 and before August 1545, appears to have been the prototype for the state portrait of Eleonora, as it was for the 1546 anonymous double portrait of Cosimo and Eleonora now in the Erlanger collection and many others to follow. Giulio Clovio's miniature of circa 1551–3 (fig. 22) stands as the only other significant original portrayal of Eleonora from life in this decade.[56]

If the state portrait was not painted from life, it seems likely that Bronzino was allowed considerable artistic freedom in composing the new genre of state portrait, that of a regent. His intellectual inventiveness would have been a significant factor in fulfilling the needs of a suitable decorum for her in this instance. Eleonora and Cosimo's confidence in him would not have been misplaced. His association with the new court was extremely close – he had assisted Pontormo with the Castello frescoes, commissioned immediately on Cosimo's accession in 1537.[57] His literary interests and familiarity with Florentine *letterati* are chronicled from the 1530s, and descriptions of his admired ephemeral sets and stagings for the couple's wedding in 1539 attest to his familiarity with Cosimo's propagandistic themes.[58] He was well aware of the political importance of the Medici-Toledo union. Its historical background is sketched in the next section to provide the context – a 'setting and circumstance' – for Eleonora's state portrait.

The Medici-Toledo Marriage and Eleonora's Regency

With the intention of further strengthening relations with Charles V, Cosimo had hoped to marry the emperor's illegitimate daughter – Alessandro's young widow – Margaret of Austria. Instead, Margaret was given by her father to Ottavio Farnese, nephew of the pope. Cosimo astutely turned his efforts to a marriage with the daughter of the immensely wealthy Don Pedro di Toledo, Marquis of Villafranca, the Hapsburg viceroy in Naples and prominent member of the power-wielding Alba family.[59] Cosimo's bid for Eleonora, his personal choice among the viceroy's daughters, was applauded in Florence. (His mother too was influential in this choice.)[60] It was a love match, but most importantly a strategic alliance, Don Pedro having great authority in Italy and very close relations with the Hapsburg emperor, Charles V.[61] He also had troops at his command.[62] Through his marriage, Cosimo consolidated his ties with the Austrian and Spanish houses and gained a powerful imperial protector.

Election to the papacy of two Medici cardinals, Giovanni (1475–1521) in 1513 as Leo X and Giulio (1478–1534) in 1522 as Clement VII, had already led to a wider international forum for Medici interests. Shrewd foreign marriage alliances became a Medici tradition, but Madeleine de la Tour d'Auvergne (Lorenzo, Duke of Urbino's French bride) and Margaret of Austria (Alessandro's Hapsburg bride) had each left Florence on being widowed shortly after their marriages.[63] It fell to Cosimo, with Eleonora's help, to establish the first court in Florence that could reflect increased Medici political power and dynastic pretensions. Her credentials were impressive. Naples was the Italian peninsula's only kingdom. Known simply as 'Il Regno,' the viceregal court had traditions of royal pageantry and rigid protocol going back about four centuries. Eleonora's father, Pedro, had surprised the high nobility there by his Spanish manners: for example, when giving audience, he remained as immobile and expressionless 'as a marble statue.'[64] The Alba of Toledo had long been trusted affiliates of the Spanish monarchy and court, and during her father's reign as viceroy (1532–53), Eleonora witnessed the lavish Neapolitan reception for Charles V in 1535.[65] Predictably, this environment produced in her an overweening imperiousness and love of luxury – qualities distinctly lacking in Cosimo's background.[66] Lessons learned by Eleonora in this crucible of extravagance, prestige, rank, privilege, and propaganda would reflect the couple's intention to be outdone only by the Hapsburg stronghold itself.[67]

Appropriate decorum for the ducal couple was designed to express suzerainty, and Eleonora was singularly qualified to impel its manifestations. Her *altezza*, as duchess, and Cosimo's stoicism contributed to a persistent demeanour of unapproachability by even their closest associates in the court, disconcertingly furthered by his tendency to 'duke and unduke' himself at whim.[68] The Florentine court became dominated by the exasperating formality of Spanish etiquette.[69] This outcome would inevitably have created its own context for decorum in Medicean portraiture.[70] The new rules of court etiquette permeated society, as the republican Giovanni della Casa complained: 'Our land has received them badly ... for such meticulous distinction between degrees of nobility is bothersome to us.'[71]

Eleonora's obstinate Hispanicism and imperious nature eventually alienated her subjects.[72] In the early years, however, the aura of privilege created around her served Cosimo's purposes well. The pomp of her *entrata* and wedding in 1539 was described as 'astounding' ('cosa da stupire').[73] The casa Medici on Via Larga was decked magnificently with pictures – including Raphael's *Leo X* – sculpture, and rich hangings in cloth of gold and silver. These, Eleonora's youth and beauty, her jewels, her peacock-liveried retinue, and the magnificence of the festivities and spectacles all contributed to the high esteem in which the couple was held, and to the pride of contemporary Florentines in their city-state.[74] Mannucci, in Cosimo's posthumous history of 1586, records:

> During the whole of the journey they were greeted with incredible jubilation, and with the happiness of the people who saw them, and they were received with the most sumptuous and noble *apparati* that each of the territories and nearby towns could prepare ... [T]here was a great concourse of people [in Florence] who went to look at the magnificence of the *apparati* and principally at the new Lady, who was received and honoured by all with great acclaim.[75]

Eleonora was young and intelligent, in robust good health, and prodigiously energetic. Her independent wealth and imperial favour provided vital insurance against further turmoil in Tuscany. Her ancient, Alba pedigree was impeccable –

a matter of some import for ceremonial occasions. Florentines, as witnesses to the emergent dynasty's public, official face, were primed by Eleonora's wedding for a continuing panoply of propaganda as the regime progressed. As 'setting and circumstance' in the scheme of Eleonora's decorum in an official state portrayal, these early manifestations of power, too, merit attention. Tribolo created a large statue of *Fecundità* for her wedding *entrata*. Placed at the entrance to the city, it declared Eleonora's role in a Medicean dynastic scheme:

> Tribolo was given the task of making a triumphal arch at the Porta al Prato, through which the bride would enter on her journey from Poggio ... [F]ull of figures and scenes ... the principal figure ... was a statue of a woman five *braccia* high, representing Fecundity, with five *putti* ... [A]nother was of Security, who leaned on a column, with a slender twig in her hand; the other was of Eternity, with a sphere in her arms. Below her was the white-haired old man, Time, holding in his arms the Sun and the Moon.[76]

The twig held by *Securità* was the *broncone*, the lopped but sprouting laurel symbolizing Cosimo as the redemptive new Medici branch, as confirmed in the inscription: 'Enter, enter, under the most favourable auspices, Eleonora, your City. And, fruitful in excellent offspring, may you produce descendants similar in quality to your father and forebears abroad, so that you may guarantee eternal security for the Medici name and its most devoted citizenry.'[77] Notions of Medicean dynasty and eternal security for Tuscany, and references to the governing deities of Sun and Moon are metaphors woven into Bronzino's portrayal of Eleonora as regent that continued to have currency well beyond her death.

Her dynastic role was further stated at the wedding festivities. In the lunettes of the first courtyard of the Palazzo Medici, *Fecundità* was depicted as a 'beautiful lady, rich with many children,' acompanied by a motto from the *Aeneid*: 'We shall bear your descendants up to the stars.'[78] Another related theme, 'joyful fertility with modesty,' existed in almost every future context for Eleonora. Her advanced pregnancy, wearing Medici green-and-red armorial colours in the chapel frescoes, has been noted, and she would be personified on Bartolomeo Ammannati's fountain (fig. 63) as Juno the chaste, fecund consort of Jupiter, goddess of matrimony and patroness of childbirth.[79] Giovanni's presence in the state portrait expresses her role as dynastic mother, but Cosimo and Eleonora were also perceived as joint rulers.[80] In time, Cosimo would have Eleonora remembered as 'madre della repubblica fiorentina,' a title that expressed fulfilment of the sentiments represented in the wedding *apparato*. Her personal identification with Juno would also express her regency: as queen of deities, Juno commanded worldly dominion and riches.[81]

The *Eleonora with Her Son Giovanni* as State Portraiture

The eulogizing of Eleonora as mother of a new dynasty and of the republic at her wedding, in her chapel, and in later iconographic cycles is a logical pendant for his regent to mirror symbolism in the duke's state portrait, *Cosimo I in Armour* of 1543 (pl. 3), which cloaks him in the role of defender and commander of his subjects.[82] In an extended, lengthened version of the portrait of about 1545, the sprouting Medici *broncone* supplied dynastic context – expressing, too, the moral imperative for portraiture prescribed by Francisco de Hollanda: to perpetuate the memory of ancestors and instruct descendants to glorify their family tree.[83] But portrayal of a regent cannot be expressed in militant absolutes, and must account for more complex, dynamic aspects of merit on which her power and authority depend.[84] Valour was as yet little promoted, even for queens assertive of sovereignty or active militarily, for whom it was still necessary to emphasize wifely modesty, chastity, piety, and fecundity.[85] Bronzino's challenge was to formulate an appropriate persona for Eleonora as regent. The duke's official portrait had been inspired by Titian's now-lost portrait of Charles V, painted 1532–3 in Bologna.[86] The most current portrait of Charles's empress that might serve as inspiration – one possibly circulated to the Medici court – was the model, probably by Seisenegger, of about 1538–9, for Titian's *Empress Isabella in Black*, of 1543–4, or even the latter, already known to Aretino in 1544. Several of many copies survive (fig. 23).[87]

When he finally viewed it in 1545, Titian's posthumous *Isabella in Black* disappointed Charles, but its interesting history provides insight into a rapid evolution in state portraiture of decorum for queens and regents at this time. Titian asked the emperor to point out its faults and imperfections so that he might improve it, to which Charles responded that the empress's nose needed straightening, and this could be attended to on one of his visits to Italy. The panel was probably worked on by Titian during the artist's visit to the Augsburg court in 1548.[88] The refined *Isabella of Portugal in Red* of 1548, now in Madrid (fig. 24), seems to have been Titian's final opportunity to compose a portrait of the empress without any encumbrance. It was greatly treasured by Charles, and taken by him to the Monastery of Yuste in 1556, after his abdication.[89]

A copy of the *Isabella in Black* of 1544–5 (or the earlier Seisenegger prototype) may, however, have been circulated to the Florentine court before Cosimo's investiture by imperial proxy in August 1545, and its 'shortcomings' also made evident to Bronzino before he embarked on the portrait of Eleonora with Giovanni. From comparison of the *Isabella in Black* with the new *Isabella in Red* of 1548 (figs. 23 and 24), the earlier version's offending elements were not only her nose, but the intrusively large crown placed on the window sill behind the empress, her less-than-majestic posture, her dull costume, her unprepossessing expression, and an uncorrected, pronounced squint. (We should not blame Titian, who may have followed his model, as instructed.) Bronzino's *Eleonora with Her Son Giovanni* – and, within three years, Titian's *Isabella in Red* – each reflect the general compositional format of surviving copies of the *Isabella in Black*. But Bronzino, and later Titian, each dispensed with overt accoutrements of dominion such as the crown, preferring instead to stiffen the posture of their respective sitters, to idealize their features, to provide more removed expressions, to garb them sumptuously, and to include a landscape as background.

A decorum of regency seems to have rapidly evolved for this genre of portraits of consorts after Titian's 1548 version, but it may have depended on Bronzino's *Eleonora with Her Son Giovanni*, painted just three years earlier.[90] Isabella is posed similarly to the 1545 *Eleonora* but in reverse, and seated erect on a bench with her right hand posed to rest lightly on her elaborate gown. Each woman is lavishly bejewelled. Titian's *Isabella in Red* holds a prayerbook in her left hand, but in both his and Bronzino's portraits, the spaces between each of the posed hands and the head of the sitter form a triangle in precisely the same plane as in the *Isabella in Black*. A landscape appears through the window in Titian's revision, filling the space left by the absent crown. Isabella, who died nine years earlier, looks dreamily distant, but her grandeur is now manifest. The expression in Eleonora's portrait, like Titian's later *Isabella in Red*, is detached and serene. Compared to the *Isabella in Black*, the decorum of Bronzino's and Titian's sitters has been suffused with majesty, the abstract characteristics of which Charles had been eager to impart to the retrospective state portrait of his late empress in black. It was the *Isabella in Red* that he finally embraced as the ideal representation of his wife, to whose memory he was devoted.[91]

In its particulars and style, Bronzino's *Eleonora* is more formal, more sumptuous, more hypnotic by virtue of its optical effects, and more directly confronts the spectator than Titian's final, posthumous *Isabella in Red* (fig. 24).[92] Eleonora was a living, official regent. Her portrayed decorum stands as a paradigm of European portrayals of female rulers and regents for centuries to come – formal in pose, rigidly but lavishly costumed, removed in expression, and posed before an expansive landscape.[93] She is made vividly present before Bronzino's airy, open loggia, which allows her to loom before the scene – a wide realm of watery plains and distant hills – without the confining wall that Titian would retain from the *Isabella in Black*. Eleonora's regency is visually expressed by her dominion over a broad vista (pl. 4 and fig. 15) uninterrupted by walls or an enframing window.[94]

Her portrayal as Regent of State could carry no weight without reference to a wider context of patronage: that of imperial protection of its Florentine fiefdom.[95] Central to Bronzino's composition is the stylized pomegranate motif of Eleonora's gown (pl. 4 and fig. 15), where its size and his fastidious rendering of every warp and weft of its gold-bound threads make it a commanding focus. Vasari suggests that this acutely optical rendering of sumptuous textures and gleaming surfaces was characteristic of state portraiture and was intended to create awe.[96] During Cosimo's reign, the traditional use of prominently embroidered or brocade motifs arranged as *imprese* or *divise* on clothing to denote rank had, with livery, become an *instrumentum regni* to declare the exclusiveness of the court.[97] The pomegranate had been especially associated with Eleonora in her role as *genetrix*, as the fruit and symbol of marriage and fertility.[98] It was an *impresa* she had appropriated from Charles's late wife, the Empress Isabella.[99]

In this case, the sumptuous textile may carry subliminal messages of access to imperial power. Charles habitually made lavish gifts of gold-loomed brocade throughout his reign.[100] Although a thriving textile industry existed in Florence, Eleonora's brocade may be of Spanish design, close to others gifted in association with Hapsburg alliances.[101] For her marriage in 1526, Charles's empress was clothed in brocade very similar to Eleonora's.[102] A Hapsburg state portrait of Catherine de' Medici's daughter, Isabella of Austria, shows her costumed in brocade of almost identical pattern to Eleonora's. Mary Tudor, wife of Philip II is attired in different Spanish brocade in Antonis Mor's betrothal portrait, Charles's gift in 1554 to her to celebrate the English queen's marriage contract.[103] Eleonora's may have been an imperial gift made to mark Cosimo's impending investiture with the Imperial Order of the Golden Fleece, along with territorial concessions.[104]

According to Equicola, *imprese* such as the emblematic pomegranate functioned to 'quietly make our [the ruler's] will known to those who have to take cognizance of our intentions.'[105] Throughout the Hapsburg Holy Roman Empire – in this period, territorially vast and politically invincible – the many seeds in the pomegranate signified unity under one authority.[106] Medici destiny and ambitions were effectively controlled by Charles V, and imperially approved marriage alliances were strongly encouraged.[107] Blazoned centrally on Eleonora's bodice, the pomegranate proclaims imperial patronage and favour, just as the insignia of the Golden Fleece on the duke's breastplate proclaims imperial connections in the Kassel version of Bronzino's *Cosimo in Armour*. Here it especially reinforces Eleonora's role as his surrogate in a chain of imperial command.[108]

Sumptuousness, an essential element in state portraiture, is also manifested through the duchess's robe of state. Eleonora regarded expression of rank through majestic clothing to be an abiding duty: letters record her directives on the design of clothing – her own, her children's, her ladies-in-waitings', and that for triumphal entries or official appearances at other courts, for Cosimo, too. Indeed, her efforts in this regard created considerable nervousness in the court about her stringent expectations. Predictably, for portraiture, destined to circulate in copies to other courts, her instructions were punctilious.[109]

Figured designs on damascened or brocaded cloth were understood to be charged with subliminal meanings: authority, respect, and moral and political influence were gained through motifs signalling nobility, *magnificenza*, and, implicitly, virtue.[110] The ducal couple was well aware of its potential. Lorenzo Pagni's letter of 23 October 1549 to Bronzino instructs him that portraits of Cosimo and Eleonora destined for the Bishop of Arras are to be finished quickly; the artist is *not* required to render a gown in brocade, but instead some other ornate cloth that makes a fine show ('non si facci di broccato riccio, ma di qual altro drappo ornato che facia bella mostra').[111] Evidently, the depiction of *broccato* was reserved for portraits intended as gifts to only the more influential and important recipients. Second, in Bronzino's hands, brocade was time-consuming to render, so that a degree of ostentation was associated even with the cost of execution of an official portrait depicting a subject in brocaded robes of state. Third, the existence of an actual gown in brocade was not essential for the artist to render one in paint. Conversely, the artist apparently had licence to insert or substitute motifs to fortify a symbolic theme and enrich an existing, figured design. Studies of cloth patterns in late-fourteenth-century panels indicate that brocaded designs offered scope to bring motifs within the metaphorical context of the whole painting.[112] Whether Eleonora's robe of state was precisely as it appears in the Tribuna portrait or not, the potential of figured textiles to carry symbolic implications suggests that a contemporary viewer would approach a state portrait with a heightened awareness of its import and intrinsic value.[113] In the fictional exchange in Vasari's *Ragionamenti*, the boy-prince Francesco de' Medici expresses awareness of brocade's special status.[114]

(Embellishment in art is echoed in contemporary literary theory: in his third *proemio* Vasari described the ornateness of mannerist *disegno* in terms that align it with *elocutio* in rhetoric.)[115] We may assume that mesmerizing optical effects and subliminal associations of brocade with rank and privilege were calculated by Bronzino to inspire *stupore* in the contemporary viewer and for posterity. The panel manifestly fulfils requirements for state portraiture and its decorum. Its illusionistic, complex style, emphasis on gold-woven brocade, and idealization of the sitter, with her expression of awe-inspiring rigidity and inscrutability were intended to convey the young duchess's powerful rank as regent. A tendency in state portraiture to isolate the sitter from the commonweal is further conveyed by the panel's size, monumentality, lavish use of lapis lazuli, and time-consuming, highly wrought detail.[116]

As this portrait is the source for about forty extant derivatives in far-flung locations, its importance as an official state portrait can scarcely be exaggerated. Two extended versions, one in Detroit by Bronzino, the other by Lorenzo della Sciorina for the important *Serie Aulica* (figs. 17 and 18), also make it clear that Bronzino's majestic prototype enjoyed continued esteem throughout the sixteenth century. Bronzino copied the Detroit version precisely but lengthened it slightly to create a deeper perspective, thereby increasing the distance between Eleonora and the viewer.[117] Lorenzo extended the portrait to almost full-length.[118] Its visual progression begins at the lower pomegranate, creating a step-like 'approach' reminiscent of advance to a throne. In other demonstrably official images of the duchess, the brocaded robe of state was precisely copied: for example, in the bust-length Wallace Collection version, or Haelwegh's 1675 engraving, with the motto 'CVM PVDORE LAETA FOECVNDITAS' ('Joyful fertility accompanied by modesty') and the inscription 'ELEONORA TOLETANA / PETRI A VILLA FRANCA PROREGIS NEAP:F: COSMI I·MAGNI DVCIS ETRVRIAE VXOR,' identifying her as daughter of Pedro, Viceroy of Naples, and as the wife of Grand Duke Cosimo of Tuscany.[119]

Today, Leonardo's exhortation on the suitability of dress to indicate rank and dignity may not carry as much force as it did in an era of strict social hierarchy and sumptuary laws supporting seigneurial privilege. Curbs on dress enacted in Cosimo's sumptuary legislation in 1546, in 1562 and again in 1568 show his determination to reinforce the role of clothing to codify the social order his court had established. Cloth of gold had been a target of sumptuary laws in Florence from the end of the fourteenth century.[120] Eleonora's dress affirmed her rank and marked her exemption from such laws and elevation above common humanity. Even today, few garments in Western portraiture have captured the historical imagination as has this sumptuous, brocaded state gown. Popular myth has obstinately linked it to Eleonora's burial attire – a claim that forensic study has recently disclosed as false.[121] The urge to mythologize the dress, however, demonstrates the hold it has had on the historic imagination, implicitly endorsing its wearer's decorum, and ensuring the absolute success of this state portrait as a vehicle of propaganda and its perpetuation. It is a tribute to Bronzino's invention of this state portrait of a living regent that he ensured the sitter's majestic persona would remain unimpaired for posterity.

Majesty and Divinity in the State Portrait of Eleonora with Her Son

Sixteenth-century art theorists advised the painter to attend especially to the decorum of majesty in portrayals of royal sitters, described by Lomazzo as 'that artificial decorum, that when the prudent painter paints an Emperor, or a King, makes their portraits grave and full of majesty, whether they have these qualities or not.'[122] Francisco de Hollanda, portraitist to the Lisbon court before his late-1530s immersion in Rome and author of the first treatise on court portraiture, would allege in 1549 that the quality of majesty was the most difficult to impart, one for which the artist needed divine guidance from the outset. It must be palpable 'with God's help' in the outlines of the first sketch – even before features are added – 'so that anyone will know this is a queen or a king.'[123] (Concurrent with de Hollanda's writing, Titian, at Charles V's request, was working in 1548 to advance this very quality in his *Empress Isabella in Red*.)

Suggestions of divinity were imperative in state portraiture. The idea originated in classical writings such as Pliny's, who implied that the portrayal of the great had evolved from sacred imagery. This iconic emphasis is repeated in essence by sixteenth-century theorists such as Biondo, Dolce, and Lomazzo. The latter's exhortation to the artist to effect majestic decorum for the high-born or great in their portraits expressly calls for an awed response from the viewer: 'The function of the portrait from life, that is the making of images of men, reproducing them as they are, [should be] so that whoever sees them may recognise ... the portraits of great men as of idols on earth.'[124] De Hollanda makes the association of royalty with divinity equally clear. He tells of distractions while portraying the king of Portugal, 'a divine work' needing 'more attention than I usually have [due to the] perfection the work requires.' Assuming reflected glory for himself as a royal familiar, he relates that the queen alone understood the intellectual demands exerted on him by this genre – she ordered the room cleared of an audience of gawking courtiers.[125]

In Eleonora's case, overtones of the divine were to embed themselves in the public consciousness on state occasions. Antonfrancesco Cirni Corso recorded the triumphal ducal *entrata* into Siena of 1560, with a detailed inventory of Eleonora's attire and demeanour:

> [Cosimo] was dressed in *bertino* velvet embroidered in gold with the Golden Fleece hanging from a gold chain, and with a golden collar. [Eleonora] appeared more as a chaste, beautiful earthly queen and of exquisite virtue all mixed with queenly goodness, of superhuman majesty dressed in white velvet embroidered with gold enmeshed with points of precious gems such as diamonds, rubies [and] emeralds, with necklaces of pearls, a girdle full of jewels, and with a sable around her neck, all of which is valued at three-hundred thousand *scudi*.[126]

This sum translates to about $10,500,000 U.S. in today's values. Her extraordinary grandeur made a similar impression on the diarist Agostino Lapini, who recalled her lavish, solemn entry into Rome on 6 November 1560, her piety in kissing the feet of Pius IV, and her inexpressible majesty ('si gran grandezza che non si può esprimere').[127]

Her portrait anticipates this 'superhuman majesty' and the wonderment created around her. Divinity is implied, first, by association of mother and son with the canonical pairing of Mary with the infant Christ. The state portrait of Eleonora appears to be the first of a female consort with her son, and Bronzino was probably without precedents to inspire him for such a double portrait.[128] The canonical reference is hardly accidental: Francesco, the ducal heir – now nearly five – was not chosen as adjunct to his mother for this portrait, the most dynastically important portrayal of the duchess ever commissioned.[129] His omission in this case suggests that the choice of a younger child allowed Bronzino to evoke a divinity for Eleonora associated with the Madonna and Child, a Child usually depicted in His early years in devotional paintings. For Florentines, it would also have evoked Fra Angelico's sumptuous images of the enthroned Madonna, the *Maestà*. In his S. Domenico altarpiece in Fiesole (circa 1425), for example, the Virgin's haloed head is posed before a lapis-blue cloth of honour.[130] Eleonora's stilled, majestic remove advances this association with the *Maestà*.[131] She is enthroned on a long cushion but almost standing, her infant son beside her, posed against a deep 'Virgin' blue that lightens to form a nimbus around her head.[132] (Several of Fra Angelico's expensive, lapis-wrought *Maestàs* had been commissioned by Cosimo the Elder, incidentally allowing a subtle dynastic association to be made between this mother and child and continuity of the main Medici line.)[133] In northern European portraiture, the use of royal women – or even mistresses – as models for the Virgin has precedence in Jan Van Eyck and Jean Fouquet's *Madonna and Child* panels.[134] Eleonora's may be the first to promote its corollary – the monarch or regent as Virgin Queen. Virginal associations were not taken literally in the case of female regents – Battista Sforza is not only deified by luminescence in Piero della Francesca's portrait of her as regent, but her *Trionfo* on the reverse shows her carriage drawn by harnessed unicorns, which Alciati reminds us was an animal that traditionally would not allow itself to be tamed except by a virgin.[135] Rather, such borrowed superlatives of chaste faithfulness, Petrarchan exclusion, and deification were evidently coined to endorse the legitimacy of bloodlines, to create awe, and to instil confidence in claims of a regent's divine right to rule.

Exclusiveness and divinity were associated with ultramarine because of its source, precious lapis lazuli. Bronzino's entreaty for more lapis suggests that artistic responsibility was associated with its use; he stipulated that the saturation had to be very concentrated ('I cannot do with less, since the ground is large and has to be dark').[136] Its extravagant, deep saturation in the Tribuna portrait's expansive background places the panel literally beyond the power of most patrons to commission. Copies, even of miniatures, seldom included it.[137] Cennino Cennini believed that *azzurro* reflected honour on both patron and painter: 'illustrious, beautiful, and most perfect beyond all other colours ... [Y]ou [the artist] will gain great honour and service from it.'[138]

There had, however, been a shift from appreciation of gold and high grades of blue in Renaissance paintings to an appreciation of skill. In the effort to effect a new form of official portrait for women in the Florentine milieu, a blending of Bronzino's skill and the earlier traditions associated with these pigments were probably seen as fortuitous by his Medici patrons; what mattered to viewer and patron was subject matter *and* intrinsic value, which could be read in the preciousness of lapis, gold, or other rare pigments.[139] In his *Dialogo di Pittura* of 1548, the Venetian Paolo Pino deplored 'those who smear them about' ('empiastrar facendo') for facile effects. Firenzuola, the translator of Horace's *Ars poetica* and arbiter of manners who was closely associated with the early court, cautioned that 'ultramarine blue at sixty *scudi* the ounce' could be used meretriciously by the 'ravishing type of painter' ('il pittore vago'), and was no guarantee of imparting charm to a painting. Bronzino's own poetry mocks vainglorious painters, who work too quickly; every blemish and blot on a surface must be accounted for.[140] Evidently, colours were considered beautiful only when they conformed to expectation.[141] In effect, a degree of decorum attended appreciation of *colore* by patrons and *cognoscenti*; Firenzuola even appears to propose a propriety of demeanour for the artist when using ultramarine, most likely because, at its most expensive – a heavy saturation yielding a deep, inky blue – it had traditionally been the pigment of choice for draperies of the Blessed Virgin.[142]

Symbolically, the pigment's lavish use for background and sky places Eleonora in the realm of the Virgin. Eleonora's backdrop is nocturnal, the inky hue allowing her to be deified by the contrasting corona of light against the starry, dark empyrean. It associates her, too, with a contemporary invocation from the Litany of the Blessed Virgin Mary, *Stella mattutina* (Star of the Morning).[143] Eleonora's placement in the environment of Mary had already been enshrined in Sandoval's elegy for Maria Salviati of 1543, where in the closing lines he refers to Eleonora as sent from heaven.[144] Such instances of the use of known, beloved models for the Virgin had a long tradition.[145] A decade after Bronzino's *Eleonora with Her Son Giovanni*, Giulio Clovio's portrait miniature of Eleonora (fig. 22) seemingly inspired the features of his contemporary miniature *Annunciate Virgin*, now in the Uffizi.[146]

Bronzino had earlier created Marian overtones of chaste virtue for his *Lucrezia Panciatichi* (fig. 27); Eleonora, if not loved by Florentines, was always praised for her virtue.[147] Lucrezia's piety is hinted at by the niche in which she is framed, and her breviary, open to the feast of the Purification of the Virgin, links her to Mary's purity. Surpassing this, Bronzino emphasizes Eleonora's official role as regent by recalling the regal, iconic, Madonna enthroned on a long red cushion as on the medieval Throne of Wisdom, the *Sedes sapientiae*.[148] A more erect, hieratic pose than the chair-bound Lucrezia's, a further remove in expression for the duchess, and a more sober portrayal of Giovanni than for Bronzino's portrait of him in April 1545 all suggest that this iconic association with the ancient, regal manifestations of Mary was the artist's intention.

Reminders of the iconic *Sedes sapientiae* alert us to another association: the pairing of wisdom with virtuous chastity that existed as a precise iconographical attribute in official portraiture for a female consort. De Hollanda, arguing in 1549 for near-royal exclusiveness in portraiture, allowed that 'a famous princess or a queen ... due to her wisdom and virtue is worthy of being known to posterity.'[149] Mary's virtue and divine regency, symbolically appropriated by Bronzino to further Cosimo's promotion of his consort in her role as chaste guarantor of his dynasty, simultaneously promotes her as a wise, surrogate ruler. Indeed, Eleonora's chosen *impresa*, the peahen with chicks, is associated with God-given wisdom. The bird is contrasted with the neglectful ostrich: 'Which leaveth her eggs in the earth, and warmeth them in the dust / And forgetteth that the foot may crush them, or that the wild beast may break them. She is hardened against her young ones, as though they were not hers ... God hath deprived her of wisdom.' (Job 39:13–17).[150] Classical references invoke wisdom for Eleonora, too. Backlit by moonlight in her portrait, she is cast as Diana, the divinity who accompanies Athena-Wisdom as she routs Venus and the Vices in Mantegna's *Triumph of Wisdom over the Vices*.[151] Royalty and wisdom for Eleonora would later be made explicit by Cosimo for their contemporaries. In 1560 a translator of the *Aeneid* written for the duke took the liberty of 'prophesying' Eleonora's birth, placing her in the realm of the gods centuries before her arrival on earth, and conferring divinely ordained dynastic status on her descendents: '[T]he sky is closing now, and shuts off view / of where she who is not yet born is admired and honoured / the splendid, the royal, the wise Leonora.'[152] Finally, Vasari, describing her interchangeably with her chosen deity, Juno, in the now-lost frescoes for Eleonora's *Loggia di Juno*, makes reference to her majesty and serenity, the latter virtue, *tranquillitas*, being an attribute desired in consorts of stoic emperors in late antiquity.[153]

In addition to the iconic and artistic references to Mary and Christ, confirmed by the luminous nimbus about her head, Eleonora's 'divinity' is furthered by Bronzino's deployment of several other 'radiant' metaphors. Ambiguous lighting, whereby Eleonora is frontally lit by daylight but posed against a night sky and landscape associates her with the Apocalyptic Woman clothed with the Sun and the Moon. The association had given redemptive overtones to Isabella of Castile's reign (1474–1504), perhaps here used as a subtle reminder of Spanish exemplars in Eleonora's background.[154] It is a conceit that Bronzino borrowed from Petrarchan poetry.[155] This simultaneous diurnal and nocturnal illumination recalls Petrarch's setting for the remote, regal 'Vergine bella':

> Beautiful Virgin who, clothed with the sun
> And crowned with the stars, so pleased the highest Sun
> That in you he hid his light:
> Love drives me to speak words of you
> But I do not know how to begin without your help
> And His who loving placed Himself in you.
>   I invoke her who has always replied
> To whoever called on her with faith.
> Virgin, if extreme misery of human things
> Ever turned you to mercy, bend to my prayer;
> Give succour to my war,
> Though I am earth and you are Queen of Heaven.[156]

The metaphorical reference to the Sun as the ruler whose light is reflected in his regent ('sommo Sole / piacesti sì che 'n te sua luce ascose') brings to mind Cosimo's mirror-like armour in his pendant portrait.[157] By placing Eleonora in daylight, but depicting her as a Heavenly queen having dominion over the moonlit landscape behind her, Bronzino especially gives form to ideas expressed in his own poetry, as when 'sweet darkness' serves as a reminder of the return of the Sun: 'Alla dolce ombra dell'amata pianta ... Membrando il Sol ... Che quanto stette a ritornar l'Aurora.'[158]

Pagan deification is implied in the portrait, too, in luminous metaphors in paint of the coexistence of night (Diana) and Day (Apollo). Such reminders in Bronzino's poem of the return of the sun suggest Apollonian meaning linked directly to the duke. 'Cosmic' puns on Cosimo's name had currency from at least 1539.[159] Eventually, his 'deification' as Apollo would be pursued at length by his artists in sculpture and bronze.[160] Possibly this was because, in this period, Apollo had become associated with the divine right to rule.[161] Further, the court sculptor, Baccio Bandinelli, identified Apollo with the triumph of Reason in a neo-Ficinesque theme for a 1545 engraving.[162] Later, in his account of the triumphal state entry into Siena in 1560, Cirni referred to the ducal couple as demigods ('due Semidei').[163] Within a few years, Cellini proposed a seal depicting Cosimo as Apollo, 'Lucerna dell' Universo', to honour the Duke's patronage of the arts when the Accademia del Disegno was founded in 1563.[164] Other 'divine' associations were more broadly stated by Cosimo's artists. In Stoldo di Lorenzo's relief, *Cosimo I as Victorious Ruler of Florence and Siena*, Eleonora flanks Cosimo, each dressed *all'antica*, as he receives tributes.[165] Cosimo's 'deification' increased, and Vasari's 1565 Sala Grande ceiling tondo, the *Apotheosis of Cosimo*, crowns a welter of tributes to Cosimo as a divinely appointed ruler.[166] Deification of the ducal couple, however, had its roots in Giambullari's inventions for the very public wedding celebrations of Cosimo and Eleonora in 1539.[167] Indeed, Medicean pomp and cultural policies following Tuscan elevation to a Grand Duchy in 1569 have been recognized as precursor in miniature to those of Louis XIV as Sun-King.[168]

Association for Eleonora with Apollo, this time as his consort, may be made with confidence. Her haloed deification against a moonlit plain transforms Eleonora into a sternly chaste Diana, goddess of the Moon. Her attribute – and Juno's – a crescent moon encircling her brow, is implicit in the moonlit nimbus encircling Eleonora's head.[169] It is a timely visual metaphor for dynasty and rule – Diana, also known as Artemis, Lucina, or Luna, was Apollo's twin, a goddess who rules the child and develops it in its mother's womb.[170] In the court of the early 1540s, the association between Diana and Apollo expressed a peculiarly dynastic association with human regeneration. In a Ficinesque philosophy currently being revitalized in the Medicean circle, Apollo-Sol and Diana of Ephesus-Natura were protagonists in an elemental theme linked to Genesis.[171] These pre-Greek, Hermetic deities had fascinated the Umidi, the lively Neoplatonic forerunner to the Florentine Academy in which Bronzino was a founding member and luminary.[172] The Hermeticism adhered to by the Umidi was very much the esoteric philosophy of an inner circle presupposing a knowledge of the 'secret affinities of the harmonies of the universe.' We find embedded there the reason why Cosimo felt affinity with its themes of divinely imparted authority and absolutism for earthly rulers: 'Thus let us praise God; but from Him we will pass down to those who have received the sceptre from His hand ... the praise of those who rule on earth ... our kings, whose rule provides safety and peace for all ... to whom God has given the topmost height of sovereignty, and on whom victory has been conferred by God's right hand.'[173]

The legendary Hermetic Hercules – Cosimo's most frequent 'alias' – who ruled Italy and founded Florence, was the protagonist of Lucio Paolo Rosello's *Ritratto del vero governo del principe dal l'esempio vivo del gran Cosimo de' Medici*, in which Cosimo is interlocutor. The theme recurs in Varchi's *Storia fiorentina* I, in Baccio Baldini's *Vita di Cosimo de' Medici Gran Duca di Toscana*, 1578, and in Giovan Battista Gelli's writings. Its association with the court and its artists persisted.[174] When Cosimo's Accademia del Disegno was founded in 1563, Cellini used the Hermetic Apollo-Sol and Diana of Ephesus-Natura as its *imprese*.[175] Consequently, Eleonora's portrayal as a nocturnal deity – implicitly as consort to Cosimo-Apollo – may be interpreted in cosmic contexts of universality and dominion.

The Landscape

The dynastic implications of Eleonora's 'divine' regency are strengthened by Bronzino's water-infiltrated landscape (pl. 4 and fig. 15) and its associations. In a cosmic scheme adhered to by Cosimo's neo-Ficinesque Hermeticists, Earth was female and Water the generative element; Fire matured them, and Ether breathed life into them. In imitation of the first creation, Nature then created bodies in the form of man.[176] Hermeticism's pre-Greek pantheon honoured Diana as patron of wildlife, who kept watch over the Earth. In Bronzino's portrait, Eleonora-Diana physically looms over the Earth, so that the watery, moonlit landscape behind her may be interpreted as Earth and Water's generating forces, giving life and form to Giovanni.[177] Cosimo, portrayed in gleaming, armoured splendour in his state portrait, is implicitly present here as Fire-Sun-Apollo, a 'presence' that explains the daylit foreground of Bronzino's *Eleonora with Her Son Giovanni*: as his consort, she is bathed in his reflective, life-giving light, source of all order.[178] Aria – the proper realm of Juno-Eleonora in elemental topoi – nurtures Giovanni.[179] Portrayed together, mother and son represent Earthly Venus and her congenial son, Amor.[180] One interpretation of Ammannati's *Juno* fountain that is dependent on alchemical notions was that Eleonora (Air) and Cosimo (Earth) had united to form water, alluding to the new life brought by Cosimo and Eleonora to the Medici family.[181] Giovanni and the watery vista in the background of Bronzino's state portrait may also mutually support this interpretation. Eleonora's watery environment also reflects a widespread artistic usage in the sixteenth century of water as a metaphor of essential womanhood, based on the theory of humours understood to be inherent in the sexes.[182]

Eleonora-Juno's role as regent was to become ever more explicit in the hands of Cosimo's iconographers.[183] Juno is the presiding deity on Ammannati's fountain, planned for the main hall of state, the Sala Grande, from 1555 but never fully installed there.[184] On the fountain, Juno is mounted on the arc of the sky, with her subjects, the personifications of earth ranged below her.[185] Similarly, the portrait's setting provides a heavenly, airy realm for Eleonora-Juno, confirming her dominion over the land.[186] Vasari aligned the Eleonora-Juno-Aria persona with territorial jurisdiction: 'The illustrious Lady Duchess ... as Juno, goddess of the air, of riches, and of kingdoms.'[187] Soon, in tandem with Vasari as Cosimo's artistic director, Vincenzo Borghini restated Cosimo's intentions to emphasize his late consort's regency through judicious placement of the *Juno* fountain in the elaborate schema that was *the* official forum of Cosimo's right to rule. His gaze from the throne was intended to centre on Ammannati's fountain, which was to be mounted on the opposite wall.[188] The symbolism of Eleonora's regency endured. In Francesco's tiny Studiolo, and in a miniature commission (pl. 15), Juno brandishes Jupiter's thunderbolts, declaring again the duchess's role as consort to Cosimo-Jupiter.[189]

His *Eleonora with Her Son Giovanni* is the single portrait in which Bronzino has placed a female sitter in an open landscape setting.[190] Its Tuscan landscape is bound to his Florentine artistic heritage, with its broad, irrigated terrain behind Eleonora inevitably recalling the universe of Leonardo's *Mona Lisa*. Although Bronzino's evolved elemental symbolism is the antithesis of Leonardo's scientific vision of Nature, it has not gone unnoticed that he transmuted *Mona Lisa*'s pose and expression into a ceremonial icon for Eleonora's state portrait.[191] It is infused with overtones of Leonardo's compositional scheme. Leonardo's lighting is, of course, pragmatic, but the silhouetting of Eleonora's frontally lit figure, set high over an expansive, irrigated landscape, echoes the *Mona Lisa*.[192] Leonardo's *Ginevra de' Benci* has been recognized as influential, too, notably for a psychological impenetrability and ambivalence characteristic of Bronzino's female sitters. (She, too, has been seen as a personification of Nature, an inescapable inference in Bronzino's contexts for this portrait of Eleonora.)[193] Bronzino's artistic deference to the *Mona Lisa* as a canonical model for the first state portrait of a female consort is eminently appropriate for court portraiture – it had by this time acquired an exemplary authority akin to the antique.[194] It was the ranking portrait of a woman.[195] Bronzino's landscape is an artistic reminder, too, of his youthful association with the Urbino court in Pesaro, in whose cultured milieu he had painted the impressive *Guidobaldo della Rovere*. Piero della Francesca's double portrait of the Montefeltro Duke and Duchess of Urbino depicts them against their idealized domains, their heads monumentally posed against the sky.[196] Battista's portrait is constructed, through the binding of links in the landscape to her own form, to suggest the successful results of *buon governo* in which she had shared.[197] Eleonora's placement binds her to the Tuscan realm over which her position as regent allows her to rule.

The landscape before which Eleonora is posed also provides a concrete context for her surrogate authority. The silted, watery vista appears under high magnification to depict the estuary around Pisa, linking it to the Erlanger *Cosimo and Eleonora with Maps* of 1546 (fig. 21), where they study the newly reclaimed water systems of that region.[198] Allusions to real domains would necessarily carry territorial import, and Bronzino here avoided the flat lapis backdrop of the Prague *Eleonora*, but instead anchored Cosimo's consort to lands over which she governed in his absence. Landscape in the portrait is not Boccaccio's mythical domain, but possibly an idealized rendering of Tuscany itself.[199] Its irrigated plains closely anticipate a description of Cosimo's Tuscan realm eulogized by Vincenzo Fedeli in 1561:

> This beautiful countryside is bathed by royal currents and beautiful rivers and is everywhere full of springs and lakes teeming with excellent fish, so that, because of the occurrence of so much water, it provides for everyone a plenitude of all the fruits

of the earth; and the stretches of woods and mountains are truly fruitful, lovely and filled with all delights.[200]

Tuscany had been both real *and* intellectual *patria* from the time of Cosimo the Elder – a symbol of the Etruscan origins of Italy, Dante's birthplace, and a place of myth in Pindaric odes. Deeply committed to the history and archaeology of his realm, the duke in 1541 also instituted the Accademia Fiorentina to convey the supremacy of the Tuscan language as an expression of the politico-cultural hegemony of the new state.[201] It was a concern that the next Medici generation, Cosimo and Eleonora's children, took to themselves, with a circle of *letterati* devoted to promoting Tuscan under Medici patronage until Grand Duke Francesco established the Accademia della Crusca ('chaff') to sift and codify its grammar.[202]

Tuscan poetry, too, is celebrated in the portrait. Petrarch's search through all forms of beauty to evoke the ethereal grace of Laura had a powerful effect on the way poets and painters looked at nature.[203] Even in landscape, Petrarch's lyric tradition is central to understanding Tuscan concepts of beauty and their representation. His classicism – and Bronzino's imitation of Petrarch – is reflected in the velvet-blue, ordered environment of Diana, chaste inhabitant of the bounteous Tuscan countryside and controller of tides. The landscape is also Bronzino's eulogy to beauty itself.

Poetic and visual tributes casting Tuscany as Arcadia was a tradition that had been a Medicean refrain from the fifteenth century, when Lorenzo de' Medici's retreats with Renaissance humanists Ficino, Landino, and Poliziano to the Villa Careggi imitated Plato's *Symposium*.[204] Another Medici villa, Poggio a Caiano, was consciously cultivated as a neo-Virgilian refuge, a reception point for new brides (including Eleonora) and an idyllic refuge for the family, especially newly wed couples.[205] Further acquisitions in the fifteenth and sixteenth centuries of Medici villas set in enormous tracts of territory across Tuscany were perceived as both strategic and sentimental.[206] The 1565 *apparato* for the marriage of Francesco to Giovanna of Austria made Medici dominion over the Tuscan *bel paese* one of six Tuscan themes for the ephemeral arch constructed at the Porta al Prato, celebrating *Agricoltura*, or the abundance of Tuscany. By virtue of land aquisition and drainage, patriotic pride in Tuscany was now invested in a Medicean realm in fact and in reverie. Cosimo's iconographer in 1565, Vincenzo Borghini, turned to Landino for inspiration and declared a pan-European reputation for its fertility ('talché questo paese si potè meritamente chiamare il Giardino d'Europa' – 'so that this countryside may justifiably be named the Garden of Europe').[207] Throughout his reign, Cosimo never lost the opportunity to convey his territorial jurisdiction, and carefully controlled visual evocations of it.[208] Perhaps it was in this climate that Bronzino selected a recognizable corner of Cosimo's realm as a backdrop to honour Eleonora. His watery terrain pointedly calls attention to the new duchess's loyalty to Tuscany in the face of overwhelming earlier Spanish domination of the region, and also to her role in establishing its economic growth.

Magnification of the right background (pl. 4 and fig. 15) shows a marshy, watered vista around a wide river-mouth with considerable silting, with a further body of water beyond, suggesting an estuary. Hills are dimly visible in the background. In 1543, with the help of his wife's considerable personal fortune, Cosimo had purchased back the low-lying Tuscan estuary around the port of Pisa, to which the Appenine foothills form a backdrop to the north, along with fortresses in the region that had been held in fief by Charles V.[209] (Cosimo complained in 1541, 'This is not the stall and stables of all this wandering riff-raff, nor is it the sewer of His Majesty's States in Italy,' wisely adding that he could afford to defend the region and serve His Majesty in other occurrences.)[210] For the Florentine viewer in 1545, the watery landscape would especially signify Eleonora's actual contribution to the security, comfort, and prosperity of Tuscan citizens, to whom wintering-over of Spanish troops in the region had been a constant irritant for over a decade. By 1545 Eleonora had a personal stake in the region. She was astute in buying marshland (the 'Palude della Duchessa') and having it drained, enriching the duchy considerably in the process.[211] The Erlanger double portrait of 1546 (fig. 21), showing the ducal pair with an unfurled map of Pisa and environs spread before them, appears to commemorate this achievement; their descendants, too, paid tribute.[212] The two were now also joint owners of the merchant navy, based in Pisa, and it may be pertinent that Diana, goddess of the moon and controller of tides, personified here by Eleonora, makes her, ipso facto, controller of tides as well.[213] As Diana, Eleonora is by implication also represented as secular patron of mariners and shipping.[214] Bronzino's landscape, testament to Eleonora's tangible contribution to Tuscan stability, served ultimately as a most persuasive argument for her acceptance by Tuscan subjects as his regent.

Love, Virtue, and Varchi's 'Due Lumi'

Eleonora's portrayal as Regent of State was sanctified by association with Christian themes of regency, pagan allegory, dominion, and allusions to imperial power. Her dynastic role as consort to Cosimo-Apollo also subsumes expression of the theme of Love. Eleonora may be viewed as the universal courtly, Petrarchan, and Neoplatonic female paradigm. In Pietro Bembo's poem *Gli Asolani* (1505 and 1530), Gismondo, the advocate of Love as a positive force in society, 'draws' a portrait of his beloved – imagined or actual – as an assemblage of features thought to characterize a lady *deserving* to be loved. The notion was to be echoed as a model for the painter in Lodovico Ariosto's (1474–1533) poetry, and by Ludovico Dolce.[215]

It was notably with respect to Love that the Neoplatonic, Ficinesque revival continued to provide inspiration in the court and to its satellite Florentine Academy throughout the 1540s and beyond. The Neoplatonic symbolism of light continued to be the fulcrum for interpretation in this revival. Turning on the cultural concerns of the court, dual illumination in Bronzino's portrait has special implications. Benedetto Varchi, head of Cosimo's Accademia Fiorentina from the early 1540s, would expound on Love in 'I due Lumi' (Two Lights) in his *Lezzioni sopra L'Amore* (1554). Light is Love's regenerative force. One is natural, the other infused into man by God. Both are 'pregnant.' The first turns us towards earthly, generative functions, the other towards contemplative love of God, each desiring to reproduce and stimulated by love to do so. This hearkens to the Neoplatonism of the brilliant circle of Lorenzo 'the Magnificent' de' Medici (1449–92). Marsilio

Ficino's 'two lights' were linked to 'two beauties,' the internal and the external.[216] Varchi's prose synthesized that of Petrarch, Dante, Ficino, Pico della Mirandola, and Francesco Cattani da Diacceto.[217] Eleonora's patronage of this revival, translations of classical works, drama, and of Varchi, too, is documented.[218] The infusion of these influences into her portrait may have resulted from Varchi's close friendship with Bronzino, or Eleonora's belief that her literary, Neopetrarchan court artist was likely to infuse her portrait with visual references that promoted the court as a new Laurentian-Ficinesque centre and cultural hub of Italy.[219] Her portrait especially reflects Varchi's own assertion that the doctrine of ideal love symbolized by a beautiful woman could be even more perfectly expressed in her portrait than by her actual physical presence.[220]

Petrarch's influence on Bronzino is certain. An accomplished and prolific Neopetrarchan poet, he genuflects in this state portrait of Eleonora to the unattainable, virtuous woman of Petrarchan love lyrics. In his own sonnet, *Bell'alma, e saggia, e sovr'ogni altra accorta* (appendix B), he coins Petrarchan similes of beauty and wisdom for the virtuous woman he addresses. She must always be approached from afar. He pleads with her to extend her white hand to him; meditation on her image transports the poet-spectator from the Inferno to the sky. The topos of the beautiful face emitting its own radiance, an effulgent grace, was a commonplace of such poetic discourse; in Petrarch's sonnets the glance that bears love, the *sguardo*, is often a ray of light: 'the sky takes fire with shining sparks / all around and visibly rejoices / to be made clear by eyes so lovely' (*Canzone* 192); and 'I know not what in her eyes / which in an instant can make bright the night, darken the day / embitter honey, and sweeten wormwood' (*Canzone* 215).[221] The radiant face that outshines the sun was a simile that had long had currency in Florentine madrigal settings, too, including Petrarch's *Canzone* 119, *Una donna più bella assai che'l sole* (A woman much more beautiful than the sun), set to music in the 1520s.[222] Identical in spirit but nearer in time are the lines 'ella / è più che'sol assai lucente e bella' ('she is brighter and more beautiful than the sun'), which conclude Varchi's *Quando col dolce suono* (When with sweet sound), set in madrigal form by Philippe Verdelot in 1534.[223] These Petrarchan inferences in Bronzino's *Eleonora* are freighted with implications from two centuries of now standard literary metaphors in celebration of the ideal woman.[224] The unadorned, ivoried hand resting weightless on the elaborate gown is loaded with allusions to the ideal grace of women, *leggiadria*, and to notions of effortlessness linked to an elevated Neoplatonic *serenità*.[225] Stemming from this tradition was the intensely emotive power of the Petrarchan ideal to carry rhetorical overtones promoting Laura's beauty, her *grazia* and associated goodness, her elevation above the mundane weal, and especially an implicit invitation to admire her beauty from afar and to recognize her power. In effect, Bronzino's *Eleonora* is presented in her portrait as a 'Laura' for Cosimo.[226]

Eleonora's portrayal as a deity presiding over Nature also finds parallel expression in Cattani's description of concord and perfection in nature, analogous, he suggests, with the nature or persona of the ideal woman:

[J]ust as the divine Plato described the body, it exists still, and the soul is certainly very different from it. The soul has intellect, the body does not have this. The soul, like a woman, has command over the body; this, as a servant, is subject and ruled. The spirit is the fountain of unity and of feeling, and of all the other affections that we perceive in the body; this by its nature is fitting to accept, and to bear, [and] we may conclude that the soul, by far more perfect, has superior rank in the universe.[227]

Cattani, direct successor to Ficino's Neoplatonism, was much admired by Varchi, literary *capo* in the court circle.[228] The lines echo Petrarch's presentation of his beloved ideal as a woman, as a composite of Nature's elemental order, and ultimately as a mirror of virtue:

> The stars, the sky, and the elements, contending with each other
> Placed all their skill and most excellent care
> In that shining light in which Nature
> And the sun are mirrored, which does not find its equal elsewhere.[229]

Mirror metaphors are particularly apt in the early Medicean court circle, when promotion of Cosimo as the 'mirror of princes' was current.[230] His official portrayal in dazzling, luminous steel – a true mirror – is a visual expression of his role as exemplar in a period when the terms 'ritratto' (portrait) and 'specchio' (mirror) each had exemplary connotations.[231] More importantly, Eleonora herself had been nurtured in the Spanish pedagogy of woman as bright mirror of prudence, wisdom, valour, and chastity, perhaps as expressed in the nimbus of moonlight behind her head, and echoed by a shaft of light that illuminates the watery landscape behind her. This in turn 'mirrors' the sky.[232] She is simultaneously paradigm of the beloved, chaste consort, regent of Cosimo's earthly dominions, the ideal, unattainable Petrarchan woman, and virtuous mirror of heaven on earth.

The Spectator's Decorum

It would be imperative for the painter of official court portraits to incorporate in them an appropriate approach for the spectator; this is implicit in the sixteenth-century understanding of decorum, which demands that the audience apprehend characteristics appropriate to the subject's rank, age, and sex. With respect to conventions of women's exclusiveness, especially for those of rank, Bronzino has responded with great subtlety. Strictures against male attention to women were far-reaching in sixteenth-century Italy, almost ludicrously so to moderns.[233] In Petrarchan spirit, the spectator of *Eleonora with Her Son Giovanni* is deliberately curbed from the act of fond gazing, *vagheggiare*.[234] Even while called upon to admire Eleonora's virtue and beauty, the notional spectator should be kept at a respectful distance. Here, the artist's control over the spectator is maintained through strategically placed areas of complexity in the compositional structure, through pattern, and by subtle iconographical references. For Bronzino's *Cosimo in Armour* (pl. 3), for example, the spectator's spontaneity will be repressed by Cosimo's averted gaze and overtones of ferocity suggested by the dangerously sharp besaques of his armour.[235] A ferocious demeanour for Eleonora would be wholly inappropriate here; in sixteenth-century Italy, the virtue of a woman resided not in her bravery but in her chastity.

For Castiglione, chastity was *the* imperative virtue for women. Manifested iconographically in Maria Salviati's and Lucrezia Panciatichi's portraits (pl. 1 and fig. 27), the currency of this maxim is enshrined in every treatise on manners for women. Vives's pedagogy for girls is dedicated to its inculcation. Chaste abstinence for young women or widows, or absolute faithfulness to a husband – even a dead one – was the unwavering ideal. Lodovico Domenichi, author of *Nobilità delle donne* (1549), discoursing in Lucca in 1564 on decorum for the woman of the court, stated: [E]ven if worldliness is commendable among men, it cannot be a virtue for women. Therefore another virtue is found, that is to say the ultimate virtue, such as virginity, chastity, and holiness, and other suchlike.'[236] Bronzino used considerable artifice in this complement to the *Cosimo in Armour* to reaffirm Eleonora's chastity and uprightness in the eye of the beholder. To effect this, appropriate degrees of removal for the spectator are in this instance staked out in a tour-de-force of design around the sitter.[237] First, the effect of encasing Eleonora in the rigid bodice has been recognized as evocative of the carapacing of Cosimo in steel armour (pl. 3).[238] Emblazoned with the imperial pomegranate, it augments Cosimo's engraved blazon of Medici shield and *palle*. The cuirass-like bodice with its imperial blazon also echoes contemporary descriptions of Eleonora at state ceremonial occasions such as her *entrata* into Rome in 1560, the tenor of which convey the impact of lavish robes of state for suggesting her virtue (*honestà*) and for inducing awe in the spectator.[239] The role of the stiff bodice in evoking these responses becomes evident if the soft, silken surfaces of the bodice in the small Prague *Eleonora* (pl. 5 and figs. 19 and 20) or in the 'private' Clovio miniature of Eleonora (fig. 22) are compared to the official Tribuna portrait. Clovio poses her hand to touch her bodice. Her fingers dent the silk, conjuring for the viewer the yielding softness of her flesh beneath it. In both the Prague portrait and Clovio's miniature, soft folds suggest the undulating movement of breathing, and promote greater intimacy and closeness between viewer and subject.[240] In the Tribuna portrait, the cloth 'cuirass' entirely suppresses her breasts, but nowhere so tightly as to evoke the appeal of the malleable softness of female flesh.

The opportunity to describe an intense male response to soft flesh swelling against such confinement had to be slyly contrived to be dwelt upon by Firenzuola's audience. In his dialogue *On the Beauty of Women*, Selvaggia, a female member of Celso's circle to whom he has paid the safe compliment that her bosom is fairer than that of the long-dead Helen or mythical Venus, drops her coyness to allow him to expound on the effect of confined female flesh:

> Selvaggia: ... nonetheless, I beg you to describe its beauty, if only for my sake, since I cannot see my own bosom.
> Celso: If only you let others see it! Well then, since I am your prisoner, I must do as you please. [*He goes on to describe its whiteness, its breadth – 'its chief ornament' – its perfect fairness ... tinged with roses.*] In this bosom the fresh and lively breasts, heaving as though ill at ease at being constantly oppressed and confined by the garments, showing that they want to escape from their prison, rise up so resolutely and vigorously that they force the viewer's eyes to rest firmly upon them, and thereby thwart their escape.[241]

These are the very responses to be avoided in a state portrait. It must leave the chaste virtue of the subject inviolate to public view. Eleonora is armoured against the concupiscence of the viewer's eye, and fortified in her role as consort and regent.

There are no known portraits of the young duchess that give her even a modicum of sexuality; there is no Eleonora as Eurydice to act as pendant to the strikingly erotic *Cosimo as Orpheus*. Eleonora has passed to posterity without a hint of private, licit sexuality as found in the voluptuous Florentine *Woman with a Statue of Eros* (fig. 26), who is shown in slight *déshabillé*, her basque untied and her chemise loosened. Although posed in luxurious surroundings, she is divested of jewellery, the usual signifier of rank, further confirming that the panel was intended for private, not public, viewing. A lively *Eros* dominates the composition and has just loosed his dart at her breast, leaving little doubt about the erotic value of her tempting state of slight undress and momentary distraction from her book of prayers.[242] The portrait belongs to a genre associated with sexuality sanctioned by marriage.[243] As for the *Cosimo as Orpheus*, its audience would appear to be strictly limited to a spouse. Indeed, in his *Libro della bella donna* (Book of Fair Women) of 1554, Federigo Luigini asserted that private enjoyment of a woman's beauty and erotic appeal was enhanced by the assurance of her high moral standing.[244] In short, the erotic tension of the devout *Lady with a Statue of Eros* of about 1530–5 relies on an unusual revelation of physical and emotional unguardedness, a decorum with which Bronzino has emphatically not imbued his contained *Eleonora*.[245]

The distance created by Eleonora's iconic, hieratic pose is also assisted by the extreme formality and symmetry of the brocade design. The weaving, hypnotic effect of its repeated arabesques serves to visually restrain the spectator from immediate access to the duchess's beautiful face (pl. 4).[246] Its smooth, ivoried planes and her steady gaze do not invite a response. It has been observed that such perfection of forms and preciousness of surface in Bronzino's portraits has the effect of fixing the persona in a perennially uncontaminated Neoplatonic and Petrarchan atmosphere: she is protected from the corrosion of time and the banalities of the viewer's mundane sphere.[247]

Eleonora's exclusiveness is also symbolically stated in Medicean terms. Lavishly decorated sleeves – subject to sumptuary laws – had long been a locus for conspicuous reference to wealth, rank, and family blazons.[248] Gold fasteners with pyramidal centres function as closures along Eleonora's sleeves; they were restricted to one row in sumptuary laws re-enacted by Cosimo in 1562.[249] Hers incorporate the traditional Medicean *diamante impresa*, associated with the motto 'SEMPER.' (The spiked besaques of Cosimo's armour [pl. 3] recall the *diamante*, too.) Just as the motto 'JAMAIS AUTRE' and the *diamante* declared Maria Salviati's faithfulness to her dead husband, it asserts Eleonora's chaste loyalty to Cosimo.

Significantly, Cosimo was reputed to own a huge pyramid-shaped diamond once lodged in the temple of Apollo.[250] The enormous diamond at Eleonora's throat would reverberate with reminders of the duke, who had so often had himself personified as Apollo. Together with the equally large topaz centred in her girdle, it may further symbolize her exclusiveness. As an acknowledged Petrarchan devotee, Bronzino was aware that Petrarch had enshrined the association of the diamond and the topaz with the doe, sacred to Diana. Petrarch related his vision of the doe, who appeared, two hundred years after Caesar's death, when the sun rose, between two rivers in the shade of a laurel, and wearing a collar of diamonds and topazes (emblems of steadfastness and chastity, respectively), inscribed 'Do not touch me, I am Caesar's' ('Noli me tangere, Caesaris sum'):

> A white doe on the green grass appeared to me,
> with two golden horns, between two rivers in the shade
> of a laurel, when the sun was rising in the unripe season.
>
> ...
>
> 'Let no one touch me' she bore written with diamonds and
> topazes around her lovely neck,
> 'it has pleased my Caesar to make me free.'[251]

Cosimo's personification as Caesar Augustus was a propagandistic promotion from the earliest years of his reign, and the radiance about Eleonora's head may link her to him.[252] Several subtle allusions to Eleonora as the *canzone*'s 'doe' are evident: the watered landscape and suggestion of pre-dawn illumination evoke Diana's nocturnal realm; the *diamante* and topaz inset at the centre of her *cintura* as described in Petrarch above; and, discussed below, her reticulated, pearled hairnet and *fichu* (pl. 4), which make reference to the Petrarchan laurel. Together, these suggest that Bronzino has declared Cosimo her Caesar, using Petrarch as his reference. Eleonora is untouchable to anyone but the duke.

Piccolomini's *Instituzione morale* (1542) details clothing acceptable for a duchess or queen and *no* other woman: brocades and cloth of gold, ornamented and embroidered with pearls and gems. In 1546 Cosimo enacted sumptuary laws that seem peculiarly designed to make Eleonora's taste in jewels exclusive to her.[253] The diamond set in the pearl necklace at her throat is hung with a large pearl, and a necklace of large pearls hangs down to her breast. The golden mesh fichu about her shoulders, and her matching hairnet – specially made for Eleonora by a Spanish lady-in-waiting – are strewn with pearls.[254] Her *cintura* ends in a tassel of pearls. Their profusion in her state portrait is appropriate. First, they were then the most precious of gems and carried royal association in official portraiture.[255] Second, given Eleonora's notorious attachment to pearls – her pursuit of outstanding specimens is recorded – their excess in the portrait would have assisted in the viewer's recognition of the sitter.[256] Recognition through accessories is enshrined in de Hollanda's treatise on portraiture; it is also implicit in Leonardo's advice that rank be made evident.[257] Wealthy Neapolitans had a passion for pearl-decorated clothing, which perhaps identifies her viceregal origins; before Eleonora's arrival from Naples for her wedding, Maria Salviati was charged with purchasing a large quantity to present to her.[258] Finally, as an attribute of earthly Venus or Profane Love, pearls associate her with Cosimo – as his beloved.[259] Ficino describes pearls as the gems closest to the nature of the moon, and thus associated with Diana, consort of Cosimo-Apollo.[260] They were also associated with chastity, and were a customary gift to brides.[261] As protectress of brides, Juno was associated with pearls, as witness Cellini's bronze, where her forehead is adorned with a large pendant pearl.[262]

Eleonora's pearl-studded fichu and matching hairnet recall Petrarch's 'gay net of gold and pearls,' linked in his poetry to a *broncone* of evergreen laurel, metaphor for eternal love:

> Love set out amid the grass a gay net of gold and pearls
> Under a branch of the evergreen tree that I so love ...[263]

In Cosimo's Kassel portrait, the *broncone* is the Medicean emblem of dynastic continuity. Giovanni is, of course, the living 'branch of the evergreen tree' ('ramo dell'arbor sempre verde') in Eleonora's. Soft, melting maternal tenderness is less evident here than iconic presentation of dynasty and continuity. Possibly a hint of Castiglionesque maleness, 'un certa virilità soda e ferma' ('a certain substantial and firm virility') intentionally conveys Eleonora's potential as regent.[264]

In the spirit of Cosimo's revived Ficinesque Neoplatonism, Eleonora, as the setting suggests, presides here as goddess of Celestial and Earthly Love. To the humanists both are virtuous, *Venus vulgaris* (Earthly Venus) being regarded as a stage on the way upward to *Venus coelestis* (Heavenly Venus).[265] *Venus vulgaris*, representative of profane love and distinguished by her rich attire, also incorporates the procreative principle as goddess of love and fertility.[266] It is the little boy, in apparent awe of his exquisite mother and in seeming imprecation to us to share his admiration, who serves to remind us of the procreative element celebrated in her personal motto, 'CVM PVDORE LAETA FOECVNDITAS' ('joyful fertility with modesty').

Joyful Fertility

By 1545, when Bronzino portrayed her with Giovanni, Eleonora had produced a child annually since her marriage in 1539. Her fecundity was a source of great rejoicing. Diego di Sandoval's eulogy of late 1543 for Cosimo's mother, Maria Salviati, counselled Cosimo to dwell on the good fortune of a fecund wife in his hour of desolation:

> From whence I pray to the great King of Heaven that
> My years are taken away and yours all multiply
> And the dear one your Consort and your children
> Who were created and those who will be, give you reconciliation.[267]

Contemporary commentaries express a similar spirit. In Adriani's *Istoria*, women are rarely mentioned except in contexts of politically astute betrothals or when their fecundity is a concern. He comments on the speed at which Eleonora produced first a daughter (Maria, 1540) and then a son (Francesco, 1541) as a sign of the couple's increasing good fortune. Mannucci, Cosimo's biographer, recalled their enormous family in 1586, again celebrating her fecundity.[268] Should the existence of two sons by 1545 not sufficiently guarantee dynastic promise, there is perhaps a hint of Cosimo's potency in the profuse 'seed' pearls lying in a swirling cascade in her lap that form the tassel of Eleonora's jewelled girdle.[269]

As related, the 1539 wedding *apparato* had urged Cosimo to found a new dynasty, 'under the auspices of the gods and with a favourable Juno.'[270] Juno's familiar was the peacock, and *pavonazzo* (peacock-blue) was the colour for livery at Eleonora's wedding, all emblematic of the peahen *impresa* she would later assume as duchess. Overtones of this theme existed in the early 1540s. In Salviati's *Triumph of Camillus*, Juno-Eleonora is borne in triumph under a pediment crowned with two peahens.[271] There, as regent to Jupiter, she holds a sceptre and rests her foot on an orb. It was Giovio who proposed Juno's symbolic peahen as Eleonora's official *impresa* a few years later; it appears on Domenico Poggini's medal of 1551 with a clutch of six peachicks beneath its spreading wings. The associated motto, CVM LAETA FOECVNDITAS encircles it.[272] In his elegy to Eleonora (appendix B), Bronzino refers to her as 'the chaste Juno' ('la casta Giunon'), and Bandini's bronze *Juno* set in her son Francesco's Studiolo is accompanied by a peahen.[273] Not surprisingly, Bronzino has portrayed Giovanni in gold-shot, peacock-blue silk – he is Eleonora's 'peachick' and principal representative of Eleonora-Juno's fecundity. In infancy, he also recalls a *putto or amorino*, five of which appeared with *Fecundità* in the wedding *apparato* as symbols of dynasty.[274] Finally, the fertile, irrigated landscape is a macrocosmic metaphor of fecundity.

The *Eleonora with Her Son Giovanni* is replete with evidence of Bronzino's apprehension of Medici propagandistic traditions. Much of the complex, symbolic layering in Eleonora's Tribuna portrait is a corollary to propagandistic mythology designed to exalt Cosimo, coined after the triumphal routing of his enemies at Montemurlo in 1537, their wedding *apparato* of 1539, the *Mosaic* chapel frescoes, and the heroic *Joseph* tapestries of the mid-1540s. Giovio had served as a source for the iconographic structure of the *Cosimo in Armour*, but Bronzino's intellectual tendencies suggest that he alone conceived Eleonora's portrait. First, Petrarchan poetry – his applauded avocation – was already an established source of inspiration for women's portraiture. Second, Bronzino's association from boyhood with the Medici had schooled him for the court's propagandistic intentions. Third, his literary circle was one intimately bound with its promotion.

Artifice and *Proprietà* in the Portrait of Eleonora and Her Son Giovanni

Bronzino's singular ability to infuse *bellezza ed onestà* (beauty and virtue) into women's portraits was recognized by his circle.[275] Vasari also cited Bronzino's portraiture as a benchmark for 'naturalism.'[276] Yet, Eleonora's appearance in the Tribuna double portrait may be the least mimetic likeness of the duchess.[277] Mimesis and naturalism were not to be confused, however: in Vasari's philosophy, it was the representation of Nature in its perfected forms for which the artist should strive.[278] Bronzino did so in his *Lucrezia Panciatichi*, as would Titian for his *Isabella of Portugal in Red*. To infuse grace in a portrait was to suggest such a spiritual quality in the sitter. In the same spirit, Grifoli's Neoplatonic reading of Horace, produced under Cosimo's aegis in 1550, would insist that imitation of Nature must strive for perfection of its highest forms.[279]

Bronzino did adjust Nature to express perfection, and degrees of adjustment were evidently dictated by reference to the desired effect on an intended audience. The Eleonora depicted in the *Crossing of the Red Sea* in her chapel is mythologized by portraying her with classical coiffure and Petrarchan-inspired golden tresses.[280] In his 'Of the Perfect Beauty of a Lady,' Firenzuola, writing between 1537 and 1540, 'in the reign of the Most Illustrious and Excellent Cosimo, Duke of

Florence,' cites Apuleius: 'Hair ... should be fine and fair, in the similitude now of gold, now of honey, and now of the bright and shining rays of the sun; waving, thick, abundant.'[281] (Wisely, perhaps with his patroness in mind, he was also careful to celebrate darker hair for its own peculiar beauty.)[282] He goes on to describe bound hair 'in comely order' on the authority of Apuleius: 'So great is the dignity of the hair that if ... [she arrays] herself most sumptuously in gold and pearls ... [and] not have disposed her hair in a fair order with pleasing skill, never shall it be said that she is either beautiful nor elegant.' Perhaps Eleonora was his inspiration; in Bronzino's official state portrait her hair in its reticulated cap is indeed disposed in fair order.[283]

In a state portrait destined for widespread dissemination, Bronzino could not make dramatic alterations to his sitter's customary appearance, but was constrained, nonetheless, to idealize her in this portrait to a greater extent that in any other. Comparison of degrees of idealization in Eleonora's portraits are particularly interesting. Idealization in each appears to have been fine-tuned for effect on a specific spectator or audience. Clovio's miniature *Eleonora* (fig. 22) shows the Duchess attired in white, posed before an ultramarine drape with a hand-on-heart gesture suggestive of love or modesty.[284] Unlike the aloof *Eleonora* of the Tribuna, she looks out engagingly. Raised to frame her face, the curtain of deep ultramarine is finely heightened with gold.[285] (The resulting *pavonazzo* effect echoes Giovanni's iridescent costume in the state portrait.) Vasari classified Clovio's miniatures as a genre intended for private viewing and unlikely to be seen by any of his readers ('che l'opere di si fatti uomini non sono publiche').[286] As they were intended for intimate viewing and even worn on the person, Giovio's miniature must stand as the least official version of Eleonora.[287] Here her relaxed decorum does echo the Castiglionesque 'soft and delicate tenderness' so absent from her state portrait.

Clovio's miniature is also probably the closest portrayal of her actual appearance. By comparing Bandinelli's bust of 1544 (fig. 25), the Prague *Eleonora* of 1545 (pl. 5 and fig. 19), the Tribuna *Eleonora with her son Giovanni* of 1545 (pl. 4), the Erlanger 1546 version (fig. 21), and Clovio's *Eleonora* of 1551–3 (fig. 22), it is possible to draw some conclusions on adjustments made by Bronzino to arrive at an appropriate decorum for his Uffizi *Eleonora*.[288] The enormous disparity between Bronzino's *Eleonora with Her Son Giovanni* and Bandinelli's contemporary *Eleonora* bust has been seen as expressive of the two artists' different temperaments and divergent modes of idealization.[289] But Clovio so closely reproduces the features of Bandinelli's bust of 1544 that it also seems likely that both sculptor and miniaturist worked close to the live model, Bandinelli perhaps from a life-cast.[290] In this respect, Eleonora's official portrait is at several removes from the Prague, Bandinelli, Erlanger and Clovio versions. The heavy jaw, strongly dimpled chin, and protuberant forehead of Bandinelli's and Clovio's portrayals have been greatly smoothed and refined for Eleonora's state portrait, and a distinct squint, visible in the Erlanger double portrait, has been corrected. (Titian would do no less for Charles V's *Empress Isabella in Red* of 1548.)

Her relaxed decorum in the Prague *Eleonora* compared to its derivative, the state portrait, has been discussed. In turn, the captivating, easy grace and warm tonality of the Prague portrait is striking compared to its copy, the Erlanger *Eleonora*, made a few years later (fig. 21) – a pastiche, workshop piece that divests the ducal couple of all *grandezza*. Degrees of formality or informality in this diverse group of portraits of Eleonora suggest that Bronzino's presentation of hierarchy and rank, as demanded in Leonardo's precept, was finely adjusted according to his awareness of an intended spectator. Eleonora's riveting 'presence' as Cosimo's regent is much advanced by his technical virtuosity. His *trompe l'oeil* effects – especially noticeable in the gold-laden warps and wefts of the gown's brocade – evoke amazement even today. His intent is to provoke the spectator's awe – *stupore* – as recorded for the lavishness of Eleonora's retinue and the inventiveness of the *apparato* for her wedding and for state *entrate*. Bronzino's vivid optics evince astonishment and reverence for an office, allowing reason to be suspended and freeing the viewer's imagination to conjure absent 'realities' of speech or breathing. In an illusion begun by the artist, the spectator tacitly assents to a magical emanation of life made present.[291]

For literary luminaries of the court, marmoreal qualities in Eleonora's portrait may have enhanced this effect in contexts of Bronzino's involvement in the current debate concerning the *paragone* between painting and sculpture. This was expressed in Benedetto Varchi's lectures to the Accademia Fiorentina in 1547, which followed on his invitation to artists, sculptors, and painters to defend their individual callings.[292] (Issues surrounding the *paragone*, or contest, between painting and sculpture may have moved Cosimo to have both his chief painter, Bronzino, and his chief sculptor, Bandinelli, make portrayals of himself and his wife in 1543 to 1544.)[293] In the court's circle of *letterati* and artists, the discussion became intense and adversarial; arguments concerning the relative merits of *scultura* over painting and *disegno* over *colore* appear to have reflected Michelangelo's preference for sculpture. Varchi carefully sought to support both branches of art, but still aligned appreciation of sculpture with intellectual superiority: painting could imitate a wider variety of things, 'but not more perfectly [than sculpture] ... [T]hinking men may perhaps find greater beauty in sculpture and derive greater pleasure from it, even though painting achieves greater similitude and better deceives the eye.' Endurance in stone was seen as 'sempiterno' (everlasting); painting was a 'cosa caduca' ('ephemeral thing').[294] Bronzino's defence to Varchi of his vocation was, unfortunately, left incomplete. He upheld it, but a deferential awareness of the 'higher' rank of *scultura* is implicit in his apologia.[295] The marbled and ivoried effects in the Tribuna state portrait may be seen as a visual manifestation of his concession to sculpture's accepted ability to infuse a persona with life and to suggest perfection, of Michelangelo's stature, and of the current debate within court circles in which sculpture was clearly held in higher esteem. It was a theme with which Bronzino had long been familiar. In 1530, his cover for Pontormo's *Halberdier* [*Francesco Guardi*] illustrates the mythological *Pygmalion and Galatea* from Ovid's *Metamorphoses*, in which the imploring sculptor brings his creation, *Galatea*, to life by sheer force of yearning and through Venus's favour.[296]

Art treatises also argued the merits of different media and their relative artistic standing, often couched in moralizing terms that move deftly between pronouncements on propriety for painter, sitter, and viewer. Colour is a case in point. Saturated hue was believed to transmit subliminal messages, and the discourse about the merit of *disegno* over *colore* is rooted in notions of painterly *proprietà*. Leonardo despised painters who brashly used colour to seduce the eye and to cater to the tastes of the 'common herd' ('l'ignorante vulgo').[297] In Venice it was an especially sensitive issue. Dolce co-opted his 'Aretino' to castigate colourists who go beyond the bounds of painterly *convenevolezza* – a term synonymous with Leonardo's *convenientia* or *decoro*. Such colourists are unlike Titian, who had shown in his works no empty gracefulness but a palette that fulfils painterly *proprietà* ('proprietà convenevole di colori').[298] Pino, writing in Venice in 1548, disdained painters who worked with fine colours just to earn a little money, implying a concern about a devaluation of art by less sophisticated artists.[299] He praised Bronzino as the consummate colourist of his day.[300] In 1586, Armenini castigated painters who

> think only of creating an effect among common people, and gaining the favour of the majority ... [T]hey entice [them] with bright colours ('adescano quelli per le tinte vivaci') and make them approve their ways ... [by using] undiluted colours ('i colori schietti') to please fools. In short, they pervert the good technique which ought to be employed in fine paintings.[301]

These cautions against indiscriminate use of brilliant colour echo medieval admonitions against occasions of sin and concupiscence of the eyes. Bronzino would have been especially obliged to control his palette in her official portrait so that Eleonora's image would not entice the common gaze. This was staunchly asserted by Dolce: the desired intense contemplation of painting, 'discovered principally for delight,' was not one that 'feeds the eyes of the vulgar.'[302] Evidently, Bronzino was constrained not to put his patron's connoisseurship in question and his own aesthetic reputation at risk.[303] Vasari, Bronzino's friend, court painter, and theorist, was explicit: the control of *colore* by the painter was difficult and burdensome, but absolutely necessary.[304]

Possibly in this spirit of strict *proprietà* by patron and painter, colour in the Tribuna panel is less intense than the flickering crimson and purple lights of the sitter's satin gown in Bronzino's *Lucrezia Panciatichi* (fig. 27), or the Prague *Eleonora* (pl. 5), where a background saturation of lapis lazuli intensifies its brilliance. The Panciatichi panels were destined for viewing by family and close acquaintances.[305] As suggested, the Prague panel was most likely for Cosimo's own delectation. Exposure to the 'ignorante vulgo' – the common herd – was not at issue there.

In the state portrait, her ivory skin contributes to Eleonora's majesty, and pallor of the face and hands perhaps reflected proscriptions against the use of cosmetics for patrician castes.[306] In his *Cortegiano*, Castiglione has Lodovico da Canossa state the case: '[H]ow much more attractive than all the others is a pretty woman who is quite clearly wearing no make-up on her face ... God's work and his creations must not be meddled with in any manner ... [especially with] *colore*.'[307] Luigini, in *The Book of Fair Women*, published in 1554, concurred: '[Only] bold courtesans (*meretrici*) anoint and put colour on their faces.'[308] Firenzuola has his Celso link pallor to a healthy balance of the humours, observing that 'cheeks must be fair (*candido*) ... a colour that, besides being white, also has a certain lustre, as ivory does ...'[309] Eleonora's lack of colour here betokens rank, good health, and disposition, all contributing to her beauty. (For the private Eleonora, recourse to cosmetics was a matter for her to reveal or conceal as she wished – and records reveal that she did use them.)[310]

Sculpture, even in this respect, was Bronzino's point of reference for this most formal of Eleonora's portraits. Its restrained colour carried with it certain safeguards, as Varchi knew. Colour could be too sensuous and seductive; pristine, marmoreal sculpture was more stringent: 'Men of intellectual inclination derive more beauty and greater pleasure from sculpture.'[311] Petrarch, yearning, had also suggested sculpture's chastening effect: 'and I would see the scarlet roses moved by the breeze amid the snow, and the ivory uncovered that turns to marble whoever looks on it from close by, and all for the sake of which I am not a burden to myself in this short life.'[312] Bronzino's marmoreal or ivoried forms 'chill' flesh in the living *Eleonora,* an accentuation of bloodlessness that safeguards her from a viewer's carnal response.[313] For any except Cosimo, Bronzino's *Eleonora* reverses Pygmalion's response by substituting marble for living flesh and placing his subject beyond the reach of desire. Firenzuola's Celso leaves us in no doubt about the desired chaste response:

> I too am a man, I too seek my other half, I too crave to rejoice in the beauty of her who hath been set before me as a radiant sight for my adventurous eyes and for the consolation of my intellect, but I enjoy it in silence and in my soul, inasmuch as the end of my love, which is pure and chaste, having its roots in the well-tilled soil of virtue, contents itself with the sight of that lady.[314]

The formal idealization of Eleonora extends to the whole composition. Her beauty apart, Bronzino used extraordinary acuity of textural rendering and beauty of surface to evoke Petrarchan, classical, and religious inferences. The mesmerizing minutiae of Eleonora's gown, its variations of line, texture, and lighting, engross the spectator; its jewelled embellishments induce awe for the office of regency it represents.[315] This perfectionism recalls Neoplatonic maxims of beauty stemming from the time of Lorenzo the Magnificent, and explicit in the inscription on the back of Leonardo's *Ginevra de' Benci* and on Domenico Ghirlandaio's panel portrait of *Giovanna degli Albizzi.*[316] In Cosimo's circle of Ficinesque revival, Beauty *is* Goodness. The moral imperative of decorum, to sway the audience, suggests, too, that beauty and implicit goodness were expected to move the viewer to contemplation of greater Good, here inextricably woven with portrayal of regency.

It is a tribute to Bronzino's powers of invention that his portrayal of Eleonora as an unearthly paradigm denies nothing of the strength of character of a regent on whom Cosimo evidently did depend, and to whom he was remarkably faithful.[317] Writing in 1561 – a year before her death – Fedeli, the Venetian ambassador to the Florentine court, reported that Cosimo 'never had relations with anyone but the Duchess' ('abbia mai conversato se non con la Signora Duchessa').[318] (Cosimo handed over government, nominally, to Francesco in 1563, a year after her death, and his 'unsuitable' later attachments suggested to contemporaries that qualities of constancy and continence during his reign were all due to Eleonora, seen in hindsight as guiding spirit of all his policies.)[319] Bronzino, imbued with the spirit of Petrarch and its entrenched codas of interactive response, could design a remote portrayal of office but still provide Cosimo with a Medicean 'Laura':[320]

> Love has joined himself with chastity in her
> With natural beauty, gracious habit
> And gestures that speak in silence,
> And I know not what in her eyes that in a moment
> May make bright the night, darken the day ...[321]

Bronzino's own sonnets, the *Cortese Donna* and especially the *All'Amore Supremo* (appendix B), where the subject radiates a holy light or fire, are Petrarchan portrayals of love reflected in his state portrait of Eleonora.

Conclusion

The *Eleonora with Her Son Giovanni* is a state portrait that, in a period when decorum of dignity and rank were forced to new extremes in the ambitious Florentine court, grandly fulfils the precept's 'moral imperative,' to sway the spectator.[322] Arresting in its formal qualities, refined, idealized and sumptuously embellished, it was a portrayal made to persuasively glorify Medici rule through formalising Eleonora's role as Regent of State. Here the individual has become a sign of the objective, desired order, of the essential stereotype.[323] The world beyond the portrait was the ambitious Medici court at an especially auspicious moment of political consolidation. As in all ruler portraits, its aura was magically intended to persuade the viewer of the legitimacy of its claims. The painting is a tissue of expressions of Medici power, ideology, cultural hegemony, wealth, imperial affiliation, moral superiority, and assertion of Cosimo's court as a nexus of culture, artistic excellence, and humanism. Cosimo's republican antecedents perhaps made it overweening for him to overtly invest himself in his state portrait with a strong message of *religio regis*.[324] Eleonora's lineage and imperial association, however, provided a signal opportunity to express this God-given right to rule. Her depiction as Madonna, with additional classical, godly associations, confers just this aura of divine authority around his consort.[325] The portrayal of Eleonora as *regina mundi* as early as 1545 make the ducal couple's growing pretensions to absolutism very evident. The overall preciosity, her iconic *portamento* or carriage, the beautiful, Christ-like child, the fertile Tuscan landscape, and the many associated subliminal messages all serve to promote virtue, wisdom, rank, sovereignty, dynasty, and the claim to divinely conferred absolutism. Eleonora becomes a paradigm of queenly perfection. These superlatives reflect courtly standards recently instituted in Florence with Eleonora's help. They draw on impeccable traditions, old and new: Christian Mariology; Petrarchan tropes of exclusiveness; Tuscan patriotism; classical and biblical allusions; ancestral exaltation; and an incipient declaration of divine right to rule with implications of absolutism.[326] The purpose, of course, was to promote an aura of *persona sacra* around the portrait of the duchess in lieu of the status neither she nor her consort could properly claim as anointed rulers. Instead, they came to be invested with particular forms of sacrality, revealed in the symbolism and ritual created around them.[327] Bronzino's portrayal of majesty is achieved by his evocation through abstract means of the dominion, authority, dignity, and near-divine personal perfection by which Eleonora as regent and dynastic mother could be proposed as protector and exemplar to Medici subjects.[328]

The timing of the portrait's completion was particularly portentous. Even as the almost-finished panel stood drying on its easel, Eleonora may have taken her place in the proxy ceremony of her husband's investiture with the Golden Fleece, enacted in the Duomo on 11 August 1545. Whether she was dressed for that occasion as she appears here or is simply commemorated as Cosimo's consort and regent at this moment of elevation in their fortunes is not certain, but multiple copies of the portrait were disseminated to make claims for her regency, and their intended audiences were to be reminded of her potential as ruler for decades to come. In an era when portraiture carried overtones of ancestral *virtù*, her contemporaries understood that a portrayal expressing her role as 'Madre della repubblica fiorentina' would have to be impeccable and enduring.[329] If dynastic propaganda embodied in Bronzino's portrait seems esoteric today, it was not so in their time. The paired symbols of dominion, *Sol* and *Luna*, for example, are expressed in the composition's dual illumination, and the Apollonian *Sol* topos had long association with Cosimo in contexts of dominion.[330] Also, *Sol* and *Luna* had been paired with Time to give dynastic overtones to Tribolo's ephemeral triumphal arch for the wedding *apparato* in 1539, and were recalled in Bronzino's 1549 *Joseph* tapestry series. One episode, *Joseph's Dream*, comes from Genesis 37:50: 'the sun, the moon and the eleven stars made obeisance to me.'[331] The *Sol* and *Luna* iconography of tapestry and portrait appear on the engraved dedication page of Mannucci's eulogistic biography of Cosimo of 1586 (fig. 28). There the dynastic theme, allusions to dominion, dual illumination, and the portrait's watered Tuscan landscape and empyrean are succinctly recalled.[332] Trophies of crowns and sceptres are displayed in the foreground of an irrigated, expansive landscape and harbour, over which *Sol* and *Luna* shine simultaneously; the word 'AETERNUM' is inscribed in the sky above.[333]

Bronzino as Court Portraitist

The commission of state portraits is likely to be a pivotal event in reflecting an artist's standing with a noble patron. Evidently these, especially Eleonora's portrait as regent, were important in heralding the foundation of what Cosimo earnestly hoped was a true Medici dynasty. Vasari suggests that Bronzino had achieved the rank of court portraitist in the early 1540s.[334] We need not doubt this. His artistic talent, literary abilities, erudition, and affability raise him to the rank of artist-courtier. Indeed, Vasari concludes his admiration of Bronzino with a tribute to his Castiglionesque refinement: 'Agnolo, known as Bronzino, painter of Florence, [is] truly exceptional and worthy of great praise ... a very gentle and most courteous friend, of pleasant conversation, and in all his endeavours greatly honoured ... He has always been by nature quiet, has never caused injury to anyone, and has always loved all able men of merit of his profession.'[335] His potential as court painter had been recognized well before Cosimo came to power, as witness his

Guidobaldo della Rovere of 1532. His sojourn at the Pesaro branch of the della Rovere court may have refined his native gentility to a courtly edge, but his recorded love of Tuscan literary traditions may also have added to his credentials in the emerging effort to establish the Florentine court as a ranking centre of cultural (especially linguistic) revival.[336] By 1539 Varchi had paid tribute to Bronzino's deep knowledge of Dante and Petrarch; Vasari, too, cites links to poets and poetry in his early artistic production.[337] Some of his early sitters were prominent in Florentine literary and cultural circles.[338] Bronzino's prodigious output of Neoplatonic poetry and parodic *berneschi* attest to an erudition and wit typically valued in a courtly milieu. His intimate links to the Neoplatonism and Petrarchism of the Umidi and to literary protegés of the duke such as Giovio and Varchi as denizens of Cosimo's Florentine Academy, the Umidi's more formal successor, mark him as a new breed of court painter in Florence. In short, he seems to have been predestined for the position.

The allure of Bronzino's portraits rests on his ability to raise his subjects beyond mere documentation of appearance, social caste, place, or social context. Artifice raises them to the rank of exceptional presences, creating an aura of greatness in place of the mundane traits they possessed. His brush pretends to record but instead weaves subliminal messages of otherworldly perfection into his subjects. Poetic, classical, or religious infusions apart, his technique greatly contributes to this elevation. His perfectionism and subtlety may be assessed even from his depiction of his sitters' hands. From the innate strength expressed through Cosimo's large, well-formed hand at rest on his helmet; to the unadorned, virginal hands of his adolescent girls; to the ivoried, Petrarchan perfection of Eleonora's weightless touch on her brocade gown; Bronzino's portrayed hands are insistently individual even if idealized – and they appear, nevertheless, as anatomically convincing as Leonardo's.

His success in portraiture also depends on his ability to layer his imagery with a tantalizing allusiveness that flatters both ruler and viewer. For the viewer, if the portrait's complexities are solved, admission to an informed, elite, inner courtly circle is implied. Instead of the inflated content used in triumphalist programs for weddings, tapestries, state rooms, or funerals – all of which demanded a kind of visual equivalent to the rhetoric of praise – Bronzino refined and distilled the associated 'abundant' style (*copia*) for his portraits, providing intellectual challenge with a wide variety of compositional tropes and visual, even literary, tactics.[339] Perhaps this subtle distillation of content and expression was what Giovio had in mind when he relayed to Cosimo a consensus of Roman prelates and painters on Bronzino's 'blessed' mastery in portraiture over his master, Pontormo.[340]

Borrowing from popular Horatian poetics, Leonardo had codified for the artist a version of the humanist precept decorum, which directed his attention to presentation of a convincing persona, an essential in state portraiture. Even if it may be assumed that its essentials were widely understood and applied by artists, it is interesting to speculate on how much of Bronzino's artistic background would have been informed by Leonardo's writings. His artistic borrowings from Leonardo in Eleonora's state portrait have been discussed and more will follow here; cumulatively these show an overwhelming evidence of Bronzino's admiration for him.[341] Around 1560 Cosimo commissioned a copy of a Leonardo *Madonna* from Bronzino along with a copy of a portrait of Eleonora, as diplomatic gifts, suggesting that his imitative skills were highly valued.[342] Bronzino's admiration for Leonardo would have been more than a passing one – his master, Pontormo, trained briefly with Leonardo around the time that Leonardo recorded his theories.[343] His further exposure to Leonardo's ideas is possible during his two-year immersion, from 1530 to 1532, in the Pesaro branch of the Urbino court, the latter the setting for Castiglione's *Cortegiano*. Castiglione had been in the service of the Sforza court during Leonardo's stay from 1496 to 1499, and was probably informed of his theories at first hand.[344] (Leonardo's tenure at the Milanese court in the late 1480s has even been associated with the notion of court-linked academies.)[345] No court portraitist could have dispensed with the tenets of the *Cortegiano*.[346] With decorum of rank at its core, the *Cortegiano* adopts several of Leonardo's theories, including the *paragone* between painting and sculpture, which Varchi would later make his own. Bronzino's first court portrait, the impressive *Guidobaldo delle Rovere* of 1532, may be viewed as an epitome of decorum. There the Castiglionesque poise, aura of rank, overtones of innate bravery expressed in dress and posture, and intimations of humanism in its Greek inscription all combine to define a new courtly ideal.[347]

In the late 1530s, Bronzino's links with scholars familiar with Leonardo's writings included men who would be drawn into the Medici court in the early 1540s. Of these, his friend Benedetto Varchi is the most important. Even as a *fuoruscito*, or political exile, Varchi's ties with Florence had never been severed. Significantly, in spite of legislation outlawing contact with Cosimo's exiled enemies, Varchi's correspondents in the late 1530s had included Bronzino and other luminaries in the Umidi.[348] Benedetto's immediate literary circle had included Paolo Giovio from at least as early as 1537;[349] Giovio, Leo X's official historian when Leonardo was living from 1513 to 1516 in the Vatican Belvedere apartment provided him by the future pope, Cardinal Giuliano de' Medici, was also author of Leonardo's biography. Giovio claimed first-hand knowledge of Leonardo's writings, and indicated that he knew Leonardo well.[350] A famed connoisseur of portraits, he, like Varchi, would presently be iconographical adviser to Cosimo and to Bronzino.

During his banishment Varchi also knew Lodovico Dolce, the Horatian scholar later turned art theorist. On his repatriation to Florence from Venice and Bologna in 1543, Varchi kept up an extensive correspondence with Dolce, who, it will be recalled, translated Horace in 1537.[351] Dolce's *Aretino* of 1557 includes a lively exchange on decorum.[352] By the time Varchi came to Florence in 1543 to steer Cosimo's new academy and to rekindle his friendship with Bronzino, both friends must have been well aware of the precept and its already-popular literary applications.

Even if we ignore these circumstantial links to Leonardo's ideas, Bronzino could not have avoided them. Scores of copies of Leonardo's writings were in circulation. Although it has been found difficult to chart precisely the spread of his ideas to Florence during the sixteenth century, one direct source in Florence in the 1540s was the court sculptor Benvenuto Cellini.[353] He recorded in his autobiography that he had lent his manuscript on Leonardo's theory of optics to Sebastiano Serlio around 1542 when they were at the court of Francis I, Leonardo's most important patron.

Cellini returned to become a member of the Accademia Fiorentina in April 1545.[354] Vasari saw the *Codex Urbinas*, perhaps in Leonardo's disciple, Melzi's hands, before completing his first *Vite* in 1547. He recorded an attempt to publish the manuscript in Florence, suggesting that a copy existed there.[355] There were many copies in circulation, several owned by artists and amateurs.[356] Candidates in Florence would be Bronzino, Varchi, Vasari, or Cosimo himself. Ugolino Martelli, exiled in 1537, whose critique of Michelangelo's Medici Chapel 'portraits' evokes Leonardo, may have been aware of his writings, and Varchi's dependence on Leonardo at several points in his *Lezzioni* included the precept of decorum.[357] Indeed, its comprehensiveness was implicitly expressed by Vasari in the passage where he emphasized the importance of relating all attributes and externals to the subject in his state portrait of Alessandro de' Medici.[358]

There was also the persistent tradition that Varchi had invoked Leonardo's *paragone* to persuade Michelangelo that painting deserved equal esteem to sculpture, the theme central to his *Due Lezzioni*.[359] The tenor of Varchi's *Lezzioni*, presented to the Academy in 1547, proves his familiarity with Leonardo's writings as Melzi penned them between 1530 and 1540.[360] Finally, transcriptions of the *Codex Urbinas* probably existed in Medici collections and the holdings of the Accademia from these years – four are recorded in Florence around the time of the founding of its offshoot, the Accademia del Disegno, in 1563.[361]

In all, it seems that Leonardo's axioms for artists were probably well absorbed in Bronzino's closely integrated circle. By the mid-1540s, Cosimo's Accademia Fiorentina had become under Varchi's direction a propagandistic arm of Medicean interests.[362] Cosimo's concerns shade much of the writings of its members. Vasari's Petrarchan cataloguing of the beauty of the *Mona Lisa*, for example, is probably a reflection of the Medicean court's Neopetrarchan revival.[363] (His description seems unconsciously to reflect Bronzino's recent Neopetrarchan depiction of Eleonora in the state portrait, itself a signal example of Vasari's recurring precept of 'grace exceeding measurement' as the stamp of true artistry.) The propagandistic intent in Bronzino's state portraits are prophetic of Robortello's emphasis in 1548 on a didactic outcome for decorum, with Grifoli following suit in 1550. In Lorenzo the Magnificent's time, Landino's version of Horace had emphasized pleasure and delight as decorum's desired outcome.[364] Later, Cattani da Diacceto, Ficino's spiritual disciple, proposed that man is prepared on earth through civic virtue for the ascent toward Platonic contemplation.[365] Robortello, a close friend of Varchi, seems to have arrived at the same conclusion, using Horace and Aristotle as his guides.[366] It is hardly surprising that, from his earliest years in Cosimo's service, Bronzino had been adept at promoting an elevated Medicean civic image to impress the duke's subjects.[367] Proof of his study of Leonardo's version of decorum must remain moot, but there is little doubt that decorum was a widely understood concept in sixteenth-century Florentine court circles.

It seems that, in this circle, Bronzino's impact was seen as greatly advancing the status of the panel portrait, a genre traditionally held in lesser esteem than sculpted portraits. Doubtless both Giovio, an avid collector of portraits, and Varchi, in his role as provocateur in the dialogue between painters and sculptors, were instrumental in this evolution. Giovio's tribute in 1546 to Bronzino's supremacy as court portraitist was followed by the proposal from Varchi in his second *Lezzione* of March 1547 that portraiture is superior to other painted genres and the most persuasive.[368] (Michelangelo's poem dedicated to Vittoria Colonna was the coda for this argument.)[369] As Eleonora's state portrait had by then been added to Bronzino's triumphs, it is significant that Varchi emphasized the evocative power of *women's* portraiture when he commented that ideal love symbolized by a beautiful woman was even better expressed in her portrait than by her actual presence.[370] Consequently, although his *Lezzioni* was not published as a treatise, Varchi is the first theoretician to propose women's portraiture as a genre worthy of intellectual examination. It is logical to suppose that women's portraits executed by his friend, Bronzino, were uniquely influential in forming Varchi's contemporary convictions about their status as art.

Bronzino could operate only in the web of patronage deliberately instituted by Cosimo between an absolutist court and its ducal academies, all effecting a sort of laboratory of the *avant-garde*.[371] In his *Due Lezzioni*, Bronzino's intimate, Varchi, expressed an avidly desired new philosophy of art in Florence in the 1540s, a significant 'circumstance' of the precept decorum. As principal portraitist to the court, it is reasonable to propose that Bronzino was implicitly expected to develop an art and artistic philosophy to advance the status of portraiture in the Italian arena, one that would reflect the best traditions of the genre – those of Leonardo.

In the state portrait of Eleonora, Bronzino may be seen to visually synthesize emerging art theory with his own literary and artistic talents in the service of a court consolidating its political power and dynastic assertions with great assurance. Its confidence is expressed in Bronzino's exceptional portraits of young Medici daughters, the subject of chapter 3.

3

'These tender and well-born plants': Young Daughters and Wards of Cosimo and Eleonora

Glimpses into the early childhood years of Eleonora and Cosimo's children suggest that, before their parents embarked on an intensive regimen to tutor them as young princes and princesses, moments of exhuberant delight lightened their daily round. The court retainer Lorenzo Pagni reported from the Villa Medici at Petraia on 2 November 1544 that the Duke and his young children were entertained by the beloved court jester, Morgante, who, assisted by his owl, had been catching birds in the boxwood trees beside the labyrinth.[1] The ducal nursery by now included Maria, four; Francesco, three; Isabella, two; Giovanni, fourteen months; and Alessandro's natural daughter, Giulia (pl. 2 and fig. 13), by now about nine. We have seen how Bronzino's punning portrayal of the infant Giovanni in red satin with a *cardellino* in hand, made just months later, lightly entertained ducal ambitions for a third Medici papacy. Daughters, too, had their place in furthering Medici interests.

However much he loved his daughters and wards – and indications are that he was a deeply affectionate, even an indulgent, father – they were of necessity significant in Cosimo's dynastic plans. His resolute ambition and Charles V's backing ensured that political alliances through marriage could be a means of cementing Medici power: the destinies of Medici princesses were bound up in political expediency, increasingly so as his dominion expanded. During the reign of Pope Clement VII de' Medici, Caterina de' Medici's marriage to a future dauphin in 1533 led to her becoming Queen of France; Cosimo's own to Eleonora in 1539 secured Tuscan prosperity, a foothold in Naples, and Hapsburg favour. Similarly, the marriage of his heir, Francesco, to Giovanna of Austria in 1565 consolidated imperial connections, and Ferdinando's to Princess Christine of Lorraine in 1589 procured a Medici alliance with France as French power rivalled Spain's. In the Italian sphere also, Cosimo's role in his daughters' unions reflected his astuteness. For Lucrezia (1545–61), for example, one betrothal replaced another when political fortunes reversed: at thirteen she unexpectedly had to replace her deceased sister Maria as future Duchess of Ferrara.[2]

A pictorial record of their rapidly increasing family was important to the ducal couple. In May 1545, Pagni advised major-domo Riccio to summon Bronzino to be lodged in Volterra, to execute portraits of the ducal children. Records show that by 15 March 1545, a portrait of Princess Maria, then five, was destined for Caterina de' Medici of France. The exuberant *cardellino* portrait of Giovanni was completed in April 1545; by August he was portrayed again for inclusion with his mother in her state portrait.[3]

For a state's survival and hegemony, succession was *the* paramount concern. All Europe had watched the acute religious and political upheavals in England, where a young, sickly boy, Edward, was sole heir to the ageing Henry VIII, with all that implied for the body politic. With Medici succession now assured, attention was focused on the daughters. Portraits of unmarried princesses could play an important role in Medici pretensions to absolutism. Prenuptial and betrothal portrayal of high-born girls was a genre with its own traditional canons in the royal courts of Europe, and its development in this court testifies to Cosimo and Eleonora's grandiose ambitions. Alliances could be sealed through betrothals, and the sooner these were effected the easier it became to secure continued peace between principalities and interested nations, and to secure buffer zones around Cosimo's Tuscan borders. To this end, likenesses of Medici girls could be circulated to make their faces familiar in the courts of Italy, and possibly even abroad.

Cosimo and Eleonora's two eldest daughters, Maria and Isabella, were painted when they were around eleven (pl. 7 and fig. 32). No childhood or early adolescent portrait of Lucrezia survives, and there are none recorded for her at that age. (Her portrayal as Duchess of Ferrara is discussed in chapter 5.) Nor are further childhood portrayals known of Cosimo's ward, Giulia, or of Eleonora ('Dianora') di Toledo, Eleonora's orphaned Spanish niece, who was raised at court from birth.[4] In the *Maria* and *Isabella* girl-portraits, their decorum reflects what the great courts prescribed for portrayals of eligible princesses.

Bronzino's *Bia de' Medici* (1536/7–1542)

The first known portrait of the duke's children to come down to us is Bronzino's portrait of Cosimo's illegitimate child, Bia, when she was about six (pl. 6), born before his marriage and raised in the Medici nursery under Maria Salviati's care. It is far in spirit from those of Eleonora's daughters, but breathtaking in its preciousness, grace, and beauty. It enshrines the almost hallucinatory beauty described by a favoured court poet, Tullia d'Aragona, 'a grace that entices, absorbs, and captivates whoever experiences it' ('una grazia che alletta, tira, e rapisce chi la conosce').[5] The *Portrait of Bia* hangs today in the Tribuna of the Uffizi in Florence, where her charismatic image still evokes delight.[6]

As Caterina Cibo recorded, 'bastards' in the court's nursery were accorded equal treatment to ducal offspring. On her marriage in 1539, Eleonora had warmly accepted the little girl Bia, born to an unnamed Florentine noblewoman and Cosimo between 1536 and 1537.[7] Maria Salviati's many reports to the ducal couple attest to the universal affection in which Bia was held. She was a lively, entertaining little girl. Her grandmother – who seems to have adored her – proudly wrote from Arezzo in July 1540: 'No news to report ... [T]he Lady Bia is the solace of this Court' ('Non c'è nuovo ... la S.ra Bia sia il sollazzo di quella Corte').[8] Bia's nursery companion, Alessandro's natural daughter Giulia, survived the illness they shared in 1542.[9] The longing of Maria, Eleonora, and Cosimo for Bia's recovery is recorded in almost daily bulletins as Maria Salviati kept vigil. Even court officials were affected when she failed to rally. 'Tomorrow will be a much sadder day' ('Domani è il giorno più tristo'), concludes Grifoni's final bulletin to Pagni, Cosimo's major-domo in Pisa, written as her condition worsened between 25 and 28 February.[10] She died on 1 March 1542, and was buried with honour in San Lorenzo, memorial sanctuary of the Medici from the time of Cosimo il Vecchio.[11]

Vasari, immediately following his record of Bronzino's *Eleonora with Giovanni*, noted that '[h]e portrayed also the little girl Bia, natural daughter of the Duke.'[12] Her image is recorded twice in the 1553 inventory, the first by Bronzino, 'A panel portrait of the dead Lady Bia, in a gilded walnut frame' ('Un ritratto in tavola della S^ra Bia de' Medici morta, con ornamento di noce tocco d'oro'). A record of her death mask in gesso follows: 'il getto di gesso della S^ra Bia morta.' The 'Bià ... morta' description of Bonzino's panel could either mean 'the late Bia,' or it could refer to a posthumous portrait.[13]

Until 1893, when Conti produced copious archival evidence to show that a 'Bia' really existed, the portrait was thought to be of Maria, born in 1540, 'Bia' being assumed to be a contraction of her name.[14] Logic prevailed. Conti pointed out in 1893 that Maria was not deceased ('morta') at the time of the 1553 inventory. The Tribuna portrait has always been attributed to Bronzino.[15] Some scholars believe that Bia's death in 1542 provides a *terminus post quem* for the panel, in which she appears to be about six years old.[16] Here her portrayal, 'still as a statue,' will be proposed as posthumous, but before 1545.[17]

In this, possibly the earliest of his portraits from the new ducal court and one of Bronzino's most compelling, Bia is posed to the left in three-quarter view, seated on a chair set diagonally to the picture plane. It has aptly been described as 'an infantile version of his Lucrezia Panciatichi' (fig. 27).[18] In place of Lucrezia's breviary, Bia holds in her right hand the terminal of a *cintura* of gold links. She is dressed richly but not ostentatiously in white silk, and adorned with pearls – a vision in white, a metaphor for her name, Bianca. Her Medici paternity is stated by a large pendant medal on her breast showing a youthful, unbearded Cosimo as he appeared before his marriage, on Domenico di Polo's medal of the late 1530s.[19] Her 'tear-drop' diamond earrings with pendant-pearl terminals carry no hidden reference to a personal motto, as do the elaborately figured earrings in portraits of Maria and Isabella (pl. 7 and fig. 32), which recall their personal *imprese*. Bia was presumably too young to carry the symbolic freight of womanly virtues expressed in them. Her demeanour is sweetly serious, and a certain seigneurial self-awareness is expressed in her upright pose. An aura of calm exudes through the overall compositional scheme of white and blue, but Bronzino has ensured that a certain starkness in the scheme detracts not one whit from Bia's recorded charms.

The panel supports Caterina Cibo's private claim that illegitimacy was not a stigma for 'natural' children at this court. Her rank is established by her evident link to the duke, and her dignity advanced by ancestral associations and artistic precedents. If the *Lucrezia* is evoked in her pose, the angle of the chair and her quiet self-containment of expression suggest that Bronzino ultimately derived this portrait format from Raphael's *Leo X* of about 1518, currently in Cosimo's Guardaroba. It had only recently been exhibited at Cosimo and Eleonora's wedding.[20] Evocation of ancestral *virtù* was a tradition enshrined in Renaissance portraiture. Leo was her great-great-uncle, Maria Salviati's uncle, Cosimo's affable godfather, and the first Medici pope. His well-loved niece, Maria, probably instilled in her granddaughter some pride in her Medici lineage.

On the basis of style alone, a date later than the *Lucrezia* is likely for this portrait.[21] Lucrezia's sculptural rendering has been seen as the beginning of a development in which Bronzino began to shed some Venetian influences acquired at Pesaro early in the 1530s. Her geometrically strict features are rendered with the clarity and power of form that will characterize Bronzino's portraiture in the 1540s.[22] In his *Bia*, the sculptural effect is further advanced by the strong plastic volumes of head, neck, and bare shoulders, and the stark separation of the figure from its azure background.

The question of whether the portrait is posthumous or not is an important 'circumstance' attending its decorum. It is proposed for several reasons here that it is based on Bia's recorded gesso death mask, now lost. First, it is the only Bronzino portrait of a young girl composed in a three-quarter-length, seated pose. Portraits of Maria, Isabella, and the related, mysterious *Girl with a Book* in the Uffizi (pls. 7, 9, and fig. 32) are each frontally posed in long-bust format. (The *Isabella* is a short-bust copy, probably of a longer original.) Second, they are all depicted in early adolescence – in effect almost nubile – which allows the portraits to be categorized as a prenuptial genre of portraiture of girls.[23] Third, in spite of the record that Bronzino was summoned to paint the Medici children in May 1545, there are no extant single portraits of Cosimo and Eleonora's daughters in early childhood and none appear in inventories; this is true for Caterina de' Medici's requested portrait of Princess Maria at the age of five, which may have been a sketch.[24] Probably Bia's death occasioned the commission of a commemorative portrait, for which her death-cast was made.

Elements internal to the composition support Bia's posthumous portrayal. Although the adolescent portraits of Maria and Isabella (pl. 7 and fig. 32) have plain backgrounds and omit any suggestion of location, Bia's sumptuous lapis-lazuli setting and the nimbus around her head are unique in Bronzino's child-portraits, and deny any impression of terrestrial existence. Bia's head casts no shadow. Rather, the nimbus of light around it seems to radiate from her. As in the later *Eleonora with Giovanni*, the expanse of lapis and the preciousness of the setting elevates her to very exalted rank. The metaphysical overtones of a halo, the child's extraordinary aura of stillness, the perfection of her forms, and the lapis background all by symbolic association place Bia, too, in the realm of Heaven.

In addition, sculptural overtones discussed for the *Maria Salviati with a Book* with cast-plaster *imagines* touch this portrait, too. This impression arises from abstraction and regularity in Bia's face and figure, and the extremely optical presentation of every form. The uniform whiteness of the entire figure and lack of colour in the dress come close to the crystalline effects of marble. Scientific examination shows that the field of lapis lazuli was painted from the outer edge of the panel, including the lightened area of the nimbus, to surround the already completed figure, and re-fortification of the contoured oval of the head creates a strong separation of the figure from its background.[25] But sculptural effects in this portrait are different from those of the Praxitelean Lucrezia or the magisterial chill of Eleonora's later state portrait. The taut, doll-like rendering of the child's dressed body makes her appear inanimate. Bia's dress style follows Lucrezia's, but the flickering lights on soft wrinkles of crimson silk on the latter's bodice suggest Lucrezia's breathing and potential for movement – consistent with Vasari's comment that the Panciatichi portraits were so alive that they 'only lacked breath.'[26] Compared to the Prague *Eleonora* of 1543 (pl. 5 and figs. 19 and 20), the suppression of the potential to breathe in the *Bia* is particularly noticeable, and the little girl's extreme stillness and unearthly removal is especially poignant compared to Titian's contemporary, vivacious *Clarice Strozzi*, at play with her puppy.[27] Significantly, a treatise of 1539 regarding dress proposed that colour must harmonize with the colouring and the 'portatura,' or bearing, of the wearer.[28] Bia's winsomeness is not enhanced with vivid colour. Perhaps the 1553 inventory entry, 'Bia morta,' properly describes a posthumous portrayal, just as the term describes her death mask in gesso.

In sum, *Bia*'s link in spirit to the aura surrounding the traditional, sculpted *imagines* exhibits elements in common with the posthumous *Maria Salviati with a Book*, notably in a degree of petrification of form, neutral tonality, and indeterminate setting. But the lowered perspective, three-quarter-length format, and less frontal presentation bring the little girl somewhat closer to our world. The formality of the portrait makes this more than a sentimental commemoration of a beloved little girl, however, and if less marmoreal than Maria's, her face is waxen under a light blush of vermilion on her cheeks.

For whom was this portrait intended? Although a definitive study of the placement of portraits in interior settings has yet to emerge, women's portraits were apparently placed in company with religious exemplars.[29] As Bia's portrait is not an official one and would have been hung in the private Medici quarters of the Palazzo Vecchio, it may be assumed that it was intended to keep her memory fresh for the immediate members of the ducal family, including the sorrowing Maria Salviati. But an exemplary role for it is certain. De Hollanda was emphatic that *all* portraits were inherently exemplary and were perceived as such; too many portraits were being painted, and he would limit all portrayals to the great and virtuous. He does allow that a princess of notable virtue may be recorded for posterity, and asserts that children ought to have portraits of parents and ancestors before them, in order to find comfort in them and as a reminder to be virtuous.[30]

Bia's virtue is eminently displayed by her decorum and her beauty. Her upright posture, her composed face, and her stilled hands all conform to Alberti's and later pedagogical writers' notions of modesty to be *demonstrably* evident in young girls. An erudite humanist, Leon Battista Alberti (1404–72) exhorted women in his *Della famiglia* to consciously promote this decorum: 'Unless they have the highest example of chastity and decorum in you, do not expect them to show ... reverence toward yourself ... [M]ake it your concern to be and *to appear* in gesture, word and deed most modest and virtuous ... [D]isdain the frivolous mannerisms, the habit of tossing the hands about.[31] In the sixteenth century, the pedagogy of the Spaniard Juan Vives swept Europe. Within a few years, his *Instruction of a Christian Woman* (1523) enjoyed pan-European appeal, and was widely translated. Specifically discussing ideals of conduct for girls like Bia just past infancy, he advises:

> Let the maid learn [no] ... uncomely gesture and moving of the body, no not so much
> as when she is yet ignorant what she doth, and innocent ... Let all her bringing up be
> pure and chaste in the first years, because of her manners, which take their first form-
> ing of that custom in youth and infancy.

Further, he dwells on the virtue of detachment:

> [She should] ... counterfeit her excellent virtue, soberness and humility of mind ...
> [L]et a young woman be indeed as she showeth, demure, humble, sober, shamefast,
> chaste, honest, and virtuous; *both let her seem so, and be so.*[32]

Firenzuola, that arbiter of manners and contemporary satellite of the court, proposed that a reining in of ebullience may also be effected by the suppression of
laughter and the cultivation of *quietas*.[33] Evidently, the posthumous portrayal of
even a very young girl of high rank would be expected to express these exemplary
maxims.

Leonardo's elements of decorum are fully observed here by Bronzino. The setting for the subject is a now quasi-royal court, and Bia's rank, dignity, dress, pose,
and gesture are in accord with an exemplary noble daughter – beloved, virtuous,
but deceased. She has been admitted to full paternal ancestry, and made a suitable exemplar for the descendants of her house. Her purity is symbolized by her
being dressed in white, as is Ripa's *Innocenza*. The symbolism was promoted, perhaps euphemistically, for another Bianca, Grand Duke Francesco's new duchess,
Bianca Cappello, his former mistress. In a 1582 commentary on a *mascherata* – a
celebratory costume parade – Bianca was declared purer than the legendary
ermine, which would expire if its fur became soiled:

> The nymph Driada ... carried an ermine ... with the motto saying 'MOST SPOTLESS,'
> denoting that even if it was white and pure, and this is why it symbolizes chastity, it
> nevertheless bowed to greater purity, alluding yet again to the name of the Great
> Bianca ... white in thought, white in appearance, white in sincerity of spirit, and
> white finally in name.[34]

Bia's purity is expressed through the luminosity of white satin and pearls, which
emit and increase light. Bronzino's *Bia* epitomizes his own 'Nuova Angioletta':

> Oh new little Angel who, free from your graceful human veil,
> Flew happy to your celestial abode,
> Leaving us behind, lost and in pain,
> And with such a heavy burden.[35]

This radiant, angelic, light-emitting vision has descended from Heaven to comfort
and delight, as Petrarch described in *Canzone* 106, the opening line of which provided Bronzino's title:

> A new little angel on agile wings came down from Heaven to

> the fresh shore where I was walking alone by my destiny.
> Since she saw me without companion and without guide,
> a silken snare which she was making she stretched in the grass
> wherewith the way is green.
> Then I was captured, and it did not displease me later, so sweet
> a light came from her eyes.[36]

The effulgent light from an image disengaged from earthly matter and so evidently open to contemplation is replete with Neoplatonic overtones. The illusionistic perfection and optical sharpness of forms and surfaces characteristic of Eleonora's state portrait are already evident in the *Bia*. All the forms are flawless, and few Bronzino portraits exhibit such extraordinary precision of rendering. Each hair is accounted for – individual strands like spun gold drift free from the overall orderly arrangement of her hair to emphasize the intense blue of the lapis background. Her azure setting and radiant halo suggest an individual already released from matter. Bia is depicted as a riveting emanation of the Divine, and the portrait, directed to those who love her, invites their contemplation and longing for spiritual ascent with her purified, sinless spirit to God.

Consideration of Bronzino's Petrarchism and Neoplatonism has implications for our understanding of the ways in which Renaissance viewers experienced works of art.[37] Such studies show the great importance of the abstractions inherent in Renaissance portraits, the revelation of inward, deeper qualities of character, the 'virtues' they are felt to possess. The capacity of painted figures to project qualities such as 'strength,' 'humility,' 'grace' or – as in Bia's case – 'purity' and 'innocence' has recently been proposed in contexts of style and decorum as the supreme achievement of art, elevating it to the realm of moral philosophy.[38]

To the delight of literary contemporaries, Bronzino's giftedness as a Petrarchan poet extended to parody. He would exploit this moral element in his *Bia* in an artistic about-face, when he combined her beauty and purity in painterly parody to compose the kind of anthropomorphic, beastly hybrid invented by Horace. In his London *Allegory* of 1545, his *Bia* is recalled for an elliptical personification of *Fraude* (fig. 29), who as part of her armour of deceit and fraudulent impulses of the flesh has Bia's angelic, innocent face even as she conceals a hybrid, beastly body and envenomed tail. *Fraude*'s ultimate source is Dante's *Inferno*, but Ariosto's *Orlando Furioso* was probably Bronzino's source:

> She had a pleasing face, a humble gaze;
> Of grave demeanour, grave in speech as well,
> And modest in her dress, beyond all praise,
> She might have been the Angel Gabriel.
> And yet deformed and ugly in all ways
> Her body is, which ample skirts conceal,
> While under them she clutches at her hip
> A dagger which is poisoned at the tip.[39]

Through his exercise of antidecorum in the *Allegory*'s *Fraude*, we understand that Bia's face represented for Bronzino the very essence of purity and goodness.

In the *Portrait of Bia*, this exemplary outcome brings into focus Bronzino's awareness of his potential audience. An audience belongs to a specific environment, and carries attitudes to portrayals of a deceased, an ancestor, or, in this case, a beloved child, all rooted in cultural attitudes to death, love, and memory. Although she is almost palpably accessible to those who loved her, Bronzino's Bia, by virtue of her halo and subtle references to perfection, is bathed in a purer, more refined spiritual essence than any she experienced in life. Her surreal presence is a reminder of the accepted power of portraits and effigies to move the emotions or to induce awe in an intended audience. Francesco Bocchi even asserted that the aim of art was to provide contact with such essences or absolutes.[40] It was a phenomenon that the Medici had traditionally exploited in the public arena for their own ends.

Bronzino's *Portrait of Bia* and the Medici Tradition of the *Fallimagine*

Bronzino's *Bia*'s waxen face, vermilion-tinted cheeks, and inset eyes, the doll-like smoothness of form on the neck and shoulders, and the torso with its too-smoothly fitting bodice all evoke the tradition of the *boto*, or popular votive figure. Her unusual demeanour has provoked the response that for Bia, 'in spite of her childish features, her cold gaze and her gravity belong to a person with neither age nor youth nor spirit,' and the observation above that, in spite of the hallucinatory detail in the portrait, Bia appears to be 'as still as a statue.'[41] Her stillness, the lowered perspective, and consequent ease of 'approachability' is balanced by an illusionism that creates a magical aura of 'presence' around Bia that makes her seem to materialize into the viewer's own space.[42]

'Image magic' had a special place in sixteenth-century portraiture. Its manifestations have been explored by David Freedberg and Hugo Van der Velden in Medici contexts. Life-sized effigies in wax made as Medici votive figures had an impressive history in Florence. The best of them achieved a high degree of verisimilitude, furnished with real hair, open eyes, and normal clothing. The craftsmen in this now venerable genre were known, not surprisingly, as *fallimagini*. The genre had become an extracurricular interest for Verrocchio, releasing him from the routine casting of effigies from life and death. Initially providing friendly tutoring to craftsmen, he had ended by outdoing the *fallimagini* at their trade. Vasari emphasized the importance of verisimilitude as essential to the *boto*'s votive function, and greatly regretted the deterioration of Verrocchio's survivals, 'all of extreme beauty ... very few have equalled them.' Bronzino's doll-like rendering of the child's body in the *Bia* is echoed in Vasari's record of Verrocchio's use of split canes over a wood frame for the body, over which cloth was then stretched and waxed. The practice persisted, and Vasari comments at length on its traditions and functions.

Medici effigies – *boti* – had for decades been set up close to ex-voto centres in Florentine churches, often in the vicinity of miraculous shrines to the Virgin.[43] The origins of the practice, and variations in skill of the *fallimagini* in achieving verisimilitude to effect palpable, 'magical' Medici presences, have received some attention. Wax *boti* of Lorenzo the Magnificent had been set up in several churches after his escape from the bloody 1478 Pazzi conspiracy – ostensibly to render thanks for his preservation, but assuredly they reaffirmed Medici hegemony and Divine favour over their enemies. Life-sized, wearing wigs and real clothing, their evocative power was of a very high order.[44] Just a few years before Bia's death, as Vasari executed his *Duke Alessandro de' Medici in Armour*, a counterfeit or *boto* of Alessandro was constructed by the sculptor and *fallimagine* Giovanni Montorsoli for installation in Santissima Annunziata.[45] The church, which had near-territorial votive meaning for the Medici, housed the miraculous *Virgin of the Annunciation*, believed to be painted by angels of the Holy Spirit in 1252. (It is still one of the most important shrines in Italy.) Its cult, and the setting up of Medici *boti* around the shrine, was now embedded in Florentine religious and political identity and had deep implications for Medici control. On the establishment of Medici grand-ducal rule from 1569, veneration of the miraculous *Annunziata* was elevated to a national cult.[46]

Boti had venerable European roots. The casting of the face of a deceased had medieval, royal connotations, when a deceased ruler was copied in effigy by his *valet-de-chambre*. This was the *repraesentatio*, which stood in place of the dead ruler until a successor was crowned. Lifelike effigies of royalty were still employed for state funerals in France and England well into the sixteenth century. The aura of *sacralità* that royal *boti* evoked depended on their verisimilitude, and the sheer charismatic force of *boti* and portraits as 'presences' provoked some dramatic responses in Florence.[47] Wax figures of the Medici were periodically exalted – and villified – according to the family's political fortunes, throughout the Renaissance. When Giuliano, Duke of Nemours (1479–1546), was in exile from Florence, his sisters Maddalena and Lucrezia placed full-scale wax effigies of him in Santissima Annunziata in 1504 after his recovery from an illness. The incumbent monks, the Servites, were pressed to remove them, and did so: such 'presences' were understood as implicitly partisan declarations that social bonds and political powers were being reaffirmed around a surrogate persona. In 1512, having forced the resignation of the republican head of government, Piero Soderini, Medicean henchmen demolished his *boto*. In 1527, wax effigies of Lorenzo, Giuliano, and Popes Leo X and Clement VII de' Medici were violently wrenched from the Annunziata and ground to dust underfoot. Benedetto Varchi remarked that, 'having slaughtered him in wax [i.e., Clement, the current pope], they would all the more readily have killed him in fact.' So strong was the perception of Medici *boti* and portraits as enduring, talismanic presences that a contemporary, Busini, did describe this destruction of Clement's image as his 'murder.'[48]

Boti could survive for centuries. An engraving circa 1850 after Marco Moro (fig. 30) shows the nave of Santa Maria delle Grazie, in Mantua, with many secular votive figures mounted in the upper arcades. A cross-section of humanity is included, with children, knights, widows, a pope, and even the condemned in various attitudes – one figure hangs by his wrists, another kneels in contrition with a noose about his neck. To judge by their dress, some were at least two hundred years old. Praying laity below confirm that the tradition of wax images, votive portraits, and donor portraits of living and dead Medici set up in churches functioned also to elicit prayers to speed posthumous subjects to Paradise.[49]

The painted portrait enjoyed a measure of this aura, too. In discussing the 'image magic' of verisimilitude in portraits and wax *boti* and their efficacy, Cosimo's iconographer, Prior Vincenzo Borghini, referred interchangeably to both genres of representation in correspondence with his monks; his colleague, Vasari, was fulsome in his praise for portraits that could effect this response.[50] It had a long history. If we have become inured to the talismanic power exerted by images, the fifteenth-century writer Giovanni Dominici bears witness for us to the Renaissance response, one that he especially emphasized was efficacious in raising virtuous children. The effectiveness of imagery, he believed, proceeds from a kind of identification between the spectator and what is represented by the image. Girls would acquire girlish virtues by seeing those qualities exemplified in the appearance and action of female saints. So well understood was this premise that children were presented with 'holy' dolls to aid the association.[51] (Their cost and beauty can only be supposed. Versions after a prototype by the ranking sculptor, Desiderio da Settignano [1430–64] were available into the late fifteenth century.)[52] The evocative power of these divine familiars was widely understood – Dominici was in favour of the use of 'holy' dolls on make-believe altars for boys playing the role of priest, nuns were known to embrace images, and young postulants of religious orders could own Christ-dolls along with sets of clothing and a play altar. The Dominican Savonarola protested against young women's 'idolatry' in association with these *bambinetti* at the end of the fifteenth century to no avail: there is evidence that they were highly prized to the end of the sixteenth century and beyond.[53] Medici children were no exception. Among the effects listed after Maria Christina de' Medici's death in 1632 were whole wardrobes in miniature, with garlands, crowns, glass necklaces, and other accessories to dress statuettes of the Madonna and infant Jesus, who is described as '[a] baby boy seated on an ebony chair dressed in worn taffeta, decorated with a silver cord with a little pearl necklace around the neck.' Judging by their worn state, Maria had enjoyed many hours of play with the *Bambino* and its accessories.[54]

Bia's portrait enshrines an angelic innocence. Taken from the world with her soul unblemished, she is implicitly an uncanonized saint, and her beautiful, haloed head in its lapis-lazuli environment evokes this. Overtones of a votive figurative tradition or the evocation of beautiful holy dolls blended with *effigie* associations would have heightened the effect of her painted presence. Even in death she is made accessible forever to the impressionable gaze of Medici children, and her talismanic appeal serves to promote her role as saintly exemplar. The contemplation of examples, images, and stories illustrating the lives of good men and women to be used as 'mirrors,' and the comparison of their behaviour to one's own, were familiar childhood exercises throughout the Renaissance.[55] As seen in the Introduction, mirror analogy in relation to exemplars had enjoyed a long history in both portrait theory and literary references. It was one much subscribed to by Cosimo for himself and his children in future years.[56] Bia's vivid presence still evokes admiration. For the sixteenth-century Medici viewer, her waxen face, and the striking quality of *quietas* projected by her haloed presence against an azure empyrean, had multiple associations with sainthood and the kinds of *effigie* and *bambinetti* that allowed intense identification by a viewer with tangible exemplars.

The evocative power of the portrait as a surrogate presence is well documented. In a scene conjured in Baldassare Castiglione's poem, his wife, Ippolita, 'cheats the long days' by 'making tender approaches' to Raphael's image of him in his absence. She talks to it, hoping for a response; their little son greets the portrait by 'laughing and playing with it.'[57] In an age when portrayal was rare, a portrait was magically evocative. Distance and separation added poignancy to this. In 1466, Ippolita Sforza requested portraits from her mother 'for continual consolation and pleasure.'[58] Isabella d'Este received a letter from a friend in 1495 recording that the marchioness's portrait was placed before her at mealtimes so that she could pretend to be in her company, and Eleonora Gonzaga's daughter reproached her for not furnishing her with a portrait to help bring her vividly to mind. Maria de' Medici (1600–33) wrote to her sister Caterina Gonzaga (1593–1629) on 28 November 1628 from Siena on the longed-for return of her husband, 'even though his portrait and my reciprocal love allows me to have him continually before my eyes.'[59] In recognition of this practice, when the zealous Cardinal Gabriele Paleotti sought in 1582 to curtail near-idolatrous adulation of portraits, he conceded that distance between mutually loving partners was a legitimate reason to commission portraits of either for the other's consolation.[60] An intrinsically beautiful portrait could claim charismatic powers of transference. Paleotti exhorted pregnant women to gaze upon images of beautiful people to help them to produce beautiful children, and also advised 'holy images' as prizes for children who could recite their *Credo*.[61] In all, transference and edification of a very exalted kind would be the outcome of viewing Bia in her rarified envelope of light. Brightness, purity, otherworldliness, tranquillity, and unblemished, ethereal beauty invoke Ficino and Petrarch, too, in whose literary tropes Bronzino was thoroughly versed.[62] Her exemplary image expands the canon of classical divinities instituted by Cosimo for himself to include a Medicean, Christian iconology.[63]

Early Adolescent Portraits of Maria (1540–1557) and Isabella (1542–1576) de' Medici

The documented luxury of the court's nursery belies the seriousness with which Eleonora and Cosimo approached the education of their rapidly expanding family.[64] Daughters were prepared for cultural prominence in courts as illustrious and sophisticated as Ferrara's, where Isabella d'Este's erudition, humanism, and social accomplishments had been nurtured.[65] Their efforts were rewarded. Maria's precocious intellect was encouraged through a regimen of pedagogy directed by Eleonora and set for the three eldest children by Riccio, Cosimo's former tutor. At eight she was fluent in Spanish, and could read and translate Latin. By the age of twelve she was praised for her acumen and fluency in reciting speeches from Cicero and Virgil. Pier Vettori had her help Francesco with his studies – he was no mean intellect as a child – exposing her to Homer and Aristotle, a novelty for girls.[66] Her tragic death in 1557 at seventeen when she was betrothed to the future Alfonso II d'Este deprived the Estense and the Medici of a significant scholar and woman of letters.

Under the humanists Antonio Angeli da Barga and Vettori, the exceptionally gifted Isabella joined the same intensive regimen.[67] Study began after daybreak and continued throughout the morning, after which the girls were sequestered with Eleonora and her Spanish ladies.[68] Both girls, however, engaged in equestrian competition with Francesco, and their sturdiness was applauded. The vivacious Isabella had prodigious musical gifts as well, and delighted everyone by improvising on the lute, singing, and composing madrigals.[69]

Not coincidentally, this humanist education for girls recalls the liberal education pursued by the daughters of Thomas More.[70] The English court and aristocracy, and soon all of Europe, were under the sway of the philosopher Juan Luis Vives (1492–1540), Spanish author of a radical program of humanist pedagogy devised in 1523 for the English queen, Catherine of Aragon's daughter, Mary.[71] The learned Catherine, daughter of Ferdinand and Isabella, had sought Vives as Mary's tutor, probably with the encouragement of her cultured husband, Henry VIII. Born in Valencia, Vives had been educated in France and met More during a visit to Bruges. A 'common star' was said to link their souls – like Vives, More was an avowed believer in *ardor intellectualis* for women. Through More's intervention, Vives arrived in 1523 to hold a readership at Corpus Christi College, Oxford, and quickly attracted royal patronage. Richard Hyrd's English translation of his *Instruction of a Christian Woman* gave this royal pedagogy widespread appeal, and by mid-century, pan-European translations popularized it across Europe.[72]

By 1545, Eleonora and Vives were linked in the Italian sphere – Pietro Lauro Modenese dedicated his translation of Vives's *De l'ufficio del marito, de l'instituzione de la foemina* to her in 1546.[73] Vives's ties to the Hispanophile court would have inspired an opportune blueprint to prepare Medici girls to take positions in a wider forum, one in which Spain was the dominant global power. Francesco's evident Hispanic education, philosophy, and dress must lead to the conclusion that Eleonora fulfilled an important goal for her daughters: to bring them, too, to a level of full international acceptance.[74] Together with his modern, itemized humanist curriculum for each sex, Vives paradoxically gave precise instructions for a rigid, devout, sober, and overwhelmingly segregated upbringing for princesses.[75] If the meticulous Hispanic decorum Eleonora brought to Florence was disdained by della Casa, and she drew criticism for assiduously isolating her children, she seems in spirit to have followed Vives to the letter.[76]

Cosimo is said to have been immensely proud of his children's achievements. Maria, prospective Duchess of Ferrara at fourteen, was highly regarded by contemporaries for her humanism, intelligence, grace, and noble bearing.[77] As mentioned, Isabella's betrothal to the Orsini heir would seal a strategically important alliance. Lucrezia (pl. 10), physically and emotionally frail, became at thirteen a substitute wife to Alfonso d'Este a few months after Maria's unexpected death in 1557.[78] Sadly, as Duchess of Ferrara from October 1559, when Alfonso succeeded his father, Ercole, she lived only two years to enjoy her unexpected elevation.[79]

Bronzino's Portraits of Maria (1551) and Isabella (circa 1552–1553)

Among a dazzling array of women's portraits by Bronzino, three are of young adolescent girls, one of which is of Maria, painted in 1551 when she was just eleven (pl. 7), now in the Tribuna. The *Portrait of Isabella*, painted in 1552 or early in 1553 at about the same age, is known from a panel in Stockholm (fig. 32), typical of inscribed, short-bust workshop copies in Medici family sets. There is also the tantalizing *Girl with a Book* of ca. 1541–5 (pl. 9), not a Medici daughter but still in the Tribuna, and the earliest of the trio. These are solemn children. No brilliant satins or lapis-lazuli backgrounds enliven these compositions; Bronzino's portrait of Eleonora in Prague (pl. 5) is warm by comparison.

With these three panels, Bronzino introduced a distinct genre of court portraits of nubile girls. Maria's, painted with her brothers' in 1551, is well documented. In December 1550, Pierfrancesco Riccio called the artist to Pisa to make a portrait destined for Pope Julius III of the future Cardinal Giovanni, now aged seven.[80] Cosimo was now determined to have a full record of his family, and was dedicated to circulating their images on the wider political stage. (One impetus behind the 1550–1 portrait commissions was his study of Paolo Giovio's *Vitae illustrium virorum* [*Lives of Illustrious Men*] and Seutonius's *Lives of the Emperors*.)[81] Bronzino soon embarked on a series of portraits of the older ducal children.[82] The first *Maria* was completed by 27 January 1551, when he wrote to Riccio from Pisa and recorded for us his unforgettable impression of these 'perfect angels':

> I find myself painting [where] they are being taught Latin and Greek and take great pleasure in seeing that these tender and well-born plants are so well raised and tended, and perfectly guided and directed to an excellent result ... I have completed the portrait of Lord Giovanni and that of Lady Maria and so tomorrow or so I will have provided Lord Garcia's ... and, when their Excellencies return, I [will] make Lord Francesco's.[83]

Luca Martini duly recorded delivery of the first three panels in duplicate on 31 July.[84] Bronzino's praises provide useful insight into what he might have been expected to convey in portrayals of ducal children in this rarified environment: they are healthy, well born, scrupulously guided, and well educated. Their location in Pisa may even hint at seclusion.

The 1550s ushered in a deep awareness of the propaganda value of portraits. Paolo Giovio's famous collection of illustrious men especially claimed Cosimo's attention, and in 1553 Cristofano dell' Altissimo was sent to Como to copy Giovio's *uomini illustri* in toto. Soon, in Giovio's posthumous *Elogi: vite brevemente d'uomini illustri di guerra antichi e moderni* (*Elegies: Brief Lives of Illustrious Men of War Ancient and Modern*) of 1559 seven Medici appeared, including Cosimo – they had not appeared in the 1547 edition; and Lucio Paolo Rosello made him an *exemplum virtutis* in his *Portrait of True Government of the Prince, with the Living Example of Great Cosimo ... with two of Isocrates' Orations*. Cosimo's efforts to immortalize his family were bearing fruit, and in these years portraiture enjoyed greater standing in Florence than it ever had. Its proliferation in the Medici court reflects the patronage given to it at the royal courts of France, Spain, and England.[85] Giovanni's aspirations are expressed in his impeccable exercises in Greek, quoting Isocrates' 'Mirror of Princes' speech to Nikokles; a version of the portrait (in Oxford) shows him tonsured for his visit to Rome in the autumn of 1551.[86] Giulio Clovio, the renowned miniaturist, was housed in Florence by the duke from 1551 to 1553, when he executed an *Eleonora* (fig. 22), a *Francesco*, and several other miniature portraits.[87]

Maria's 1551 portrait is universally accepted as the half-length version now in the Tribuna (pl. 7), where her right hand is placed over her heart.[88] Vasari records it with Bronzino's portrayals of the ducal children: 'and afterwards, some new ones, and some the second time, of all the Duke's children; the Lady Maria, [now] a big girl, truly beautiful.'[89] Copies of the 1551 commissions were made. A miniature on tin, in short-bust format and part of a family set, inscribed 'MARIA. MED.COS. / FLOR.ET.SEN.DVCIS F' (pl. 8), is a faithful copy of the Tribuna *Maria*. Vasari records Cosimo's deep attachment to this set, located outside his study, the Scrittoio di Calliope, in the apartment of Leo X:

> [T]here is a great number of antique statues of marble and bronze, and tiny modern paintings, rare miniatures, and an infinity of gold, silver and bronze medals, arranged with exquisite order. These portraits of the illustrious men of the Medici house are so natural, [and] alive, as to be true likenesses.[90]

Another *Maria*, 'framed in walnut in the manner of a mirror' and recorded in the Medici inventory of 1562, five years after her death, is lost. It may have been a copy of the Tribuna *Maria* of 1551, or perhaps the older *Maria* Vasari alludes to, among others now lost.[91] The possibilities for it include a figured allegorical, sliding cover, a portrait designed to slide over a mirror, or one covered by a sliding mirror. Could this *Maria* have been intended for her prospective husband, Alfonso d'Este, at some time between 1551 and 1557, when she died? An allegorical cover must remain in the realm of conjecture, but amorous associations did surround a mirror-covered portrait of Castiglione's love, Elizabetta Gonzaga, behind which two *Sonetti dello specchio* (Sonnets of the Mirror) by him were concealed, and other amorous themes are found in association with mirrors.[92] Gazing on oneself in a mirror that concealed an absent love could be a piquant experience for a prospective bridegroom, allowing a sense of exclusive access to the prospective bride he had yet to meet. A mirror would also suggest Maria's exemplary status, in tandem with Giovanni and Cosimo's current promotion as princely 'mirrors.' The enframing of this portrait 'in the manner of a mirror' and its meaning in the context of Medici court portraiture remains a tantalizing mystery.

A seventeenth-century engraving by Adriaen Haelwegh (fig. 31), in which Maria's hand held to her breast is omitted, is based on the 1551 *Maria*.[93] As she died unexpectedly in 1557 at seventeen, the unusual use of her portrait as a girl of eleven as its source may suggest that she was not portrayed from life between 1551 and her death in 1557.[94]

Vasari makes no mention of a childhood portrait of Isabella, but the panel in Stockholm shows her at about eleven, and must have been painted around 1553 (fig. 32).[95] Inscribed 'D.ISABELLA. DE.MEDICE' [*sic*], it follows the short-bust format of the miniature series on tin (pl. 8), in which each of the ducal children appears, but from which Isabella's portrait is missing. As miniatures of infant boys were included in the miniature set, while those of girls appear only from about the age of eleven, Maria and Isabella's portraits appear to mark a rite of passage into adulthood, and at the same time declare their suitability and availability as marriage prospects.[96]

Because of its dimensions, 44 × 36 cm, the inscribed Stockholm *Isabella* panel cannot belong to the miniature Medici set on tin, each 15 × 12 cm, from which hers is missing, but must belong to another, dispersed, workshop set. Probably Bronzino's original *Isabella* was in longer format, similar to the Tribuna *Maria*. She may have held her hand to her heart or held a book, like Bronzino's mysterious *Girl with a Book*, circa 1541–5 (pl. 9), Bronzino's prototype for the *Maria* and *Isabella* compositions.[97] (The strongly plastic treatment of her face comes closest to the *Bia*'s.) Her identity as a younger sister of Eleonora might be considered, as her features, especially her eyes, resemble hers (pl. 5), and the silvery gown with dark blue velvet banding exhibits the Toledan armorial colours, silver and dark blue. Eleonora (1522–62) was fourth of seven children and second daughter of Pedro and Maria di Toledo; Isabella was the eldest girl and the names Juana, Ana, and Francesca are variously mentioned. If Maria, their mother, had further children after 1522, some of her daughters may have been born between 1522 and 1530.[98] This would allow for a Toledan daughter as the *Girl with a Book*, perhaps painted on a visit to Florence or from a sketch. She, Maria, and Isabella are all adolescent, and they share a commonality of decorum that may suggest a strong infusion of Spanish canons for the portrayal of young girls.

They are all dressed in restrained colours, which adds to the impression of sober temperament for each.[99] Their *proprietà* – decorum – would have found favour with Vives, who quoted Democrates in support of silence and of modesty of dress for women: 'The decking of a woman standeth in scarcity of speech and apparel.' His advice to parents was to instigate a stoical upbringing of self-denial ('cherishing marreth the sons, but it utterly destroyeth the daughters'), with one precept to the fore: 'a woman hath no charge to see to but her decency [*onestà*] and her chastity.'[100] Even a religious virgin (the classical Quinta Claudia), he admonished, was reputed an evil woman when she wore gay raiments. ('God made neither purple nor crimson sheep.')[101] Showiness could lead to lust in a beholder, he intoned, and could occasion a loss of chastity in the wearer.[102] Chastity was to be demonstrably visible.

In Florentines, Vives had an audience of the converted. In 1549 a Welsh visitor, William Thomas, recorded the unusually sober dress and cloistered lives of girls there: 'Florentines ... love a modesty in their women's apparel and ... they keep their maidens so strait that in manner no stranger may see them.'[103] Indeed, it seems that Medici princesses' attire epitomized what was 'solid, noble and seemly' in 1588. When a costume was sought for Lepida, the young, chaste heroine of Girolamo Bargagli's *La Pellegrina*, due to be enacted for Grand Duke Ferdinando and Christine of Lorraine's wedding in 1589, it was delicately proposed that a Medici princess's dress could be borrowed if this was allowed – the part was for a man – or perhaps one from a Rucellai girl.[104] This 'solid, noble and seemly' decorum infuses Bronzino's portraits of aristocratic, unmarried girls. Traditionally, flattering colours and lavish jewellery could wait until after marriage: in 1465, Alessandra Strozzi advised her son Filippo that his prospective wife could 'turn out to be good looking – particularly when dressed as a young woman rather than as a girl.'[105] Bronzino's *Maria Salviati with a Lapdog*, *Lucrezia Panciatichi*, and Prague *Eleonora* (pl. 1, 5, and fig. 27) were married when portrayed. Each is dressed in brilliant crimson and bejewelled.

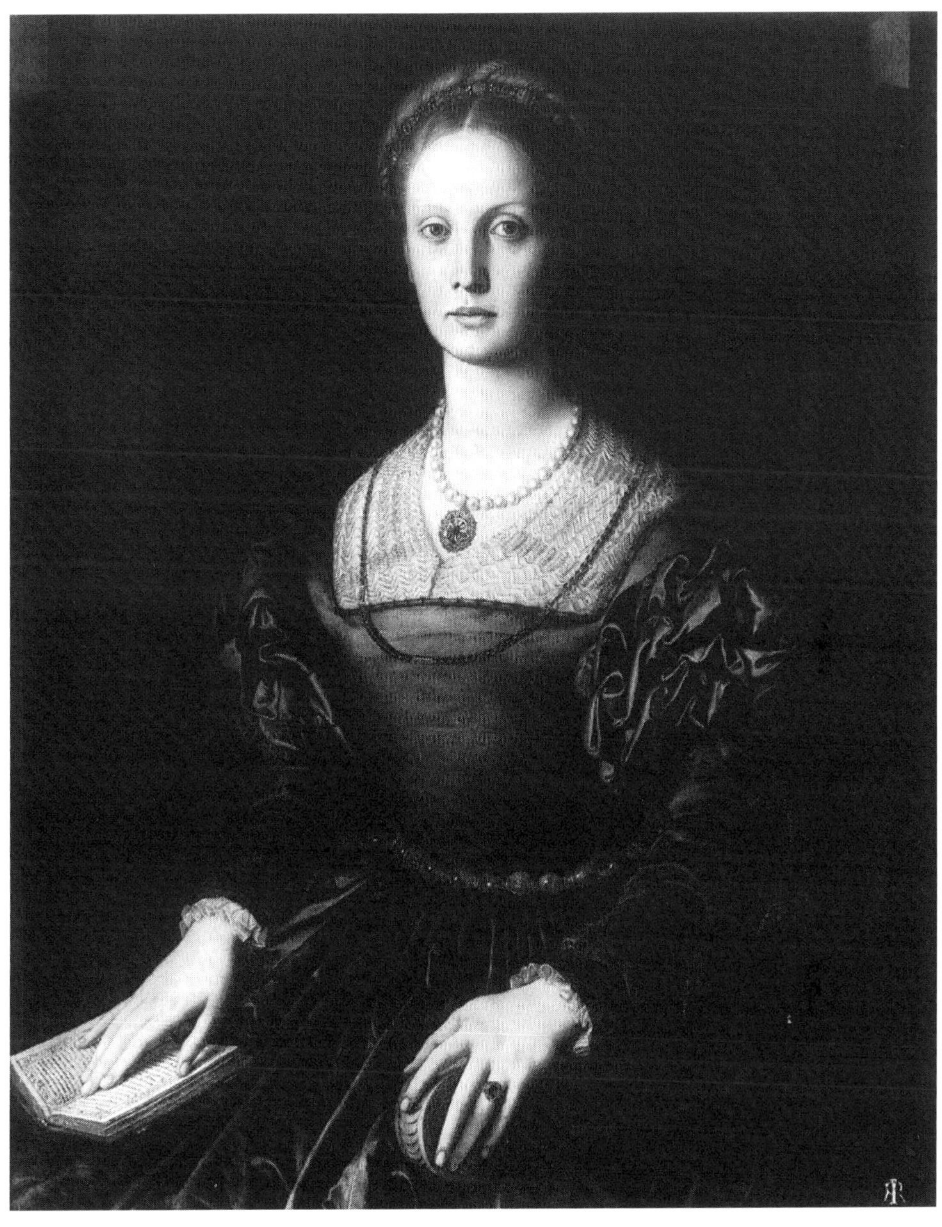

Figure 27 Agnolo Bronzino, *Lucrezia Panciatichi*, circa 1540. Oil on panel, 102 × 85 cm. Florence, Galleria degli Uffizi.

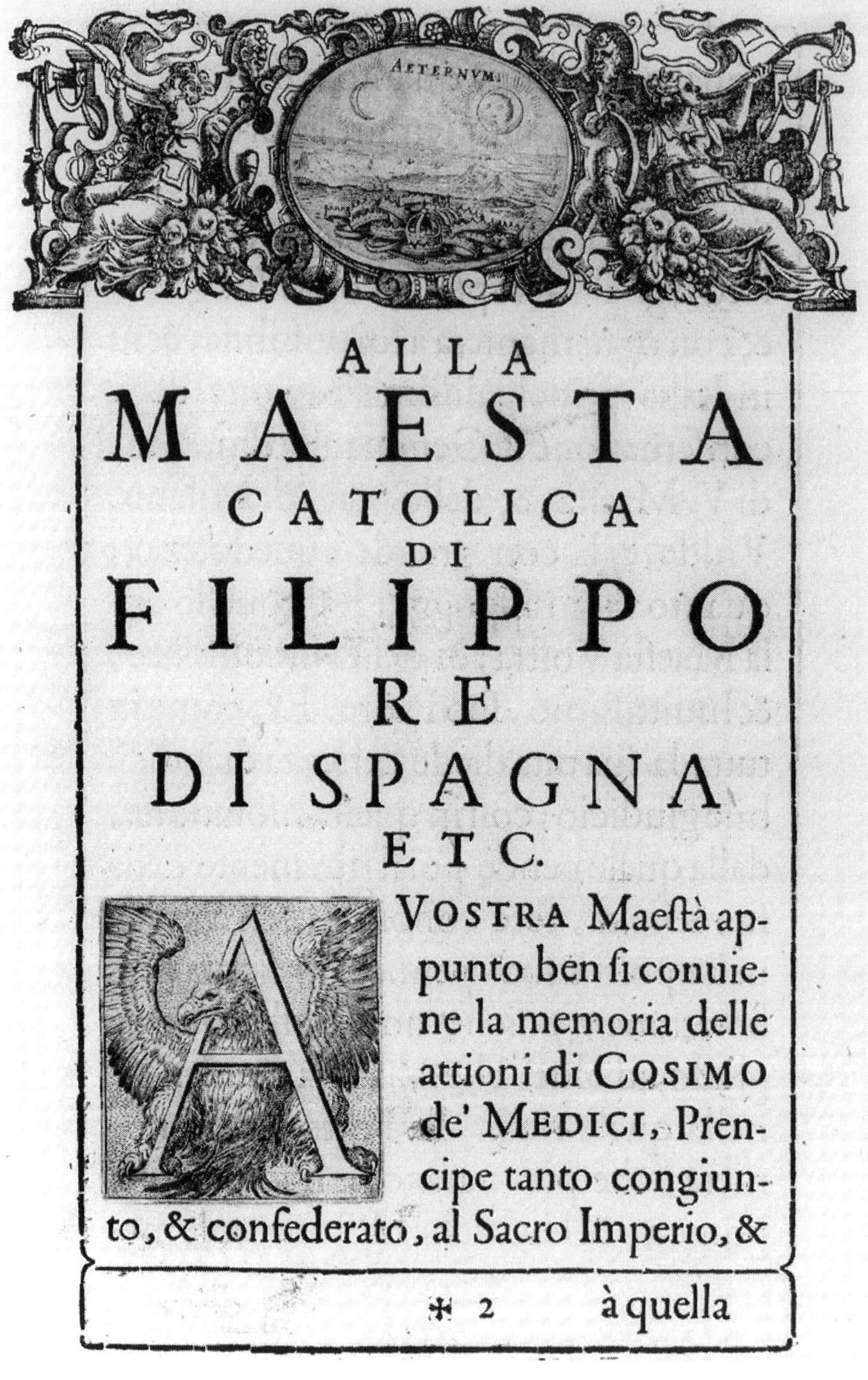

Figure 28 Title page, Aldo Mannucci, *Vita di Cosimo de' Medici Primo Gran Duca di Toscana descritta da Aldo Manucci*. Engraving. Bologna, 1586.

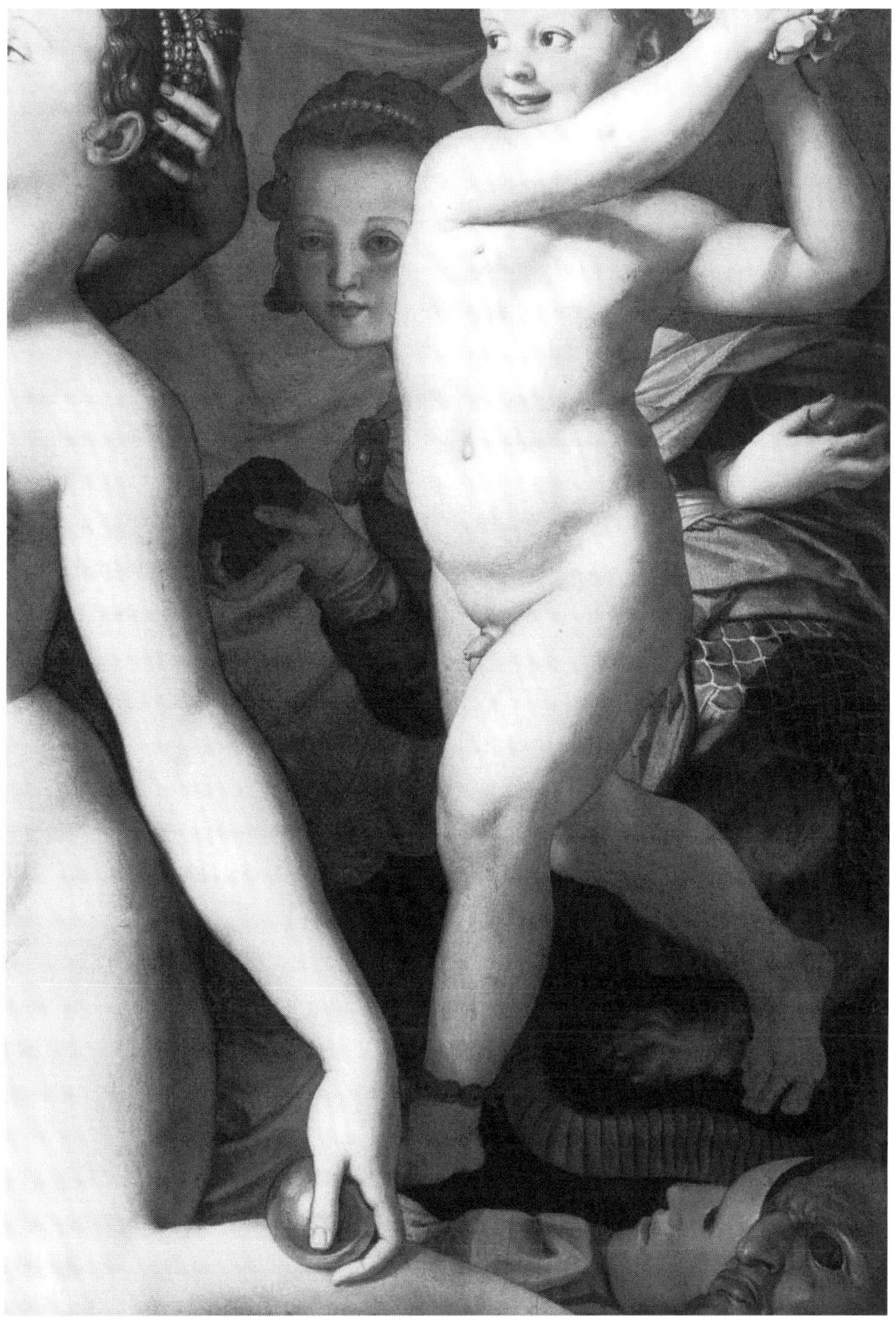

Figure 29 Agnolo Bronzino, *Allegory of Venus and Cupid*, 1544–5. Oil on panel, 146.5 × 116.8 cm, detail: *Fraude*. London, National Gallery.

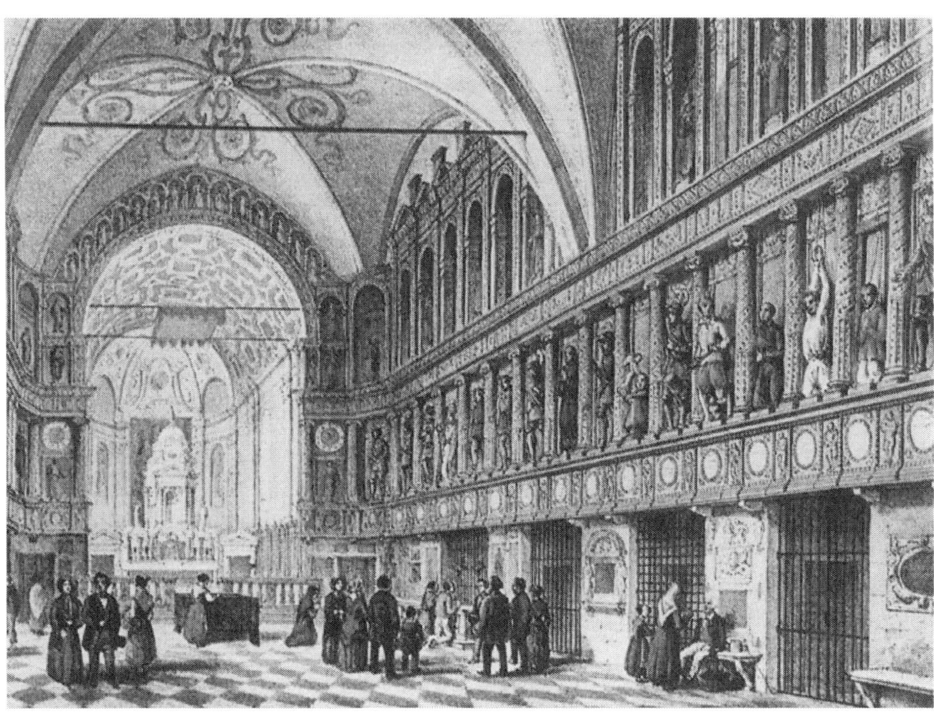

Figure 30 After Marco Moro, *View of the nave of the Santuario di S. Maria delle Grazie, Mantua* (before removal of *boti* figures in armour), circa 1840. Engraving. Santa Maria delle Grazie, Milan.

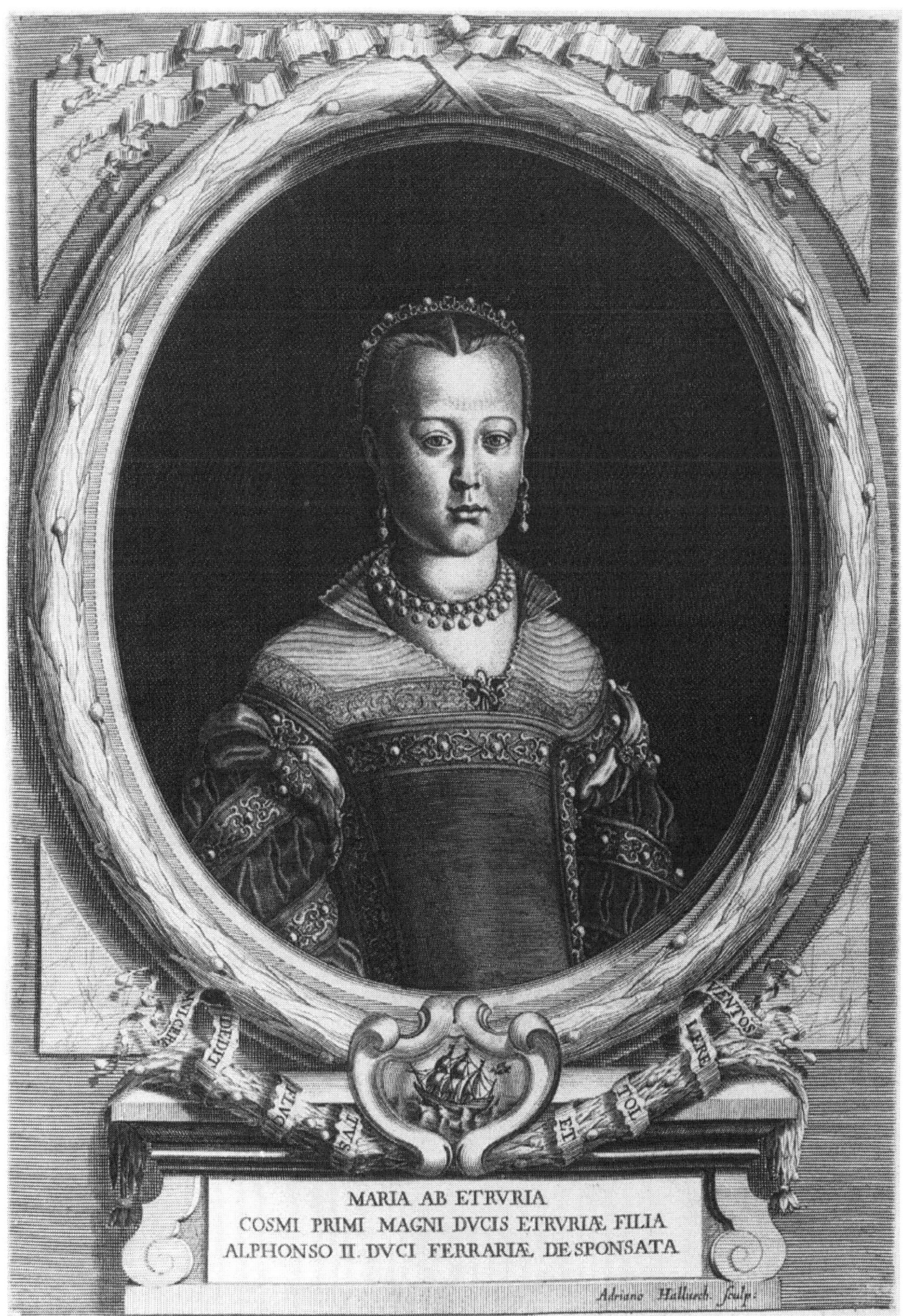

Figure 31 Adriaen Haelwegh, *Maria de' Medici*. Engraving, 1675. Giuseppe Zocchi, *Chronologica series simulacrorum regiae familiae Medicea*, Florence, 1761.

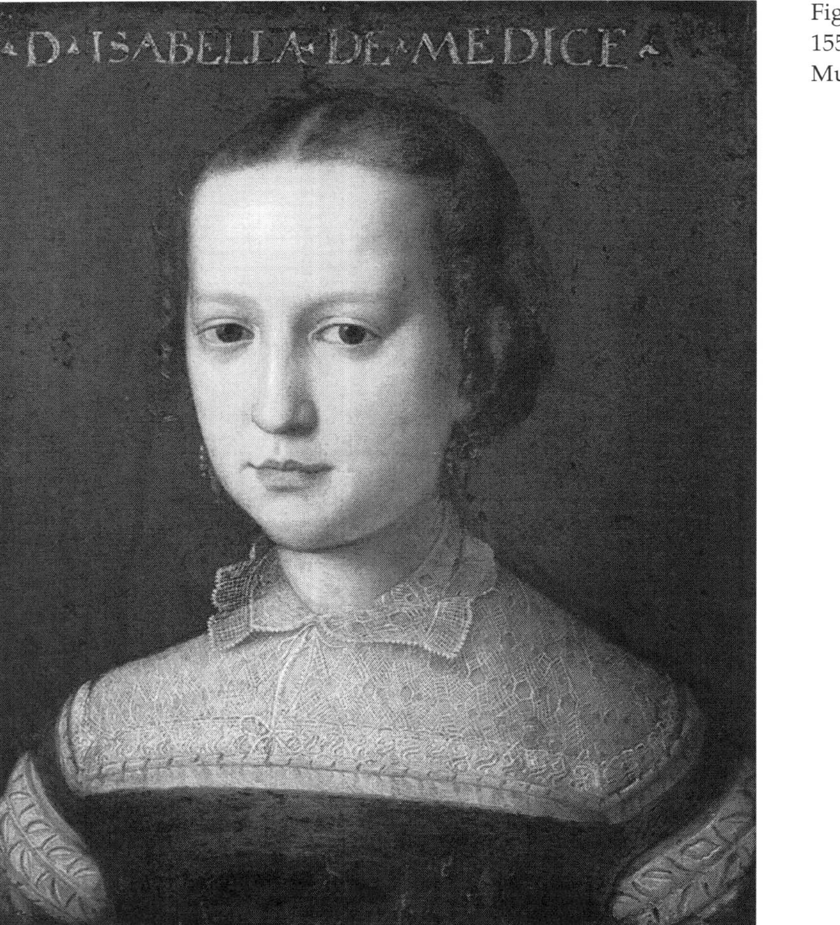

Figure 32 After Bronzino, *Isabella de' Medici as a Girl*, circa 1552–4. Oil on panel, 44 × 36 cm. Stockholm, National Museum of Fine Arts.

Figure 33 Diagram, 'cornucopia' earring, after figure 32, *Isabella de' Medici as a Girl*.

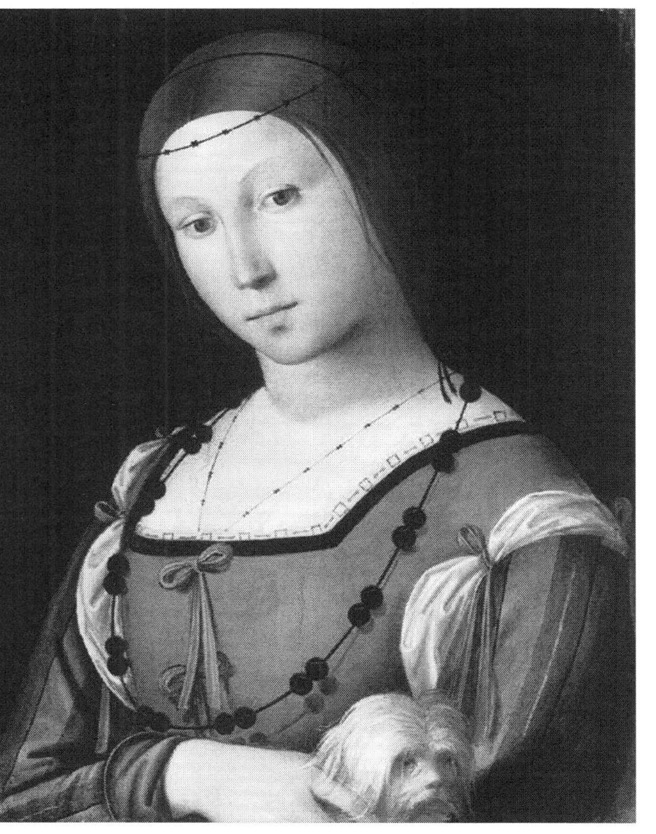

Figure 34 Juan de Flandes, *Infanta*, circa 1495. Oil on panel, 31.5 × 22 cm. Madrid, Thyssen-Bornemisza Collection. © Museo Thyssen- Bornemisza, Madrid.

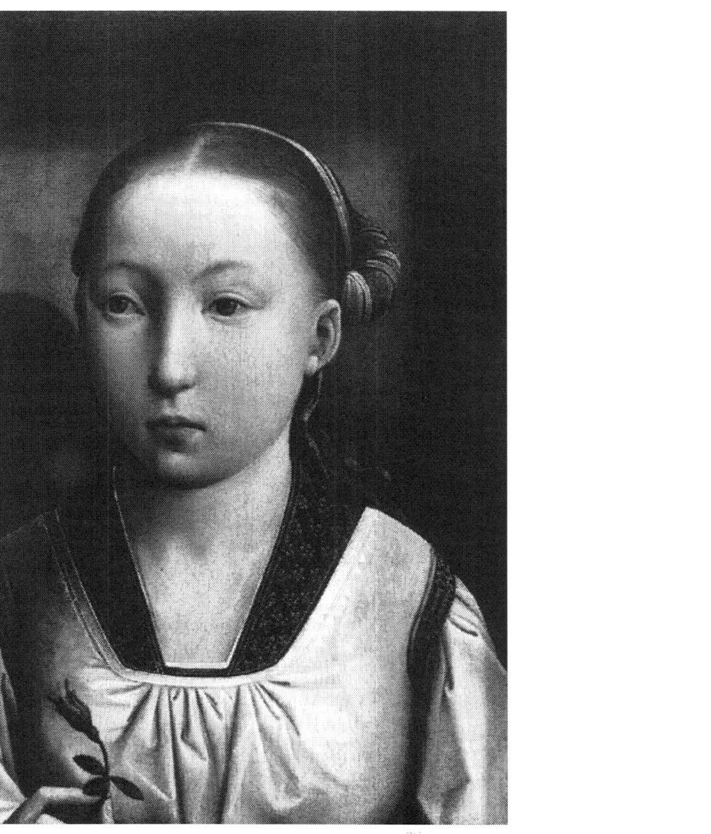

Figure 35 Lorenzo Costa, *Woman with a Lapdog*, circa 1500. Oil on panel, 45.5 × 35.1. Hampton Court, The Royal Collection © 2004, Her Majesty Queen Elizabeth II.

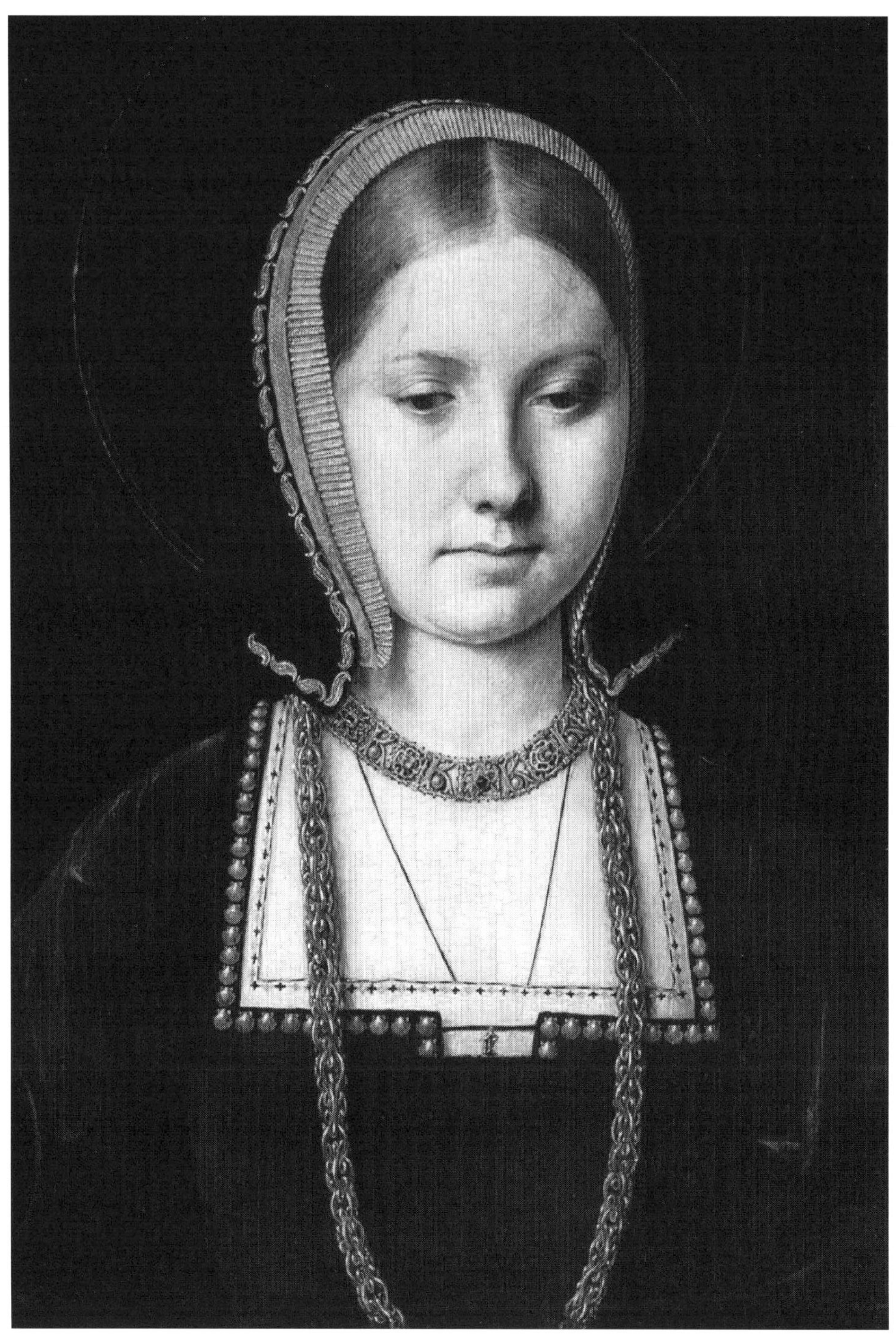

Figure 36 Michel Sittow, *Catherine of Aragon*, circa 1501. Oil on panel, 29 × 20.5 cm. Vienna, Kunsthistorisches Museum.

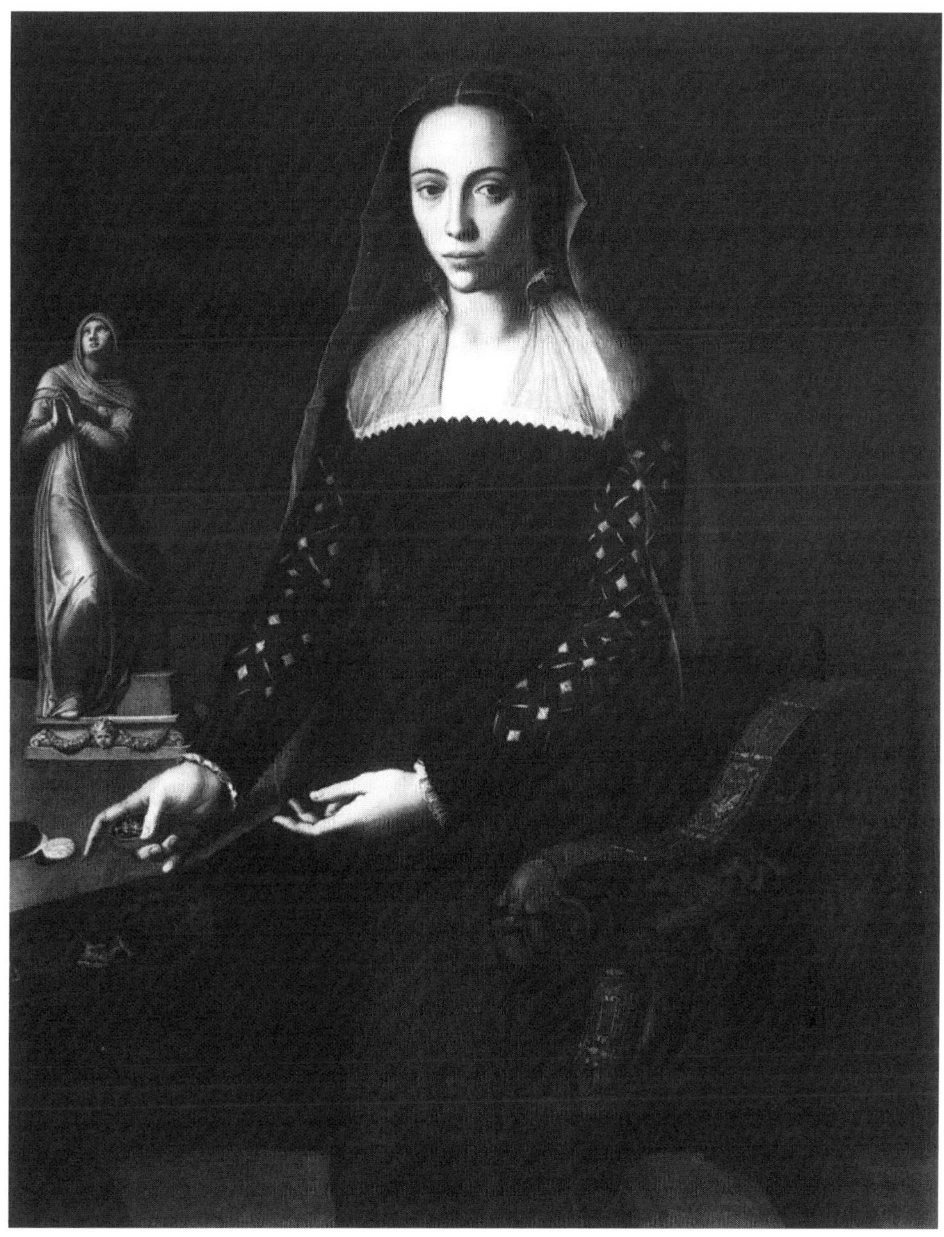

Figure 37 Alessandro Allori, *Portrait of a Woman* (here identified as Giulia d'Alessandro de' Medici), 1559. Oil on panel, 121 × 95 cm. Florence, Galleria degli Uffizi.

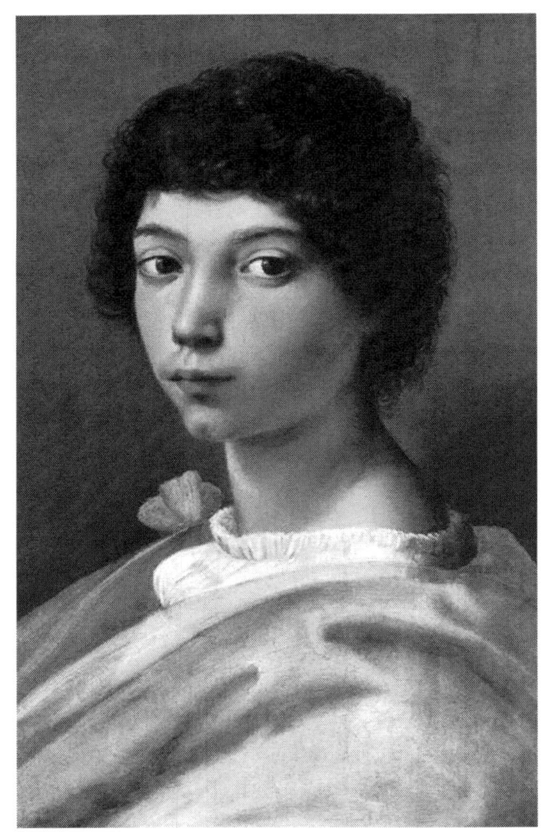

Figure 38 Alessandro Allori, *Portrait of a Woman* (here identified as Giulia d'Alessandro de' Medici), detail of figure 37: face.

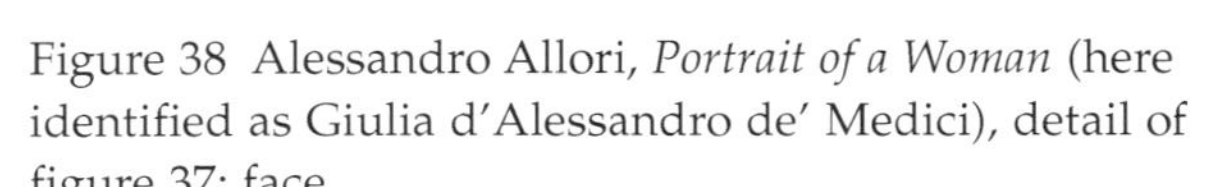

Figure 39 Raphael / Giulio Romano. *Alessandro de' Medici as a Boy*, circa 1520. Oil on panel, 44 × 29.5 cm. Madrid, Thyssen-Bornemisza Collection. © Museo Thyssen-Bornemisza, Madrid.

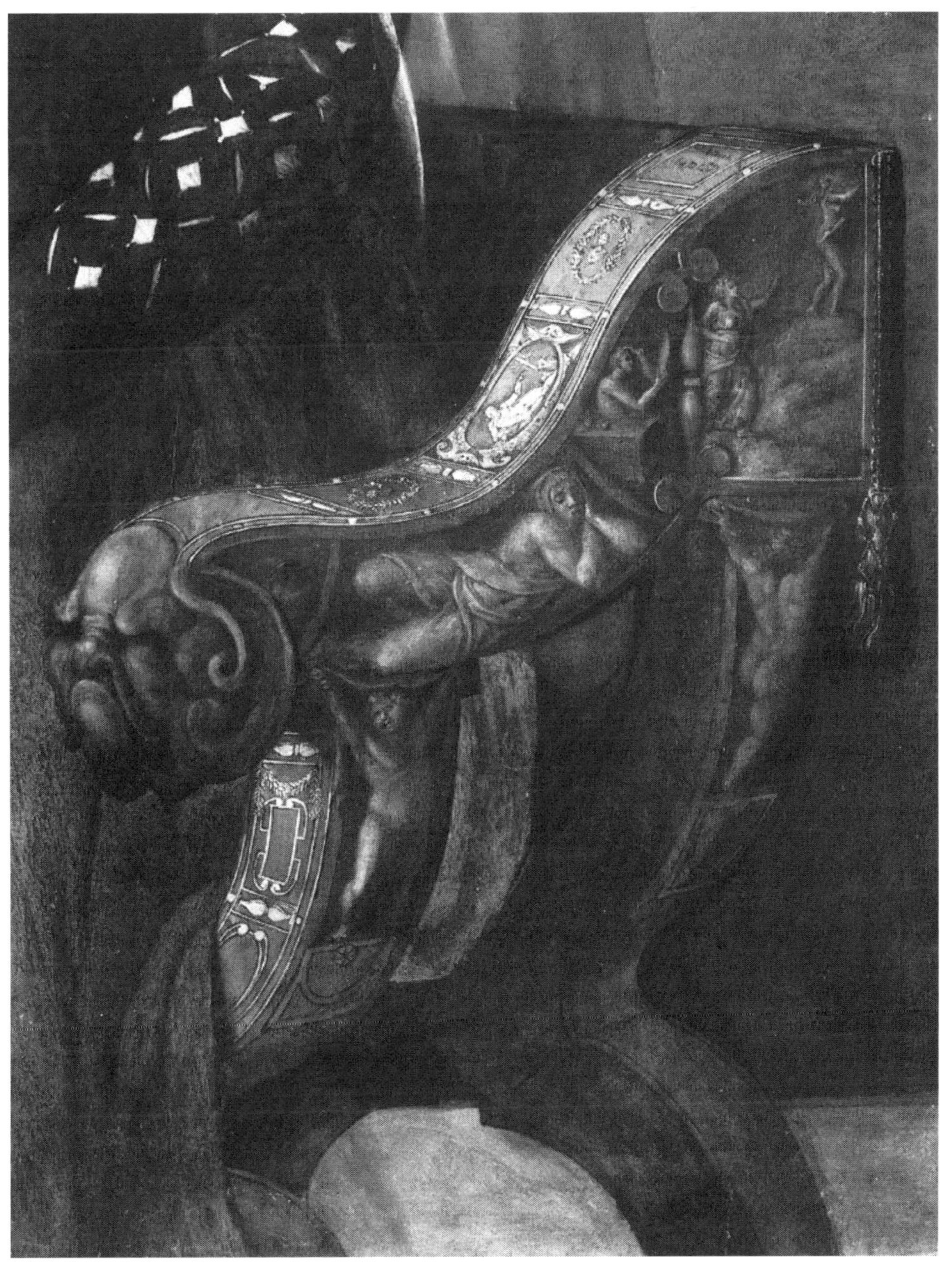

Figure 40 Alessandro Allori, *Portrait of a Woman* (here identified as Giulia d'Alessandro de' Medici), detail of figure 37: chair.

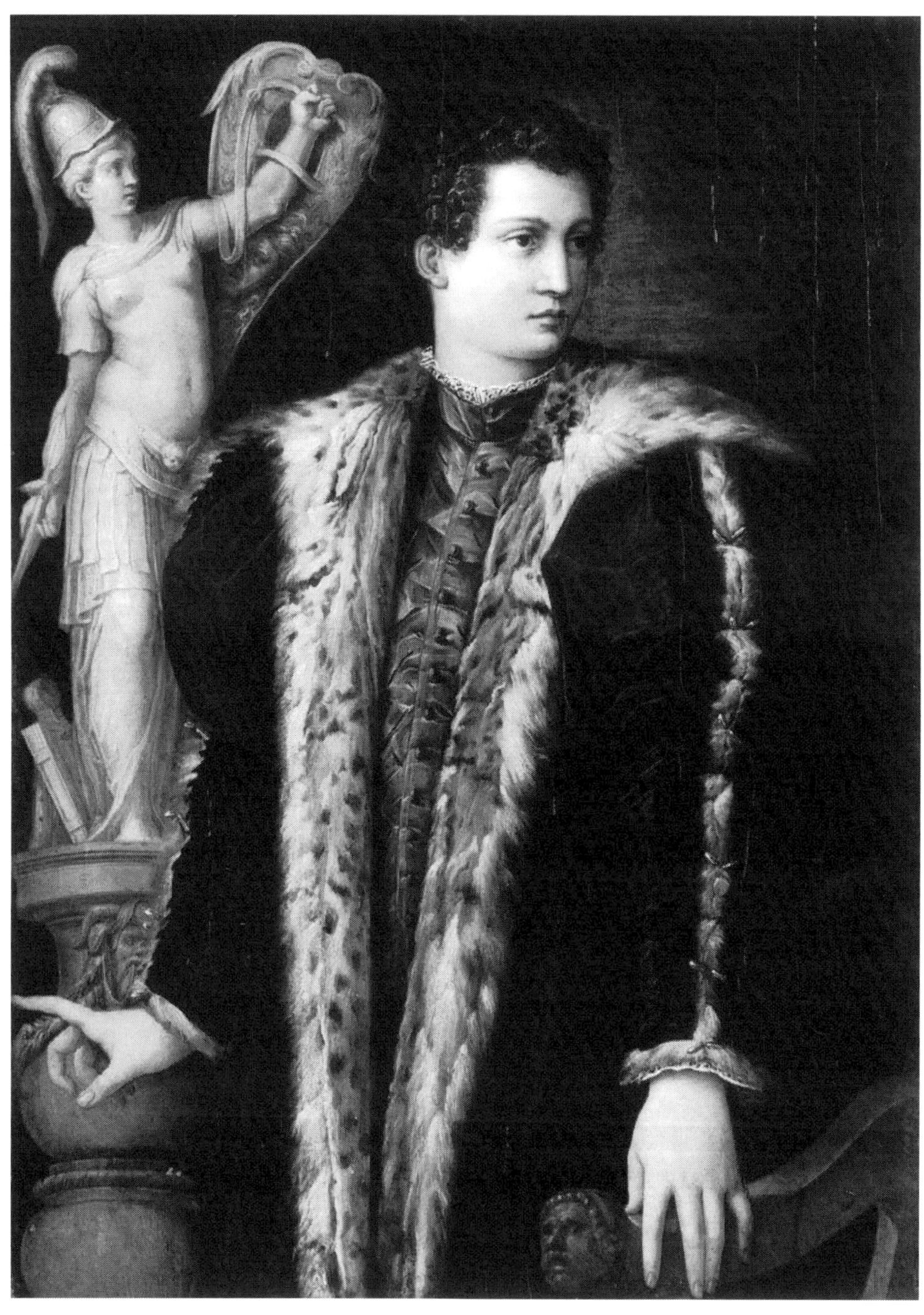

Figure 41 Giorgio Vasari, *Bernardetto de' Medici*, 1549. Oil on panel, 133 × 95 cm.
Berlin, Staatliche Museen, Gemäldegalerie.

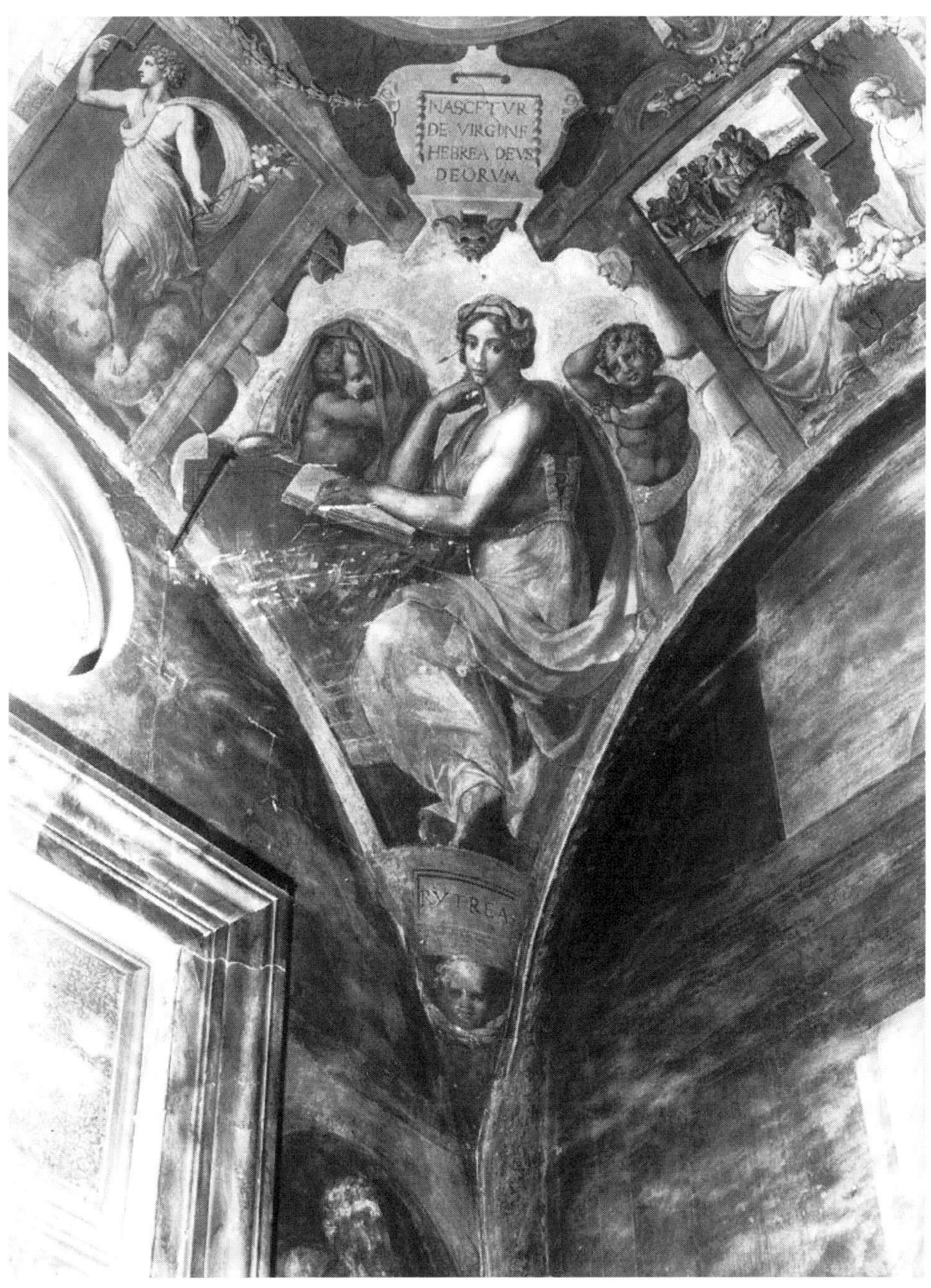

Figure 42 Alessandro Allori, *Erythraean Sibyl*, 1560. Fresco, vault pendentive, Montauto Chapel, Santissima Annunziata, Florence.

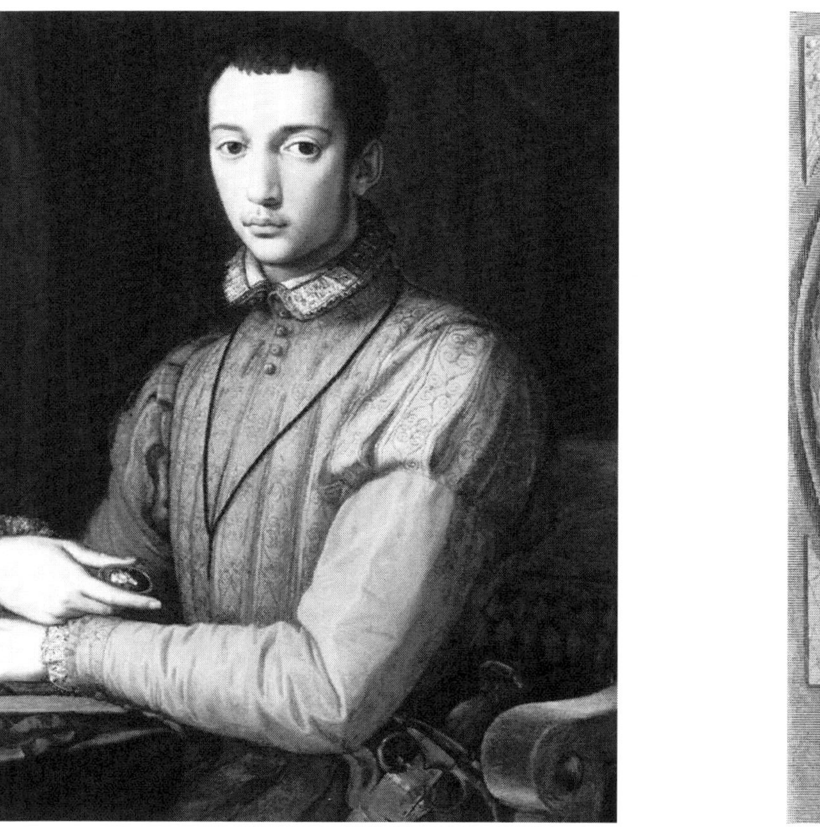

Figure 43 Alessandro Allori, *Francesco de' Medici with a Miniature of Lucrezia de' Medici*, circa 1560. Oil on panel, 82.7 × 65 cm. Private collection.

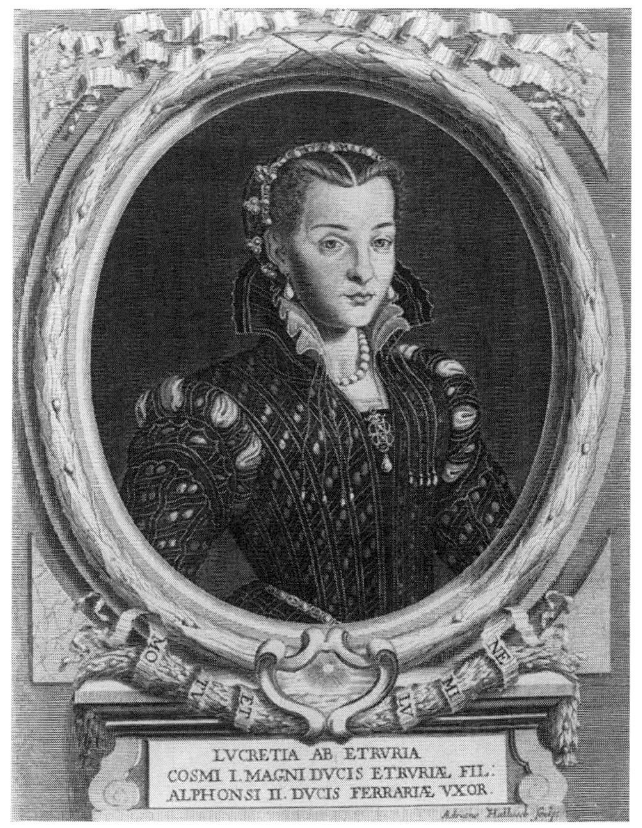

Figure 44 Adriaen Haelwegh, *Lucrezia de' Medici*. Engraving, 1675. Giuseppe Zocchi, *Chronologica series simulacrorum regiae familiae Medicea*, Florence, 1761.

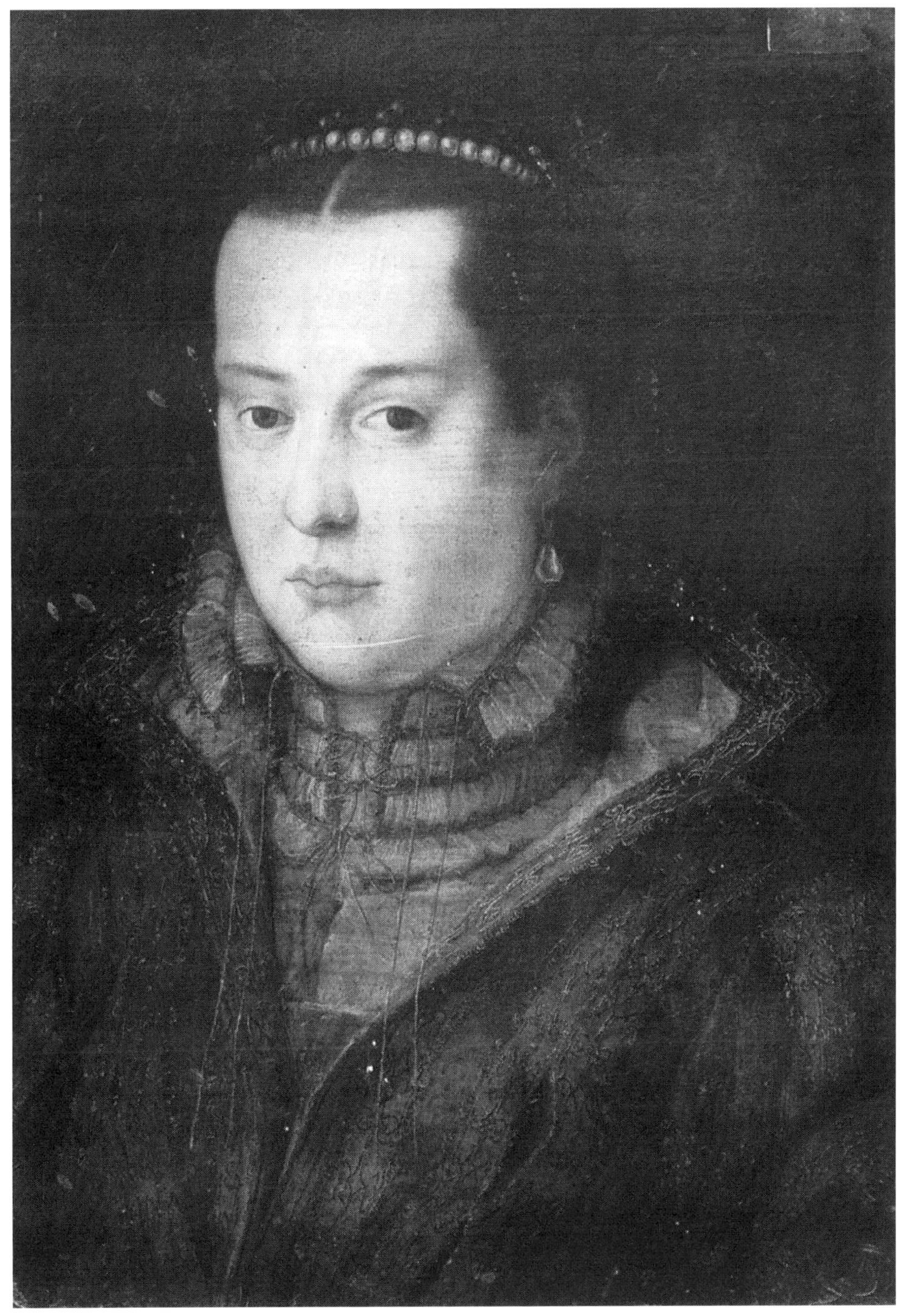

Figure 45 Allessandro Allori? *Lucrezia de' Medici*, before 1559. Oil on panel, 58 × 44.5 cm. Florence, Galleria degli Uffizi, Florence.

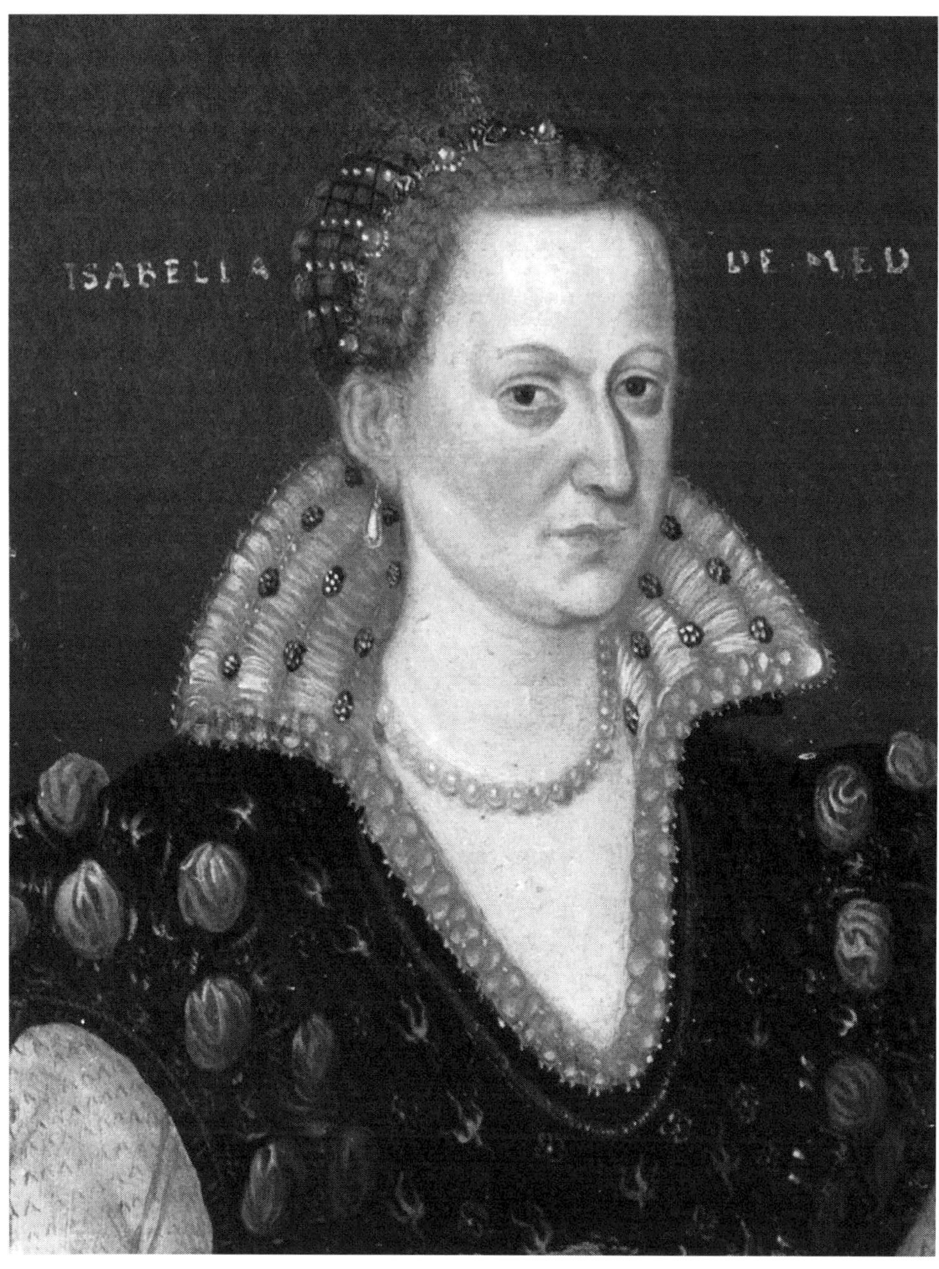

Figure 46 Anonymous, *Isabella de' Medici Orsini*, 1587. Paper on cardboard, 13.5 × 10.5 cm (Ambras Series). Vienna, Kunsthistorisches Museum.

Nunlike habits for girls were urged by the classicist Andrea Alciati (1492–1550) in his popular *Emblemata* of 1530, who advised close quartering in their homes: 'A woman's reputation, not her beauty, should be known to the world' ('Mulieris famam, non formam, vulgatam esse oportere,' from Plutarch's *Conjug. praecept.* no. 32); girls should mark the tortoise's habits, who keeps silent and never leaves its house.[106] Demure expressions and dress were paramount for presentation of eligible aristocratic girls. In Bronzino's *Maria*, the *Isabella* copy, and his *Girl with the Book*, no hint of a fleeting smile breaks through. Curtailment of laughter was advised, and dictated the extent of the slightest smile or of a decorous trill of delight, even proscribing the degree to which teeth should be uncovered while smiling. Laughter could make ugly a lovely face and, above all, it was associated with loss of control.[107]

This is not to say that rank and power could be overlooked by Bronzino in portraying Medici children, whose parents had struggled mightily from the outset for precedence in rank over ruling Italian houses.[108] Maria's heritage is evoked by the Medici armorial colours, her dress in dark green and her tiara, a *grillanda* set with rubies and emeralds; pearl spheres separating these supply the Medici armorial *palle*. Copious *palle* form her necklace, and more are interspersed in the gold-embroidered banding on her dress of stylized lilies, the emblem of Florence.[109] As her mother's were in her state portrait, her sleeves are secured by gold *diamante* fastenings, the Medici emblem linked to the motto 'SEMPER' ('forever'), with connotations of steadfast loyalty.[110] This recalls Quattrocento identification for women in profile portraits, proclaimed through blazons worked on sleeves or woven into rich dress fabrics.[111]

But portraits were also freighted with subliminal messages of character and exemplariness. Maria's figured golden earrings symbolically affirm her individuality and moral worth. On them, the Florentine lily is suspended from a ring with a large, pendant diamond enframed by two feathery arcs that cross at the base, possibly palm fronds, but hinting of laurel, too. Palm was a common signifier of victory, of peace, of virgin martyrs, and of chastity.[112] Laurel would hint at the dynastic Medici *broncone* and simultaneously express her learning and sterling character. Eulogistic references to palm, or laurel had a precedence in Florentine portraiture. Leonardo's *Ginevra de' Benci* was painted on the reverse with laurel, palm and juniper (for 'Ginevra') intertwined with the scrolled inscription, 'VIRTUTEM FORMA DECORAT' ('Beauty Adorns Virtue').[113] This association of persona and *impresa* was highly valued in portraiture: it is recorded that, after her death, the heartbroken Cosimo kept Maria's portrait and *impresa* together in his study until he died.[114]

The formation of the two feathery arcs on Maria's earrings evokes, too, the upswept wings of a swooping bird. This is probably not accidental, but typical of Bronzino's adept layering of meanings. The halcyon, the bird assuredly included in the personal *impresa* enshrined on Maria's commemorative engraving and medal, was understood to embody the qualities of a perfect mate in Giovio's *Ragionamenti sopra i motti, e disegni d'arme, e d'amore* (Discourse on mottoes, armorials and amorous designs), published in 1556, four years after he died. (When Bronzino painted Maria's portrait, Giovio had been Cosimo's valued guest, from 1551 to 1552, in Florence.) He alluded to Pliny's halcyon, fabled to breed in a floating nest on the sea at winter solstice, which could charm the wind and waves into calm for the purpose.[115] The reverse of Antonio Selvi's 1740 *Maria* medal depicts a halcyon in flight over a turbulent sea with a galleon in full sail, encircled with the telling inscription 'MVLCERE.DEDIT.FLVCTVS.ET.TOLLERE.VENTOS' ('I granted [you] to quieten the waves or to drive the winds away'), adapted from Virgil, *Aeneid* 1: 65–6 ('Aeole namque tibi divom pater atque hominum rex / et mulcere dedit fluctus et tollere vento'). The variant form, 'ventos,' on the medal was also inscribed on Adriaen Haelwegh's 1676 *Maria* engraving (fig. 31), where Haelwegh's image of Maria is copied directly from Bronzino's 1551 portrait of her (pl. 7), and includes the galleon, tempestuous sea, a halcyon, and the identical inscription. The substitution of 'ventos' for Virgil's original 'vento' for the inscriptions on both medal and engraving must be seen as peculiar to Maria's own motto. It has significant implications. Virgil's phrase translates to 'I granted [you] to quieten the waves or raise them with the wind,' whereas the variant accusative form 'ventos,' to 'drive the winds away,' emphasizes Maria's role as peace-maker, one directly linked to the halcyon's ability to charm the wind and waves into calm.[116] The bird had significant Medicean association with marriage. Two halcyons had signified marital tranquillity and peaceful rule, as Giambullari recorded for Eleonora's wedding *entrata* in 1539, when the pairing was used in the decoration of the Palazzo Medici. There the inscription 'VENTOS CVSTODIT ET ARCET AEOLUS' ('Aeolus locks up the winds and does not allow them to escape') referred to Ovid's account of the winter calm that allowed Alcyone and Ceyx to mate (*Metamorphoses* 11: 747–8); it implied that Cosimo and Eleonora's union would be accompanied by peace and fertility. It was a popular idea. Valeriano included the emblem in his *Hieroglyphica* in 1556, citing Pliny as his authority for its association with divinely ordered tranquillity.[117] Cosimo's iconographer, Borghini, used it in the wedding celebrations for Francesco and Giovanna in 1565 to proclaim the duke's peaceful governance.[118] Maria's association with the halcyon promises her as a supportive partner, assures her fertility, and promotes a pacific nature, one ready to weather the storms of matrimony, a recurring theme in Medici wedding celebrations.[119] As Maria's gesture promises her love, the *impresa* so subtlely worked into her earrings praises her goodness, applauds her learning, implies her fertility, and connotes her potential as a compatible consort. She is the exemplary potential bride.

In Bronzino's Medici portraits the *impresa* probably played an important role in the exercise of *vagheggiare* – warmly pleasurable gazing. *Imprese* were personally chosen emblems distinct from family mottoes on crests or coats of arms. Devised to express dimensions of the persona that include the metaphysical *animus* or soul, an *impresa* allowed expression of a unique reciprocity between the real and the ideal self-image towards which the bearer would strive. It was an eloquent vehicle for declaration of personal mores and character.[120] The inherent challenge was to create a message that was not immediately clear, but which did not require formidable intellectual effort to unravel its implications. Exposure in Medici circles to this courtly, implicitly learned pursuit came directly through Cosimo's patronage of Giovio, whose discourse on *imprese*, centred on arms and love, appeared a year after Bronzino's *Maria* and just before his *Isabella* were executed. Fascination with *imprese* among the educated and the noble ranks of Europe was widespread.[121] To the informed, courtly viewer, the unlocking of the meaning of Maria's *impresa* would immeasurably add to the visual delights of Bronzino's painted record. In addition to their inherent intricacy, the prevalence and increased interest in Egyptian hermeticism at mid-century now imbued the *impresa* with an occult, magical aura. Treatises abounded – notably Giovio's, Valeriano's and Scipione Ammirato's – and Vincenzo Borghini's herculean efforts as Medici iconographer would soon expand the repertoire. Ammirato defined the *impresa* as carrier of interwoven aspects of personality, outlook, spiritual qualities, and magical aura, and of their inherence in the person to whom the *impresa* belonged and for whom it had been created. It constituted 'a signifier of our thought as a knot of word and image ... [H]e will interpret it, who sees both soul and body together, and reads the author's hidden thought almost as a hieroglyph, explained under the guise of these two things.' The complexity of *imprese* was utterly suited to the opaque language of the ambitious ducal court.[122]

The inclusion of *imprese* on portraits destined to travel to a distant court and be scrutinized by an unmet potential suitor would be hard to overestimate. Maria's credentials, in effect a symbolic portrait of her moral aspirations and the familial renown that she would strive to honour, could travel weightlessly with her image. With time and use, an *impresa* could even gather new layers of significance around it.[123] If the halcyon used for Eleonora and Cosimo's wedding in a public forum in 1539 heralded a prosperous and tranquil future for Florentines, it would by 1551 have resonated with connotations of acquired Medicean power and a tranquil rule, which was its message when it was reused on the Arch of Florence in street decorations for Francesco and Giovanna's wedding in 1565.[124]

This expansive portrayal of Maria functions as a prospective 'wooing' portrait – long a tradition in royal houses – to be viewed with growing familiarity and delight by a suitor or future husband. At fourteen, she was betrothed to Alfonso d'Este, future Duke of Ferrara, then twenty-one. Alfonso's reveries should he view her portrait, surrogate for the girl he had never seen, would be flooded with such associations. It is easy to imagine that the alliance of the Medicis' cultured, beautiful child with the courtly, humanist scion of an illustrious Italian dynasty caused elation in the ambitious Florentine court.[125] Sadly, the first great personal tragedy of Cosimo and Eleonora's lives intervened. Maria died unexpectedly of fever on 17 November 1557 at the Castello Mediceo, Livorno. Cosimo, inconsolable, was seen to weep bitterly on the castle terrace and heard to reproach his unfortunate wife that Maria had been like him, a lover of the outdoors, and should never have been so cloistered. Muzio lamented that she was beautiful, humane and gentle – as exemplary as her *impresa* implies.[126] (Scurrilous rumours were circulated by *fuorusciti*, [political exiles], and revived by Settimanni, that Cosimo poisoned Maria on finding her in the arms of Iacopo Malatesta, a page at court, but these are widely discounted.)[127] According to her parents' wishes, there were no solemn obsequies in Florence. Maria's body was placed in their private oratory at Livorno, and it was through her portrait and *impresa* that Cosimo sought to ease his grief.

In her inscribed portrait (fig. 32) in Stockholm, Isabella, who was noted at court for her infectious gaiety, and later for her finery, her talent, and high-spirited escapades, is portrayed as soberly as Maria, but is even more simply dressed and adorned only with earrings. Her motto, 'FLORES FRVCTVSQUE SIMVL' ('Flowers and fruits together'), is implicitly alluded to in them, each a highly wrought cornucopia overflowing with fruit and flowers (fig. 33), and it is inscribed in Antonio Pazzi's *Isabella* engraving of 1761.[128] Quite apart from identifying her and heralding her fertility, the cornucopia was linked in contemporary *imprese* to the nymph Amalthea, source of Mercury's gifts of letters and eloquence, with overtones of virtue.[129] The Muse Rhetoric was portrayed with cornucopias flanking her.[130] For Isabella, 'la stella di casa Medici,' the *impresa* probably alluded to her erudition and giftedness in languages, philology, and music.[131] The date when Bronzino was commissioned to paint the original *Isabella* is unknown, but she appears to be around the same age as Maria in her portrait. At eleven, in 1553, she was betrothed to Paolo Giordano Orsini, an alliance made to protect Cosimo's southern borders and a strategic buffer in anticipation of his looming conquest of Siena.[132]

The almost invisible *impresa* in her earrings makes an enlivening foil to the seriousness of her decorum. Offering surprise, delight, and a privileged engagement in unravelling its nuances, the *impresa* would lightly flatter Orsini as a Medici 'insider' and as the connoisseur of courtly allusiveness in art and music that he was. The panel would allow a degree of chaste intimacy, not least because the time taken to unravel its messages would keep attention focused on Isabella's face. For Isabella, the serious, direct gaze and seeming lack of idealism recorded from Bronzino's lost original echo the decorum of her sister and the young *Girl with a Book*. Typical of the inscribed sets, the short-bust Stockholm *Isabella* is missing the extended, lower expanse of panel found in the *Maria* and *Girl with a Book* (pl. 7 and 9). Maria's hand, posed over her heart, is acutely delineated and mimics the pose of Bronzino's Prague *Eleonora* (pl. 5 and fig. 20).[133] Isabella may have held a book or, like Maria, conveyed a gesture of faithfulness or loyalty.

The loss of the original *Isabella* is a significant one. Bronzino's meticulous attention and individualization of his sitters' hands is a hallmark of his portraiture. Women's (and men's) hands are suprisingly large, often unadorned, with long tapering fingers and nails cut straight. *Sprezzatura* might have been coined by Castiglione to describe their cultivated but unaffected grace and strength. Often they are posed close to the picture plane in full light, between subject and spectator and against dark areas of dress – as is Maria's – which enhances their pallor and emphasizes an understated elegance of shape.[134] For every Bronzino sitter, hands are a mark of their owner as much as are the subject's face and decorum.[135] Cosimo's hand at rest on his helmet (pl. 3); the surprisingly strong hand of the *Girl with a Book* (pl. 9); Eleonora's, weightless on the sumptuous folds of her robes of state (pl. 4); or Maria's are each unique to its owner. In Leonardesque tradition, every nuance of anatomy is delineated and the essential *quietas* of the pose of the sitters' hands is infused with organic truth and with a suppleness that brooks no suggestion of rigidity or indolence. Bronzino's Medici hands are probably visible evidence of high breeding and, in the case of the women, are perhaps indicators of seclusion and exclusiveness, but they always retain an innate capability. The straight-cut nails for both sexes subtlely suggest utility and sound common sense. Maria's stilled hand, or the prominent hand of *Girl with a Book*, are each as capable as Cosimo's posed 'at the ready' on his helmet, or as Ludovico Capponi's as he grace-fully holds a cameo of his beloved (fig. 56). Ultimately, Bronzino's inspiration for such individualization, anatomical truthfulness, purposefulness, and overt presen-tation of hands derives from Leonardo's devotion to anatomy, evident in the draw-ing linked to the *Ginevra de' Benci* (1474–8) in its original state, and in the *Lady with an Ermine* (1485–90).[136] Above all, the unaffected, anchored hand pose in the *Maria* and the *Girl with a Book* echo Vives's rule for the public decorum of a princess: 'Let her show great soberness, both in countenance and in all the gestures of the body.'[137]

Collectively, these portrayals of adolescent girls appear to mark a rite of pas-sage. They have survived childhood to become viable prospects in marriage alli-ances. Bronzino's defining expression for this genre of Medici court portraiture is encapsulated in the solemn, cool gaze (*sguardo*) of Maria, Isabella, and the *Girl with a Book* – hers so stark as to be slightly unsettling – their plain dress, tightly dressed hair, and stilled gestures. Their contained decorum may reflect an intense scrutiny to be expected of prenuptial portraits exchanged between distant courts.[138] According to Vasari, the move to oil on canvas had enabled paintings to be carried from country to country; traffic in portraits, whether on panel or on canvas, had increased.[139] Posthumously, a copy of Maria's portrait did travel to the royal court of France. Whole Medici sets of inscribed copies destined for other courts included images of Isabella as well.[140] Their unique decorum and proliferat-ion tells of the introduction of a traditional royal genre that reflects diligent atten-tion to dynastic interests.

The unusual directness of gaze and frontal presentation of these young sitters may be explained by the implication of not needing to 'hide' anything from geo-graphically distant marriage prospects. Records inform us that this genre of por-traiture had to meet exacting expectations: a pragmatic approach to portrayals of prospective brides had a long pedigree. Henry VIII's patronage of Holbein to make 'truthful' records of prospective brides immediately springs to mind. His father, Henry VII, had despatched ambassadors with an elaborate questionnaire, cautioning that they

> marke the favour of hir visage whether she bee paynted or not ... whether there appere any here aboute hir lippes or not ... [and approach her closely when she has been fasting] ... to fele the condicion of hir brethe whether it be swete or not ... Dili-gently enquere for some conynge paynter havying good experience in making and paynting of visages and portretures and such a oon they shall take with theym ... that the said paynter maye drawe a picture of the visage and semblance of [her] ... and marke it in every pointe and circumstance soo that it agree in similitude and like-nesse as nere as it may possibl[y] be ... [and] to renewe and reforme the same picture till it be made perfaite and agreable in every behalf with the veray Image and visage of the said Quene.[141]

Henry VI had provided similar instructions in 1422, when he sought a bride from among the daughters of the Count of Armagnac: 'Portraie the iii daughters in their kertelles simple [everyday dress] and their visages like as ye see their stature and their bveaulte and colour of skynne and their countenances with al maner of fetures.'[142] In need of a replacement wife in 1538, Henry VIII sent Thomas Hoby with Holbein to Brussels to record Christine of Denmark, the widowed sixteen-year-old Duchess of Milan. Frontal, sober, demure, steadfast – and wholly unadorned – her portrait epitomises the required full, physical record and expression of good character. (The match fell through.) Holbein then portrayed Anne of Cleves. His hopes dashed on sight of the real Anne, Henry fumed that he had requested a record of *exactly* what she looked like; he felt bitterly deceived and even suspected that Holbein had been bribed.[143] In 1605 Frans Pourbus II was cautioned by his Gonzaga patron to depict prospective brides 'just as they are' and not to add anything of his own.[144]

Bronzino's mandate for this court genre was verisimilitude. Peachlike down is visible on Maria's temples, and such exactitude does conform to recording the face 'with all maner of fetures' to appear 'just as they are.'[145] Versimilitude in Medici girls' portraits is the antithesis of the idealization and abstraction seen in Eleonora's state portrait. Significantly, Elizabeth I, Henry VIII's humanist daughter bravely (and uncharacteristically!) acknowledged her plainness in William Scrots's (?) portrait of her at thirteen, which she despatched to her brother, Edward VI around 1546, noting: 'The face, I grant, I may well blush to offer, but the mind I shall never be ashamed to present.'[146] Vanity and idealization were purposely set aside for candour in this genre.

Vives would approve. He particularly cautioned prospective noble brides – and wooing husbands, too – against any deceit of self-presentation in the course of this endeavour: 'Therefore let the maid neither catch and deceive by subtilty [*sic*] him that should be her inseparable fellow ... but take and be taken by honest, simple, plain and good manner, that neither of them complain with [on account of] both their harms, or say they were deceived or compelled.'[147] Vives was writing for the instruction of an Anglo-Spanish princess, at a time when Spanish power was at its height. Eleonora of Toledo also adhered strongly to her links with the court of Spain, and her children spoke fluent Spanish. We may take Vives's admonitions on royal decorum to heart. If the written word could deceive, the potential for 'harm' would be even greater for the conjured likenesses in paint intended for repeated viewing by a future spouse. Court dispatches to Charles V in 1551 reveal that Queen Catherine de' Medici's daughter, Elizabeth of Valois, was trained at the age of five to salute a portrait of her prospective consort, the delicate future boy-king Edward VI of England (1538–53), which was hung to be visible from her bed.[148] (He died in 1553 at fifteen; in 1560 Elizabeth became the third wife of Philip II of Spain.) The comment of the Italophile portraitist and retainer of the Lisbon court, de Hollanda, that full frontal presentation was rarely used, but that certain persons must be portrayed in this way when it was most advantageous, suggests that it was reserved for a distinct portrait genre or genres. This appears to be one of them.[149] Bronzino's portraits of Isabella, Maria, and the *Girl with a Book* are all youthful and all frontally posed. The implicit end for this genre was candour, expressed in wholeness and directness of presentation.

This cautionary approach was *de rigueur*. Classical literature, courtly romance, and oriental fairy tale had long sentimentalized the portrait that 'set the heart on fire.' The motif occurs in sonnets, where artists are thanked for pictures of the beloved that 'compel love.'[150] Eroticism was always inherent in the 'presence' a portrait of youthful beauty could elicit, and the introduction of oil pigments, which gave added lustre to eyes, could now increase a viewer's enchantment.[151] Fears that a beautiful, idealized portrait could *of itself* charm a viewer into infatuation and ultimately lead to deep disappointment are expressed in many commissions of portraits of prospective brides. This was one important sphere in which relations between likeness and idealism, or a Petrarchan 'higher idea,' could not be pushed to extremes. The painter's responsibility in these situations was a heavy one and led to a degree of worry about the outcome. When a portrait of Juana of Naples was not forthcoming, Henry VII suspected that she might not be beautiful and vowed that, if so, he would not marry her for all the treasures in the world. Elizabeth I of England's portrait was found wanting by Queen Catherine de' Medici when a bride was sought for Charles IX; charitably, Catherine pronounced the portraitist to be at fault, and offered to send her own portraitist to do the job. (Taking no chances in 1574, she sent Nicolas Belliart to Sweden and Denmark to portray prospective brides for Henry III.) With hindsight, Queen Maria de' Medici's pride in her prenuptial portrait's charismatic effect in such a chancey endeavour was worth recording – precisely because this was secondary to its role in advancing a crucial political alliance, her marriage to Henry, King of France in 1600. The genre introduced by Cosimo and Eleonora had been consolidated by her father, Francesco: Maria and her sisters – Cosimo's granddaughters – had each been portrayed around the age of eleven by Bronzino's successor, Alessandro Allori.[152]

The pedigree of these direct, tangibly realistic, but modest portrayals of Medici princesses is one that would have had particular appeal for Eleonora of Toledo. It was at the court of Isabella and Ferdinand that the demand for prenuptial portraits of putative brides seems first to have taken hold; Spanish power, able monarchs, and a thirst for strong alliances across Europe after the Reconquest spurred the new genre's creation.[153] Northern painters, steeped in the tradition of verisimilitude and exactitude, were in demand, were highly paid, and moved between the courts from the end of the fifteenth century. Juan de Flandes, Michel Sittow, Joos van Ghent, Holbein, William Scrots, and possibly Jean Clouet are among them; an affinity in Bronzino's portraits with works of Holbein and Clouet has been observed.[154] The Burgundian Juan de Flandes/Jan van Straet's *Portrait of an Infanta*, dated usually around 1490 to 1495 – probably either Maria or the unfortunate Juana 'the Mad' – shows a girl just past puberty, who holds a red rosebud, to symbolize either her youth or her love (fig. 34).[155] Her hair is tightly bound and severely tied back with a simple, woven ribbon. She is unadorned and plainly robed in white – perhaps to symbolize chastity – with a modest black bodice trim embroidered in gold. Although her presentation is almost fully frontal, her deflected gaze is distantly focused beyond the viewer, allowing close scrutiny of her impassive face but little psychological access. In contrast, Lorenzo Costa's *Woman with a Lapdog*, circa 1500, in Hampton Court (fig. 35), which shows a striking resemblance to Juan de Flandes's *Infanta*, implies a different approach. As a lapdog appears exclusively in portraits of young, married Medici women (pls. 1 and 12), Juana's (?) pert expression, tilted head, and more revealing décolletage suggest a more intimate engagement by the viewer – who, if this is Juana, would be her husband, Philip the Fair.[156]

Juana's sister, Catherine of Aragon, was meticulously observed by Michel Sittow, an imperial portraitist currently 'on loan' from the Tudor court to portray her in 1501 just before she left to marry Prince Arthur of England (fig. 36). Her necklace identifies her by its alternating intials, 'K,' and stylized Tudor roses. In 1501, at the age of sixteen, she married Arthur, to whom she had been betrothed since infancy. (Widowed in 1502, she married his brother, King Henry VIII, in 1509.) She is further proclaimed as a Spanish princess by an embroidered trim of scallop shells on her bodice, emblem of St James, patron of Spain, to whose shrine at Santiago de Compostela she made a visit in August 1501, three months before her departure for England.[157] Ever proud of her lineage through Ferdinand and Isabella, Catherine is nevertheless unidealized, frontally presented with marked realism, with her eyes modestly lowered.

In Bronzino's paintings, more imposing effects than those seen in Spain's early-sixteenth-century *infanta* portraits were instituted at the Florentine court in 1551. Maria de' Medici's gaze is self-assured, seeming almost to assess the viewer's in return. The steady, unsmiling expression of Bronzino's young girls, their tightly dressed hair, stilled gestures, and sober clothing – even the reference to their individual *imprese* to suggest exemplary intellectual and moral qualities – all combine in extended metaphors to express Vives's precepts of decorum for noble girls and to reflect the traditional royal idiom for the portrayal of young European princesses. The essential canons of this genre were carried between the courts by peripatetic northern artists and transferred, too, by an increasing traffic of portrait copies between European courts.[158]

Cosimo and Eleonora's pride and aspirations for their two highly intelligent daughters are unquestioned, but their institution of this courtly, dynastic genre was in the spirit of securing a place for the Florentine court in a wider forum of powerful marriage alliances. By his own account, these were an important commission for Bronzino, and they doubtless had Cosimo and Eleonora's close attention. In addition, the portraits commissioned in 1551 were duplicated immediately, marking the beginning of workshop manufacture of 'ancestral' sets (pl. 8). They appear in inventories, and were sent as gifts to other courts.[159] This proliferation of portraits of girls is characteristic of royalty and seigneurial favour. It marks a moment of great self-confidence in Cosimo's promotion of his dynasty and his claims of absolutism.[160]

4

A 'Medici' Papacy and a Counter-Reformation in Portraiture: Allori's *Giulia d' Alessandro de' Medici*

'La casa del signor Duca e la nostra è tutt'una.'

Pius IV, 1563[1]

Three years after the portrait series of Maria and her brothers was executed at Pisa in 1551, Bronzino's chief workshop assistant, Alessandro Allori (1535–1607), left Florence for Rome for five years' training, from 1554 to 1560. Bronzino had been his guardian – indeed, a surrogate father to him – and in court circles Alessandro's sojourn was perceived as the capstone to the artistic career for which Bronzino had groomed him. In Benedetto Varchi's poetic tribute on the occasion, Bronzino is cast as Apelles and play made on Allori's first name as Alexander the Great. Varchi implies that Allori's artistic succession at court is assured:

> My dear Alessandro, who in the first flower
> Of greener years [do] not only of your great name
> Become proud, but of your fine last name
> Which I hold sacred in the centre of my heart.
> Follow the Tuscan Apelles, the eternal honour
> Of the Arno, and be so, that if [you are] renamed
> The second BRONZINO before your hair greys,
> The world honours you after him.[2]

Raffaello Borghini recorded young Allori's departure 'at the age of nineteen for Rome, where he studied antique statuary ... the works of Michelangelo and of other worthy artists: and in the same period he made more portraits.' Vasari, too, noted his output in portraiture.[3] He returned early in 1560 with his artistic reputation and his future in the Medici domain secured.

Ever hard-working and dedicated artistically to his Medici patrons as he was throughout his life, Allori would never match Bronzino's brilliance as a portraitist. His star rose in the 1550s period of Rome's entrenchment as moral lightning rod in the face of spreading Protestantism, and his works would document winds of change felt across Europe in philosophical, political, religious, and social spheres throughout the second half of the century. The protean efforts of the Council of Trent were formulated at its final session, from January 1562 to December 1563, and its doctrinal promulgations legislated by Pius IV in January 1564.

This reform period, known through the Council's venue as 'Tridentine,' affected Florentine art, religious and secular. Its effects are equally traceable in Allori's portraits from his return from Rome in 1560.

A prelude to Allori's welcome arrival in Florence and probably one of the last of his Roman portraits is a panel of Medici provenance in the Uffizi collection, once known as Bronzino's *Lady with a Cameo*, inscribed 'ROMA MDV[IIII]' ('Rome 1559') (figs. 37, 38, and 40). She is identified here as Duke Alessandro de' Medici's daughter – Cosimo's ward Giulia – and the panel's commission is linked to her marriage that year to Bernardetto de' Medici, Cosimo's cousin. For over two decades the portrait has been firmly attributed to Allori.[4] It bears signal witness to his immersion in the Holy City at a momentous turn in European fortunes, when Cosimo's unrelenting manoeuvring for a 'Medici' papacy was fulfilled.[5]

Giulia's identification has had a long gestation. My investigation of the panel began two decades ago, culminating in 1989 in a reattribution to Allori, but frustratingly without full identification of its sombrely beautiful subject.[6] Copious iconography linking her to Cosimo, Trent, two Medici popes, and the 1559 conclave and election of a 'Medici' pope all suggested a Medici identity – the panel's provenance to Cardinal Leopoldo de' Medici was of interest, too – but ducal daughters were still young and none resembled her.[7] In 1584 Raffaello Borghini listed several male portraits by Allori, followed by Ortensia Montauto and Aurelia Manelli, along with other unnamed subjects, during Allori's Roman period. The sitter's sombre gaze and very dark clothing, relieved only by her transparent dark-gold veil and fichu, had often suggested to scholars that she was a widow. Restoration reports released as this study went to press reveal that her dress is dark blue, not necessarily that of a widow.[8]

As Ortensia was in Rome in 1559, and Allori had frescoed the Montauto chapel on his return to Florence, her identity has been proposed.[9] Vasari's 'Vita' for Michelangelo provides an orderly chronology of the months after Pius IV's election in December 1559: Giovanni de' Medici's consecration as cardinal in 1560; Cosimo and Eleonora's *entrata* and reception by the pope in November 1560; and the Florentine colony's hopes in this heady period after the 'Medici' pope's election to rebuild their church of San Giovanni on the Strada Giulia. For this they elected Tommaso Bardi, Ortensia's husband, to a committee of three. Now elderly, Michelangelo took on the project and ordered plans and a model from Tiberio Calcagni; the account progresses to the period, in 1563 and early 1564, of Michelangelo's last illness and death. There is no other reference to Tommaso in the latter passage, but it confirms that he was alive in November 1560 in Rome when the committee was nominated.[10] Ortensia was, therefore, in Rome with her husband in 1559.

There was, however, a Medici woman also known to Allori who may have been in Rome, twenty-five-year-old Giulia, Duke Alessandro's illegitimate daughter, the child who appears with Maria Salviati in Pontormo's portrait (pl. 2).[11] Giulia and her husband Bernadetto de' Medici (Cosimo's cousin) were probably absent from Florence during the months of the lengthy 1559 papal convocation, as were many Medici partisans. As Borghini credited Allori with other, unnamed portraits while in Rome, however, and some scholars had argued for Ortensia Montauto, caution – and much probing research – was in order.[12] For reasons set out below,

my investigation favours Giulia de' Medici as Allori's subject, but let us engage at
the outset with Allori's attractive subject.

Giulia is recorded to have been 'the living image of her father.'[13] As the only
record extant made before his manhood, the beautiful, boyhood portrait in Madrid
of about 1520 (fig. 39) is a pertinent choice for comparison with Allori's sitter (fig.
38). A very long nose, slightly pouting mouth, short, dimpled chin and black,
tightly curled hair identify him as Alessandro (figs. 11 and 12). Attributions to
Raphael or Giulio Romano are not incongruous, as Alessandro spent much of his
early and adolescent years in Rome, and he was nine or ten when Raphael died in
1520.[14] Giulia's face, too, is posed from the left in three-quarter's view, showing
that the contours of each, the shape of their eyes, their sweeping brows, their long
noses, short upper lips, and small chins are indeed very close in form, and Alessandro's tightly curled hair is echoed under magnification in the few tightly curled
wisps visible above Giulia's left ear. Giulia's paternal resemblance may not be fortuitous, but may respond to Renaissance traditions of honouring ancestry in portraiture. My earlier study identified copious Medici references in the panel.
Gleanings from archival records that help sketch Giulia's life after her childhood
portrayal with Maria Salviati record her intimate ties to Cosimo and Eleonora, their
blessing on her marriage in 1550, a brief widowhood from 1555, and her remarriage
to Bernardetto de' Medici in 1559. The long period of convocation leading to the
vitally important 'Medici' papal election in Rome that year parallels the couple's
apparent absence from Florence, and makes the Medicean iconographical references in the panel especially significant. Finally, archival records reveal Giulia's
armorial colours to have been dark blue and orange/gold, the colours of her dress
that were unequivocally revealed in the 2005 cleaning. The Montauto heraldic
colours are bright blue and gold.[15]

The Fortunes of Giulia d'Alessandro de' Medici

Giulia's unbroken presence at the Medici court proves her status as a well-loved
ward and intimate of Eleonora's children. It will be recalled that, following her portrayal with Maria Salviati around 1540 as Cosimo's ward (pl. 2 and fig. 13), Caterina Cibo's blunt commentary in 1541 on the lavish Medici nurseries recorded that
Medici children, 'both legitimate and bastards,' were in Maria's care. Maria's
reports to Cosimo and Eleonora during Bia's decline had duly included news of
Giulia's recovery. Following Maria's death in 1543, court rolls record Giulia as an
integral member of the expanding ducal family, listing her *en famille* with Maria,
Francesco, Giovanni, and Isabella.[16] It seems, too, that the duchess was as notoriously demanding about Giulia's appearance as she was for her own children. A
retainer, Mariotto Cecchi, reported in 1548 (when Giulia was twelve or thirteen)
that Eleonora had flown into a passion because the girl's riding cloak was unkempt
as a result of her orders about its decoration and length being ignored or not met.
('Master Agostino knows that when this was made, there was more uproar than in
Hell.')[17] Bernardo Segni chronicled Cosimo's wardship and promotion of her
brother, Giulio, in those years, and in 1582 Francesco Sansovino would describe
him as one of Cosimo's closest relatives.[18]

Ducal wardship of Giulia was above reproach, and contact by Eleonora and her family with another of Alessandro's illegitimate children, her half-sister Porzia, was maintained. Porzia, placed as a child in the Augustinian convent of San Clemente in Via San Gallo – founded by Maria Salviati to house Alessandro's other illegitimate daughters – was now Abbess.[19] She was a confidante of the inner ducal circle: a now-lost mural there depicted her in company with Francesco, Ferdinando, Giovanni, and Garzia. This appears to have been a close-knit, extended family in which Alessandro's daughters were honoured, and every allusion to Giulia strengthens the impression that she was raised as a Medici princess.[20] After her portrayal as a *puttina* by Pontormo (pl. 2 and fig. 13), however, there is no record of an adolescent portrait of her, perhaps because her first marriage in 1550 was before the burst of portraits of Medici offspring began in 1551.[21]

Documentation of her marriage in 1550 at about fifteen to Francesco Cantelmi, heir to Giovanni, Lord of Abruzzo, testifies that Cosimo and Eleonora's personal involvement and generosity – not to speak of their pride – marked this first marriage in the ducal family. Under Charles V's protection, the Cantelmi, Dukes of Popoli (capital of Abruzzo and located about ninety miles from Rome), had amassed wealth from enormous feudal holdings, mercenary stipends from the Viceroy of Sicily, and as viceroys to provinces of the principalities of Neapolitan Citra and of Basilicata. Giulia's father-in-law, Giovanni, Counseller Collateral to the Kingdom of Naples, was Lieutenant General to the Duke of Alba. Clearly, this alliance strengthened links between the Cantelmi, Eleonora's Alba family, and the viceregal court. Vital links to Rome were also consolidated: Francesco was related to Cardinal Giovanni Caraffa, shortly to become Pope Paul IV (1555–9).[22]

This highly advantageous alliance quickly won exposure for the couple in high places. On 2 September 1550 Eleonora ordered a reception for Francesco when he was en route to Rome to marry Giulia at Altopascio.[23] On 10 October the Florentine embassy in Rome reported on elaborate ceremonies and preparations for the occasion: Francesco was currently lodged with Archbishop Francesco Colonna, in company with one hundred and fifty horses in his train, all liveried in black velvet trimmed with white taffeta; Giulia's retinue numbered two hundred, and were liveried in her personal colours of orange/gold velvet striped with peacock blue. Expenditures for the event, reported to cost eighty to one hundred *scudi* daily, about thirty thousand dollars in equivalent value today, were directed by Eleonora.[24] The celebrations extended into November, when Cosimo's satisfaction with reports of the reception and entertainments for Cantelmi and Giulia during their lavish progress to Altopascio is confirmed.[25] The duke's dowry to Giulia was twenty-five thousand *scudi*, equal today to about eight million U.S. dollars.[26] It was an auspicious beginning to her married life. After the marriage, the Cantelmi allied themselves even more closely to Cosimo by helping with the Sienese War. When Giulia was widowed in 1555, Francesco had left no male heir and, when a new marriage was arranged for her, it cemented her Medici connections. Her union in 1559 with Bernardetto, son of Ottaviano and Francesca Salviati and Cosimo's first cousin, returned her to Florence.[27]

Bernardetto had extremely close ties to the court. His father, Ottaviano (d. 1546), had for decades acted as Medici diplomat and papal intimate. Bernardetto too became a ranking functionary at portentous Medici alliances – he and his brother Tommaso were recent witnesses at the 1557 wedding of Isabella, Cosimo and Eleonora's brilliant daughter, and Paolo Orsini. With Giulio, Giulia's brother, he would serve as pall bearer at the funeral of Cardinal Giovanni, Cosimo and Eleonora's most promising son, in November 1562. (Giulio carried Eleonora's coffin at the solemn obsequies for her only weeks later, in December.) In 1565 Bernardetto would be sent as Medici ambassador to Bologna to receive Francesco's intended wife, Giovanna, daughter of Emperor Ferdinand I. He was also an inaugural member of Cosimo's Knights of St Stephen, to which the Council of Trent reported its progress.[28] Later, he was Medici minister of state to the viceregal court in Naples.[29]

Giulia and Bernardetto were married on 14 August 1559. The dates when it seems they were absent from Florence late that year are of enormous interest for the location and date inscribed on Allori's panel – Rome, 1559 – and for copious Medici and Tridentine iconography depicted in it and described below. The widowed Giulia had often stayed at the Augustinian convent of San Clemente on Via San Gallo, where her sister, Porzia, was abbess. From May 1558, records of the nearby Regina Coeli, also called Chiarito, on Via San Gallo, another Augustinian foundation, show that she paid frequent visits there, too. Her patronage is recorded, and she is referred to with great respect as daughter of Florence's first duke, Alessandro. Ill late that year, she came to San Clemente but was advised by her doctors to move to the Chiarito on 1 December, where she remained until 2 April 1559. Her marriage on 14 August to Bernardetto is recorded by the nuns without comment; perhaps her former widowhood made her remarriage a rather quiet affair. Bernardetto may have departed from Florence within weeks, as she again boarded at the Chiarito from 18 to 26 September. The nuns recorded that she was angry with Bernardetto – whether during her stay or on leaving is unclear. Perhaps this marked an absence from Florence, as a long break in her recorded visits then occurred, marked by a recorded devotional visit to the Chiarito on 4 May 1560. The couple was evidently now setting up house: orders were in hand for pages' and coachmen's livery to be embroidered at the convent. On 10 September when embroidered bed furnishings were commissioned for Giulia's room, it was noted that she was pregnant. When her son was born on 17 December, the nuns recorded that he was named for her father, Alessandro – a votive image of whom was kept on view in their convent.[30]

The timing set out in these records is important in the context of Bernardetto's – and Giulia's – possible presence in Rome in 1559 during the conclave, the longest in history. As Bernardetto's diplomatic role in the Florentine court was already well established before 1559, it could be that their marriage on 14 August took place in anticipation of this conclave so that Giulia could accompany him on an impending diplomatic mission to Rome. The elderly, terminally ailing Paul IV died on 18 August, and the conclave to elect his successor began on 5 September. It was soon evident that it would be a protracted affair – not least because of Cosimo's stake in electing his favourite, Cardinal Giovan' Angelo de' Medici, and his manipulation of powerful factions within the conclave. Anticipating this, Bernardetto may have returned to Florence to take Giulia back with him to Rome on 26 September. The conclave lasted until 26 December, with the election of 'Cosimo's' pope, Pius IV. The success of this crucial Florentine alliance with Rome may in turn have delayed their return until May 1560. Their household established, they entertained lavishly as intimates of the younger Medici circle: Francesco attended a feast and musical recital in his honour in their home that year.[31]

Giulia's paternity was not viewed as shameful in Medici circles – illegitimacy notwithstanding, she was directly descended from the main Medici branch of Cosimo Pater Patriae, a bloodline that even the duke himself did not claim. (It is significant, too, that Giulio was a ranking courtier.) Cosimo had commissioned a portrait of Alessandro to exhibit at his wedding; Vasari proudly recalled his mythologizing of Alessandro in his Palazzo Vecchio frescoes – all done under Cosimo's patronage; and Giulia named her first child for her father.[32] Medici mythmakers came to align Alessandro's murder with Caesar's by Brutus, and cast Cosimo, the new duke, as Augustus.[33] (To add to the lustre of Medici rank, Giulia was related to the last Cibo pope, Innocent VIII [1484–92] through her mother, Taddea Malaspina.)[34] This complex genealogy and the panel's date are important in understanding the iconography woven through Allori's portrait of her.

The Historic Moment

The inscribed date on the panel, 1559, stood as a landmark year to cement Cosimo's political heft. His fortunes now began to be integrated with wider European interests and were set to make an impact on the entire Italian pensinsula. The Treaty of Cateau-Cambrésis, signed on 3 April 1559 between Henry II of France, Philip II of Spain, and Elizabeth I of England, put an end to the wars between these 'superpowers' and closed the sixty-year-long struggle between France and Spain for control of Italy. France formally withdrew from Italy, and Cosimo, already allied with Spain, gained a strong alliance with Savoy, restored as an Italian duchy under Emmanuel Philibert. Following his acquisition of Siena from Spain after he had infamously starved it into submission in 1555, Cosimo's possession of the vanquished city was formally ratified and his new status as Duke of Florence and Siena officially confirmed by the European powers.[35] Spain, his powerful ally, remained in possession of both the north and the south of Italy; Cosimo now held the centre. It was crucially important to consolidate Medici interests by a strong papal alliance, the better to pursue his bid for title of Grand Duke and permanent hegemony over all Italian principalities. The wheels were set in motion by Cosimo's adroit gerrymandering of the papal conclave, when Cardinal Giovan' Angelo de' Medici – not a relative but deeply loyal – was finally elected Pope Pius IV on 26 December. In conclusion, the year 1559 marked signal political triumphs for Medici supporters, and set fair Cosimo and Eleonora's determination to consolidate the new Medici dynasty.

Allori's *Giulia d' Alessandro de' Medici*, Rome, 1559

Perhaps the most striking features of Allori's engaging portrait are those of Giulia herself (figs. 37 and 38). Her pallor is striking, and the sitter's 'sloe-eyed beauty' has not gone unnoticed. Her beautiful oval face, lustrous almondine eyes, and distinctive features may record her descent from her grandfather, Pope Clement VII, and his rumoured youthful liaison with a servant, perhaps of Moorish descent, in Alfonsina de' Medici's household in Rome in 1510.[36] Lightly veiled and sombrely dressed, she exhibits a cameo of Mercury in her right hand and points to a medal on the table portraying a Bacchus. She is flanked by a large statuette of Rachel set on a table to her right. Her dress, which until recent cleaning appeared almost black, can now be recorded as deep blue, and her veil and modest fichu are painted in a transparent glaze of gold/orange, the hues of her personal livery. White puffs of her linen *camicia* visible through her slashed sleeves enliven the composition.

Although the panel is inscribed 'ROMA MDV[IIII]' ('Rome 1559') in a slightly marred inscription on the upper arm of the chair (fig. 40), inlaid emblems there and on the table make extensive references to Medicean Florence. Honouring Clement's Medici patronage, Michelangelo's *Day* and *Night* in the Medici Chapel appear on the table edge at the lower left; they also affirm Allori's admiration of the great Florentine's genius. On the armrest, classical busts flank a bearded river-god reclining on the usual flowing urn, who points to a lopped laurel that has sprouted bilaterally – the *broncone* used to signify the return of Medici power from the time of Leo X's triumphal procession into the city in 1513.[37] It shelters a docile lion, who begs at the river-god's feet. Ripa explains Arno's attributes, and the inclusion of Florence's *marzocco*, the lion symbolizing justice:

> A bearded old man with long hair, who reclines with his arm on an urn from which issues water, this figure having around his head a garland of beech, and nearby is seen a lion who holds in his paws a red lily, both denoting the ancient name of Florence, principal City of Tuscany ... [Florentines] chose among the animals the lion, as King of all animals, and [also] among men of excellence, the great Hercules ...[38]

Reference to Hercules recalls entrenched salutes to Cosimo's valour and to his lineage as founder of the new Medici dynasty.[39] In 1559 his personal seal, an emerald worked with an intaglio 'Hercules' by Domenico di Polo, was in use.[40] Unusually, Hercules' ferocious feline has been replaced here by a lion cub. The docile little lion represents more than mere whimsy on the artist's part: a peaceable lion with Arno was planned early in 1538 to be included in Tribolo's statuary in the garden at Castello; Stoldo di Lorenzo's relief *Duke Cosimo as the Victorious Ruler of Florence and Siena* shows Arno at the duke's feet with an amiable little cub tucked in the crook of his elbow, and Pierino da Vinci's relief *Cosimo as Patron of Pisa* depicts a deferential Arno seated at Cosimo's feet with a small, contented lion resting at ease behind the river-god's arm. In Vincenzo Dandini's tapestry *The Felicity of Cosimo's Rule of Pisa*, commissioned by Ferdinando II de' Medici in 1655–66, a large, docile lion lounges across Arno's lap.[41] These disarming versions of *Marzocco* with Cosimo may draw on the biblical myth of Adam presiding before the Fall over docile animals in the Peaceable Kingdom (Gen. 2:8–20). Undoubtedly, they mythologize Cosimo as benevolent, protective ruler of Florence and justify his subjugation of Siena and Pisa.

On the chair, Arno is flanked by wreathed busts of Caesar Augustus, the antique hero most frequently featured in Cosimo's battery of mythological aliases. (Soon, he would have medals struck of himself as Augustus, dressed *all'antica*.) Long associated with the Medici, Augustus's laurel crown serves to honour Cosimo, but, as 'Caesarean' was a term often used for Charles V, Alessandro, and Cosimo, it may be Alessandro, Giulia's father, who is referred to here.[42]

In tandem with these Florentine references, carving on the side of the chair (fig. 40) teems with symbolic references to Allori's Roman environment at a critical moment in Cosimo's plans. He had manoeuvred secretly from the moment of Pope Paul IV's election in 1556 to position the Medici cardinal as prospective successor. Following the pope's death on 18 August 1559, France and Spain sought to influence the outcome as the conclave dragged on. Cosimo's partisans infiltrated it, notably undermining the powerful Cardinal d'Este faction, while feigning Florentine support for him. (Cosimo's daughter Lucrezia was now married to Alfonso d'Este.) Intrigues were rife in the interminable conclave. Towards the end, Cosimo moved to decisively swing votes to 'his' cardinal: in a cunning hoax, he had spurious promissory letters 'leaked' to the late pope's nephew, Cardinal Caraffa, that expressed his intent to approach Philip II to secure indemnification for disputed Caraffa lands; in the event that this did not transpire, he would pay 300,000 *scudi* himself in reparation – (about \$105 million U.S. today) – if Caraffa would relinquish his candidacy. After hasty familial wrangling, Caraffa capitulated. With Caraffa's cadre securely on Cardinal Medici's side, Cosimo's 'Medici' pope, Pius IV, was duly elected on 26 December.[43]

In the rebus-like imagery on the chair (fig. 40), Allori records his Roman sojourn and Giulia's presence there. It further expresses ducal support for the recall of the Council of Trent, promised by his favourite candidate, and expresses a Medici 'return' to the papacy. Reading the imagery from lower left to upper right, detailed relief carving first features a vase in a cramped, shadowy recess; it introduces a slumbering figure posed in a second, draped recess supported by two *putti*. By far the most dominant element, the recessed figure commands our attention at the outset. Like de Hollanda and Heemskerk, Allori – as Borghini recorded – had diligently studied antique statuary during his sojourn in Rome.[44] His painted recess recalls *nymphaea* in several Roman gardens where antique, sleeping nymphs, male and female, had been installed as features in Roman 'grotto' fountains, including one in the Vatican Belvedere Court recorded in de Hollanda's sketches.[45] Coveted by wealthy collectors, these antique garden features had assumed Christian overtones in early-sixteenth-century Rome following a poetic blending of Neoplatonic and Christian funerary associations in Renaissance writings. Porphyry's *De antro nymphaeum*, featuring naiads as water spirits, had served as a metaphor for transmigration of the Christian soul.[46] Expressions of these symbolic transformations are found in Baccio Bandinelli's unused tomb design for Pope Clement VII from the 1530s, which borrows the *nymphaeum* format. In it, Clement assumes the same slumbering pose as Allori's entombed figure, flanked by torch-bearing, nude youths.[47] The pope's pose in that case derived from a *nymphaeum* then installed in the Pio da Carpi gardens.[48] Baccio had infused a Neoplatonic overtone of purification and spiritual ascent to signify Redemption: in the level above the recumbent pope, angels bear his 'Soul' – a traditional *ignudo* in a mandorla – towards the third, upper heavenly realm with a Trinity, Virgin Mary, and saints.

Allori's dormant male figure, 'entombed' in the lower register, recalls a more contemporary *nymphaeum*. He would have witnessed the protracted reinstallation in the Vatican of the antique *Dying Cleopatra*, known also as the *Sleeping Ariadne*. Its fame extended even to the court of France. It was acquired in 1512 by Julius II for the Belvedere fountain, and relocated in a new *nymphaeum* in the 'Stanza della Cleopatra,' constructed by Daniele da Volterra from 1550 through 1558.[49] Its new location subsumed the Ariadne myth into a context of Christian redemption through Baptism.[50] During these years of reconstruction, free access was allowed to these Vatican areas, and Allori would hardly have missed this opportunity to view Michelangelo's most important pupil at work.[51] Moreover, the *Ariadne*'s pose had inspired a male version, Michelangelo's *Blinding of St Paul* for Paul III's chapel, painted in 1542. Allori's inspiration for his 'entombed' male, its pose, musculature, and drapery, are directly borrowed from that source and merged with his painted *nymphaeum* to evoke these themes of Christian redemption.[52] Doctrinal underpinnings for the slumbering figure were well established.

In Allori's *Giulia*, the narrative action and compositional direction in the reliefs wend upwards to the right to 'emerge' into the light – the top surface of the arm-rest with its panoply of symbolism representing Cosimo's realm. This scheme echoes another Vatican project planned by Paul IV, the Casino in the Vatican gardens ultimately named for Pius IV, who put the project into effect. Its stuccoed façade and decorations were designed by Pirro Ligorio, who drew on his own writings. He had recently posited that the evils of this life are circumvented by the Soul when led by Truth, expressing Rome's denunciation of Protestantism's pre-destination. Also, the tipped vase, prominent on the Casino's stuccoed façade and the first image on the lower left on Giulia's chair, is emblematic of God's benevolent protection and of transmigration of the Soul. Pirro describes a dark vase shattered by Mercury, who released Truth, until then miserably confined there with all the evils, again suggesting the Counter-Reformation ethos. Man's own responsibility lay in the choice between Good and Evil. The theme is again promoted in the Casino's interior *nymphaeum*, symbol of Baptism, where a frescoed *Choice of Hercules* depicts the hero as he disdains the attractions of Vice before he embarks on the hard upward path of Virtue.[53]

In the portrait, a variant on the *Choice of Hercules* fills the upper-right area on the chair (fig. 40), where a graceful female figure, presumably the released *Anima* or 'Soul,' passes a seated, preening *Vanitas* – complete with her attributes, a sceptre, purse, and mirror.[54] The Soul embarks at that junction on a rocky, upward path towards a beckoning nude figure. This tiny figure seems to combine the attributes of *Occasione-Fortuna*, and sports the forelock and bald-naped skull recorded for *Occasione* by Alciati in 1531.[55] Ripa's nude *Occasione* is similar. The forelock streams ahead to signify that once she speeds past, the opportunity to grasp her is forever lost. The merging of the two expressed the dogmatic view that *Occasione-Fortuna* is potentially malleable, and that man is responsible for deciding his own fate.[56] In her total nudity, Allori's figure approximates *Veritas*, too, described as 'adornata in modo con le parole,' that is, as nude and unadorned as her words.[57] Allori has placed a yoke, emblem of Pope Leo X de' Medici – and of *Matrimonio* – on her shoulders.[58] This composite *Occasione-Fortuna-Veritas* points to the lighted area above, into which she and the Soul are destined to emerge; her role for spiritual guidance is implied. A taste for this type of involved *invenzione* would derive from Allori's years with Bronzino, but this assiduously worked parable is all his own.[59]

Alciati's dialogue for *Occasione* – Opportunity – emphasizes that she offers only one chance to be seized. Timing was everything:

> [Interlocutor]: 'Why is there a lock of hair on your brow?'
> [*Occasione*/Opportunity]: 'So that I may be seized as I run towards you.'
> [Interlocutor]: 'But come, tell us now, why ever is the back of your head bald?'
> [*Occasione*/Opportunity]: 'So that if any person once lets me depart on my winged
>   feet, I may not thereafter be caught by having my hair seized.'[60]

Allori's *Choice* composition draws on Cartari's 1556 *Fortuna buona*, inspired from Greek stelae, in which a dejected woman is shown seated, accompanied by a young girl; they are approached by a graceful young woman, who offers her right hand and indicates *Fortuna buona*'s path. The girl follows, but the woman, unpersuaded, remains seated.[61] Allori's *Fortuna buona* has made the hard ascent and stands atop a rocky mound. Bronzino would use the nude *Fortuna buona*, complete with streaming forelock, in his *Allegory of Happiness*, painted for Francesco in 1567.[62]

The Church's emphasis on free will and the benevolent help of divine grace in man's salvation had been the subject of Tridentine condemnations of heresies against the doctrine of original sin when it convened session 5 on 17 June 1545, which, with session 7 of 12–22 February 1546, condemned Protestant errors concerning the sacraments, particularly Baptism. This offensive was to counter Luther's teaching that original sin is not effaced completely by Baptism, as well as the heretical Protestant adherence to predestination.[63] The council had been prorogued by Paul IV, another 'dark' period that coincided with Allori's sojourn in Rome, perhaps symbolized by the confinement of Truth in her vase. This extended allegory records the prelude to a critical moment in Cosimo's political fortunes, his bid to grasp *Occasione*-Opportunity.[64] The expectation that a 'Medici' Pope would effect Trent's recall is implicit in the iconographical program of Allori's *Giulia*. Not coincidentally, Allori's entire allegory of upward movement by *Veritas* toward the light may be subsumed in Psalm 85:11, 'Veritas da terra orta est' ('Truth shall spring out of the earth'), a psalm that seems to have had particular meaning for Allori and his patrons. His nude figure here is almost identical to a nude *Veritas* on a cameo held by Francesco de' Medici in a portrait painted around 1560. His is inscribed with the closing words of the preceding verse, Psalm 85:10, '*OSCULA-TAE SUNT*,' depicting the meeting of Mercy and Truth. The two verses, Psalm 85:10–11 read: 'Mercy and Truth are met together; justice and peace have kissed each other. Truth shall spring out of the earth; and justice shall look down from heaven.' The crux of Allori's painstaking allegory may reside in the *Mercury* cameo so prominently displayed in Giulia's right hand. Its message is twofold: Mercury's caduceus – the snake-entwined staff – had signified the Medici destiny to rule all of Italy in the wedding celebrations of 1539, and Pastorino's medal for Francesco I, before 1560, shows Mercury wearing his winged cap or petasus and carrying his caduceus.[65] In contemporary emblematic lore Mercury is also Christianized by Alciati.[66] His emblem, *'Quà Dij vocant eundum'* ('Go where Heaven calls'), illustrates yet another 'Choice' allegory in which Mercury, with his caduceus, presides over a mountain path where a traveller proceeds towards a junction. Its text explains:

> At a parting of the ways, there is a hillock of stones. Rising above it is a half-statue of a god, fashioned as far down as the chest. So the hill is Mercury's. Traveller, hang wreaths in honour of the god who points out the road to you. We are all at the cross-roads, and on this track of life we go wrong, unless God himself shows the way.[67]

These associations suggest that the conclave's divinely inspired choice is pivotal to the political future of the duke. The third 'Medici' pope's election in 1559 ushered in a period when Cosimo's relations with the papacy reached an acme of mutual intimacy and goodwill. The grateful new incumbent of St Peter's chair began his reign by exaggerating his family ties with the Florentine house, and declared his alliance with Cosimo in short order by adopting the Medici *palle* for his arms and by the appointment of the first papal nuncio to Florence, Giovanni Campeggio.[68]

His loyalty was bound, of course, to raising Cosimo's claim to hegemony over Italian principalities. He first attempted to have Cosimo raised to the rank of king, to no avail. When Francesco married Giovanna of Austria, Pius proposed that Cosimo be entitled Grand Duke, with similar rank and prerogatives as the Austrian princes. The proposal was kindly considered by her brother, Maximilian II, but resisted by others in the Hapsburg house. When Cosimo's staunch ally died in December 1565, to be succeeded by the less sympathetic Pius V, Hapsburg loyalties cooled. (It was not until 1569 that Cosimo was created Grand Duke.[69] Ultimately, his title was awarded by Pius V – after years of dogged Medici jostling for precedence over the Este of Ferrara – in recognition of Cosimo's ignoble gesture of support for the Inquisition.)[70]

Pius IV de' Medici was appropriated by Cosimo's iconographers into the duke's genealogy, notably in 1565, when he joined the two Medici ancestral popes, Leo and Clement, on the *Theatre of the Medici* arch, a backdrop to the intensively propagandistic *apparato* that filled Florentine streets for the *entrata* of Giovanna of Austria for her marriage to Francesco that year. Pius's historic stature as pope was commemorated in a painted panel on the arch, which showed him receiving the decrees of the Council of Trent. The inscription of elegiac verse makes him appear to be a blood relative: 'PONTIFICES SUMMOS MEDICUM DOMUS ALTA LEONEM/CLEMENTEM DEINCEPS, EDIDIT INDE PIUM.' ('Supreme pontiffs have sprung from the lofty house of the Medici: Leo, then Clement, then Pius [IV]'). The west façade of the Arch of Religion showed a Medici coat of arms with the papal tiaras of Leo, Clement, and Pius.[71]

The topos of longing for a Medicean 'return' is expressed in Allori's *Portrait of Giulia*, where the Medici papacies of Leo X and Giulia's grandfather, Clement VII, are each commemorated. The yoke worn on the nude *Occasione-Fortuna buona-Veritas*'s shoulders was Leo's *impresa* ('Jugum meum suave' – 'My yoke is sweet').[72] The emblem had been mined for its iconographical flexibility from the time of

Cosimo the Elder, and Paolo Giovio's 1556 edition of family arms and mottoes linked the *impresa* especially to Leo's election and the immediate, triumphal return of Medici power to Florence in 1513.[73]

Reminders of the second Medici pope, Clement VII, inhere in the composite figure of *Occasione-Veritas-Fortuna buona* and her gesture towards the light. He was commemorated in Bocchi's *Symbolicarum* of 1555, where a nude *Fortuna buona*, her sphere at a standstill, is urged by an antique warrior with the aegis of Julius II to pass the papal tiara to Cardinal Giulio, later Pope Clement. Giulio holds the shining sun of *Veritas*, an attribution also given to her by Ripa. Bocchi's reference to a Medici papal succession also suggests Cosimo and Eleonora's hopes for their young son, soon to be Cardinal Giovanni.[74]

Beyond the current hopes for a third 'Medici' papacy, this prospect for a fourth Medici pope was probably the one most deeply felt. This is evoked in the reference to Leo, the first Medici to wear the tiara. Affable, cultured, and urbane, Leo had taken orders early, was promised a cardinal's *biretta* at thirteen, and was groomed for the papacy by Pope Julius II. (He succeeded him in 1513.)[75] Cosimo and Eleonora's son, Giovanni, the little boy named for Leo and portrayed around the age of two in red satin with a *cardellino* in hand (fig. 16), had been groomed for the papacy since childhood. Now sixteen and living in Rome, Giovanni was equally *papabile*. Prospects for him during the 1559 conclave were momentous, and were fulfilled: Pius promptly created him cardinal in January 1560. (Unfortunately, he died in 1562 before realizing his promise). Allori's imagery constitutes, in effect, a pantheon of Medici popes, past, imminent, and to come.

The Medici papal references and Tridentine ideology in Allori's *Giulia* would narrow the date when the portrait was executed to the period of the long papal conclave between early September and 26 December 1559 – or in the ensuing weeks of Medici exultation if the old Florentine calendar is taken into account, when the new year started on 25 March. Alessandro's daring letter petitioning the duke to procure a sitting with Pius is evidence of a victory in which he and Cosimo's Florentine supporters in Rome must have revelled:

> Illustrious and Excellent Lord Duke, my Lord and Patron:
> The great willingness that I have to serve your Excellency [makes] me look for what to my soul is an auspicious opportunity, and this being, as I myself believe that your Illustrious Excellency would wish, as many others wish, [to have] a portrait of our Lord Pope Pius IV, [and] I entreat you, that if I be deemed worthy to create such portrait, to deign to let me have the opportunity to have one or two occasions to see him: and I hope by our Lord God, that your Illustrious Excellency may grant this request, [and] not be displeased at all with these intentions; and I devotedly kiss your hands to ask you anew to grant me this favour, ever begging our Lord God's blessing on it.
> From Rome, December 29th, 1559.
> From Your Illustrious Excellency's humble servant
> Alessandro Allori, pupil of Bronzino.[76]

The speed of Allori's request so soon upon the papal election, his opening address, and his tone all confirm that he was a confident retainer in the duke's cohort of partisan expatriots. Giulia's densely figured chair summarizes the feverish atmosphere of Florentine ambitions during the protracted election process of the Medici favourite.[77]

In her portrait, Giulia's mostly dark apparel as a remarried matron may emphasize her respectability. During widowhood, she would probably have been heavily veiled in *de rigueur* widow's 'weeds,' such as Maria Salviati always wore. The desire to remarry was often taken to indicate some taint of unseemly sensuality. Florentine matrons were in any event noted for their sober appearance, and Giulia's adherence to a light veil, dark blue dress, and lack of adornment are in keeping with that decorum.[78] (Bronzino's *Laura Battiferri*, also a remarried matron, is dressed in dark colours, is lightly veiled, and wears a minimum of jewellery.) A woman's marital identity was traditionally of tremendous importance in portraiture, of course, and pride in Giulia and Bernardetto's shared Medici ancestry and name would explain the exclusively Medici references. His branch, too, had strong roots to the principal Medici line. His mother, Francesca Salviati, was Cosimo's aunt and niece of Leo X. (His brother, Alessandro, became the next Medici pope, Leo XI, in 1605.)

Giulia's resemblance to Alessandro, her age – now around twenty-five – her Medici lineage, her quiet remarriage in 1559, and a seeming absence from Florence during the long 1559 Vatican conclave all accord with the panel's date, as do its Roman location, Bernardetto's usual role as ambassador in important Medici missions, and with the wealth of symbolic content assiduously woven into the panel by young Allori at the end of his Roman sojourn. It is possible that Giulia commissioned the panel – her personal wealth would have made this feasible – and her limpid gaze, and the biblical reference to the faithful Rachel, would suggest a pledge of her love. It is possible, too, that the panel was commissioned as pendant to one of Bernardetto, originally with the intention of commemorating their marriage on 14 August 1559. A three-quarter-length portrait of Bernardetto in Berlin (fig. 41) shows him with a statue of Minerva behind him. The panel measures 133 by 95 cm – identical in width and only twelve centimetres longer than the *Giulia* (121 × 95 cm). It has been identified with Vasari's *Ricordanze* of a portrait of Bernardetto with a Minerva, recorded for 10 August 1549. Errors or 'slips' in Vasari's *ricordanze* dates are not unknown, but a second possibility could be that Vasari's earlier portrait of Bernardetto with a Minerva was reworked or copied as the basis for a portrait to commemorate Bernardetto's marriage ten years later.[79] The panel's style, and Bernardetto's costume, do suggest a date in the 1550s: beneath his cloak he wears a ruched, satin doublet with a standing collar, around which a narrow edge of shirt ruffle projects, similar to Ludovico Capponi's (fig. 56). Moreover, very close links to the *Giulia* are evident in the prominent statue, pointing hand gesture, and similar style of chair. As Bernardetto's *Minerva* statue echoes that of Giulia's *Rachel*, the two Medici especially complement each other as *vita attiva* and *vita contemplativa*. The *Bernardetto with Minerva* appears to have been the model for the compositional organization and pose of Allori's *Giulia*, 1559, and for his *Portrait of Pietro Palma / Young Collector* in Oxford, dated 1561. Usually attributed to Vasari, the Bernardetto panel was once believed to be Bronzino's work – not an unusual circumstance for Allori's works until about twenty years ago.[80] On 10 August 1559 Bernardetto was in his twenties, and would shortly marry Giulia, on 14 August, a significant rite of passage. Possibly a new or revised *Bernardetto with Minerva* was painted in 1559 by Allori, following his superior, Vasari's 1549 prototype because the new version was intended to have a pendant *Giulia*. This would necessarily have been postponed if she was absent from Florence from 24 September, and would eventually be executed later that year in Rome by Allori; or, possibly both portraits were painted in Rome – Bernardetto's lynx-trimmed cloak suggests a winter engagement between patron and artist.

Bernardetto and Giulia's commission to Allori would continue a family tradition of promotion of young artists. Ottaviano, collector and connoisseur extraordinary, had acted as mentor to the young Vasari on his arrival in Florence; Vasari blesses his memory – Ottaviano had treated him like a son. It seems that Allori's first important Medici commission had come from the family, too, and it may be significant that Bernardetto chose Minerva, goddess of the arts, as his companion.[81] Also, the couple would probably have known Allori during his childhood years as Bronzino's assistant. These mutual links would have made him a trusted choice of portraitist and, being close to him in age, Giulia may even have viewed him as 'modern.' His copious, assiduous iconography suggests that Allori would certainly have seen himself as in the vanguard in this field.[82] Also, Bronzino's assistant was ingrained with the iconographical traditions of the Florentine court and could be relied upon to represent Medicean interests. For religious content, Allori's use of a female portrait for detailed dogmatic imagery was opportune – it was in women's portraiture that overtones of piety held a traditional place.

Whether we may assume Bernardetto's fervour is not so easy to plumb. His personality is revealed to us in somewhat contradictory impressions that give interesting insight into Cosimo's astuteness in administering Florentine affairs and in the control of his extended family. In 1555, as a youth, Bernardetto was a member of the Accademia del Piano, a group whose members hovered on the margins of non-conformity. Domenico Zanrè gives engrossing insight into this less-official side of life in ducal Florence. Most *Pianigiani* were scions of ranking Florentine families; some were political dissidents, others perhaps relished their notoriety as revellers. A degree of intellectual liveliness was required, and many of these aristocratic 'lords of misrule' enjoyed letting off steam in antics designed to parody the social and intellectual aspirations of Cosimo's autocracy, or of ecclesiastical power. Above all, the *Pianigiani* took aim at the high aspirations of Cosimo's official cultural cohort in the Accademia Fiorentina.[83] All operated under nicknames to cover themselves – Iacopo Pitti, for example, was 'Pontefice Massimo,' his house named 'the portals of Bacchus' when used as a venue. Bernardetto's pseudonym was the very paradoxical 'Marchetto Massimo.'[84] (Perhaps this ridicules his pomposity: his arrogance is recorded by the notoriously truculent Benvenuto Cellini.)[85] His participation in an elaborate pantomime with other *Pianigiani* is recorded. In 1555 the duke's diligent factotum, Lorenzo Pagni, expressed his displeasure in a letter to the Duke in which Bernardetto is prominent in a group of forty-five to forty-eight men involved in a macabre mock funeral for the recently deceased bishop of Pisa, Onofrio Bartolini. Mock 'esequies' were enacted at Bartolomeo Panciatichi's house, and the bishop's effigy for this event was composed of turnips, leeks, and carrots. This carnivalesque parody of the *laudatio funebris*, a staple of the Accademia Fiorentina's orations for leading Florentines, was held on Twelfth Night, 6 January, a date on which ribaldry was usual, but which Pagni held was significant as the anniversary of the assassination of the first duke, Alessandro. (Pagni, who 'with his own eyes' had spied on activities at Panciatichi's house, was perturbed by the adornment of the exterior windows with cabbage stalks, and ordered officers of the Bargello to investigate their 'significance.')[86] Cosimo wisely remained unruffled in the face of this ponderous sleuthing and decided not to enforce his Polverini Law, which forbade unauthorised meetings. He could be implacably swift to quash rebel *Pianigiani*, but ordained that in this instance no improper conduct or interference in the affairs of state arose.[87] Probably this was because Bernardetto was his kinsman; and Panciatichi was a valued intimate. (Bartolomeo, renowned humanist poet of the Accademia Fiorentina and Cosimo's emissary to the French court, was active in cultural affairs from the early days of Cosimo's reign. His religious unorthodoxy, possession of banned books, and his suspect French connections had led in 1552 to his trial and that of his wife, Lucrezia, by the Inquisition for heresy. She is seen here in Bronzino's portrait, fig. 27.) Bartolomeo, who brilliantly succeeded Benedetto Varchi as consul of the Florentine Academy in 1545, was made senator by Cosimo in 1567.[88] Cosimo's tendency to cloak himself with the aura of Solomon in adjudicating his own harsh laws was not unusual, and lent an illusion of judicious mercy to his carefully crafted image.[89] Bernardetto's links to the *Pianigiani* notwithstanding, he was soon given significant rank in Cosimo's administration, perhaps to bring him firmly into the inner Medici circle. His marriage to Giulia in August 1559 cemented this link in any event.

Some scholars believe that relations were eventually severed between Giulia and the duke. Giulia identified herself very strongly with her father, Duke Alessandro. It is told that in the early years of her marriage to Bernardetto she insisted that she be treated as the equal of Cosimo's mistress, Eleonora degli Albizzi, in matters of protocol, which caused a rift between Cosimo and the couple.[90] Bernardetto and Giulia did relocate in 1567 to Terra di Lavoro, Ottaiano, near Naples, having purchased the principality from the Gonzaga at enormous expense – fifty-thousand *ducati*, the equivalent of $20 million dollars today – with Giulia's personal fortune. (Their descendents are princes of Tuscany and Ottaiano.)[91] Caution is called for, however, in accepting that this signified any rift; Naples and its dependencies were allied to the Hapsburgs and implicitly to Cosimo; given Bernardetto's role as diplomat to the viceregal court in Naples, their relocation suggests an important diplomatic appointment and elevation for the couple rather than involuntary exile. If there is any grain of truth in the story of a rift with Cosimo, it either healed somewhat or the demands of kinship kept these convoluted relationships in equilibrium. In February 1574, a few months before Cosimo's death, Giulia sent a relic of St Andrew to the devout Giovanna, Cosimo's daughter-in-law.[92]

The portrait of Giulia stands at the beginning of what we know of the development of Allori's portraiture of women. Its style reflects the young artist's Roman immersion, and Giulia's engaging gaze and spiritual accessibility to the viewer contrast strongly with the aloofness and subtlety of Bronzino's court portraits.[93]

During his sojourn, Allori had absorbed a Roman directness of expression. In 1549, after his own immersion there, de Hollanda identified darkness and expressiveness in portraiture as peculiarly Roman. Italians used lamp-black, he professed, 'in order to make shadows blacker and lights more transparent, and to stress the emotions strongly.'[94] The overt blend of dogma, propaganda, and solemn, direct expression define the *Portrait of Giulia de' Medici* as essentially Tridentine in spirit. Tellingly, for his first important commission on his return to Florence early in 1560, Allori recalled Giulia's features for an *Erythraean Sibyl* in a frescoed vault pendentive of the Montauto chapel in Santissima Annunziata (fig. 42).[95]

The *Portrait of Giulia* is infused with Counter-Reformation ideology, and her expression heralds a phase in which candour and clarity in communication will come to characterize Allori's mature court portraiture. Just such changes for religious art were demanded by the Holy See in its final Tridentine session in 1563.[96] Inevitably, the new climate affected art in general, including portraiture, as post-Tridentine writers Paleotti (1582), Lomazzo (1584), and Armenini (1586) reveal.[97] Its influence was abroad long before Paleotti codified his curbs on portrayal in 1582: Allori had absorbed its ethos before his return to Florence in 1560.[98]

Florence was well primed for Counter-Reformation ideology. By the late 1540s Eleonora had exchanged correspondence with Ignatius Loyola and his Jesuit representatives in Tuscany, who hoped to establish a school in Pisa or Florence. They moved into the San Frediano area in 1551 and, with ducal sponsorship, occupied S. Giovannino in 1553. The duchess had been instrumental in their establishment.[99] Counter-Reformation affairs were also set in motion by Cosimo – by no means a religious fanatic by the standards of his time – when in 1557 he ordered the burning of books banned by the Inquisition.[100] In 1559, a few months before Allori painted Giulia's portrait, he proposed a second bonfire.[101] Cultivation of papal interests would put a grand-ducal crown within reach at last, and the Medici were enjoying the closest alliance with Rome since Leo and Clement's papacies. This pivotal point in Medici fortunes was proclaimed when the ducal couple made their lavish state visit to Rome for Cardinal Giovanni's investiture in November 1560, when Eleonora's 'inexpressible majesty' and her piety in kissing the pope's feet are recorded.[102]

Remaining studies of portraits of the second generation of Medici in this climate attest to the keenly sympathetic response of Allori's patrons to Counter-Reformation ideology as generated by the Holy See, and to the adjustments Allori would make to reflect this new philosophy and to accommodate it to a radical change in courtly style.[103]

5

The New Medicean Cosmos:
Lucrezia de' Medici, Duchess of Ferrara

Politically, Cosimo and Eleonora could revel in the extraordinarily rapid ascent they had secured by 1560. Privately, however, harrowing family losses were to mark the new decade. Iron-clad alliances were forged when Isabella married the Orsini scion, Paolo Giordano, in June 1558, and when Lucrezia married Alfonso d'Este in July 1558 as Maria's replacement. With hindsight, however, Maria's untimely end in 1557 stands as a fateful signal of severe buffeting within the family over the next twenty years that would erode the preordained roles planned for Medici daughters to further ducal ambitions.

The duke's longstanding favour with the Hapsburgs was reinforced by extremely cordial relations with Philip II (1527–98), papal ally and 'most Catholic king.' Proclaimed King of Spain by his retired father, Emperor Charles V, in 1556, Philip was the dominant colonial power in Europe after the Treaty of Cateau-Cambrésis in 1559. The territorial reach of the Hapsburgs was now enormous: Philip ruled Milan, Naples, Sicily, the Netherlands, and Portugal, and had consolidated a vast empire in Mexico, Peru, and the Caribbean. At this moment, Cosimo appeared to have the simultaneous support and trust of the two European powers most critical to his interests, the Hapsburgs and the pope.

In 1560 Francesco was nineteen, of an age now to be made regent for the duration of Eleonora and Cosimo's two-month absence in Rome to formally celebrate Giovanni's investiture as cardinal.[1] It was deemed time for the prince's initiation into affairs of state, and he was soon caught up in Tridentine affairs in Rome and in Spain.[2] Pius's promise to reopen the prorogued Tridentine council had Cosimo's enthusiastic support, and the Counter-Reformation quickly became an important focus in Florence. The prince's role was an active one, but relative to the mood of the times, Francesco, like his father, was no fanatic. Writing from Spain in 1562 after one of his gentlemen was castigated by the Inquisition for uttering an oath, he registered his opinion with his father that moderation would be more appropriate in Florence in applying its strictures: such extreme responses brought only grumbling against their house and no profit to religion.[3] In time, however, Cosimo would cynically use the Inquisition to further his obsessive bid for a grand-ducal crown.[4]

Allori's stock too had risen. He had maintained his contact with Bronzino and the court during occasional return visits to Florence – acting as Medici portraitist a few times.[5] From the extant artistic evidence – an important fresco commission for the Montauto chapel in Santissima Annunziata, portraits of Cosimo's heir, Francesco, and of his daughter, Lucrezia, and, arguably, the splendid *Deposition of Christ* altarpiece for Santa Croce – we can conclude that his standing as a mature artist with the court was set in motion immediately on his return. Allori remained devoted to Bronzino, but the prodigious growth in the duke's political fortunes must have led him to envisage a future as painter to a greatly expanded court. By 1560 he was official portraitist to Francesco, who may have perceived him as 'modern' and suitably 'Roman' by inclination as the new papacy was launched.[6] Roman tendencies in Allori's art were quick to find acceptance at the Medici court, and his portraits of the younger Medici in the early 1560s are characterised by the same direct gaze, uncomplicated perspective, and darkly expressive tonality as in his *Giulia d'Alessandro de' Medici* (figs. 37, 38, and 40).

One panel in Allori's *Francesco* portrait series is usually dated to 1560 by a miniature in the prince's hand that he extends to our gaze (fig. 43). It portrays his sister Lucrezia (1545–61), who became the replacement bride for Alfonso d'Este (1533–99) after Maria died in 1557. They were married on 33 July 1558, when Lucrezia was thirteen and Alfonso twenty-four. On Ercole II d'Este's death on 3 October 1559, Lucrezia became Duchess of Ferrara at the tender age of fourteen.[7] She departed Florence for a lavish official *entrata* into Ferrara on 10 February 1560, never to return. The miniature *Lucrezia* held by Francesco is thought to mark his journey to Ferrara to escort her there in February 1560.[8] It was evidently copied from a three-quarter-length *Lucrezia* panel now in the North Carolina Museum of Art, once attributed to Bronzino but almost certainly by Allori (pl. 10). An attractive miniature copy on tin exists in the Palazzo Pitti.[9] Because several inscribed Medici derivatives of the North Carolina panel exist – all small – its identity and its official status are secure.[10] One copy, in short-bust format, appears in the Medici miniature family set on tin (pl. 8).[11]

Curiously, a portrayal of Lucrezia in the Schloss Ambras miniature Medici series sent to the court in Vienna in 1587 seems to bear only slight resemblance to the North Carolina portrait (pl. 10), but it is inscribed on the back LUCRETIA DE' MEDICI DUCHESSA DI FARARA [*sic*]. It derives from a short-bust *Lucrezia* panel in the Uffizi (fig. 45), probably by Allori, where she is dressed in bright red and her ruched, high-collared *camicia* is fastened with drawstrings and tied in a series of bows at the front.[12] Her hair is covered by a pearl-strewn mesh haircover similar to those favoured by her mother, and she wears drop-pearl earrings. Her casual decorum in this portrait, her naturalism, but especially her plumpness compared to her official portrayal as Duchess of Ferrara (pl. 10), is striking. It must have been made before her decline from consumption, symptoms of which were apparent before she left Florence. It could be an informal portrait made after her wedding in July 1558, probably after court mourning concluded on the anniversary of Maria's death, 19 November, but before October 1559, when she adopted official mourning again on her father-in-law, Ercole II's death. The more robust *Lucrezia* contrasts greatly, too, with the imposing 'pre-nuptial' portrayals of Maria, Isabella, and the *Girl with a Book* (pl. 7, fig. 32, and pl. 9), and her brilliant red costume is not in the spirit of that prenuptial genre, where costume is in drab tones, expression aloof, and pose severely frontal. Allori, whose hand is evident in all of these *Lucrezia* portrayals, must have painted this panel during a return visit to Florence in the late 1550s. Was this perhaps commissioned by her parents as a sentimental record in anticipation of her inevitable departure for Ferrara, between July 1558 and February 1560? Medici inventories do not record any Lucrezia portraits, and the occasion for its execution remains somewhat mysterious.[13]

Pastorino's 1558 medals for Lucrezia, inscribed 'LVCRETIA MED./ESTEN. FERR.PRINC. A.A. XIII,' commemorate her marriage, and show her posed in profile, the first with a blank reverse; another reverse in the series has an illegible inscription but depicts the legend of the love-struck nymph, Salmacis, and her Hermaphroditus; a third medal reverse shows a draped female figure near musical instruments and an armillary sphere, with the inscription NEC.TEMPVS.NEC. AETAS ('Neither the Passing of Time nor the Passing of the Years'), perhaps referring to the Muse Erato and signifying harmonious and everlasting love.[14] Domenico Poggini's medal that year depicts her in profile and is inscribed 'LVCRETIA MED./ESTEN.FERR.PRINCEPS,' with Alfonso on the reverse. On an anonymous copy of it, the reverse depicts an Apollo in his *quadriga*, travelling high over a reclining river-god Po who is posed to embrace a nymph with a cornucopia; it is inscribed 'NOVA.ERIDANO.FVLXIT.LVX' ('Eridanus Shone with an Extraordinary Light'), referring to the myth of Phaeton, who fell into the river Eridanus (Po) after he lost control of his father Apollo's chariot. The River Po, representing Este territory, presumably will be illuminated by the presence of Lucrezia and Alfonso and their union made fertile.[15]

The North Carolina panel (pl. 10) also inspired the retrospective official commemoration of the young Duchess of Ferrara engraved by Haelwegh around 1675 (fig. 44).[16] In this she is identified as Lucrezia, daughter of the Grand Duke of Tuscany and wife of Alfonso II, Duke of Ferrara ('LVCRETIA AB ETRVRIA/COSIMO I. MAGNI DVCIS ETRVRIAE FIL:ALPHONSI II DVCIS FERRARIAE VXOR').[17] Her motto, 'MOTV ET LUMINE' ('With Energy and With Light'), appears on it above her *impresa*, a sun shining over water. It also appears on Antonio Selvi's *Lucrezia* medal of 1739, where the sun beams over waves breaking against rocks.[18] The *impresa* symbolized steadfastness, and was used also by Vincenzo Gonzaga during Lucrezia's lifetime.[19]

The Marriage of Alfonso d'Este and Lucrezia de' Medici

The negotiations for Lucrezia's marriage had a chequered history that demonstrate Cosimo's parallel, Machiavellian climb to power. They began with the house of Montalto when she was four.[20] In 1553, at the age of eight, Lucrezia was betrothed to Pope Julius III's nephew, Fabiano del Monte. These plans were abandoned as Cosimo moved towards the acquisition of Siena and, on Julius's death in 1555, that alliance was dropped. Cosimo's rapid ascendency among Italian principalities went apace. Maria's death was undoubtedly a deeply painful loss to Cosimo and Eleonora, but, as a result of the duke's usual talent for dealing decisively with every political contingency, the frail, thirteen-year-old Lucrezia was suddenly destined to become duchess of a powerful rival court.

The Medici-Este alliance had to be honoured. It stood as a landmark détente in a protracted contest for precedence between the two houses, and augured well for maintaining the delicate and outwardly civilized balance of power that had long existed between the two courts. One dynasty could claim antecedents stretching back to Charlemagne and august connections with the royal house of France – Alfonso's mother was Princess Renée, daughter of King Louis XI and Anne of Brittany. The other was only recently ennobled, rapidly aggrandizing, and assiduously striving for hegemony in Italy.[21] Ercole, in a personal letter written to Cosimo at the culmination of negotiations for Lucrezia's replacement of Maria diplomatically avoided any mention of the ancestral divides that underlay the Este house and the parvenu Florentine duke's. Writing in 1558, before the Treaty of Cateau-Cambrésis, he eloquently expressed the political significance of this union, 'not only for the increased importance of our houses, but also perhaps for some benefits to the public good, and at least for the calming of poor Italy.'[22]

Cosimo's overarching ambition made such diplomatic niceties moot. The opportune substitution of Lucrezia as bride for the Este scion was fortuitous, and her life seems to have drawn little contemporary comment until she was precipitously thrust into the marriage arranged for her gifted, highly presentable older sister, Maria. Lucrezia was said to have been unprepossessing, lacking in vivacity, and less physically appealing than her sisters; some scholars note, however, that in her official portrait (pl. 10), she is dignified and does express the grace and fine appearance recorded of her in court correspondence.[23] Widely admired for his humanistic learning and personal gentility, Alfonso gallantly accepted his child-bride as replacement for Maria, whose brilliance might have shone as much as the cultivated patronage and able diplomacy of his ancestor Isabella d'Este (1474–1539), who had so famously graced the Gonzaga court. Lucrezia, hardly past childhood, was infatuated, but Alfonso by all accounts was not attracted to her – hardly an unusual state of affairs in such alliances.

Cosimo's stake in the Este alliance is expressed in his extravagant dowry for Lucrezia of two hundred thousand gold *scudi* – about $70 million in today's currency. The Medici-Este nuptials were a protracted affair, beginning with Alfonso's giving of the ring on 11 May 1558 at Pisa, his solemn *entrata* into Florence on 18 June, and his first meeting with Lucrezia sometime before 25 June. No personal correspondence between Alfonso and Lucrezia exists to describe his deeper feelings, but Estense courtiers were pleased with the appearance of his young bride.[24] Festivities included a public football match on 2 July, the eve of the wedding, in Piazza Santa Maria Novella, in which one side was dressed in gold, the other in silver. (The Orsini arms include silver, and the Este arms extensive fields of gold.)[25] Clearly, much of the delight enjoyed by spectators arose because the distinguished houses of Cosimo's new sons-in-law were pitted against each other. No record of an elaborate public *apparato* for either Isabella's or Lucrezia's wedding such as marked Eleonora's has been found.[26] The reason for this could not be other than rigid codes of mourning observed at Renaissance courts. Both weddings took place before the requisite year of mourning for Maria's death was over in November 1558, forcing the court to restrict ostentatious or carnivalesque public celebrations.

Lucrezia and Alfonso's marriage took place on 3 July 1558 in Santa Maria Novella, followed by a feast and an exotic masquerade with music, dancing, and other diversions throughout the night.[27] Alfonso left three days later to lead military campaigns for Henry II of France. Saddened by his long absences on campaigns that left her sequestered and fretting under her mother's close quartering until 1560, Lucrezia's life was to run a downhill, miserable course to a tragic conclusion. Eleonora, who died in 1562, was herself already in decline from tuberculosis. She may have recognized its ominous symptoms in Lucrezia, and dreaded to release her forever to Ferrara at so tender an age. Her marriage of less than three years – wholly marred by her pathetic, lingering death in exile in Ferrara, under sympathetic Este care but mostly isolated from her family – informs the brief historic traces there are of her.[28]

Bronzino was moved to pen two elegies on Lucrezia's death, each expressing the horror felt in the court at the grievious loss now of two beloved Medici daughters (appendix B). In each he concluded with expressions of the imponderables of life and death, and profound unease at what may lie ahead: 'What will bring consolation to us wretched ... Alas, vain hopes, alas blind life, shadows and fear' ('Chi fia, miseri noi, che ne console ... Ahi viver cieco, e solo ombra, e spavento').[29] Historically, what few vestiges of her pathetic life are recorded reflect this recognition of dashed hopes for greater unity in Italy. On her death in 1561, the precedence controversy between the Medici and the Este broke out anew.[30] Its latent presence is subtly made evident in the official portrait made during the interval of her reluctant detention at the Florentine court.

Allori's *Portrait of Lucrezia de' Medici d'Este*

There are several overt expressions of Medici *dominio* in Lucrezia's official portrait as Duchess of Ferrara that may rank it as one of the most politicized images of Medici women from Cosimo's court. This, the North Carolina panel, shows her with her hand on a crystal sphere in the foreground (pl. 10). The sphere may refer to the sun in her *impresa* and the motto exhorting her to energize and lighten, but the emblematic globe and its relative the sphere (*palla*) had long served as the supreme Medici symbol. It allegorized Cosimo to express overtones of *cosmos*, universality, and dominion, and was apt for the position in which he strove to place himself. The Sun-god Apollo was one of the most enduring of the duke's chosen personifications, and it was currently enjoying considerable use. Domenico Poggini's statue of *Cosimo-Apollo* of 1559 is one instance.[31] Lucrezia's hand over the sphere is also a reminder of the bronze *genio Mediceo*, accompanied by Cosimo's Capricorn *impresa*, the goat, probably by Stoldo di Lorenzo and now in the Palazzo Pitti, who raises the Medici *palla* aloft in triumph.[32] Even as a symbol of marital harmony in her portrait as Duchess of Ferrara, the Medici *palla* injects an ambiguous freight into Lucrezia's portrait as Duchess of Ferrara in the light of Cosimo's persistent intention to gain hegemony over the Estense house.

Even at the height of cordiality between the Este and Medici, the détente between the two houses seems not to have been entirely made in good faith on Cosimo's part. The precedence controversy between the two houses had commenced early in his reign. It was made public in Lucca in 1541, when Ercole II of Ferrara was allowed to ride on Charles V's right, with Cosimo relegated to his left, and protocol favoured Ercole at the imperial banquet. It continued to be waged throughout the courts of Europe, gradually coming to favour the Medici. Records reveal that Lucrezia's marriage to the Este heir in 1558 had not served as a brake to temper Cosimo's ambition as he grasped for supremacy. It was during the period of the papal conclave, from September to December 1559, that the duke infiltrated its sessions and covertly frustrated Ferrara's hopes for an Estense papacy.[33] Intermarriage by the Medici with the Este was nevertheless extremely important in maintaining a balance of power, and Lucrezia's death in 1561 was a harsh political blow for both families.

The theme of *dominio* in Lucrezia's official portrait (pl. 10) as Duchess of Ferrara expresses an era of aggressive power play as her father's best hopes rose for his promotion by Pius IV to Grand Duke of Italy. Its setting and circumstances reside precisely in the glow of triumph that must have pervaded the court throughout 1560.[34] As noted, Lucrezia was already in decline in 1559, and looks thinner than in the informal, bust-length portrait in the Uffizi (fig. 45), probably painted around the time of her marriage in 1557. As she became Duchess of Ferrara in October 1559, her official portrait (pl. 10) can only have been painted during the last weeks of the conclave that year or after Giovanni Angelo Medici's election as Pius IV on 24 December, but certainly before she departed for Ferrara on 10 February 1560. The portrait has often been attributed to Bronzino, but its facial modelling is similar to that in Allori's *Giulia* and *Francesco* portraits (figs. 37 and 43) and their direct, expressive gaze and extremely dark tonality are all legacies of Allori's recent Roman immersion.[35] His slightly inept handling of drapery around Lucrezia's poorly foreshortened left forearm in the North Carolina portrait is an artistic lapse fated to persist in his portraits (see pl. 11 and 16). These, like his *Giulia de' Medici* (fig. 37), also show his tendency to reuse stock hand poses from subject to subject. But Allori brings a winsome seriousness of expression to his portrayal of the child-duchess, and accentuates her small-featured, oval face and the desired high forehead. Her very dark hair and eyes distinguish her from her sisters, the grey-eyed Maria and the dark-eyed but fair-haired Isabella (pl. 7 and fig. 32); of the three Medici daughters, she appears to have most closely resembled her mother. Even if Lucrezia was described as unprepossessing by some contemporaries, her portrait may support Estense courtiers' descriptions of her as 'noble, well-formed, and of attractive appearance.'[36] Her expression in the portrait is composed but not remote, and perspective places her accessibly close to the viewer. The young Este duchess has none of the seigneurial aloofness that Bronzino infused into his *Eleonora with Her Son Giovanni* (pl. 4) in 1545.

The diarist Agostino Lapini recorded Lucrezia's departure in mourning from Florence, 'vestita tutta a bruno per la morte del padre del suo marito' ('dressed all in dark [clothing] for the death of her husband's father'). This is confirmed in the North Carolina portrait and the miniature on tin in the Palazzo Pitti.[37] The young duchess is dressed in black. She is, however, bedecked in Medici and Ferrarese jewels, some part of her dowry, others probably recording a portion of the inalienable Estense treasury released by her father-in-law, Ercole II, and ceremoniously loaned to her by Alfonso on the occasion of their wedding.[38] Ercole is explicit on the traditional association between family jewels and a wife's integrity as collateral for the privilege of wearing them. In seigneurial tones and using the majestic 'we' to refer to himself, he had gone so far as to grudgingly caution his son that there were no guarantees Lucrezia would bear Alfonso's children, or certainty of her *onestà* – a term that could imply chastity as well as integrity when describing women. The Medici had long been a thorn in his side, and his barely concealed disdain for the parvenu duke's family is loaded with subtle insult and mistrust that attest to his understandable bitterness at the loss of precedence in noble rank endured by his aristocratic house as a result of Medici manoeuvring:

> It can be evidence of the fact [of his approval] that we have given to her the triangular diamond, which our Lord Duke our father did not want to give to our [bride], to whom (when I went to France to marry her), our father the Duke did not want to give anything if not in the manner that I have told you, and that is the habit of princes. And truthfully we do not know that it matters if we give her the jewels so that she may enjoy them and wear them, on the understanding that they must remain in our house if she has no children by you, or, if we give them to her in another way, if she does not have in mind to alienate them [from us], [something which] does not seem honest to us.[39]

Although the pendant Lucrezia touches with her hand is somewhat obscured, her gesture as she holds the magnificent jewel to her breast conveys heartfelt faithfulness to her husband, with the usual implication of exclusiveness and chastity. Her hand-over-heart gesture suggests that the enormous jewel was either a gift from Alfonso (or loaned from Estense holdings), and the *cintura* of precious stones that girdles her waist may well record the one released from Ferrarese coffers by her begrudging father-in-law for her wedding.[40]

Her persona is not, however, subsumed in Ferrarese symbolism, and, as suggested, the prominence of a *palla* in the foreground manifestly proclaims the interests of her father's house. As with almost every portrait of Medici women examined here, the emphasis on Medici lineage is almost overstated, and Medici artistic patronage remained implicitly tied to propagandizing the Florentine house. Her grave expression and demeanour may be real and not merely a formal expression of mourning for Ercole (who had died in October 1559). Her situation was poignant. Alfonso used his military campaigns as a *condottiere* as an excuse to delay his child-bride's move to Ferrara. She was wan after nearly two years of her husband's absence: following his hasty departure after their wedding he was, in spite of his reputation for gentility, resolutely incommunicado with his new bride while on campaign. His Estense retainer at the Florentine court, Francesco Susena, detailed her plight in troubled letters to Alfonso, who, apparently, could not be moved to write to his young wife: 'I try to say as much as I can to make her say something, but without your warmth I cannot: you need to learn a little bit to [express] love a little, at least in writing' ('Il mi vado ben facendo più cantafavola alle mani che posso, per indurla a dir qualche cosa, ma senza il vostro caldo non posso: bisogna che impariate di far un poco d'amore, almeno in scritto').[41] Also, her status as a wife and duchess of an illustrious house in her own right was undermined in spirit. Sickness, loneliness because of her husband's absence, and close quartering by her mother made her continuously fretful. Susena reported that his lord's wife, now fourteen, was hardly eating, pined for letters from him, and scarcely smiled or spoke, 'a sad woman compared to her sister [Isabella] and the others' ('una donna grave apresso alla sorella et agli altre'). By March 1559, De Fiaschi reported to Susena: 'The Princess wishes to be free of her mother's control, since she feels her incarceration to be too long and harsh' ('La Principessa desidera uscir di mano della matre, parendole troppo lunga et aspra la prigionia in cui si trova' [sic]). Susena's plaintive letter of 15 June indicates how desperate she had become to establish her rightful position in Ferrara: 'Our Princess has said that, once the Lord Prince is here, she wants to show [him] with a stratagem how she ardently wishes to go from where her mother keeps her, and will throw herself at his feet and beg him to take her away from this prison' ('La principessa nostra ha detto che, giunto il Sig. Principe, vuol con arte a vedere dove la matre la tiene, et gettarseli a' piedi, et supplicarlo a levarla di questa prigionia' [sic]). In July she was ill, but in October Susena expressed hopes of a pregnancy. These soon faded.[42]

Lucrezia's entreaties to leave Eleonora's zealous care were eventually success-ful. She left in a litter for Ferrara on 10 February 1560 with a retinue of five hun-dred and fifty and arrived in a weakened state seven days later, dressed in silver and black, for her magnificent *entrata* into the city. Este celebrations for her arrival were unstinting, and included a banquet where a personification of Flora recited verses to praise the young duchess, and Muses of matrimony sang eulogies to the couple. This was followed by a masked ball. Ominously, Francesco wrote from Ferrara that day to report that she was feverish.[43] In exile and now desperately ill – as moving letters to Florence reported – Lucrezia's sad saga of decline was to bring great anguish to Cosimo and Eleonora. For a brief time, her symptoms were again thought to be due to pregnancy, a dashed hope that only added to the con-fusion and grief of her parents and the Este as she sank into terminal decline. Faced now with the seriousness of his wife's condition, Alfonso and his family proved to be deeply caring during her final months of futile, agonizing treat-ments. The dispatch of the reputed Medici physician, Andrea Pasquali, on a hur-ried, four-day journey to Ferrara on 31 March 1561 was comforting for her but fruitless.[44] (He was elderly and arrived exhausted by the rushed journey.) She died on 21 April from consumption, at the age of sixteen. Pasquali's distress at breaking the news of her death to Cosimo and Eleonora is harrowing. They were inconsolable, and both courts entered a period of deep mourning. Cosimo's letter to Alfonso of 4 May records their grief, thanks him for his dedication to Lucrezia in her last months, and regrets the loss of kinship between their houses. These inter-court documents dispel forever rumours by Medici enemies that Alfonso poisoned her, as later recorded by the disaffected Settimanni (circa 1720).[45] The loss of promised accord between the two houses, and of an alliance that boded well for greater peace in the Italian peninsula, was mourned by all.

The grave, direct expression that characterizes Allori's *Giulia* and *Lucrezia* por-traits defines him as instigator in Florence of a radical, new artistic force. Exposed to Bronzino again in 1560, his palette lightened, but Allori's own Roman immer-sion had primed him in advance of a rapid change in artistic philosophy in Flo-rence in the 1560s. His patrons, now strongly allied with Rome, were instrumental

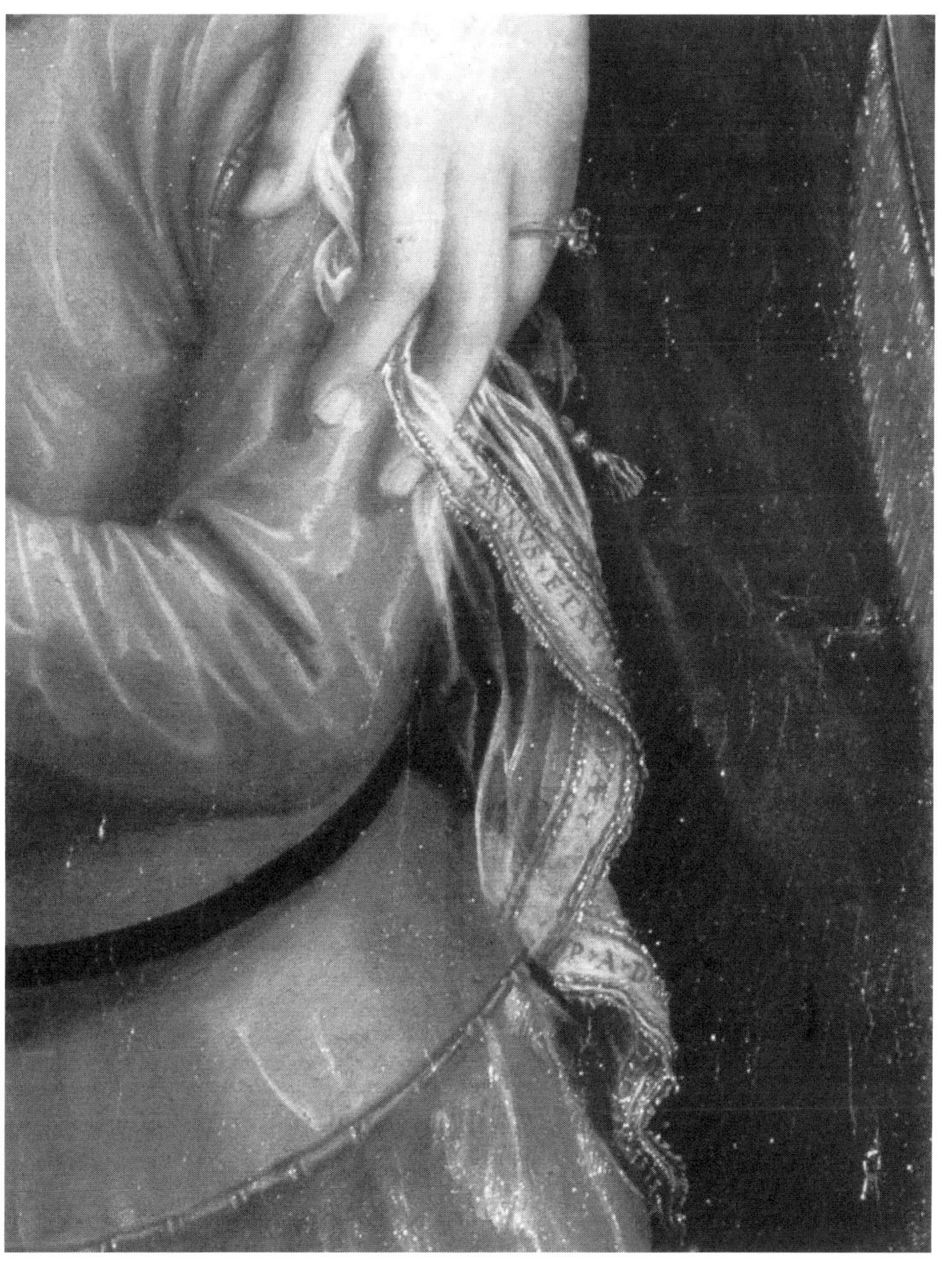

Figure 47 Alessandro Allori, *Isabella de' Medici Orsini with Her Son Virginio*, detail of plate 11: kerchief inscription.

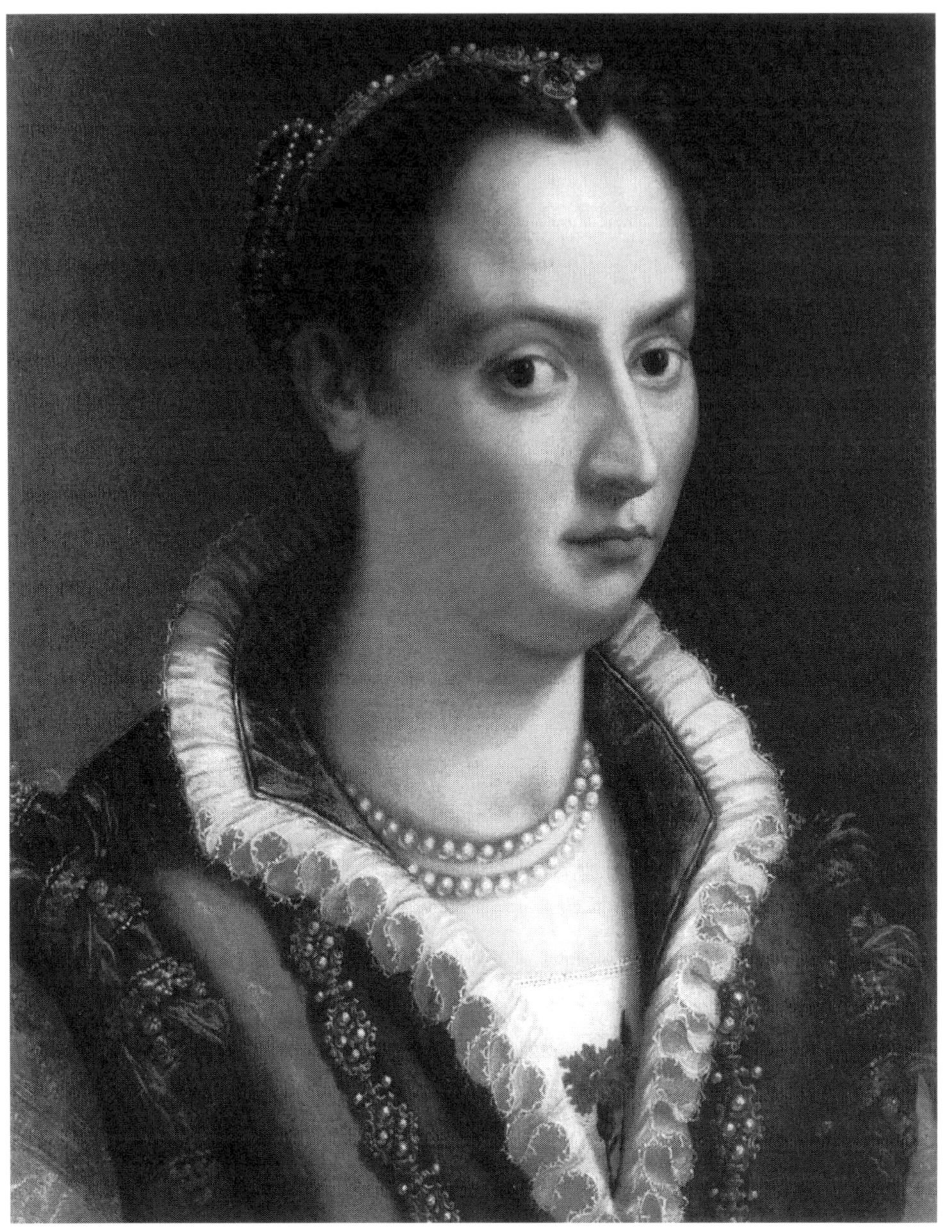

Figure 48 Alessandro Allori, *Isabella de' Medici Orsini*, 1574. 46.8 × 37.8 cm. Formerly New York, Piero Corsini Gallery.

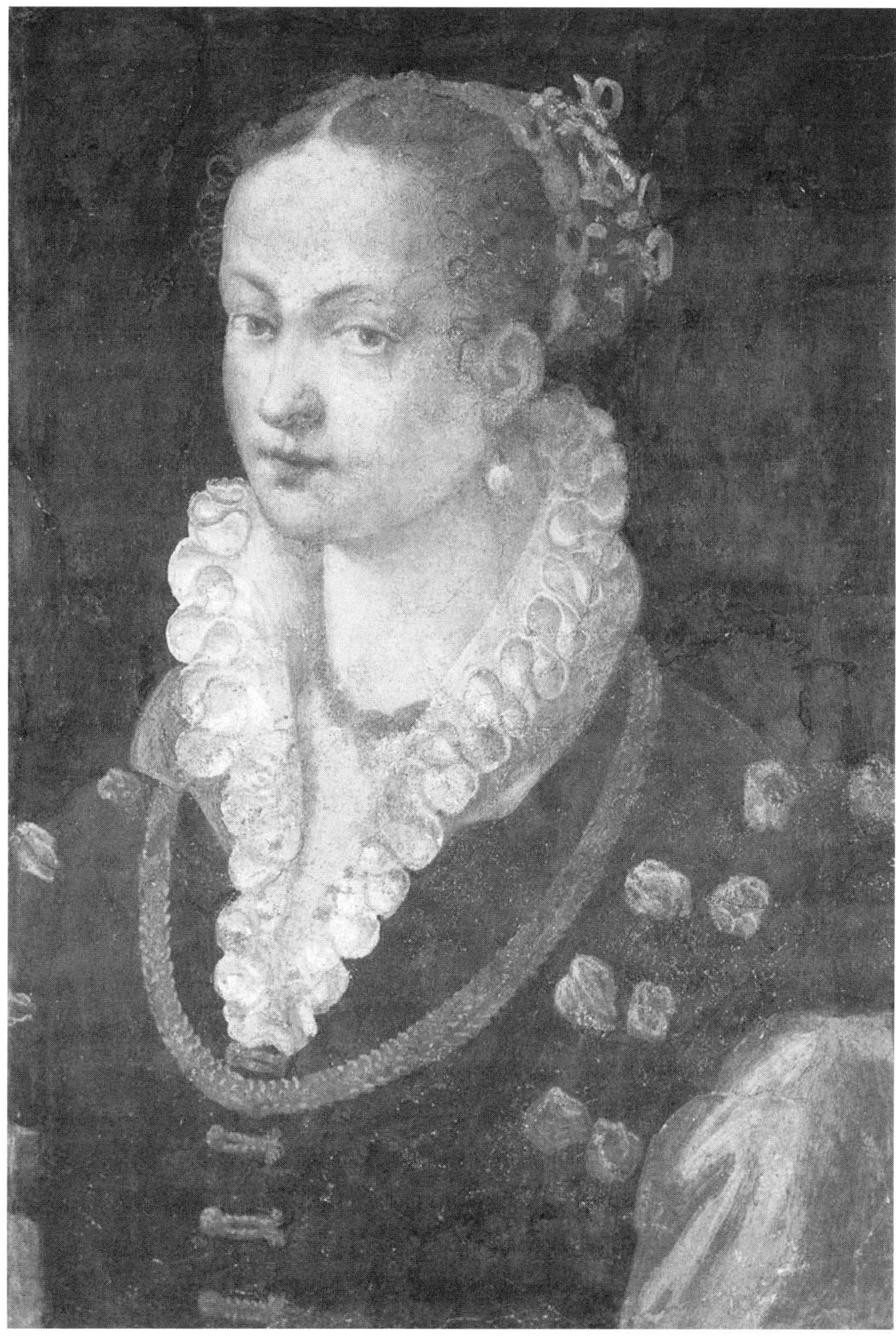

Figure 49 Anonymous, *Isabella de' Medici Orsini*, after 1563. Fresco fragment, 75 × 52 cm, from Santa Maria ad Olmi, Mugello. Florence, Galleria degli Uffizi.

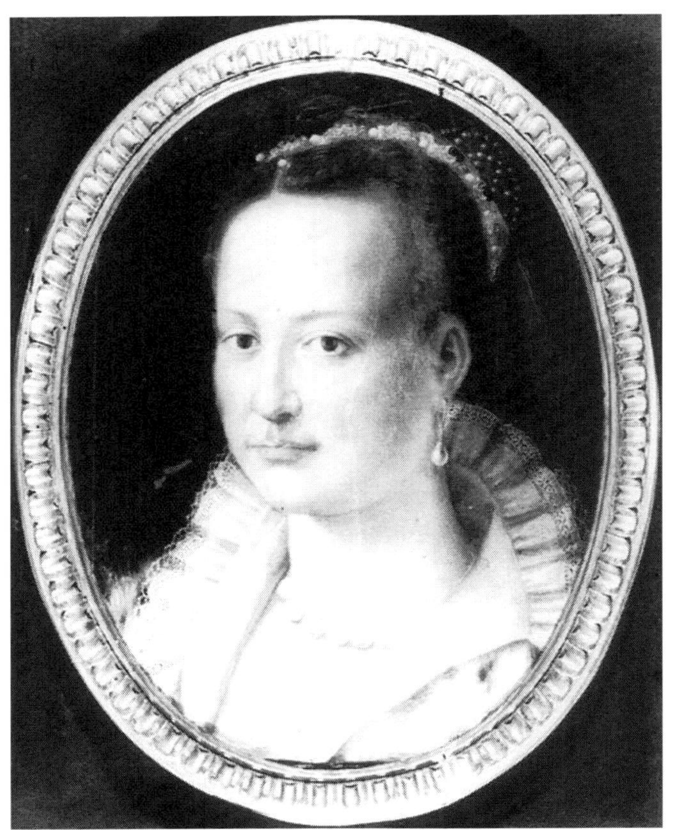

Figure 50 Anonymous, *Isabella de' Medici Orsini*, 1587. Tempera on parchment, on cardboard, 13.5 × 10.5 cm (Ambras Series). Vienna, Kunsthistorisches Museum.

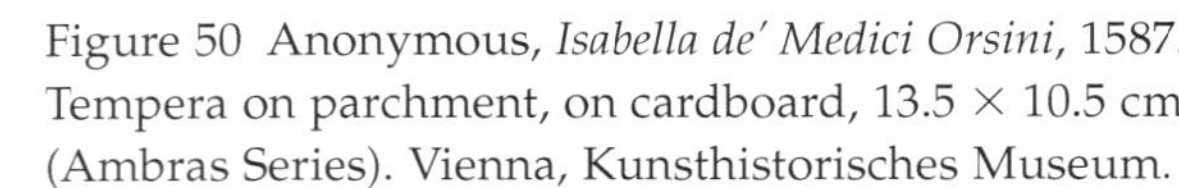

Figure 51 Alessandro Allori workshop (Santi di Tito?), *Isabella de' Medici Orsini*. Oil on panel, oval height circa 35 cm. Florence, Medici Villa, Poggio Imperiale.

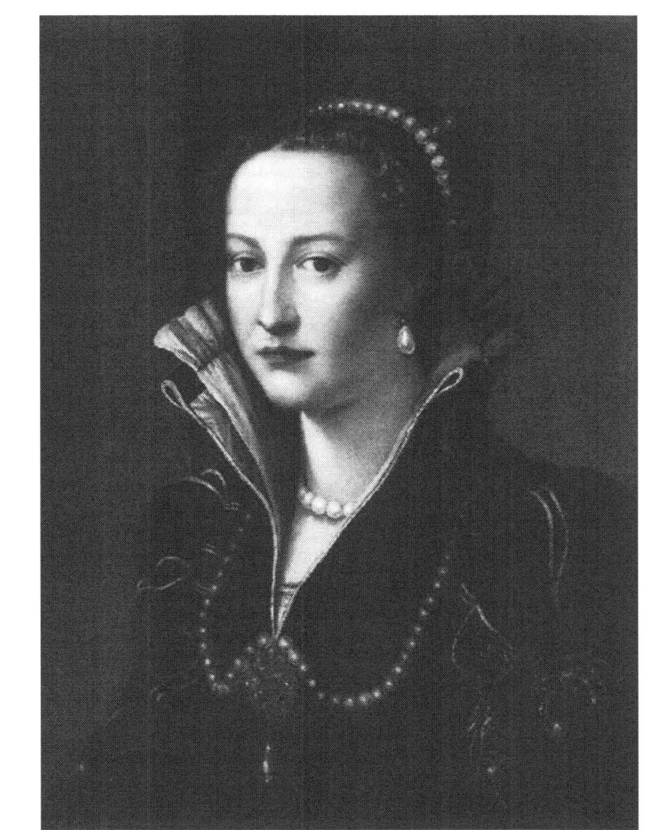

Figure 52 Alessandro Allori workshop, *Isabella de' Medici Orsini with Music*, circa 1565. Oil on canvas, 96 × 70 cm. Florence, Medici Villa, Poggio a Caiano.

Figure 53 Alessandro Allori, *Isabella de' Medici Orsini*, circa 1565. Rome, Palazzo Corsini.

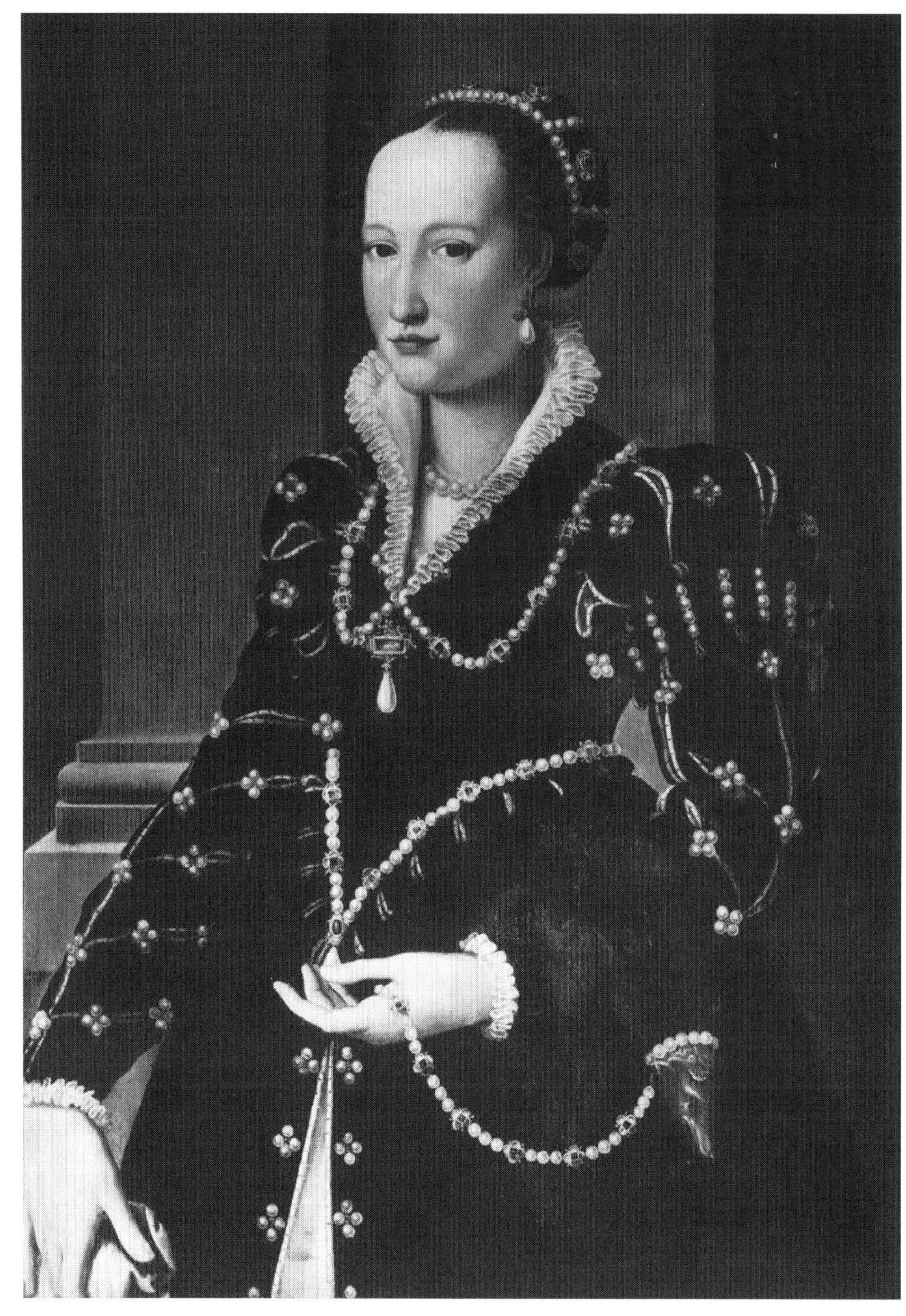

Figure 54 Alessandro Allori, *Isabella de' Medici Orsini with a Fur Pelt*, circa 1565.
Oil on panel, 99 × 70 cm. Florence, Palazzo Pitti.

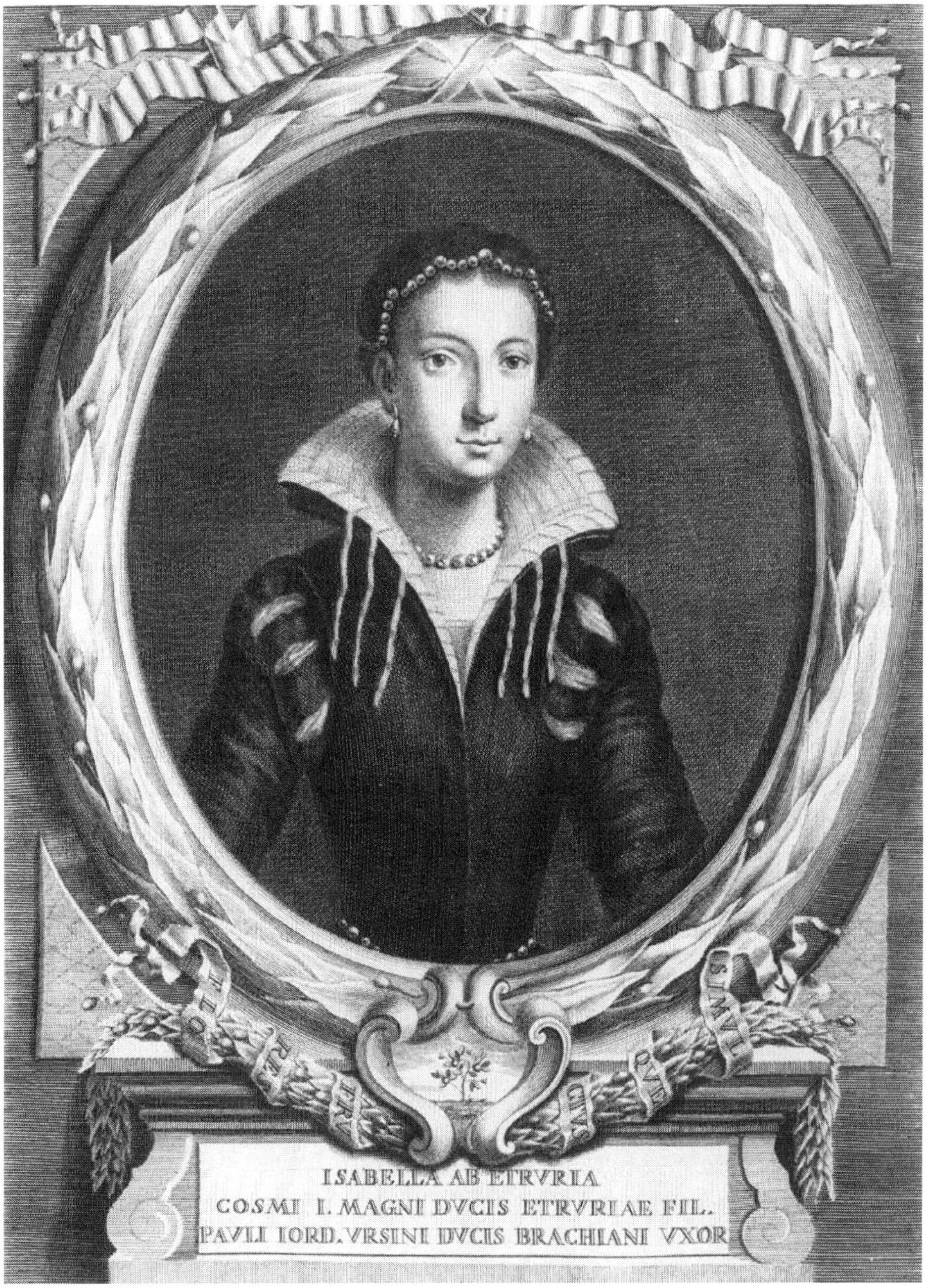

Figure 55 Antonio Pazzi, *Isabella de' Medici Orsini*. Engraving. Giuseppe Zocchi, *Chronologica series simulacrorum regiae familiae Medicea*, Florence, 1761.

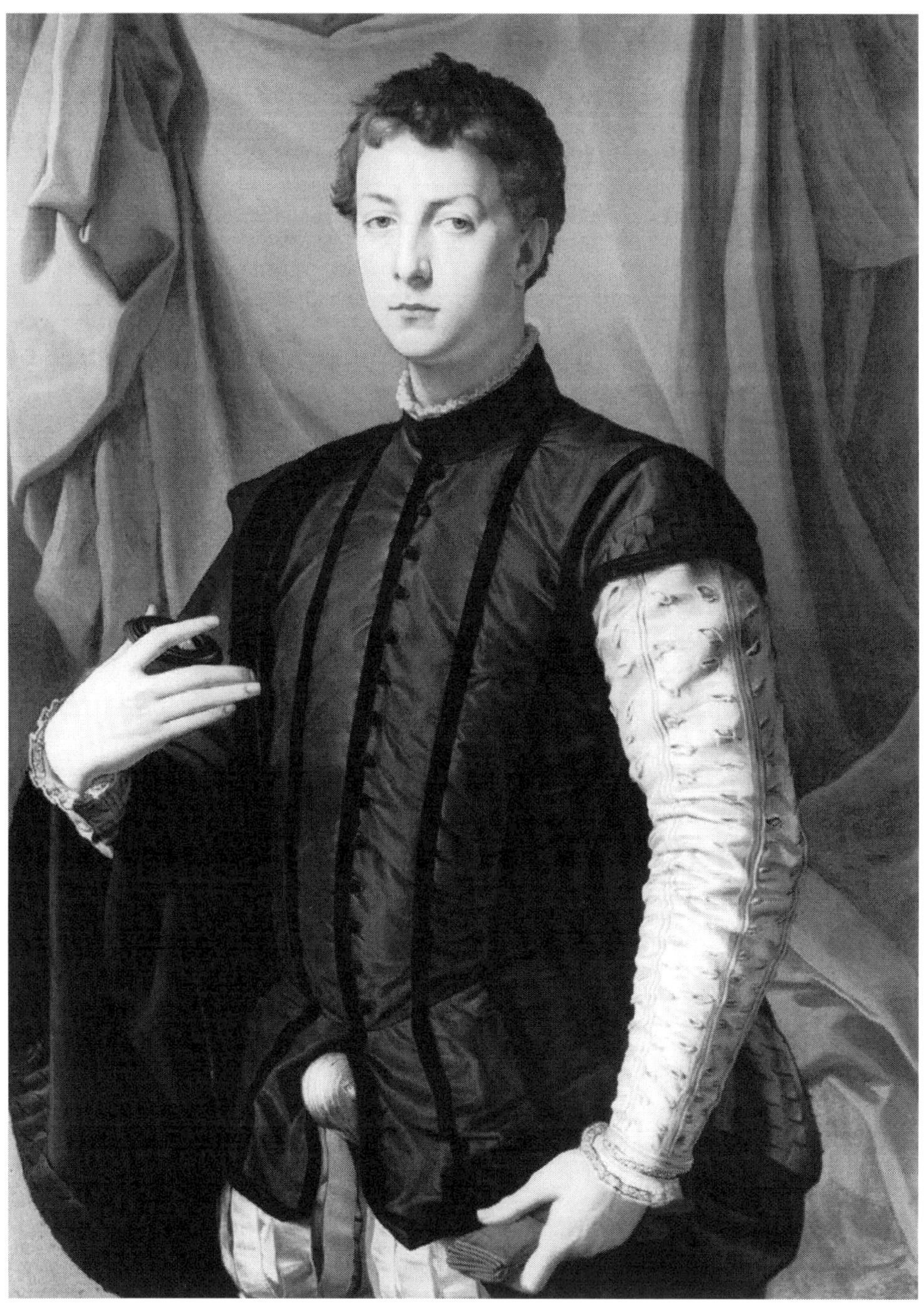

Figure 56 Agnolo Bronzino, *Ludovico Capponi*, circa 1555. Oil on panel, 116 × 85 cm. The Frick Collection, New York.

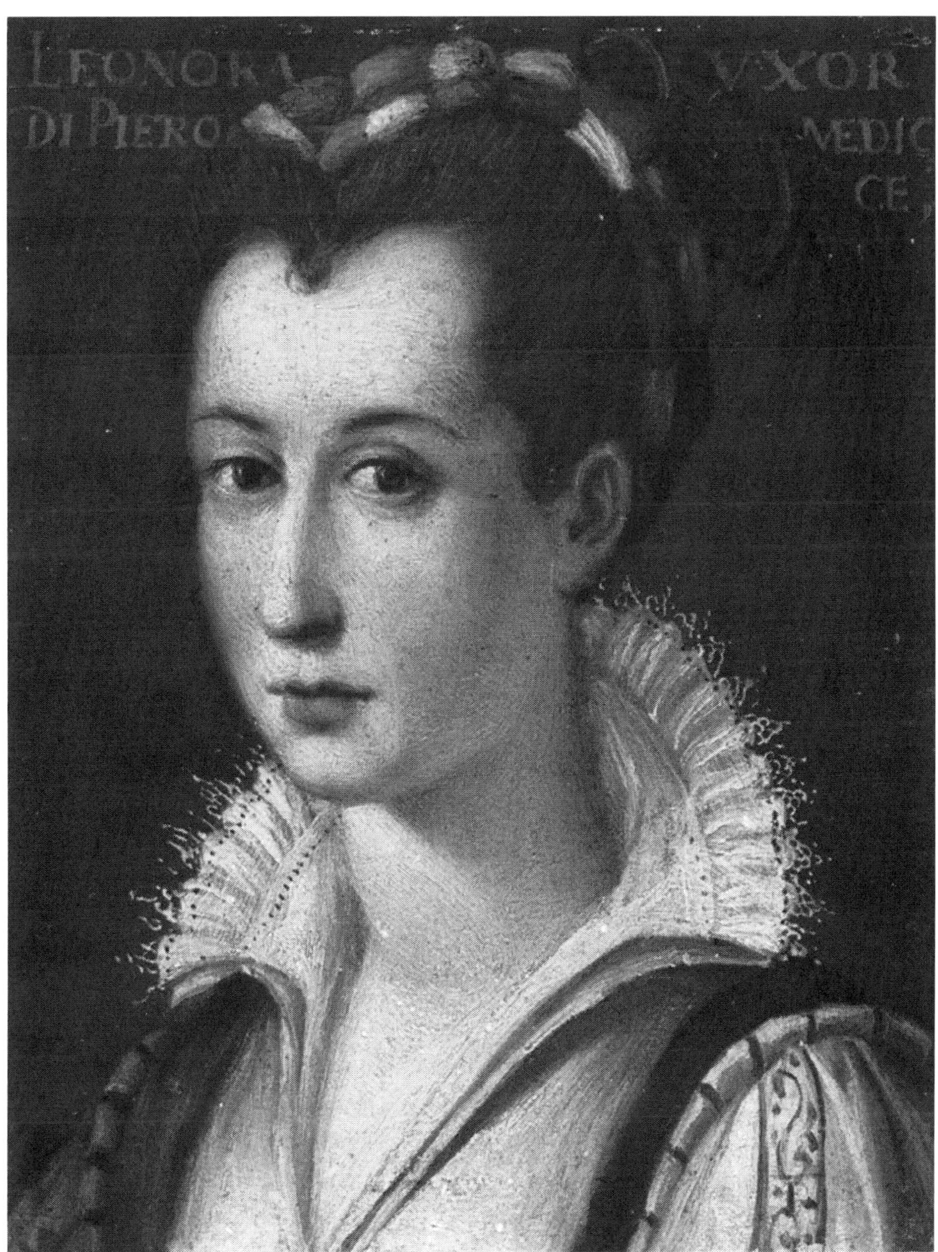

Figure 57 Anonymous, *Eleonora ('Dianora') di Don Garzia di Toledo di Pietro de' Medici*, 1587. Paper on panel, 13.5 × 10.5 cm (Ambras Series). Vienna, Kunsthistorisches Museum.

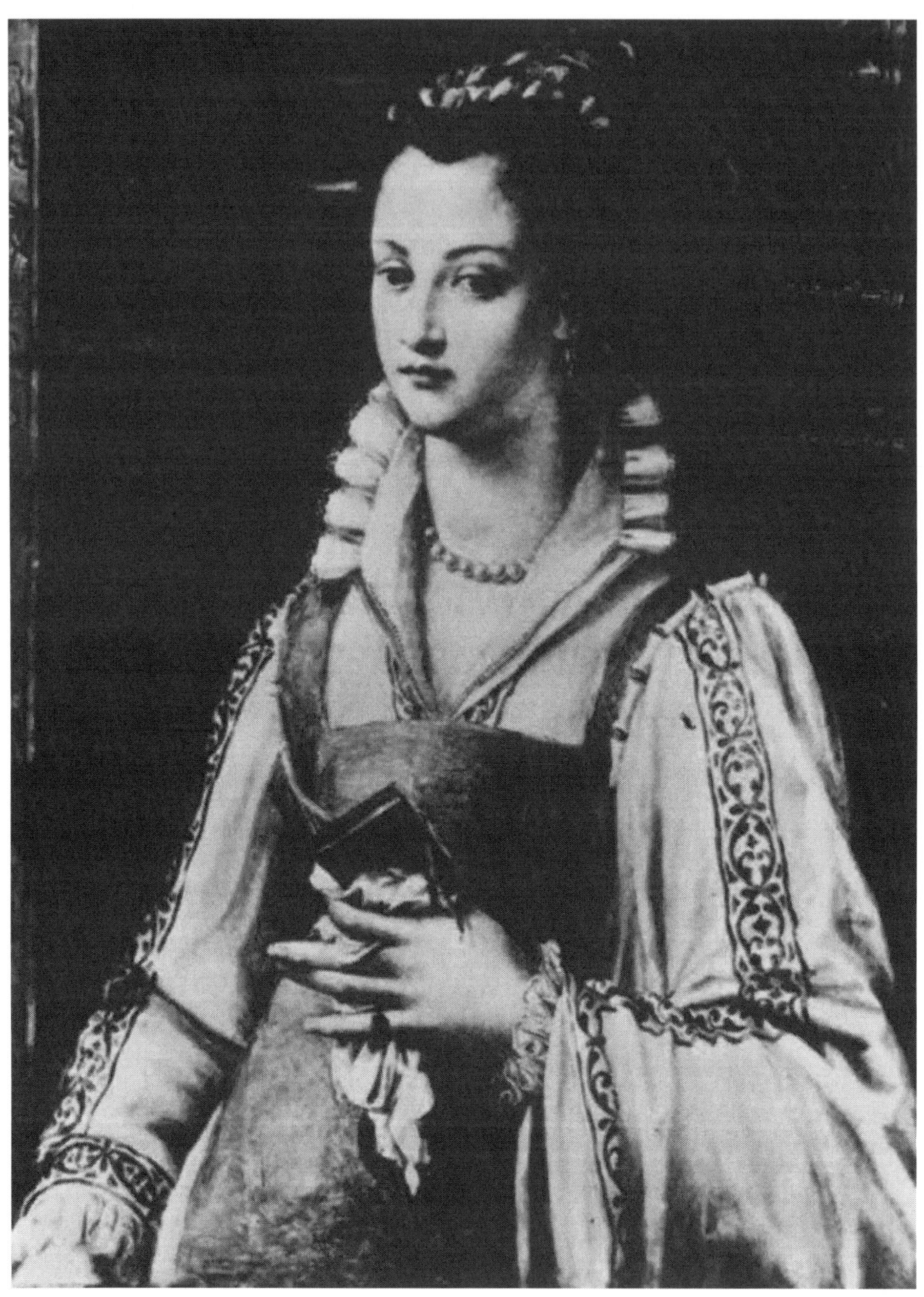

Figure 58 After Francesco Brina (?) *Eleonora ('Dianora') di Don Garzia di Toledo di Pietro de' Medici*, late 1572. Oil on panel, 86 × 70.5 cm. Private collection, Florence.

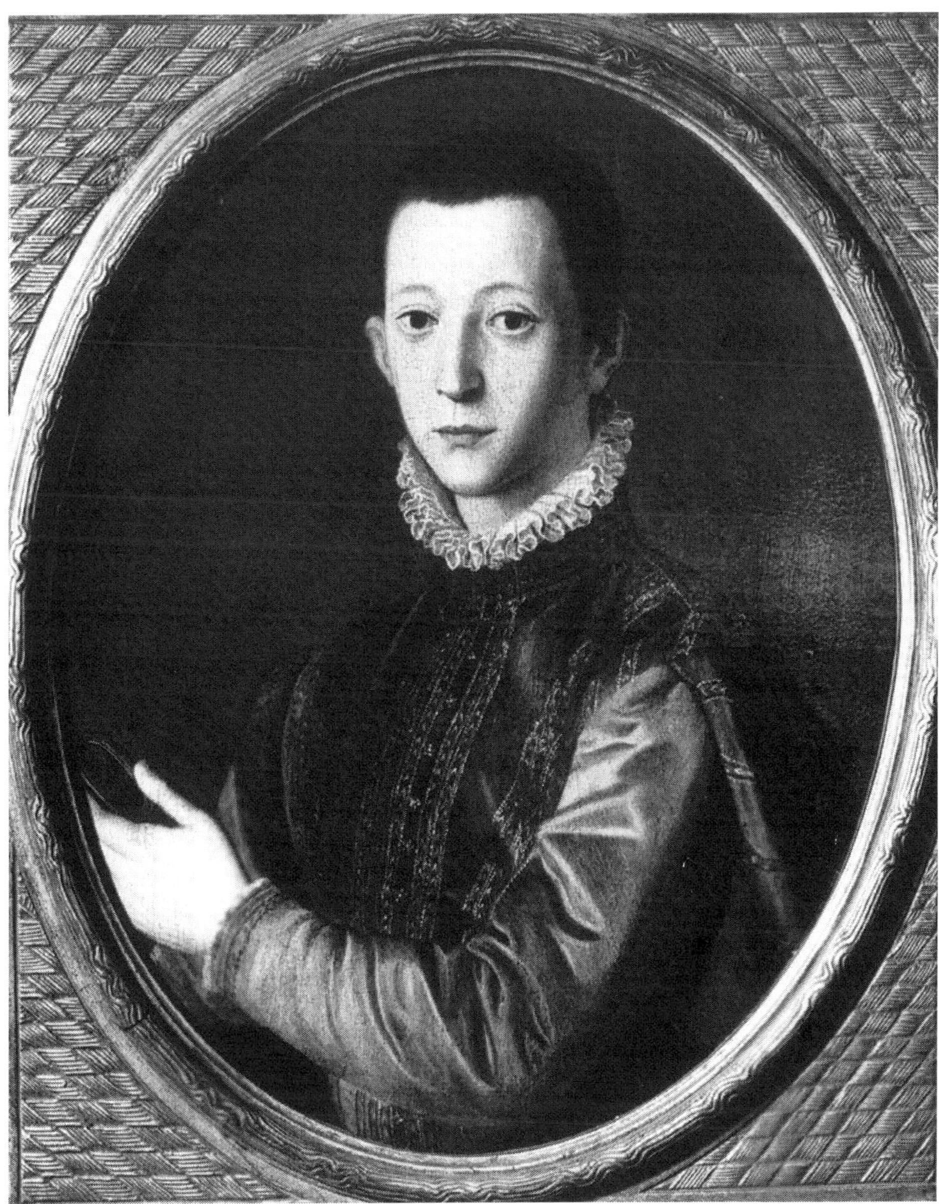

Figure 59 Alessandro Allori, *Pietro de' Medici with a Miniature*, circa 1571. Oil on panel, oval, 67.5 × 52 cm. Private collection. (Formerly Sotheby's, 7 June 1978, lot 6.)

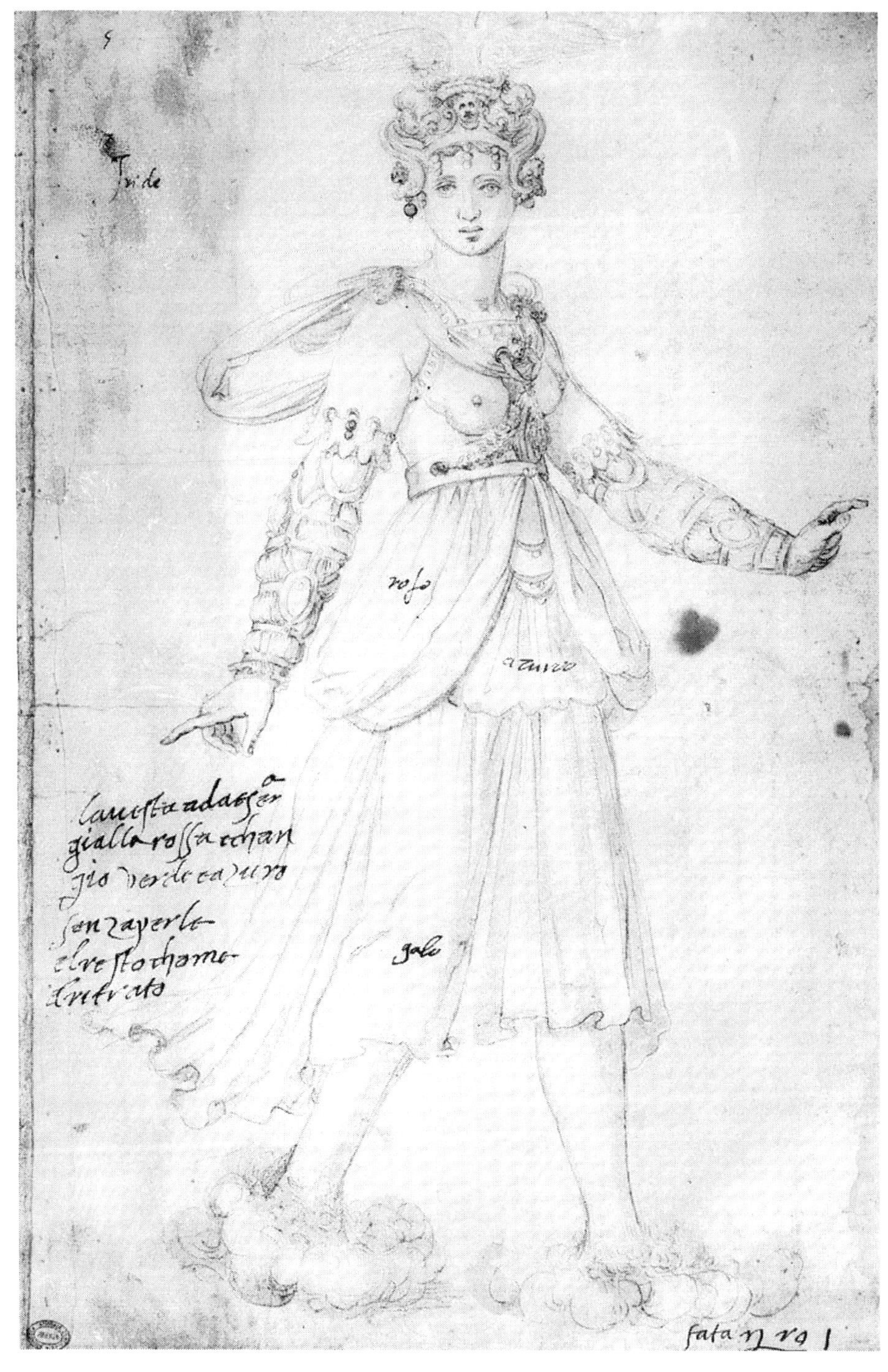

Figure 60 Alessandro Allori, *Iris*, 1565. Black chalk, heightened with watercolour, on paper, approx. 45 × 30 cm. Florence, Biblioteca Nazionale Centrale, Ms. Pal. CBIII.53, I, f. 115.

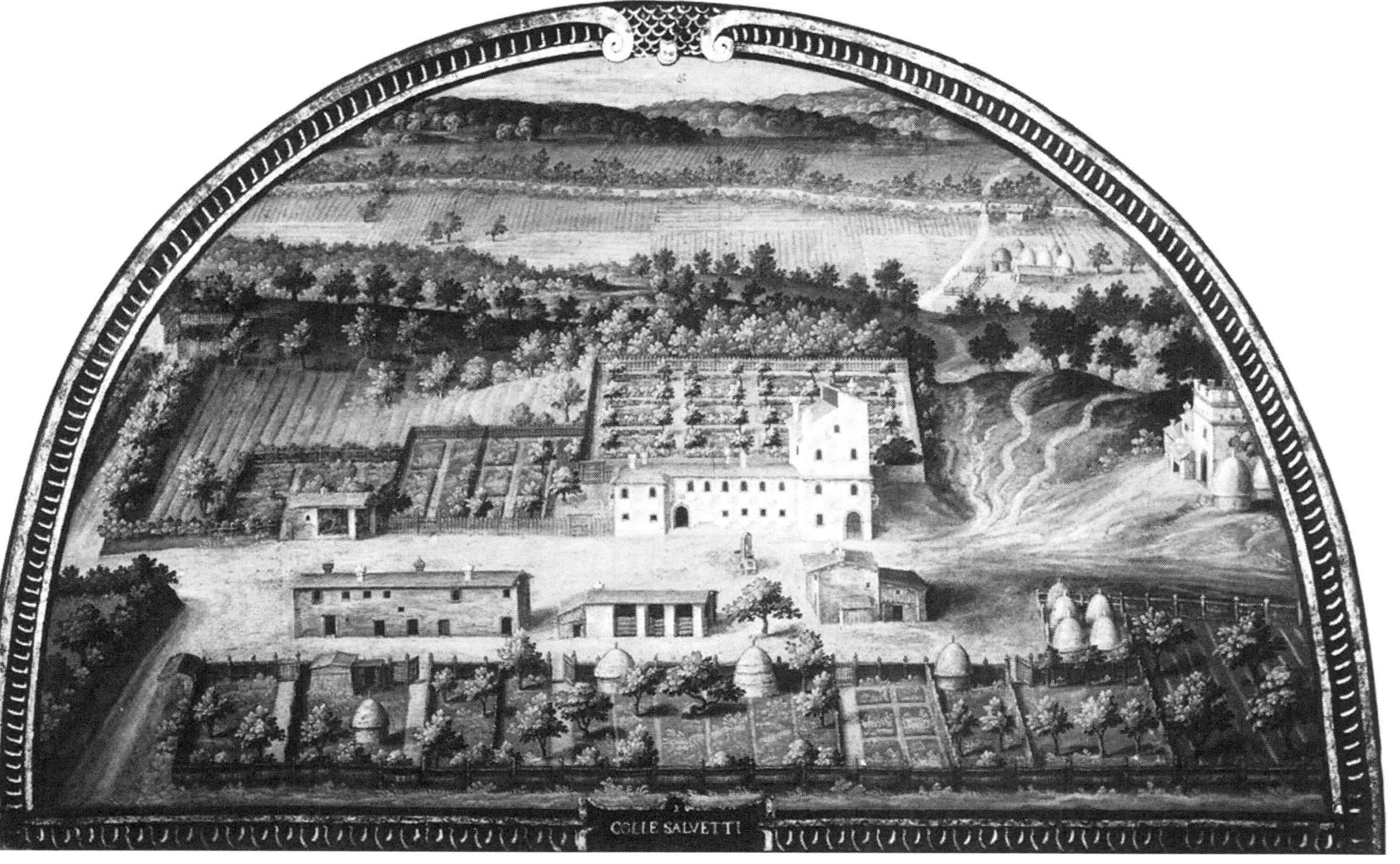

Figure 61 Giusto Utens, *Villa Medici, Collesalvetti*, 1599. Tempera on canvas, 144 × 235 cm. Florence, Museo Topografico 'Firenze com'era.'

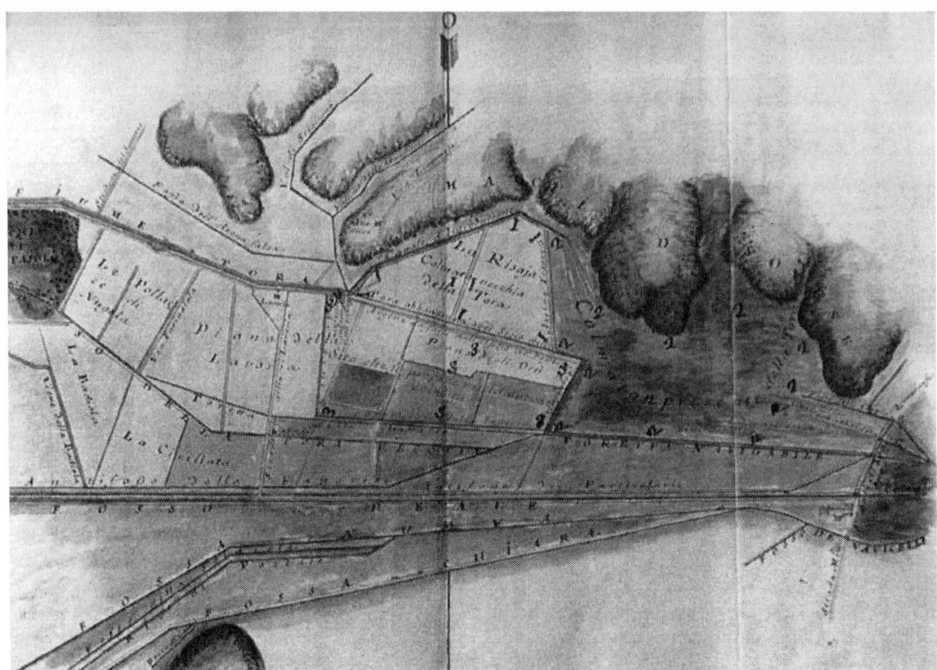

Figure 62 Angiol Maria Mascagni, *Irrigation Plan for the Tora at Collesalvetti*, 14 April 1756, marking the path to the Badiola and holdings (left), and the road to the Villa Medici, Collesalvetti (centre) and dependencies, 18th century. Archivio di Stato di Firenze, Regie Possessioni, f. 1350, ins. 17.

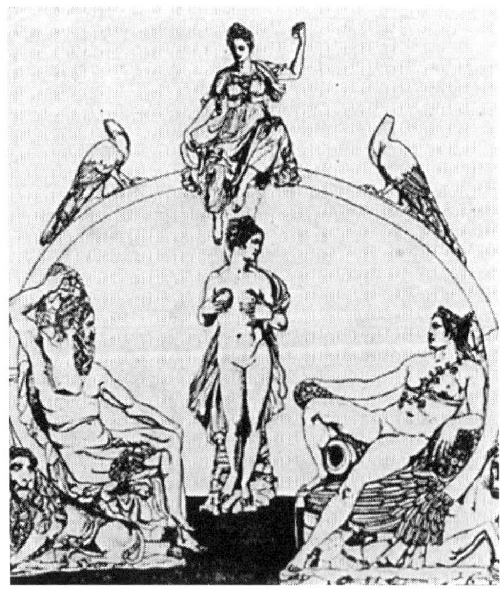

Figure 63 Bartolomeo Ammannati, *Juno Fountain*, circa 1565. Reconstruction by Detlef Heikamp.

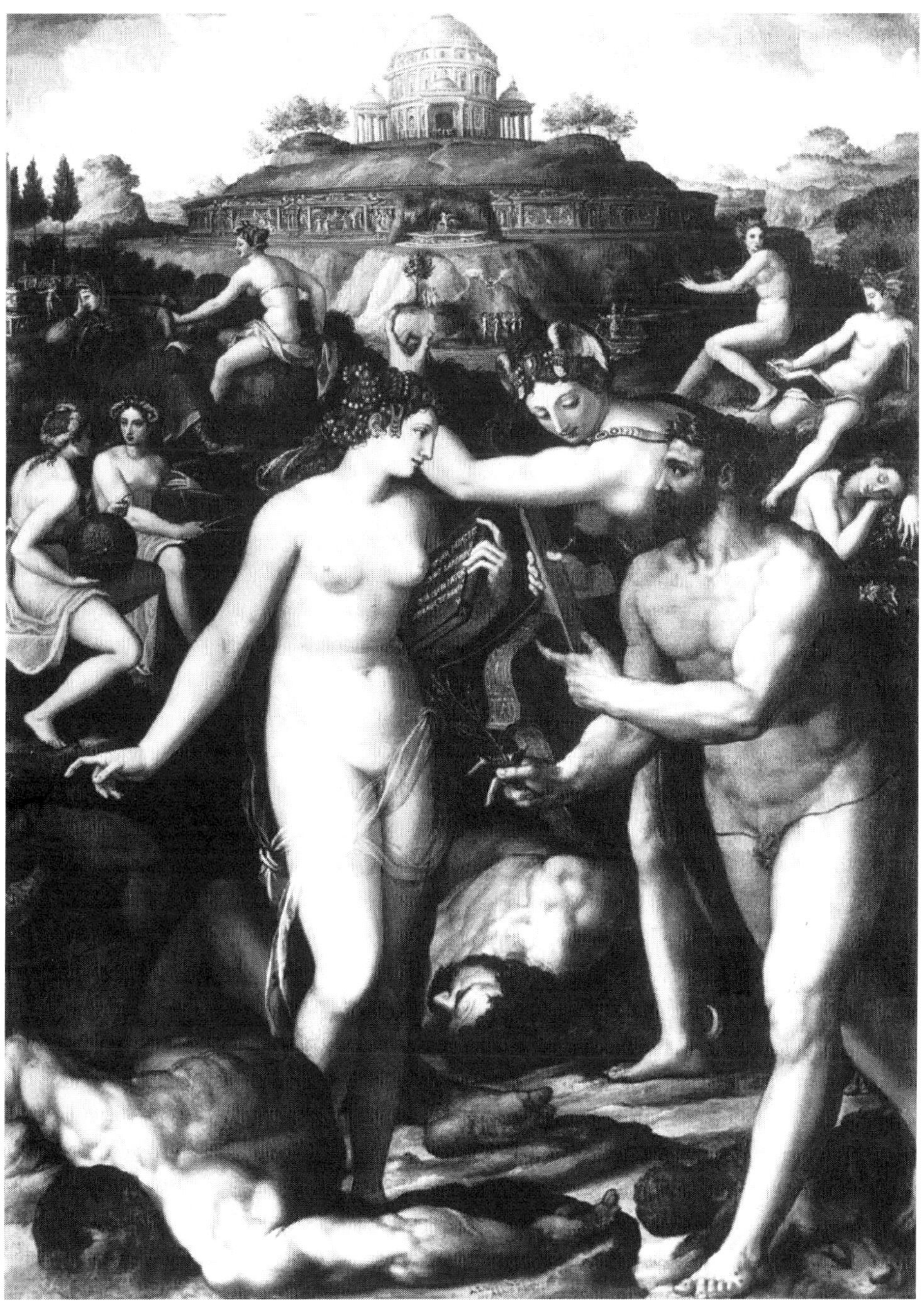

Figure 64 Alessandro Allori, *Hercules Crowned by the Muses*, 1568. Oil on copper, 37 × 27 cm. Galleria degli Uffizi, Florence.

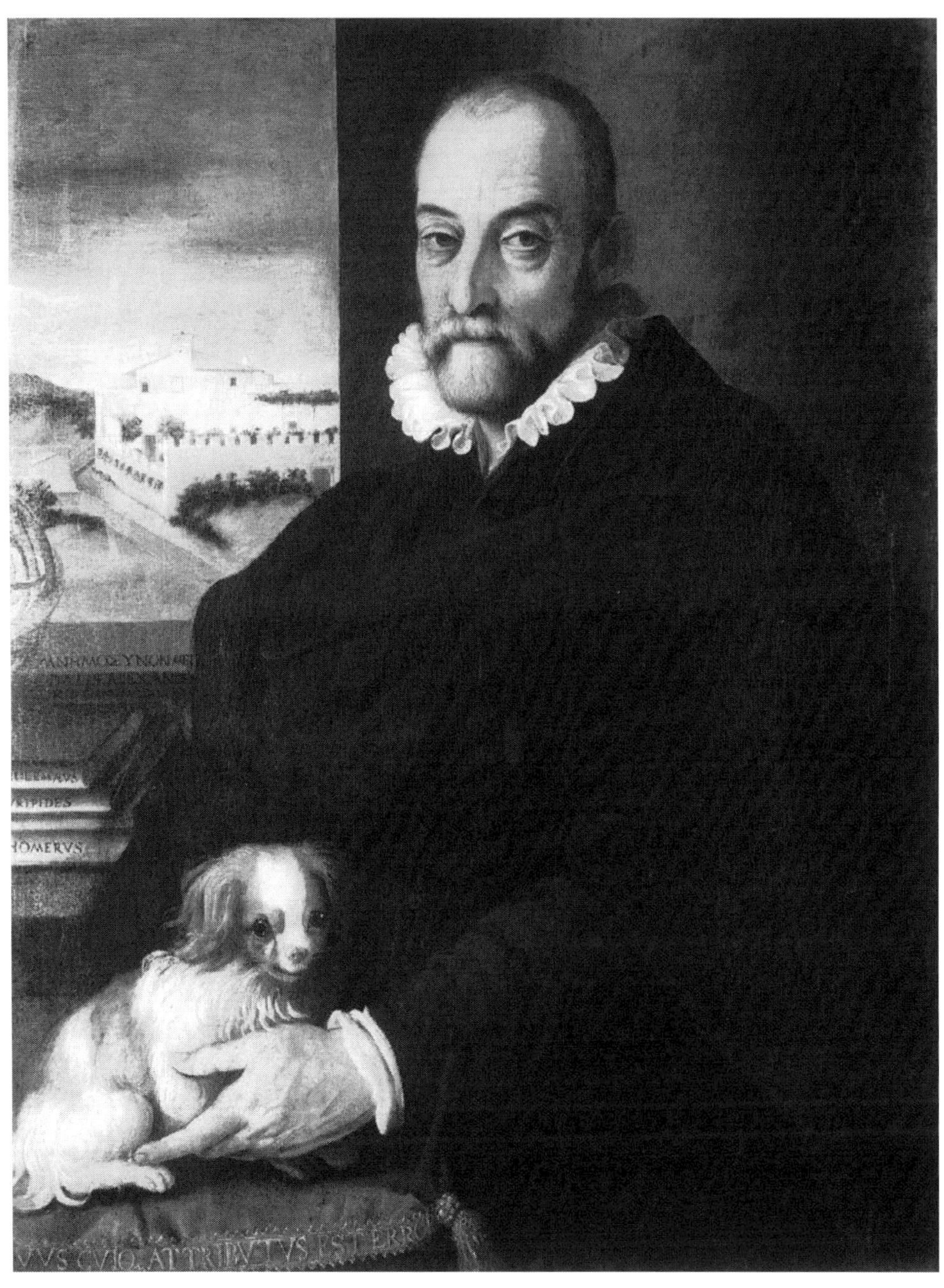

Figure 65 Anonymous, *Alessandro Allori*, or Alessandro Allori, *Self Portrait*, 1580. Oil on panel, 95 × 70 cm. Private collection. (Formerly Christie's, 14 May 1971, p. 11, cat. no. 18.)

during those years in promoting Counter-Reformation directions in the city.[46] By
1565, Allori had become one of the foremost artists in Vasari's group of Counter-
Reformation renovators in the churches of Florence.[47] He had been court portraitist of choice to Cosimo's children, dating from about 1557 and before his return to
Florence from Rome in 1560. Stylistically he breaks from Bronzino's high-manner-
ist portrait style and ushers in a more pragmatic mode. This is more readily traced
in his images of the brilliant but tragic Isabella de' Medici Orsini, which were
made throughout the remaining years of Cosimo's reign.

They were to be years of further, crippling family losses.

Damnatio Memoriae: Isabella de' Medici Orsini, 'La stella di casa Medici'[1]

Wit, beauty and talent made her conspicuous among all the women of the day, and she captivated every heart except her husband's. Speaking Spanish, French and Latin fluently, a perfect musician, singing beautifully, a poetess and *improvvisatrice* by nature, Isabella was the soul of all around her, and the fairest star of the Medici.[2]

The contrast between the gifted Isabella and the unfortunate Lucrezia could scarcely be greater. As a child she excelled intellectually, was versed in Virgil and Homer, and was vivacious to a fault. Among ducal daughters her future was essentially bound up in territorial acquisition and the consolidation of power when she was formally betrothed to Paolo Giordano Orsini on 11 July 1553. She was then almost eleven.[3] Paolo was scion of one of the mightiest baronies in Italy: based in Rome, it counted several popes, statesmen, and renowned *condottieri* to its credit. The Orsini were allied with Venice, had been favourites of Leo X and Clement VII, and had vitally contributed to the strengthening of Rome and the entire peninsula. Vast territories north of Rome were in their power, including the independent county of Pitigliano, which involved them in constant border disputes with Siena. As Cosimo had his sights set on Sienese conquest, this alliance promised territorial security and renewed historic links between the two families.[4]

The Duke's obligation to rise to the occasion to cement Medici interests with one of the most august baronies in the peninsula and to bless the marriage of his adored daughter was expressed in a munificent dowry of 50,000 gold ducats and more than 5000 ducats in jewels from his purse. In today's currency, this would amount to about \$20 million.[5] Isabella and Paolo were married in June 1558. When Lucrezia and Alfonso's wedding followed in July, Orsini bore the full expense of the elaborate football game in the Piazza Santa Maria Novella to celebrate the two alliances with the Medici. Courtiers, pages, valets and servants appeared in lavish livery, with onlookers filling a temporary amphitheatre.[6] His gesture was prophetically grandiose and extravagant.[7] The Orsini marriage was officially consummated at the Villa Medici, at Poggio a Caiano, on 17 September 1558, Isabella having completed her sixteenth year.[8]

Orsini was ennobled by Cosimo's ally, Pius IV, in 1560. In gratitude for the duke's crucial role in his recent election, Pius raised the immense, lucrative, feudal

Orsini Principality of Bracciano to the status of duchy, and the Orsini *contea* of Anguillara to a marquisate for future, firstborn Orsini sons. All of these honours did nothing to move the young duchess to be domiciled on Orsini estates. Because of his military reputation after the war between Paul IV and Spain, Paolo was in demand by the Spanish and papal courts, leading to frequent, prolonged absences. Isabella resolutely remained at her father's court throughout the eighteen years of her marriage and became the hub of its cultural life.[9]

Catastrophic family losses had followed Maria's and Lucrezia's deaths. Late in 1562, Giovanni, Garzia, and Eleonora died within three weeks of each other. Bereft of Eleonora and four of his adult children, Cosimo lavished unquestioning love and wealth on Isabella, his remaining daughter, until his death in 1574. For her part, she assumed the role of consort to Cosimo, organizing feasts, recitals, balls, and other court celebrations.[10] She brought a vivacity and cultural lustre to the Medici court that ushered it into its second phase of development, as a flourishing centre for music, literature, and intensely patriotic linguistic endeavours centred on the codification of vernacular Tuscan as the official language of Italy.

Isabella's wit and brilliance were magnetic. ('Non lascia mai vivere con quella sua vivacità, che è in lei natia,' reported Francesco Susena, a retainer of Alfonso d'Este.)[11] The young Orsini spent prodigally. They lived in great pomp, maintaining ostentatious households in the old Medici palace, the Antinori palace, the Villa Baroncelli (Poggio Imperiale), and later at Pisa. By 1564 Isabella's enormous dowry was gone, Cosimo was forced to honour a staggering shortfall in household expenditures, and Paolo was forced now to go on campaign to repay their debts. It became a recurring pattern.[12]

The calamitous tragedies that had struck the family must have deeply shaken Isabella's 'native' vivacity. Nevertheless, she met the ensuing demands on her strength to rally her family and maintain the ducal household with courage and resilience. Following Cardinal Giovanni's death, Cosimo's able son, Ferdinando, was made cardinal by Pius in 1563 at fourteen; he departed for Rome to occupy the place in church politics that had been Cardinal Giovanni's destined preserve. This left Francesco, Cosimo's reclusive heir, and two young children, the deeply troubled Pietro and their cousin, Eleonora's Spanish niece 'Dianora,' who had been raised at the court from infancy. They were only eight and nine years old when Eleonora died. It is a tribute to Isabella that she rallied to act as surrogate consort to her father, conducting his affairs and directing Pietro and Dianora's upbringing.[13] In 1565 she supervised the protracted extravaganza planned for Francesco's wedding to Giovanna of Austria. Above all, she enjoyed Cosimo's absolute confidence and trust.[14]

Isabella was the emotional mainstay for the family.[15] As a result, Paolo was obliged to return to Tuscany to see his wife, an arrangement on which Cosimo persistently dissembled – and which, no doubt, suited his purposes. Her life as a young wife can be only lightly sketched. She had several children, but their identities, except for the future Duke Virginio Orsini and his sister Leonora, are uncertain. Born in 1560, Leonora survived to adulthood and was a musician.[16] Another daughter, born in 1564, died in childhood.[17] (It was around this time that Isabella began a protracted love affair with Paolo's cousin, Troilo.) A girl referred to as

Francesca in Cosimo's will was perhaps born in 1568.[18] After Isabella briefly visited Bracciano following her father's coronation in Rome as Grand Duke of Tuscany on 13 March 1569, she returned to Florence. Orsini departed again on campaign; he would distinguish himself at the Battle of Lepanto in 1571.[19] A daughter born in 1571 died one month before the Orsini heir, Virginio, was born in 1572, and another daughter as born around 1576.[20]

Cosimo was known to readily 'duke and unduke' himself at whim ('si inducava e si sducava a suo piacimento') with courtiers.[21] Towards Isabella he was, however, deeply indulgent, and his love was repaid with unwavering loyalty.[22] She was a wise, sympathetic mediator when Cosimo married Camilla Martelli in 1570, a morganatic match that displeased his family and incensed Cardinal Ferdinando.[23] (Her tolerance of Francesco's mistress, Bianca Cappello, is also recorded.)[24] It was at Isabella's table that the first of two incapacitating seizures overtook the duke in 1571, leading to gradual paralysis and death in 1574.[25] He had jokingly warned her that he could not live forever. ('Isabella, io non ho a vivere sempre.')[26] Bereft of his protection, she survived him by only two years.

During her lifetime, considerable notoriety attended her name. Her escapades in the popular, new-fangled vehicle of the age, the coach, caused one outcry:

> At that time [1565] there was a big increase in Florence of a great number of coaches, particularly at night, [so] that there was then a rumour that seemed to spread all over Florence that the Lady Isabella, daughter of the Duke and wife of Lord Giovan Paolo Orsini who, after coaches leave the palace, of which there were four, spent close to two hours inside hers, singing, shouting, and whistling so that they seemed as many demons; she with young men, not considering anything else, creating scandal.

Isabella was then twenty-three, about the time when her liaison with Troilo Orsini had begun. Flouting of the traditional exclusiveness and isolation of women of the court would cause outrage in any event. Compared to the usual means of transport of aristocratic women by litter, a coach provided privacy and a venue for intimate trysts. Its destination could be dictated by its passengers at will, putting its occupants in contact with street life. This would endanger the very aura of exclusiveness and privilege so carefully nurtured by Cosimo and Eleonora for the early ducal court. But darker, spurious, and outrageous accusations of incest, abortion, and infanticide were routinely made by enemies against Cosimo and his daughters.[27]

Isabella's suspicious death in July 1576 at the age of thirty-four took place during a visit to the new Medici villa at Cerreto Guidi, probably designed by Bernardo Buontalenti for Cosimo in 1566, to provide a country retreat for her close to Pisa.[28] Her twelve-year-long liaison with Paolo's cousin, Troilo Orsini di Monterotondo, had finally become too public a scandal for the Medici and Orsini to support. The couple was deeply in love, and some of her passionate but decorous letters to Troilo are signed 'Your Lordship's slave forever' ('Schiava in perpetuo'). Both Isabella and Troilo paid for their indiscretion with their lives.[29] A year after her murder in 1576, Troilo was murdered by Francesco's henchmen in Paris, where he had been sheltered by Queen Catherine de' Medici.[30] These events shocked contemporaries and promoted Isabella to legendary status for generations in novels, theatrical plots, and opera, all hinging on her alleged affairs, her murder by her long-philandering husband, and his subsequent notoriety.[31]

Sadly, a seeming *damnatio memoriae* on Isabella by the Medici, pan-European myths surrounding her untimely end, and her notoriety – in its extreme forms due to anti-Medicean libels – all conspired eventually to obscure her genuine contribution to Tuscan scholarship and the arts.[32] Some hitherto unidentified portraits presented here may help to shed light on her role in the vanguard of literary taste, as does her patronage of composers and descriptions of her in madrigal texts, eulogistic poetry, and musical dedications to her by contemporaries. It is in these contexts that her decorum in portraiture may be better understood.

The Portrait of *Isabella de' Medici Orsini with Her Son Virginio*

The dearth of portraits of Isabella so puzzled Langedijk that she suspected a *damnatio memoriae* against her.[33] Here, two exceptionally fine portraits of her from life by Alessandro Allori are newly documented (pls. 11 and 12). It will be shown that these are related to portraits of Isabella already documented by Langedijk, and proposals will be made to locate the newly discovered *Isabella*s in this study within the chronology of Langedijk's existing Isabella portrait series.

The starting point for any proposed new adult portrait identification of Isabella is the small, crudely painted portrait inscribed *ISABELLA/DE MED.* (fig. 46), one of the Schloss Ambras set of small Medici portraits sent by Duchess Giovanna of Austria to her brother, Archduke Ferdinand, in Vienna in 1587, eleven years after Isabella's death.[34] The inscribed Ambras version is evidently derived from a late portrait of Isabella dated 1574, painted when she was in her early thirties (pl. 11, three-quarter-length, and fig. 48, a bust-length version of the latter), securely identified here. Some portraits already included in Langedijk may also be confidently linked to an earlier, youthful *Isabella with a Dog* in a private collection (pl. 12), evidently painted in the early 1560s, and introduced in this study. The expanded *Isabella* group also allows insight into Allori's mature portraiture after 1560, when Counter-Reformation pronouncements on religious art continued to inform this secular genre, too.

Isabella's distinguishing features may be described from the two secure, inscribed portraits of her in Langedijk's Isabella series, the Stockholm adolescent portrait (fig. 32) and the mature Ambras portrait of her (fig. 46). She had curling, dark-blond hair; a high, domed forehead with slight bony prominences at the temples; well-arched, slightly quizzical brows; very large, round, dark eyes; a large 'Roman' nose; a short upper lip, and a slight double chin. In spite of the crude rendering of the mature Ambras version, an impact of staunch individualism and intelligence is strongly conveyed.

The three-quarter-length double portrait of a woman with a little boy acquired by the Wadsworth Atheneum Gallery, Hartford, Connecticut, in 1988 (pl. 11 and detail, fig. 47) matches the inscribed Ambras *Isabella*.[35] Dated 1574, it is securely identified here as *Isabella de' Medici Orsini with Her Son Virginio*. The portrait has been attributed to Allori, but the provenance of its ownership is unhelpful.[36] A companion version in short-bust format – also of mysterious provenance – is in a private collection (fig. 48).[37] This is so exceptional in finish but close to the three-quarter-length Wadsworth Atheneum version that it seems probable that Allori painted the two almost simultaneously, with the bust-length portrayal painted directly from life.[38] A copy of that bust-length version also exists in the Casa Vasari, Arezzo; it does not have an embroidered carnation on the linen *camicia* and has less elaborate hair jewellery. Its execution exhibits less finesse and a somewhat blunter delineation of Isabella's features, and it may be by Allori's assistant, Giovanni Maria Butteri (1540–1606).[39]

In the *Portrait of Isabella with Her Son Virginio* of 1574, Isabella appears as a mature woman of about thirty posed with a boy of about three to the right of the panel. She looks directly at the viewer, but the boy glances out to the right. Her left arm is curved about his shoulder, and she clasps his right hand in hers. His left hand gestures towards his mother. A sumptuous green taffeta drape balances and enlivens the composition, in which Isabella is posed off-centre, and a duller tone of green is adopted for her dress. Reddish-gold stripes on her sleeves alternate with silver, and are elaborated with gold and silver *passementerie*, a type of embroidery native to Florence.[40] The silver bands are embroidered with Florentine lilies. A deeply ruffled collar frames her face and opens at the breast to reveal a *camicia* embroidered with a red carnation, symbol of fidelity.[41] It reverberates with import for the presence of Virginio, the Orsini heir, whose legitimacy is conveyed through this strong compositional accent. Red is the armorial colour common to each house, and Medici and Orsini bloodlines are combined in him. Isabella's costume combines the Medici armorial green and red, while her sleeves carry the Orsini gold and silver.[42] The child – who so touchingly resembles his mother – is dressed in the Orsini gold, confirming his individual identity to posterity as Virginio, the Orsinis' only son, born in 1572. Allori adopted this disguised heraldry from Bronzino, and manages here to convey crucial messages of legitimacy, merged bloodlines, and dynastic promise.[43]

Medici armorial references are extended in Isabella's magnificent jewellery. In the gold and pearl necklace, each segment is inset with six pearls to prompt association with the six *palle* of the Medici arms. The clasp of her weighty gold *cintura* is inlaid with a bust of a young woman wearing a yoke, an attribute Cesare Ripa supplied for *Matrimonio*, *Obedienza*, and *Patienza*.[44] Yoke symbolism was rooted in classical and Christian marriage lore: in Statius's *Silvae*, the bride is urged to submit to the husband's yoke.[45] Because of its balance of two equal halves the Roman version symbolized harmony.[46] Such emphasis on Isabella's fidelity and wifely perfection scarcely tallies with her long-standing liaison with Troilo and rumours of her many affairs, but it underlies the essential purpose of official portraiture, to conjure an exemplariness that extolled the subject's rank and office. Isabella's presentation as chaste, dynastic mother perforce declares the legitimacy of the Orsini line. (It was not in doubt – Virginio was apparently conceived during Orsini's furlough after his signal triumphs at Lepanto in 1571.)[47] Leo X's 'Medici' yoke would be evoked, too – and would be again in designs for Cardinal Ferdinando's new villa in Rome in 1588, where the yoke is accompanied by Leo X's motto, *SUAVE*, and a papal tiara.[48] Again, Medici identity is consistently stated in women's portraits to emphasize the ancestral past and papal power.

In her left hand, Isabella's flowing, transparent kerchief embroidered in gold carries a slightly marred inscription, '*ANNUS ETATIS/SUAE.../P.A.D. MDLXXI-III*,' lettered in majuscule (fig. 47). In 1574 she was at the peak of her influence in the court, and she is depicted here at that moment, when her father was still alive – before 21 April 1574. (She would have worn mourning clothing in the months that followed his death.)[49] The visible gap in the inscription after the words *ANNUS ETATIS SUAE* is curious. This was invariably followed by the sitter's age.[50] Isabella died in 1576, and her age – thirty-one until August 1574 – would suggest that the letters XXXI were inscribed, but must have been obliterated inside the borders of the inscription. This element is so precisely excised – the borders are undamaged – that the obliteration can only have been deliberate. Virginio was not inserted later, when a date might have been adjusted, as the compositional organization, with Isabella placed slightly to the left of the swirling, green taffeta drape, accommodates the little boy and balances the overall design, as do the serpentine rhythms of their mutual gestures of affection.[51] The obliteration is provocative, but until the panel is X-rayed, speculation on it must be inconclusive. Evidence at the moment suggests an attempt to obfuscate a vital clue to Isabella's individual identity and her place in history.

Allori's *Isabella with Her Son Virginio* is a propagandistic statement of rank and privilege. Even without the confirmation supplied by the Ambras face of 1587 (fig. 46), the sumptuousness and high quality of a double portrait entirely by so important an artist as Allori at this time would be telling. By 1574 he had worked on the decorations for Michelangelo's funeral (1564), Francesco and Giovanna's wedding (1565), and Francesco's *Studiolo* (1571–3). He was a moving force in Cosimo's Accademia del Disegno, and read the oration to its members on Bronzino's death in 1572. (Bronzino had been made Consul of the Academy that year.)[52] Allori was responsible for decorations for the grand duke's solemn funeral in 1574 and, on Vasari's death that year, he assumed the unchallenged role of premier artist to the court for which he had been groomed by Bronzino from childhood.[53] The *Isabella with Virginio* is one of his most magnificent portraits, painted as Cosimo's reign drew to its close. Its official status is manifest: it is sumptuous in conception, majestic in setting and expression, important by virtue of its subject and author, and generous in size; and there are several versions extant (fig. 48, its bust-length prototype, a copy of the latter in the Casa Vasari, and one in the Ambras set [fig. 46] inscribed with her name).

As a dynastic statement, Allori's *Isabella with Virginio* does, of course, recall the *Eleonora with Giovanni*.[54] Bronzino's ability to infuse exquisite grace and to elevate his subject was supreme, but his rarified, iconic air had become outmoded in the growing climate of rationalism and naturalism now promoted at the Florentine court. Hagiographic overtones do not inform this composition. The easy gracefulness with which Isabella holds the kerchief owes nothing to Bronzino's Petrarchism, but responds to a current imperative to manage the body and its movements in a civilised manner.[55] Bronzino's *Eleonora with Giovanni* represented the Petrarchan ideal – iconic, unattainable, removed, abstracted, and exquisitely elevated above the common weal. There, a shining-eyed Giovanni entreats our adoration of his nearly beatified mother, as an infant Christ might for Mary. Steeped in the Counter-Reformation ethos of emotiveness, clarity of expression, and telling gesture, Allori instead makes Isabella and Virginio's association an earthly one. Idolatry had no place in the Tridentine philosophy of self-presentation. Bronzino's petrifaction of form and pallor of skin has been abandoned; Isabella's face is flushed with rosy health. Absent, too, is Eleonora's enthroned, artificial rigidity. Isabella's chastity is suggested through the symbolic carnation and yoked *Matrimonio* on the clasp of her jewelled girdle.

All suggestion of transcendence or Neoplatonic ideology is absent now. Lighting is noticeably logical, unlike the coexistent diurnal and nocturnal effects in the *Eleonora with Giovanni*.[56] Here, the enveloping space is ours, the child's, and Isabella's all at once; a lower perspective places the viewer within it, and lighting gives clarity to palpable realism.[57] Neither pose, gesture, perspective, nor setting elevate Isabella beyond mortal existence, and Allori's composition is markedly uncluttered compared to his *Giulia* (figs. 37 and 40). Now in his artistic maturity, he speaks for a new era of circumstances and contexts.

The later sixteenth century witnessed gradual abandonment in the arts of the poetic, Neoplatonic saturation of Cosimo and Eleonora's court and its satellite academy. Instead, Isabella's presentation as a reassuringly earthly matron parallels a growth in literature in the late sixteenth century of anti-*petrarchismo*. The great poet's model for centuries – the aloof, unnattainable, chillingly exquisite 'Laura' – no longer dominated poetics: Ercole Tasso voiced the new pragmatism in his *La Virginia* when he vowed that his verses would *not* revolve around the cruelty of a beloved's cold remove – or the destruction of the poet's peace of mind. Contrary to Petrarch's Laura, Virginia is nurturer of his soul and spirit, *and* of his body.[58] The clarification of pictorial space in the Hartford *Isabella* is a tendency that has been linked to the growth in interest in the physical sciences in the post-Tridentine period, which was thought, consciously or unconsciously, to have served the post-Tridentine demand for less artfulness and obfuscation in painting.[59] The *Isabella with Her Son Virginio* is an uncomplicated presentation of a woman of high rank. Her gaze is candid. Virginio seems to have spontaneously run into her outstretched arms, and his backward gaze suggests a return to other pastimes, unlike the entreating Christ-like child so elegantly esconced behind Eleonora's gown. The expressive effect of the Hartford *Isabella* is one of gravity without metaphysical overtones, of an alert intelligence and sensibility dispassionately rendered. One senses that the real Isabella is truthfully – even prosaically – recorded.

Allori's *Isabella with Virginio* and the Tridentine Philosophy of Portrayal

Tridentine activity initiated in Florence during Pius IV de' Medici's reign fulfilled the premise of Allori's *Giulia de' Medici* (fig. 37) of directness of expression and didacticism. When Allori became chief assistant to Vasari in 1564 to initiate the Tridentine renovation of Florentine churches, it reinforced his position as a court artist fully in tune with the much-proclaimed alliance of his ducal patrons with the new 'Medici' papacy in Rome. The distinct changes that occur in the *Isabella with Virginio* express Allori's mature Counter-Reformation ethos with greater sophistication and economy than his *Giulia*. Clarity and accuracy were called for in the Tridentine edicts on religious art. It affected even such arts as music.

Andrea Gilio da Fabriano, vociferous critic of decorum in Michelangelo's *Last Judgment*, held in his *Due dialoghi* of 1564 that 'a thing is beautiful in proportion [only] as it is clear and evident.'[60] Vincenzo Borghini, the churchman and brilliantly erudite iconographer who worked in close partnership with Cosimo and Vasari, held fast to the same idiom, and Allori's rationalization of space and lighting, directness of expression, and less abstracted portrayals for Isabella are almost literal interpretations of this outlook.[61] Tridentine pragmatism, directness and expressive gesture infused into his altarpieces in Florentine churches were already present in his portraits of Lucrezia and Francesco (pl. 10 and fig. 43). Secular portraiture at this court had anticipated the Counter-Reformation's winds-of-change.[62]

Even Allori could not have envisaged how fanatical the official Tridentine stance on portraiture would become. Pronouncements to curtail 'lapses' in portraiture came from the See of Bologna, testily penned by its Jesuit cardinal, Gabriele Paleotti. Curbs proposed for portraiture in his *Discourse Concerning Sacred and Secular Images* reveal as much about the general status quo of mid-Cinquecento portraiture as they express about the prelate's dogmatism. Its retrospective slant is a touchstone to understanding the ethos brought to bear on court portraiture from the 1560s in the closing years of Cosimo's reign. When Paleotti emphasizes that the dignity of mature and exemplary persons must not be demeaned ('non in altre maniere poco degne di persone mature et essemplari'), he codifies the long tradition of the exemplary function of portraits.[63] Even as he holds forth on who may be portrayed, how, and to what purpose, he states a general neo-medievalism of Tridentine thought concerning the self and the body: '[It shows] no little weakness of the intellect, especially if one considers that that individual had to spend no less than two or three hours idly allowing himself to be observed by the painter, in order for him to portray a bodily form which in a small span of time will be dissolved into dust by death.'[64] Obliged to defend itself against charges of idolatry by the Reformation, the Church now held that portraits of those of high rank should not recall graven images and evoke adulation. The zealous Paleotti was warned by the Jesuit Francesco Palmio that if he asserted this notion in print he would cause offence and, bowing to expedience, Paleotti promised to make the comment more palatable for his readers.[65] His fellow Jesuits – pillars of the Inquisition – recognized that Paleotti had flown too blatantly in the face of the traditional norms for portrayal of the powerful. This reining in of his zealotry is further evidence that a fine balance of decorum was needed in the official portraiture of princely patrons. Admiration and awe were implicitly expected – indeed, entrenched – as a raison d'être in the exemplary role that this genre was believed to fulfil.[66]

Tridentine philosophy had affected portraiture throughout Europe long before Paleotti's pronouncements in 1582.[67] Paleotti's, Lomazzo's, and Passerotti's precepts of rigid social categorization, exclusion of less than virtuous subjects, and eschewing of the silly or vain (all embodiments of decorum) flooded European portraiture in the second half of the sixteenth century. Immutable rules were framed by Passerotti for distinctions of rank in portraiture (nobility, ecclesiastics, warriors, etc.). De Hollanda's treatise on portraiture, 1549, had already expounded on selectivity according to rank and virtue, and on the importance of the high-born as exemplars. What infuses late Cinquecento ideas is a rigidity of categorization and dogmatic enforcement.[68] Raffaello Borghini's outrage in 1584 against Pontormo's and Bronzino's 'offences' proves that the laity, too, were deeply affected by moralistic fervour.[69] Perhaps in response to a demand for stricter observance of propriety, Leonardo's precept, decorum, was expounded at length in Giovanni Battista Armenini's secular treatise for artists of 1586.[70] Indeed, few areas of patronage in art would be so sensitive to decorum as portraiture. As de Hollanda declared, portrait artists had long been on guard to respond to notions of 'suitability' and 'dignity' that implicitly reflected on the moral status of the persona and the exemplary role of the genre. The *gravitas* and directness of Isabella's portrayal is in accord with an ethos that was already entrenched.

Alessandro Allori's *Portrait of Isabella de' Medici with a Dog*

With Isabella's identity in the Wadsworth Atheneum Gallery panel (pl. 11) secured through the inscribed Ambras derivative (fig. 46) and made evident in symbolic references in the composition itself, other identifications devolving from it may now be made. Three more portraits supplement Langedijk's identifications for adult portraits of Isabella. The first, from a private collection, again by Allori, was known simply as the *Portrait of a Young Woman with a Dog* (pl. 12).[71] It shows a younger Isabella than the mature woman in the Hartford version. Besides the close facial resemblance, Isabella's identity is confirmed by the appearance in her hair of the same tiara seen in her maturer portrait with Virginio, composed of large gems separated by pearls. Its rubies and emeralds represent Medici armorial colours, and the tiara was possibly part of Cosimo's dowry on her marriage. The earlier portrait (pl. 12) shows alternating rubies and emeralds, separated by two pearls. The portrait of 1574 (pl. 11) and its copy (fig. 48) show that the emeralds were later replaced by rubies in the tiara's setting, supplemented by a dominant emerald at the front that accentuates the pronounced 'widow's peak' of her hair.[72] She wears the same ruby ring seen in the maturer portrait, and a *cintura* of rubies, emeralds, and pearls adds to her rich adornments and defines her high rank. As in that portrait, her dress combines the Medici and Orsini armorial colours. Her gown is of dark green velvet – a fabric then associated with sumptuousness and dignity – with touches of silver embroidery on the bodice and shoulders.[73] A gold stripe embellishes the white sleeves and the gown is worn over a reddish-gold underskirt. As in her portrait with Virginio, a red carnation (in her hand) supplies the armorial colour common to each house.[74] The pose in the *Isabella with a Dog* is almost mirrored in the Wadsworth Atheneum version, executed in 1574, but here a younger Isabella's right hand caresses the affectionate lapdog. This is an exceptionally compelling portrait, painted when Isabella was about twenty and not long married. Allori's frank observation of her features is sweetened with a softness of modelling and youthful mutability of expression missing in her mature, official 1574 portrait, where the fashionable plucked hairline of the decade heightens her forehead and sharpens the oval of her face.

The *Isabella with a Dog* also has a place in helping us understand the retroactive vision of Cardinal Paleotti as he pronounced on traditional lapses in decorum for portraiture and cautioned against worldly vanity: 'Moreover, in portraits of people of rank and dignity patrons should make sure that the gravity and decorum appropriate to their condition should be portrayed, not with little dogs or flowers or fans in hand, nor with birds or parrots or monkeys nearby.[75] The *Isabella with Her Son Virginio*, painted in 1574 when she was thirty-two, has indeed dispensed with dogs and flowers, both of which had been inserted by Allori into his *Isabella with a Lapdog* of the early 1560s.

Amusing instances abound to illustrate the widespread, sometimes even public association of dogs, fans, flowers, birds, parrots, and monkeys in amorous contexts. Birds can only be lovebirds in such environments of dalliance and lovemaking as Allori's own design for a large *spalliera* (headboard) for a tester bed. It was painted in 1572 for a Medici patron, and is now in the Bargello, Florence. Birds coexist with *grottesche* such as herms, apes, a Pan, a Flora with a cornucopia, a musician resting on a viola da gamba, *putti*, and garland-crowned male and female nudes surrounded by copious greenery. All of them play as gracenotes to enframed erotic vignettes: a *Ganymede* at the centre, flanked by a *Leda and the Swan* and a *Europa and the Bull*. The whole troupe presides over a reclining nymph.[76]

Parrots had more paradoxical meanings, as Paleotti was doubtless aware. Vasari's *Eloquenza* (1546) in her frescoed niche in the Sala dei Cento Giorni of the Cancelleria in Rome is accompanied by one, as is François Clouet's *Francis I as John the Baptist*, to align his eloquence with that of the preacher-saint. The literary Marguerite d'Angoulême, Francis's sister, was portrayed by Clouet in 1527 with a parrot perched on her finger.[77] But parrots appear in carnal contexts, too, to suggest 'parroting' of Satan's urgings to indulge the flesh, and the bird's imitative, mindless chattering also gave it currency in contexts of deceit. Its presence in Dürer's engraving *The Temptation of Adam and Eve* of 1504 mocks their 'parroting' weakness in the face of the Serpent's golden-tongued invitation to sin. As a symbol of carnal pleasure it appears in Vasari's *Adoration of the Magi* (1547). A male figure clad *all'antica*, who sports a monkey on his back and a parrot tethered to his wrist, retreats into a crypt-like opening as Balthazar's hound snarls menacingly at them.[78] The parrot is here the familiar of the ape, traditional emblem for base human lust, each hitherto shackled to humanity, and the vignette may symbolize a routing of sin, with the Nativity being a redemption from the burden of original sin and the weakness of the flesh. The parrot, seen as an unorthodox element in Veronese's *Feast in the House of Levi*, was, of course, one of the 'scurrilities' to which the Inquisition objected in 1573.[79]

Ripa's first edition appeared in 1593 and records the familiars for *Passione d'Amore* as dogs, monkeys, bears, lions, etc., following the Ovidian legend of Circe's transformation of Odysseus's men into lower animals subject to unbridled sensuality.[80] Evidently, Paleotti had trawled popular iconology for ambiguous, wayward connotations to illustrate his proscriptions. His strong denunciation of dogs, flowers, or hand-held fans suggests that there is more to small dogs in Italian portraits of women than meets the eye. Perhaps his fanatical censure of them was prompted by the association of dogs as emblems of fidelity and fecundity in lighthearted marriage celebrations. Dogs had traditionally signified faithfulness. Paleotti's reference to the 'cagnuolo' [*sic*] or small male dog describes the lapdog, the modish, pampered plaything of women.[81] In fact, a genre of portraiture can be proposed where young men appear not with the usual impressive hound, but in the act of welcoming and stroking an adulatory lapdog, surrogate for an absent *inamorata* or wife – absent, that is, from the composition, but implicitly present as the intended viewer before the frame.[82] The dog could also be legitimately present to promote sensuousness in a more serious context of desirable fertility in marriage.[83]

Dogs and fans were also part of the argot of sexual innuendo among the population at large in the late sixteenth century. Fans have traditionally allowed for some covert flirting, an 'occasion of sin' that Paleotti may have decided was within his jurisdiction. They were a commonplace in the new age of print. Cheap paper versions were printed in quantity for sporting events, spectacles, and other outdoor entertainments held in warm weather. Parallel to lampoons on printed broadsheets, they were ideal mass conveyers of parody and, perhaps for its tendency to mate indiscriminately, the dog was a handy symbol on them to mock chastity. An excited dog appears on a cheap, copperplate-printed fan circa 1600 on which doggerel verse archly cautions against carousing and prostitution – illustrated by a drunken client embraced with abandon by an importuning prostitute outside an inn. Her delighted lapdog jumps against the woman's skirts.[84]

The potential of such farcical, lascivious, humorous content on fans had long been frowned upon by the Church. Fans had been censured by Cardinal Carlo Borromeo (1538–84), a Medici associate, who had been made Archbishop of Milan at twenty-two by his uncle, Pius IV de' Medici, in 1560. As Secretary of State to the Holy See, he dominated the papal court and, as a rigorous upholder of the current Tridentine ethos, was notoriously alert to the subversive power of symbolism.[85] The dog came to symbolize an increasingly wide range of amorous contexts in later decades. In the pageant organized by Isabella's cultured son, Virginio Orsini, for Ferdinando's wedding to Christine of Lorraine in 1589, a carnival float allegorized the vanquishing of lust by expelling dogs and animals from an Arcadian scene to illustrate the institution of legitimate, conjugal love.[86]

Isabella's lapdog – hardly a blunt reference to sensuality – probably celebrates faithfulness and physical love sanctioned by marriage. In court circles, the lapdog had a traditional, decorous place in the portrayal of wives.[87] The portrait by Lorenzo Costa – probably of a former infanta of Spain – shows her fondling a lapdog (fig. 35). Her decorum suggests that it was made soon after a marriage, around 1500; it is a direct contrast to the remote, severe adolescent girl in Jean de Flandes's *Portrait of an Infanta (Juana?)* in Madrid (fig. 34), of the same subject. Older in the Hampton Court panel, she smiles slightly and her gaze connects readily with the viewer's. Her glance, and almost pert expression, may express both seigneurial confidence and high intelligence, but it also invites an intimate response. The small dog in her arms is, of course, a traditional and appropriate symbol of fidelity, which did not exclude sanctioned sexuality in marriage. Her husband was probably intended to gaze at this portrait of a wife rather differently than he would have done as a suitor to the virginal young girl in the Madrid portrait.

The *Isabella with a Dog* was painted when Isabella was a young wife. She does not look much past twenty, and the portrait is not in such sombre tones as Allori's

Giulia or the *Francesco* series of the late 1550s. Allori's palette began to brighten on his return from Rome: his *Susanna and the Elders* in Dijon (1561), shows the process well under way; the tiny *Allegory of Human Life* of about 1564 is stylistically close to his *Hercules and the Muses* (fig. 64), mentioned in Vasari's *Vite* in 1568. These two, mid-1560s examples are brilliant in tone.[88] Circumstances at court help to narrow the date of the *Isabella with a Lapdog*. She would have been in mourning for Lucrezia from 21 April 1561 to April 1562, for Giovanni and Garzia from November 1562, and for Eleonora from December 1562 until the end of 1563.[89] It follows that a date between April and November 1562, or beginning in 1564 – when Isabella was not in mourning – is very likely for the *Isabella with a Dog*, where bright reds, gold, and white contrast with her deep-green velvet dress.

The youthful *Isabella with a Dog* celebrates Isabella's married state, but it may also celebrate her fertility, and hopes of an heir. She had a daughter in 1560, but this portrait is bright in tone, suggesting that Allori worked it a little later. Official mourning for Lucrezia ended in April 1562. It is certain that Isabella was pregnant that summer – in July 1562, she suffered a miscarriage as a result of a fall from her horse. Her recovery was a lingering one. In correspondence to Cosimo in November 1562, she recorded continuing visits to make votive offerings to the miraculous *Virgin* of Santissima Annunziata, held to have been painted by an angel in the twelfth century, in hope of a recovery.[90] It was in November 1562 that extended court mourning commenced – not to speak of distress and deep grief – on the sudden deaths of Giovanni and Garzia, followed within weeks by Eleonora's from consumption. Mourning ended only in early 1564. This period between April and July 1562 allows time for the brightening of Allori's palette. It would account for a portrayal to mark a significant rite of passage such as a pregnancy, and explain Isabella's evident youth in the portrait. A careful chronological reordering below of Langedijk's catalogued portraits of Isabella to include those discovered in this study tends to confirm that the youthful *Isabella with a Dog* belongs in the early 1560s.

A Proposed Chronology for Newly Identified Portraits of Isabella

The two newly discovered portraits are the *Isabella with a Dog* (pl. 12) and the *Isabella de' Medici Orsini with Virginio*, inscribed 1574 (pl. 11). These support and expand Langedijk's identifications as follows. An unidentified woman from the Ambras set rejected as Lucrezia in Langedijk's catalogue (fig. 50 here) is the same woman as the *Isabella with a Dog*. She wears identical jewellery and jewelled *grillanda* in her hair, but with the addition of a bow to secure a short veil to it.[91] In an oval portrait at the Medici villa at Poggio Imperiale catalogued by Langedijk (fig. 51), she again wears identical jewellery to that in the *Isabella with a Dog*, also seen in the later *Isabella with Virginio*.[92] Langedijk identified a fresco portrait from Santa Maria ad Olmi, Mugello, as Isabella (fig. 49); it too matches the *Isabella with a Dog*.[93] The young *Isabella with a Dog* ranks here as the earliest adult portrait of her, but lost images of her as a younger woman did exist.[94] Langedijk identified an *Isabella with Sheet Music* – once believed to be Bianca Cappello – in a workshop panel in the Villa Medici at Poggio a Caiano, in which she holds a bifold of musical notation (fig. 52).[95] It matches an attractive, bust-length portrait now in the Palazzo Corsini, Rome (fig. 53) in Langedijk that, judging by its superior rendering and delicacy of form, was probably the prototype that inspired both the *Isabella with Music* and the *Isabella with a Fur Pelt* (fig. 54).[96] The 'freshness' of this *en buste* portrait and the older *Isabella en buste* (fig. 48) exhibits the vital spark of warmth that sets a prototype apart from copies. As proposed in other chapters, recorded instances of aversion to the arduousness of posing explain why shorter formats appear to have been usual for portraits made from life, and records from Allori's workshop do confirm that state robes and jewels were loaned for completion of a more sumptuous official portrait.[97] Possibly the workshop retained preparatory drawings or a copy of a shorter, original panel when needed for further copies – a bust-length *Isabella* by Butteri in the Casa Vasari or its prototype, the bust-length version of the *Isabella with Virginio* (fig. 48) – may have served in this capacity. Such bust-length prototypes are intrinsically important art-historically; the two *Isabella* examples (figs. 48 and 53) are as compellingly infused as the Prague *Eleonora* (pl. 5) is with the elusive *fiato* – the breath of life that Vasari owned was crucial, but lamentably missing in his own portraits.[98]

Chronological ranking to give the new *Isabella*s a place in Langedijk's listing may now be attempted. The Palazzo Corsini *Isabella* (fig. 53) in Langedijk's group – then in the Villa d'Este – probably dates to around 1565: she looks slightly older than in *Isabella with a Dog*. That *en buste* portrait also served the workshop for the rather 'wooden' *Isabella with Sheet Music* (fig. 52).[99] A second Palazzo Corsini derivative is the three-quarter-length *Isabella with a Fur Pelt* (fig. 54), also included by Langedijk. These two derivatives probably belong to the late 1560s. Finally, the *Isabella with Virginio* (pl. 11) is dated 1574 and celebrates his birth as Orsini heir in 1572.

Considering Isabella's longevity compared to her sisters, her rank, and her fame, it would be logical to suppose that her identity would be as secure for her images as other Medici women's are in their portraits. But traditional *misidentifications* discovered by Langedijk for her portraits are intriguing. The *Isabella with a Fur Pelt*, formerly in the Corridoio of the Uffizi and later in the Accademia, had traditionally been identified as Laudomia de' Medici (1518–after 1558), but costume in this panel would place Laudomia's age at over fifty, which is patently not so. The uninscribed Ambras *Isabella* (fig. 50), rejected by Langedijk as a 'Lucrezia,' matches the *Isabella with a Dog*; the *Isabella with Sheet Music*, traditionally named 'Bianca,' was simply identified with another patron of music, Francesco's mistress, Bianca Cappello. The similar fresco fragment from Santa Maria ad Olmi, Mugello, is also misidentified as Bianca, who was corpulent and was grey- not brown-eyed, as all of these are. The unusual degree of confusion in these identities – all actually Isabellas – may be explained, as Karla Langedijk proposed, by a *damnatio memoriae* enacted by the Medici after her death. Its ramifications are far-reaching in art as well as in historical myth.

Collectively this expanded group of portraits provides a range of iconography that portrays Isabella as a young wife (pl. 12), as a mother and dynastic figure (pl. 11), and – for the first time in this series of studies of Medici women – with an attribute commemorating her status as a musician-composer (fig. 52). She is always dressed and adorned sumptuously, leaving no doubt about her high rank and, in spite of contemporary commentaries on her vivacity, she is portrayed as serious and does not appear to be much idealized. In the late, official portrait, *Isabella with Virginio* (pl. 11), Allori's pragmatic recording of her fulfils the necessary *gravitas* of the genre and suggests strength of character and high intelligence.

Setting and Circumstances for Allori's Portraits of Isabella

Eleonora's death in December 1562 removed a patroness who had brought more influence to bear on Bronzino's portraiture of her family than has been previously suspected.[100] Records indicate that Isabella in turn directly patronized Allori.[101] Webs of patronage and their links to the 'Big Man' Cosimo's interests will be discussed in the next chapter, but it is clear that if Isabella commissioned portraits and took an active part in their fruition they would be expected to reflect a current, 'modern' ethos – all the more as Allori was associated with Isabella's humanist circle.[102] Interest in the esoteric strains of Varchi's writings and Cosimo's revived Ficinesque Neoplatonism had waned, to be replaced by Aristotelian pragmatism. Isabella's passion, literary criticism and philology, came to the fore, and her giftedness and erudition in music and languages was acclaimed. She principally devoted herself to preserving original writings and codifying the speech and grammar of the Tuscan vernacular. This gave her an authoritative role as leader of a widely respected literary circle.[103] Her salon drew statesmen, magistrates, and rhetoricians from the courts of Ferrara and Spain; churchmen (including Vincenzo Borghini and Simone da Fortuna of the Florentine Academy); ambassadors from the court of Urbino; humanists and philosophers such as Pier Vettori; and philologists of repute such as Lionardo Salviati and Giovan Battista Deti.[104] Satellites drawn to her also included poets, musicians, and artists of note.[105] The sculptor Giambologna, Francesco's favourite architects Bernardo Buontalenti and Bartolomeo Ammannati, and Allori were included.[106] Even the absent had enthusiastic support – at Isabella's salon, a revised version of Torquato Tasso's (1544–95) *Gerusalemme Liberata* was recited to invite judgment for the poet's enlightenment before its completion in 1575.[107] To judge by his age – about thirty – in a putative portrait, Allori probably portrayed him around this time.[108] They shared a mutual intellectual affinity: Tasso was the orthodox Counter-Reformation poet par excellence and had great appeal for this court.[109]

The *questione della lingua*, the impassioned debate being carried on across the peninsula on the nature and philological standards to be agreed upon to codify Italian, was pivotal to Cosimo's promotion of Florence as the cultural capital of Italy. It was the birthplace of Dante, with close links to Boccaccio and Petrarch – Tuscans all three. Petrarch's poetry and Boccaccio's prose had been proposed in the early sixteenth century by Pietro Bembo's disciples as the purest expression of a universal Italian language. On the other hand, Dante's unfinished treatise on language, written circa 1305, had argued for the elegant idiom of chancery and courts, which both Lodovico Ariosto (1474–1533) and Baldassare Castiglione (1478–1529) had promoted. The effort to codify Italian had continued unabated. Cosimo commissioned a new grammar of the Tuscan vernacular in 1550, and the *questione della lingua* became *the* cultural focus of the new Medici generation. Isabella's contribution is especially associated with the founding of the Accademia della Crusca ('chaff') by Francesco de' Medici in 1582, six years after her death. (Its principal mission culminated in the first great Italian dictionary, the *Vocabolario*, in 1612.)[110] Isabella's scholarly stature in this process was recorded in 1573 by Giovanni Battista Strozzi, who quotes Isabella's document of arbitration for the unequivocal use of the negative 'mai' (never), for which she cited Boccaccio's *Decameron* as her authority.[111] Literary patronage was *de rigueur* for the younger Medici generation. In 1575, Dianora, then twenty-two, is the only female patron recorded for the Accademia degli Alterati.[112]

An enormous curiosity in Aristotle's pragmatic, empirical philosophy existed in tandem with these efforts. Its Latin translations were the foundation of university-based scholasticism and arts curricula throughout the Renaissance, and interest had not abated in the Cinquecento.[113] After the arrival of the Jesuits in Tuscany at the end of the 1540s, Aristotle was adopted across the duchy as the major philosophical authority in the Order's educational institutions.[114] The implementation of Tridentine decrees on religious art in 1564 also advanced this authority. Cosimo had already acquired an 'authentic' Aristotle work for the Laurentian Library in 1548.[115] Vernacular translations from ducal presses fanned this trend: Piccolomini translated Aristotle's *Poetics* into Tuscan in 1572, following publication in Florence of several Latin versions, all directly associated with the court.[116] Decorum was debated anew in this revisionist literary climate. Vincenzo Borghini, Cosimo's brilliant humanist-iconographer, preferred Aristotle over Horace, and pronounced that, in Dante, the rules of decorum are observed with clarity and appropriateness.[117] By the last third of the Cinquecento, Aristotelianism had permeated Florentine religious and secular philosophy.

It was a sea-change that was bound to influence portraiture.[118] The essential coda of Aristotelianism was the direct imitation of nature, which explains the great difference between Bronzino's metaphysical, poetic style and Allori's artistic pragmatism. Lionardo Salviati's addresses to the Academy in 1564 and 1565, dedicated to Francesco, were symptomatic, too, of the new philosophical outlook in court circles.[119] (Aristotelian 'naturalism' also affected Isabella's other love, secular music.)[120] In recognition of artistic genius as a distinct cultural entity, Cosimo founded the Accademia del Disegno in 1563, with Vasari and Vincenzo Borghini as leading lights.[121] With Borghini as the intellectual head of its artistic endeavours and Vasari, Allori's immediate superior, as artistic director to the court, Aristotelianism was bound to affect its principal portraitist, Allori. Portraiture had enjoyed further ducal attention in the 1550s, when Cosimo, in imitation of Paolo Giovio's collection, had commissioned whole family 'trees' of portraits for circulation, from the earliest recorded Medici to his own children.[122] Rooms were frescoed by Vasari in the Palazzo Vecchio from the early 1560s in a titanically ambitious programme to proclaim Medici prestige and dynasty, and each was filled with medallion portraits of Medici past and present.[123] The duke further commissioned about three hundred portraits of popes, emperors, kings and princes, cardinals, saints, soldiers, and *letterati*. The 1568 edition of the *Vite*, which would include wood-cut portraits of each artist – an arduous undertaking for the ageing Vasari – reflects this enormous interest in a visual record of both the living and the dead.[124] An inventory of 1574 listed two hundred and twenty-eight portraits, including portraits by Titian of Charles V (1500–58), the late Hapsburg emperor, and of his son, King Philip II of Spain. Portraiture now enjoyed high status as a genre of art.

The *Portrait of Isabella de' Medici Orsini with Sheet Music*

Tridentine and Aristotelian reflections in portraiture should not, however, lure us into a delusion that life in the inner circle of the court was arcane or staid. Music was an abiding interest for the new generation of Medici, and subtle distinctions between sixteenth-century attitudes to music and those to court portraiture are illuminating. Music was a more private, intimate, and usually more ephemeral branch of art than it is today, and it exhibited fewer conventional constraints than portraiture for its time. Probably due to Eleonora's encouragement, Isabella excelled from childhood in vocal recital, improvisation, and instrumental performance.[125] This is commemorated on the *Isabella with Music*, in which she appears with a bifolded sheet of faked mensural notation (a kind of notation used to notate vocal music) in her hand (fig. 52). While not of high artistic quality, the portrait is of great art-historical interest.[126] Musical accomplishment was expected of women of the courts, but the rarity of portrayals of them celebrating this talent deserves some comment, as do the musical texts associated with Isabella herself.

Madrigal texts that eulogize Isabella are interesting for the reflections their verbal 'portrayal' of her might offer. The madrigal, the verse set to music, was *the* absorbing interest in the courts of the mid- and late sixteenth century. It had its impetus in Florence from the 1520s.[127] From the time of Cosimo and Eleonora's wedding, madrigal performances were an established feature of the court's entertainment.[128] Aristocratic women cultivated music as a social grace and, before an informed *coterie*, some sang and played with a certain professionalism.[129] The vivacious, brilliant Isabella was at the hub of Medici musical affairs, an accomplishment she would instil in her children.[130]

It was with Francesco's reign as regent from 1564 that the Medici consolidated their role as ranking patrons of music in the peninsula, a position driven by their intention to wrest even this status from the rival Este of Ferrara.[131] Isabella's role as doyenne of the court's musical circle was fully established by then.[132] Tasso's epic texts were also widely adapted for madrigals (*laude*), and were warmly received: Simone Fortuna recorded that in Isabella's house he listened to 'songs of Signor Torquato Tasso's which were divinely interpreted.'[133] It was, however, in the sphere of frankly hedonistic *poesia per musica* that Isabella was renowned – perhaps even notorious. This was a typical product of aristocratic culture, its chief characteristic being a refined voluptuousness, the erotic double meanings of the poems being delicately underlined by the music.[134]

'Naturalism' was also part of its character: musicalized images – effects such as the rise and fall of flight, audible emotional tics such as sighs, even the employment of 'blackened' notation when *notte* (night) came into a text, and erotic innuendo in musical rhythms to echo amorous passages – were typical.[135] The Petrarchan *laude* madrigals of the *Vergine bella* of the earlier court would have been outmoded in Isabella's avant-garde salon.[136] Younger, well-published madrigalists like Cipriano Rore put their own emotive stamp on secular Petrarchan lyrics from the 1550s.[137] In turn, Rore influenced Alessandro Striggio, the enormously popular young Mantuan nobleman who joined the Medici household as court musician in 1559.[138] Isabella's husband's musicians also infused new life into Florentine musical developments: through Striggio they transmitted the comical, raffish *villanesche napolitane* into the court.[139] Amorous burlesque madrigals – a genre parodying canonical Petrarchan forms – found particular favour with Isabella.[140] (Later, Tasso would denounce *burleschi* as a 'degenerate' genre that catered to 'lascivious young people.'[141] His comment echoes Cardinal Paleotti's contemporary censure of any portraiture with an amatory message, some of which also ranged from mildly suggestive to salacious.)[142]

Decorum presented in *madrigali* is noteworthy when women of the courts are its patrons and its subjects, when they pen their own versions, or when they are dedicatees. Isabella's stature in music appears to have cut across all of these categories. The Flemish *émigré* Filippo di Monte, patronized by the younger Medici as well as by the courts of London and Vienna, composed a festive madrigal for Isabella and Paolo's wedding in June 1558 that gives them equal merit and praise:

> The strongest of Rome
> Flora's wisest and most beautiful
> [Are] Paolo and Isabella.
> Heaven has joined this branch
> Who can adorn it
> With pearls, gold, and diamonds
> [Which] are nothing [compared] to the twinned virtues
> That surpass all other honours.[143]

It was the beginning of a long assocation for di Monte with Isabella. He dedicated a book of madrigals to her, and in 1600 dedicated his *Secondo libro a 7* to the younger members of the Medici court, with whom he had practised in 1566.[144] They were halcyon days, when Isabella was enjoying her ascendancy as 'la stella della Casa Medici.' Her adoring father was still in his prime and she was well established as a cultural force in the court. Di Monte's madrigal, penned in 1567, gives voice to a Roman's lament – possibly one from the Orsini stronghold – for her absence:

> Another dawn brings such happy days
> And so sweet and happy a north wind
> To beautiful Tuscany
> That Heaven openly shows
> How to rejoice with his friend Flora,
> In whose rich valley
> Frost is no longer feared
> Winter produces there grasses and flowers
> And Nymphs and Shepherds
> Weave a noble crown with her spheres.

> Istro has filled the Arno with such joy
> Which carries golden sand to the Etruscan sea –
> Only I always have damp eyes from weeping
> Because I no longer rest on that pleasing knoll
> Which raises its summit above the seven hills.[145]

Einstein hazarded that Isabella may be the 'bella Toscana' referred to here. This is confirmed by the words 'Flora' and 'l'herb'e i fiori' – one to Florence, the second to Isabella's *impresa*, the cornucopia and 'fruitful' mottoes associated with her. Bronzino portrayed her wearing cornucopia earrings in the year of her betrothal to Orsini, 1553 (figs. 32 and 33); Domenico Poggini's reverse for his 1560 *Isabella* medal featured a Ceres/*Abbondanza* under a beaming sun; Antonio Selvi's eighteenth-century *Isabella* medal reverse is inscribed '*FLORES.SIMUL.ET.FRUCTUS*' ('Fruits and Flowers Together') around a fruit-laden tree in a flowery meadow; and Antonio Pazzi's engraving of Isabella of 1761 is similarly inscribed '*FLORES FRUCTUSQUE SIMUL.*'[146] Di Monte knits together Medici and Orsini associations. 'Ch'alza la cima sopra i sette colli' refers to Rome, City of the Seven Hills; 'palle' (spheres) and 'Arno' refer to Medicean Florence. The 'nobil corona' probably refers to Cosimo's continuing struggle for a grand-ducal crown of Tuscany. (It would finally be awarded by Pius V two years later.) These metaphors echo Allori's clustered symbols in his *Giulia de' Medici* of 1559 (figs. 37 and 40), alluding to Cosimo, Augustus, and Arno.[147] Goddesses, Arcadia, and the grand-ducal crown will be found also in the *Allegory* on the reverse of Dianora's miniature (chap. 7 and pl. 15).

The composer Stefano Rossetto's output under Isabella's patronage was prolific. He dedicated two madrigal books to her, the first in 1566.[148] A second, in 1567, contained stanzas from Ariosto's *Lamento di Olimpia* set to music at her request. It has been proposed that she may have identified with Olimpia, and that the commission was meant to draw attention to her husband's abandonment of her when she contracted smallpox in October of that year. (Orsini declined to visit her, claiming that he had to take a cure for his obesity.)[149]

Other composers eulogized her.[150] One composition included in the renowned Maddalena Casulana's collection of *madrigaletti*, dedicated to Isabella, is written in a female 'voice,' and has long been identified as Isabella Orsini's:

[1] Lieta vivo et contenta	I live happy and content
Dapoi che 'l mio bel sole	As long as my handsome sun
Mi mostra chiari raggi come suole.	Shows me his bright rays, as is his wont.
[2] Ma così mi tormenta	But I'm so tormented
S'io lo veggio sparire	When I see him fade away
Più tosto vorrei sempre morire	That I would yet readily die.[151]

'Sun' (sole) was synonymous with husband/lover in these lyrics. (Erotic innuendo on dying was a commonplace in madrigals.)[152] These few surviving lines of Isabella's reflect a new development. The 'voice' is a woman's, who has moved beyond the Petrarchan unattainable, unyielding, ideal object to an assertion of herself as an earthly object of male desire.[153] This tendency towards naturalism and expressiveness in musical arrangements reflects the parallel Aristotelian 'naturalism' found in Allori's portraiture.[154]

Isabella's popular love poetry and madrigal compositions have been lost almost without trace. Possibly much of her improvised music, played on the lute and other stringed instruments, was committed to memory by contemporaries. As codes of behaviour prescribed modesty, women's contributions were rarely recorded.[155] It is surmised, too, that Isabella's poems were destroyed because they included rumour and satire.[156] A more sinister reason may arise from a Medici *damnatio memoriae* against her, discussed below.

As the bifold sheet was a format in which many composers informally circulated works, the stiffly posed *Isabella with Music* is certain to record her musical inclinations.[157] Portrayals of aristocratic 'musical' women are rare, however, and a comparison with the decorum of Domenico Puligo's (1492–1527) renowned, musically gifted courtesan 'La Barbara' provides a useful counterpoint. Barbara Raffacani Salutati was Machiavelli's beloved, cultured mistress from 1523 until his death in 1527 (pl. 13).[158] In his *Vita* of Puligo, Vasari recorded the panel, painted around 1525: '[He] painted on panel Barbara Fiorentina, famous at that time, a beautiful courtesan, and much loved by many, not only for her beauty but for her elegant manners, and particularly for being a very fine musician and divine singer.'[159] Machiavelli's ardour for 'La Barbara' is expressed in a love song inscribed by Puligo in the painting.[160]

Both Barbara and Isabella enjoyed high reputations as composer-madrigalists, but the two women are poles apart in rank and decorum. Compared to the stiffly rendered Isabella, 'La Barbara' is far more accessible to the spectator. Sumptuously bejewelled, Isabella stands in perspective from below as her hand extends the notation to view. Barbara's jewellery is modest and she gazes candidly at the viewer. Thanks to Puligo's level perspective, we 'sit' in Machiavelli's chair as an intimate of her musical circle, seemingly in direct conversation with her as she sits perusing a musical part-book. Its pages open on two compositions eulogizing mutual love, one from the *Song of Songs* ('How beautiful you are, my love, how beautiful you are and how lovely, and how lovely your voice'), the second, beneath her left hand, is the well-known 'J'ayme bien mon amy de bonne amour certaine' ('I love my friend well / With a fine and true love / Because I well know that he loves me'). Machiavelli, fifty-four when they met in 1523 – she was in her twenties – was besotted with her. Seventeen years after his death she still recalled their love.[161] Beside her, a volume of Petrarch opens to *Canzone* 213, which eulogizes its subject as of humble birth but high intellect, musical giftedness, and impeccable moral standing – perhaps not too apt a description for Barbara, who was generous with her charms! Her decorum personifies rather the role of a beloved *cortigiana onestà*, the faithful and 'decent' courtesan.[162] The portrait subtly invites physical and intellectual intimacy, just as does the lovely *Lady with a Statuette of Eros* (fig. 26), also posed at her desk in a moment of unguardedness and made visible to the loving gaze of a close intimate who is implicitly positioned 'outside' the frame.

Distinctions in societal attitudes allowed the musical creativity of 'La Barbara' to be fully acknowledged in this warm, candid portrayal. By contrast, Isabella's appearance as singer or instrumentalist could have provoked censure, so that any token of laxity is countered by her containment and stiffly formal presentation.

Also, the music is a fake, a token of her talent. Authors of conduct books held that the mere presence of female musicians in masculine gathering places inspired destructive physical passions. They were perceived as suspiciously seductive Sirens.[163] (According to Vasari, Puligo's sudden death from plague was brought about through his association with 'fast' company, musicians, and 'loose' women.)[164]

The very characteristics to be avoided in court portraiture – improvisation, spontaneity, and emotiveness, even sensuousness – were integral to musical accomplishment and now rooted in performance of the secular madrigal.[165] Court portraiture marched of necessity to a different drummer, a tradition imbued with exclusiveness, exemplariness, ancestral *virtù*, and dynastic and propagandistic overtones. Its decorum drew on sterner canons and had a more public face, and thus the *Isabella with Music*, a derivative portrait of poor quality, could not have been intended for circulation beyond her circle. Freely interpreted naturalism that could find expression in the private sphere of musical recital is not visible in any of Isabella's portraits.

Allori's unfinished *Ragionamenti delle regole del disegno* of about 1565 demonstrates his disinterest in the metaphysical.[166] He wrote no poetry, and his interests appear to have been in empirical observation expressed in his dedication to anatomy, for which he was praised by Vasari.[167] His was the new artistic philosophy and mandate of the Accademia del Disegno, a forum for theoretical and practical refinements that had the stamp of state approval.[168] His portraits of Isabella, with their steady gaze, realistic illumination, and direct recording of physiognomy, are characteristic of a new cultural ethos in the court circle, one that reflects the dedicated intellectual concerns of Cosimo's children as his reign drew to its end. He died on 21 April 1574, at the age of fifty-four. Loss of his protection was to have a profound effect on Isabella's fate.

Damnatio Memoriae and the Legend of Isabella de' Medici Orsini

Tragically, Isabella's career as leading intellectual light in the late Medici court was abruptly cut short when she was thirty-four. She died suspiciously at the Medici villa at Cerreto Guidi on 16 July 1576. Rumours of her murder by her husband because of her long liaison with his cousin, Troilo Orsini, spread rapidly in court circles, even to the Hapsburg court in Spain.[169] Her affair with Troilo began in 1564 and was even alleged to have resulted in the births of two children who were lodged in the Ospedale degli Innocenti. From 1567, Cosimo sent Troilo on protracted missions abroad, including to the French court of Caterina de' Medici. From 1574 Francesco, too, made efforts to contain the scandal, to no avail.[170] On 29 July 1576, Ercole Cortile, the Ferrarese ambassador to the Florentine court, vividly described Isabella's appalling death in secret documents to his patron, Alfonso II d'Este.[171] Their animation and immediacy suggest that he had direct knowledge surrounding the event, perhaps through household retainers:

> The Lady Isabella was strangled, having been called by Lord Paolo when she, the poor woman, was in bed. She arose immediately, and as she was in a nightgown, drew a robe about her, and went to his room, passing through a room in which the

priest known as Elicona was with several other servants; they say that her face and the set of her shoulders told that she may have known what was in store for her. Morgante and his wife were in his chamber, and Lord Paolo hunted them out and bolted the door with great fury. Hidden under the bed was a Roman Knight of Malta, Massimo, who helped to kill the lady. He did not remain more than a quarter of an hour locked in the room before Paolo called for a woman, Donna Lucrezia Frescobaldi, telling her to bring vinegar because the lady had fainted. Once she had entered, followed immediately by Morgante, she saw the poor lady on the ground and propped against the bed, and overcome by her love for her, said, 'Oh, you have killed her! What need have you of vinegar or anything else?' Lord Paolo threatened her and [urged her to] hold her tongue or he would kill her. Like the Lady Eleonora [Dianora], the lady was placed in a coffin already prepared for this purpose, and this was taken at night to Florence and placed in the Church of the Carmine and was forced open for anyone who wished to see. And it is said that there was never seen a more ugly monster. Her head was swollen beyond measure, the lips thickened and black like two sausages, the eyes open [and] bulging like two wounds, the breasts swollen and one completely split, it is said because of the weight [of] Lord Paolo who threw himself on her to kill her as quickly as possible. And the stench was so great that no one could go close. She was black from the middle up and completely white below, according to what Niccolò of Ferrara told me, who had lifted the covers, as others had done to see her. She was buried the following night in San Lorenzo.[172]

The horror of this account is outstripped only by its realism, and the lurid conclusion recalls the vilification of Alessandro de' Medici after his death in 1537, that his body had fouled and blackened the whole interior of his tomb. Probably such descriptions were reserved for those who had 'sinned': in 1536, Protestant supporters of Henry VIII's remarriage reported that his stubborn, erstwhile Queen the steadfast Catholic Catherine of Aragon's postmortem revealed her heart to be 'completely black and hideous.'[173]

Adultery by women was a blot on family honour and brought pressure to bear to make public the family's disapproval. Isabella's fate was sealed when Ferdinando raged to Francesco that her liaison was widely bruited: both Isabella and Dianora were subjects of the witty, scurrilous or derisive commentaries posted around the colossal sculpture fragment 'Pasquino,' a popular Roman gathering point.[174] It was only when the scandal became public that Orsini – who had secured a legitimate heir from Isabella in 1572 and who had long known of her twelve-year affair – acted on Medici 'outrage.'[175]

The circumstances of Isabella's 'dishonourable' demise may have had repercussions for the survival of her portraits. She is not represented in the set of miniatures on tin painted in 1553 that are copied from original portraits, to which images of the other ducal children would later be added. As noted, many counterparts of this inscribed set were circulated. One, as witness the inscribed *Isabella as a Girl* in Stockholm (fig. 32), is evidence of her portrayal when young, and although her name first appears in the 1560 inventory, it is omitted in a similar entry listing Cosimo's children in the 1595–7 inventory.[176] Allowing for her high rank, prominence, and longevity compared to her sisters, and her persistent presence in Florence with Cosimo's court as foremost figure in the city's cultural life, this hiatus is highly significant. Langedijk wondered if Isabella could have been the subject of a *damnatio memoriae* because of her conduct, which 'drove her husband to do away with her.'[177] As Grand Duke Francesco is believed to have abetted Orsini in her murder, a *damnatio memoriae* could have been instituted by him.[178]

Damnatio is not romantic fiction. The custom was established practice in Florence and throughout the courts of the sixteenth century. Grand Duke Ferdinand instituted a *damnatio* immediately on Francesco's former mistress, Grand Duchess Bianca Cappello's death, too. (They died within hours of each other in 1587.) Ferdinando – who had loathed her elevation – immediately ordered any vestige of her existence destroyed. A moratorium was declared on spoken reference to her title, Grand Duchess, and her family arms were obliterated throughout Tuscany.[179] *Damnatio memoriae* had royal currency and sanction. Images of Henry VIII's queen, Anne Boleyn, executed in 1536 on trumped-up charges of adultery, are rare in spite of Henry's prodigious patronage of ranking European portraitists such as Hornblut, and notably of Hans Holbein. Portraits of Katherine Howard, Henry's other doomed queen, are unknown. In the aftermath of their beheadings, their escutcheons were erased across the realm.[180] (Paradoxically, pursuit of an official *damnatio memoriae* is likely to have the opposite effect: Anne and Isabella would each pass into folklore and inspire literary fiction and opera.) Adultery by women often carried the ultimate penalty – death – presumably because it implicitly called into question confidence in bloodlines, the legitimacy of heirs, and succession to high-ranking titles, vast riches, and inheritances. The casting into darkness of their names served to restore family honour.

Langedijk conjectured that proof of a *damnatio memoriae* instituted against Isabella may be inferred from the extraordinary paucity of acknowledged Isabella portraits in Medici collections. Indeed, this is highly significant in light of the didactic, commemorative role expressed for portraiture by de Hollanda, and reiterated by Paleotti and Lomazzo, among others.[181] It is noteworthy also that Antonio Pazzi's inscribed *Isabella* engraving of 1761 (fig. 55) bears no resemblance to any of Langedijk's *Isabella*s or to securely identified portraits of her in this study, whereas engravings of Maria and Lucrezia are faithful to well-known likenesses of them (pls. 7 and 10).[182] Their portraits are still in Medici collections, in the Tribuna of the Uffizi and in other locations. Second, Langedijk's painstaking identifications of Florentine portraits of Isabella were made from portraits culled in Medici holdings that had erroneously been identified as Bianca Cappello (*Isabella with Music*, fig. 52), or Laudomia de' Medici (*Isabella with a Fur Pelt*, fig. 54).[183] In other words, even *Isabella* panels that had remained in unbroken Medici possession appear to have been kept hidden from view and ultimately from recognition – their identity was lost to memory. Finally, those documented in this study, the *Isabella with a Dog* (pl. 12) and *Isabella with Her Son Virginio* (pl. 11), have mysterious provenances. Were these very important adult portraits of her, both originals and painted from life, deliberately dispersed from Medici collections? Did this happen soon after her death, or in the climate of growing anti-Medicean sentiment and infamy surrounding Isabella's notoriety in the seventeenth century? Certainly, it seems that there were no secure portraits of Isabella in Florence from which the engraver Pazzi could work to contribute to the eighteenth-century Medici set.

Because of the expansion of known portraits of Isabella furnished by this study, the problem of *damnatio memoriae* seems to have great probability. In the *Isabella with Her Son Virginio*, the letters of the inscription that would allow a correct Medici identity – her age – were deliberately expunged. It was probably defaced not long after her death – it seems that, as this portrait and the *Isabella with a Dog* were not in Medici collections in the 1580s, they were probably removed to obliterate her memory. Support for this premise can be inferred from the circumstances in which the Ambras set of small Medici portraits was painted in 1587. The inscribed Ambras portrait identifying the adult Isabella (fig. 46) was executed in 1587 during the former cardinal, Grand Duke Ferdinando's reign.[184] Isabella and Ferdinando had been close through most of her life, and it seems that he allowed a second, uninscribed adult portrait of her to be included in the Ambras set (fig. 50). The series is uneven in execution, but the inscribed *Isabella* is remarkably crude and at many removes from its source, the impressive *Isabella with Virginio* (pl. 11).[185] It suggests that the prototype, painted only twelve years before, was not available to Medici court copyists.

Langedijk's justification for a *damnatio memoriae* of Isabella is the omission or removal of Isabella's image from Cosimo's own set of miniatures on tin that remained permanently in Florence (pl. 8). This omission is pivotal to accepting or rejecting a *damnatio memoriae*. In 1568 Vasari remarked on the excellence of those likenesses and had emphasized the importance to the duke of this ancestral and dynastic record. The group was hung outside Cosimo's study door in the Palazzo Vecchio, and it has remained with unbroken provenance in Medici collections. Vasari, in the 1568 edition of his *Vite*, describes the set at the end of his *vita* of Bronzino as including 'all the great men of the Medici house ... as well as Cosimo and his children.'[186] With the exception of Isabella, each of Cosimo and Eleonora's children – alive and deceased – appear there from infancy to early adulthood, with their names inscribed on each portrait to ensure preservation of their memories. This loss of an *Isabella* from that commemorative family series on tin takes on added significance now that several scattered portraits of her have come to light in this study. Isabella had been portrayed with considerable frequency during her life, ranging from the lost (or destroyed) childhood portrait when she was about eleven to the portrait of her with Virginio of 1574 (pl. 11) and several in between. (See pl. 12 and figs. 32, 49, 51, 52, 53, and 54.) Further, at the time of Vasari's writing, only Giovanna of Austria outranked Isabella, who, at the time of her death held a distinguished place in Italian cultural circles. This was a status that had been assiduously cultivated by Cosimo and Eleonora for each of their children and one that, it is logical to expect, Cosimo would have wished to commemorate forever for Isabella, both as a child and as an adult. His deep love for his only surviving daughter at the time of Vasari's writing makes it certain that she would have had pride of place in the important series that was visible to all who entered his apartments.

Two records, however, may help to assess the extent of the *damnatio memoriae*. In 1584, only eight years after her death, the arch-moralist Raffaello Borghini listed extant portraits of Isabella, Ferdinando and Pietro by Santi di Tito.[187] Second, the 1621 Medici inventory records a bust-length portrait of her in oval, perhaps related to the Palazzo Corsini version (fig. 53). It appears that some lesser portraits of Isabella escaped destruction or were stored. It could be argued, too, that a *damnatio memoriae* was instituted because of later growth in mythologizing her notoriety by the mid-seventeenth century, but the absence of records of her portraits in earlier inventories seems to obviate this proposal.[188] Adultery by a woman was a blemish on Medici family honour carrying with it centuries of historical and visual ostracism of one of the most gifted of Medici women.[189]

Allori as Court Portraitist

A testament to Allori's intellectual standing and social elevation is recorded in the *Portrait of Alessandro Allori*, dated 1580 (fig. 65), a portrait apparently painted when he was forty-five, soon after the deaths of Bronzino (1572) and Vasari (1574). It marked his now-unchallenged status as chief artist to the court. To affirm his humanism, he is surrounded by volumes of Ptolemy, Euripides, and Homer. A Latin quotation from Catullus is inscribed on a cushion in the foreground, '*SVVS CIVQ.ATTRIBVTVS EST ERROR*' ('To each is attributed his own fault'), a Greek inscription is found on the window sill behind him, and a cushion in the foreground is inscribed '*MNHMOΣYNON MEI SODALIS ALEXANDRI ALLORI ANN. MDLXXX*' ('Record of my friend Alessandro Allori in the year 1580'). A view of his villa at Peretola appears through the open window behind him. This pragmatic portrait, perhaps a self-portrait, makes him an exemplary man of his times.[190] The artist-courtier, and evident humanist, Allori had risen to affluence undreamed of by Bronzino.[191] Allori had 'arrived.'

The years of Isabella's prominence as cultural doyenne in Florence were also those of Allori's artistic ascendency. His landmarks are evident: childhood apprenticeship to Bronzino and, soon, his chief assistant; portraitist to the younger Medici even before his return from Rome in 1560; a founding member of the Accademia del Disegno in 1563; and chief artist from 1564 under Vasari's Tridentine renovation of Florentine churches. He was prominent in Michelangelo's obsequies in 1564 and, under Vasari and Borghini's direction, in Francesco and Giovanna's wedding in 1565, for the *Studiolo* from 1571 to 1573, and for Cosimo's state funeral in 1574. On Vasari's death that year, he was uncontested chief court artist. His prescience was extraordinary. He anticipated the 1564 Tridentine demands for 'naturalism' and pragmatism: his was a pivotal role in introducing Aristotelian directness and logic to Florentine portraiture. His *Il primo libro de' ragionamenti delle regole del disegno* of 1565 records his pursuit of empiricism and the science of anatomy. His unwavering ascent was clearly well deserved.

But if Bronzino's transcendent, exquisite Petrarchism held little appeal to the second Medici generation, Allori was no Leonardo, nor could he match Bronzino's genius for the portrayal of charismatic grandeur and for economy of means. Try as he might, Allori's posed figures have the stamp of repetition. Gestures are often stiff and articulations awkward. Bronzino's ability to infuse even one hand of a sitter with extraordinary organic truth and supreme grace was lost on Allori, who reused hand poses from sitter to sitter and never quite mastered the logical movement of drapery over the articulation of the elbow, or graceful foreshortening of arms that, in his portraits, are often bulky and dominate the foreground. Some of his best efforts are realized in more contained formats – the bust-length *Isabella*s (figs. 48 and 53), for example. It is, however, in his unsuspected gifts as a portrait miniaturist of outstanding talent, described in the following chapter, that we may appreciate his special powers of artistic concentration – and the degree of saturation of Medici propaganda into all spheres of its artistic patronage.

7

Up Close and Personal: Patronage and the Miniature *Eleonora ('Dianora') di Toledo de' Medici*

[S]he was twenty-one years of age, beautiful, gracious, genteel, becoming, charming, affable, and above all had two eyes in her head which were like two stars in their beauty.[1]

If Isabella's life has been overlaid with myth and notoriety, the tragically brief life of her cousin and sister-in-law, a second Eleonora di Toledo, has been virtually ignored by biographers for a century.[2] Yet, her entire life was spent at the Medici court, and portraits of her are not unknown.[3] Emphasis in this chapter will be on the exceptionally fine Florentine miniature in the Thyssen-Bornemisza Collection, Madrid, bearing a portrait of a beautiful young woman on its face backed by a detailed allegory of Juno in her role as Protectress of Brides on its reverse (pls. 14 and 15). Its painted, oval, silver support measures only 5.5 × 4 cm (2.2″ × 1³/₈″).[4] Its engaging subject is identified here as Eleonora ('Dianora') di Toledo the Younger (1553–76), born at the Florentine court and raised there by her aunt, Eleonora di Toledo, and her uncle, Duke Cosimo. Celebrated by Florentines for her vivacity and exceptional beauty, she married her first cousin and childhood companion, the youngest ducal son, Pietro de' Medici (1554–1604) in 1571, when she was eighteen.

Dianora was an intimate, beloved member of Eleonora and Cosimo's family with close ties to Medici political and cultural concerns, and an attempt is made here to place the tragic circumstances of her murder in 1576 in context. She is proposed as patron in the commission of the miniature, and the miniature allegory interpreted as an implicit, personal plea to Pietro for marital accord around the time of their wedding. Its iconography extols the two highest points of Medici ambition: imperial favour cemented through Francesco's marriage to Giovanna of Austria in 1565 and Cosimo's successful bid in 1569 for the title of grand duke.

The miniature *Dianora* belongs to a genre quite removed from the contexts and intent of official court portraits. Their minuscule dimensions ensured that miniatures would be intimately viewed by a very restricted audience, in this case Pietro. They had implications of mutual love and deeply talismanic associations. Perhaps their power to enchant was served by immediacy in their execution – there is ample evidence that they were invariably painted from life to capture the vivacity of the subject.

Double-sided versions are rare and, unusually, this one carries a heavy freight of propaganda. Exploration of its allegory reveals comprehensive links to Allori's colour-coded, annotated drawings of 1565 for a Juno float, twelfth in the lavish pageant to celebrate the genealogy of the gods – the *Mascherata della geneologia degli dei de' gentili* – that wound through Florence in February 1566 to mark Francesco's marriage to Giovanna of Austria.

Despite its minute proportions, the allegory ranks as a significant historical document. It is layered with themes that reach back over the years of Cosimo's reign and combine with those of larger artistic cycles and courtly ritual at its culmination. The Juno allegory is infused with contexts of current Medici patronage, when Vincenzo Borghini was iconographer with Vasari, and later Allori, as principals of an artistic team entrusted with Cosimo's most ambitious propagandistic programs in the Palazzo Vecchio, from the 1550s until the duke's death. Allori's authorship is evident from comparison with his annotated drawings for the *mascherata* and is reinforced by comparison with his figure style in contemporary miniatures. It was an era of intensive propaganda that has generated widespread scholarly study, and the minutiae of the allegorical group and the landscape in which it is set richly support contexts of setting and circumstances for Medici concerns at the close of Cosimo's reign.[5]

The miniature's iconography also fleshes out a context for women's patronage and less-documented psychological and social dimensions attending the personal life of a woman of high rank. In all, this miniature's private nature admitted an intimacy and frankness to be conveyed about one woman's tragic predicament that abandons the mask of conventional self-presentation so typical of more widely viewed panels. Its detailed allegory also expresses the traditional ancestral and familial ties of portraiture codified in the earlier Renaissance, and enduring here in the portraits of other Medici women. Dianora's closeness to her father-in-law, Cosimo, suggests that this minute work bears witness to a saturation of intellectual patronage and propaganda into artistic endeavours that radiated from the duke himself. This 'minor' decorative commission exposes a web of ideology at the core of Medici dynastic aspirations that transcends a very intimate work of art, but one that expresses the heady ambiance of Cosimo's new grand duchy.

The Italian Miniature Portrait

The independent miniature portrait was a relatively new European development. It had its genesis in portrait roundels of patrons or illustrious exemplars painted in illuminated manuscript margins in the earlier Renaissance.[6] Study of its Italian development has been somewhat neglected, probably because of its ambiguous status. Few genres of art have suffered more from relegation to trivial ranking: the portrait miniature is generally categorized as a 'minor' art and evaluated as jewellery or as an *objet de virtu*.[7]

This was not the case in the mid-sixteenth century. It stood then as a recent production of the greater courts, as an exclusive possession, and, as a genre of portraiture, implicitly the most vivacious. Marked by a high degree of artistic virtuosity, it ranked intrinsically as an art form of specially high repute. Francisco de

Hollanda boasted of a miniature of Charles V by his father that the emperor had ranked as superior to his now-lost state portrait painted by Titian in Bologna in 1533.[8] Vasari held that tiny images executed by master *miniatori* such as Giulio Clovio were luxury items, and a branch of portraiture that was almost exclusively a court genre:

> [Giulio's miniatures] cannot be seen, because nearly all are in the hands of great lords or of men of high rank: I say almost all, because I know some private citizens who have beautiful portraits in tiny cases from his hand, of lords, friends, and women beloved by them. But such works are not for public viewing, and cannot be seen by everyone, such as paintings, sculpture, and architecture by our other artists.[9]

Miniatures were fashionable keepsakes exchanged between the sexes; and spouses and lovers demonstrably did so, as Spanish, English, and Florentine portraits attest.[10] This was a notably personal art form: miniatures in costly settings were worn on the person rather than being the collectible items they later became, when they were locked away in cabinets as curios.[11]

The evocative power of portraits then ensured that, because of an aura of intimacy and secrecy associated with individual viewing of them, miniatures held a peculiar fascination.[12] Bronzino deftly suggests this in his *Ludovico Capponi*, painted about 1555–60 (fig. 56). Ludovico stands in a curtained space holding a miniature of his forbidden love, Maddalena Vettori – visible to him, but tantalizingly averted from our intrusive gaze.[13] It would have provided exceptional opportunity for enthralment of a kind held by Leonardo to be the special province of the painted portrait:

> And if the poet claims that he can inflame men to love ... the painter has the power to do the same, and indeed more so, for he places before the lover's eyes the very image of the beloved object, [and the lover] often engages with it, embracing it, and talking with it; which he would not do were the same beauties placed before him by the writer ... [S]o much more [does painting] conquer the hearts of men.[14]

De Hollanda, miniaturist to the Lisbon court, recorded his products' irresistible appeal, 'due to the perfection of the drawing being so powerful, even on so small a space,' and Vasari marked the genre as a benchmark of artistic excellence.[15] In every sense, the miniature was esteemed as a precious commodity.[16]

The Miniature *Dianora di Toledo de' Medici*

For its size – an oval measuring 5.5 × 4 cm, just over 2.2″ × 1³/₈″ – and considering the complexity of the scene on its reverse, the Thyssen-Bornemisza miniature stands as a tour-de-force of the miniaturist's art. In superb condition – it is painted in oils on silver – it still provokes the detailed perusal and wonder that de Hollanda and Vasari described. On the front (pl. 14) a wide-eyed, red-haired young woman, turned slightly to the right of the composition, smiles gently. She is bedecked in costly jewellery. Her tiara, a *grillanda* formed by pairs of large pearls alternated with rubies or garnets set in gold, crowns her elaborate coiffure. This is dressed with two small pink bows and, over her right ear, a corsage is surmounted by a blue lily. Pear-drop pearls decorate her ears. She wears a deep-blue gown with a high collar on which the lily motif is embroidered on a yellow ground. Over her shoulders rests a lavish gold collar set with large, table-cut emeralds and rubies, each divided by two pearls; it terminates in a pendant composed of a single ruby and an enormous cabochon emerald.

Her decorum should be noted. She is sumptuously dressed and bedecked in jewels befitting a state portrait, but her demeanour is relaxed, even engaging. There is no trace of effeteness here, however. In spite of her lavish costume, a vivid, warm presence is expressed by the slight tilt of the sitter's head, her dawning smile, the fresh rendering of her complexion, and, not least, a certain mutability conveyed by the varied lighting of the irises of her light-brown eyes. The miniature appears to have been painted *ad vivum* – from life – as the ranking European miniaturist, Nicholas Hilliard (1547–1619), would insist, and it fulfils his maxim for the miniaturist: to 'catch those lovely graces, witty smilings, and those stolen glances which suddenly like lightning pass.'[17]

Eleonora di Toledo II, ('Dianora') di Pietro de' Medici

Since the pendant appeared on the market in 1975, the sitter's identity has proved to be perplexing.[18] The miniature *Dianora*'s features, brown eyes, and reddish-brown hair are, however, identifiable from her several portraits in Langedijk, all tied by her to the inscribed miniature (fig. 57) from the ancestral Medici 'Ambras' set made in 1587. In each she is dressed in a peacock-blue gown – the *pavonazzo* hue so prized by her aunt, Eleonora di Toledo. Another shows her pregnant (fig. 58).[19] Apart from her inscribed name, her Toledo-Medici links are proclaimed in the Ambras version by a hair ornament of twisted blue with white/silver ribbons (the Toledo armorial colours), which are entwined with red and green ribbons (those of the Medici).[20] Her warm, appealing expression in the miniature portrait reflects affectionate contemporary descriptions of her: 'This Eleonora was a tall young woman, charming and beautiful, of becoming presence and endowed with courtly manners and virtuous habits.'[21] Unfortunately, apart from a brief interval at the end of the nineteenth century, information about her life and tragic death seem to have passed into obscurity.[22] Her story is valuable in revealing attitudes and legalities attendant on the lives and decorum of women in the early-modern Italian court. Also, the miniature unlocks a fresh aspect of Medici patronage – that of women – and implications of this for its intended viewer. In turn, the allegory expresses webs of political and intellectual patronage in the Medici sphere radiating from the persona of Grand Duke Cosimo and entrenched in decades of input from court *letterati*-iconographers, all dedicated to mythologizing his right to absolutism and hegemony and to asserting dynastic pretensions anew as his life drew to a close.

The encoding of identity has been found to be a feature of many portraits examined here. The *Dianora* miniature is no exception. Even without the supporting evidence of the inscribed Ambras portrait, intrinsic clues in it reveal her identity and rank. Dianora wears the dark blue of the *stemma* of her Alba family's principal Spanish seat, Toledo.[23] The lily motifs on her collar and in her hair proclaim Florentine connections, as they do on numerous Medici portraits.[24] Her priceless jewellery confirms her high rank and exhibits the colours of the Medici *stemma*. The long-standing Medici *impresa*, the *diamante*, appears on her right shoulder, as it does on several Medici women's portraits as pyramidal, gold sleeve fasteners (pls. 4 and 7).[25] Moreover, this Eleonora is linked to her aunt and namesake, the late duchess, by virtue of her peacock-blue gown – the *pavonazzo* of Eleonora's *impresa*. (It associated the duchess with Juno and was the colour of her personal livery.)[26] Dianora is copiously decked in pearls, Eleonora's favourite adornment.[27] In the miniature, she becomes, through ancestry and familial association, a second Eleonora di Toledo de' Medici. Finally, on the frame, imitation emeralds supply the main colour of the Medici *stemma*, while black enamelled scrollwork, small blue stones, and white imitation diamonds between each set combine the Alba colours with the 'emeralds' in a heraldic merging of armorial colours for both houses.

This now almost-unknown second Eleonora di Toledo was the only daughter of Don Garzia di Toledo and Vittoria d'Ascanio Colonna, niece of Vittoria Colonna, the poet. 'Dianora' – named to distinguish her from her aunt – was born at the Florentine court in March 1553. That year her father, Garzia (1514–78), son of Emperor Charles V's viceroy in Naples and brother-in-law and ally of Cosimo de' Medici, had assumed command of the castles of Valdichiana. His tour of duty successfully completed, he returned to Naples with Vittoria. The journey was considered too arduous for their newborn daughter, however, and she was left in the care of Duchess Eleonora. Sadly, Vittoria died a few months later. Lovingly raised and educated with her Medici cousins, Dianora became, in effect, a *menina* – one intended for courtly life – in the Spanish tradition of courtly fostering, a custom intended to reinforce aristocratic hierarchy.[28] She was totally integrated into the Medici family. After Lucrezia's wedding in 1558, Dianora, then five, was reported to be always by her side, suggesting that she was a comfort to her during her separation from her new husband, Alfonso d'Este. Eleonora di Toledo's death in 1562 left Dianora motherless again at the age of nine. Cosimo, charmed by her vivacity, ready ripostes, and physical vigour, adored her. As a woman, she delighted in arms and horsemanship. It is said that Cosimo would half-heartedly caution her to behave with 'Florentine' decorum, concluding 'you were indeed born in Florence.'[29] There is no record of an adolescent portrait of Dianora, who was betrothed at the age of fifteen to Pietro, her close contemporary in the Medici nursery. The numerous portraits of her as a young woman attest to her standing in the court as a well-loved member of the ducal family; no doubt they also pay tribute to her celebrated beauty and personal appeal.[30] As she matured, Dianora became a close companion to the liberated Isabella. Isabella's biographies and archival searches have made it possible to piece together the extremely tragic life of her young cousin and sister-in-law, Dianora.[31]

It was with imperial approval, and to reaffirm the long-standing Medici-Toledo alliance, that Cosimo betrothed Dianora in 1568 to Pietro (1554–1604).[32] Her father, Garzia, who later distinguished himself as Philip II's commander at Lepanto in 1571, provided her dowry of forty-thousand ducats of gold, five thousand of which was to provide jewellery – fifteen to eighteen million dollars in today's currency.[33] In August 1568, Cosimo responded by deeding enormous wealth to Pietro. This included the Medici villas and *poderi* (agricultural holdings) of Careggi, Trebbio, Castagnola, Fiesole, Livorno, Massa Maritima, Pisa, Mugello, and Montepaldi, the Medici palace in Via Larga, and mills and tracts of lands across Tuscany.[34] Mutual family goodwill, imperial favour, great wealth, and their acquaintance since birth did nothing, however, to cement Dianora and Pietro's union. On their marriage in April 1571, it was known in Medici circles that Pietro had been compelled to consummate the enforced marriage ('fatto per forza torre in moglie la Toledana'). He had been deeply disturbed from childhood, and there was widespread awareness in court circles of his maltreatment of Dianora.[35] The crucial issue in this union was Medici succession, and their son Cosimino, born in 1573, was sole legitimate Medici heir in this generation until his death in 1576.[36] Cosimo's hopes for curbing the unstable youth had appalling consequences: Pietro murdered Dianora in cold blood at the Medici villa at Cafaggiolo on 10 July 1576.[37] She was twenty-three. The diarist Agostino Lapini, who knew her, recorded: '[S]he was twenty-one years of age [*sic*], beautiful, gracious, genteel, becoming, charming, affable, and above all had two eyes in her head which were like two stars in their beauty; everyone said that she was murdered ... She was buried with rites in S. Lorenzo.'[38]

Just before her death, an admirer with whom she had been infatuated, Bernardino Antinori (1537–76), courtier, poet, Knight of S. Stefano, and hero of Lepanto, was murdered in his cell on Francesco de' Medici's order.[39] The hot-headed Bernardino had composed love poetry to Dianora from prison in Elba (appendix C), where he had been incarcerated for repeated brawling. Its Neopetrarchan mode echoes the conventions of the day and, paradoxically, Antinori's poetry also serves as a touchstone to reveal Petrarchism in her miniature portrait.[40] In his opening lines, 'Eyes accustomed to working great miracles / with the Sweet rays of your light / you move the inner powers of him/who dares to look at your light /...,' her eyes powerfully radiate a transforming light on him. This Petrarchan trope is echoed above in the diarist Lapini's sorrowing comment on her death, that she had 'two eyes in her head ... like two stars in their beauty.' The simile had widespread currency.[41] The covert yearnings that underlie Petrarch's addresses to his unattainable beloved would have a special resonance for privately viewing a miniature of a woman, and the larger, wider eyes and emphasized catch-lights in this intimate portrait of Dianora conjure up the Petrarchan trope of the reciprocal 'threading' together of eyes in mutual attraction and love.[42] (Compare her eyes here to the Vienna *Dianora* [pl. 16], a far more formal portrait.) This trope of reciprocal magnetism is suggested in Dianora's personal *impresa*, a sunflower turned to a radiant sun, and combined with the motto 'PVLCHER DVM SIMILIS' ('Beautiful and Simultaneously Alike').[43] Antinori evokes a poetic, mutual transformation to make explicit a charged eroticism and merging of lover-beholder through intent mutual gazes:

> Oh what perfect joy! oh what bliss!
> Oh what pleasure, to see two trusting lovers
> as each, intent on the other's eyes

sees there his own image!
Oh what sweet oblivion of all torment,
when the holy spirits of sight go out
and with a miracle so rare and so welcome
transform the lover into the beloved!

Leonardo's assertion of the power of the painted portrait to entrance the beholder could scarcely be better expressed. The largeness and brilliance of Dianora's eyes in the miniature may have been emphasized to invite an intended *vagheggiare*, or mutual, fond gazing.

Antinori refers to Dianora's 'alabaster throat' and 'polished ivory' hands in his Petrarchan cataloguing of her entire form.[44] Her throat in the miniature is noticeably white, and her pallor is enhanced by the luminosity of the silver support, which avoids the underlying ruddy glow typical of the more commonly used copper.[45] The miniature carries all the conventional associations of the love token as gift from subject to beloved – here of bride to bridegroom. Ironically, the Petrarchan stanzas written a few years later by her incarcerated, lovesick admirer are one of the very close pairings we may make between the painted image and literary or poetic portrayal of a beloved woman.

Antinori's tragedy played itself out and led inexorably to Dianora's own. He was treacherously implicated by Pierino Ridolfi, a rival admirer, who confessed under torture that Dianora had aided and abetted his own escape after an abortive Pucci-led, anti-Medicean vendetta. Possibly, his perceived act of treason and his persistent, compromising correspondence with Dianora during his two-year incarceration from 1574 to 1576 on Elba cost Dianora and the innocent Antinori their lives.[46] Other, political implications surround his death. He was an inaugural member of the Order of San Stefano, founded in 1562 by Cosimo with papal approval, whose stringent trappings of rank, decorum, and ritual were intended to lend an aura of feudal legitimacy and chivalric status to the Medici court in the new era of *Ecclesia Triumphans* and religious crusades.[47] Antinori's brawling and recidivism made him a *persona non grata* in the elite, newly founded Order. In the crusading temper of the times, violence was now a state monopoly channelled into a quasi-religious, feudal ethic directed towards warfare. For that reason, duelling for personal retribution had been condemned by popes from Julius II on – most recently by Pius IV – with automatic excommunication as penalty. It was condemned again by the Council of Trent.[48]

Dianora's own beauty and vivacity drew admirers, a situation that put her at grave risk and led to some comparisons with devouter Medici exemplars. The poet Felice Faciuta eulogized the pious Giovanna of Austria's peregrination in 1573 to the shrine of Loreto, but mused that the beautiful Eleonora di Pietro and Isabella probably would have preferred a procession devoted to music, dance, a hunt, or a light adventure to participation in a pilgrimage.[49] This is misleading. By 1575, when she was twenty-two, Dianora had already fulfilled the intellectual patronage devolving on younger Medici by serving as patron to the Accademia degli Alterati. It had been founded in 1568 and met twice weekly, its principal raison d'être being the *censura* of verse and prose past and present, criticism of comedies, lyrics, discourses, works of members, and translations, and *annotatione* on antique texts. (All this was to promote Tuscan as the 'purest' form of Italian.)[50] These smaller academies were semi-official, and Dianora was one of the rare women admitted to any of them.[51] Pseudonyms were used for Alterati members, and in the academy's *Diario* Dianora, the only female member, was named 'Ardente.'[52]

Cosimo died in 1574, and Dianora's dalliance with Antinori that year and its aftermath of correspondence with him during his incarceration brought matters to a head. As related above, Medici defensiveness against scurrilous rumours was already taxed by widespread bandying about of Isabella's 'indiscretions.'[53] Codes of family honour and the chastity of wives were invoked for Dianora's murder, which followed within days of Antinori's. She was taken under guard to the Villa Medici at Cafaggiolo, where Pietro strangled her, apparently with Grand Duke Francesco's tacit approval – a classic honour killing.[54] (Isabella's murder followed on 16 July.) Their only child, Cosimino – heir now to the grand duchy – died at the age of three within weeks of his mother's funeral.

Dianora's dreadful death at the hands of her husband on 10 July 1576 is reliably documented, most graphically by the Ferrarese ambassador to the court, Ercole Cortile, who reported it secretly to Alfonso II d'Este on 29 July 1576. His dispatch also announces the suspicious death of Cosimo's adored daughter Isabella within days of Dianora's murder:

> I advise Your Excellency of the announcement of the death of Lady Isabella [16 July]; of which I heard as soon as I arrived in Bologna, [and] has displeased as many as had the Lady Leonora's; both ladies were strangled, one at Cafaggiolo and the other at Cerreto [Guidi]. Lady Leonora was strangled on Tuesday night; having danced until two o'clock, and having gone to bed, she was surprised by Lord Pietro [with] a dog leash at her throat, and after much struggle to save herself, finally expired. And the same Lord Pietro bears the sign, having two fingers of his hand injured by [them being] bitten by the lady. And if he had not called for help to two wretches from Romagna, who claim to have been summoned there precisely for this purpose, he would perhaps have fared worse. The poor lady, as far as we can understand, made a very strong defence, as was seen by the bed, which was found all convulsed, and by the voices which were heard by the entire household. As soon as she died, she was placed in a coffin prepared there for this event, and taken to Florence in a litter at six o'clock [in the morning], led by those from the villa, and accompanied with eight white tapers [carried] by six brothers and four priests; she was interred as if she were a commoner.[55]

A scrawled letter to Francesco from Pietro, written on 11 July, tersely refers to his wife's death during the previous night:

> Last night at six hours an accident occurred to my wife and she died. Therefore Your Highness be at peace and write me what I should do and if I should go over there or not. Your humble servant and brother, Don Pietro de' Medici.[56]

Francesco dutifully relayed news of the 'accident' to his brother, Cardinal Ferdinando.[57]

Dispatches to Italian and European courts asserted that Dianora had died of a heart attack, but the truth was immediately bruited as far as Spain, where the Florentine ambassador, Baccio Orlandini, registered 'enormous disturbance ... and infinite torment ... [This news] sharply pierced my soul,' he wrote, on reliable confirmation of her death.[58] In Florence, Medici power over legal matters was absolute.[59] But Dianora was a ranking Spanish subject and member of the powerful Alba house.[60] Francesco eventually was forced to admit to Philip II that Pietro had killed her, for behaviour 'unbecoming to a lady':

> Although in the letter I had told you of Donna Eleonora's accident, I have nevertheless to say to His Catholic Majesty that Lord Pietro our brother had taken her life himself because of the treason she had committed through behaviour unbecoming to a lady ... We wish that His Majesty should know the truth ... and at the first opportunitity he will be sent the proceedings through which she should have known with what just reasons Lord Pietro acted.[61]

On the strength of her past letters describing her husband's cruelty, her brother Pedro di Toledo disdainfully responded in April 1577 that her death was reprehensible.[62] By 15 May, on the strength of the promised records of her 'treason,' however, the Hapsburg court absolved Pietro de' Medici of her murder, assured Francesco that there were no hard feelings or sinister opinions harboured towards Pietro, that preparations were under way to receive him as a courtier, and that he was to stand as godfather to Philip's newborn heir.[63] Uxoricide appears to have been accepted if a wife's continence was even suspect.

This brief sketch of her life gives special poignancy to Dianora's unusually warm, 'accessible' expression in this intimate portrait. Pietro's reception of it appears to have been recorded on panel. A *Pietro* in oval (not in good condition), dated to about 1571 (fig. 59), was identified by Langedijk, and is now in a private collection. He holds a miniature in his hand, with a barely decipherable surface made visible to the viewer that shows the formal essentials of the *Allegory* to be present.[64] It appears then to have been in a simple wooden frame, similar to the miniature held by Ludovico Capponi (fig. 56). Possibly it was originally boxed, as is believed for another Medici portrait that portrays a prospective bridegroom with a miniature donated to him by his bride, Raphael's *Lorenzo de Medici*.[65]

In order to interpret the *Allegory* (pl. 15), it is crucial first to accept Dianora's role as patron and Pietro's as recipient. Despite the frustratingly marred pictorial evidence in Pietro's portrait, the present disposition of the miniature's frame serves to provide the strongest evidence of his ownership, tied to his notoriously disreputable career in Spain, where he lived in exile from 1577. His portrait shows that a jewelled frame was not in place around 1571, but Hackenbroch believed that a frame set in precious gems preceded the present one. Reframing of miniatures was common, either for retrieval of gold and gems, or because of changes in taste.[66] From the back (pl. 15), the jewelled frame is clearly not a good fit and its workmanship only fair.[67] Of roughly cast silver-gilt enamelled in black and white, it is secured to the slim, gold rim of the silver support by two crudely placed struts. Table-cut doublets of green glass in 'box' settings imitate emeralds, which in turn are set in silver-gilt and roughly bolted through the frame with tiny cotter pins.[68] The present frame is thought to be Spanish and dates from the early seventeenth century.[69] Medici goldsmiths enjoyed a high reputation, and it is unlikely that even a paste-set frame would have been so ill matched to the double miniature – the reverse was meant to be seen, but the crudeness of the frame does not respect this. If this is indeed a replacement frame, the less careful work and the use of glass settings could indicate that its former precious stones were sold to recover their value, suggesting a reversal of fortune for its owner. Spanish jewellery design lagged in this period,[70] and its paste sets do conform to the heavier Spanish settings of the later sixteenth and early seventeenth centuries.[71]

These Spanish associations for the miniature tend to confirm proposals that Pietro had been its intended owner. In December 1577, just over a year after he murdered Dianora, the Hispanophile Francesco exiled Pietro to the Spanish court 'to see if he makes [of himself] a man of this house and rises above the indolence that vainly consumes the best years of his youth.'[72] From Madrid, a Medici retainer at the court, G.B. Lupi, confided to Francesco's secretary Antonio Serguidi on 8 October 1578 that 'when nature and intellect are of this temper, it is not possible to rely on him more than somewhat.'[73] Pietro continued to be unbridled and reckless, and his manners and behaviour at court were described as 'fastidioso' (repugnant); Prospero Colonna's letter from Spain of 3 August 1578 noted that his entourage was filled with scoundrels.[74] He lived out his years as a Spanish grandee, returning intermittently to Florence to plead for funds to offset his overwhelming gambling debts.[75] On his death in 1604, dozens of creditors' appeals – among them some of the most illustrious names in Florence – appeared in the petition prepared by the Pietà della Città di Firenze, dated 13 June 1605. His debts amounted to 148,374 *scudi*, about thirty to forty million U.S. dollars converted to today's values. The original gems in the miniature's frame may have accrued to his creditors in their bids for compensation. Devalued, the miniature's appeal is likely only to have been sentimental; possibly it was redeemed by members of the Alba family or others who then framed it with imitation gems.[76] Another possibility is that it remained unframed until after Pietro's death, having been sold *as* art and framed by a buyer around 1605. (Item 454 of the creditors' appeals lists 'quadri pitture di più sorte,' so the miniature could have been subsumed in this group.) Unfortunately, a decisive conclusion on why the present frame came to be attached is impossible. Provenance is unhelpful – miniatures were highly portable and sought far and wide by collectors, even in the seventeenth century.[77] It is clear, however, that all of the circumstantial evidence upholds Pietro's original ownership. It strongly suggests, too, that the miniature probably remained – perhaps simply stored – with his effects for decades: the miniature *Dianora* is Florentine and dates to around 1571; Pietro lived largely in Spain after 1577 and the present frame is typically Spanish; the frame dates to about the end of the sixteenth century, corresponding to his lifespan; and the enamels and imitation jewels of the frame combine the armorial colours of her Toledan and his Medici origins.

Dianora would have been patron in the commissioning of this conventional keepsake on her betrothal or marriage, between 1568 and 1571, and its Spanish frame places it in Pietro's ambit later. Bearing in mind the traditional role of miniatures as love tokens and the unusual commission of an allegory on its reverse, the scene was clearly intended to have deep, personal import for Pietro. A horrible irony inheres in its allegorical theme. It seems that it was to her new husband that she made a plea for her own safety.

The *Allegory of Juno, with Nymphs of the Air*

The immediate impact of the allegory lies in the artist's impressive management of a detailed group of seven figures, and a landscape, on such a tiny surface (pl. 15). In the centre, a slightly larger nude female is posed on an airborne throne. The peacock stationed at her left leg identifies her as Juno, patroness of brides and guardian of marriage and childbirth.[78] She and her attendants float above a landscape featuring a walled building on the shore of an estuary behind which a pale, dawn light breaks over low hills. Two *putti* personifying wind-gods flank the upper scene, each blowing a stream of air.

As *governatrice* of brides and childbirth, Juno was a recurring protagonist in sixteenth-century Medici wedding *apparati*, and this must date the miniature to Dianora's betrothal in 1568 or to her wedding in 1571.[79] Her aunt's lavish *entrata* and wedding to Cosimo de' Medici in 1539 had initiated the chaste, fecund goddess and her peacock as an enduring *impresa* for Medici brides. References to Juno emphasized Eleonora's hoped-for fecundity in establishing a new dynasty.[80] In the lavish street procession, the *Mascherata della geneologia degli dei de' gentili* (Masquerade of the Genealogy of the Gods of the Gentiles) on 21 February 1566 to celebrate Francesco and Giovanna's wedding in December, Juno presided over unfelicitous Nymphs of the Air, signifying her ability to avert marital catastrophe.[81] In 1589 Juno's nymphs cleared the sky of darkness and shadows when she made wedding felicitations to Virginia de' Medici and Cesare d'Este in the fifth intermezzo of Giovanni Bardi's *L'Amico fido*.[82] In 1600, in 'La contesa fra Giunone and Minerva,' Juno and the warlike Minerva competed in an intermezzo enacted during the wedding feast for Maria de' Medici and Henry IV of France.[83] (Maria had Rubens include Juno and Minerva in the scene recording Henry IV's reception of her prenuptial portrait, fig. 1.) Expressions of Juno's role in promoting triumph over marital discord were a tradition for Medici wedding *apparati* by the end of the century.

Variations in the choice of Juno's supporting players, however, always distinguish one Juno wedding *apparato* from another.[84] With minor changes, the grouped nymphs in the miniature's *Allegory of Juno* (pl. 15) match accounts by Domenico Mellini, Baccio Baldini and Giovanni Battista Cini of Juno's attendants in 1566.[85] Her *carro* was the twelfth of twenty-one processional floats designed for Francesco and Giovanna's stupendous *mascherata*:[86]

Adorned with a superb royal crown and glittering, transparent clothing, Queen Juno was seen after Vulcan's [chariot] had passed, in great majesty in the twelfth [position], not the least of the elaborate carts taking part, which was pulled by two gorgeous peacocks; [its decoration] was divided into five paintings of her deeds ... Following on foot with the cart were to be seen the better part of those atmospheric disturbances which are generated in the Air: first among them was seen Iris, believed by the ancients to be the messenger of the gods, daughter of Thaumas and of Electra, slim and with her hair unbound, clothed in red, yellow, blue and green, signifying the rainbow, [and] wearing two sparrow-hawk's wings on her head to signify her speed. Accompanying her then was Comet, dressed in red and with reddish unbound hair, presented as a young woman, who wore a bright star on her forehead. With them [was] Serenità, looking virginal. Her face was azure, as was her wide gown, with a white dove on her head signifying the air. After them followed Snow and Fog, who looked as though they had come together, one dressed in tawny robes on which many trees covered in snow seemed to have been placed, and the other, almost shapeless, appeared as a walking, great white mass. With them came green Dew, depicted with this colour because it is usually seen on the green grass; she had a full moon on her head, signifying that when the moon is full, dew falls from the sky on to the green grass in the greatest quantity. Rain followed, dressed in white, albeit somewhat murky, above whose head, signifying the seven Pleiadi, were seven stars arranged in a garland, some bright, some dimmed, like the seventeen that glittered on her breast, signifying rainy Orion. Three virgins of various ages followed adorned in white garments and crowned with olive garlands, representing the three ranks of virgins that used to run [in] Juno's ancient games. Finally, last in their group was the goddess Populonia, in rich matronly clothes, with a garland of pomegranate and bee-balm in her hair and a small altar in her hand, who beautifully closed up the group of creatures of the air.[87]

The miniature's Juno allegory corresponds to Cini's description above of the 1566 Juno *carro*, drawn by peacocks. She wears a crown on her head over a transparent veil, and a decorous strip of blue drapery crosses her lap – the 'cestus' or magical girdle loaned by Venus to make Juno irresistible to her erring husband, Jupiter. She brandishes thunderbolts, his attribute, in her left hand.[88] Her entourage is almost entirely drawn from that of the Nymphs of the Air in the 1566 *mascherata*. Iris, first on the left, is clothed as described by Cini, but with a complete bird on her head, and in addition has a small rainbow above her, details that later appear in Ripa.[89] Each foot is encased in swirling forms. Next on the left, her companion Comet is dressed entirely in red, as Cini narrated, but she holds in her hand a piece of sulphur, an attribute also given to her by Ripa, who describes her malevolence and sinister plottings of grave mishaps for the world.[90] Snow next appears, at Juno's right elbow, wearing snow-sprinkled branches on her head. Grey and indistinct, Fog looms beneath the thunderbolts in Juno's left hand. Beside her, just as Cini described, Rain is dressed in murky robes and wears her starry, Pleiadian crown; the seventeen stars on her breast representing the showers of Orion are included. Ripa's description for her is identical.[91] Lastly, Dew appears to the right of Rain and, as in Cini's account, is dressed in green with a full moon over her head; Ripa includes dew-drenched branches mounted on her head, and they too appear in Cini's account.[92] Magnified, these droplets – not much larger than pinpricks – are individually painted with breathtaking illusionistic effect on the miniature's surface.

Changes on the miniature are few, but significant. Serenità, the bluish, veiled figure with a dove on her head now plays a leading role as Juno's attendant, and occupies the foreground. It was Populonia, listed by Cini with her three attendant virgins, who had the culminating role in the 1566 pageant. The ideal of an antique republic of popolani had been juxtaposed with the notion of Cosimo's sovereignty in the so-called *Apotheosis of Cosimo* in the central ceiling tondo of the Sala Grande of the Palazzo Vecchio in 1565, executed in the stateroom to celebrate Francesco's wedding.[93] Populonia and her attendants were probably omitted in the miniature because her role would have been redundant for intimate viewing. Cini and Baldini were, after all, describing a public wedding float with enormous dynastic import for the Medici, the momentous alliance of the Florentine house with a legitimate member of the imperial house.[94] (Cini's *ragguaglio*, or prospectus, for the 1566 *Mascherata* procession was especially conceived as a guide for the imperial court.)[95] A sceptre-carrying Populonia had civic significance in the mascherata: civil obedience and tribute to a ruler are signified on Allori's annotated costume drawing for the deity.[96] The 1565 marriage alliance was part of Philip II's grand scheme for a network of Italian control, and the Populonia theme implicitly promoted this to all Florentines. Each nymph is precisely described later in Ripa's group of Nymphs of the Air, and it is not his Serenità, but specifically Serenità della notte, wearing blue drapery with peacock-blue and silver veils, who occupies the foreground here.[97] Her prominent placement and wide gesture appear to signal that all stormy, inclement elements of marriage may be brought under her control.

Two full sets of drawings for the 1566 *mascherata* are still extant, one in the Biblioteca Nazionale, Florence, the other in the Gabinetto dei Disegni e delle Stampe of the Uffizi. Each set includes the designs for the twelfth *carro*, Juno's costume and attributes, and those for her attendant Nymphs of the Air.[98] Drawings for the peacock-harnessed *carro* and personifications of the nymphs are more detailed than a miniature could allow, but they correspond in the individual costume designs, colours, and attributes for each.[99] Baldini's descriptions of literary sources and symbolism for the latter correspond to annotations found on the Biblioteca Nazionale drawings, the superior group attributed to Allori.[100] Annotations for Iride (Iris, fig. 60), for example, describe yellow, red, blue, and green robes, and her hair is adorned with a prominent set of bird's wings, presumably to represent her attribute, the sparrow-hawk, which denoted her speed as messenger. In the miniature scene, she appears on the extreme left with an entire bird on her head. Swirls of wind about each foot appear in both drawing and miniature – also signifying her speed, according to Baldini.[101] On his drawing for La Pioggia (Rain), Allori noted: 'A maiden clothed in murky white ... with seven stars on her head ... and seventeen stars on her breast ... [holding] in her hand a spider who makes its web.' (There the web is spun on a diviner's rod held by La Pioggia, apparently Allori's own invention, and the spider and web described in Baldini's 'eyewitness' account make a consistent appearance later in all of Ripa's illustrated editions from 1603. It seems that Ripa was directly inspired by iconographical descriptions of the *mascherata* of 1566.)[102] La Neve (Snow) and La Nebbia (Fog) were described by Baldini as dressed entirely in cotton wool, and the two are decidedly impressionistic in the *mascherata* drawings and on the miniature.[103] Although neither Cini nor Ripa recorded tinted skin for any *mascherata* personae, Baldini observed La Rugiada (Dew) to be 'una femmina tutta verde'; in the miniature she has green skin, and Comet's skin is red. The complementary colours help distinguish the tiny figures in the composition, but they also assert the Medici armorial colours in the allegorical scheme. Serenità della Notte's dark blue robes and silver veils are no accident: these are Dianora's Toledan armorial colours, familiar in the Medici court since Eleonora di Toledo's arrival in 1539.

The larger scale of the miniature Juno to the figures around her also ties the miniature directly to the *mascherata*. Vincenzo Borghini's *invenzione* probably informed the program, and floats were under Vasari's artistic direction.[104] Gods who presided over each float were statues designed by him to be integral to the structure.[105] Like the miniature version, the Juno of the 1566 procession was probably larger than the live actors personifying her nymphs.[106] As Juno's handmaid, the figure of Iris is the most consistent attendant in all of the *apparati* for Medici weddings; on Ammannati's fountain, Juno lays aside her thunder-making tambourine on the sculpted rainbow – Iris's attribute – that supports her. In the miniature, Juno's tambourine – visible under strong magnification – rests in Iris's lap.[107] As Juno's assistant, Iris symbolically brightens the sky after a storm has subsided. She may allegorise the emotional balm of forgiveness in the wake of marital discord.

From comparison with the written descriptions and drawings, there is no doubt that the iconography and cast of players in the miniature allegory are 'lifted' directly from the *mascherata* pageant enacted on 21 February 1566.[108] The few omissions and additions to the cast of personae respond to the private nature of this genre, in this case a tiny miniature intended exclusively for Pietro's eyes and designed to engage him in a private reverie with the sympathetic gaze of a woman who knew him intimately.[109] Pietro became, in effect, an interactive beholder and participant in its message. Under Juno's guidance, it is the unpredictable Nymphs of the Air, some protective, some malevolent, who project their collective gaze to his; Serenità della Notte, dressed in Dianora's armorial colours, leads and guides them by her unifying gesture.

To clarify Juno's patronage in the miniature scheme, we may turn to Vasari. In his *Ragionamenti* he describes the Loggia di Juno, the late duchess's private terrace and its lost frescoes of 1555–6, with Eleonora-Juno, Goddess of the Air, as its principal persona. Majestic, beautiful, and serene, she graciously banished the vicissitudes of passion and sad sighs in her subjects with the assistance of Iris. Vasari reminds his interlocutor, Francesco, that as Juno, Eleonora had arranged Lucrezia's marriage to the Este, and Isabella's to the Orsini.[110] The scenes were familiar to Dianora from infancy, who in turn would have adopted Juno-Eleonora in spirit as *patrona dea* on her betrothal.

Talismanic touching associated with the miniature portrait was somewhat akin to handling a religious relic, and Pietro's intent gaze on Dianora's beautiful face would have been both an aesthetic experience and a transforming, psychological one.[111] It is useful to pause here in consideration of what Elizabeth Cropper describes as the *io–tu* (I–you) relationship for a portrait's spectator. The Petrarchan ethos of beauty embedded in sixteenth-century portraits of women inevitably partakes of the speaking *io* of the conventional Petrarchan lyric with its reflexive *si*.

Through Allori, Dianora defines herself in the miniature portrait as a persuasive distillation of beauty itself. Pietro's response, is not, of course, without erotic possibilities: the nude figure of Juno presides over their marital domain, and Serenità della Notte's presence inevitably implies the bond of physical love as safeguard against marital discord.[112]

Pietro's engagement with the allegory's underlying *psychomachia* would be different. It called for an exercise of reason and free will, much in the spirit of *Hercules at the Crossroads*. Looming around Juno are the Nymphs of the Air, poised momentarily in equilibrium. Juno-Eleonora, with a clutch of her consort Jupiter-Cosimo's thunderbolts in hand, is a potent reminder to Pietro of his parents as spiritual guides to him and as protective guardians to their charge, Dianora. But as her thunder-making tambourine rests in Iris's lap, her pointing gesture towards Dianora–Serenità della Notte, the most prominent member of her entourage, suggests deference to her. Pietro must enact a Herculean decision to choose Serenità della Notte, veiled in the armorial colours both of his late mother and his bride.[113]

The poignant recall of Eleonora di Toledo, mother to her orphaned niece Dianora until she was nine – and, of course, to Pietro – is especially timely and locates the miniature in an interwoven network of current Medici patronage. By 1571, the year of Dianora's and Pietro's wedding, work was in progress in the Studiolo to commemorate the tenth anniversary of Duchess Eleonora's death.[114] On the left of its 'Air' wall, which is dedicated to her, Giovanni Bandini's bronze *Juno*, her associated *dea*, stands in a niche with her peacock.[115] Although she died in 1562, Eleonora presides in Allori's tondo above, costumed in 1570s style, no doubt to suggest a living presence and influence on Francesco.[116] (Cosimo presides above the opposite wall.) Similarly, in the miniature, Juno-Eleonora stands as a guiding spiritual force to her youngest son. For the Studiolo, begun in 1570, Vincenzo Borghini, the prolific Medici fountainhead of *invenzione*, was chief iconographer, Vasari artistic director, and Allori a leading artist.[117] Although Borghini's input into the *mascherata* pageant is undocumented, it is thought that Cini, his disciple and author of its *ragguaglio* commentary, may have acted on his behalf.[118] Thus, Allori's strong links to the *mascherata* Juno's inventors persisted. In tandem with these, his artistic contribution to the pageant, his designs for each of its players were available. It was to these that he turned for the miniature's figured allegory and its message of marital accord.

The Miniature Landscape

The evocative landscape beneath the allegorical group has links to the *mascherata* and to the Studiolo. The minute scene includes two puffing wind-gods on either side (pl. 15). Opposite *Juno* in the Studiolo is Elia Candido's *Boreas*, the North Wind. In a letter to Vasari of 7 October 1570, Borghini was at pains to differentiate Boreas from Zefiro: 'Take note then, that where the statue of Zephyr is, it must be Boreas, and in my writing it is otherwise and in error, because the crystals he makes are from across the mountains and not from the sea ... [I]t is the person of Boreas who has the other quality from that of Zephyr.'[119] Boreas and Zefiro had also appeared in the *mascherata* pageant – on the Neptune float, which followed immediately on

Juno's.[120] Placed on the right, below the Juno figure group, Boreas must be the *putto* who blows a stream of frosty crystals. The *putto* opposite, whose breath is unfrosted, who presides over the mouth of the estuary, must be his brother Zefiro, whose western breath comes from across the sea. Their role is twofold: they further the theme of *psychomachia* – Zefiro is associated with spring and renewal, either physical or spiritual, and Boreas presaged terrible storms and winter.[121] Their more practical function is to act as geographical markers. Zefiro is positioned at the estuary on the left, that is, westerly, which makes our viewing position a southerly one. As the low hills in the background are typical of the foothills of the Apennines north-east of Pisa, this estuary is surely the Arno emptying to the west at Pisa, as it would be if viewed from the south. Pietro, soon to be admiral of the Tuscan navy, and his new wife were domiciled in Pisa, a then-unsilted port on the Arno serving as base for the Tuscan fleet.[122] The single building in view is placed in an open, rural setting, incorporated in a walled enclosure situated in the lower middle of the scene, surrounded by a wide plain. On the right foreground ('east') is a prominent clump of trees.

One of Cosimo's gifts to Pietro to mark his betrothal was the 'palazzo di signore' of Collesalvetti and its dependencies (figs. 61 and 62), remnants of which are now incorporated into the hamlet of Collesalvetti, southeast of Pisa and a few miles east of the port of Livorno. Then – and now – a *palazzetto rustico* set in the plains south of wooded hills, it was a principal resting point for the Florentine court en route to Livorno, and was used as a winter hunting lodge by the younger Medici. It was unique among Medici villas in having westerly views to the sea across an open plain.[123] In 1571 the abbot of the adjoining Badia of Santa Maria dei Dodici Apostoli, reached by a footpath along Collesalvetti's western boundary (see figs. 61 and 62), recommended to his community that the monastery's estates be deeded in perpetuity to Dianora.[124] In the miniature, the gabled building in a walled enclosure 'near' the estuary – a typical *murate* foundation – corresponds to the Badia's location and commemorates the abbot's gesture, surely marking Dianora's marriage. A *terminus post quem* of 1571 for the miniature seems certain.

Landscapes in women's portraits are rare, their absence reflecting a general status quo in women's existence – an interior or blank background expressed the traditional decorum of chaste circumspection and devotion to family and home. The *Eleonora di Toledo with Giovanni* was the exception, and its landscape is freighted with territorial emphasis (pl. 4 and fig. 15). Here the intention is similar. Medici control and rationalization of material resources in creating the modern state now extended to city, theatre, arts, engineering, and to Tuscany itself. Its landscape was patterned in this period by country villas built or refurbished for the Medici, with extensive acreages of orchards, farmlands, vineyards, forests, and hunting and fishing. Less now the arcadian retreats of antique tradition held dear by Cosimo il Vecchio – who had once owned Collesalvetti – they had become strategic, reciprocal satellites of such major centres as Florence, Siena, and Pisa. They acted as a network of command-and-supply posts at short distances from each other, as places to garrison troops, and to maintain rural government.[125] The prospect of the Medici *fattoria* at Collesalvetti to the sea is not merely sentimental. Rather, it demonstrates a political entity with sentimental and intellectual overtones of Medici governance, suzerainty, expansion, patriotism, and religion, just as did Bronzino's Tuscan landscape in Duchess Eleonora's official portrait (pl. 4). Indeed, Cosimo's use of landscape as carrier of propaganda was emphatic in 1563, when the ceiling *tondi* of the Sala Grande were initiated. Archaeological, historical, and literary allusions to Florence were rigorously assessed for authenticity: the duke kept Borghini and Vasari's ideations under strict control, prompting most of the major revisions to these programs himself.[126] (In 1565, he proposed the northern landscapes for the *cortile* of the Palazzo Vecchio to have emotive and territorial import for Princess Giovanna of Austria on entering her new sphere as his daughter-in-law and future duchess.)

Neither was landscape in this circle of patronage merely decorative. Its inclusion, and the challenging meticulousness of technique demanded of the artist in *miniatura* makes its significance in this case certain. Cosimo's preferred residence after 1568, Pisa and its environs enjoyed an increasingly important status as a strategic Medici administrative centre and family gathering point.[127] The Collesalvetti scene is replete with reminders of seventeen-year-old Pietro's impending maritime jurisdiction as admiral of the fleet. Tuscany is eulogized as a secure, idyllic haven now under grand-ducal rule.

The miniature also advances ducal propaganda expressed in Ammannati's *Juno* fountain, currently important in the scheme of renovations in the Palazzo Vecchio. Partially installed in the Sala Grande for the 1565 wedding, the fountain conflates Eleonora-Juno and alludes to her matriarchal role in the new Medici dynasty.[128] The miniature portrait also vaunts the ancestral emulation that was typical – even imperative – in portraiture. Dianora wears the Toledan dark blue and copious amounts of pearls associated with her aunt. This emphasizes her ancestry and identifies her as the second Eleonora di Toledo de' Medici.[129] This theme is repeated in a second portrait of Dianora that the miniature may depend upon, but which it most likely inspired. When the miniature appeared on the market in 1975, Detlef Heikamp drew attention to its similarity to a large, three-quarter-length portrait by Allori in Vienna (pl. 16).[130] The brown-eyed sitter with reddish-blond hair wears the same coiffure and gown with its lily-embroidered collar, and the jewelled collar is identical to that worn in the miniature. Allowing for the enormous disparity in scale, it is evident that the two works portray the same person. This is Dianora, and in the three-quarter-length Vienna portrait, long arms and neck emphasize her tall stature. There the face is more abstracted, less winsome, and lacks the intimacy and 'accessibility' of expression of the miniature. These are just the kinds of differences in decorum that might be expected between miniature and panel portraits, the latter intended to be viewed at a greater distance from the viewer.[131]

Dianora and Isabella, the daughters to whom Cosimo was so deeply attached, each died violently within two years of the duke's death in 1574. Dianora was a particular favourite with Cosimo, who was paternal in his protection of her during her short, miserable marriage to his unstable son.[132] Symbolism in the *Dianora* miniature reflects a period when his protection was assured. Given these close family ties, Cosimo's love for her, and his deep involvement in all significant Medici iconography, it seems likely that he at least informally approved the Juno allegory with Dianora. For this minute surface, Allori drew on decades of entrenched propaganda to convey its personal message. The thunderbolts brandished by Juno make her Jupiter-Cosimo's emissary.[133] The court's 1540s Ficinesque revival had established the Jupiter link with play on Cosimo's 'cosmic' name:

> You, however will fashion a better image within yourself when you know that nothing is more orderly than the heavens and that nothing can be thought of that is more temperate than Jupiter. You should hope at last to attain benefits from the heavens and from Jupiter if you have rendered yourself very orderly and temperate in your thoughts, emotions, and mode of life.[134]

Jupiter's attributes include his role as protector of the weak, and Jupiter-Cosimo's implied presence is intended to spur temperance in his wayward son and to remind him of Cosimo's benevolent protection of his beloved ward, Dianora.

The duke's greatest triumph is recorded even on this minute surface. Now his most important piece of regalia, Cosimo's grand-ducal *corona radiata* is worn by the miniature Juno over her bridal veil. His coronation by Pius V on 15 March 1570 was in Isabella and Dianora's presence.[135] The design was confirmed by papal bull, but a version had been been anticipated by Cosimo himself some years earlier – it appears on the central Sala Grande tondo and on Juno's head in the drawing for her *carro* in the 1565 *mascherata*.[136] Cosimo's coronation was the victorious realization of all of his striving against formidable political odds to become principal Italian ruler in the peninsula.[137] Dianora's Alba family had been his staunchest ally in his bid in the struggle for precedence.[138] Enormous resentment ensued in Italy over this Medici elevation; the pope's unilateral decision strained international relations and infuriated the Hapsburgs – who as representative of the Holy Roman Empire could hardly countermand papal authority.[139] This pinnacle in Medici fortunes is flaunted on a minutely painted surface through which Pietro can savour his family's triumph. Replete with Cosimo-Jupiter's grand-ducal crown and thunderbolts, Eleonora-Juno evidently proclaims Eleonora as regent grand-duchess.[140] (Eleonora was dead, but a later portrait of her exhibiting a *corona radiata* beside her attests that it was tacitly understood that she shared Cosimo's distinction.)[141]

The rippling effect of patronage from its absolutist epicentre, Cosimo, is remarkably evident in this minute, personal expression of familial ties and political trumpeting of Medici ascendancy that had persistently accompanied portraits commissioned in this court. Its effects are discussed a little later, but the development of yet another Italian portrait genre in his court deserves some exploration.

Allori as Medici Miniaturist

The European portrait miniature seems to have sprung Athena-like from the illuminated manuscript page by around 1520. In a biography of Lodovico Sforza, Duke of Milan, of about 1490, a margin roundel portraying him shows that transformation to have been only a historic heartbeat away: it even includes an illusionistic, fictive frame.[142] Jean Clouet of Flanders included roundels of Francis I in the margins of the *Commentaires de la guerre gallique* and on the title page of a treaty with Henry VIII, but tiny, framed versions on vellum were being produced by his *atelier* by 1525. Soon, Clouet and his son, François's services were in demand by French nobility.[143] Giulio Clovio executed his miniature *Eleonora di Toledo* (fig. 22) in this Northern tradition of watercolour on vellum during his stay at the Florentine court from 1551 to 1553. As a result, Vasari praised Clovio and *miniatura* highly and recorded the currency of these tiny portraits in the courts. He chronicles, too, that Bronzino made 'in a small panel a *Nativity of Christ* in tiny figures, incomparably fine, in everyone's opinion.' Had Bronzino been experimenting with miniaturisation, perhaps inspired by Clovio, the preponderence of whose work was of religious scenes?[144] It was during the following decade that the Medici *ritrattini* in oils on tin were being produced by Bronzino's workshop, each 15 by 40 cm (pl. 8). By 1555–60, Bronzino's *Portrait of Ludovico Capponi* was thematically conceived to show Ludovico in the act of privately viewing a small, framed miniature in his hand (fig. 56), as was Allori's *Francesco de' Medici with a Miniature of Lucrezia* (fig. 43), made by 1560.[145]

Clearly, there was some Florentine involvement in miniaturization by Cosimo's artists by 1560, and it was one that did not imitate the overwhelming preference for watercolour on vellum in courts elsewhere. At some time between 1551 and 1560, the choice was made to use oils on a metal support, a preference that came to set Italian miniatures apart from other European developments and fully emancipated the genre from the illuminator-miniaturists' purview.[146] Oil's superior luminosity and endurance may utimately have influenced this choice. Bronzino may have initiated this move, or overseen its adoption for the Medici *ritrattini*, the small, labelled portraits on metal (pl. 8). His meticulous talents and expertise in oils were honed for just such a transfer, and there is no evidence that he was drawn to watercolour. Vellum would not support oil-based pigment without seepage of the oily base and, to effect the extreme precision *miniatura* called for, it may be that in an age of printing the metal plate readily presented a support that was smooth and enduring. His position as chief court portraitist in the 1550s would have allowed him to advance workshop experimentation in the miniature format, one that was clearly gaining ground in the French court and had rich potential for personal exchanges between rulers. Apart from a competitive urge to be in the vanguard of artistic developments in court portraiture, Cosimo may ultimately have preferred not to rely on Northern artists, but to give impetus to an Italian development within his own domain. Vasari claimed to have executed a scene 'in the manner of a miniature' for Francesco – sent to the late Eleonora's sister in Toledo – suggesting that he too wished to be seen as an *aficionado* of miniaturization at the court.[147]

When precisely Allori became adept at miniaturization is uncertain, but his Pitti *ritrattino* of Lucrezia and its replica *en buste* on the miniature in Francesco's hand (fig. 43) suggest that this must have been by 1560. Vasari, who describes the young academician's success in painting the *rilievi* and paintings for Francesco's nuptials from 1565 to 1566, tacitly predicts his future excellence in miniature production: '[H]e executed a little picture full of small figures after the manner of a miniature for Lord Francesco, Prince of Florence, which is highly praiseworthy; other pictures and portraits he has painted with great study and diligence in order to obtain facility and to form a fine manner.'[148] Italian miniaturists were generally not specialists in the genre, but artists more accustomed to executing easel paintings.[149] Allori was an able miniaturist by 1571. Signatures on miniatures in oils are rare and, if Allori did not sign his work in this instance, it was doubtless because an area of about twenty-two square centimetres left little space for a legible signature.[150] In his *Dianora* miniature, he appears to have initiated the rare use of silver for the genre. Copper was the usual Italian support, as was the case for the larger miniature series such as Allori's *Allegory of Human Life* backed by the *Portrait of Bianca Cappello* of the mid-1560s.[151] In later decades, the more economical silver-coated copper was used when special effects of luminosity were desired.[152] Why silver was chosen to support this portrait miniature can only be conjectured, but Bronzino's previous, Petrarchan tendencies in portraiture may have influenced the choice of a paler, 'cooler' ground that silver would provide.[153] Bronzino died in 1572, and, as Vasari and de Hollanda held that miniatures of the *Dianora* type were greatly esteemed, a commission by a ranking Medici patron to mark so important an occasion as a wedding would most likely have gone to Allori if he had mastered *miniatura*.[154]

It seems that he had. His densely populated, small-scale works on copper from the late 1560s, and his Studiolo works soon after 1570, provide a logical range of work to assess his mastery and to serve for comparison of his style in the Juno allegory.[155] The signed *Hercules Crowned by the Muses* (fig. 64), painted around in 1568 for Francesco de' Medici, was praised for its miniaturization by Vasari and Raffaello Borghini.[156] Its principal muse, Clio, is posed similarly and exhibits precisely the same figure style as the miniature's *Juno*. In each a small, wedge-shaped head widens at the brow and is set on robust, broad, shoulders and upper chest. Limbs are long, smooth but well covered, with the knees round and prominent. Clio and Juno are each given nearly identical poses for arms, hands, and fingers – predictable repetitions of Allori's perennial hand pose where the index finger points and the other fingers curl under the large hands. Allowing for a difference in scale, Juno's left arm with the hand grasping thunderbolts is only a slight variant on Clio's as she holds her book. From the *Hercules Crowned by the Muses*, Allori merged Clio's body with Terpsicore's head to compose the miniature Juno, and her left arm and hand grasping thunderbolts is only a slight variant on Terpsicore's as she rests her viol.[157] Allori's *Ricordi*, begun in 1579, further confirm his now-established role as court miniaturist.[158]

The very impulse to combine miniature portrait and allegory on the recto and verso of a metal ground links the *Dianora* miniature to Allori's *Portrait of Bianca Cappello*, with the populous *Allegory of Human Life* on its reverse, which measures only 37 by 27 cm (14.8 × 10.8"). Painted on copper in the mid-1560s, its small-scale portrait with conjoined allegory and its intimate associations – Bianca and Francesco were clandestine lovers at this time – show that it is a forerunner of the miniature *Dianora* portrait backed by its Juno allegory.[159] As Hackenbroch observed, Allori's tiny landscape in the Juno allegory with its pearly, dawn light is typical of his contemporary *Pearl Fishers*, painted for the Studiolo in 1571.[160]

Allori's association with wedding iconography was soon reinforced. It is thought that the *spalliera* or bedhead painted by him in 1572, decorated with an erotic repertoire of amorous themes, was a Medici commission. As there were no other Medici weddings of note at this time, it is possible that its commission was to honour Dianora and Pietro's marriage in 1571, perhaps – as was the case with the famous Borgherini bed – as a lavish gift from the groom's father.[161]

Allori's tiny masterpiece proves that mastery in this courtly genre had been achieved as the grand duchy was launched in 1569. Its beauty and technical excellence express the widespread aesthetic of preciousness in the greater courts but, most touchingly, it provoked revelations about the life of an almost forgotten, much-loved woman of Cosimo's court, Dianora di Toledo de' Medici. In spite of public adulation of her beauty, genuine affection for her in court circles, and the dreadful circumstances of her death, her life has been largely overlooked for over a century.[162] In the commission of what was intended to be a keepsake and talisman for her husband, 'image magic,' beauty, and private reveries to flatter Medici sensibilities were all bound up in an appeal for love and harmony. Unknowingly, she also added her name to a long list of Renaissance women who commissioned their own portraits.[163] Its date, about 1571, situates it in the vanguard of the late-sixteenth-century emergence of the private miniature portrait painted in oils on metal, peculiar to Italy, which Bronzino probably initiated and Allori mastered in the ducal court. The tiny double format shows Allori at a high point in his artistic abilities. In the allusive tradition of the court, the allegory on its reverse depicting Juno with Nymphs of the Air, was charged with secret meanings and a freight of propaganda extraordinary in the history of this genre. For this, Allori drew on Medici expressions of ostentatious masquerade and propaganda consolidated over a period of almost four decades and now at its zenith on the birth of Cosimo's new grand duchy.

Conclusion

More than any other work discussed in these chapters, the miniature epitomizes and summarizes the development of Medici power and its influence on women's portraiture within this evolving absolutist dynasty. It confirms that Cosimo's self-fashioning of his own role as protector and leader had penetrated deep into the consciousness of his own family. The tiny portrait exhibits the covert ancestral and familial references found in all portraits of Medici women in Cosimo's ambit, includes Medici triumphalism, and expresses deference to the social heirarchy that rippled from the persona constructed around the new grand duke.[164] This ambiance radiating from the 'Big Man' is inextricably connected to him as ideological patron, in which the present leader is mythologized to become 'part of a great continuum, extending deep into the past and far into the future.'[165] Portrait and allegory together also enshrine the 'Juno' mythology that had accorded the role of dynastic mother and spiritual patroness to the late Duchess Eleonora.[166] It records, too, a scene that conjures the lavishness of the 1565 *mascherata*, seen as axiomatic in establishing regal ceremonial for this ambitious court.[167]

Cosimo's role as affectionate surrogate father to Dianora suggests that he may have been directly involved in the commission of this tiny decorative work, which may have expressed his desire to curb his son's already difficult psyche.[168]

Dianora's relaxed decorum belies the fact that, in this intimate commission, Allori drew on a very current Medici concern. Critical hopes turned on this Medici-Toledo partnership because, in the absence of an heir for Francesco and Giovanna after six years of marriage, a successful union between Pietro and Dianora was crucial to Cosimo's dynastic aspirations.[169]

But the Juno allegory also confirms the notion that the early modern European court was both institution and ethos, a complex entity built around ruler and regent.[170] Its character was determined not only by them, but by the nature of its inner entourage.[171] Monarchical society had always perceived its social organization as a series of concentric rings around the prince, with the other classes revolving around him. Cosimo's recent elevation to Grand Duke – supreme Italian ruler – now called for even greater demonstrations of exclusiveness.[172] The growth in grandeur of this successful, streamlined, absolutist court and its retinue had involved extensive shorings by literary eminences, extravagant ceremonial, and symbolic declaration of autonomy in jurisprudence and rule. Medici renovation of the republican stronghold, the Palazzo Vecchio, its expansion of territory, creation of symbolic ritual and pageantry, and the eventual unfurling of the banner of Counter-Reform under the aegis of Rome were all depended upon now to hold both grand-ducal subjects and the regime's overseers, the Hapsburgs, in a thrall of conviction about its raison d'etre and its mystique.[173] The new court's genres of portrayal for women were drawn, too, from the greater European courts and infused with the ideology of absolutism.

It has also been proposed that the typical court of the sixteenth century was an entity that sought to transform the medieval baron-culture of earlier ages into a civilizing force. Its cultural significance lay precisely in its vaunted exemplary status, its self-conscious place in the 'process of civilisation.'[174] Cosimo blended the knightly ethos with that of a centralized political system on his institution of the Knights of San Stefano. In support of this carefully constructed expression of absolutism, mystique, and distinctiveness, the conscious promotion of the exclusiveness of women was cultivated by adopting large retinues and involved pageantry for them that fostered elitism and *stupore* – awe – of them, too.[175]

Onus for maintenance of a unified front would weigh on all the court's members, but it is evident that chastity for women was strictly upheld. Males could break rank in this ethical construct with impunity – Francesco and Ferdinand each had their paramours, one while married to the emperor's daughter, the other as a prominent cardinal sworn to celibacy – and Isabella's husband Paolo Orsini was a fixture in the stews of Rome.[176] Dianora's liaison was not proven as adulterous, but it was disastrously ill advised. Women who admitted male outsiders to an inner circle of power and trust appear to have threatened a rarified mystique constructed over two generations around its prince, and this was a lapse that Medici 'honour' could not admit. At an elemental level, the determination of dynasty was threatened; simply put, bloodlines had to be above question.

Within two years of Cosimo's death in 1574, a fatal fracturing of paternal protection occurred, leading to the violent deaths of the two women who had been the duke's closest and much-loved female companions. Francesco, less gifted in statesmanship, less tenacious than his father in promoting the court as a supreme nerve centre, appears to have bowed to pressure from Cardinal Ferdinando in Rome to make evident Medici control over the conduct of women in his court.[177] The tragic *delitti d'onore* – 'honour' uxoricides – of Dianora and Isabella demonstrate that implacable codes of conduct and ferocious justice prevailed for even the most privileged of women in sixteenth-century Florence.[178]

Epilogue[1]

Still annually celebrating his successful deliverance from 'the stone,' the energetic Samuel Pepys, His Majesty Charles II's rising naval personality, lapsed into unaccustomed disgruntlement on 4 October 1661. On his return to Hart Street, he confided in his diary that he had never had so little pleasure in his life as at the theatre that evening. Arriving late to an almost full house, he had been badly placed to view a performance of *The White Devil; or the Life and Death of Victoria Corombona* (1612), John Webster's dramatized version of events surrounding the infamous murder of Isabella de' Medici, Duchess of Bracciano. Scenes where an impassioned, wronged Isabella kisses her unfaithful husband's portrait each night – and is poisoned by doing so – were perhaps not played with sufficient conviction or aplomb by the boy who played her role. (On one such occasion, a lad had had his ears boxed, to the delight of an unruly audience.) Pepys neglected to record the reason for his dashed hopes, but his expectations would have been high. Webster's version of events had stood the test of fifty years, and still brings in a good house after four centuries. Pepys enjoyed Webster's *Duchess of Malfi* (vaguely based on Isabella) so much on 3 September 1662 that he swore in his diary to forego his addiction to the boards for at least a year to atone for his lapses. (It was a vow he had broken many times.)

It was all a fiction, of course, a mask that good theatre allows, but interest in legends and infamy about Isabella would not wane for centuries. It was five years after her murder that her husband Paolo and Vittoria Accoramboni actually met, in 1581. Their tragedies fuelled many dramas, among them Stendhal's *Italian Chronicles* and Alexandre Dumas's *Les Médicis*. The *Risorgimento* patriot Francesco Guerrazzi's melodrama *Isabella Orsini, Duchessa di Bracciano* (1845), on which Brogi's operetta *Isabella Orsini* (1921) is founded, even made its heroine Isabella the metaphor for his beloved Italy's political ills.

The truth had been far more tragic. Fate itself had taken retribution for Isabella's murder when Paolo and Vittoria embarked on their notorious affair. Vittoria's husband, Francesco Peretti, had been content to turn a blind eye because the affair allowed him access to Orsini's powerful circle, but he was soon murdered by Orsini's henchmen to make way for a marriage. This outcome found no favour with the Medici – no strangers to murderous solutions themselves – who were committed to young Virginio Orsini's legitimacy and had the support of Pope Gregory XIII, who immediately prohibited the new Orsini marriage. Recklessly, the couple married ten days after the pope's death in 1585. Disastrously for them, the Curia elected the relentless reformer Pope Sixtus V Peretti, uncle of Vittoria's murdered husband, Francesco. Faced with threats of internecine war with the pope, they fled – Orsini to Venice and Vittoria to Padua. Orsini died soon after. The newly widowed Duchess of Bracciano was in turn murdered within a few months by her brother-in-law, Lodovico Orsini, to enable him to recover the enormous Orsini wealth that she had inherited. Lodovico was executed by order of the Paduan authorities. This swamp of political and moral scandal broke the Orsini grip over Roman affairs forever.

Virginio Orsini, Isabella's young son, became Duke of Bracciano in 1587. He had been raised after her death at the Medici court with great affection by Grand Duke Francesco and his successor, Grand Duke Ferdinando, who had become his tutor. Showered with honours, Virginio was one of the most prominent and well-respected lords in Italy. Invested in the Order of the Golden Fleece, he became a grandee of Spain and went on to hold the secular title of Assistant to the Pontifical Throne – comparable to the rank of cardinal. He married Princess Flavia Damasceni Peretti of Piombino, grand-niece of Sixtus V Peretti, in 1589. (They had eleven children.) Virginio, acclaimed as a gifted military man, humanist, poet, and patron of the arts and music, became diplomat of the Holy See to the courts of Germany and Norway, and to the English court of Elizabeth I.

Perhaps Isabella's truest legacy was that left to the Italian language. The winnowing in the 1560s and 1570s of the linguistic beauties of Dante, Petrarch, and Boccaccio in her salon in the Medici court to refine Tuscan and its grammar into a lingua franca for Italy was prophetic. Francesco, a devotee to the cause, too, founded the Accademia della Crusca ('Bran' or 'Chaff') six years after her death. Its *impresa* was the sieve, to symbolize the Crusca's mandate to separate the grain of linguistic purity from its 'husk' or accretions. This effort culminated in the first great Italian dictionary, the *Vocabolario della Crusca*, published in Florence in 1612.

Buontalenti's Villa Medici at Cerreto Guidi, near Empoli, where Isabella died so violently, has been absorbed into the nearby hamlet. It is set opposite a peaceful, tree-shaded piazza, and is open to the public. A rope hung from the villa's dining room ceiling is intended to further a legend that Orsini strangled his wife with the help of an accomplice who, on signal, let down a noose through the ceiling as Orsini embraced Isabella after they dined.

More verifiable is the fact that Cosimo's obdurate efforts to gain precedence over the House of Ferrara may be proven with hindsight as being somewhat unnecessary. Lucrezia, whose rumored pregnancies so raised the hopes of an Este heir before her miserable death in 1561, could not have borne Alfonso a son even if fate had spared her. Contrary to his father, Ercole's pessimism regarding her desired fecundity, it was Alfonso who failed to continue the illustrious Estense line: his second and third wives, Barbara of Austria and Margherita Gonzaga, also remained childless, leading to recurrent anxiety concerning the succession until his death in 1597. The outcome of this misfortune was far-reaching: his designated successor Cesare d'Este, an illegitimate cousin, was unacceptable to the papacy, under whose grant the Estense ruled as vicars in Ferrara. Ferrara became a papal fiefdom after Alfonso's death.

Cosimino, Dianora and Pietro's three-year-old son, died only weeks after his mother's murder in 1576. As he was the only prospect at that moment to secure the Medici succession, rumours that he was poisoned by his father, Pietro, are probably not to be taken seriously. (His body was later buried near Dianora's in the splendid but gloomy Cappella dei Principi mausoleum in San Lorenzo.) Giovanna and Francesco's son, Filippo, was born in 1577 after twelve years of marriage, but he too died young, in 1582. Paradoxically, the deaths of Grand Duke Francesco and his former long-standing mistress and wife, Grand Duchess Bianca Cappello, within hours of each other in 1587 undid the family's strategy for a third Medici papacy: to save the dynasty, Cardinal Ferdinando had to be released by Sixtus V from Rome to marry Christine of Lorraine in 1589. The French alliance enriched Medici coffers by the equivalent of between $100 and $200 million U.S. dollars and, in the wake of the defeat of the Spanish Armada in 1588, it marked a turning away from the half-century of Hapsburg domination of Medici affairs.[2] The continuation of the dynasty was guaranteed by Ferdinando's able rule and their many children. Hopes for a Medici pope never were fulfilled. Leo XI de' Medici died only eleven days after his election in 1605, the last of that name to occupy the throne of St Peter.

Giulia left Florence with her husband, Bernardetto de' Medici, in 1567 – it is said over a rift between her and the duke because of her pique at having to give precedence at court to Cosimo's mistress, Eleonora degli Albizzi. Probably the two events are not connected, as she and Bernardetto were evidently in good standing with the court after they left to found the Principality of Ottaiano, to which their heirs hold title today.

If the portrait has its 'masks,' so does history. Some time after 1612, Giulia's childhood face as a *puttina* with Maria Salviati was painted out. Whether this was because her grandmother had reputedly been a Moorish slave and her features were unacceptable to posterity, or because in time her identity was no longer congruent with Maria's historic role as mother to Grand Duke Cosimo, will remain mysterious. Perhaps the panel was simply more saleable if the duke's mother was its sole subject. In any event, Maria was alone when the panel found its way to the Walters Art Museum in Baltimore in 1902, and the actual date of Giulia's obliteration has never been determined. Her restoration to light came about only in 1940 after X-rays and cleaning revealed her presence, when 'Cosimo' seemed the only likely identity for the child with Maria. Berenson soon wryly recorded, eighteen years before the 1612 inventory 'una puttina' record was discovered by Keutner, that it was 'certainly a girl, not the *boy* destined to become Cosimo I.' A significant document to a decisive turning point in Medici history, her portrait hangs in the Walters Art Museum, today labelled as Pontormo's *Portrait of Maria Salviati with Giulia de' Medici*. It was recently titled as such in Medici exhibitions at the National Gallery, Washington, in Florence, and in Philadelphia. Press interest in academic controversy over her race and sex brought Giulia brief celebrity at the outset, but scholarly approaches to the loss of 'Cosimo' are often tentative. That the inventory of 1612 recorded a little girl with Maria is sometimes followed by equivocal identification, or proposals that this brown-eyed Medici child of probable African descent – who so resembles her father, Duke Alessandro – is the grey-eyed Maria or the blonde Bia. A modern *damnatio memoriae* on Giulia may 'paint her out' for the second time in history.

Eleonora has been Bronzino's triumph. It has been through her sumptuous state portrait that the stubborn legend grew, after exhumation of her body in the nineteenth century, that she had been buried in the lavish robes of state so vividly rendered by him. This was another fiction, one finally put to rest by a moving exhibition at the Palazzo Pitti, Florence, in 1994. There were no robes of state. Her painstakingly restored burial dress was exhibited with a replica of it dressing a mannequin of her graceful proportions, in company with the grave clothes of her husband, Cosimo, and of Garcia, one of the two sons she had just mourned. The erratically laced bodice of the mended, pale-gold satin gown showed that Eleonora was hastily dressed in everyday apparel for that final journey to Florence in November 1562. A muted trace of her historic role as Duchess of Florence is recognizable only in the gown's embroidered bands of Florentine lilies.

Academic interest in the new millennium has revealed a more sympathic, less enigmatic Eleonora than before, but one no less complex. Medici disinterments have recommenced, with science now promising to flesh out our knowledge of the founders of a dynasty whose cultural and political reach extended for two centuries over European affairs.

Appendices

APPENDIX A
Genealogical Table: The Medici to Cosimo II*

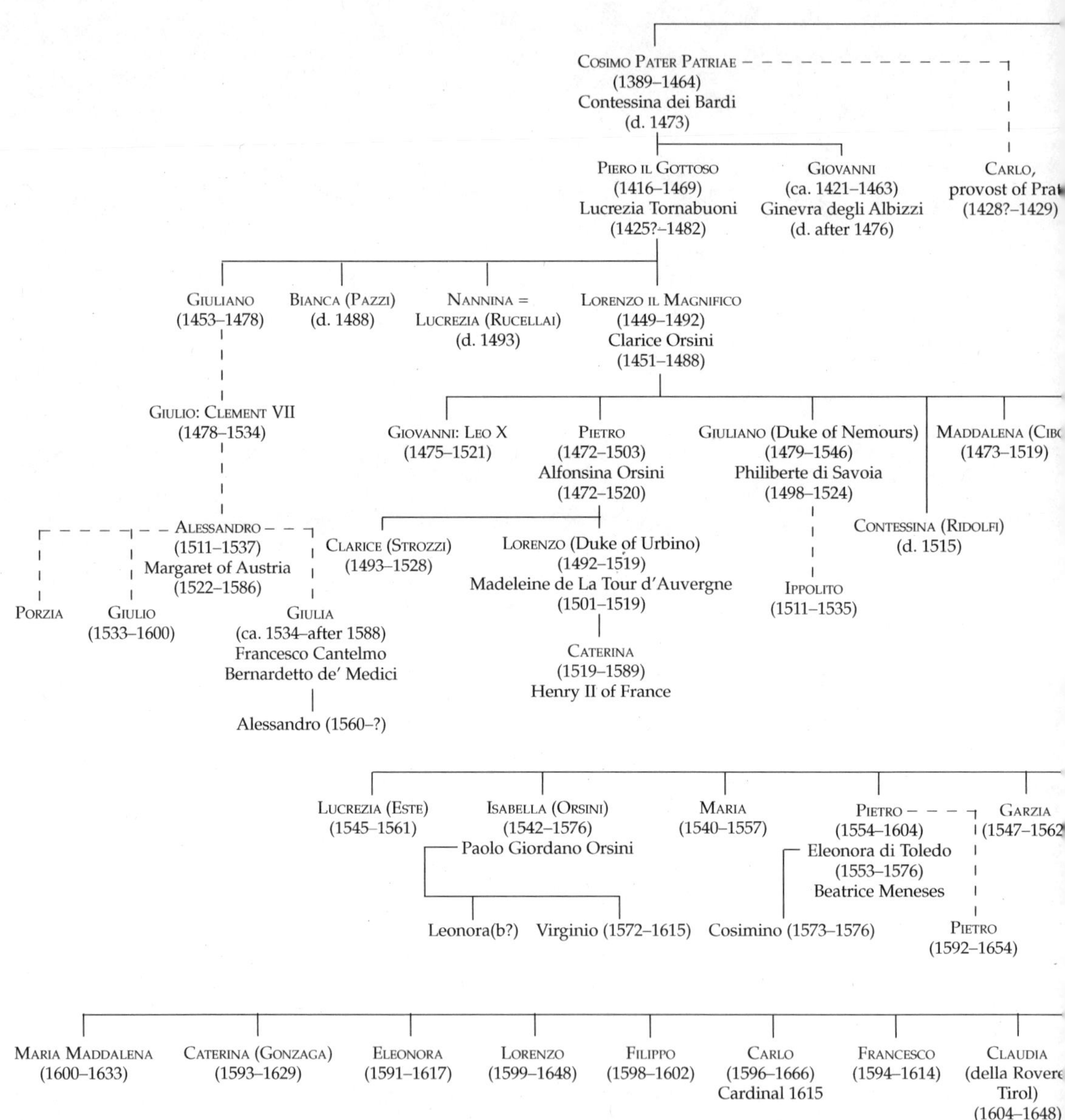

*After Langedijk 1981, 1: 10–11, with my additions.

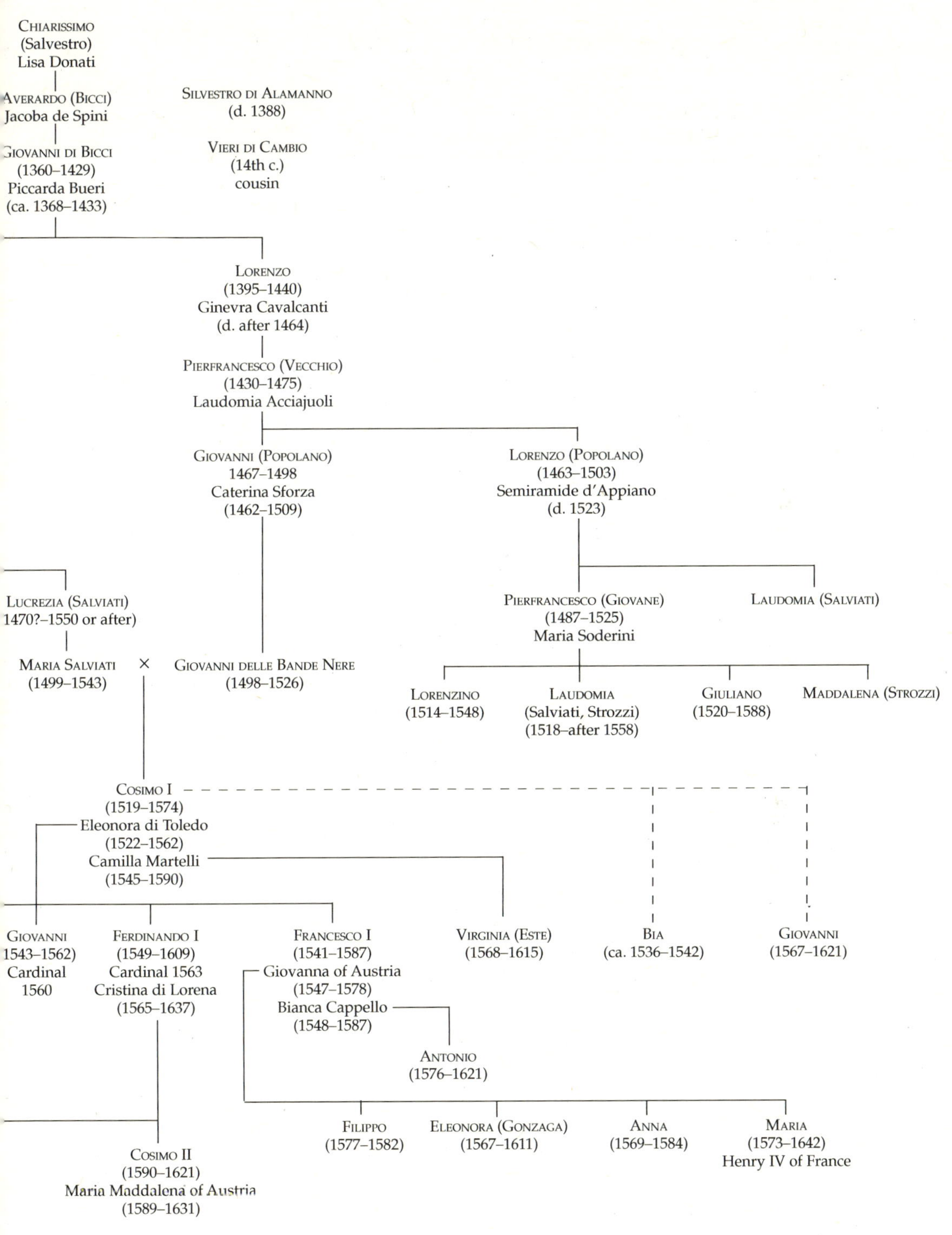

Chiarissimo
(Salvestro)
Lisa Donati

Averardo (Bicci)
Jacoba de Spini

Giovanni di Bicci
(1360–1429)
Piccarda Bueri
(ca. 1368–1433)

Silvestro di Alamanno
(d. 1388)

Vieri di Cambio
(14th c.)
cousin

Lorenzo
(1395–1440)
Ginevra Cavalcanti
(d. after 1464)

Pierfrancesco (Vecchio)
(1430–1475)
Laudomia Acciajuoli

Giovanni (Popolano)
1467–1498
Caterina Sforza
(1462–1509)

Lorenzo (Popolano)
(1463–1503)
Semiramide d'Appiano
(d. 1523)

Lucrezia (Salviati)
1470?–1550 or after)

Maria Salviati   ×   Giovanni delle Bande Nere
(1499–1543)   (1498–1526)

Pierfrancesco (Giovane)
(1487–1525)
Maria Soderini

Laudomia (Salviati)

Lorenzino
(1514–1548)

Laudomia
(Salviati, Strozzi)
(1518–after 1558)

Giuliano
(1520–1588)

Maddalena (Strozzi)

Cosimo I
(1519–1574)
Eleonora di Toledo
(1522–1562)
Camilla Martelli
(1545–1590)

Giovanni
1543–1562)
Cardinal
1560

Ferdinando I
(1549–1609)
Cardinal 1563
Cristina di Lorena
(1565–1637)

Francesco I
(1541–1587)
Giovanna of Austria
(1547–1578)
Bianca Cappello
(1548–1587)

Virginia (Este)
(1568–1615)

Bia
(ca. 1536–1542)

Giovanni
(1567–1621)

Antonio
(1576–1621)

Cosimo II
(1590–1621)
Maria Maddalena of Austria
(1589–1631)

Filippo
(1577–1582)

Eleonora (Gonzaga)
(1567–1611)

Anna
(1569–1584)

Maria
(1573–1642)
Henry IV of France

APPENDIX B

Bronzino Sonnets*

Bell'alma, e saggia, e sovr'ogni altra accorta

Bell'alma, e saggia, e sovr'ogni altra accorta,
   Come scorgeste a sì grand' uopo il vero?
   Quando di se vi diè l'arbitrio intero
   La Donna, che'l mio cor nel viso porta!
Piana diceste voi la strada, e corta
   Fia per condurve al desìo vostro vero,
   E me già freddo col mio foco altero
   Giungeste a me la sua man bianca porta,
Ben fu pietà d'Amor, ch'a ciò v'indusse
   Com'anco fe' l'altrier quella, che'l gielo,
   Ch'oggi per voi per se sola distrusse.
Cosi d'Inferno mi poneste in Cielo,
   Ond'io partimmi, e chi cagion ne fusse
   Ella ben sa, ch'a tutti gli altri il celo.

Fair spirit, prudent, and above others wise,
   How did you perceive such great need for the truth
   When the Lady who carries my heart in her face
   Gave you absolute power over herself?
You told me that the road
   Leading to your true desire was easy and short
   And, already cold with my proud fire,
   You joined her white hand to mine.
It was certainly pity of Love that led you to it
   As also did, in the past, that coldness
   That today through you destroyed only herself.
Thus from the Inferno you transported me into Heaven
   From whence I had departed; who was the reason for this
   She, whom I hide from all others, knows well.

All'Amore Supremo

   Quant'io d'Amor nella fiorita etate
   Scrisse e cantai, mentre che 'n cieco ardore

---

*Bronzino 1823, 109, 62, 81, and 29 respectively. I warmly thank Paola Tinagli and Konrad Eisenbichler for suggested refinements to my translations.

Per terrena beltà struggeasi il core,
    Posto ha in oblio di me vera pietate.
Ma queste rime, o voi che l'ascoltate,
    Sebben d'altezza e dolce stil minore,
    Avran però di santo e puro amore
    Degno subbietto in casta alma beltate;
E sebben di sospir sovente e pianto
    Sonar l'udite, e guerra, e morto, il senso,
    Che troppo chiede, ancor, che onesto il face:
L'alma non già, che 'n dolce foco, e santo
    Gioisce, e quant'io dico, e quant'io penso,
    Così 'l gustasse ognun, m'è vita, e pace.

True compassion has made me forget
    How in my flourishing youth
    I wrote and sang of Love, while in blind passion
    My heart was consumed with earthly beauty.
But these lines, oh you who listen to them
    Whether [they be] in lofty and sweet style
    Shall nevertheless have a worthy subject of holy and pure love
    Shaped in the beauty of a chaste soul.
Although often resounding with sighs and tears,
    War and death, you hear my sentiment
    Which still asks to be chastened.
Not so the spirit, which rejoices in sweet and holy fire.
    And what I proclaim and what I reflect
    And [I wish] everyone could experience it, is for me life and peace.

Cortese Donna

Cortese Donna, in vera alta onestade
    D'Amore accesa, alteramente schivo
    D'alto core, e bellezza esempio vivo
    Saggia, e perfetta in fresca acerba etade.
Di se mi degna, e sì dal cor mi rade
    Ogni basso voler, ch'io non arrivo
    Pur col pensiero in parte, ond'io sia privo
    D'un raggio sol di sua chiara bontade.
Buon tempo è gia, che, sua mercede, impresi
    Sgombrar del falso, s'l cor di vero amore
    Empiendo farmi a lei pari, o simile.
Cruda mi fu del primo, e nel dolore
    Mostrommi, oh che pietà, quant'era vile,
    Finchè d'altero, e santo ardor m'accesi.

A gracious Lady, in true high probity,
    Lit with love, loftily elusive
    A vivid, splendid example of a sublime heart
    Wise, and perfect in fresh youthfulness
Condescends to me, and so from my heart strikes out
    Each vile desire so that I do not
    Dwell on this even a little
    In case I should be deprived of even a ray of her bright goodness.
It is a long time since, thanks to her, I began
    To free myself from deceit, by filling my heart with true love
    To make myself equal to her or alike.
She was severe to me from the first, and in sorrow
    She revealed, oh what pitiful [sight], how lowly I was
    Until I was lit up by lofty and holy love.

In morte della Sig. Donna Lucrezia Medici, Duchessa di Ferrara

Chi fia, miseri noi, che ne console,
    O pur n'ancida in così gravi, e tanti
    Danni? o dar possa a così doppii pianti
    Rime con già, ma pur tronche parole?
L'alme due luci, oimè, felici, e sole.
    Gli almi due soli, oimè, si chiari, e santi
    Sono spariti, e l'alte glorie, e i vanti,
    E lo sperar di lor divina prole.
Poco t'era, o ria morte, il primo germe,
    Il più bel fiore, anzi l'aprir del giorno,
    Avere svelto, e scolorato, e spento?
Che l'altro ancor mentre sì chiaro, e adorno
    Rendea'l gran Po troncasti? ahi spemi inferme;
    Ahi viver cieco, e solo ombra, e spavento.

What will bring consolation to us wretched,
    Or what, amongst so much destruction and grievous loss, will kill us?
    How to find rhymes to these tears, with words which are yet broken?
    Alas, those two divine lights, happy and shining.
Alas, those divine suns, so clear and holy,
    Have vanished, together with [their] noble glory and merits,
    And hopes for divine progeny.
    Was it not enough, evil death,
To have extirpated, discoloured, and extinguished
    The first seedling, the most beautiful flower, in fact, the dawning of the day?
    What more did you cut short,
    While she brightened and adorned the great Po?
Alas, vain hopes! Alas, blind life, shadows and fear.

Sopra la Signora medesima

Nuova Angioletta, che l'umano scarco
    Leggiadro velo, al tuo celeste albergo
    Volasti lieta, noi smarriti a tergo.
    Lasciando in doglia, e con si grave incarco;
Poichè'n breve ora il Ciel di largo in parco
    S'è volto, e'l caro don rapito, aspergo
    D'amaro pianto il sen, ma più il sommergo
    Nel duol, di doppia, e giusta tema carco;
Che bellezze, onestate, e cortesìa,
    Chiaro sangue, alma saggio, altero ingegno
    Veggendo, e'n somma, ogni ben nostro, e speme,
Che teco venne, esser fuggito via
    Così repente, è chiaro orribil segno
    Di quel, che, di te privo, il mondo teme.

Oh new little Angel who,
    Free from your graceful human veil,
    Flew happy to your celestial abode, leaving us behind,
    Lost and in pain, and with such a heavy burden.
Because in a short moment Heaven,
    Once large, has become small,
    And the dear gift has been stolen,
    I flood my breast with bitter tears.
But the more I submerge it in my pain, [the more I am] oppressed
    By a double and just fear,
    That beauty, chastity, courtly refinement
    Famous blood, wisdom, lofty spirit,
In fact, seeing all of our blessings and hopes which accompanied you,
    Fly away so suddenly, is a clear horrible sign
    Of what the world, bereft of you, fears.

APPENDIX C

Love Poetry from Prison, ca. 1574–1576, from Bernardino Antinori (1537–1576) to Eleonora ('Dianora') di Pietro de' Medici (1553–1576)*

I
Occhi ch'alti miracoli solete
far con i dolci rai del vostro lume

*Excerpted by Saltini 1902, 6: 173–5. I thank Susan Scott-Cesaritti for refining my translation.

e le potenze interne in quel movete che di mirar vostra luce presume;
con quel poter che i cori altrui prendete,
fate in me d'Elicona sorger fiume,
ch'io dica il bel che in voi chiaro si vede,
e 'l gran valor ch'ogni valore eccede.

II
Oh che goder perfetto! oh che contento!
oh che piacere, veder due fidi amanti
mentre ciascuno è ne'begli occhi intento
dell'altro, e scorge in quelli i suoi sembiati!
Oh che soave oblio d'ogni tormento,
quand'escono i visivi spirti santi,
che con miracol si raro e sì grato
fan trasformar l'amante nell'amato!

III
Testa sostien si bella e si divina
in cui del Cielo il gran valor si scorge,
la delicata gola alabastrina
che dalle larghe spalle dritta sorge
nel bianco petto Amor gli strali affina;
...
La membra ond'ha composta la persona
son con proportion si ben formate
ch'ogni sua parte con l'altra consuona,
e tutte con tal' arte collegate
che si può dir che non fu mai persona.
ossia delle presenti ovver passate,
che avesse corpo si leggiadre e bello,
cercando il mondo in questo loco e in quello.

IV
Nella candida man pose natura
ogni suo studio per farla perfetta,
E lungo alquanto, senza vene, e pura
qual terso ivorio, poi morbida, schietta,
in cui non par che sia sforzata cura,
ma per se stessa bianca, molle e netta:
sottil le dita, senza nodi e grate,
'unghia grandette, pulite, inarcate.

V
Stupisce ogn'uomo ai graziosi gesti
se va, se posa, o balla, o parla, o ride.
Sono i bei modi in un dolci e modesti

co'quai da vita in un tempo e uccide;
gli atti, tutti amorosi e tutti onesti,
fan che onestà da amor non si divida.
Lieta si mostra e grata in ogni parte,
ascosta umil, risponde con grand' arte.

VI
Poi ch'io pur dir nol so, dicalo amore
donna, qual sia maggior mentre vi miro,
o la beltade in voi e in me l'ardore!

VII
Qual si possente e si benigna stella
ornò voi di si pregiati onori
per farvi sopra l'altre altera e bella.

I
Eyes, accustomed to working great miracles
with the sweet rays of your light
you move the inner powers of him who
dares to look at your light;
using that power with which you capture others' hearts
make a river of Helicon spring forth in me
so that I may tell of the beauty that in you shines so clear
and of your great worth exceeding all worth

II
Oh what perfect joy! oh what bliss!
Oh what pleasure, to see two trusting lovers
as each, intent on the other's eyes
sees there his own image!
Oh what sweet oblivion of all torment,
when the visible holy spirits go out
and with a miracle so rare and so welcome
transform the lover into the beloved!

III
Holding up a head so lovely and so divine
in which Heaven's great worth is revealed,
the delicate alabaster throat
rises erect from broad shoulders.
In her white breast Love sharpens his darts.
The parts of her body
are so well formed and proportioned
that every part harmonizes with the others
and all are connected so skilfully

that one could say never has there been anyone
     past or present
who had a body so graceful and lovely
though one searched the world over.

IV
Nature took every care
To make her white hand perfect,
rather long, veinless and pure
as polished ivory, and soft, flawless,
so it seems not formed by art
but in itself white, soft, and pure:
slender fingers, unbent and graceful
with generous nails, clean and curved.

V
Every man marvels at her graceful ways
as she walks or pauses, dances, or talks or laughs.
These are her lovely manners, at once sweet and modest
with which she at the same time gives life and kills;
her actions, all loving, all sincere,
Make virtue inseparable from love.
Happy she appears, and pleasant in every way,
modest, she responds masterfully.

VI
Since I don't know how, let Love say,
Lady, which is greater as I gaze on you,
the beauty in you, or the ardor in me!

VII
What powerful and kindly star
adorned you with such glorious gifts
to make you above all others so exalted and beautiful.

Terminology and Abbreviations

all' antica	in antique style/guise
Ambras group	A series of small portraits ('ritrattini') of the Medici family commissioned in 1587 by Archduke Ferdinand of Austria, brother of Archduchess Giovanna de' Medici, for his collection at Schloss Ambras, near Innsbruck
ASF	Archivio di Stato, Florence
BNF	Biblioteca Nazionale, Florence
braccio	braccio fiorentina (plural braccia) = measuring 53.3 cm
c.	carta, page
f.	folio, sheet
GDSU	Gabinetto dei Disegni e Stampe degli Uffizi, Florence
ins.	inserto
MAP	Medici avanti il Principato: ASF documents dated before 1537
MAPD	Medici Archive Project Database: documents transcribed and accessible through www.medici.org
MDP	Mediceo del Principato: ASF documents dated after January 1537
ms.	manuscript
n.d.	no date
n.p.	no page
r.	recto
scudo	= 1 fiorino = 1 ducato = 7 lire. Modern equivalents are proposed by Hollingsworth 1996, xii, and Saslow 1996[1], 18, based on typical earnings; based on their findings, the equivalent value of the scudo as used here is about $350 U.S. (A skilled worker earned about 100 ducats/scudi per annum.)
Serie Aulica	Medici portrait series, begun in 1584–5, of family members from its beginning until its extinction in the eighteenth century, in Florence
v.	verso

Notes

Introduction

1 See Woods-Marsden 2000, 3. On Michelangelo's genius as context for Medici art, see Florence, Palazzo Strozzi 2002, exh. cat., or Chicago and Detroit exh. cat., 2002.

2 Paris, Louvre. The twenty-four panels (1621–5) were designed for the Luxembourg Palace. See S. Cohen 2003; Millen and Wolf 1989, 49–52; Saward 1982, 51–7; and Held 1980, 1: 189, 202; and Spinelli 2005, 137–40, fig. 3.

3 Millen and Wolf 1989, 50, quoting ASF MDP 4615, f. 296r. For other early Marias, see Langedijk 1981, 2: cats. 86,5, 86,11, 86,12, and 86,17; see also Florence, Palazzo Pitti and Museo degli Argenti 2005, cat. no. I, 1–6 and I, 35. Maria's was the first betrothal of a Medici daughter to a reigning king. Caterina de' Medici was betrothed by Clement VII in 1532 to Francis I's second son, Henry, Duc d' Orléans, whom she married in 1533. As the Dauphin, Francis, died in 1536, Henry became king on his father's death in 1547, making Catherine Queen of France. For her wedding and these events see Young 1910, 393–405; see also Zerner 1999, 10–12.

4 On love-inducing portraits, see Kirkham 2001, 49, and see 271nn150–1 below.

5 Sansovino 1670, 200–1. (First published in Venice, 1582.)

6 See chap. 2, on Cosimo's wedding to Eleonora; chap. 7 on Francesco's to Giovanna of Austria, 1565; and, on Ferdinando's to Christine of Lorraine, 1589, Saslow 1996.

7 On his 'mania' for portraits, see Alazard 1968, 226; on Giovio, see n. 31 below.

8 See Forster 1971; Simon 1982, 1983, 1985, and 1987; and Langedijk 1981, 1: 79–120 and cat. series 27. Robert Simon's studies of Cosimo's portraits included many aperçus on women's portraits that prompted deeper investigation here. They are acknowledged in turn.

9 Several instances of the surrogacy of portraits for the absent occur in chap. 3.

10 Bronzino left for the Villa Imperiale, Pesaro, in 1530 to portray Guidobaldo della Rovere, future Duke of Urbino (Florence, Palazzo Pitti, dated 1532; see Cecchi 1996, pls. 18 and 19; Brock 2002, 48–52). Allori was groomed by Bronzino for his role. See text, 121. On the complexity of court life, see especially Cropper 2004.

11 See esp. Cropper 2004, 6–7; Hale ed. 1981, 135–7; and see also Eisenbichler ed. 2001, x–xii for a useful summary.

12 See Langdon 1992², passim; and Crum 2001², 50. The event is related here in chap. 1.

13 Margaret of Austria (1522–86) married Ottavio Farnese. See Firenzuola 1992, 74, and Eisenbichler 2001 on her life and poetry.

14 See Cox-Rearick 1993, 23, citing ASF MDP 2, ff. 121v.–3r., of 11 January 1539.

15 Francesco Salviati's *Triumph of Camillus* fresco in the Palazzo Vecchio depicts Eleonora as Juno, as fêted booty borne aloft to Florence. See Cox-Rearick 1993, figs. 2 and 27.

16 See discussion, text, 63 and 98, of Bronzino's *Giovanni with a Goldfinch* (fig. 16).

17 Fernando Alvarez de Toledo, Great Master of the King's Household, was a dominant influence on Charles's son, Philip II. Rodríguez-Salgado 1991, 209–23, 234–5; Maltby 1983, passim.

18 He was in Madrid; Cosimo's letter is quoted in Franceschini 2004, 199. See n. 20 below.

19 On his betrayal of Pietro Carnesecchi, 1567, see Cleugh 1975, 289; see also Hibbert 1980, 272–3.

20 On Maria's death, see text, 115; Lucrezia's, 144; and Eleonora, Giovanni, and Garcia's, 147 and 157. On Cosimo's dependence on Isabella and his delight in Dianora, see 147–8 and 175.

21 Jacopo de' Medici, one of two ambassadors sent to Naples for Cosimo's marriage by proxy, wrote back to Major-domo Pierfrancesco Riccio that they were ill equipped in terms of finery and courtly demeanour as well as gifts expected of them. See Adelson 1983, 148, citing ASF MDP 1169, ins. 4, f. 109–10. (29 March and 2 April 1539), Cox-Rearick 1993, 23–6, and, on the Neapolitan court, Edelstein 2000, 2004[1], and 2004[2].

22 Della Casa 1994, 19 and 61; see also Pinelli 1993, 113.

23 On their triumphal entry as conquerors into Siena in 1560, Francesco Cirni referred to the couple as 'due Semidei.' See text, 72 and 76. See text, 60, for Eleonora's complex personality.

24 See Richelson 1978, passim. Contemporary observers praised Cosimo's gravity, his beautifully modulated voice, his modesty and dignity. He detested adulators; ibid., 14 n. 4. On his self-propagandizing as symbol of state, see Kempers 1992, 284 and 290; the researches of Starn and Partridge 1992; Williams 1988, 1997, 1998; Scorza 1981, 1995, 1998; van Veen 1986, 1998; and contribution to Jacks ed. 1998 and Eisenbichler ed. 2001 as cited in chapters throughout this book.

25 On this ideology and its relation to power, see Woods-Marsden 2000, 2 and n. 3.

26 See chap. 2 for an expanded discussion of Eleonora's role in this ethos and Edelstein 2004, 187–8 on the court of Naples as its model.

27 See especially monographs on this topic by Shearman (1967) and Pinelli (1993).

28 On longing and love as implicit, appropriate responses to women's portraits see, among many references throughout this study, Rubin 1995, 406–7.

29 See Scorza 1988, 18, and A. Ricci 2001, 103–20, on his presses and cultural programs. See esp. Scherberg 2003, 26–8, who traces Cosimo's assumption of control over the informal, humanist Umidi group of *letterati*, and his merging of it with his new Accademia Fiorentina in 1541.

30 Starn and Partridge 1992, 189 and 191–2.

31 See chaps. 1–3. Giovio was a court satellite from 1551–2. Vasari added woodcut portraits to his revised *Vite*, printed on Cosimo's presses in 1568. Rubin 1996, 200–8. See Costamagna 2002, 193, on Cosimo's aristocratic court, and its pivotal influence on the development of portraiture.

32 See Cox-Rearick 1993, Edelstein 1995, Edelstein 2001 and 2004, Brock 2002, and Eisenbichler ed. 2004 on Eleonora's cultural patronage.

33 Fantoni 1999, 262.

34 For Alessandro and his 'court,' see text, 43.

35 For these criteria, see Asch and Birke eds. 1991, 8–9.

36 See ibid., 10, for these essential elements, and Warnke 1993, 225.

37 See Fantoni 1999, 255–73 and 334–6, on Cosimo's visionary ambition, the court's legacy, the dynastic extinction in 1737, and Florence as courtly centre to the nineteenth century.

38 Pietrosanti 1991 (13–16, 23–9, and 42–4) comments that religious overtones of the ducal couple's *entrata* into Siena recalled Christ's entry into Jerusalem on Palm Sunday.

39 Maria di Francesco married Henry IV in 1600. See n.3 above.

40 For Varchi, see Barocchi ed. 1998 and Mendelsohn 1982. Corrias 1993, 169–72, summarizes Borghini's role; see also Barzman 2001, 177–88.

41 Winspeare 1961, 147, quoting Giovan Battista Cini, Cosimo's contemporary biographer, contrasts this amusing *'sducarsi'* with his customary *gravitas*. On Cosimo as *paterfamiglia*, see D'Addario 1972, 301 and Darr 2002, 5.

42 See Woodall ed. 1997, xiii and 18, on this problem.

43 Kemp ed. 1989, 26. On Leonardo's landmark three-quarters pose, the eye as the 'window of the soul,' and the connected gaze of the sitter's eyes to the viewer's, see Garrand 1992, 59–61. See Shearman 1992, 118; and Land 1994, 81–97, for poetic 'captivation' by portraits in Bembo's, della Casa's, and Aretino's verses. Castiglione visualizes his wife, Ippolita, playing, laughing, and joking before Raphael's portrait of him (now in the Louvre); Land 1994, 85–6. See also Rosand 1981, 294–6, Syson 1998, 13–14, and Langdon 2001 and 2004.

44 See Leonardo da Vinci 1956 1: xi–xiii; on this circulation, see Armenini 1977, 11–12.

45 Heydenreich 1956, 1: xi–xiv, and Barzman 1989, 27 n.6.

46 Blunt 1940, 35 and 124; Leonardo 1956, 1: 147, varies slightly. The *Codex Urbinas Latinus 1270*, a compilation made around 1550 of Leonardo's writings, was seen by Vasari and Lomazzo in the 1550s. The precept appears on folio 125v.

47 'It would be absurd if the hands of Helen or Iphigenia were old and gnarled ... [A]ll the members should conform to a certain appropriatness ... [I]t would be unsuitable to dress ... Jove in the clothes of a woman. Antique painters ... [were diligent] in expressing the function, kind and dignity of whatever they painted.' Alberti 1956, 74–5.

48 Written in the first century BC. Langdon 1992[1], 25–9, traces its Cinquecento appeal: Cristoforo Landino's commentary appeared in Florence in 1482; Badius Ascensius's edition in Paris in 1500 and Milan by 1518, with Tuscan and French versions circulating from the 1530s.

49 For decorum of age, rank, fortune, etc. in Horace's *Ars poetica*, see Brink ed. 1963, lines 73–8, esp. 99ff. and 153ff., 176–80, 201ff., and 312f. Advice to the poet to effectively move his audience occurs in lines 333ff. In *Rhetoric*, III, Aristotle concurs: 'Each class of men, each type of disposition, will have its own appropriate way of letting truth appear. Under "class" I include differences of age, as boy, man, or old man; of sex, as man or woman; of nationality, as Spartan or Thessalian ... [A] rustic and an educated man will not say the same things nor speak in the same way.' Plato examines noble decorum in *Republic*, IV, 420; and Giovanni Pontano's *De Principe* (Naples, ca. 1490) urged Cicero's ideal of princely decorum on dress, speech, and expression to effectively proclaim majesty. For these see Schmitt et al. eds. 1988, 424–5.

50 Weinberg 1961, 1: 81–2. Of interest with respect to sixteenth century appreciation of the transformative effects of dress is Machiavelli's memorable description of the effect on

him of donning royal and curial robes to feel *appropriately* dressed when he sought to commune itellectually with the ancients during his writing of *The Prince*. Scherberg 2003, 48 reproduces and translates the letter, written on 10 December 1513 to Francesco Vettori.

51 Ibid., 1: 77. Horace (1963) implies this in lines 333ff.

52 Ibid., 1: 75, 77; Horace, ll. 333ff., emphasizes the poet's intent to profit or to please.

53 Ibid., 1: 45, 89–90. Rensselaer Lee's exposition on 'ut pictura poësis' of 1940 stands as the foundation study. See Langdon 1992¹, 25–47 on this precept in poetics and art treatises; see also Ames-Lewis 1992, 7–14.

54 Weinberg 1961, 1: 127, quoting Dolce's *Osservationi nella volgar lingua*.

55 L. Dolce, *La Poetica d'Horatio tradotta per Messer Lodovico Dolce* (Venice, 1535).

56 See Weinberg 1961, 1: 127; and Feinberg 1991, 9–10. On Bronzino as poet-painter, see Parker 2000 and 2003; and Brock 2002, 6–17.

57 See Kemp 1992, 15.

58 Pino's *Dialogo* is typical of the genre. Fabio, a Florentine 'didactic' voice, and Lauro, a Venetian gallant, are each posed to give resonance to the other's complementary point of view – or the witty undermining of either. See Pino 1983, 121–31. On the *Cortegiano* as a 'portrait of Urbino,' and Castiglione as the 'portraitist's' voice, see Rosand 1981, 293.

59 See Langdon 2004, 55–6, on Eleonora as earthly reflection of Mary and as Petrarchan ideal in her state portrait (pl. 4); on other sacred overtones, text, 72–7.

60 Vasari 1878–85, 7: 688, on his portrait of Luigi Guicciardini; of his friend Antonio de' Nobili, Cosimo's treasurer-general, which he was 'compelled to do against my inclination ... [but did] with great diligence.' Rubin 1995, 394, notes Vasari's aim, to improve on his infusion of '*fiato*' – the 'breath of life' – by copying Raphael's *Leo X*, owned then by Ottaviano de' Medici. See esp. Shearman 2003, 1: 904–5.

61 Rubin 1995, 208. For Vasari's other portrait interests, see n. 31 above.

62 Blunt 1940, 89.

63 See Pommier 1998, 79; Rubin 1990, 42; Simons 1995, 263–311; and Langdon 2004.

64 Blunt 1940, 89, citing Vasari's life of Domenico Puligo; Vasari 1878–85, 4: 462–3.

65 Blunt 1940, 89, quoting Vasari 1878–85, 9: 171.

66 Vasari 1878–85, 4: 352.

67 See ibid., 7: 637. On damask and brocade robes, see text, 70–1.

68 Syson 1998, 10, citing G. Rouillé's introduction to his *Prima parte del Prontuario delle medaglie* (Lyons, 1553).

69 Shearman 1992, 112; on infusion of 'the breath of life' see also Pommier 1998, 75–92.

70 Implications of Bronzino's *trompe l'oeil* effects are examined in chaps. 2, 71, and and 3, 144.

71 He criticizes earlier art: 'In proportion there was wanting a certain correctness of judgment ... *a grace exceeding measurement*.' Vasari 1878–85, 4: 9. Firenzuola's dialogue, completed in 1541, appeared posthumously in 1548.

72 Blunt 1940, 87, 91–2, scathingly comments on Vasari's emphasis on *grazia*.

73 See Barocchi ed. 1960–2 1: 207–69, and 1971–7, 2: 1690. Pardo 1983, 153, supports Summers 1979 and Rossi 1977 in linking Vincenzo's theories to Michelangelo's. Vincenzo was in Florence from 1557. See Vasari 1878–85, 7: 630–3.

74 Summers 1981, 58. See also Barocchi 1971–7, 2: 1688ff.

75 On *grazia* and poetics in decorum at mid-century, see Weinberg 1961, 1: 434–7.

76 See Rossi 1977, 128, on Michelangelo and Varchi as its inspirational sources. Vincenzo is seen to supremely unify diverse streams of Neoplatonism. Barocchi 1971–7, 2: 1689.

77 Rossi 1977, 130, quoting Castiglione (1528), book 1, xxvi; see also Rossi 1977, 131.

78 Castiglione 1959, 41. On Vasari and *grazia*, see Pinelli 1993, 110–14.

79 Furno 1902, 11, 47, 69, and 102; see also Summers 1979, 221.

80 Ultimately, however, Vincenzo is seen as a modern eclectic, as the Aristotelian maxim of portraying 'things as they ought to be' strongly informs his treatise. See Rossi 1977, 147.

81 On consciously produced effects in portraits of beloved women, and the 'io' who addresses a 'tu,' with its locus in the Petrarchan lyric tradition, see Cropper 1995, 197–9.

82 See Goldstein 1988, 30–2, citing Bellori's theory of Ideas; Langdon 1992[1], 46 n. 74; and, on *grazia*'s contemporary Christian context and meanings, Mendelsohn 1982, xix.

83 Varchi, *Libro della beltà e grazia*, written after his pardon and return from exile, 8 March 1543. See Mendelsohn 1982, 190–1; see also Blunt 1940, 93.

84 Mendelsohn 1982, 277 n. 157, citing Varchi's dependence on Bembo's definition of beauty. On its roots in Petrarch and Ficino, see Barocchi 1971–7, 2: 1671–81.

85 Firenzuola was tied to Varchi's circle by Aretino in a postscript to a letter to Firenzuola in 1541 from Venice. See Aretino 1957–60, 1: no. CXXXVI, 199–201.

86 Bronzino corresponded with Varchi during his political exile in Padua. Prior to its amalgamation by Cosimo into the Accademia Fiorentina in 1541, the artist belonged to the light-hearted Accademia degli Umidi, where his output was dialogue, vernacular sonnets, and especially burlesque poetry. See Mendelsohn 1982, 14–15, and 25. For Bronzino's poetry, see Bronzino 1823 and 1988, and Furno 1902; Parker's critiques, 1995, 1997, and 2000; and Langdon 2004 on his Petrarchan infusions into women's portraits. See Nencioni 1983, and Sherberg 2003 for Cosimo's new Academy, and his political motives for its foundation.

87 For Varchi's influence on Medici cultural endeavours see text, 80–1, 89, 91, 95–7. See also Pommier 1998, 84–7, on a painter's power to create an implicit dimension of the *anima* of the sitter.

88 Warnke 1993, 208.

89 Mendelsohn 1982, 84.

90 See Paleotti 1971, 2: 117–517. De Hollanda's claim to have moved in Michelangelo's circle is accepted in de Hollanda 1979, viii, and 1998, 5; Deswarte-Rosa 1991; Sohm 1994, 775; and see Clements 1969 and Pommier 1998, 47.

91 Summers 1981, 137. See de Hollanda 1998, 1–8, on his Roman writings.

92 'What a lofty thing is Decorum; and how little painters who are not painters work at it, and how much the great painter attends to it.' This was spoken in the wake of virulent attacks on his *Last Judgment*, after 1541. See Hartt, 644, and Blunt 1940, 118–24.

93 De Hollanda 1868. Fournier notes the original's clumsy syntax and punctuation. It was translated into Spanish by Manuel Diniz in 1563; for the Portuguese, see de Hollanda 1984. On de Hollanda, see John Bury 1989, and Lorne Campbell 1990, ix and 86; I thank them each for useful discussions on de Hollanda.

94 De Hollanda 1868, 339–40.

95 Ibid., 344 and 355.

96 Ibid., 336–9. Because of the excellence of Apelles's portrait of Alexander's favourite concubine, Campaspe, she was given in gratitude to Apelles – a comment on the portraitist's challenge to improve on nature. Great patrons nobly express their appreciation

through Francisco's interlocutor 'Fernando'; and an assertion that the court portrait-ist's burden was almost superhuman is also a theme in the treatise.

97   He relates that, to avoid distraction, his father, Antonio was allowed to work alone on a portrait of Charles V at Toledo. Likewise, the Queen of Portugal thoughtfully ejected intrigued courtiers as Francisco worked on the king's portrait. Ibid., 341.

98   Ibid., 336–9. He deplores proliferation of execrable portraits of lesser nobility – excellence of noble character was not served by poor artistic quality.

99   Blunt 1940, 103–36; Shearman 1967, 165–70; and M. Hall 1979. See n. 106 below on the Council of Trent.

100   Paleotti 1960–2, 2: 370.

101   Ibid., 2: 372.

102   My italics. Ibid., 2: 332, treating of the official portraiture of princes.

103   See Pommier 1998, 81–2. When drying, Titian's *Paul III* was deferentially saluted.

104   See 105–6, 263nn43–7 on Van der Velden's analysis of Aby Warburg's pioneering study (1902) on Medici *boti*, wax images of living or dead members set up in Florentine churches to maintain an aura of power or to commemorate them. In 1527, Clement VII's *boti* were ground to dust by enraged citizens. See Pommier 1998, 92–4, on their hyperrealism and function.

   'Magical' perceptions of portraits were widespread. In 1586, an Irish rebel insulted an image of Elizabeth I: Sir Brian O'Rourke 'fell with such spiteful and traitorous speeches to rail at it, and otherwise so filthily to use it ...' Abject devotion was equally possible – prostration before her portrait is also recorded. L. Campbell 1990, 222.

105   See Rogers 2000[1], 375, review of Woods-Marsden (1998), and of Mann and Syson eds. (1998).

106   At the nineteenth ecumenical council, held at Trento (1545–7, 1551–2, and 1562–3), certain Catholic doctrines were reformulated to counter Protestantism.

107   Pino's *Dialogo di pittura* (1548), Dolce's *Aretino* (1557), Danti's *Il primo libro de trattato delle perfette proporzioni* (1567), and Lomazzo's *Trattato dell'Arte della Pittura, Scultura, ed Architettura* (1584) provide many instances and are further cited here.

108   Aristotle, *Poetics*, Else ed. 1978, 4–7; on Borghini and Aristotle, see Corrias 1993, 171.

109   *Poetics*, 1978, 44.

110   Paleotti 1971, 2: 344. See also Kemp 1992, 15–23, for Alberti, Leonardo, and others on the painter's *virtù*.

111   See Kempers 1992, 5, on the dominant role of the client and implications for a painter of a court environment; see Rubin 1995, 22, on Vasari's pursuit of courtly ideals and rank.

112   For codification of decorum as axiomatic in portrayal by Roger de Piles in Dom Bernety, *Dictionnaire ... de peinture, sculpture et gravure* (Paris, 1756), see Saisselin 1963, 5.

113   On the period's 'willing submission to enjoyable deceptions on the part of the spectator,' see Rogers 2000[1], 375, and 2000[2], 375, rev. of Woods-Marsden (1998), and of Mann and Syson (1998). See also R. Williams 2000, 357, on audience susceptibility to illusion.

114   See Cropper 2001[3], Washington (2001), cat. no. 36, for inscriptions on front or verso of panels as expanded reference for a subject; D.A. Brown, ibid., cat. no. 16 (Leonardo's *Ginevra de' Benci*, 1474–8), and cat. no. 30 (the *cartellino* in Domenico Ghirlandaio's *Giovanna degli Albizzi*). See Brock 2002, chap. 2, 'To Each Their Own Mask,' on Bronzino's female portraits; Cropper 1997, 92–8, on his *Pygmalion and Galatea* cover for Pon-

tormo's *Halberdier, Francesco Guardi,* and Cropper in Ottawa 2005, cat. no. 81, who observes that the connection between cover and portrait often resembled that between the two sides of a medal, in which an allegorical image on the reverse commented ingeniously on the appearance of the figure on the obverse. See also Simons 1995, 270–1; Barolsky 1998, 451; and Brock 2002, 52–8.

115 See Syson 1998, 12–13.

116 Cropper 1997, 80, describes such prompts as 'visual hieroglyphs' for identification.

117 See Fantoni 1999, 272.

118 See Langdon 1992², expanded here in chap. 1 for examples of such incongruities and defacement; Cropper's probing monograph on Pontormo's *Halberdier* refuted another 'Cosimo' in 1997.

119 See Pinelli 1993, 110, in the context of Vasari's *grazia* especially.

120 See Cox-Rearick's studies on Medici art since 1984 and authors listed in n. 24 above; Fantoni 1989; Pietrosanti 1991; and Pinelli 1993. Simon's studies of Bronzino's *Cosimo* portraits since 1984 are rich in context of the ducal environment. For festivals, see Wisch and Munshower eds. 1990; Starn and Partridge 1992; and Saslow 1996.

121 Notably, Janet Cox-Rearick's *Bronzino's Chapel of Eleonora* (1993) expanded Medici ducal contexts and enriched awareness of Eleonora's role as regent, as have the writings of Bruce Edelstein. Konrad Eisenbichler's 2004 edition is devoted to her cultural milieu.

122 See Warnke 1993, 194–6 and 212; and Cropper 2004, 1–32.

123 See Woodall 1989 and 1991; L. Campbell 1990; Schneider 1994; Tinagli 1997; Pommier 1998; Woods-Marsden 2001; and contributions to Johnson and Matthews Grieco eds. 1997; to Woodall ed. 1997; and to Mann and Syson eds. 1998. Especially, see Shearman's chapter 'Portraits and Poets' in 1992, 108–48; and recent, important exhibitions in Washington (2001), Ann Arbor (2002), and Philadelphia (2004). See also n. 113.

124 See Cropper 1985, 1986, 2000, and 2004, and Rogers 1986, on Petrarchism. See Rogers 1988 on conduct books: principal authors were Trissino, Firenzuola, and Luigini. These scholars spurred my earlier study of decorum in Medici womens' portraits (Langdon 1992¹).

125 Both pioneers continued to widen the scope of enquiry in these fields: see Cropper 1995, 1998, 2001, and 2004; and Rogers 1991, 1998, and 2000. Important contributions were made by Wiesener 1993; and Tinagli 1997, who cut across a range of genres to reveal cultural ideology and apprehensions for women's decorum. Relevant collected editions are Johnson and Matthews Grieco eds. 1997; Woodall ed. 1997; Lawrence ed. 1997; Mann and Syson eds. 1998; Panizza ed. 2000; and Reiss and Wilkins eds. 2001. See, too, D.A. Brown 2001; and Dixon ed. 2002. An exposition of Italian sixteenth-century issues surrounding decorum by Robert Williams appeared in 1997; portraits are not a focus, but see chap. 2: 'Style, Decorum, and the Viewer's Experience.'

126 See Brock 2003; and Cropper 2004.

127 See Plazzotta and Keith 1999, for X-ray revelations of dense reworking of its figures and interpretation of Bronzino's revisions.

128 See Rogers ed. 2000, 14. Rabb and Brown 1986, 4–6, argue that in teasing out the complex implications of symbols, mental patterns, and cultural structures, scholars 'hope for the tangible and the concrete that flows eternal in the land of the implicit.'

129 See Welch 1997, 22–3; Holly 1998, 476; and Langdale 1998, 479–97, on responses to the

concept, noting Baxandall's deep anthropological analysis of a society's visual culture; Cropper 1995, 164–5; and Ames-Lewis and Rogers eds 1998, xv–xvi.

130 Tinagli 1997, 8–9, and see next note.

131 See Reiss and Wilkins eds. 2001, xix, n. 12, and xx, n. 18, supporting Tinagli; Elam 1996 and Barolsky 1998 on more nuanced positivism; Panizza 2000, xviii, and Sohm 1994, 759–60, on misplaced modern applications; Winn 1981, 123–4, pleading interdisciplinary approaches and historicity; and Rabb and Brown 1986, 6, refuting 'temporal imperialism.'

132 On Gombrich, see Tinagli 1997, 7; and Mann 1998, 12, on historicity in portrait study.

133 Tinagli 1997, 7.

134 See especially Cropper 1995, passim, and notably 160–74 and 190–205.

Chapter 1

1 Vasari 1878–85, 4: 281–3. See text and n. 6 below, on the lost Castello frescoes.

2 For Maria's genealogy, see appendix A. On Giovanni, see G. de' Rossi 1997, 24–5; on Aretino and Giovanni, see Booth 1921, 13–21.

3 See Tosi 1906, 106–7. See also Adriani 1583, 1: 195. For her direction of Cosimo's humanist education as a child, see Mannucci 1586, 33–4.

4 Baia 1907, 32. She died at her villa at Castello, near Monte Morello, north of Florence. Conti 1893, 44–5, 275–6, quotes Francesco Campana's letter to Pier Francesco Riccio of 12 December 1543 arranging transfer of her body and relocation of the children there: 'Since at this time Lady Francesca, her sister, and Lady Cassandra, returned in the Lady [Maria]'s litter, it will be necessary to send it back to convey these three little children, although someone told the coachman to keep it [the coach] waiting at the door to send it out again, and I commend myself thoroughly to your Lordship. From Castello, December 12th, 1543.' See also Simon 1982, 196, and n. 59 below on her death mask. Her body was removed to the Dominican convent of S. Caterina in Piazza S. Marco, to which she was attached as a tertiary member of the Order. See Cox-Rearick 1993, 398, quoting Settimanni (1681–1763) ASF Manoscritti, 126, II, I, 301.

5 Pieraccini 1986, 1: 479–85, describes her final illness.

6 Vasari 1878–85, 6: 283. Borghini 1584, 484, reported them almost indecipherable.

7 Pilliod 2001, 17, nn. 13, 14, and fig. 18, proposed a Pontormo sketch as a study for a portrait of Maria made between 1537–42 (British Museum, Inv. P p. 1–57 verso), but the face is indeterminate. An *Enthroned Madonna and Child* might also be considered, as there are clouds about its baldacchino and elaborate throne. Perhaps it was a study for Pontormo's lost *Nostra Donna*, which Cosimo acquired in 1564. Cox-Rearick 1981, 127–30, 230, and cat. no. A212, 395, who did not propose any identification for the drawing.

8 Vasari 1878–85, 7: 598. The list is not chronological; Ferdinando was born six years after Maria died.

9 Beck 1974[1], 64–6, citing ASF Guardaroba, 45, f. 59v., who notes a recurrence in ASF 65, f. 161a, the latter a copy of filza 45, which was continually updated until 1567.

10 See Langedijk 1981, 2: cat. 87,12; and Beck 1972, 10, 1974, 66, and 1974[2], 61–2. Another entry, a 'ritratto della Signora Maria' by Luigi Fiamingo, separate from those of Cosimo's children, is presumably lost. Langedijk, ibid., cat. 87.13, notes also a 1666 guardaroba entry for a *Maria Salviati*, 1¼ × 1 *braccio* (73 × 58 cm), which does not con-

form to any extant portrait of her. For those proposed here, see nn. 11, 71, and 181 for measurements. Perhaps the reference was to a copy. Falciani 1995, 131, gives the Baltimore *Maria with a Child*, to Bronzino's circle.

11 Frankfurt, Inv. 1136, Städelsches Kunstinstitut, 89.7 × 70.5 cm. See Cropper, 2001[3], cat. no. 39; Brock 2002, 61–2, 69–72; and Strehlke 2004, cat. no. 24. Berti 1973, no. 117, tied it to the Riccardi inventory 1612: 'A portrait of similar height from the hand of Jacopo Pontormo, showing a lady with a small dog, with a gilded frame.' In 1802 its attribution was to Bronzino; Berenson's in 1896 to Pontormo gained acceptance for a few decades, with cautious support from Hiller von Gaertringen 2004, 492. Baccheschi 1973, cat. 164, lists Smyth, Shearman, and Cox-Rearick for Bronzino. Berti 1993, 265; Costamagna 1994, 296; Cecchi 1996[1], 18; and Cropper 2001[3], cat. no. 39, all agree on Bronzino.

   Smyth 1955, 113–15, gave a lucid account of its style with his attribution to Bronzino: '[T]here is many an indication of Bronzino here, not only in the general aspects like the strict composition and the clean luminous volume, but in morphological details and minute matters of handling ... One should observe the symmetrical formation of the face, its flat contours, the shaping of the forehead, brows, eyebrows and the eyes with their encasing lids, the ears and nostrils, the flat plane above the lips, the lighting around the mouth.' On identification as Maria, see Simon 1982 at n. 15 below; Costamagna 1994, 297, proposed Francesca Salviati, found to be inconclusive by Cropper 2001[3], cat. no. 29, and Hiller von Gaertringen 2004, 494.

12 M.H. de Young Memorial Museum, 127 × 100 cm, Kress Collection. Baccheschi 1973, cat. no. 30, linked it to the 1560 inventory entry. Langedijk 1981 omits it; Simon 1982, 190, repudiates a Maria identification. Cecchi 1996[1], 46, believes it shows Maria before her death; also Brock 2002, 79–80, dating it to the year of her death, 1543, but her three-year-long illness would probably have precluded protracted sittings. See nn. 4 and 5.

13 Note especially the thin lips of the San Francisco *Lady*. Possibly this is Maria's mother, Lucrezia Salviati (ca. 1470–1553), whose letters in 1540 suggest a vital seventy-year-old. See ASF ff. 429 and 435 (MAPD 345); on Lucrezia, see also Maguire 1927, 175.

14 See Langedijk 1981, 2: cat. 56,3 and 87,3.

15 Simon 1982, 197–200, detailing similarities in all facial features. For Hiller von Gaertringen's (2004) recent return to a Pontormo attribution, see n. 11.

16 C.H. Smyth 1955, 112–15. Baccheschi 1973, cat. nos. 3, 10, 29, believed that Bronzino had seen Parmigianino's *Gian Galeazzo Sanvitale*, 1524. See McCorquodale 1981, 25. Cropper 2001[3], cat. no. 39, notes a 'republican' austerity combined with Bronzino's courtliness of the 1530s, and disputed Costamagna's identification with Francesca Salviati.

17 Nigro 1994, caption to pl. X3, who sees this as uncharacteristic of Pontormo.

18 The Capponi Chapel decor was begun in 1525. For the ceiling *tondi*, see Cecchi 1996[1], colour pl. 5, who saw their saturated colours reflected in the *Lady with a Lapdog*, ibid., 15–16; he assigned the panel to Bronzino's Pesaro period. See n. 19.

19 Cropper 2001[3], cat. no. 39, dated the Frankfurt panel to ca. 1533, and noted comparisons to Bronzino's *Young Man with a Book*, New York, dated ca. 1529, before his Pesaro sojourn. Cox-Rearick 1982, 78 n. 14, surveyed its wide dating: C.H. Smyth 1955, 117–24: 1527–9; Shearman 1963: early 1530s (she agrees); Burroughs 1909: early 1530s with additions ca. 1545; Forster 1965 dates it to 1542–6. Berti 1993, 265, dates it ca. 1540; Costamagna 1994, cat. no. A58, to 1533; Cecchi 1996[1], 18, to the early 1530s, but see

n. 18. Brock 2002, 69, summarizes the dating to the onset of the 1530s; Hiller von Gaertringen 2004, 490–2 dates it to the early 1530s; Strehlke 2004, cat. no. 24 concurs.

20 See Capretti in Florence, Palazzo Pitti, 2002 exh. cat; and Berti 1993, 136–7. Loved by Machiavelli and others, the cultivated courtesan, Barbara Salutati, was portrayed by Puligo (1492–1527). See Vasari 1878–85, 4: 465, an identification for the panel that is widely accepted; Slim 2002[1] is the fundamental study. Barbara's costume, hairstyle, and headdress parallel the style of the Frankfurt woman's, and a brilliant red dress also dominates the composition. Puligo's *Portrait of a Woman as the Magdalen* (Ottawa) is dressed in similar style, and has been dated to ca. 1520–5. See Elena Capretti in Ottawa 2005. cat. no. 50. For Pontormo's *Woman with Spindles*, Uffizi, Florence, see Berti 1993, 138, and Costamagna 1994, 280, cat. no. A27, summarizing scholarly dating, mostly to the mid-1520s; and Nigro 1994, colour pls. X2, X3; her costume is strikingly close to the Frankfurt woman's, as is that for the *Woman in Yellow*, Windsor, late 1520s. Shearman 1983, cat. no. 3, suggests that the latest date would be 1530 for Bronzino's *Woman in Green* (*Dianora Sofferoni?*) in Windsor, ibid., cat. 55, the outlines of whose dress and headdress follow those of the Frankfurt woman's. See Strehlke 2004, cat. no. 20, 98–9. For del Sarto's *Girl with a Volume of Petrarch*, Uffizi, Florence, and drawing for a woman with a book, Uffizi, Florence, see Pope-Hennessy 1966, figs. 258 and 259; Costamagna 1994, 280, cat. no. A26, agrees with general dating of around 1525. (Andrea died in 1530.) Bacchiacca's *Lady with a Nosegay*, 1520s, also wears a high-waisted dress, square neckline, and billowing sleeves. See Cropper 2001[3], cat. no. 37. See also Giulio Romano's *Isabella d'Este*, Hampton court, ca. 1524, where the high waist, enormous sleeve, and wide *balzo* or headdress echo the trend, L. Campbell 1990, fig. 139.

21 All appear in Cecchi 1996[1], figs. 47, 51, 58, 65, and 69; see also Brock 2002.

22 See the discussion below of the contemporary widow's costume and demeanour, and of Maria's strict adherence to the custom, in context of Pontormo's *Maria Salviati with Giulia*.

23 She is heavily veiled and unadorned as witness in the Sala di Clemente VII scene, Palazzo Vecchio, *The Marriage of Catherine de' Medici to the Dauphin of France*, 1533. For the prescribed widow's costume, see Sangiorgi 1973.

24 See Harbison 1990, 285–6, and here, 154–7.

25 The Counter-Reformation churchman Gabriele Paleotti proscribed the inclusion of dogs in women's portraits as indecorous frivolities, asserting that the dignity of the sitter, especially a mature one, was thereby undermined. Paleotti 1971, 340. The topic is discussed at length in chap. 6, with regard to portraits of Isabella de' Medici with and without a dog. In Bronzino's *Joseph Tapestries*, Potifar's seductive wife has a tiny lapdog stationed at her knee, at the leg of an ornately carved bed. See Cox-Rearick 1993, fig. 69.

26 For the motto on Allegrini's *Maria* engraving, see fig. 8 and n. 39. (On Allegrini, see Langedijk 1989, 3: appendix D.) For strictures on widows by churchmen, see Valone 1992; for books of manners on widowhood, see below, in the context of *Maria Salviati with Giulia de' Medici*. See Vaccaro 2001, 183, on exhortations for widows to eschew remarriage for chastity and piety – as ordered by St Jerome, a patron invoked by widows.

27 These are contentious: see Forlani-Tempesti and Giovannetti 1994, cat. no. 41, 127, for the scholarship to date; Cecchi 1996[1], 6, gives *St. Matthew* to Bronzino, as did Baccheschi 1973, cat. no. 6; Pilliod 2001, fig. 60, prefers Pontormo for it; Brock 2002, 24, gives Saints *Mark* and *Luke* to Bronzino.

28 For analysis of Bronzino's stylistic emergence in the 1520s from Pontormo, see C.H. Smyth 1949[2], 191, and 1955, 114; Pilliod 2001; and D.A. Brown 2004. Bronzino's *Lady in Green* (Windsor Castle), Brown 2004, cat. 20, proposed by Shearman and Pilliod as Matteo Sofferoni's daughter, is close in date to the Frankfurt panel, as the general lines of costume suggest; stylistically less emancipated from Pontormo's idiom, it may date to about 1525. For *Guidobaldo* see Brock 2002, 48–52, and Philadelphia 2004, 23 and 90.

29 Krystof 1998, 112, fig. 104; see also A. Wright 2001.

30 Vasari 1878–85, 7: 596. See Cecchi 1996[2], 370, for Bronzino about this time, and Cropper 2004, 1–25.

31 On his urge to return to his early master Raffaellino del Garbo's linearity and decorativeness, which was native to his own artistic bent, see C.H. Smyth 1949[2], 190–205. See Costamagna 1994, 296, cat. A58, and Cropper 2001[2] on Bronzino's 'new' style.

32 Black chalk, 20.2 × 12.3 cm, Florence, Uffizi, Gabinetto Disegno e Stampe no. 6680F. See Langedijk 1981, 2: cat. 87,15 (Pontormo), noting Maria's youth. She is a young wife, lightly veiled, as is Isabella (fig. 50), who was never widowed; see also Cropper 2001[3], cat. no. 35, dated 1508. Compare Maria's widowly, opaque, long veil over a dark, nondescript dress, Langedijk ibid., cat. 87,1–14; her dress in the Baltimore panel (pl. 2) is characteristic.

   See Cox-Rearick 1981, 305, cat. 335, fig. 333 (Pontormo); Cox-Rearick 1989, 18. *Pace* Strehlke 2004, cat. no. 46 (Pontormo) see Langdon 2005, on the drawing as a live record of Maria, not a youthful (male) workshop model, by Bronzino.

33 See Strehlke 2004, cat. no. 13, for the *Ippolito* drawing. Forster 1965, 224, gave the youthful Uffizi *Maria* drawing to Bronzino, dating it 1527–30, before his Pesaro sojourn, 1530–2. Its style is consistent with the Chatsworth drawing, Bronzino's *Man with a Lute*, ibid., fig. 24, dated before Pesaro by McCorquodale 1981, 44. Maria's cool gaze and the domination of the left eye over the right is reflected in the composed, sharp glance of the Lutenist. In contrast to Pontormo's mid-1520s *sfumato*, Bronzino's graphic 'handwriting' approaches an engraver's: sharp, contained, delicate, and precise. G. Smith and Tofani 1988, 66.

   Cox-Rearick 1981, cat. no. 335 (Pontormo), concluded that the young *Maria* drawing was not for the lost Castello portrait (after 1537) nor for the *Maria Salviati with a Book* ibid., cat. no. 346. She surmised that this *Maria* related to another portrait. *Pace* Cox-Rearick, it appears to be Bronzino's, and earlier than the Frankfurt panel.

34 The results of these calibrated comparisons were confirmed when the three images were subjected to photogammetry in 2003 by forensic artist Giuseppina Orsatti of the Forensic Identification Services of Toronto Police. Photogammetry is a computer-generated application used in forensic identification to plot key points on the adult face (heights of upper, lower, and full face; height of the mandible; intercanthal width; soft-nose width; and width of mouth). A unified scale is produced that allows a suspect's image/images to be matched – or proved unrelated – to a securely identified image, or to a computer-generated image of a suspect. The process of aging is integral to the application. Orsatti reported precise correspondence of the key facial points – and revealed others – between the secure Maria Salviati in the Baltimore panel (identified by King 1940, 74–84 from her image on the ceiling of the room dedicated to her husband, Giovanni de' Medici 'delle Bande Nere,' in the Palazzo Vecchio), the *Lady in Red / Lady with a Lapdog*, and the youthful drawing of Maria. The identification of these two

as Maria was assigned to the category of 'highly probable' (91–9%). The co-authored study continues, and it is hoped to publish expanded research on these and other identifications, including implications arising from there that touch on attribution, artistic style and influence, dating, workshop procedures, and other matters.

Overlay procedures have been used by Cropper 2001[2], 499–504, who used mylar-overlay tracing and X-ray that confirmed suspected close relationships between Pontormo's *Halberdier (Francesco Guardi)*, Bronzino's *Portrait of a Young Man*, and Bronzino's *Portrait of Guidobaldo della Rovere*. A second study recently appeared, by Cox-Rearick and Westerman Bulgarella 2004, 101–59, that includes an extensive exploration of suspected portraits of Cosimo (National Gallery, Ottawa) and Eleonora (Galleria Sabauda, Turin). It included a technique similar to Cropper's, coupled with computerized calibration to a unified scale to demonstrate that these two portraits appear to correspond at vital points to the facial features of securely identified portraits of the ducal couple. Each of these studies includes far-reaching implications for portraiture. Catherine Johnson in Ottawa 2005, cat. no. 85, with figs. 85.1 and 85.2, has proposed that the Ottawa portrait is of the prominent Florentine banker Pierantonio Bandini, and that the Turin panel portrays his wife, Cassandra Cavalcanti, on the basis of Vasari's reference to Bronzino portraits of them, of the panels' possible links to recorded Giugni family inheritance of Cassandra's estate and the Ottawa panel's Giugni provenance, and of resemblance to the Bandini funerary busts.

35 Gauthiez 1901, 324–6. See also Cheetham 1982, 199–202, in the context of Clement VII's disastrous statesmanship in the European arena.

36 See Cropper 1997, 23–4, and 2004, 7. See Mannucci 1586, 33–4, on Maria's flight to Venice (Cosimo followed with Pierfancesco Riccio, his tutor); Gauthiez 1901, 211, 233; Booth 1921, 15–20; and Pieraccini 1986, 1: 470–2. Gauthiez documents her astuteness: she had already persuaded Clement in 1524 to bring Cosimo to Rome to keep him in the public eye – a move also calculated to eclipse Clement's illegitimate son, Alessandro. Gauthiez 1901, 324–6. Further on Maria's political activities, see esp. Tomas 2004 145–9. For the upheavals in Florence and Rome under Clement's papacy, see Cleugh 1975, 250–62; Cecchi 1996[2], 370; and Cropper 2001[3], 6–8.

37 See Langdon 1992[1], 75–111, and 1992[2], 20–40, on evidence in portraits of Pontormo's association with Alessandro's circle at this time; Pilliod 2001, 31–2, asserts that Alessandro and Cosimo exclusively patronized Pontormo in these years. See Cropper 2004, 1–33, for a political, cultural, and artistic study of this unstable decade in Florentine history of plague, siege, depopulation, and loss of its republican status.

38 Alciati 1996, emblem no. 205; the illustrated, expanded Aldine version was first printed in 1546. The lapdog as emblem of conjugal love is further discussed in chap. 6.

39 For the Medici armorial colours of red, white, and green, and the *diamante* emblem with its associated motto, SEMPER, see esp. Gelli 1928, emblem no. 1555, 437–8. The colours signified the cardinal virtues: faith (white), hope (green), and charity (red). See also Acidini Luchinat 1993, 363–70, who observed that in Benozzo Gozzoli's *Procession of the Magi* in the Medici Chapel, Palazzo Medici, Via Larga, a retainer is included 'wearing livery with the Medici colours of red, white and green and hose in the same colours … with the device of the ring with the *cartiglio* (scroll) with the motto SEMPER.' Cole Ahl 1997, 93 has noticed that Baldasar wears a gold crown 'decorated with green, white and red feathers, the colours of the Medici.' She also (295 n. 83) credits Ames-Lewis 1979

with the most systematic analysis of the Medici colours and their heraldic devices. I thank Paola Tinagli for sharing her observation that the three Magi are dressed in the Medici colours: white for Caspar, green for Balthazar, and red for Melchior. Medici armorials and emblems are combined on the title page to Conti 1893, who records their currency for the new ducal court: five plain red *palle* or spheres in triangular formation, the central, sixth sphere blue with lily motifs, all on a green field. The whole in this case has been surrounded by a diamond ring with the traditional pyramidal stone identical to that worn on the finger of the *Lady in Red / Lady with a Lapdog*.

Maria's *diamante* ring is identical to that seen on Piero the Gouty's *impresa* as shown on the reverse of Selvi's medal of her, a soaring falcon with a ring in its beak, with the motto 'IAMAIS AUTRE' ('Never another'), a variant on SEMPER; triple *diamante* rings also appear on Allegrini's 1761 *Maria* engraving. See Langedijk 1981, 2: cat. 98,6a, 98,14, 87,5a, and 87,7. The *diamante* appears, among other instances for Leo, on the bell in Raphael's portrait of him. See Minnich 2003, 1019.

For extended *diamante* discussions, see Cox-Rearick 1984. On Cosimo's association with a legendary *diamante,* see chap. 2. On the consolidation of the repertory of Medici motifs from 1494 to 1537 of the *broncone* (sprouting laurel), *diamante,* and Virgilian return of a Medici Golden Age, see M. Campbell 1985[2], 385. Costamagna 1994, 297, cat. A58, proposed Francesca Salviati as the Frankfurt subject, tying it to her marriage to Ottaviano de' Medici, 1533, but costume here is of the early/mid-1520s. See also n. 16.

40 On the resemblance, see Settimanni, ca. 1720: 'Fu alta di statura, bianca di volto, occhi grossetti, come quella chi ritrarreva a Papa Leone X[e], essendo nata di Madonna Lucrezia de' Medici sua sorella.' ('She was tall, pale-faced, with large eyes, which she had inherited from Pope Leo X, having been born of Lady Lucrezia de' Medici, his sister.') See also Cox-Rearick 1993, 261; Pieraccini 1986, 1: 473, and Booth 1921, 6–7.

For Raphael's *Portrait of Leo X with Two Cardinals,* see Minnich 2003; and Beck 1994, colour pl. 37, and 39, 120. See also Alazard 1968, 181, and Langedijk 1981, 1: 42. It was exhibited at Lorenzo de' Medici, Duke of Urbino's wedding to Maddalena de la Tour d'Auvergne, in 1518, and again for Cosimo and Eleonora's in 1539.

Cropper 2001[3], cat. no. 39, detailed the Frankfurt portrait's compositional links with Raphael's *Leo X* and Parmigianino's *Galeazzo Sanvitale,* 1524.

41 Ottaviano stored it until 1537; for its status as a Medici symbol, see Cropper 2001[3], cat. no. 39. On current Florentine upheavals, see Cleugh 1975, 254–30.

42 See Langedijk 1981, 2: cat. 74,72 for Selvi's medal of Lorenzo and verso with three feathers, a *diamante* and the inscribed 'SEMPER'; and Gelli 1928, emblem 1555 (second version), showing these with two dolphins beneath. Verrocchio's *Boy with a Dolphin,* 1470, was a Medici commission; also Leo X's Vatican inlays (n. 45); and one beneath Francesco de' Medici's foot in Caccini's statue, Palazzo Vecchio, 1592/4. Langedijk ibid., cat. 42,74, notes its meaning, the attribute of a good prince. See nn. 45–9 for more on Medici dolphins.

43 Mannucci 1586, in his *Vita di Cosimo,* 33–4, noting her diligence in tutoring Cosimo in Latin, Greek, and Tuscan; many letters to her son attest to her literacy. See also n. 130.

44 Until Cosimo's birth, the illegitimate Alessandro (1511–37) and Ippolito (1511–35) were contenders for the Medici succession. See Gauthiez 1901, 117–18, and Booth 1921, 10. For the adoption by the Medici of the vivified *broncone,* its source in Vergil's *Aeneid* (6.143), its use in Medici iconography by the 1520s and into the early years of Cosimo's

reign, see Simon 1982, 117–34, and Cox-Rearick 1984, 49–51 and 1993, 278 (the Poggio a Caiano fresco). Cox-Rearick and Westerman Bulgarella 2004, 101 recognized the *broncone* necklace elements on the *Lady in Red* / *Lady with a Lapdog*. A crossed, twin-twig arrangement must, however, symbolize the conjoined Medici 'branches' of Maria and Giovanni delle Bande Nere in Cosimo. Cox-Rearick and Westerman Bulgarella's naming of the *Lady in Red* as Francesca Salviati follows Costamagna 1994, 297; this did not find favour with Cropper 2001³, cat. no. 29, or Hiller von Gaertringen 2004, 494. (See n. 11 above.)

45 Leo's dolphins were inlaid in the Sala dei Pontefici. On its endurance as a Medici symbol from Lorenzo the Magnificent's era, see Mandel 1990; it was also linked to Venus and happy marriage. For Verrocchio's bronze, see Olson 1992, 117–18, fig. 85. Dolphins appear on Ammannati's *Neptune* fountain; as emblematic of Neptune in Vincenzo Borghini's iconography; and on the *Arch of the Maritime Empire* in the *apparato* for Francesco and Giovanna's wedding. See also Starn and Partridge 1992, passim, and figs. 68, 77, 86, and 89. See Edelstein 2004², 197 on the transfer of Verrocchio's *Boy with a Dolphin* from the Villa Careggi to the courtyard of the Palazzo Vecchio to celebrate the wedding of Francesco to Giovanna of Austria in 1565.

46 Alciati 1996, emblem no. 156. See also Kiefer 1979, 15, on the dolphin as rescuer of men.

47 It had also stood for the redemptive notion associated with Jonah and the Whale, Schneider 1994, 175 n. 183. This redemptive association may reaffirm renewal of the Medici line through Maria.

48 See Mandel 1990, 83, 87, 91, 95, and 99, on the dolphin-anchor theme in Verrocchio's *Putto with a Dolphin*, the motto *festina lente*, and Cosimo's Augustan astrological sign.

49 Mandel 1990, passim, scrutinizes the dolphin's much-conflated symbolism in these contexts, including linkage with Prudence. See her fig. 5, from Typotius's *Symbola divina* 3:37.

50 For these claims and related isues, see nn. 36, 44, 93, and 153.

51 Cropper 2001³, cat. no. 39, marks the 'shocking' red expanse of the dress. For the important discussion on vermilion, on Titian, and on Aretino, see Freedman 1995, 77–84. Hiller von Gaertringen 2004, 490, reports the pigment used to depict the dress in Bronzino's *Lady with a Lapdog* was cinnabar, or vermilion.

52 C.H. Smyth 1955, 114. Hiller von Gaertringen 2004, 488–9 recalls Bernard Berenson's claim that this portrait exhibits a new expression of ideal, social position; he also notes that the triangular composition serves to provide equlibrium, inner stability, and a hieratic effect on the sitter.

53 Cropper 2001³, cat. nos. 39 and 40, citing Keutner. Both appear in the 1612 Riccardi inventory, as does Pontormo's *Francesco Guardi*. See text below. Cropper 1997, 17, lists portraits in the lunettes: *Maria Salviati with a Little Girl* ('una puttina'); *The Woman with a Dog* (Maria); *Duke Cosimo de' Medici as an Old Man*; *Grand Duke Ferdinand with Duchess Christine of Lorraine*; a *Duke Cosimo I*; and Gian Paolo Pace's *Giovanni delle Bande Nere* (see n. 63). See Strehlke 2004, cat. 30; and Hiller von Gaertringen 2004, 479–94.

54 See n. 40.

55 Langedijk 1981, 2: cat. 87,10. See Simon, 1982, 193, on Vasari or Michele di Ridolfo as author.

56 See Allegri and Cecchi 1980, 160, and Frey 1923, 1: CCLXV, 462, for Vasari's letter to Cosimo of 26 December 1556: the ceiling tondo was complete, but the walls unfinished

at that date. The portrait of Giovanni (Bargellini 1968, 2: ill. 344), a copy of Ghirlandaio's
Cosimo at Age Twelve (E. King 1940, fig. 3), and a portrait of Giovanni di Pierfrancesco de'
Medici (1467–98) had been finished, all on the ceiling. Two more in ovals had yet to be
placed on the walls: Cosimo's maternal grandmother Caterina Sforza, Duchess of Imola
and Forlì (1462–1509) (Bargellini ibid., 344), and Pierfrancesco de' Medici. See Allegri
and Cecchi 1980, 155–8, and Lensi-Orlandi 1977, 166, for the program.

57 Vasari 1878–85, 8: 187, quoted below. On the *Ragionamenti*, see Tinagli 1985 and 2001.

58 Vasari 1938, 260–1. See Simon 1982, 187–8.

59 Her death mask was made by Santi Buglioni under Tribolo's direction. Conti 1893, 44.

60 Caterina Cibo, Duchess of Camerino, to her sister Eleonora Gonzaga, Duchess of
Urbino, 8 July 1541. Booth 1921, 117; Firenzuola 1992, 69. The court moved from the
Palazzo Medici to the Palazzo della Signoria (Palazzo Vecchio) in May 1540. Baia 1907,
24–5 describes the apartments, their occupants, the ducal nursery, and the children's
instruction. Maria's frugality was a stark contrast to Eleonora's love of luxury. See also
Cox-Rearick 1993, 55–6. On the leather hangings, see Orsi Landini, Florence, Palazzo
Pitti, 1993, 44. Further on Caterina, see Strehlke 2004, cat. no. 26, 115.

61 Conti 1893, 44–5.

62 See Allegri and Cecchi 1980, 167–74, pl. 34.3, for related figures and documents; and
Langedijk, 1981, 2: cat. 87,11; Pieraccini 1986, 1: 473, and Booth 1921, 44. For Jacopo's
version, see Langedijk ibid., cat. 17,14. See Falciani 1995, fig. 5, for a preparatory drawing for its *Maria*, which he believes is based on the Baltimore portrait of her with the
child.

63 Uffizi, Inv. 1890, no. 2232 (Serie Aulica), Langedijk 1981, 2: cat. 56,5 and 87,3; and colour
pl., Scalini ed. 2001, 231, fig. 2. Giovanni's portrait, too, is from a death mask, by Giulio
Romano; he died in the arms of his boon companion, Aretino, who wrote to console
Maria. Booth 1921, 13–14. (On a posthumous medal made from the cast, see n. 199.) See
Langedijk 1981, 1: 110–11, and cat. nos. 56,5 and 6; and Ferrai 1891, 330, no. 1, for Gian
Paolo Pace's *Giovanni*, which Aretino passed as Titian's – as attributed in *guardaroba*
records. For Giovanni, see Scalini ibid.; on Maria's unhappy marriage, see Gauthiez
1901, 62, 78–80, 100–25, and 332, and Pieraccini 1986, 1: 466ff.

64 The Serie Aulica was the first of two sets of family portraits commissioned by Grand
Dukes Francesco and Ferdinand, continuing until the eighteenth century. Langedijk
1981, 1: 137. The Ambras set of 1587 for the Vienna court had each subject's identity
superscribed.

65 Langedijk 1981, 2: cat. 87,2.

66 Ibid., cat. 87,5a.

67 For a discussion on the Medici *diamante imprese*, see n. 39 above.

68 Langdon 1992[1], 1: 89–127, and Langdon 1992[2]. Further, Cropper 1997, 3–5, proposed
reassessment of the 'Cosimo' identification, and 2001[3], cat. no. 40, concluded with additional independent research that it is Giulia de' Medici. Florence, Palazzo Strozzi 2002,
cat. no. 33, 'Pubblicazioni recenti (Langdon, Cropper, Spicer) sostengono con copiose
argomentazioni l'identificazione del fanciullo con Giulia' resulted in the title *Ritratto di
Maria Salviati e di un fanciullo (Cosimo I?)*; scholarly debate is aired there, and the text
includes reference to Giulia and to her possible African ancestry. The references to
Cropper, Langdon, and Spicer are missing from this entry in the Chicago-Detroit version of the catalogue, 2002, still no. 33 ('Cosimo'), and scholary enquiry is directed to

Costamagna's 1994 *Pontormo* catalogue entry. Further, in the bibliography my 1992 dissertation, 'Decorum of Medici Women,' is redated 1994, and my 1992 article 'Pontormo and Medici Lineages,' Cropper 2001[3] ('Giulia'), and Spicer 2001 ('Giulia') have been dropped. Spicer, Curator of Renaissance and Baroque Art, Walters Art Museum, indicates that the title *Maria Salviati with Giulia de' Medici* has been used there since 1994. The child is identified as 'Giulia,' citing the scholars above, in Strehlke 2004, cat. no. 30.

69 Vasari 1878–85, 6: 71ff., 281–2. For the victory and the slaughtered *fuorusciti* – banished political exiles – see Young 1910, 553–5. Cosimo eagerly adopted the combined image of an ideal prince; symbolic personifications used by the Emperor Charles V; and Caesar Augustus, the latter believed predestined to rule. Langedijk 1981, 1: 80. For this theme on commemorative medals, see Richelson 1978, fig. 5, and Langedijk ibid., cat. 27,156. For the Castello (1537–43) garden statuary, 'symbolizing all the virtues possessed by His Excellency,' see Vasari, ibid.; Forster 1966, 87ff.; Cox-Rearick 1984, 253ff. and fig. 20; and Adelson 1983 and 1985. See also Giambullari in Minor and Mitchell, 75ff. For Cosimo's adoption of constellations of Augustus and Charles V, see Fedeli in Albèri 1839–63, II, 1, 350ff. For Cosimo's self-propagandizing programs, see Forster 1971, 65–104, Richelson 1978, Simon 1982, and Cox-Rearick 1984. For Pontormo's profile portrait of 1537 for Castello, see Berti 1993, 174–8; Cropper 1997, 5, fig. 4; and Pilliod 2001, figs. 8 and 9.

70 Cropper 1997, 22, argues that Vasari's wording, that Pontormo 'received for this eight *scudi* a month from His Excellency; whom he portrayed, young as he then was at the beginning of that work, and likewise Donna Maria his mother,' suggests that the portrayals were inclusive in the fresco program. (For the value of the *scudo*, see Hollingsworth 1996, xii and 28: on the basis of her translation of its value into present U.S. currency, one *scudo* was worth about $350, which would make a monthly salary for Pontormo equivalent to about $2800, or an annual income equivalent today to about $33,600.)

71 Baltimore, Walters Art Museum, 87.6 × 71 cm, cat. no. 37.596. It was recorded in the Riccardi inventory in 1612, passed from the Riccardi to the Masserenti in 1881, and acquired in 1902 with the Masserenti collection as *Vittoria Colonna* by Sebastiano del Piombo. Clapp's re-attribution to Pontormo in 1916 has not been challenged. See nn. 73 and 77, recording a wide range of scholarly dating. See Langedijk 1981, 2: cat. 87,5; Forlani Tempesti and Giovannetti 1994, cat. 46, recorded the continued wavering of scholars on the sex of the child; see Strehlke 2004, cat. no. 30 and Washington 2001, cat. no. 40 for recent bibliographies.

72 Decorum for the conduct and dress of widows was prescribed in Fusco's *La Vedova*, 1570, and in Vives's *De institutione feminae Christianae*, written for Catherine of Aragon in 1523 for her guidance of her daughter, Mary Tudor. It enjoyed pan-European popularity for the rest of the century. C. Murphy 1997, 129ff., refers to Vives as the supreme contemporary writer on widowhood. See Sangiorgi 1973, 90–7, and Valone 1992 on widowhood.

73 Forster 1965, 223ff., and 1966, cat. 33, believed Bronzino painted it in 1527. E. King 1940, 74–5, identified her from an identical *Maria* tondo in the Palazzo Vecchio. See text below.

74 See Berti 1955, 53ff.; Gamba 1956, 15ff.; and Zeri 1976, 2: 325.

75 On her death, see n. 4 above.

76 E. King 1940, 74–84, announced Cosimo, described as about seven to eight years old, followed by Cox-Rearick 1964, 311, and 1993, 261; Forster 1965, 223ff., and 1966, cat. 33; Langedijk 1981, 1: 81–2, and 2: cat. 87,5; and Costamagna 1994, cat. 77. Berti 1993, 119, posited either Cosimo or Bia. Bia, however, was blond. (See pl. 6.)

77 Berti 1955, 53; Zeri 1976, 2: 326; Cox-Rearick 1982, 74; Forlani Tempesti and Giovannetti 1994, 139–41, all opted for 1537, with Cosimo retrospectively portrayed; see also Pinelli 1993, 135–7. Berti 1964 and 1973, cat. 127, preferred 1540 and believed the 'puttina' was Bia; Berti 1993, 119 (see n. 76) summarized scholarly dates ranging from 1537 to 1543; Langedijk 1981, 1: 81–2, and 2: cat. 87,5, believed this *Maria* was posthumous. Costamagna 1994 ('Cosimo') dated it 1537; Cox-Rearick 1997, rev. of Costamagna, held to 1526. Florence, Palazzo Strozzi 2002, cat. no. 33 cites Langdon, Spicer, and Cropper's documentation of Cosimo's ward, Giulia, in Maria's care in 1540.

78 E. King 1940, 76–7.

79 Cropper 1997, 4, referring to Berenson's postcard to Melvin Ross, 30 March 1941.

80 Gamba 1956, 15. Zeri 1976, 2: 325, dismisses any possibility but Cosimo, but lists scholars who noted the child's girlish appearance and notes Giulia and Bia in Maria's circle.

81 'A panel of 1½ *braccia* of the Lady Maria Medici with a little girl by the hand of Jacopo Pontormo.' ('Un quadro di br.ª uno e mezzo della Signora donna Maria Medici con una puttina per mano di Jacopo da Pontormo.') Keutner 1959, 139–54.

82 Cropper 1997, 112 n. 10 records Freedberg's vacillation: S. Freedberg 1971, 484 n. 20, has Cosimo as 'certainly erroneous,' but, expressing his considerable discomfiture at length, he reluctantly abandoned his opinion: Freedberg 1993, 688–9, n. 20. Forlani-Tempesti and Giovannetti 1994, 139–41 record Berti's vacillations on the child's identity; see next note.

83 Berti 1973, cat. no. 127, summarising scholarly arguments on dating and the child's sex; Berti 1990, 44–5, reiterated that the child's sex was problematical, but in Berti 1993, 119, identified the child as 'Cosimo,' with a summary of scholarly positions: a retrospective portrayal of Maria and Cosimo made in 1537; probably the child Cosimo ('not Bia'); or, possibly, posthumous portrayals of Maria, Cosimo's mother, and Bia as 'two "spirits."'

84 Simon 1982, 194. For 'Giulia' identifications, see n. 68 above.

85 See the Introduction for sixteenth-century idealization in portraiture; scientific evidence for Pontormo's idealization of Alessandro is detailed in Philadelphia 2004, 43–4.

86 Langedijk 1981, 2: cat. 87,15. See text and note 34 above. The drawing may be a few years earlier.

87 E.g., Battista Naldini's portrait, painted 1585–6. See nn. 4 and 59, recording the death mask that inspired it. On the drawing, see Langedijk 1981, 2: cat. 87,14a; see Philadelphia 2004, cat. no. 46, for both drawings, with current bibliography.

88 Vasari 1878–85, 8: 183–6. Giovanni delle Bande Nere's life follows, for Francesco's edification. On the *Ragionamenti*, see Tinagli 1985, 83–94, and Tinagli 2001, 63–76.

89 For the 1537 profile portrait of Cosimo, see n. 69 above.

90 See Langedijk 1981, 1–2, for entries for Cosimo and children; and Baccheschi 1973, cats. 134–57, workshop sets based on existing panels (pl. 8 here). Cropper 1997, 14, refuting Cosimo as Pontormo's *Halberdier*, reasoned also that absence of a copy of it there was significant.

91 Christie's sale cat., New York, 31 May 1989, compiled by Cox-Rearick, 26–7.

92 Gauthiez 1901, 117–18, 327–8. On Giovanni's stoic, agonized death, Clement VII lauded the legendary *condottiere* and urged that all Maria's hopes be placed in Cosimo. The Bande Nere wished her to hand the boy over to be raised on the field, but she demurred. Giovanni's fame led the Duke of Urbino to solicit a cavalry company for Cosimo from Francis I.

93 Christie's sale cat. 1989, 11, citing Baccio Baldini's *Vita di Cosimo*, Florence 1578. Clement's irritation was well founded: Cosimo's martial demeanour attracted some Giovanni delle Bande Nere loyalists to the boy's side. Cosimo stubbornly remained secluded until Alessandro allowed him to revert to his unusual dress ten days later. Booth 1921, 45–6.

94 See Simon 1983, 527–39 and figs. 9–13, for Cosimo; and fig. 15, for Giovanni in similar armour by a Florentine artist, ca. 1545, Galleria Sabauda, Turin. Giovio, who devised the iconography of the *Cosimo I in Armour*, received an autograph Bronzino version from Cosimo in 1546, and acknowledged the 'mirabile ritratto', 'I am greatly obliged to the Lord Duke [and] I advise your Signoria that in the three parts of four of the panel it seemed to me the portrait of the excellent Lord Giovanni, his father, whom I remember as vividly as a man alive.' Giovio to Pierfrancesco Riccio, Rome, 30 July 1546. See Simon 1987, 387–8.

95 It is mentioned in Vasari 1878–85, 6: 545. The inscription on the upper right of the panel reads 'COSMO.MED.'

96 See Mannucci 1586, *Vita di Cosimo*, 33–4. Langedijk 1990/91, 290, notes 'veiled allusions to Cosimo's future greatness' in Ridolfo's portrait.

97 Alciati 1621, 233a. Charles warmly addressed Cosimo at the Neapolitan court in 1536 as son of 'a cavalier who made France and Spain tremble.' Booth 1921, 50.

98 Langedijk 1981, 1: 81.

99 See Albèri 1839–63, II, 1: 350ff., quoting Fedeli (1561).

100 Castiglione 1959, 32: '[T]he reputation of a gentleman whose profession is arms, if ever in the least way he sullies himself through cowardice or other disgrace, always remains defiled before the world and covered with ignominy.'

101 Albèri 1839–72, II, 1: 335, citing Fedeli (1561), posited childhood seclusion with Maria. See also Booth 1921, 21–2.

102 See n. 36. Giovanni was famed as *condottiere* and Captain General of the Republic. Gauthiez 1901, 211 and 233; Booth 1921, 15–20; and Pieraccini 1986, 1: 470–2.

103 Litta 1899–1902, Serie I, G–O 'Medici'; Booth 1921, 27; Pieraccini 1986, 1: 472.

104 ASF MAP 140, ins. 1, p. 7; also Pieraccini 1986, 1: 467; Langedijk 1990/91, 288; and Saltini 1898, xx–xxi. Maria had instructed his tutor, Pierfrancesco Riccio, to arrange Cosimo's appropriate attire for his meeting with Charles V. See Edelstein 2001, 250 n. 10.

105 Booth 1921, 38, quoting Cosimo's letter to Maria, 28 January 1530.

106 Vives 1912, bk. 2, chap. 9, scorns 'coddling' or overt motherly love.

107 Gauthiez 1901, 117–18, 327–8. Leo had enthusiastically named Cosimo for his 'wise, prudent and most valorous' ancestor, Cosimo the Elder. See also n. 92 above.

108 See text above.

109 Maria was responding to her brother, Cardinal Salviati's concern for Cosimo's safety. Saltini 1898, xxviii. The conniving of the Cibo cadre is described in my text; Cox-Rearick 1993, 255–6, lists other factions who sought his downfall. Sforza reputedly

exposed her genitals from the ramparts at the siege of Forlì to convey her ability to replace two sons held hostage by the enemy. See Cleugh 1975, 222–3, and Gundersheimer 1994, 41–2.

110 For this pedagogy, see Vives 1912, bk. 3, chaps. 1–3; Fusco 1570, 36; and Kelso 1977, 128. For Sandoval, lines 140ff., see Tosi 1908, 74–5. Sandoval arrived with Eleonora's retinue in 1539.

111 Variously attributed to Justus of Ghent or Pedro Berruguete. For the *Federico da Montefeltro and His Son* see Levey 1971, 47, pl. 28; Rosenberg 1986; Eisenbichler 1988, 21; and Mateer ed. 2000, 199–222, fig. 3.15. For *Federico and Guidobaldo Listening to a Lecture*, see Eisenbichler ibid., pl. 29; Clough 1967, 281ff.; and Woods-Marsden 1987, 211.

112 See Eisenbichler 1988[2], 21. The future Ferdinando II de' Medici is recorded with his mother, Maria Maddalena, by Justus Sustermans at about four, in robes of state; he grasps a sword, and the grand-ducal crown is nearby. See Ann Arbor 2002, colour pl. 52.

113 See also Wethey 1971, 2: pl. 165, cat. no. 91, and pl. 113, cat. no. 31, the 1542 *Ranuccio Farnese as a Knight of Malta*, who is girded with a sword and the Order's insignia.

114 Adriani 1583, 1: 195.

115 Sandoval, in Tosi 1908, lines 140–50.

116 Fusco 1570, in *La vedova*, 41–2, cites Lavinia Colonna as an exemplary widow, who '[widowed] when she was in the flower of her youth, very beautiful and virtuous, contented herself with that one husband ... and raised her son Marc' Antonio to such sublimity of virtue that he above every other patrician of his age these days is found for that reason to be refined and illustrious.' Contessa Clelia, Fusco's dedicatee, also faithful from youth to her dead husband, is praised.

117 See nn. 81–4 for challenges to the 'Cosimo' identity. Cropper 1997, 2–5, carefully set out the Baltimore panel's controversial status; her fresh appraisal, favouring identification of Giulia de' Medici (Cropper 2001[3], cat. no. 36) is discussed below.

118 In her tightly argued monograph on Pontormo's *Halberdier*, Cropper (1997) identified the figure as Francesco Guardi, recorded by Vasari as costumed as a soldier in a Pontormo portrait.

119 Langedijk 1981, 1: 3. Ferdinando abandoned his cardinalate in 1586 when Francesco died without heirs; he was succeeded by his son, Cosimo II (1590–1621) in 1609.

120 Zeri 1976, 2: 325. On obliterations, see Kaplan in Posner 2001.

121 For example, Titian's *Filetto and His Son* (now separated into two panels) in Vienna, 1538–40; *Ranuccio Farnese*, 1542, in Washington: the six boys in *The Vendramin Family* group, and *Guidobaldo II della Rovere and His Son* of 1552 (location unknown). See Wethey 1971, 2: pls. 133, 113, 136, and 165. Parmigianino's *Countess of San Secondo with Her Three Sons* in Madrid, 1533–5, is another case in point; see S. Freedberg 1950, pl. 143, 213–14.

122 See Baccheschi 1973, colour pls. XXI and XXIII, pl. 29, and colour pl. LXIII.

123 Simon 1982, 194, lists them but favours Cosimo. See n. 4 on Maria's nieces and n. 171 for her links to Alessandro's daughters; see Keutner 1959, 147, and Berti 1973, no. 127.

124 Florence, Uffizi 1980, no. P299. See Baccheschi 1973, colour pl. XLIII, and Cecchi 1996[1], cover and colour pl. 47. (See chap. 3 here for Bia, who was born ca. 1535–6.)

125 Florence, Uffizi 1980, no. P306, and Baccheschi 1973, cat. no. 87.

126 See Saltini 1898, 2–4, and documents quoted in Booth 1921, 116–17. Bia, a favourite at court, was buried in San Lorenzo on 1 March 1542.

127 Clement's parentage of Alessandro was tacitly acknowledged by Cosimo and Vasari: In Vasari's *Supper of St. Gregory*, 1540 (Bologna), Clement is enthroned, with Alessandro leaning at ease on the back rail of the chair. See Conti 1989, cat. no. 11, and Le Mollé 1995, pl. 11. Alessandro is prominent in Vasari's Sala di Clement VII frescoes in the Palazzo Vecchio of 1556–61. See Langedijk 1981, 1: 1,49, for about fifty portraits of him, many posthumous. See also Pieraccini 1986, 1: 316 and 429ff.; and the genealogical tree in Langedijk 1981, 1: 10–11 (adapted here for appendix A).

128 Albèri 1839–72, II, 1: 75 n. 1.

129 Adriani 1583 I, 25, 99. It is argued that Giulio's infancy, not his illegitimacy, made the Florentine senate choose Cosimo over Giulio. See Sansovino 1670, 152–5, and Saltini 1898, xvff. Cibò (1499–1550) had wielded influence from Leo's pontificate and was a formidable political player until Cosimo's accession. See Hollingsworth 1996, 14, 32, 75, and Le Mollé 1995, 62–4.

130 Adriani 1583, 1, 101. See also Saltini 1898, XLV; Ferrai 1882, 392ff.; Arditi 1970, 43–6, 63, and 119–21; and Pieraccini 1986, 1: 414ff. Giulio was raised at court (*Bibliografia Universale Antica & Moderna*, 36, 478), and Cosimo's letters to him document promotion of him through his youth, marriage, and career. Loving reports to Cosimo from Maria Salviati concerning the boy (ASF MDP 3, I, ff. 70 and 70v., for example), and correspondence between Cosimo and Giulio in later years (Cosimo to Giulio, ASF MDP 6373, f. 28v.), and concerning armaments, 1561, ASF MDP 6373, f. 36); and, on Giulio's wedding, 11 August 1561, ASF MDP 6373, f. 36v.) confirm a mutual affection. In 1562, he was one of the first Knights of Santo Stefano to be invested by the duke, and was made First Admiral of the Order, founded to fight the Turks. Booth 1921, 214. Giulio bore the young Cardinal Giovanni's coffin in November 1562. Saltini 1898, 180–1.

131 See n. 167 below, where Cosimo's agent promises to comfort the temporarily relocated little girl in 1539; the ducal couple's abiding care of her is evident in Maria Salviati's letters to Cosimo, ASF MDP 345, ff. 364 and 380.

132 Booth 1921 trans., 117. The illegitimate children were Giulio, Giulia, and Cosimo's daughter Bia; for Porzia, another Alessandro daughter, see n. 171, and 274n19.

133 See Fantoni 1999, 256, on Cosimo's reinvention of Medicean identity to initiate a princely court and persona. On the redoubtable Caterina (d. 1557), see Sansovino 1670, 155–6; and Philadelphia 2004, 20–1.

134 Conti 1893, 117–23.

135 See D.R. Wright 1976, 2: 601–3, quoting ASF MDP 616f., 614ff. ins. 21, dated 1543. She is listed with Maria, Francesco, Giovanni, and Isabella. Segni (1504–55) 1805, 2: 389, recorded Cosimo's wardship of Giulio; in 1561, Giulio was given a commission in Pisa with an income of 1000 ducats per annum – worth today $400,000 U.S. (see also n. 130). Sansovino (1582) 1670, 154, records Giulio as one of the closest ducal relatives. Cox-Rearick 2004, 228, records that he bore Eleonora's coffin in solemn procession in 1562.

136 See ASF MDP 6357, f. 8, 29 December 1549. (For Giulia's relations with Cosimo as an adult, see chap. 4 here.) Her second marriage, in 1559, was to Cosimo's cousin, Bernardetto d'Ottaviano de' Medici. See Litta 1899–1902, Serie IA, Medici.

137 On the dynastic import of the name Romolo, see Cox-Rearick 1984, 234. For Eiche's findings, see Cropper 2001[3], cat. no. 40, citing Archivio dell'Opera del Duomo, Florence, Registri di Battesimo, *Femmine*, 1533–42, fol. 46v., and *Maschi*, 1533–42, fol. 14. Giulio

and Giulia were presumably born of the same mother, argued below as Taddea
Malaspina.

In 1550 Giulia married Francesco Cantelmo, Conte d'Alvito and Duke of Populi
(Litta 1899–1902, Serie I, G-0), at about fifteen, to judge by Medici daughters' marriages: Maria's was intended to take place when she was seventeen, Isabella's at fourteen, and Lucrezia – replacing the deceased Maria – at thirteen, all suggesting that
Guilia was born around 1534–5. See Langdon 1992², 26 and n. 71. These proposals are
in accord with Eiche's findings.

138 See Langdon 1992². The provenance of the Lucca panel is undisputed: it had been
recorded as a 'Lord Giuliano de' Medici' when it was located in the Tribuna of the
Uffizi from 1635 to 1678, but scholarly efforts to match the boy to any known Giuliano
de' Medici have been frustrated. Because several scholars pondered its perceived
resemblance to Alessandro in spite of the boy's red hair – Alessandro's was certainly
black – I proposed in 1992 that it could be his son Giulio, and that it could have been
painted in the early 1540s. However, its exhibition with other Pontormo panels in Philadelphia recently suggested that, stylistically, it probably should be assigned to the
late 1520s, which predates Giulio's birth. On the Lucca panel, see Strehlke 2004, cat.
no. 14.

Pace Strehlke, in consultation with Niccolò Capponi, the attempt to date the Lucca
portrait by comparison of the boy's wide pink cape with the clothing of male figures in
Pontormo's *St. Anne Altarpiece* tondo, ca. 1528–9 in the Louvre (ibid., fig. 60) may be
misleading. The altarpiece likely records an associated religious procession, not a civic
one. Half of the group is dressed in voluminous pink capes, hardly pages' dress –
there was no court in Florence at this date. Rather, the robes of a religious sodality
come to mind, regalia that is not likely to respond quickly to changing modes of fashion. Berti 1993, 161 notes Vasari's description of the scene, which represents an association of the Signoria of Florence when it went in procession, a description that does
not exclude a religious affiliation. Also, wide-collared, voluminous cloaks teamed
with flat berets similar to the Lucca boy's are seen in Bachiacca's Florentine street
scene (now in Amsterdam), dated 1540 (?) by Berti ibid., 167. The problems of secure
identity and dating of the Lucca panel have yet to be resolved.

139 Tenhove 1747, 2: 388, unfortunately without documentation or portrait references. For
Alessandro's Philadelphia portrait (fig. 11) see Strehlke 2004, cat. nos. 14 and 15, with
recent bibliography. A long nose, pouting mouth, short, dimpled chin, and black,
tightly curled hair identify him. See also fig. 39, his beautiful childhood portrait in
Madrid; see Langedijk 1981, 1, cat. no. 1, 12. If it was painted by Raphael and not by
Giulio Romano, Alessandro would be about nine. (Raphael died in 1520.)

140 Segni 1805, 1: 165, reports Niccolò Capponi's contemporary record of her as a Moorish
slave. Pieraccini 1986, 1: 397–8, denies Alessandro's African ancestry, but records posthumous descriptions: Ceccherelli (1587), 'curly black hair and a dark face' ('capelli
ricci neri e bruno in viso'); and Ammirato (1647), 'dark in colour, with large lips and
frizzy hair' ('colore bruno, labbri grossi e capegli crespi').

Scholars are divided on the issue today. Le Mollé 1995, 28 cites the Uffizi *Alessandro*
as evidence (fig. 12 here). Brackett fully accepts the same evidence. Micheletti 1983, 41,
notes Alessandro's nickname, 'Il Moro,' but Duke Lodovico 'Il Moro' was not black,
and today this is a sobriquet for a dark complexion, not proof of ethnicity. However,

overtones of racism – subtly expressed in Ceccherelli and Ammirato's comments on Alessandro above – tend to support Segni's opinion that Simunetta was Moorish, or of slave descent. Further on Simunetta, see Ferrai 1882, 449, and Young 1910, 322; Strehlke 2004, cat. 30, however, locates her Italian dialect in Lazio, which suggests that she was perhaps born in Italy. Lorenzino de' Medici, Alessandro's killer and self-styled 'Brutus,' excuses his tyrannicide by denying Alessandro's Medici paternity; he describes her as a housemaid 'of the lowest and basest class' whose coachman husband fathered Alessandro. (This would hardly explain Clement's fondness for him.) Lorenzino de' Medici, Brown trans. 2004, 6–7. Ammirato, a Medici historian, paired Clement with a servant; Marco Foscaro, Venetian ambassador in 1527, and his successor, Carlo Cappello, in 1529, each make Alessandro his nephew; see Albèri 1839–63, II, 1: 74–5 – who opines that he was Clement's son. Langedijk 1981, 1: 221, agrees, as do most modern scholars. See also n. 127.

On Eleonora's slaves, see Pieraccini 1898, I, 82, and Franceschini 2004, 183. G. de Ricci 1972, 131, 143, 175, and 300 records instances of hundreds of slaves captured as booty in Tuscany's Mediterannean skirmishes with the Turks, but their origins are seldom referred to. Antonio, a galley-slave found to be the illegitimate son of Prince Luigi of Portugal, was ransomed for 3000 *scudi*; Francesco de' Medici was presented with a tame lion accompanied by a Turkish slave, who was immediately baptised. Ibid., 253–4, and 388–9. For slavery in the courts, see Earle and Lowe eds. 2005; I am indebted to Paul Kaplan (on Isabella d'Este's slaves), and John Brackett (on Alessandro, as black ruler) for discussion prior to publication. For a wide range of Alessandro's images, see Langedijk ibid., cat. series 1; and see Cox-Rearick 1981, fig. 310a; Cropper 1997, 6; and Strehlke 2004, cat. nos. 25–7.

When entombed in San Lorenzo, Alessandro was vilified, perhaps racially, by the diarist Agostino Lapini, who recorded a resulting 'phenomenon': 'The same Duke Alessandro was buried in San Lorenzo in the New Sacristy, in the tomb on the left side, which is foul and black because of his body.' The republican Varchi loathed him for his tyrannical cruelty, and for procurement of 'nuns as well as lay women, virgins, married or widowed, noble or ignoble, young or mature' and for insatiable sexuality. Cropper 2004, 19–23; and see Cleugh 1975, 274–81. See M. Campbell 1985[1], 355 and n. 50, on his libertine circle. Others view him more kindly. Ferrai 1882, 163, records his benevolence to the poor – and to his young relative and rival, Cosimo. Rubin 1995, 100, praises his efforts to restore and protect Florence.

Costamagna 2002, 206, and Strehlke 2004, cat. no. 30, infer that Giulia's identification in the Baltimore panel (Langdon, 1992[2]) was founded on a foregone observation that the child 'looked black.' This is baseless; see Langdon 2005. Identification arose as described in this chapter: Maria's middle age, widowhood, and a feminized, too-young 'Cosimo' were incongruous; the inventory recorded 'una puttina'; the child resembled neither Bia nor Cosimo's Maria, but archival documentation confirmed Maria's other charge, Giulia; and political contexts explained her presence. Her resemblance to Alessandro is evident; his rumoured ethnicity – recorded by Segni – was then discussed. (The child's obliteration on the panel in the historic past may be crucial to this discussion. Forensic science may one day solve these conflicting opinions of Alessandro's and his children's ancestry.) Cropper 2001[3], cat. no. 40, augmented my archival sources proving Maria's links with Giulia – all researched in the late 1980s and extrapolated from my dissertation. (Media attention during the 2001 Washington exhibition focused on Giulia's ethnicity, with some muddling of the research – and credit for its findings.)

141 Recent scientific analysis of the Philadelphia and Chicago *Alessandro*s reveal degrees of idealization – notably elimination of the neck fold. See Tucker et al. 2004, cat. nos. 40–54. The later Medici miniature (fig. 12 here), which clearly exhibits the fold, may have been made directly from a preparatory drawing from life (see ibid., 40). See Feinberg 1991; Florence, Palazzo Strozzi 2002, cat. no. 34; Chicago-Detroit 2002, cat. no. 34; and Strehlke 2004, cat. no. 25. All resemble the Baltimore Giulia. In *Alessandro* armoured *all'antica*, Sala di Leone X, Palazzo Vecchio, his features mirror the child's expression. See Langdijk 1981, 1: cat. 1,48.

142 Adriani 1583, whose *Suoi tempi* is dedicated to Francesco de' Medici, without hazarding Giulio's mother's name. Segni 1805, 2: 137–8, who names her as 'una Pratese' and a nun, ibid., 2: 19–20 and 59–60; see Ferrai 1882, 159–60; and Litta 1899–1902, Serie IA, Medici. Alessandro had a liaison with Taddea Malaspina, whose sister was a nun, from the early 1530s to 1537. I will argue Taddea's parentage of Giulio and Giulia below.

143 See Strehlke 1985, 5, and 2004, cat. no. 26; Nigro 1994, 157; and Costamagna 1994, cat. no. 72. Alessandro's limpid glance and his sketching of a woman's head support Vasari's claim that the panel was destined as a gift for Taddea. Vasari 1878–85, 6: 278. (Ricciarda Malaspina, too, was reputedly his lover, and Taddea had other admirers. Strehlke 2004, ibid.) Alessandro's air of wistfulness and gentility, and his artistry, promote him as a connoisseur of feminine beauty; see Langedijk 1981, 1: cat. 1,75, and Williams 1997, 48; Strehlke 1985, and Tucker et al. 2004, cat. nos. 43–4, also reflect on Leonardesque and Petrarchan implications; furthering these, see Cropper 2004, 21–2. The portrait was painted 'at the time of the death of our good Pope Clement,' as noted by Constantino Ansaldi in a letter to Francesco de' Medici, 23 November 1571; Nigro 1994, *sub* pl. X,9.

144 The poet Francesco Berni satirized the frivolous and pedestrian Alessandro-Malaspina-Cibo circle and mocked its neo-Petrarchan pretensions. Strehlke 1985, 11 and 2004, cat. no. 26.

145 M. Campbell 1985[1], 340; see also n. 143 above. The small study is more restrained. See Lloyd 1993, 197–202 with colour pl., and Strehlke 2004, cat. no. 25. The Palazzo Pazzi was Cardinal Cibo's residence, where Alessandro amused himself with Ricciarda Malaspina and her sister, Taddea. Cibo's sister Caterina, the excommunicated Marchesa of Camerino, was also in residence in the early 1530s. The independently wealthy Ricciarda, Marchioness of Massa and Carrarra, Cibo's separated sister-in-law and mother of several of his children, had extremely influential links to Charles V – and a child by his papal ambassador.

Linkage of the nun Angelica Malaspina's name rather than her sister Taddea's to Alessandro probably grew from rumours of Alessandro's forays into convents (see n. 140), but Taddea was Alessandro's companion over several years, and Giulio's links to the family remained unbroken into adulthood. (See 230n135.) Taddea, who did not remarry after Alessandro's death, was almost certainly Giulio and Giulia's mother.

Relations between the Medici and the Cibo Malaspina family were convoluted. In 1532, Maria Salviati petitioned Pope Clement to provide a wife and estates for Cosimo

– then thirteen – apparently proposing Maddalena Cibo, niece of Cardinal Innocenzo and Caterina Cibo, but Caterina was obstinately opposed. Booth 1921, 32. In spite of this snub and mischief by the Cibo-Malaspina family over Giulio on Cosimo's succession, Caterina was a ranking courtier in Cosimo and Eleonora's court.

146 See Clapp 1916, 280–2, for Ansoldo's indignant letter to Francesco, 23 November 1571, ASF MDP Carteggio Universale 567, f. 187; see also Nigro 1994, *sub* pl. X,9, and Strehlke 2004, cat. no. 26. (Taddea had a legitimate daughter, Giulia, also, but the link with Giulio is telling.) On Cosimo and Giulio's relations, see n. 135.

147 See Segni 1805, 2: 137–8.

148 Ferrai 1882, 156 n. 1, quoting G. Viani, *Memorie della famiglia Cibo* (Pisa, 1808).

149 Minor and Mitchell 1968, 1: 129 n. 58. Gamba 1956, 14–15 and fig. 13, claims that the *Portrait of a Cardinal* in the Galleria Borghese (by Pontormo or Salviati) is of Cibo.

150 Albèri 1839–63, II, 1: 75 n. 1.

151 Adriani 1583, 1: 410. See also Simon 1982, 25–6.

152 On the currency of this message, see G. Smith 1982[1], 187, 191, and 193.

153 See Kuehn 2002, esp. his important chap. 1 on legitimization and legal rights of illegitimate children. On legitimization of Federigo da Montefeltro to allow him to succeed his murdered half-brother Oddoantonio in 1444, and of his own natural son Buonconte, see Rosenberg 1986, 218. Charles V arbitrated the illegitimate Ippolito's challenge to Alessandro's dukedom after Clement's death in 1534. Strehlke 1985, 3, and Booth 1921, 53–98. For instances of papal legitimizing, see Hallman 1985; on related bulls, see ibid., 125. On the Malaspina-Cibo, see Baia 1907, 1–2. After his election, 9 January 1537, Cosimo waited six months before the emperor declared his ducal title legitimate. Cox-Rearick 1984, 238, citing Cantini, *Vita di Cosimo de' Medici* (Florence, 1805): 73–4, notes delivery of documents on 30 September 1537; Cosimo proclaimed his status on 16 October. See also Saltini, 1898, XXVff.

154 See Cropper 2001[3], cat. no. 40.

155 Kelso 1977, 129–30.

156 See pl. 6: Bia is bedecked in white satin, diamond-and-pearl earrings, a pearl collar, a heavy gold chain with a pendant cameo of Cosimo, and a heavy gold girdle.

157 Fusco 1570, 6–10, 22–7, 61, 164. The infant girl should be taught the paramount virtues of chastity and of obedience to her father, by her mother or another lady. He quotes Petrarch on decency and humility, advises on strict seclusion from public view or entertainments 'where the greater numbers of men congregate.' The proper upbringing of adolescent girls follows. Among classical exemplars is Giulia, Pompey's stoic wife; Porzia too is included. On Giulia's sister, Porzia, see n. 171 below, and chap. 4, 124

158 Kelso 1977, 129–30; on Vives and Fusco 1570, see nn. 72 and 110. For Alessandro, see Langedijk 1981, 1: cat. 1,21. See Giovio (d. 1552), *Elogia*, Basle, 1575, 319.

159 See Fusco 1570, 24, 38, and 112–20.

160 Lavinia Fontana's *Portrait of a Young Widow and Her Child*, with the mother holding an open book to the child's gaze, has been seen as reminiscent of portrayals of St Anne teaching the Virgin by C. Murphy 1997, 134–5.

161 Cropper 1997, 81, notes Pontormo's onomastic, i.e., visual, punning on Francesco Guardi del Monte's name in the *Halberdier*, who stands guard for his community, Florence. Here, Bia (pl. 6) is dressed in white (bianco), and in *Eleonora di Toledo with*

Her Son (pl. 4) Giovanni is Eleonora's peachick in gold-shot, *pavonazzo* taffeta, the peahen being her *impresa* and blue the Toledan armorial colour, as visual clues to their identities.

162 Caterina Cibo reported Maria's ill-health to her sister, 8 July 1541. Booth 1921, 117.

163 Cox-Rearick 1964, 310 proposed the separate head and torso on one sheet, Uffizi 6503F (fig. 9), as posthumous studies. I discuss physiognomical evidence for this in the *Maria Salviati with a Book* below. See also Strehlke 2004, cat. no. 46.

164 Cosimo, through Marchese d'Anguilar, imperial ambassador in Rome. Trans. by Booth 1921, 93–4.

165 Albèri 1839–63, 1: 99–101; Tenhove 1747, 2: 386–7; Booth 1921, 93–6.

166 Albèri 1839–63, II, 1: 101; Booth 1921, 94–8 records Cosimo's Machiavellian moves in this episode.

167 Florence, ASF MDP 4068, f. 210, Pyrro Musipsilo to Cosimo from Naples, detailing hostilities with the Turks. It concludes with a passage coded in numerals, with a halting, truncated gloss inserted in a different hand above; several words are indecipherable: 'I have a great secret of a good place to live. A practical move has been made [...] concerning the apartment house with Lady Giulia and nothing at all has been concluded thereby except for a [...] thus through the [...] year[?]. I'll dwell there until her manservant returns. This is what he said about the coming and going ever from S. Mra, and to deal with her apartment with the very young wife of the [castle?] of the Nas. sao, we may thus conclude. [*End of gloss.*] The L'ma ... affectionate entreaty [to] your Excellency ... I kiss your hands and in your good grace recommend me to the Lady Duchess and the Lady mother Maria. From Naples, January 10th, 1540.' (Ho un' gran secreto di buon luogo come al vivere. Stato mossa pratica [...] del casamento con la signora Donna Giulia e in si e concluso cosa alcunna ne nunca, exclusa una sin[...] cosi tra il si ... l'anno[?] fino abito c l'huomo suo tornera. C'e questo lui ha detto ch'il viavi[?] mai da S.Mra e per trattare suo casamento con la mona di gioventù moglie fu già del [cast...] del Nas. sao [...] si jiusta conclude portrebbe. [*End of gloss.*] La L'ma haver affetto suplico v. Ex[cellento] ... basio li mani et in sua buona gratia mi rac.^do. [...] S^{ra} Duchessa et S^{ra} m^a Maria. Di Napoli alli X di Jiniaro MDXXXX. [*sic*]). (On the modern calendar, this would be January 1541. In the sixteenth century, the Florentine year began on 25 March.)

168 Van Veen 1986, 15–17, demonstrates that Cosimo's power was consolidated gradually, beginning with the confirmation of his dukedom by Charles V.

169 On the symbolism of the *broncone* see Langedijk 1981, 1: 68 and 86; Sparrow 1967, 163–75; G. Smith 1977², n. 18; Cox-Rearick 1984, 237–8; and M. Campbell 1985¹, 356–7. See also my text and n. 44 above, on a *broncone* reference in Bronzino's *Lady in Red*, here identified as Maria Salviati.

170 Cox-Rearick 1984, 43.

171 Later, Giulio spent time at Massa with the Malaspina family, presumably also with Taddea. In 1538, Maria Salviati had founded the convent of S. Clemente in Via San Gallo for Alessandro's other illegitimate daughters, all entered 'al servizio di Dio,' Segni 1805, 214. These included Porzia, Giulia's sister or half-sister, later an abbess, who was portrayed in a lost mural there; for this and Allegrini's engraving, 1761, see Langedijk 1981, 2: cat. 104, 1a.

172 Segni 1805, 214 and 138ff.

173 Baia 1907, 65, refers to Eleonora's role as regent, 'especially after the death of her
     mother-in-law, Lady Maria Salviati.'

174 Langedijk 1981, 2: cat. 87,5, proposed that the plaque Maria holds may have shown the
     joining of the two branches of the Medici, which seems appropriate.

175 See chap. 4, 135.

176 See Cropper 1997, 102, listing Medici portraits in the Riccardi inventory.

177 Uffizi Inv. 1890, no. 3565, oil on panel, 87 × 71 cm. Langedijk 1981, 2: cat. 87,14. See
     Becherucci 1964, 21; Falciani 1995, 130–1; and Strehlke 2004, 150, fig. 84.

178 Purchased in 1911 as an anonymous Sienese work from Signora Ciaccheri Bellanti, it
     was attributed to Pontormo first by Berenson in 1933; Lanyi 1933 identified the sitter
     as Maria, and dated it 1537–43. E. King 1940, 80–2 concurred, as have many scholars.
     Cox-Rearick 1964, 310–11, believed it was done close to her death in 1543, perhaps
     posthumously, and both scholars repudiated it as the 1537 *Maria* for Castello men-
     tioned by Vasari. Berti 1973, cat. no. 128, revised his 1956 Pontormo attribution in
     favour of a Sienese master using Pontormo's posthumous drawing of Maria, Uffizi
     6503F. See fig. 9 here. See also Cox-Rearick 1974, no. 346; Simon 1982, 191–2, won-
     dered if the painting might be Beccafumi's after the same drawing. Following recent
     restoration of the panel, Cox-Rearick's 1997 review warmed to Costamagna's 1994
     attribution to Pontormo.
         Langedijk 1981, 1: cat. 87,14, concludes the identification as uncertain, with a com-
     prehensive bibliography that includes some early identifications: Berenson 1963, 180,
     attributed it as *Maria* by Pontormo; Berti 1966, *sub* pl. CLXII, proposes a *Maria* based
     on the Baltimore portrait; Forster 1966, as *Maria*, *sub* lost pictures, no. 33, and not the
     1537 portrait; Zeri 1976, *sub* no. 211, *Maria*. Gamba 1956, 15–16, and Keutner 1959, 144–
     6, disallow a *Maria* and doubt Pontormo's authorship.
         Berti 1993, Nigro 1993, and Forlani-Tempesti's 1994 monographs omit the panel.
     Costamagna 1994, cat. A35, 284–6, believes that this is Maria, by Pontormo. Pilliod
     2001, 17, tied it to a Pontormo drawing in the British Museum because of similar drap-
     ery patterns; it confirms authorship of the panel, but its subject is unlikely to be Maria.
     See n. 7 above.

179 See n. 180. Forster 1965, 224, gives the earlier drawing, Uffizi 6680F, to Bronzino, and I
     concur. (See fig. 6.)

180 Uffizi, Gabinetto Disegni e Stampe no. 6503F, in red chalk. Langedijk 1981, 2: cat.
     85,14a, who gives annotated bibliographies for this and for no. 6680F (ibid., 85,15),
     identifying common features in each, but both under 'uncertain identifications' of
     Maria, both by Pontormo. Identification and dating are debated.
         Dating for no. 6503F is wide, Clapp 1914, 230, and 1916, 86, allowing a date as late as
     1540, when Maria was forty. Forster 1965, 153, thought it was a Bronzino study for the
     Baltimore panel, which he dates to 1527. This is untenable. The Baltimore sitter's much
     advanced age over the drawing would be an unprecedented reversal of painterly ide-
     alization from preparatory drawing to panel portrait.
         Uffizi 6503F (fig. 9) is almost certainly the same woman as the youthful drawing of
     Maria, Uffizi 6680F (fig. 6), as Langedijk noted, and see n. 34 above. The oddly intense
     gaze of the sitter's left eye in each, and the deep-set eyes with well-delineated lids
     under high, smoothly arched brows are common to both, as are the proportions of the
     features to the face, and a pronounced roundness of the nares in each. For Maria,

Uffizi 6503F (the later drawing) see Berti 1973, cat. no. 128[1]; Costamagna 1994, 237–8, who dated it shortly before Maria's death in 1543; Natali ed. 1995, concurs, also Falciani 1995, 119, but her illness was chronic after 1540, and she would hardly have been fit to pose. Cox-Rearick 1989, n. 8, reiterates in her 1997 review of Costamagna 1994 her belief that no. 6503F may record studies for a posthumous portrait.

181 The Baltimore and Uffizi panels are identical in size, 87.6 × 71 cm.

182 See Langedijk 1981, passim, for copious Medici engravings that often match their subjects' portraits and were clearly sourced from them.

183 Pieraccini 1986, 1: 473; and see n. 40 above on her resemblance to Leo X.

184 De Hollanda 1868, 344. See also de Hollanda 1984, 22–3.

185 De Hollanda 1984, 23–4. I thank Prof. Zilpa Howard for refining this translation.

186 Badius Ascensius's Horatian commentary appeared in Paris in 1500, in Milan by 1518. See Weinberg 1961, 1: 82–3.

187 Firenzuola 1848, 278–9.

188 Ibid.

189 G. Smith 1982[1], 183. See Tinagli 2004, 119–35; and Hoppe 2004, 98–118.

190 G. Smith 1982[1], 183 and 193, on the *Joseph* tapestry cycle, celebrating the life of Joseph, saviour of his people, model ruler and statesman. (Bronzino's Chapel for Eleonora, detailing the Life of Moses, casts him in similar vein. See Cox-Rearick 1993.)

191 See the Introduction, n. 21. Hauser identified Eleonora's extreme grandeur as central to Bronzino's peerless style of court portraiture. De Logu and Marinelli 1975, 88.

192 Her role as arbiter of protocol may be inferred from Jacopo Salviati's deference to her when urging his daughter, Maria, to go with Cibo to Marseilles for the wedding of Caterina de' Medici to the Dauphin in 1533. See n. 104 above.

193 Becherucci 1964, 21; and see also Falciani 1995, 130–1.

194 These exhumations were ordered by the state in 1857 because the Medici Tombs had been pillaged for jewels in the early-nineteenth century, and were in considerable disorder. Some of the reports seem to have been romanticized. Eleonora was reported to have been buried in the dress in which she is portrayed in Bronzino's state portrait (pl. 4 here), which is a fallacy. See Picenardi 1888, 340; Young 1910, 550 and 588–9; Simon 1982, 197; Gauthiez 1901, 341; and Cox-Rearick 1993, 263 and 398. For shrouding of Dominican tertiaries see Francesco Bonsignori's 1519 altarpiece, Tinagli 1997, 62–63, fig. 19; on widows, see Valone 1992, 61.

195 Cropper 2001[3], cat. no. 36, refutes the title for Bugiardini's *La Monaca* (The Nun) for its revealing dress, and notes that laity did not wear the Franciscan habit in life.

    Tribute may have been made to Maria Salviati if she inspired Bronzino's nun-like Virgin in his *Lamentation*, begun soon after her death. See Cox-Rearick 1993, 261–4.

196 See also Cox-Rearick 1989, n. 8.

197 De Hollanda 1868, 346–51; he also prescribes correction of a slack jaw and protruding lip – signs of nobility, he asserts, no doubt to placate his Hapsburg patrons. See Lari 1995 on refinements to the *Maria with a Book*; Ainsworth 1990, on Holbein's refinements from drawing to panel; and Cox-Rearick 2004, 243, on Bronzino's posthumous *Eleonora*, Wallace Collection, which combines youth and maturity from her earlier portraits.

198 Syson 1998, 10, cites Cicero on casting. See Simons 1995, 271, for Francesco Barbaro's comment on the burden of imitation *imagines* evoked for survivors. On the Accademia Fiorentina's *esequie* and her portrait, see Strehlke 2004, cat. no. 46.

199 Medical confirmation in fig. 9 of post-mortem morbidity include a characteristic slack-
   ening and lengthening of the upper lip, and Maria's eyes, 'opened' by Pontormo.
   Extremely open nares result from plugging them to prevent wet plaster entering them
   during its application to the deceased's face and neck; its weight flattens forms
   (Schuyler 1972, 115–19), as Pontormo's posthumous drawing of Maria's nose records.
   See D.A. Brown ed. 2001, cat. no. 27, for Botticelli's *Giuliano de' Medici's* 'opened' eyes,
   rigid jaw, and depressed nose tip; see also Danese Cattaneo's *Giovanni delle Bande Nere*
   medal, Davis 1978, 333–4.

200 See n. 63 on Giovanni's death mask and portraits derived from it.

201 Cf. Langedijk 1981, 2: cats. 87,3 and 87,4.

202 Schuyler 1972, 115–19. See also n. 204.

203 Museo del Bargello, Florence.

204 Schuyler 1972, 114ff. Supporting moisture, depleted in eyesockets, results in concavity
   and exaggerated protrusion of closed eyes; the neck was stretched back to facilitate
   casting. (For overt signs in Donatello's *Niccolò da Uzzano*, d. 1433, see Olson 1992, 91,
   fig. 67.) The smoothed planes and convexity of the eyelids were evident in the Uffizi
   portrait when cleaned in 1995; particulars of ageing had been removed, with broad
   brushstrokes used over the cheeks and around the eyes. See Lari 1995, 3 and reflecto-
   graph, fig. 4.

205 Laurana's terracotta death-cast is in the Louvre; in life, Battista's features and neck
   were heavier; she had a pronounced double chin. In death, her jaw and mouth were
   slack.

206 See Tinagli 1997, 77–9, for detailed analysis; see also D.A. Brown 2001, cat. no. 30, for
   further discussion and bibliography on this portrait.

207 The Elder Pliny's instructions for casting an image in wax and gesso were recorded by
   Cennino Cennini. For this, see Schuyler 1972, 135; see also Schneider 1994, fig. p. 28,
   for a life-size, marble statue of a Roman patrician of about 30 BC carrying such busts of
   his ancestors.

208 On these locations and modes of display for busts, see Schneider 1994, 25.

209 See Valone 1992, fig. 9 (Vittoria della Tolfa's tomb, in Santa Maria in Aracoeli, Rome,
   ca. 1586). Characteristics of post-mortem casting are manifest in her face and pose.

210 See n. 198 above.

211 See Langedijk 1981, 2: cat. 78,2. It was recorded in inventories from 1492 to 1609.

212 Schuyler 1972, 151.

213 Ibid., 26. Vasari 1878–85, 3: 373, records that death-casts were a source for *personae* in
   frescoes in Cosimo's palace. Verrocchio had pioneered their use for reference and
   study.

214 Schuyler 1972, 26 and 95, quoting Vasari 1878–85, 2: 416. Eleonora's was probably
   Bandinelli's *all' antica* version, 1544, in the Bargello; Schuyler 1972, fig. 36 (fig. 25 here).

215 For the panel, see Hartt 1994, 348–9, colour pl. 65. The drawing is in Stockholm.

216 Langedijk 1981, 1: cat. 10,2; Brock 2002, 78, notes Bia's posthumous 'vivification.'

217 'Una testa di Madonna d'Imola madre del Sor Giovanni,' a cast in bust form, according
   to the later inventories. See Langedijk 1981, 1: cat. 18,6; and cat. 18,12 for Vasari's oval,
   in his time in the Annalena; ibid., cat. 56,34. See also Allegri and Cecchi 1980, 158.

218 Langedijk 1981, 1: cat. 18,7, anonymous, ca. 1490. De Hollanda 1984, 24, cites the profile as the noblest pose of all. For elongation of the neck, see n. 204 above.

219 See Berti 1973, 6; Varchi had orated the artists' responses in his *Due Lezzioni* to the Accademia Fiorentina in 1547.

220 McManamon 1989, 31.

221 For Vasari, Bronzino, and Pontormo's responses in full see Barocchi ed. 1971, 1: 492–507.

222 Berti 1973, 6: '... Ma quello che io dissi troppo ardito, ch'è la importanza, si è superare la natura in volere dare spirito a una figura e farla parere viva, e farla in piano.'

223 Mendelsohn 1982, 154.

224 See the Introduction, 15, and Mendelsohn 1982, 3–6.

225 Weinberg 1961, 1: 54–5, 122–6, 257–77, and 418–20, quoting the Neoplatonist Jiacopo Grifoli. In a Neoplatonic vein, Carlo Lenzoni referred to the Medici Chapel as a standard for unity and beauty. Ibid., 2: 825. Varchi's disciple, Ugolino Martelli, recorded that Michelangelo improved on nature, giving Lorenzo and Giuliano 'a grandeur, a proportion, a decorum, a grace, a splendour which it seems to him bears them more praise.' See Summers 1981, 337.

226 Summers 1981, 54.

227 Mendelsohn 1982, 154, 269, referring to Varchi's *Due Lezzioni*, Florence, 1550.

228 Simons 1995, 271, quoting the Camaldolan general Delphin on his predecessor's death mask, which he gazed upon daily. See n. 198 on the burden of imitation of *imagines*.

229 Bronzino had just completed Eleonora's chapel and received important portrait commissions; see text, 60.

230 Sandoval, lines 21–7; see Pratesi 1909, 9–17.

231 He borrows the three phases of epideictic oration. In his 'exordium,' he proposes that Arno assume his voice to express the collective grief of Florentines. 'Arno' then moves to the second aspect of funeral oratory, praise, in which he eulogizes Maria's elevation to God, describing her charity, her virtues (*onestà, pietà, grazia*) and, predictably, gives praise for benefits she has bestowed. Her piety, *grazia*, and role as mother to all preface his opportunity to refer to Cosimo's fame. In the third element, the peroration, he repeatedly deplores her loss. Finally, he addresses Cosimo, who is urged to allay his grief in this earthly prison by counting his blessings; in the tradition of Medici orations, this passage dwells on his alliances, political strength, benefits bestowed on Florentines, and the continuation of his line. For Quattrocento and Cinquecento funeral oration, and Medici versions, see McManamon 1989, 12ff., and 49–53.

232 'Tu allato del Fattor alta sedendo / In lui solo mirando ed ei splendendo / In te ...' Sandoval, lines 93–5. See Pratesi 1909, 13.

233 Pratesi 1909, 13, citing Dante, *Paradiso* 1: 64–7.

234 Sandoval, lines 1–5; see Pratesi 1909, 10.

235 See Langedijk 1981, 2: cats. 74,25 and 25a, a lost death mask with similar inscription.

236 Benedetto Varchi, *Orazione funebre per la Salviati, recitata nell'Accademia Fiorentina* (Florence, Torrentino, 1549), quoted in Pratesi 1909, 11.

237 McManamon 1989, 31.

238 *Oratio habita in funerere Leonardi Laurentani Venetiarum principis* (Venice, 1521), 24–53. See McManamon 1989, 47.

239 Sandoval was on safe ground: Eleonora, married in 1539, had four children by 1543.

240 Sandoval in Pratesi 1909, 17.

241 L. Campbell 1990, 195, and 265 n. 18, paraphrasing the original passage.

242 Castiglione 1959, 31.

243 Zollner 1993, 125: women's portraits were privately hung with religious works. A sole *'Nostra Donna* antica' is recorded for private Medici rooms in 1533. Conti 1893, 75–6.

244 National Gallery of Art, Washington. Cox-Rearick 1981, 308–10, links the style of Pontormo's Uffizi 6503F studies of Maria's head and torso (fig. 9 here) to his studies for the portrait of della Casa.

245 Della Casa's keen gaze is evidently captured from life in the drawing, however. For a bibliography and discussion on both drawing and panel, see Strehlke 2004 cat. nos. 44 and 45, where they were exhibited together.

246 Vasari 1878–85, 7: 597–8, on Bronzino: 'The Lord Duke, having seen the excellence of this painter in these and other works, particularly that it was his habit to portray from life with the most diligence that can be imagined, commissioned a portrait of himself while then young, armed completely in steel armour and with one hand over the helmet [Vasari then lists Eleonora, the ducal children, Francesco di Toledo, Ercole II of Ferrara and] ... Signora Maria, mother of the Duke.' See also Simon 1982, 44.

247 For Giovanni delle Bande Nere's portraits, see n. 63.

248 Mendelsohn 1982, 6: See Sherberg 2003, 50–1 on Cosimo's attempts to claim precedence for Lorenzo's *letterati* in the *questione della lingua*, and Nencioni 1983 on Cosimo's political intentions for the Accademia.

249 See the Introduction, 15; Cecchi 1996[1], 20, quotes Varchi: '[Bronzino] ... has memorized the whole of Dante and a very great deal of Petrarch'; see 251n155.

250 Alessandro de' Medici, Amerigo Antinori, and Maria Salviati were among them. Vasari 1878–85, 6: 260–79, also includes Ottaviano de' Medici as his patron.

251 Studies by Pilliod, 1998 and 2001, expose Vasari's disdain for Pontormo, and explore his motivation. Hope 1980 had signalled some unreliable aspects of his writings.

252 See Vasari 1878–85, 6: 259–64. Pontormo's diary reveals deep sensitivity. See Mayer et al. 1982

253 On this, see Cox-Rearick 1981, 8–9, 69–70.

254 Simon 1982, 23–5 cites his intractability when Clement renewed the Poggio a Caiano commission in 1530. In 1535, Alessandro's commission for Careggi stipulated that he should not work alone. Vasari 1878–85, 6: 276–81; see Cox-Rearick 1964, 287–92, and Forster 1965, 84–90.

255 See Cox-Rearick, 1993, 1.

256 See n. 246: Vasari suggests Cosimo 'noticed' Bronzino's talent as portraitist at this time, but Cosimo was surely familiar with the *Maria Salviati with a Lapdog* (pl. 1).

257 Notably, his Germanic borrowings at Galuzzo, and a *fumus heresiae* around the San Lorenzo cycle (1545–56). See n. 251 above; Pinelli 1993, 5–30; and Cox-Rearick 1997, 127. Cropper 2004, 12 and 17–23, defends this northern influence as an artistic quest to evoke devotion, and notes Pontormo's humanism, scholarship, and familiarity with chancery script.

258 De Hollanda 1979, 11.

259 Pontormo's emulation of Michelangelo is evident in his response to Varchi; see 53, and n. 219 above. Michelangelo's only portrait was the drawing of Andrea Quaratesi, ca. 1530 (London, British Museum, exh. cat. by John Gere, 1974, no. 45). For Vasari's unenthusiastic attitude to portraiture, see Introduction, 13, and 214n60.

260 Ronald Firbank coined the term 'unglimpseable.' See Parker 1997, 1013. On Bronzino's

superb ducal portraits, see Richelson 1978, 2–5 and passim; Simon 1982 and 1985; Cox-Rearick 1989, 37; and Brock 2002, 155–9. Cropper 2004, 30, also holds that Bronzino was more adaptable to the new regime.

261 Cox-Rearick 1993, 115, believes that Cosimo's powerful major-domo, Riccio, was instrumental in promoting this decorum, also noting Francesco Salviati's decline from favour. See S. Freedberg 1993, 430–3 for an exceptional analysis of Bronzino's 'high artifice, which serves as a mask for passion or as an armour against it.'

262 Turner 1986, 141, and see Freedberg 1993, 430–3.

263 On receipt of a gift of a Bronzino *Cosimo I in Armour*, circa 1544, Giovio records the praises of members of the papal curia, and concludes: '[B]lessed is the hand of Bronzino, who to me seems to have surpassed that of Pontormo his master' ('... benedetta sia la mano di Bronzino qual mi pare che avanzi quella del Pontormo suo maestro'). See n. 94.

Chapter 2

1 Portions of this chapter are reflected in Langdon 1992[1] and Langdon 2004. I thank Ashgate Publishing for permission to include excerpts from the latter in this study.

2 Tosi 1910, 162–5. On her regency, see Booth 1921, 119–22; Langdon 1992[1], 1: 196; and Cox-Rearick 1993, 355; see Edelstein 2001, 235, for Pagni's, Riccio's, and other exchanges. Eleonora may have been regent from her wedding in 1539: Apollo's eulogy, by Giovanni Battista Gelli, guaranteed good rule by Cosimo *and* Eleonora. Rousseau 1990, 422. On artists, and Major-domo Riccio's powerful role as intermediary to Cosimo, see Cecchi 1998 and Cox-Rearick 2002, 37.

3 Cox-Rearick 1993, 34–5 and 354; Edelstein 2000, 301–7 and 2004[2], 74; and Booth 1921, 121 (on her fortitude and astuteness as Regent). See also Segni 1805, 2: 218; Baia 1907, 43–6, 65; and Tosi 1910.

4 Edelstein 2001, 255–6 and passim, details Cosimo's early struggles, his precocious statemanship, his adroit treatment of enemies, his absolutism, and his avoidance of reference to a principato. See also Fantoni 1994. See D.R. Wright 1976, 2: 806, on Charles V's granting of the title of Duke after the Battle of Montemurlo, August 1537.

5 See Cox-Rearick 1987 and 1993, 217–37 and 294–319; and Edelstein 2001, 236–7. The *Crossing of the Red Sea* and *Moses Appointing Joshua* express dynastic success on Francesco's birth. In 1579, Venetian ambassadors opined that the chapel's symbolism ranked Cosimo 'on par with kings.' Fantoni 1999, 270, who sees its focus as princely majesty, with quasi-royal status. (By 1545, Maria [1540], Francesco [1541], Isabella [1542], Giovanni [1543], and Lucrezia [1545] had been born. Six more children followed.)

6 Classicism was its inspiration: *The Triumph of Hercules* was included by Tribolo in the Castello program in 1537 and on Domenico di Polo's medal. For Salviati's fresco, *The Triumph of Camillus* in the Sala delle Udienze in the Palazzo in 1543, see Cox-Rearick 1987, 55. For the tapestries, see G. Smith 1982[1]; and Cox-Rearick 1993, 6, on their expression of a Medici Golden Age. On Cosimo's cultural reach across the arts, see Eisenbichler ed. 2001.

7 Langedijk 1981, 1: 82–6 and cat. 27,44; ibid., cat. 27,19 (Kassel derivative); Baccheschi 1973, cat. 54; Simon 1982, 62–135; Cox-Rearick 1993, 36; and Brock 2002, 157–9.

8 Vasari 1878–85, 7: 597–8, listing Bia, Maria, Francesco, Giovanni, Garzia, and Ferdinando, Francesco with his mother, a list spanning years – Ferdinando was born in 1549. The sequence is suspect: Maria Salviati, listed after Ferdinando, died in 1543. On Eleonora's patronage, see Edelstein 2001, 225–6; and, on her increasing power, Carolyn Smyth 1997.

9 Uffizi Inv. 1890, no. 748, 115 × 95 cm. Florence, Uffizi 1980, *Catalogo generale* no. P300; Langedijk 1981, 1: cat. 35,10, and Brock 2002, 81–4. Other child identifications include Francesco, Garzia, or Ferdinando: see Langedijk, idid. Becherucci 1964, no. 129; McCorquodale 1981, 92–3; and Simon 1982, 75. The 1553 Inventory (Conti 1893, 117) records Francesco with Eleonora, possibly the portrait of them in Pisa (Langedijk 1981, 1: cat. 35,12, 12a, and 12b). The 1560 inventory records '[t]he portrait of the Duchess from the hand of Bronzino, with Don Giovanni as a child'; Langedijk, ibid., cat. 35,6. Cox-Rearick 1993, 37, and Cecchi 1996[1], 40, agree. In Lorenzo della Sciorina's version (fig. 18), Serie Aulica, 1584, Garzia is substituted. Langedijk, ibid., cat. 35,17.

10 Jenkins 1947, 13–15, held it to epitomize the genre; see Langdon, 1992[1], 2: 196–292; Cox-Rearick 1993, 37; Tinagli 1997, 111–12; Edelstein 2001; Brock 2002, 82; and Langdon 2004. On its potential for propaganda, see Richelson 1978, 4–7; Simon 1982, 1983, 1985, 1987; Langedijk 1981, 1: 83–8 and cat. 27,29ff.; and Cox-Rearick 1993, 37, 149, 254, 259, and 321.

11 See Segni 1805, 2: 255; Pieraccini 1986, 1: 55–70 and passim; Booth 1921, 106, 114, 123, and 291; Tosi 1909[2], with documentation; see also chap. 4, 123, recording her fury with retainers. Edward Goldberg kindly advised on Eleonora's betting on the sex of courtiers' unborn children. (Elizabeth of Valois pawned jewels to cover her debts. Rodríguez-Salgado 1991, 236.) Such deep attachment also marked the marriages of Isabella of Spain – 'la reina proprietaria' for her obsessive devotion to Ferdinand – and the happy marriage of Charles V and Empress Isabella. Fraser 1992, 12–13. On contradictory reports of Eleonora's personality, see Cox-Rearick and Westerman Bulgarella 2004, 113–14, quoting Victoria Kirkham's unpublished commentary.

12 See Parker 2000, 3 and nn. 3–4; and 'evidence' in de Logu and Marinelli 1975, 1: 113–16. Eisenbichler ed. 2004, dedicated to refuting biased accounts of Eleonora, reveals her intelligence, energy, patronage, and business acumen, the latter seen as an essential stabilizing element for Cosimo's realm.

13 Williams 1997, 8 and 73–122; for decorum in portraiture, see Langdon 1992[1], chaps. 1–2.

14 Plazzotta and Keith 1999 concluded that sophisticated audiences enjoyed the resulting iconographical challenges because they allowed for flexible, layered, multiple interpretations.

15 For the portrait connoisseur Giovio's response, see chap. 1, 57.

16 For Cosimo's directives in August 1545 to speed the *Lamentation* (now in Besançon) to Charles V's minister, Nicolas Perrenot de Granvelle, and for an uncompleted portrait believed to be the Uffizi *Eleonora with Giovanni*, see Simon 1982, 71–5, and Cox-Rearick 1993, 74–7, 79–80, 333–8, and 362–5. See also Vasari 1878–85, 7: 597, and Borghini 1584, 536. Bronzino's letter of 22 August to Riccio reveals that Cosimo was torn between completion of the portrait and of the *Lamentation*. (The chapel's present *Lamentation* is a copy commissioned in 1553.)

17 For assessment of Bronzino's role and talent as court portraitist, see Brock 2002, passim (Brock's monograph convincingly repeats this theme many times).

18 Aristotle believed that in manipulating abiding truths, an orator could appeal to his audience's preconceptions rather than abiding strictly to truth. Williams 1997, 86.

19 Richelson 1978; Simon 1982, 1985, and 1987; and Brock 2002, 174–5, explore these.

20 For the blackwork, see Arnold 1993, 49 and 59.

21 On goldsmiths at the Medici court from 1545, including Benvenuto Cellini, and on Eleonora's lavish commissions, see Sframeli and Contu in Florence, Palazzo Pitti 2003, 24–35.

22 Very tiny pearls – weighing less than one-quarter grain – are graded as 'seed' pearls.

23 Baccheschi 1973, cat. 53; Cox-Rearick 1993, 37, and Brock 2002, 160–1. Begun on 21 March, it was completed 19 April 1545, when he was eighteen months old. See Marzio Marzi de' Medici, from Pietrasanta, to Riccio, in Florence, ASF MDP 1171, f. 260, ins. 6 (MAPD #2445). Soon, Bronzino was commissioned to portray 'the others' – probably Maria, Francesco, and Isabella – for which no records exist, ibid., f. 266 (MAD #2434). Eleonora proposed Giovanni's cardinalate to her Jesuit confessor in the early 1550s. Edelstein 2001, 225, 228–9, including Eleonora's patronage of Bronzino. See Brock 2002, 82, 158, 161, and 176 for other *Giovanni*s.

24 Bronzino to Pierfrancesco Riccio, 9 August 1545, in Gaye 1840, 2: 329–30, quoting ASF MDP 1170A, I, f. 36, ins. 3. See also Edelstein 2001, 226.

25 Payment for gilding the *Deposition/Lamentation*'s frame was made 31 July 1545, when it must have been completed or nearing completion. On this, see n. 16.

26 National Gallery, Prague, Inv. no. DO 880, 59 × 46 cm. See Baccheschi 1973, cat. 55d, and Brock 2002, 87, for colour pls., and see Cox-Rearick 2002, 35–6. On Cosimo's strong interest in this precious material, see Cox-Rearick and Westerman Bulgarella 2004, 119.

27 Simon 1982, 75.

28 The Fleece was a prized ducal insignia, signifying imperial Hapsburg protection.

29 Simon 1982, 68–76, quoting ASF MDP 1170A, I, f. 36, ins. 3, 9 August 1545.

30 Simon 1982, 78.

31 Eleonora's portrait was still incomplete on 22 August 1545. See nn. 16 and 25.

32 Allegri and Cecchi 1980, XXX–XXXI, provide birthdays for Eleonora's eleven children: Maria Lucrezia, 2 April 1540 [–1557]; Francesco, 25 March 1541 [–1587]; Isabella Romola, 31 August 1542 [–1576]; Giovanni, 28 September 1543 [–1562]; Lucrezia, 14 February 1545 [–1561]; Pedricco, 1546 [–1547]; Garzia, 1 July 1547 [–1562]; Antonio, 1548 [–1548]; Ferdinando, 30 July 1549 [–1609]; Anna, 1553 [–1553]; Pietro, 3 June 1554 [–1604]. See Pieraccini 1986 for biographies of each.

33 For these various past identifications, see n. 9.

34 Langedijk 1981, 1: cat. 35,10, identifies the child as Francesco; for his portraits, see ibid., cat. series 42; and Baccheschi 1973, cats. 88, 126, 130(?), 153, and 158. M. Campbell 1985, 387, challenged the Francesco identification and upheld Vasari's reference to Eleonora with Giovanni, also pointing out the child's tender age and distinctive hair colour.

35 Langedijk 1981, 2: cat. 46,2a. On identifying Garzia in Eleonora's state portrait of 1545, see Woermann 1906, 82 (Garzia or Ferdinando); and Jenkins 1947, 13 (Garzia).

36 For Ferdinando, see Langedijk 1981, 2: cat. series 37; and for Pietro, series 100.

37 Ibid., cat. series 54.

38 McCorquodale 1981, 92, notes the little boy's 'sparkling' presence. See also n. 23.

39 Baccheschi 1973, cat. 132; and Brock 2002, 171–3. See esp. Simon 1985, 30–42, who believes it to be amatory and private, the sole viewer, Eleonora, being 'Eurydice' to Cosimo's 'Orfeo.' See also Strehlke 2004, cat. no. 38.

40 See Baccheschi 1973, 83; G. Smith, 1982[1]; Pinelli 1993, 145–7; Rousseau 1990, 416–23; and Fantoni 1999, 261.

41 Langedijk 1981, 1: cat. series 27. Cox-Rearick 1993, 36–7, dates the bust-length *Cosimo in Armour* to 1543, accepts it as prototype for the Kassel version, where Cosimo wears the Order of the Golden Fleece. She links the Prague *Eleonora* to the 1543 *Cosimo in Armour* and the *Eleonora with Giovanni* to the Kassel panel.

42 Vasari 1878–85, 7: 598.

43 See Langedijk 1981, 1: cat. series 27.

44 See n. 26 for the portrait, probably that taken to Cosimo's bedchamber during his illness.

45 Simon 1982, 78–9 ties its commission to July 1543, when Cosimo gained control of Tuscan fortresses from Charles V. He links this portrait to Bandinelli's bust, 1543–4, and Niccolò della Casa's 1544 engraving, where Cosimo is more lightly bearded than in portraits of him wearing the Golden Fleece.

46 Simon 1982, 77, quoting ASF MDP 363, f. 165, and supported by Cox-Rearick 1993, 36, and Brock 2002, 87. Cecchi 1996, 46, however, dates it 1539; Lecchini Giovannoni 1991, cat. no. 188, assigns it to the 1570s as a posthumous portrayal by Allori.

47 Oil on slate, 30 × 24 cm. Simon 1982, cat. no. D1; Langedijk 1981, 1: cat. 27,32 and copy, 32a; see also M. Campbell 1985[2], 386.

48 Langedijk 1989, 3: addenda to cat. no. 35,10f.; Langedijk 1981, 1: cat. 27,32 and 35,10; Baccheschi 1973, cat. 55d; each identify the Prague panel with the 1545 state portrait.

49 Alciati 1621 (published 1531), emblems 118 (*Virtute fortuna comes*) and 47 (*Pudicitia*).

50 See Florence, Palazzo Pitti 2003, exh. cat., nos. 9 and 10 for her rings.

51 She was dressed in crimson satin embroidered with spun gold when she took her seat in the Palazzo Medici, 29 June 1539. On arrival at a temporary Doric portal at the Porta al Prato she was met by thirty-six noble youths on foot in livery of peacock-blue silk contrasted with crimson. See Baia 1907, 21–3; and Lazzi 1993, 29. 'Dianora' of Toledo (pls. 14 and 16, chap. 7) wears Toledan peacock-blue armorial colours. See also n. 67 for these.

52 Cox-Rearick 1993, 23, 36, who also records a description of Eleonora by an intimate as '[b]eautiful, fresh, with the complexion of a rose' at this time.

53 For Vasari's description, see text above. See also Florence, Palazzo Pitti 2003, 66.

54 For these and many instances, see L. Campbell 1990, 177–9; and Warnke 1993, 215.

55 Robes for Bianca Cappello's state portrait, for example, were returned to the palace by Allori on 8 November 1580. Langedijk 1981, 1: cat. 12,1.

56 For Prague-inspired *Eleonoras*, see Langedijk 1981, 1: cat. 35,2; 32,8; 32,10–i; 32,11; 32,12–12c; and 32,17; and Brock 2002, 81. For Clovio's miniature, see Langedijk ibid., cat. 35,20, and Simon 1989.

57 Vasari 1878–85, 7: 595–6, recording also his help with Pontormo's 1519 frescoes at Poggio a Caiano, when he would have been sixteen.

58 See Minor and Mitchell 1968.

59 For Margaret of Austria's role in the marriage negotiations, and her future life, see Eisenbichler 2001, 282 and 290. For Pedro di Toledo (1484–1553), see Pane 1975. Eleonora's role as a linchpin in Cosimo's push for power increased. Her family, the Alba of Toledo, grew enormously powerful through the 1550s and 1560s, with Don Fernando Alvarez de Toledo, Great Master of the King's Household, an assertive, controlling influence on Philip of Spain, Charles's successor, in state affairs. Toledo, the wealthiest

benefice in Christendom, had royal cachet: until 1560, it housed the imperial court. Rodríguez-Salgado 1991, 209–23, 234–5. Further, see Maltby 1983.

60 Maria wrote that Eleonora was closer in age to Cosimo than her sister, Isabella. ASF MDP 1171, f. 174 ins. 4 (MADP #2419), from Castello, undated, 1539. See also Eisenbichler 2004, 2–3.

61 See Rousseau 1990, 422, and figs. 11–12: in the 1539 wedding *apparato*, the actor personifying Flora wore headgear with a Hapsburg eagle to allegorize Medici protection. See Watt's (2004) expansive analysis.

62 Adriani 1583, 1: 96.

63 Lorenzo (1492–1519) married Madeleine de La Tour d'Auvergne in 1518; soon after his death she returned to France. (She was the mother of Caterina de' Medici, its future queen.) Alessandro's widow, Margaret of Austria, left for Rome after Cosimo's election in 1537.

64 Mitchell 1986, 49. An Italian who saw a later imperial viceroy in Naples carried in a litter in 1591 commented that he was so grave and motionless 'that I should never have known whether he was a man or a figure of wood.' Burke 1987, 154n4 and 1992, 82nn23–4.

65 On Toledo, see n. 59. Naples was the most populous city in Italy, around 200,000, with Pedro Alvarez de Toledo its longest-reigning viceroy, 1532–53. For Charles V's 1535 *entrata* to celebrate his victory at Tunis he was paraded by the viceroy under triumphal arches celebrating Alexander, Hannibal, Julius Caesar, Scipio, his ancestors, and his triumphs over Protestants and Turks; wondrous mechanical images of the Fall of the Giants struck down by Jupiter's thunderbolts issued from the imperial eagle. See Hollingsworth 1996, 224–7. On the impact of this event on Cosimo (who was also present), and on its political implications for him and for Eleonora as Duke and Duchess of Florence in later years, see Edelstein 2004[1], 187–8.

66 On Medici retainers' discomfiture at the Neapolitan court in 1539, see 212n21.

67 Lavish tapestry cycles praising just government and the Medici-Toledo union include the *Primavera* (Palazzo Pitti), 1545; *Justice Liberating Innocence* (Palazzo Vecchio); *La Primavera / Flora* (Palazzo Vecchio), 1546; and the *Allegory of the Medici-Toledo Union* (Pitti), 1552. See Heikamp 1968, 22–30; Baccheschi 1973, cats. 56, 57, 57[1], 58, and 90; Adelson 1985, 163–5; and Cox-Rearick 1993, 160 and fig. 107. The latter incorporates the Medici *palle* and Toledan chequered silver and blue arms, flanked by Apollo and Minerva and inscribed FUNDATA ENIM/ERAT SUPER PETRAM. Toledan arms exist under a superimposed *Trinity* in the vault of Eleonora's chapel; see Smyth 1955, 217, and Cox-Rearick 1993, 40 and 276, and 2004, 248.

Lincoln 1999, 16, sees the Medici move to the Palazzo Pitti as the ultimate declaration of autocracy, with its attendant trappings. It was purchased by Eleonora in 1549 with additional land, now the Boboli Gardens, and expanded and transformed as the official grand ducal residence by successive architects. Bartolomeo Ammannati's great courtyard was completed by 1562, the year of her death. Tribolo designed the gardens until his death in 1550, followed by Buontalenti, under Eleonora's patronage. For this, see Edelstein 2000, 80 with useful references; and Edelstein 2004[1], 187–200.

68 Pieraccini 1986, 2: 16 and 60ff.; Tosi 1909[2], 16; and Booth 1921, passim, document Eleonora's 'insupportable aloofness.' Pieraccini, ibid., 55–70, divined inferior wit from her handwriting: fig. 10, ASF MDP 338, f. 29, 15 May 1539. Baia 1907, 78–9, sympathetically

documents her intellectual patronage; see also Cox-Rearick 1993, 26, 352, 355, and passim; Edelstein 1995, 2000, and 2001; and n. 218 here.

69 Pinelli 1993, 113. On Ferdinando's marriage to Christine of Lorraine, a new sphere of influence, France, emerged; see Fantoni 1994, 265–6, on the *Diari di Etichetta*, begun in 1648, codifying strict dynamics for hierarchical access in ceremonial – including that surrounding the person of the grand duke at meals – and formalized exchange of gifts, etc.

70 On consort portraits used for propaganda, see Corradini 1998, 30, on Este medals.

71 Della Casa 1994, 19 and 61. (Pinelli 1993, 113, believes that della Casa's *Galateo* most closely reflects the world and culture of Vasari.)

72 The diarist Marucelli scathingly records her mode of transportation in 1548: '... in which litter the Duchess travelled, who owing to her pride was never to be glimpsed going on foot, nor ever seen riding, and in it she most often went as in a reliquary tabernacle, that is to say half of the litter was exposed and under the other half she remained; a woman of such great haughtiness [is] a truly marvellous thing to see.' Marucelli is unduly harsh: Eleonora was pregnant annually throughout the 1540s; she also loaned the litter to transport Bartolomeo Lanfredi's widow on 6 November 1544, see ASF MDP 1171, f. 150, ins. 3. The duchess supervised its design; payment to a swordsmith for the gilding of fittings was made 6 March 1542 (ASF MDP 600, f. 23). It was covered with green velvet and lined with crimson silk inside, the Medici armorial colours. See Pieraccini 1986, 1: 60. On green velvet's connotations with aristocratic dignity, see Saslow 1996^2, 61–2. (Another litter, of red velvet, is recorded in ASF MDP 1176, f. 44, ins 5 [MAPD no. 3177]; f. 24, ins. 6 [MAPD no. 3122]; f. 30, ins. 7 [MAPD no. 3126]; f. 43, ins. 9 [MAPD no. 3216]; f. 24, ins. 10, and f. 44, ins. 24 [MAPD no. 3177], dated 1551.)

73 Quoted in Baia 1907, 21–3; see Giambullari, passim, in Minor and Mitchell 1968, and Mannucci 1586, 79. See also Cox-Rearick 1984, 241–6, and Cox-Rearick 1993, 28–9.

74 Adriani 1583, 1: 96–7.

75 Mannucci 1586, 79.

76 Vasari 1878–85, 6: 86–7.

77 Cox-Rearick 1993, 30; on the *broncone*, see Cox-Rearick 1984.

78 Cox-Rearick 1993, 31. See also Tinagli 2000, 265.

79 See Heikamp 1978, 117–73, and Allegri and Cecchi 1980, 223–6; for Juno's attributes, see Alciati 1621, 833a,b. Cosimo appears as Jupiter in Vasari's Camera di Jove frescoes. Richelson 1978, 77 n. 79. See n. 179 below; and see text, 181–5, for the *Allegory of Juno* (pl. 15), where Juno-Eleonora brandishes Jupiter's thunderbolts. (On Henry IV and Marie de' Medici as Jupiter and Juno, see Dixon 2002, pls. 89 and 92.)

80 Cox-Rearick 1993, 42, citing Domenichi's *Nobilità delle donne* (1549): 'Tuscany may indeed be called blessed today, governed by two such exceptionally just and humane rulers.' Benson 2004, 144, analyses Domenichi's praise of Eleonora in her role as Cosimo's consort.

81 Brumble 1998, 190–2, citing Cristoforo Landino on Juno's determination to rule others.

82 See Simon 1982; see also Langedijk 1981, 1: 84.

83 De Hollanda 1868, 340. For the Kassel portrait, see n. 41.

84 ffolliott 1989, 138.

85 See Lunenfeld 1981, 157–8 and 160: Isabella the Catholic (1474–1504) aggressively asserted her destiny to rule and wore chain mail into battle, but her portraits associate

her with the Immaculate Conception and the Apocalyptic Woman clothed with the Sun and the Moon. Tomas 2000, 71–2. Elizabeth I of England famously claimed to have the body of a woman but the stomach of a king, yet her portraits similarly promote a 'virgin queen.' On this, see Baumgärtel 2002.

86 The lost *Charles V* is known from Giovanni Britto's woodcut of 1533–4. See Simon 1983, 535. On Hapsburg state portraits and Titian's influence on the emerging genre, see Jenkins 1947, 1–17, and Howarth 1993, 100.

87 Seisenegger sojourned in Spain from 1538–9, before Isabella died. Titian's panel was destroyed by fire at the Prado in 1604. For copies, see Hôtel Drouot sales catalogue, Paris, 13 March 1914 (fig. 23 here); Jenkins 1947; and Wethey 1971, 2: cat. L-20, 200; see also Hope 1980, 86. Woodall 1991, n. 38, includes an engraving of Rubens's lost copy, and links Titian's *Isabella in Red*, 1548, to his *Eleonora Gonzaga* of 1536–8. (As Bronzino's only Pesaro-Urbino visit ended in 1532, he may never have seen it. In any event, his *Eleonora* is more likely to have imitated a Hapsburg model than one from the rival Urbino court.)

88 Wethey 1971, 2: cat. L-20, 200; see also Warnke 1993, 216; and Woodall 1991, n. 38.

89 Madrid, Prado, 322 × 279 cm. Wethey 1971, 2: 111, figs. 141–4; Hope 1980, colour pl. XVIII.

90 See Lunenfeld 1981, 157–60, on the influence of portraits of Hapsburg queens on European portraits of regents, from Titian's to Antonis Mor's, in the reign of Philip II.

91 Charles had relied on Titian to infuse this majestic aura into his impressive *Charles V with a Hound* of 1533 in Madrid, an enhanced version of Seisenegger's *Charles V*, 1532, Vienna, for which see L. Campbell 1990, 235, figs. 235 and 256.

92 If customary exchange of portraits between courts occurred, a copy of Bronzino's *Eleonora with Giovanni* may have been sent to Charles V after 1545, which may in turn have provoked the commission of Titian's final, and greatly enhanced, *Isabella in Red* in 1548.

93 See Lunenfeld 1981 for an impressive analysis of this decorum.

94 Ibid., 159; more typical was an indeterminate background in the female ruler portrait, described as the 'Spagnolized body,' from the later sixteenth-century onwards.

95 For Florence as Holy Roman Empire fiefdom under Charles V, see Tanner 1993, 115.

96 See Introduction, 14, for Vasari's description of Raphael's *Leo X*, and on the gleaming armour in his own *Duke Alessandro in Armour*, Vasari 1878–85, 4, 342, and 7, 656–7. See also L. Campbell 1990, 130–3 and fig. 155; and Rubin 1995, 100–2 with colour pl. 44, citing Vasari's promotion of painting over sculpture to Varchi, especially for rendering 'satin, velvet, silver, gold and jewels with the lustre of pearls.'

97 See Lazzi 1993, 27, figs. 18 and 19: the Florentine lily appears on Garzia's collar, and on banding for Eleonora's burial dress. See also text, 103. Allori's *Isabella de' Medici* (pl. 11) is dressed to combine Orsini and Medici colours; also, Allori's *Dianora de' Medici* (pls. 14 and 16), wears the Toledo *pavonazzo* blue with a lily-embroidered collar. For armorial symbolism in portraits, see also G. Smith 1977[2], 265–9; and Tinagli 1997, 52–3.

98 Cox-Rearick 1993, 37 and passim.

99 See J. Hall 1979, 249; it also appears on Lucas van Leyden's *Maximilian I* of 1520. See Langedijk 1980 (unpaginated).

100 May 1965, 12, noting its rank as a cloth of royalty when interwoven with gold.

101 Cosimo sponsored the silk industry in Florence. See Richelson 1978, 39. The colours

portrayed are uncharacteristic of Eleonora's taste. Those most often recorded for her were crimson, black, peacock [blue], grey, and white, see Orsi Landini 1993, 38. On the Hispanic style of the dress, see Bemporad 1988, 62, and Arnold 1988, 151.

102 Orsi Landini 1993, fig. 16, and Edelstein 2001, 250–1, note brocade similar to Eleonora's in the Carrand Collection, Bargello; J. Thomas 1994, 266, and Dixon 2002, 121, propose a Spanish design for Eleonora's.

103 May 1965, pl. 5. See L. Campbell 1990, 198, pl. 216; and Woodall 1991.

104 Spanish garrisons in the duchy were ceded at this time. Mitchell 1986, 178.

105 Warnke 1993, 194.

106 See n. 99. The pomegranate also appears in Antonio Fantuzzi's engraving of Rosso Fiorentino's *Concordia*. The vast empire now stretched from Peru to the Black Sea; Minor and Mitchell 1968, 18.

107 Guarini 1999, 8. Hapsburg control over the Medici was strongest in this era.

108 See also Lazzi 1993, 28; Arnold 1993, 54; and Cox-Rearick and Westerman Bulgarella 2004, 132–6 for symbolism in Eleonora's wardrobe.

109 See Edelstein 2001, especially 227–8, and 234. For sumptuous dress as a visible sign of status for rulers, see Rodríguez-Salgado 1991, 240–1.

110 Tinagli 1997, 51. On brocade and sumptuary laws, see Rodocanachi 1907.

111 ASF MDP 1175, f. 43, ins. 4. See Edelstein 2000, 226–7. The cost of gold or silver brocade can be grasped from Cosimo's order to Antonio da Nobile to pay for such textiles at 'seicentottantuno *scudi* per CCLXX *bracchie*.' ASF MDP 1542 f. 7. This would be about $850 U.S. per yard today. For monetary equivalents, see 226n70.

112 See Monnas 1990, 41, 53, and passim, for Orcagna's use of pattern books to feign brocade.

113 See Lunenfeld 1981, 158–60, on typical female ruler portraits that blanch the face into a mask and emphasize costume, jewellery, and regalia. Elizabeth I's portraits exemplify the genre.

114 Francesco: 'Who is that in this row, dressed in rich, golden brocade? It seems from his appearance to be Lord Lorenzo de' Medici; is it he?' Vasari: 'That is he.' Beck 1975, 141.

115 Williams 1997, 73–4 and 81.

116 Jenkins 1947, 12–13, cites the *Eleonora and Her Son* as a major exercise in regal formalism.

117 Detroit Institute of Arts, 121.8 × 100 cm. See Baccheschi 1973, cat. 55a; Langedijk 1981, 1: cat. 35,9. Its background is worked in smalt, not in lapis lazuli. See Urry 1998.

118 Uffizi, Serie Aulica, inv. 1890, no. 2239, 140 × 116 cm. See Langedijk 1981, 1: cat. 35,17, with Garzia substituted for Giovanni, and with a plain grey-green background.

Fantoni 1994, 68, commenting on *religio regis* observed in the court, noted that social status determined how close a courtier or supplicant could approach, which was formalized according to rank. On such 'successive stages of spectatorship,' see Schwartz 1997, 482. See also Lincoln 1999, 17 and 22.

119 See Langedijk 1981, 1: 35,11 (the Haelwegh engraving), and ibid., 35, 10-i, the Wallace Collection portrait, which is inscribed 'FALLAX.GRATIA.ET.VANA.PULCHRITUDO' ('Grace is deceptive and beauty is vain'). For a detailed study of the portrait, see Plazzotta 1988; and for posthumous portrayals and eulogistic reference to Eleonora's wifely virtues, see Cox-Rearick 2004, 243–5, figs. 10.6 and 10.9a.

120 Rodocanachi 1907, 157.

121 A year after Eleonora's tomb was opened in 1857, Picenardi described the burial dress as 'similar to that in Bronzino's portrait.' Florence, Palazzo Pitti 1993, cat. no. 53. Scientific study, reconstruction, and its exhibition (Florence, Palazzo Pitti 1993) proved otherwise: it was of pale-gold silk with black velvet guards embroidered with Florentine lilies, worn with a red velvet underbodice and red silk stockings. She had been hastily dressed in mended everyday attire. See esp. Westerman Bulgarella 1993.

122 Jenkins 1947, 44.

123 De Hollanda 1868, 354. I thank John Bury for relevant discussion.

124 Jenkins 1947, 5.

125 De Hollanda 1868, 341, echoing Michelangelo's disdain for distractions at court. See also the Introduction, 16.

126 See Richelson 1978, 61, citing Cirni 1560, Aiii–Aiij; and see n. 164 below. On Hollingsworth's conversion of *scudi* to today's values, see 226n70.

127 Lapini 1906, 131. (Bronzino penned his Petrarchan 'Colma le glorie tue, famoso Padre' to mark the occasion; see *Sonnetti*, Moreni ed., 52.) Fantoni 1999, 272, believes that spectacles helped erase the memory of Medici bourgeois origins. Tomas 2000, 71, notes that the inclusion of Medici women had monarchical overtones: in polities imitating kingdoms, grand-ducal Florence, for example, formal roles would be designated for them in semipublic and public arenas in decades to come. For evidence of the roles of Isabella and Dianora in Florentine academies in that era, see text, 159–60, and 177–8.

128 The *Maria Salviati with Giulia* (pl. 2) is excluded here, as her status, and decorum of female guardian and protectress, being incompatible for a ruler-portrait. The *Eleonora and Giovanni* did inspire later retrospective insertions, as witness Bronzino's *Young Woman with Her Little Boy*, about 1540 with additions of 1545–6. Cox-Rearick 1982, 67–79. Three sons were added to Parmigianino's *Countess of San Secondo* (Prado), 1533–5. S. Freedberg 1950, 118, and 213–14, pl. 143.

129 For the *Eleonora and Francesco*, Pisa, around 1549, see Langedijk 1981, 1: cat. 35,12.

130 Pope-Hennessy 1981, 5–7. Giotto's *Maestà* is seated on a red cushion, as is Eleonora.

131 Shearman 1992, 82, described this exploitation of expectations associated with traditional images as the 'genealogy of the moment.'

132 Ultramarine – ground lapis pigment – was termed 'Virgin' blue by Cennini because of its traditional use in portrayals of the Madonna. See Cennini 1932, 37–8.

133 For these, see Pope-Hennessy 1981, 48–9, 70, and 72, especially the S. Marco altarpiece (1438–40) and, notably, the Medici *Bosco ai Frati* altarpiece (1450–2), in which lapis lazuli is liberally used to clothe the Virgin. On depiction of Medici grand duchesses as saints or holy, see Fantoni 1999, 270–2.

134 O'Meara 1981, 99–103. Van Eyck's Washington *Virgin Annunciate* portrays Isabella of Portugal, mother of Charles the Bold, on the occasion of his baptism. Agnes Sorel, favourite of Charles VII, posed for a *Madonna Lactans*; a secular version shows her breast identically exposed (Lorches Château). See Duby, Perrot, et al. 1992, colour pls. 98 and 99. Giulio Clovio's miniature *Eleonora* of about July 1552 inspired his *Virgin Annunciate*; see Simon 1989, figs. 39 and 42. See Levey 1971, 108 and pl. 80, on Eleonora as model for Giovan Maria Butteri's *Sacre Conversazione* with Cosimo and their family, ca. 1575. (Syson 1998, 9–14, sees the incorporation of portraits of secular personages in holy imagery as conferring 'superstar' status on a subject.)

135 For the unicorn, see Alciati's *Verginità*, Alciati 1621, 1: 233. On luminescence in Piero's

Battista Sforza (who died in childbirth), see Tinagli 1997, 58. For the *Trionfo*, see D.A. Brown 2001, cat. no. 18. On imparted divinity, and for *Marie de Medici as Astrea*, a virgin goddess, see Dixon 2002, 2 and pl. 23. Elizabeth I's portrayals, promoting her as new Virgin of a new Church, echoes elements in Bronzino's *Eleonora with Giovanni*, with profuse pearls and metaphorical reference to the star and moon. For Elizabeth's portraits, see Strong 1995, and Dixon ibid. See also Hollingsworth 1996, 317.

136 Cecchi 1996[1], 40.

137 Its source was Afghanistan, traded via Baghdad and Constantinople to Venice for processing. It was frugally eked out. Froschl's copy of Clovio's miniature *Eleonora* replaced the original's *azzurro* with green drapery. See Simon 1989, 482f., and esp. Bergstein 2001, 1598 on the intrinsic value of some pigments.

138 Cennini 1932, 36.

139 Langdale 1998, 490, citing Baxandall. For patronage and art's intrinsic worth, see Hollingsworth 1994, 8.

140 Reilly 1989, 56–7, and, citing Dolce, 183; see Pino 1983, 240 for Pardo's comments; see also Reilly 1992, 97 and Parker 2004, 163; also Reilly ibid., 87, citing Armenini and Vasari. Firenzuola dedicated his *On the Beauty of Women* to Cosimo on its completion on 18 January 1541. See Firenzuola 1992, 48. His translation of Horace is lost (see ibid., xv–xvi), but it must have been well known in this milieu. He died in 1543.

141 Reilly 1992, 90–1. Parker 2004, 161–2, in her analysis of Bronzino's *Il secondo delle scuse* (The second [poem] on excuses) also reveals the artist's keen awareness of differing levels of discernment on the part of the public. She cites also Cox-Rearick 1993, 143 on his perfectionism when working the chapel frescoes.

142 Cennini 1937, 36–7. See n. 133, on Fra Angelico's altarpieces.

143 The Litany emerged during the Avignon period of papal persecution of the Dominican Order; it became a rubric of its *Office* during Tridentine promulgations. Bonniwell 1944, 208.

144 Sandoval, lines 171ff. Quoted in full in Pratesi 1909, 9–17, and Langdon 1992[1], 441.

145 See n. 134 above.

146 The miniature technique was greatly esteemed. See chap. 7. Pino (1548) praised Dürer's abilities as miniaturist. Pardo (Pino 1983, 68, 453–4) notes de Hollanda's belief that the illuminator's delicate technique and materials enhanced portrayal of inherent *aria* and *grazia* in the figure. (For Eleonora's features on an *Immaculate Conception* in Santa Maria Regina della Pace, see Cox-Rearick 2004, 238–40 and fig. 10.4.)

147 Tosi 1909[2], 16.

148 This honorific also occurs in the Litany. On the *Sedes sapientiae*, see Forsyth 1972. Significantly, Eleonora in her portrait has been compared to 'a finished carving of ivory, with eyes of semi-opaque gems,' by L. Campbell 1990, 25; see also Brock 2002, 84. Weil-Garris Posner 1974, 42, describes the Tribuna *Eleonora* landscape as a 'hard, blue empyrean, pure and daunting as Byzantine gold,' again implying an iconic link to early paintings of the Virgin.

149 De Hollanda 1868, 340. Hilliard shows Elizabeth I enthroned, flanked by Wisdom, on the Charter of Emmanuel College, Cambridge, 1584. See Strong 2000, 170. Further, referring to Bronzino's posthumous *Eleonora*, Wallace Collection, London, see Cox-Rearick 2004, 245, on its inscription, Proverbs 31:10–31.

150 On Eleonora's dedication to her children, see Edelstein 2001, 223–31.

151 Brumble 1998, 100–1 and fig. 19.

152 Aldobrando Cerretani, *L'Eneida in toscano* ..., a translated addition to book 6 of the *Aeneid* written for Cosimo (Florence, 1560), quoted and translated in Rousseau 1990, 427.

153 Langedijk 1981, 1: 99, quotes Vasari and Thomas Aquinas on *quies aeris*, expressed in the wide blue background of the portrait, as essential to serenity for a stoic ruler's consort.

154 For Isabella, see n. 85. On her wardship of Eleonora's mother, see Gaston 2004, 159–67.

155 Varchi, writing in May 1539, commends Bronzino for having committed Dante and most of Petrarch to memory. He was known, too, for his knowledge of Pico della Mirandola. For his portraits of poets and *letterati* with verses from Virgil, Homer, Dante, Petrarch, and Bembo open to view, see Cecchi, 1991 and 1996[1], 17; and Cropper 2004, 23–5 and cat. no. 21. See Parker 2000 on Bronzino's erudition in Petrarch expressed in parodic mode (*burlesche*); and Brock 2002, 6–17. See also Langdon 2004 on Petrarchism in his Uffizi *Eleonora* and other portraits.

156 Petrarch, *Canzone* 366 (1976, 574–5). Durling (trans.) notes its traditional epithets and phrases in praise of the Virgin, and direct link to Apocalypse 12:1: 'mulier amicta sole, et luna sub pedibus eius, et in capite corona stellarum duodecim.' The Apocalyptic verse inspired at least twenty madrigals ('laude') to the Virgin. Familiar also in Florence from the 1520s, a secular madrigal setting of *canzone* 119, *Una donna più bella assai che'l sole* (A woman much more beautiful than the sun) calls to mind the illumination of Eleonora's face. On the popularity of madrigals in Florence, see Haar 1986, 66–7 and 121; and Minor and Mitchell 1968, 39–40.

157 On strong, directional lighting as implied 'illumination' from Duke Lodovico Sforza on his beloved, Leonardo's *Cecilia Gallerani*, see Shearman 1992, 120.

158 Bronzino 1823, 87. Further on Cosimo as the Sun, see Parker 2003, 234 on Bronzino's panegyrics in praise of the duke as the 'new Sun' and saviour of Florence in the aftermath of the siege of 1529.

159 See n. 158. For the wedding *apparato* of 1539, Apollo-Sol was moderator of harmony generated by the celestial Muses. See Rousseau 1990, 418, on its theme, Cosimo's destiny to rule.

160 Richelson 1978, 37–40, on Poggini's medal and statue, 1559; see also Langedijk 1981, 2: cats. 94–5.

161 See Girolamo Ruscelli's *Le imprese illustri*, 14ff., dedicated to Philip II: 'This [emblem] applies also to the king in whom resides God's intentions ... God has imbued his mind with the sun's rays.' Tanner 1993, 223. For linkage of kings to a heliocentric universe, see Filipczak 1997, 27.

162 See Brumble 1998, 28–32, fig. 1, for Baccio's *theomachia*, *The Fray of Cupid and Apollo*, 1545, where the conflict between Lust and Reason led by Apollo is superintended by the Neoplatonic Mind.

163 See Cox-Rearick 2004, 240 n. 63, and Edelstein 2004[2], 72n4. See also n. 125 above.

164 Richelson 1978, 39: 'Apollo è sol la luce / Cosmo è principio alla gran / Scuola e Duce ii F e S [*sic*].' ('Apollo is the light of the sun / Cosimo is the foundation of the great / School and second Duke of F(lorence) and S(iena) [*sic*].') In this reference, Alessandro is rightly acknowledged as first Duke of Florence, but Cosimo alone had the title Duke of Siena, from 1559.

165 Leicester Coll., Holkham Hall, England, 1550–60. Langedijk 1981, 1: cat. 27,136.

166 See Starn and Partridge 1992, 355 n. 142, on his symbolic claims to divinity there.

167 See Rousseau 1990, 418.

168 See B. Mitchell 1986, 52.

169 For Diana, see Alciati 1621, 696b. Bandini's Studiolo *Juno* wears a crescent moon diadem. (The pairing of the sun and the moon occurs in Eleonora's horoscope; see Cox-Rearick 1984, 290.)

170 Brumble 1998, 98–101; Edelstein 2004^2, 87; and see n. 162 above. She is paired with Apollo in Bandinelli's *theomachia*, *The Fray of Cupid and Apollo*; other associations are with tides, human generation, and night, as chaste and 'chilled', and with Wisdom. (See text.)

171 In 1463 Ficino translated the *Corpus Hermeticum* – pseudo-Egyptian writings – for Cosimo the Elder. Cosimo ordered a Tuscan version, Tommaso Benci's (Florence, Torrentino, 1548). The *Corpus* had been a major source of elemental themes in academic circles. See Mendelsohn 1982, 21; Kristeller 1964, 17; and text below.

172 See Mendelsohn 1982, 6. It was founded in 1540.

173 *Hermetica*, Libellus xviii (Hermes Trismegistus 1992, 113).

174 D.R.E. Wright 1976, 2: 309–11 and n. 219, 554, and 788–92. Rousseau 1990, 419, observes that Egypto-Roman symbols were already in place in 1539.

175 See Mendelsohn 1982, 21 and 205 n. 54, for Cellini's Diana of Ephesus *impresa*.

176 Ibid., 21.

177 See also Mandel 1988, 97, on the offspring of Cosimo-Water and Eleonora-Air in contexts of Medici fountains.

178 On Cosimo as the Sun in Bronzino's sonnets, see Parker 2000, 44 and 2003. See Simon 1983, 533, on visionary, reflective effects of Cosimo's steel armour: exemplars of male *virtù* in literature were personified as 'mirrors of princes.' On 'mirror' implications, see the Introduction. For current Medicean appropriation, see nn. 229–32 below, and chap. 3, 110–11.

179 For Juno-Aria, see Ripa 1988, 1: 139, citing Pliny, who provided her with a peahen, various birds of the air, and a chameleon – an animal fabled to exist on air. In Francesco's Studiolo, Eleonora presides over the 'Air' wall and its bronze *Juno* with her peahen.

Scholars observe that the topos of Cosimo-Earth and Eleonora-Air assumed ever greater import as metaphor for the 'Cosmic' scheme in public art. See Rousseau 1990, 426–7, on Ammannati's *Juno* fountain, who also refers to the metaphor's dynastic, life-giving implications; see also Starn and Partridge 1992, 181–2, for its 'Cosmic' contexts. For extensive discussion of Eleonora-Juno, see Cox-Rearick 1993, 41–5, who notes the alchemical programme of the fountain, based on the union of Air (Eleonora) and Earth (Cosimo) to produce water, alluding to Medici regeneration. Mandel 1988, 97, compares its iconography to the Piazza della Signoria fountains.

180 Panofsky 1962, 142–3 on Earthly Venus 'Vulgaris,' mother of Cupid, whose attribute, like Eleonora's, was the pearl.

181 Cox-Rearick 1993, 41–5.

182 In a good balance of the humours, men were 'hot' and 'dry,' women 'cool' and 'wet.' Filipczak 1997, 20–5 and passim. Bronzino's watery iconography, echoed in 'cool' lunar, tidal associations and water-linked pearls – profuse in this portrait – intensifies Eleonora's womanly state.

183 For his iconographers, see the Introduction, 7, 9 and 20.

184 Bargello, Florence. Begun in 1555, its completion was stalled when Vasari assumed control. Ammannati completed the statues by October 1563, a year after Eleonora's death; in 1565 Cosimo had it partially installed for the wedding of Francesco and Giovanna. On Cosimo's death in 1574, its elements were used as garden sculpture. Heikamp 1978, 129, 135; Rousseau 1990, 425.

185 See nn. 79 and 184.

186 Heikamp 1978, 129, records Eleonora's other deity, Diana's association with Fiorenza-Flora, i.e., Florence, at this time.

187 Starn and Partridge 1992, 186, and 356 n. 161; see also Langedijk 1981, 1: 99.

188 See Starn and Partridge 1992, 169, 177–8, 181, and 189–90; also Edelstein 2000, 307.

189 See chap. 7, on the miniature *Juno, Protectress of Brides*, ca. 1571; for Traballesi's *Rain of Gold* in the Studiolo, ca. 1572, see Mandell 1995, 56.

190 See Levey 1971, 105; and Cox-Rearick 1993, 37.

191 Weil-Garris Posner 1974, 42.

192 On Leonardo's use of a shaded balcony against a bright landscape to create a *contre-jour* effect in the *Mona Lisa,* and his reversal of this precept in the *Madrid Codex* 2: 71v., the *Codex Urbinus* n. 422, and *Codex Urbinus* 1270 135r.–136r., see Farago 1994, 319–20.

193 On this common trait, see Weil-Garris Posner 1974, 42; on *Ginevra,* see Cropper 1986, 188; D.A. Brown 1988, 101–22, and 2001, cat. no. 16; Walker 1968; Garrard, 1992; Tinagli 1997, 85–8; and Dale Kent 2001, cat. 43. On women as Nature, see Garrard 1992, 87–9. See next note, and text on Bronzino's dependence on Leonardo.

194 Levey 1971, 105; and L. Freedman 1989, 168 (on copious Cinquecento copies). To Lomazzo it exemplified the beloved woman. Rogers 1986, 297.

195 See Garrard 1992, 59 and Tinagli 1997, 88–93 on Leonardo's ground-breaking contributions to the three-quarter-length portrait.

196 For detailed analysis of the Urbino diptych, see Tinagli ibid., 58–9.

197 For its analysis, see Warnke 1998, 85.

198 Extended discussion of Bronzino's landscape as dynastic and territorial (Langdon 1992[1]), is echoed in independent observations in Cox-Rearick 1993, 37, who proposed Poggio a Caiano.

199 The Arcadian Renaissance landscape was a garden of delight, with literary connotations of love, innocent pleasure or desire, Eden, a shady grove to inspire poets, or a sun-drenched setting for such dialogues as Firenzuola's *On the Beauty of Women.* See Cole 1998, 28–43.

200 Albèri 1838–63 II: 1, 324, quoting Fedeli (1561). Hibbert 1980, 267, quotes Cabriani on how Cosimo had hunted and fished with his courtiers in such surroundings throughout his reign: '… [T]he Duke would catch various fish, such as trout, and would divide his haul among his courtiers and watch with great delight as they ate the fish which they had cooked in the neighbouring meadows, he himself lying on the grass.'

201 Fantoni 1994, 41; see also Scherberg 2003. On Cosimo's love of archaeology and antiquities, see Young 1910, 567.

202 Translations of Dante and Petrarch under Cosimo's patronage made Florence leader in vernacular literature by 1550; it outdid Venice in classical translations. Mendelsohn 1982, 7. For his adult children's roles in codifying the Tuscan language, see chaps. 6 and 7.

203 Cropper 1998, 1.

204 Hale ed. 1981, 15. See Kirkham 2001, 149–75: her newly discovered eclogue by Laura Battiferra mythologizes the ducal couple in a bucolic Arcadia, identified by Kirkham as the environs of the Villa Medici in Fiesole, and recalling perhaps the pastoral surroundings of Lorenzo de' Medici's literary circle.

205 Alidori 1995, 36–40.

206 Ibid., passim, and chap. 7, 186–7, here. In the early years of consolidation of his duchy, Cosimo and Eleonora moved court from one Medici villa to another. Cox-Rearick 1993, 33.

207 See Scorza 1995, 172–3, and Saslow 1996^2, 272 n. 22. The importance of land drainage is restated in Bronzino's *Luca Martini* of about 1560. See Brock 2002, 152–3.

208 During revisions for the Sala Grande ceiling in 1563, he argued the plausibility of proposed historic scenes vis-à-vis themes of invincibility, and placed Vincenzo Borghini in charge of iconography for it. Scorza 1998, 192; and Williams 1997, 168–9.

209 Eleonora provided 150,000 *scudi* – about $52 million U.S. today (see 226n70 for equivalents) – to persuade Charles V to turn garrisons over to Cosimo. Cox-Rearick 1993, 258. On her enormous contribution to the improvement of the duchy, see especially Young 1910, 586–7.

210 Cochrane 1973, 45.

211 D'Addario 1968, 54. See also Spini ed., 1976, who details Eleonora's continuing acquisition of lands and the incomes accruing from them. Further on the 'Palude,' see Nelson 1995, 295–6, and next note. Public works were an Alba tradition: as viceroy of Naples, her father funded them extensively; Pane 1975, 1: passim and Edelstein 2004. See Edelstein 2004^2, 71–97, on themes of 'Dovizia' or Abundance, seen as fundamental to assessing Eleonora's business acumen; see also D.R.E. Wright 1976, 1: 34–35.

212 Land drainage was commemorated in Vasari's Sala Grande ceiling fresco of the mid-1560s, *The Drainage of the Pisan Swamps*. See Starn and Partridge 1992, 269. Also, seven medals were struck by Pietropaolo Galeotti commemorated building and engineering projects; five others included Pisan reclamation and new aqueducts around Florence. Langedijk 1981, 1: 139. On the far-reaching effects of the latter, see Richelson 1978, 58–60 n. 31, citing Mannucci 1586; see also Young 1910, 573–4. (In Ferdinando II's tapestry series *The Life of Duke Cosimo I*, 1665–6, Vincenzo Dandini's *The Felicity of Cosimo I's Rule of Pisa*, Ceres, goddess of fertility, pays Cosimo tribute. See Harper 2001, 231–2, figs. 15.1 and 15.5.) A vital port in the Cinquecento, Pisa, silted now, lies some kilometres inland, but the low-lying, watery plain in the Uffizi portrait probably characterized it then. In Cosimo's reign, its population grew from 7000 to 22,000. Nelson 1995, 289–90 and 292, emphasized the political importance of the drainage of Pisan areas and the association with Eleonora with reference to the map of the area held by Luca Martini in Bronzino's portrait of the 1550s. See Brock 2002, colour pls. 151 and 153.

213 On the navy, see D'Addario 1968, 54; and Hibbert 1980, 266–7. On Diana as controller of tides, see Heikamp 1978, 130.

214 Marten van Heemskerk's *Luna* was inscribed: 'Those whose mistress is the Moon pass their lives as if in water ... working either in ships or fishing.' Filipczak 1997, 18.

215 Freedman 1995, 66, who cites Roskill 1968, 130–7; Cropper 1976; Pozzi 1979, 3–30; and Mirollo 1984. Pontormo's engaging *Alessandro de' Medici* in Philadelphia (fig. 11), who draws a female profile in the portrait destined for his beloved, Taddea Malaspina, gives visual expression to this composite ideal. See chap. 1, 43 and 233n143, Strehlke 2004, cat. no. 26.

216 Mendelsohn 1982, 59, noting influence from current *trattati d'amore*, a courtly tradition.

217 Ibid., 9, and passim. After Pico della Mirandola, Cattani (1466–1522) was Ficino's most important follower, whose revival is directly linked to Cosimo's court: Varchi assembled Pico's *Three Books on Love*, with biography, for publication (Venice, 1561).

218 Baia 1907, 78–9, documents her patronage of alumni of the University of Pisa from its restoration under ducal patronage in 1543, her habitual presence at reunions of the Accademia degli Elevati founded under ducal aegis to promote poetics, Varchi's translation of Seneca under her direction, and her patronage of drama as recorded by Grifoni in 1541.

219 On Bronzino and Varchi, who eulogized him as Apelles, see Gaston 1991, 255, 262–6. Pinelli 1993, 129–30, notes Neopetrarchan and Neoplatonic strains in Bronzino's poetry woven into his portraits in allusive metaphors. See G. Smith 1996; Plazzotta 1998, 254–5; and Parker 2000 on Bronzino's Petrarchan tribute in his *Laura Battiferri*, ca. 1555–60.

220 Mendelsohn 1982, 128–9.

221 Petrarch, 1976.

222 On its musical settings, see Haar 1986, 67 and 72.

223 See ibid., 72 and 180–4, which provides its verse and musical setting. See Bowen 2003, 101 and 107–9 on the contribution of northern musicians to Florentine musical development. Verdelot was associated with the ducal court in the 1540s. For essential ekphrastic elements of sonnets using similes and metaphors eulogizing women, see Rogers 1986, 291, and Quondam 1989. Important are waving, gleaming golden tresses; alabaster/lily-like skin; eyes outshining the sun or stars; ruby lips; pearly teeth; ivory hands; and white neck and bosom. Rogers, ibid., 294.

224 Lee's remains the landmark discussion of *ut pictura poesis*. More recently, see Shearman 1992, chap. 3: 'Portraits and Poets,' 108–48. On the painted portrait as metaphor for the lyric poem, and implications that *all* portrayals of women in this period are freighted with this tradition, see Cropper 1986; and see Freedman 1995, 75–87, on ekphrasis and Aretino's poems on Titian's portraits of women, which Aretino describes as expressing decency, chastity, gentleness, modesty, honour, and prudence. On this 'formidable machine' and 'hyperconnotation,' see Quondam 1989, 24.

225 See Fermor 1998 on *leggiadria*, denial of physicality, and Neoplatonism.

226 For expanded discussion, see Langdon 2004, 40–70. (Virginal associations were not necessarily taken literally; see text earlier in this chapter.) Leonardo allowed for the metaphysical in his *Ginevra de' Benci*: a laurel wreath on its reverse is entwined with the motto 'VIRTUTEM FORMA DECORAT' ('Beauty adorns virtue'). Walker 1968 includes poetry to Ginevra; see also Tinagli 1997, 88, for Ginevra's circle, notably Bembo and Lorenzo the Magnificent. On *grazia* in women's portrayal, metaphysical grace, and Castiglionesque beauty as goodness and the birthright of nobility, see Emison 1991; see also chap. 1 here.

227 Cattani da Diacceto 1561, 15–17. In the Fisher Rare Book Collection of the University of Toronto copy, a seemingly contemporary marginal gloss reads: 'That and the celestial bodies have the spirit and from that govern the whole' ('Che & i corpi celesti hanno l'anima e da quella governa il tutto').

228 Mendelsohn 1982, 6.

229   Le stelle, il cielo, e gli elementi a prova
      tutte lor arti et ogni estrema cura
      poser nel vivo lume in cui Natura
      si specchia e 'l sol, ch'altrova par non trova.
Petrarch 1976, *Canzone* 154. On Cattani's sources, see Kristeller 1961, 63–4. See also Tinagli 2000, 268.

230   The popular 'mirror of princes' genre derived from such writings as Isocrates speech to Nikokles, or Xenophon's *Cyropaedia*. Lucio Paolo Rosello's translation, *Il ritratto del vero Governo del Principe, dal essempio vivo del Gran Cosimo ... con due orationi d'Isocrate conformi all'istessa materia*, Venice 1552, makes Cosimo the exemplar. (See next note.) Erasmus's *Institutione Principis Christiani* appeared in Italian, Venice 1542. Langedijk 1981, 2: cat. 54,6. See Woods-Marsden 2000, on Cosimo's *letterati* and artists' use of the genre to promote his rule.

231   Two portraits of Cosimo's children support the philosophy of portraiture as 'mirror.' The 1562 Guardaroba inventory records a lost *Maria*, framed as for a mirror – possibly a sliding cover: 'Un ritratto della S^{ra} Maria già figliuola di S.E.I. di $^2/_3$ braccio, ornamento di noce a foggia di spera'. ('A portrait of the Lady Maria, late daughter of the Duke, of $^2/_3$ braccio, framed in walnut in the manner of a mirror.') A *Giovanni*, 1551/2 in Bowood, England, shows him as a tonsured boy-cardinal proferring a handwritten copy in Greek of Isocrates' 'mirror' speech to Nikokles, boy prince of Cyprus. Langedijk 1981, 2: cats. 85,1 and 54,6; also see Edelstein 2001, 230 and fig. 4.

232   See Weil-Garris Posner 1974, 41–2. See Benson 2004, 136, quoting a letter to Eleonora of 1560, giving spiritual advice on her role as mirror and light to other women, and ibid., 147. Her mother, Maria, commissioned a personal devotional treatise, *The Mirror of Illustrious Persons*, in 1524. Gaston 2004, 159, believes it had a formative role in her upbringing.

233   See Rodocanachi 1907, 311–19 and appendix 3. In Florence in 1525, a man who embraced a woman in public was incarcerated in the Stinche prison for a year; another impetuous gallant was banished to Pisa on penalty of two years' labour on the galleys should he return.

234   On this topic, see Hills 1988, chaps. 1 and 4, and 1990, 224.

235   On Cosimo's armour see Simon 1982, 135–50.

236   Domenichi 1564, 3. Kelso 1977, 24–8, 41–4, 53–4, 97–9, surveys the wide range of books of manners and pedagogy with respect to women. Chastity was *the* primary virtue; Luigini 1907, 299ff., even asserts that his erotic ideal had to be '*santità*' and '*onestà*.'

237   See Goffen 1995, 192–4, on the 'shape' of a work of art and the notionally present spectator.

238   McCorquodale 1981, 93.

239   See text above for Cirni's and Lapini's descriptions, and n. 127.

240   For Della Casa's poem (1543) on Elisabetta Quirini Massola, musing that Titian's portraits of women seem to speak and breathe as if alive, see Rogers 1986, 295, with her translation on 302.

241   Firenzuola 1992, 62. Celso compares the ancient vase, where 'the bust rises above the hips, and the throat above the bosom and the shoulders.' Firenzuola authored bawdy tales, such as his *Canzone in lode della salciccia* (Songs in praise of the sausage), Venice, 1545. Ibid., xliii.

242 Its text is illegible, but rubrics open each passage. I thank his Lordship, the Earl of
Wymess and March, for annotations to my sketch. Shearman linked the work to
Salviati's *Lute Player*, Musée Jacquemart-André, Paris, and its preparatory drawing in
the Louvre. Boskovits 1985, 140–1; see also Mortari 1992, 162–3 and 260, figs. 198 and
486, who dates it to the early 1530s.

243 From Gosford House, Scotland, now in the National Gallery of Scotland, Edinburgh.
On a desirable combination of chastity and voluptuousness in a bride, see Panofsky
1962, 160–1, on Titian and Rembrandt; also, Graham Smith kindly provided me with
pertinent notes taken at a Panofsky seminar on the topic.

244 On sanctioned eroticism, see Luigini 1907, n. 236 above.

245 The warm emotion existing between Cosimo and Eleonora is documented in Caterina
Cibo's letter of 8 July 1541. See Booth 1921, 117. Cosimo's faithfulness throughout his
marriage is documented by Segni 1805, 2: 217–18. Eleonora died in 1562.

246 L. Campbell 1990, 118, has observed the same effect in Giulio Romano's portrait of Isabella d'Este, whose cutwork velvet dress imitates her *impresa*, the *fantasia* of knots.

247 Pinelli 1993, 129–30, identifies formal Platonism in their crystalline lighting, refined
linearity; cameo-like faces; eyes like precious stones; ivoried, transparent skin; and
hair like chiselled bronze or gold wire; these qualities in Bronzino's paintings are paradoxically allusive, anti-naturalistic, chilled, and subordinated to a metaphorical
ethos. See also Tinagli 1997, 85.

248 See Rodocanachi 1907, 132, on Pisanello's and Piero della Francesca's female portraits;
and see Simons 1988; and Tinagli 1997, 53 and 67–70, who refers to the Pisanello and
Piero portraits in her discussion on 'dynastic' portrayals of Italian women; Baldovinetti's *Lady in Yellow*'s sleeve has the Galli arms; Domenico Ghirlandaio's *Giovanna degli Albizzi*'s brocade *giornea* exhibits the Tornabuoni diamond with doves and
sunbursts. (For Eleonora's wedding *apparato*, *Flora*'s sleeves were decorated with Medici *palle*. See Rousseau 1990, 422.)

249 Rodocanachi 1907, 157. *Diamante* buttons secure sleeves by tapes attached to the bodice, visible in young Maria's case (pl. 7). Arnold 1993, 53–4, fig. 24.

250 See Richelson 1978, 70 n. 60, citing Giovanni Franceschi, *Vita della Sig. Maria Salviati de'
Medici* (1545), 5v. Later, Cellini was asked to evaluate a diamond exceeding thirty-five
carats for a pendant for Eleonora. Florence, Palazzo Pitti 2003, 25.

251 *Canzone* 190, ed. Durling (1976), who notes the doe as sacred to Diana; two golden
horns refer to Laura's braids; the inspirational anecdote is from Solinus, third century
AD.

252 Saward 1982, 32, aligns a radiance around Maria de' Medici in Rubens's *Birth of Maria
de' Medici* with Seutonius's *Divus Augustus* 2, 94: Augustus's father dreams his son will
be born with a *corona radiata*. On Cosimo's adoption of Charles V's Augustan *impresa*
and horoscope, see Richelson 1978, 25.

253 Rodocanachi 1907, 157–8. Bridgeman 1998, 45 and 48, remarks that a garment's instrin-
sic beauty was *insignificante* unless worn by one *entitled* to wear it – social function was
all-important. See also Edelstein 2001, 225–31, on Eleonora's acute sense of the importance of clothing in expressing grandeur and rank.

254 These hairnets were of gold-wrapped thread. Lazzi 1993, fig. 9; see also Cox-Rearick
and Westerman Bulgarellla 2004, 133. In Cosimo's sumptuary laws of 1546, they were
not to exceed two ounces of gold! Rodocanachi 1907, 157–8. See also n. 283.

255 See Lunenfeld 1981, 159–61, on portraits of Margaret of Parma and Elizabeth I. See Filipczak 1997, 127 and cat. no. 56, on their profusion in Pourbus's *Infanta Isabella Clara Eugenia*; on their cost and prestige, see Woods-Marsden 2001, cat. no. 67; for Medici state portraits of grand duchesses, see Florence, Palazzo Pitti 2003, 26.

256 On her passion for pearls, see Albèri 1839–63 II, 1: 465–6, quoting Andrea Boldù, Venetian ambassador to Savoy (1561); see also Florence, Palazzo Pitti 2003, 26. New World trade swelled supply, leading to enactments to control their profuse use as adornment, see Filipczak 1997, 127.

257 De Hollanda 1868, 354–5.

258 Two hundred bought in Venice were sent to Eleonora in Naples; one hundred and fifty were to be on hand for her arrival in Florence, on Maria's orders. ASF MDP 5926, f. 8, 6 March 1539. On Neapolitans' love of pearls, see Rodocanachi 1907, 170 n. 3.

259 On their loving marriage, see nn. 245, 318, and 319. Vasari held that Cosimo resembled Augustus, who was deeply attached to his wife. Starn and Partridge 1992, 154. See n. 11 above.

260 Rousseau 1990, 419–32, citing Ficino, *De Vita coelitus comparanda*, Florence, 1489.

261 Tinagli 1997, 98. See Filipczak 1997, 128, on the pearl as emblem of chastity; oysters were fabled to rise to the surface, open, and form pearls from the pure dew that gathered in them.

262 See Cox-Rearick 1995, 299–301 and figs. 329 and 330. The pearl symbolized Mary's purity and faith, echoing the 'pearl of great price' (Matt. 13: 45). See Filipczak 1997, 127.

263 *Canzone* no. 181 (trans. Durling, 1976).

264 For Castiglione on male *virilità* and female *tenerezza*, see Fermor 1993, 132.

265 See Brumble 1998, 337–46, on the duality of Venus, especially Ficino's version. See also Firenzuola 1992, 37.

266 Quattrocento Florentine humanists' source was Plato's *Symposium*; Alciati 1621, 460, refers to Ficino's commentary of 1469. See text and n. 217. See also Panofsky 1962, 142–3.

267 Sandoval, lines 170–4. See n. 144.

268 Mannucci 1586, 79; also Adriani 1583, 1: 109 and 121.

269 See n. 22; see Woodall ed. 1997, 4, on emphasis in court portraiture on the trunk and genital area, regions associated with physical prowess or the generation of noble lineage.

270 Cox-Rearick 1987, 60.

271 See 212n15 for this scene.

272 Langedijk 1981, 1: cats. 35,30 and 35,31; and on Selvi, ibid., 1989, 3: appendix D. For other Juno-Eleonoras posing as *genetrix*, see Cox-Rearick 1987, passim, and 1993, 41–45.

273 Vasari 1878–85, 8: 73; Bronzino 1823, 41; and Cox-Rearick 1984, 290 and 1993, 41–5 on Poggini's *Juno* medal. For Bandini's *Juno with Her Peahen*, see Schaefer 1976, 1: 457, fig. E. For an important recent study on Francesco's *studiolo*, see Feinberg 2002, showing the 'Air' wall (46 and 57–61, figs. 27a and 27b).

274 On the *putto* as a dynastic fertility symbol in Antoine Caron's tapestry design, *Le Placets*, around 1560, for Queen Caterina de' Medici, see ffolliott 1989, 139–40, fig. 1.

275 Vasari 1878–85, 7: 600, on Bronzino's portrayals of Constanza da Somaia and Camilla Tebaldi in his *Christ in Limbo* of 1552. Further, see Gaston 1983.

276 Vasari ibid., 569.

277 Simon 1989, 483, comparing Bandinelli's bust of 1544 and Bronzino's *Eleonora with Gio-vanni*. On the bust, see Langedijk 1981, 1: cat. 35,23; and Cox-Rearick 1993, 36, fig. 21.

278 See Langdon 1992[1], 1: 34, on Ugolino Martelli and Giacopo Grifoli's commentaries.

279 Giacomo Grifoli, *Q. Horatti flacci liber de arte poetica* (Florence: Torrentino Press, 1550). See Weinberg 1961, 1: 122–8. On Torrentino, Cosimo's printer, see A. Ricci 2001.

280 See Baccheschi 1973, pls. XXIV–XXV; Cox-Rearick 1993, 30; and Brock 2002, 197. See n. 282 below.

281 Firenzuola 1992, ending his Preface, and 47–8.

282 See Cox-Rearick 1993, 264–5, on the range of hair colour in Eleonora's portraits. At the time of her death, her hair was reddish blond. See Cox-Rearick and Westerman-Bul-garella 2004, 108. For preliminary reports on current and projected Italian-American Medici exhumations, see Follain, 2004; and Di Domenico and Lippi 2005. I thank Paola Tinagli for alerting me to this recent publication. The exhumations will chronicle Medici medical history.

283 Firenzuola 1992, 48. The cap of gold and pearls, known as a *vespaio* ('wasps'' nest), was in various forms linked to great wealth. Orsi Landini and Westerman Bulgarella 2001, 93; and D.A. Brown 2001, cat. no. 28. See also n. 254 above.

284 Simon 1989, 481ff., discovered it and its inventory record. Clovio arrived with his patron Cardinal Farnese in the summer of 1551, and was quartered in the Palazzo Pitti by 1553.

285 Ibid., 482–3. Froschl's copy is close, with the drape rendered in brilliant green.

286 Vasari 1878–85, 7: 568–69. See Langdon 2001, and chap. 7 here.

287 On Italian miniatures, see Meloni-Trkulja 1983 (Giovio) and Meloni 1994; see chap. 7, 172–3.

288 On Cellini's lost marble *Eleonora*, see Langedijk 1981, 1: cat. 35,25. See Cox-Rearick and Westerman-Bulgarella, 2004, 112 and 109–16, where an extended study of her portraits searches the 'true' Eleonora in the process of identifying her as Bronzino's *Portrait of a Lady*, Turin. See also Langdon 1992[1], 1, 243–5, and Follain's forensic evidence.

289 Simon 1989, 483.

290 For procedures for recording from life for miniature portrayals, see chap. 7, 174, 295n17.

291 See Introduction, n. 43, on palpable 'presences.' Alberti's comment, that portraits make the absent present, is reflected in Isabella d'Este's belief in them as a kind of facsimile of the sitter. Cropper 1997, 92–8, and Ottawa 2005, cat. no. 81 discusses Bronzino's *Pygmalion and Galatea* cover for Pontormo's *Francesco Guardi* as expressive of the artist's will to bring a subject to life.

292 Mendelsohn 1982; and Williams 1997, 36–9. On Varchi and the *paragone*, see also Crop-per in Ottawa 2005, cat. no. 81 (Bronzino's *Pygmalion and Galatea*), who believes that in Cinquecento Florence, the myth of Pygmalion was inseparable from the theme of artis-tic *virtù*.

293 Cox-Rearick 1993, 36.

294 Ibid., 36. Warnke 1993, 193; see also Williams 1997, 36–7.

295 Benvenuto Cellini, in his letter to Varchi, 1546, suggested that in emulating Michelan-gelo, Bronzino surpassed painters in achieving a synthesis of the two arts. Baccheschi 1973, 11. See Barocchi ed. 1960–2, 594–9, and 1998, 66–9. For his rendering of frontal and

dorsal views of the dwarf Morgante on two faces of a panel (Galleria Palatina, Pitti, Florence, ca. 1553), see Baccheschi ibid., cat. 163A and 163B, and Brock 2002, 177–8 with plates. See Plazotta and Keith 1999, 98, on Bronzino's sculptural excurses elsewhere.

296 Getty Museum, Los Angeles; the cover is in the Palazzo Vecchio. See Cecchi 1996[1], 14–15, figs. 14 and 15; Cropper 1997, 92–4; Cropper, in Ottawa 2005, cat no. 81; and Brock 2002, 52–8. As prelude to viewing the portrait, it functions as a visual metaphor of Pontormo's infusion of *fiato* – the breath of life. Cecchi, ibid., notes that Varchi dedicated his 1539 *Metamorphoses* translation to Bronzino and Tribolo. (For Ovid's account of Pygmalion and Galatea, see *Metamorphoses* 10, 238–97.)

297 Rubin 1995, 245.

298 Dolce in Reilly 1992, 91–2; Land 1994, 156; and, on Aretino, Freedman 1995, 77–8.

299 Pino 1983, 341–2, in Reilly 1989, 61.

300 Baccheschi 1973, 11.

301 Armenini 1977, 176; and Reilly 1992, 87–90 and 94, noting Aristotelian, Albertian, and Vasarian precedents; Vasari preferred drawing to a canvas 'smeared' with colours.

302 Land 1994, 18, quoting Dolce.

303 Dolce held that the educated eye returns again and again to examine painting, as to good poetry. This reflects Dolce the translator's deep knowledge of Horace, who observed for poetics that 'once the sight doth please, this ten times over will delight.' Land 1994, 18. On the precept *ut pictura poesis*, see n. 224 above.

304 Reilly 1992, 90. (Farago 1994, 302, warns that sixeenth-century writers would have understood *colore* to inform colour, light, shadow, finish, and the handling of paint.)

305 They hung in their son Carlo's home, in 1584. Florence, Uffizi 1980, no. P298.

306 Cennino Cennini held that cosmetics were 'contrary to the will of God and of our Lady.' Reilly 1992, 95. Alberti cited the ancients. Further, see especially Rodocanachi 1907. Becherucci 1964, 46, compares the forms of the official *Eleonora* to the 'chilled' London *Allegory*; McCorquodale 1981, 92, notes the sitter's inanimate quality; L. Campbell 1990, 25, compares Eleonora to an ivory idol, and Brock 2002, 81–4, notes her mask-like mien. See also n. 247.

307 Castiglione (1528), cited by Reilly 1992, 93.

308 Quoted in Reilly 1992, 95; see Firenzuola 1992, 1 and 54.

309 Firenzuola 1992, 14–15.

310 Pagni, writing from Figline Valdarno to Major-domo Riccio on 14 September 1544, encloses a cassone key with instructions to immediately send cosmetics stored there ('terra di Portogallo rozato') and another forgotten, unnamed item. ASF MDP 1171, f. 124, ins. 3.

311 Varchi, quoted by Reilly 1989, 131.

312 *Canzone* 131 (trans. Durling, 1976).

313 Plazzotta 1988, 20.

314 Firenzuola 1992, 18; see also Rogers 1988, 66–7.

315 This is striking in the newly cleaned Bronzino Detroit copy; see Dixon 2002, cover, and n. 117 above. Warnke expounds on essential presentation of the ruler on a real and ideal plane, recognizable in form as a persona invested with suprapersonal aura. The artist was constrained to produce a likeness that was both true to nature (*imitatio*) and in keeping with convention (*decorum*). Warnke 1993, 215.

316 For Vasari on this philosophy, see Cheney 1998, 180 and passim, and D.A. Brown 1998,

101–22, and 2001, cats. 16 (*Ginevra de' Benci*) and 30 (*Giovanna degli Albizzi*), on perfection in their portraits to express womanly virtue reinforced by inscriptions; X-ray of the reverse revealed Bembo's motto, VIRTVS ET HONOR, beneath Ginevra's own (see text), implying a subliminal approach to her portrait by the poet.

317 His chastity is expressed in the *Joseph* tapestries. G. Smith 1982[1], 189 and notes below.

318 Albèri 1839–63, II, 2: 351. Fedeli implies exclusiveness since his marriage. Cosimo was reported by William Thomas in 1549 never to go abroad without Eleonora, unless to church, and was reputed 'a very chaste man.' Cox-Rearick 1993, 33. See also nn. 245 and 317.

319 See Booth 1921, 214–15, 220, quoting Priuli in Albèri 1839–72, I, 2: 76; and Segni 1805, 450, ca. 1555. Eleonora died from consumption on 17 December 1562, mourning the deaths of Giovanni on 20 November and Garzia on 12 December. Saltini 1898, 112–77. Mannucci 1586, 144, records Cosimo's heroic stoicism in the face of his losses: 'He heard through him of the death of the Duchess, who had been ill for many days and had suddenly worsened, to the infinite grief of the Duke, who had always loved and honoured her as much as is possible [any] woman ... These grave losses the Duke bore with such forebearance of spirit as can possibly be imagined. And not only did he not need consolation because of her, but he himself, quite calm and without tears, consoled all those relatives and friends who needed it, which he also did by writing to the Prince [Francesco], who was still at the Court of Spain.' Saltini ibid., 125–8 and 136–42, quotes Cosimo's moving correspondence to break the dreadful news of the three deaths to Francesco; and see, more recently, Franceschini 2004, 199. See the diarist Lapini 1906, 134–5, for their funerals and scurrilous rumours concerning Giovanni's and Garzia's deaths. (The rumour that Garzia killed Giovanni with his sword during an argument, and that Cosimo then killed Garzia, has been completely disproved during the current scientific examination of the boys' exhumed remains. See Follain 2004 and Di Domenico and Lippi 2005.)

320 The successful portrait allowed the viewer a glimpse of the sitter's soul. See 'The Poet's Eye,' Land 1994, 81–95, on Petrarch's poem on Simone Martini's portrait of Laura and others which were to follow: Bembo's on Giovanni Bellini's (lost) panel; Castiglione's on Raphael's *Castiglione*; della Casa's on Titian's (lost) *Elisabetta Massola*; and Aretino's on Titian's Urbino portraits.

321 Petrarch, *Canzone* 215 (trans. Durling, 1976).

322 The spectator of ceremonial state portraits was 'the political nation' of nobles, advisers, a few wealthy burghers, and representatives of foreign crowns. Lunenfeld 1981, 158. (I would include ranking clergy, based on references to portraits of Cosimo for Giovio's Como collection, and that of Eleonora destined for the Bishop of Arras, described above.)

323 See Williams 1997, 36–7, 89, on the need for an ideal unity to be signified in court contexts; see also Saslow 1996[2], 7, on the technologies of power.

324 Fantoni 1994, 32. It incorporates classical overtones of *virtù* and leadership, inspired by antique portrait medals. See Simon 1982, 1983, and 1987; and Richelson 1978.

325 Divinity was imparted to rulers by representing them in sacred or mythological guise, their faces endowed with traits reminiscent of Christ, Hercules, or Alexander. Warnke 1993, 213, citing Forster 1971, n.p.; Richelson 1978; and Mellen 1963, 53–8.

326 Cosimo is perceived as guardedly deferential to republican institutions by Kempers

1992, 284 and 290, but his persistent Apollonian imagery and diligent harnessing of symbols of absolutism through his iconographers, Giovio and Borghini, leave no doubt of his intentions. See Starn and Partridge 1992, Williams 1998, Scorza 1998, and van Veen 1998 studies, and, on related aspects of his cultural politics, Eisenbichler ed. 2001.

327 On this aspect, see Fantoni 1999, 268. Contemporary records of her *entrate* are replete with this extreme elevation of the duchess's public persona. See text, 72.

328 Her links to Mary implicitly promots Eleonora as protectress of Florence. See Fantoni 1999 in n. 133 above, on the increasing investment of divinity in portraits of successive grand duchesses.

329 The posthumous, official title was devised by Cosimo in the 1570s. Van Veen 1986, 18.

330 On Sol-Apollo as central to an elaborate cosmic theme at the wedding in 1539, probably the invention of Pierfrancesco Giambullari, see Wisch and Munshower eds. 1990, 418–19.

331 On the arch, see text at n. 76; the tapestries are recorded in the 1553 Guardaroba Inventory. Baccheschi 1973, cat. 65; and G. Smith 1982[1], 185, 188, 190–2, and fig. 2.

332 Cox-Rearick 1993, 258–9, summed up the portrait's essential meaning, too, as dynastic. She lists also repeated themes in 1540s Medicean programs as legitimacy, destiny, power, promise, rebirth, and return, all pertinent to Bronzino's *Eleonora with Her Son Giovanni* and to large-scale programs of the 1540s. See also Langdon 1992[1], 1: chap. 5.

333 See Mannucci 1586, 32.

334 See text, 59–60, and n. 8 above.

335 Vasari 1878–85, 7: 593ff., referring to Bronzino as 'un grande Apelle.' See Bronzino, 1988, 442, and Rogers 1998, on Vasari's notion of the 'beautiful' artist endowed with exterior grace to signal his God-given endowment. A more mundane factor was an artist's access to Cosimo through his major-domo, Riccio, Bronzino's included. See n. 2.

336 See Rogers 1998, 95, on Castiglionesque talents such as persuasive speech, charm, and intellectual pursuits as requisite for the court painter.

337 Cecchi 1996[1], 20, notes Vasari's reference to Bronzino's portraits of Dante, Petrarch, and Boccaccio. For Bronzino as painter-poet, see Parker 2000 and Brock 2002, 6–17.

338 He portrayed Ugolino Martelli before 1537, and Bartolomeo Panciatichi in the early years of Cosimo's reign. See Cecchi 1996[1], 20, figs. 24 and 57; and Brock 2002, chaps. I–III with plates; and Cropper 2004, 23–4.

339 See Starn and Partridge 1992, 166. For this background, see essays by Rousseau 1990; Cox-Rearick 2002; and Jacks, in Jacks ed. 1998, for example. Plazzotta and Keith 1999, 90, 94, and 99, provide scientific proof that Bronzino's perfectionism and immutability evolved from painstaking work; his *pentimenti* reveal 'daring and drastic revision at a late stage' concealed under the paint. See also Cropper 2001[2].

340 For Giovio, see 241n263. Idealism and flattery were expected: see text above. Hans von Aachen, was thought 'much shrewder [than others], knowing how to paint His Majesty's likeness *con bel garbo* even if he was not thought as *sincère*.' Warnke 1993, 218, with reference to Rudolf II's court painter.

341 See Weil-Garris Posner 1974, 41, for borrowings. Bronzino borrowed *Envy* in his

London *Allegory* from the screaming man in Leonardo's *Battle of Anghiari*. (Smyth 1971, 8–9, 36–8, 58, and n. 48). Smyth 1949², 201, cites dependence on Leonardo in the *Holy Family* (National Gallery, Washington), 1526–7, via Pontormo's contact with Leonardo in 1506; Levey 1971, 105, echoes this for the London version. McCorquodale 1981, 35, cites *The Lady with an Ermine* or *La Belle Ferronière* for Bronzino's portraiture. See especially Brock 2002. Marvin Eisenberg conveyed his observation that Bronzino's girl-monster in the London *Allegory* recalls the angel in Leonardo's *Virgin of the Rocks*.

342 They were for Count D'Altamira in Spain. See Gaye 1840, 3: 94, no. XCII, Bronzino to Cosimo, dated 9 February 1563. The original painting was owned by Cosimo de' Pazzi. See also Weil-Garris Posner 1974, 41 nn. 249, 252; Cox-Rearick 1993, 86; and Warnke 1993, 208.

343 Vasari 1878–85, 6: 246. On his arrival in Florence at the age of thirteen, Pontormo was sent by Bernardo Vettori to stay with Leonardo before his departure for Milan in 1506.

344 Farago 1991, 82.

345 Kempers 1992, 286.

346 On its impact, see Jenkins 1947, 30ff. and passim.

347 For detailed analysis of it, see Eisenbichler 1988, and Brock 2002, 48–52 and passim.

348 Mendelsohn 1982, 5.

349 Aretino mentions them in this context in a satirical letter. Ibid., 30.

350 Farago 1991, 82 n. 78, thought him highly reliable; also Pino 1982, 51–2.

351 Mendelsohn 1982, 5.

352 See Dolce 1968, 118.

353 On dissemination of Leonardo's writings, see Langdon 1992¹, chap. 1. Also, see Pino 1983, 53.

354 Mendelsohn 1982, 26. (Cellini penned his autobiography in 1558.) Presumably this was not the only part of Leonardo's writings to be copied by Cellini. On ease of access allowed to artists by Melzi to Leonardo's writings, see Langdon 1992¹, chap. 1.

355 See Leonardo 1956, xxi.

356 Farago 1991, 83.

357 For Ugolino, see Summers 1981, 337. Mendelsohn 1982, 126, links Varchi's writings to Aristotle and Alberti's decorum.

358 Vasari 1878–85, 7: 657; see L. Campbell 1990, 130–2, and fig. 130.

359 Mendelsohn 1982, 38 and n. 5, citing Vincenzo Carducho, Madrid, 1633, 101v.

360 Ibid., 37, 38, and 40.

361 Farago 1991, 83 and n. 87. A copy belonging to this 1564 group exists in the Accademia, Florence. For a study of other copies existing before the first published edition of 1651, see Steinitz, 1958, 39–44, and supplements in *Vinciana* (1960 and 1962).

362 See Mendelsohn 1982, 25.

363 For analysis of his description of the *Mona Lisa*, see Rubin 1990, 42.

364 Weinberg 1961, 1: 83.

365 Mendelsohn 1982, 6.

366 Robortello's *In librum Aristotelis de arte poetica explicationes* of 1548, the first great commentary on Aristotle, arose from interpretation of manuscripts in Cosimo's possession. See Weinberg 1961, 388, who also discusses Robortello's passages on moral

utility and decorum (394–5). Mendelsohn deduces increased significance for Horace's *Ars poetica* in art theory generated in the Medici milieu. Mendelsohn 1982, 8.

367 See G. Smith 1982[1], 187–8, stressing that mythology coined for Cosimo before the 1545 *Joseph* tapestries had already included *civic* exemplars such as Augustus, Alexander, Moses, Solomon, and David. 'Joseph' would again emphasize his civic role as exemplary statesman.

368 The two lectures, presented before the Accademia Fiorentina on the second and third Sundays of Lent at a public meeting in Santa Maria Novella in 1547, were published as an *editio princeps* in 1550 by Lorenzo Torrentino as *Due Lezzioni*. See Mendelsohn 1982, 90.

369 Varchi drew on it for themes of universality in Neoplatonic philosophy. Varchi is also indebted to Pico della Mirandola's ideas on beauty, love, and grace. Mendelsohn 1982, 59–62.

370 On this topic, see text, 81.

371 Pinelli 1993, 157–65, sees Cosimo's absolutism as pervasive in art and forcing a very strong bond between his artists and the court.

Chapter 3

1   ASF MDP 1171, f. 147 ins. 3, (MAPD 6020); also ibid., f. 62 ins. 2, (MAPD 6488). On the family's attachment to him and statuary of him, 292n172.

2   On crucial Medici marriage alliances, see Fantoni 1999, 256. (Noble girls usually married around the age of sixteen; Bridgeman 1998, 47.)

3   ASF MDP 1171, f. 260 ins. 6, (MAPD 2445), 11 May; f. 295, ibid., 15 March, records a *Maria* on Queen Caterina's request; only Giovanni's portrait survives.

4   For Eleonora's niece, Dianora, see chap. 7.

5   Tullia d'Aragona, 'Della infinità di amore,' 1547, on portrayals of Beatrice penned by Dante. Emison 1991, 428. On Eleonora's protection of Tullia, a courtesan, see Basile 2001, 140–1.

6   Uffizi no. P299, Inv. 1890, no. 1472, 60 × 46 cm. Baccheschi 1973, cat. 51, colour pl. XLIII; and Langedijk 1981, 1: cat. 10,2. A copy, 63 × 47 cm, exists in Kinneard Castle, Scotland.

7   See Pieraccini 1986, 2: 78. Bia's baptism was entered under Cosimo's name.

8   Ibid., 79.

9   Pieraccini 1986, 2: 80, listing archival references.

10 Ibid.

11 Pieraccini ibid., 79.

12 Vasari 1878–85, 7: 598.

13 Conti 1893, 117; Müntz 1895, 161, includes 1558 entries; see also Langedijk 1981, 1: cat. 10,2. Comparing inventory wording, Malcolm Campbell 1985[2], 388, argued for a posthumous *Bia*. Most modern Bronzino scholars agree, but see Tazartes 2003, 130.

14 Conti 1893, 119–21. Further on Bia, see also Saltini 1898, 2–3, and Baia 1907, 49.

15 See Langedijk 1981, 1: cat. 10,2, lists early scholarship; for modern scholars, see Emiliani 1960, pl. 27; Levey 1962, 170; Baccheschi 1973, cat. 94; Uffizi (*Catalogo generale*) 1980, no. P299; McCorquodale 1981, 90; Cox-Rearick 1982, 71; Cecchi 1996[1], 37; Brock 2002, 77–81; and Tazartes 2003, 130–1.

16 Emiliani 1960, 15, is equivocal, '1540–42'; Baccheschi 1973, cat. 94, allowed it could be posthumous, as did Cox-Rearick 1982, 71, and Brock 2002, 78. Simon 1982, 20, believed it was. McCorquodale 1981, 90, dated it before her death; Langedijk 1981, 1: cat. 10,2, and Cecchi 1996[1], 37, do not firmly date it.

17 See Simon 1982, 20. In Vasari's list, Bia's portrait follows on the *Eleonora with Giovanni*, 1545. The list is not chronological. See chap. 1.

18 Cox-Rearick 1982, 71, and Brock 2002, 78.

19 Cox-Rearick ibid.; and Richelson 1978, 27, fig. 5.

20 For the esteem in which the *Portrait of Leo X* was held, see 13–14, 30, and 223n40.

21 Grohn 1982, 64; Cox-Rearick 1982, 71; and Brock 2002, 72 and 78 (dating *Lucrezia* ca. 1541).

22 For analysis of this facial abstraction, see Brock 2002, 74. Smyth 1971, 83–6, links it to the Pesaro visit, and sees Piero della Francesca as contributor to Bronzino's 1540s style of containment and monumentality.

23 Piper 1957, 51, sees them as 'wooing' portraits. Woods-Marsden 2001, 64, believes they commemorate betrothals. Simons 1987, 35–8, concludes that profile portraits such as Pollaiuolo's *Young Woman* (Uffizi) and Baldovinetti's were intended for male scrutiny.

24 See n. 3 above. Langedijk 1981, 2: cat. 63,19, rejects a full-length portrait of an infant girl as Isabella – indeed, its 1560s dress would be incongruous when Isabella was this age, around 1544–5.

25 See Grohn 1982, 64, recording visible *pentimenti* as a result of this process. Brock 2002, 79, notes the halo-like nimbus; see also Langdon 1992[1], 2: 295–305.

26 Vasari 1878–85, 7: 595–7.

27 Berlin-Dahlem, Staatliche Museen. Wethey 1971, 2: cat. 101, fig. 106, dated ca. 1542.

28 Alazard 1968, 203, quoting Alessandro Piccolomini's interlocutor Raffaella in the *Dialogo dove si ragiona della bella creanza delle donne*, 1539. See also Zonta ed. 1913, 167.

29 Zollner 1993, 125; see Woods-Marsden 2001, 81, reassessing what dictates their placement.

30 De Hollanda 1868, 340.

31 My emphasis. Alberti 1969, 217, where Gianozzo describes the instruction of his new wife, and the upbringing of girls. Written in Tuscan, the treatise was still much cited. Ibid., 3.

32 My emphasis. Vives 1912, 42 and 88. Milton's Nun, 'devout and pure / Sober, steadfast and demure,' later enshrines this ideal (*Il Pensieroso*, 31–1). On Vives in England, see text in this chapter, and nn. 70–2.

33 Rogers 1988, 71–2. See Firenzuola 229; and Vives 1912, chaps. 6–8, 63–89, 98, on the curtailment of laughter. Ovid's *Ars amatoria* provides other contexts: 'Let the mouth be but moderately opened, let the dimples on either side be small, and let the bottom lip cover the top of the teeth.' O'Rourke Boyle, ibid., 715–17, citing Ovid, 'The Art of Love' and other Problems, trans. J.H. Mozley (Cambridge, 1969), 137–9. Jean de Muen's *Roman de la rose* asserted that a woman should laugh with her mouth closed; Erasmus held that unrestrained male laughter expressed 'a mind which has lost control.' O'Rourke Boyle, ibid.

34 My translation. See Barocchi and Bertelà 1993, no. 244; J. Hall 1979, 115. See Pochat 1973–4, 140, on the ermine in portraiture; and Simons 1995, 279, citing Leonardo: the

ermine 'would die rather than besmirch itself.' (Ripa's white-clad *Innocenza* [1618] holds a lamb; see Ripa 1988, 1: 120.)

35 See appendix B, Bronzino 1823, 29. See Parker 2000, 185; and Langdon 2004, 51.

36 *Canzone* 106 (trans. Durling, 1976), 215–16.

37 The influence of Raffaellino del Garbo (1466–1523), Botticelli's assistant, whose shop Bronzino entered in 1514 at eleven, may account for his Neoplatonism. On Raffaellino and Bronzino, see Smyth 1949², 184–5, and 1971, 45–6, 71. McCorquodale 1981, 13–14, credits him with Bronzino's formal clarity and technical proficiency, and sees affinities with Botticelli's linearity.

38 Williams 1997, 17–18.

39 See Cox-Rearick 1995, cat. no. VII-I on the *Allegory*, with detailed account of scholarship on the girl-monster, ibid., 229–30. On revealing pentimenti in the *Allegory*, see Plazzotta and Keith 1999. See Moffitt 1993, 309–10 and 313, for Dante's *Fraude*; Moffitt also believes Bronzino was familiar with Horace's monstrous hybrid in the opening lines of the *Ars poetica*, and notes the familiarity of his circle with Ariosto's *Orlando Furioso* (1516), referred to often by Vasari; and Ripa 1970, 188, cited Ariosto, 14:87 and revealed his source for her in Dante's *Inferno*, 17:7–15, 25–7. Langedijk 1981, 1: 312 credits Matteoli 1969, 309, for identifying Bia with *Fraude*; Simon 1982, 3, saw Maria (aged four to five in 1544–5), not Bia (age about six on her death); Gaston 1991, 258, opted for a Medici girl.

40 Cited by Williams, 1997, 21, in his discussion on didacticism in art. On the viewer's incentive to recognize prompts in art that led to this awareness, see Emison 1991, 434.

41 Alazard 1968, 116, and Tazartes 2003, 130, who comments on the child's porcelain-like bust and face. See Van der Velden 1998, 127, for Warburg's pioneering study on Medici *boti*.

42 Brock 2002, 78, accounts for this palpability through the illusionistic costume details.

43 Of interest here is Armenini's commentary on the importance of the artist's sensitivity to the nature of the place in which works of art will appear, quoted by Williams 1997, 96–7. For *boti* and Warburg's pioneering research on their potency, see Van der Velden 1998, 127–8. See ibid. for Vasari's commentary.

44 D. Freedberg 1969, 225–6; Van der Velden 1998, 127 and passim.

45 See Rubin 1995, 101–2.

46 See Fantoni 1999, 261 and 269. See especially 287n90 below. Lecchini Giovannoni 1991, cat. no. 75 describes other copies also by Allori.

47 Zerner 1999, 9, noted that the Medici eschewed tomb effigies, but kept life-sized, dressed ex-voto figures made of wax that were installed in Santissima Annunziata. See next note; and D. Freedberg 1969, 225–6. See Tomas 2003, 105–11 on visits to such Medici installations in churces all over Florence. On royal *boti*, see Warnke 1993, 214. William Forrest, present at the funeral of the abandoned Queen Catherine of Aragon in 1536, reported her robed *boto* as 'curiously lifelike.' Fraser 1992, 231.

48 Trexler 1980, 123. Further on forceful, charismatic Medici votive imagery, see Van der Velden 1998, 133–6; of interest, too, see Edgerton 1985.

49 For this, see Van der Velden 1998, fig. 1; see also Syson 1998, 11.

50 See Van der Velden 1998, 126 and 135; and see L. Campbell 1990, 60, fig. 69: Vasari reported that when Raphael's *Pope Julius II* was exhibited after the pope's death in

Santa Maria del Popolo, it was 'so wonderfully life-like and true that it inspired fear as if it were alive.'

51 Syson 1998, 4–6 and n. 7, citing Dominici's *Regola del governo di cura familiare* (1403). Part 4, 'Rule for the Management of Family Care,' recommends the use of didactic panels in the house. For 'holy' dolls and talismanic imagery for girls see Langdon 1992[1], 2: 302–4; and, for the pertinent exploration of 'icon-centred education,' Crum 2001[2], 40–1.

52 D. Freedberg 1969, 446 n. 7. Desiderio's busts of infants or *putti* exhibit a bewitching charm and an extraordinary skill in infusing marble surfaces with crystalline light. See, for example, Hartt 1994, 294–6, figs. 296–300. Brock 2002, 78, notes Bia's 'china-like face.'

53 Trexler 1980, 88.

54 Florence, Palazzo Pitti 1985, 20. Maria died at age twenty-three.

55 See Tinagli 1997, 26–9, citing Dominici on exemplars as 'mirrors.'

56 See text below and further, nn. 91 and 92, on the exemplar as 'mirror.'

57 See Shearman 1992, 37ff., on Renaissance viewing of the portrait; and Tinagli 1997, 85.

58 Klinger Aleci 1998, 74.

59 ASF MDP 6106, n.f., (MAPD 7159). For Eleonora Gonzaga, see Tinagli 1997, 85.

60 Paleotti 1971, 2: 337 and passim.

61 See C. Murphy 1997, 121.

62 On Bronzino's erudition, and the revival of Petrarch and Ficino in Cosimo's Accademia Fiorentina, see the Introduction, 15, and chap. 2, 80–1. Emison 1991, 431–4, aligns *grazia* with rank and virtue.

63 Children who would view the *Bia* in exemplary contexts would be Giulia, now six; Maria, born 1540; Isabella, born 1542; Lucrezia, born 1545; and Dianora, born 1553.

64 For the luxurious nursery, see Caterina Cibo's letter, quoted chap. 1, 41.

65 For Isabella d'Este's accomplishments, see M. King 1991, 161–2.

66 Saltini 1898, 4–6; McCorquodale 1981, 131; Saltini 1883, 55–7. In the Quattrocento, Latin was considered unfitting for women. Corradini 1998, 30; and Florence, Palazzo Pitti 1985, 18. Vettori's stature was such that in 1576 he delivered an oration on the death of Emperor Maximilian II, in San Lorenzo. G. de Ricci 1972, 203.

67 Saltini 1901–2, 1: 121 no. 23, 561; and Booth 1921, 173.

68 Booth, ibid.

69 On Giulia's equestrianism, see chap. 4, 123; on Isabella's see chap. 6, 157; and on Dianora's, chap. 7, 175. Lucrezia's delicate health may have prevented this development.

70 See Kelso 1977, 62, 63, 72–4, 118, and 288.

71 Catherine patronized Erasmus, friend of More and Vives. Vives 1912, 12, 16, and 22; see also Fraser 1992, 78.

72 Fraser 1992, 11–12 and 100; see also M. King 1991, 161; and Vives 1912, 21, on his fame. See Kelso 1977, 421–2, on widespread European translations.

73 Murphy 1997, 277 n. 68.

74 On Francesco, see Saltini 1883.

75 See text in this chapter, 115, on Cosimo's anguish on Maria's death that she should have been so cloistered.

76 See Pieraccini 1986, 2: 94; Booth 1921, 173; and Saltini 1883, 53. This did not exclude their Italian heritage – Tuscan was ardently cultivated at court. See chaps. 2, 6, and 7.

77 Saltini 1901, 1: 121 no. 23, 561–2; Saltini 1898, 55–9; see Pieraccini 1986, 1: 89–91, for doc-
    umentation. Her beauty and grace are often noted, even by the vitriolic Settimanni,
    quoted in Saltini 1898, 54. On 19 November 1557 Lapini mourned her, describing her as
    'bella e graziosa'; Lapini 1906, 118. Adriani 1583, II: 596, noted her 'costumi reali' (regal
    manners).
78 On her death and rumours surrounding it, see n. 127 below.
79 See chap. 5.
80 Probably this is the panel at Bowood; an untonsured *Giovanni* is in the Ashmolean
    Museum, Oxford, Inv. no. 105. See Heikamp 1953–6, passim, and figs. 5 and 6; Lange-
    dijk 1981, 2: cat. 54,5 and 54, 6; Cecchi 1996[1], 46; and Edelstein 2001, 226–7. The schol-
    arly Giovanni was invested as cardinal in 1560 at seventeen, but died in 1562. See
    Pieraccini 1986, 2: 116 and passim, and Saltini 1898, 122–77. His promise is reflected in
    numerous portraits. See Langedijk 1981, 2: cat. series 54.
81 See Langedijk 1981, 1: 100; and 98–117, on Cosimo's efforts to enhance Medici *virtù*.
82 See Heikamp 1953–6, 137.
83 Ibid., 138.
84 Alazard 1968, 214–15, and Heikamp 1953–6, 138, citing Martini's letter.
85 On this royal tendency, and on Giovio's and Rosello's books, see Langedijk 1981, 1:
    100–1, and 2: cat. 54,6. For *personae* as *exempla virtutis*, see Tinagli 1997, 29.
86 It enjoyed wide popularity by mid-century; Erasmus's Latin translation was added to
    his *Institutione Principis Christiani*. An Italian translation was published in Venice in
    1542; Langedijk 1981, 2: cat. 54,6. For more on these portraits, see Edelstein 2001, 230.
87 See Simon 1989, 481, 484. These were distinct from the 'tiny modern paintings' and a
    Medici portrait-miniatures set (pl. 8) that hung outside the duke's study; see text below
    and n. 90. For the miniature *Francesco*, see Costamagna 1992, fig. 2.
88 Uffizi Inv. 1890, no. 1572, 49 × 37 cm.
89 Vasari 1878–85, 7: 598. A maturer *Maria in Red* exists in Poggio a Caiano (Langedijk
    1981, 1: 128, and 2: cats. 85,2 and 3), but the nose is flatter, the facial transitions less
    modulated than Bronzino's *Maria* of 1551, and the expression 'wooden'; it is probably
    posthumous. See also n. 94.
90 See Bronzino's *vita*, Vasari 1878–85, 7: 603. They are by various hands. See Baccheschi
    1973, cats. 134–57; and Langedijk 1981, 2: cat. 85,4. (Isabella's was later removed. See
    chap. 6, 166–7.)
91 For the 'mirror,' see Beck 1974[2], 63. It measured 38.9 cm; Langedijk 1981, 2: cat. 85,1
    ('Bronzino?'). For lost (?) *Maria*s, see ibid., cat. 85,2. See n. 89 on the Poggio a Caiano
    Maria.
92 Uffizi, maybe by Raphael, ca. 1504, perhaps taken by Castiglione to London in 1506.
    Shearman 1992, 136–7. Lorenzo Lotto in 1552 owned a woman's portrait with 'a cover
    in the manner of a mirror'; Cranston 2000, 163. See also Florence, Palazzo Pitti and
    Museo degli Argenti 2005, cat. no. I, 24 1981, a mirror in the Casa Vasari concealed by a
    sliding panel depicting a nude *Vanitas with Her Mirror*, with bibliography. It is over-
    whelmingly attributed to Bronzino.
93 Langedijk 1981, 2: cat. 85,5a. Dated 1676, it reverses the Tribuna pose, omits her hand,
    and is inscribed: 'MARIA AB ETRVRIA/COSMI PRIMI MAGNI DVCIS ETRVRIAE
    FILIA/ALFONSO I DVCA FERRARIAE DESPONSATA,' followed by her motto,
    'MULCERE DEDIT FLUCTUS ET TOLLERE VENTOS,' discussed below. It is linked to

a composite drawing in which Francesco, Giovanni, and Garzia appear with her, all drawn from Bronzino's child portraits of 1551; Uffizi, Coll. Santarelli, no. 1494. See Heikamp 1953–6, 134, fig. 1, who dates it to the late eighteenth century.

94 Langedijk 1981, 2: cats. 85,3 and 85,6, proposes two other possible *Maria*s: first, see n. 89 above; second, an Allori panel, Vienna, dressed in 1570s style, identified as Maria or Lucrezia, is 'Dianora' di Toledo (1553–76) (chap. 7). See pls. 14 and 16.

95 National Museum, Stockholm, Inv. 37, 44 × 36 cm. Baccheschi 1973, cat. 171, and Langedijk 1981, 2: cat. 63,5. Its provenance is known only from 1852, from the Bryström collection.

96 Portraits of Francesco's daughters support this thesis: in 1578, Allori portrayed Eleonora, twelve, and Anna, ten; Maria had to wait until 1581, when she was around nine – by which time she was betrothed to the Dauphin of France. See n. 152 below. (On the portrayal of Florentine adolescent girls as a long tradition, see n. 138 below.)

97 Uffizi, no. P303, 58 × 46 cm. Brock 2002, 90, contrasts its sober decorum with that of the Prague *Eleonora*.

98 I thank Bruce Edelstein for discussion on Eleonora's sisters; only Isabella is recorded in correspondence. Cox-Rearick 1993, 22, proposed four sisters. See esp. Gaston 2004, 159.

99 Bronzino's Cleveland *Young Lady* is excluded here. See nn. 133 and 145.

100 Vives 1912, 34, 80, and 133. Giovanni Dominici had disdained toys, elaborate clothing, stories, cuddling, laughter, and songs as leading to sensuality in all things. For emphasis in treatises on absolute exclusiveness, i.e., chastity, to husbands, see Kelso 1977, 25.

101 Vives 1912, 74.

102 Ibid., 78.

103 W. Thomas 1963, 97.

104 See Saslow 1996², 63–4 and n. 29, for documentation on the need to provide a dress for Lepida 'di cose sode, d'abiti nobili e apparenti' ('of something solid, noble, and seemly').

105 Bridgeman 1998, 47; see also Simons 1988; Woods-Marsden 2001, 64–7; and Orsi Landini and Westerman Bulgarella 2001, 93.

106 See Alciati 1621, emblem 210.

107 See O'Rourke Boyle 1999, passim and 714–17, on Ficino's plea for moderation of these strictures.

108 See 141–2. In 1562 Francesco jockeyed with Farnese and Parma scions in the imperial Chapel, Madrid, over which pew they should occupy. Cosimo's elevation to grand duke by Pius V in 1569 ended such precedence squabbles. See Williams 1998.

109 On *grillande*, see Florence, Palazzo Pitti 2003, 71. For Eleonora's lily-trimmed burial dress, worn in life, see Arnold, in Florence, Palazzo Pitti 1993, figs. 25 and 36.

110 See 84. Sleeves were detachable; Maria's *diamante*-buttons are secured by tapes at the shoulders of her dress. See Arnold 1993, cat. 53.

111 See Simons 1987 and 1988; Tinagli 1997, chap. 2; and D.A. Brown 2001, cat. no. 30.

112 For Ripa's palm see Okayama 1992, 621, and J. Hall 1979, 231–2. For technical description of the earrings, see Florence, Palazzo Pitti 2003, no. 13.

113 See D.A. Brown 2001, cat. no. 16, with reconstruction.

114 Booth 1921, 173–5; Pieraccini 1986, 1: 90; and Winspeare 1961, 37–8. It is not known if the *impresa* was incorporated in the portrait (as in Maria's earrings, pl. 7), painted on the reverse (as on Leonardo's *Ginevra*), or was a separate object.

115 See Gelli 1928, *impresa* no. 1315, two halcyons in a floating nest, and galleons on a becalmed sea.

116 I thank Dr Maria Ausilia Pisano for alerting me to the distinction between 'vento' and 'ventos,' which is so important for the interpretation of Maria's motto in these instances. For Selvi's 'halcyon' medal, see Langedijk 1981, 2: cat. 85,8; and, for Haelwegh's engraving, ibid., 85,5a. Haelwegh's copperplate was entered with Bronzino's portrait of Maria on its return to the Uffizi, 16 December 1676, proving it had been a direct source for his engraving. Ibid. 1: 940.

117 Scorza 1981, 61–2 and 75.

118 The ephemeral Arch of Florence depicted 'two halcyons making their nest in the sea at the beginning of winter with the sun entering into the sign of Capricorn [Cosimo's *impresa*] which renders the sea smooth and tranquil ... [allowing Florence] to flourish in the greatest felicity and peace.' Vasari, in Starn and Partridge 1992, 173, and figs. 65, 26, and 79.

119 On Maria's *impresa*, see Booth 1921, 173; for control of the elements as a persistent metaphor in Medici weddings for the moderation of marital strife, see chap. 7, 181 and 184.

120 Rousseau 1989, 113.

121 On Giovio and *imprese*, see Scorza 1981, 63, and Rousseau 1989, 113–14 and passim.

122 Ammirato, in Rousseau 1989, 124 n. 5. On courtly opacity, see Cropper 2004, 28–9.

123 See Rousseau 1989 on Leo X's yoke *impresa* and its perpetuation by the Medici.

124 See n. 118 for the Arch of Florence.

125 On their betrothal, see Winspeare 1961, 37–8, and Saltini 1898, 25–6.

126 On her sympathetic, wise counsel to Maddalena Vettori, who was forbidden by Cosimo to marry Ludovico Capponi (see fig. 56 here and chap. 7), see Saltini 1898, 17–23, and G. de Ricci 1972, 379, who relates that Cosimo relented.

127 Saltini 1898, 37–8, 54–60, refutes them. Celletti 1963, 107–12, notes many calumnies by Medici enemies. See Booth 1921, 173–5; Pieraccini 1986, 1: 90; and Winspeare 1961, 37–8. For letters of condolence from Duke Ercole d'Este to Eleonora on Maria's death, and discussion of Lucrezia's dowry, see ASF MDP 2912, ff. 39–46v.

128 See Langedijk 1981, 2: cat. 63,8. Domenico Poggini's *Isabella* medal, 1560 (ibid., 63,9) shows a figure of Ceres with a cornucopia surrounded by the inscription 'DONEC MILIVS NITEAT' ('So that it may shine even more'). Antonio Selvi's medal, 1740 (ibid., 63,11) shows shows a tree with fruit and flowers together, encircled with the inscription 'FLORES.SIMVL.ET.FRVCTVS' ('Flowers and fruits together').

129 Gelli 1928, citing Alciati's *Emblemata*, 1531 and later; for which see Alciati 1996, emblem nos. 147 and 1809, with a cornucopia scrolled and inscribed 'VIRTUTI UBIQUE' ('Virtue in all places').

130 See Étienne Delaune's etching, Paris, 1557–76, in Matthews Grieco 1994, fig. 19.

131 For Isabella as the 'stella di casa Medici,' see chap. 6, 161.

132 The Roman Orsini was a *condottiere* in demand, and leader of the papal armies.

133 The pose is seen in Bronzino's *Young Woman*, ca. 1555 (Cleveland). See n. 145. The lack of any prenuptial portrait of Eleonora may be due to Cosimo having seen her in 1536.

134 See Lurie 1974, 6–8. Kennedy 2001 notes Berger's analysis of *sprezzatura*, an art 'of behaving as if always under surveillance,' apt for the decorum in these portraits of prospective brides.

135 Compare Allori's repetitious hand poses and unconvincing grasp, making inserted

objects appear weightless: fig. 38 (Giulia), pls. 11 and 12 (Isabella), and pl. 16 (Dianora).

136 For *Ludovico*, see Brock 2002, 142–3; and New York 1986, 210–15. On *Ginevra*'s hands and Leonardo's silverpoint drawing in Windsor, see D.A. Brown 1988, 106–10 and 2001, cat. nos. 16 and 17. (The hand of Bronzino's *Girl with a Book* resembles the left hand in the drawing; Cosimo's [pl. 3] echoes Cecilia Gallerani's in the *Lady with an Ermine*. See Woods-Marsden 2001, 76, on the latter's.)

137 Vives 1912, 97. See text above for Alberti on this decorum.

138 The tradition of portrayal of nubile, marriageable girls had existed in Florence before the sixteenth century. Schuyler 1972 who examined Florentine late Quattrocento sculpted busts of adolescent girls (figs. 93–6b) supports Bode's view of their execution close to the girls' marriages; a portrait of Bona of Savoy, prospective bride of Galeazzo Maria Sforza, Duke of Milan, was sent for his approval in the mid-fifteenth century. Rogers and Tinagli 2005, 124.

139 Warnke 1993, 208–9.

140 The *Maria* sent to France in 1565 in a miniature set was posthumous. Another inscribed *Isabella*, 29 × 22.3 cm, portraying her as a young woman ca. 1557 (of recent provenance) exists in a private collection, all of which suggests a number of unidentified, lost sets. See Costamagna 2002, 207, on the circulation of Medici portraits from Cosimo's court; and Cox-Rearick and Westerman Bulgarella 2004, 126–7, on workshop replication as standard practice for the court.

141 L. Campbell 1990, 159–60.

142 Piper 1957, 31.

143 L. Campbell 1990, 85; and Syson 1998, 9. When the Milanese match failed, Henry became excited by a surfeit of choices between the Duc de Guise's daughters and other noble girls, but Guise responded that his daughters were not mares for sale. Pope-Hennessy 1966, 196.

144 Warnke 1993, 216.

145 Bronzino's *Young Woman / Maddalena Vettori(?)* ca. 1555 in Cleveland is excluded here following its assessment by Brock 2002, 91, but see Lurie's valuable study, 1974.

146 See Warnke 1993, 66, and 220–3, for many instances of 'truthfulness' for prospective spouses. See London 1971, pl. 4, for this *Elizabeth*, her letter, and the 1547 inventory; see L. Campbell 1990, 222, who quotes the long passage in its original form.

147 Vives 1912, 115.

148 L. Campbell 1990, 222. It was made when Edward was twelve. See also Toronto 1988, cat. no. 25, a frontal sketch, short-bust length, of an infant Edward in 1539.

149 See chap. 1, 48–9, with regard to the posthumous *Maria Salviati*.

150 Warnke 1993, 220. See also Shearman 1992, 118; and Land 1994, 81–97, on talismanic portraits in Pietro Bembo's, Giovanni della Casa's, and Pietro Aretino's poetry, and Ippolita Castiglione's response to Raphael's *Castiglione*. See also 294nn12, 14, and 303n112.

151 On the use of oils, see Tinagli 1997, 88–91 and 124; see Goffen 1992, 111 and 117, and Pointon 2001, 48, 63, and 67, on the eroticism implicit in viewing, holding, and wearing a lover's miniature, and its having talismanic, relic-like overtones. See especially chap. 7 here.

152 For Allori's portraits of Anna, Eleonora, and Maria di Francesco at around the age of eleven, see Langedijk 1981, 1: cats. 4,1a, 4,1b, and 33; and 2: 86,11. On Queen Maria's prenuptial portrait, see fig. 1 and Introduction, 3.

153 See Eisler 1989, cat. no. 19.

154 Gaunt 1980, 5–32; L. Campbell 1985, xvii; Belozerskaya 2002, 160–76. Scrots, who succeeded Holbein, was court painter to the regent of the Netherlands. On Bronzino, see Levey 1962.

155 Oil on panel, 31.5 × 22 cm, Inv. 1930, 36. I thank Mar Borobia for copious documentation and Lorne Campbell for useful discussion. Close ages for these *infantas* causes confusion in portrait identifications: Juana 'the Mad' (1478/9–1555) married Philip the Fair in 1496; Isabel (ca. 1480–1500) married Manuel of Portugal, who on being widowed married her sister Maria (1482–1517) in 1500; Catherine (1485–1536) married Arthur of England in 1501, was widowed in 1502, and married the future Henry VIII in 1509. See Eisler 1989 and Fraser 1992. Juan de Flandes's pendant panels of Juana and Philip in Vienna were painted on their marriage. For Juana (?) with a lapdog, ca. 1500–1, see text. See Eisler 1989, 160, figs. 1 and 2; and Belozerskaya 2002, 171 and figs. 36 and 37.

156 Oil on panel, 45.5 × 35.1 cm. See Shearman 1983, cat. no. 77, 1495–1500, subject unidentified. (A copy exists in Vienna.) Lorenzo worked in Bologna then, but as Juana and Philip travelled from Burgundy to Spain in 1501, perhaps Lorenzo met them *en train* to portray them. On lapdogs in portraits, see chap. 1, 26–9, and chap. 6, 155–7.

157 She made this pilgrimage en route to La Coruña to embark for England late in 1501. Fraser 1992, 22. Lorne Campbell proposed the identification from her necklace iconography, to which I add the St James references. She is certainly unmarried, which dates the panel to before summer 1501. (A copy exists in Vienna.) Arthur died in April 1502, from when she would have worn a widow's costume until she married his brother, soon to be Henry VIII, in 1509. She became queen that year. In a National Portrait Gallery, London, portrait, she appears majestic in her role as queen, a decorum prescribed by de Hollanda and Paleotti in their portrait treatises. Another date proposed for the Sittow *Catherine* is around 1515, but her age then – thirty – and her role as a still-honoured queen, is at odds with her youth and shyness in the portrait. (See Campbell 1985, xix, and Fraser 1992, 49–71 and pl. following p. 146.) Sittow was the portraitist favoured by her mother, Isabella, which further suggests that this *Catherine* was painted before she left Spain to marry Arthur in 1501.

158 On this traffic of portraits, see Shearman 1970, 76.

159 Two of each of the Medici children's portraits were delivered to Poggio a Caiano in July 1551. Heikamp 1953–6, 134. The 1553 inventory lists the miniature set on tin; see text and nn. 90, 95, and 96. In October 1562 Cristofano dell' Altissimo delivered an inscribed set of seventeen portraits on panels measuring 1 × ¾ *braccio* to the Guardaroba, recorded as fixed to cupboards in the 1609 and 1637 inventories; another set was sent in July 1565 to Catherine de' Medici of France. Langedijk 1981, 1: 108. Other inscribed sets existed: the *Isabella* in Stockholm does not conform to any measurements for the above; see also n. 140 for an *Isabella* measuring 29 × 22.3 cm. The Schloss Ambras set was sent to Grand Duke Ferdinand in Vienna in 1587. See Langedijk 1981, 1 and 2, passim, for each.

160 Such portrait circulation involved some power play. Henry VIII restricted Princess Mary's (1516–58) portrayals and their circulation. Childhood portraits were sent on her betrothal to Charles V, from 1521–6, and to François I, in 1527, but Henry refused one in 1541. Hearn ed. 1995, 47–8. (She ultimately married Philip II of Spain, in 1554.)

Chapter 4

1 'The house of the Lord Duke and ours is all one.' Saltini 1883, 66–7. See Smith 1977[1], 28, 32, 67.

2   Caro Alessandro mio, ch'al primo fiore
    de' più verdi anni, non pur del gran nome
    superbo andate, ma del bel cognome
    vostro, ch'io porto sacro in mezzo al core
    seguite il tosco Apelle, eterno honore
    dell'Arno, e fate sì, ch'ancor si nome
    il secondo BRONZIN, pria, che le chiome
    cangiate, e'l mondo dopo lui v'honore [*sic*].

Lecchini Giovannoni 1991, 34, from *De' Sonetti di M.B.V.*, 1 and 2. For Alessandro's family as intimates and dependents of Bronzino, see Parker 2000, 10, 17, and 69 and supporting bibliography; and Pilliod 2001, 81–2 and 97–107. For the *Joseph* tapestry (1545–53) border designs, credited to Allori, see Lecchini Giovannoni, ibid., cat. nos. 1 and 2, pls. 1–3. Alessandro would have been ten when these were begun.

3 Borghini 1584, 624; Vasari 7: 606–8.

4 Uffizi 1980, P307, 121 × 95 cm, restored 1971, cleaned 2005; recorded 1675 with Cardinal Leopoldo de' Medici's inheritance from Rome as by Bronzino; Baccheschi 1973, cat. no. 111; S. Freedberg 1975, 459 ('Bronzino' in Counter-Reformation style). For the attribution to Allori, see Costamagna 1988, 24–5, fig. 25; simultaneously in press, Langdon 1989; and Lecchini Giovannoni 1991, cat. 176.

5 For his tactics throughout the conclave of 1559, see Pastor 1928, 14: 413–24 and 15: 1–65.

6 The study began as a master's seminar topic under Prof. Graham Smith's direction, at the University of Michigan, Florence, Summer 1985. I thank him for many useful insights.

7 The only Medici woman around this age in 1559 was Lorenzaccio's daughter, Lorenzina. As he was hunted down in 1548 on Cosimo's orders to avenge his murder of Alessandro, Lorenzina is an unlikely subject. Further, her husband Giulio Colonna's armorial colours and emblem, the column, are absent in the panel.

8 Langdon 1989; Kathke 1997, 281; and Pilliod 2001, for example. Piccinini 2005, 32: 3–4, believes that recent cleaning negates such interpretation. Evidence in my text shows that Ortensia Montauto was not a widow in 1559; searches for Aurelia Manelli in genealogies were unhelpful.

9 Lecchini Giovannoni 1991, cat. 176, followed Costamagna's Ortensia identification, as did Pilliod 2001, 179–82.

10 Vasari 1878–85, 7: 261ff. ASF *Carte Dei* ('Montauto'), f. 33, ins. 11, a *ricordanze* written in 1578 by Benedetto Montauto, her cousin, indicates only that Tommaso died between 1557 and 1562, when a five-year Bardi-Montauto contract could not be renewed. It does not prove, as Pilliod concluded, that Ortensia was widowed by 1559, the date inscribed on the portrait (Pilliod 2001, 179). Piccinini 2005 provides the date of Tommaso's death as 1561.

11 See 'Postscript,' Langdon 1992[2], 31.

12 My 1980s doctoral research for Pontormo's *Maria Salviati with the Child* had already con-

cluded from archival documentation and chronicles, and from portrayed resemblance, that the child there was Alessandro's Giulia, not Cosimo (Langdon 1992[1], chap. 1: see chap 1, pl. 2 here). A postscript to my extrapolated 'Pontormo and Medici Lineages' (1992[2]) recorded a recent verbal observation then that Allori's *Lady with a Cameo*, published as a Medici widow (Langdon 1989), might be tied to Alessandro. Significantly, in 1984 my fellow graduate students in Florence had observed an un-Italian beauty about Allori's limpid-eyed sitter as well. But caution was in order. The brief postscript, based on comparison of a range of Alessandro portraits with Allori's *Lady* and research amassed for the 1992 publication proving Giulia's historic role as a child, showed promise. The discussion in this chapter results from expanded archival and other researches since 1992 that I believe arrive at a plausible identification for Allori's *Lady* as Giulia.

Pilliod 2001, 269 n. 147 ('Ortensia'), seemingly overlooked my 1992[2] Pontormo study, in which the postscript acknowledged Costamagna's 'Ortensia' identification and announced my preliminary identification for Giulia as a Medici 'widow.'

13 Tenhove 1747, 2: 388, without historical references. On resemblance, see 304n129.

14 Langedijk 1981, 1: 70, cat. 1, 12, 44 × 28.5 cm. Its provenance is unhelpful.

15 Ciabani ed. 1992, 1: 141–2: 'Montauto di Ciaini': an *azzurro* eagle with six 'monti' on a gold ground – in heraldry, a strong, bright blue, not light blue (celeste) and not dark blue (blu notte). The arms appear on the Montauto chapel entrance, right side. I especially thank Paola Tinagli for this useful reference.

16 See D.R. Wright 1976, 2: 601–3, quoting ASF MDP 616, f. 614ff., ins. 21, dated 1543 for court rolls. See also 231n135.

17 Florence, Palazzo Pitti 1993, exh. cat., 31, quoting ASF, MDP 1174, n.f., 6 November 1548.

18 See Segni 1805, 2: 389; and Sansovino (1582) 1670, 154.

19 See 235n171. Allegrini's engraving shows a nun, from a lost portrait, with the motto 'MAJESTAS ET ROBUR' ('Authority and Strength'). Langedijk 1981, 2: cat. 104, 1a.

20 See Segni 1805, 2: 389.

21 See chap. 3 for Bronzino's 1551 and 1553 Medici childrens' portraits.

22 De Lellis 1654, 141–4. see also G. Alberigo, *Dizionario Biografico degli Italiani*, vol. 18, 'Cantelmo.' Giovanni's pension of 3000 *ducati* per annum as Counseller Collateral to the Kingdom of Naples would be worth about $1.6 million U.S. today. See 226n70 for equivalents.

23 ASF MDP 1176, f. 44, ins. 5 (MAPD 3117), from Tommaso de' Medici to Pierfrancesco Riccio, from an unspecified location. See next note.

24 Benedetto Buonanni, secretary to the Florentine ambassador in Rome, to Riccio in Florence, ASF MDP 1176, 24 and 44ff. (MAPD 24); for Eleonora's orders, see ASF MDP 1176, f. 24, ins. 6 (MAPD 3117 and 3122).

25 ASF MDP 1176, f. 30, ins. 6 (MAPD 3126), Lorenzo Pagni in Pisa to Riccio.

26 ASF MDP 6357, f. 8 (unpaginated); Segni 1805, 2: 389; Litta 1889–1902, vol. 3, Serie G-O; and De Lellis 1654, 143–4, record $25,000 *ducati*, about $11,250,000 today – perhaps a slight exaggeration.

27 See Litta 1899–1902, vol. 3, Serie 1A Medici, for this branch. Francesca, Cassandra, and another of Bernardetto's sisters were known to Giulia as childhood companions during visits to Maria Salviati at Castello. See 218n4.

28 For his presence at its first meeting and the council's report, see ASF MDP 1212, f. 74

(MADP 4202). See Saltini 1898, 130–4 for the funerals. For Bologna, see Saltini 1901–2 1: 567, and Litta 1899–1902, vol. 3, Serie G-O.

29 Albèri 1839–63, II, 1: 51 n. 3. For more on Bernardetto de' Medici, see Ademello 1845, 76; del Badia 1902, 2: 56; and Litta 1899–1902, vol. 3, Medici, tab. XX. Presumably Giulia's Spanish upbringing at the Florentine court was a considerable asset in both her marriages.

30 For Alessandro's votive image, see Vasari 1878–85, 6: 632, asserting that it was made in 1532 by Giovanangelo Montorsoli; Langedijk 1981, 1: cat. 1,54, citing Richa, 1971 5: 208; and see Richa, ibid., 216–18, for the Chiarito's records of Giulia's visits there. For more on the Chiarito and San Clemente, see D'Addario 1972, 394.

31 Anton Francesco Grazzini's *La Spiritata* was performed there. See Ghisi 1969, xxv.

32 See Strehlke 1985, 9, on Battista Franco's pastiche of Sebastiano's *Clement VII*, Titian's *Ippolito*, and Pontormo's *Alessandro*, for the wedding. For frescoes, see Vasari 1878–85, 7: 257. Richa 1972, 5: 216, records an entry citing Giulia's paternity warmly, and the naming of her son. (Great snobbery attached to ranking illegitimacy: in 1511, a natural daughter of the Marquess of Mantua refused Agostino Chigi's suit because he was a mere banker. Ettlinger 1994, 784–5.)

33 See D.R. Wright 1976, 2: 241–3 and 248–55.

34 See text, 34.

35 See Richelson 1978, 8; and also Young 1910, 578–9.

36 On her 'sloe-eyed beauty,' see Pilliod 2001, 149, and my n. 12 above. See chap. 1, 41–3, for discussion of Giulia's ancestry.

37 Vasari 1878–85, 6: 250. For Cosimo as Caesar, see 226n69; for Cosimo the Elder's medals showing *broncone* and yoke, see Hill 1978, cat. nos. 245–7. The emblem was adopted by Leo X.

38 Ripa 1970, no. 161, and Okayama 1992, 91 and 613. The wreath signifies beeches native to Falterona, source of the Arno, in the Appennines. Arno, accompanied by his lion, appeared again on the Arch of Florence in the 1565 *apparato*. See Starn and Partridge 1992, 269. See Parker 2003, 235–40, on Bronzino's panegyrics to Cosimo as Hercules, with a useful summation of ducal commissions on this personification for propaganda.

39 See text, 82, on its inclusion in Bronzino's *Cosimo in Armour* in Kassel.

40 See Richelson 1978, 79–106, fig. 18; it is today in the Museo degli Argenti, Florence.

41 For Tribolo's, see D.R. Wright 1976, 2: 160. Stoldo's relief is in Holkham Hall, England; Pierino's is in the Vatican. Richelson 1978, 101–2 and figs. 6 and 7; and see Louis A. Waldman in Ottawa 2005, cat. no. 106 on Pierino's relief. For Dandini's tapestry, one of eight in the series *The Life of Duke Cosimo I* (Pitti), see Harper 2001, 231–2, fig. 15.5.

42 See Richelson 1978, figs. 21 and 22 and pp. 24–78, on Cosimo's deification as Caesar Augustus in astrological references and *imprese* for the 1539 marriage festivities to its culmination in Vincenzo Danti's over-life-size statue of Cosimo-Augustus in 1574, now in the Bargello, Florence. See also A. Thomas 2000, 168, 219–20, and figs. 3.3 and 3.21 for other Medici examples. See text, 34, 266n69 and Langdon 1989, 38.

43 Pastor 1928, 15: 12–19 and 40–65. A Venetian source claimed that Pius took the Caraffa to court so that Cosimo might regain the promissory note and the affair be kept secret.

44 See text, 121. Examples in Allori's art include the Apollo Citharoedos in the Ashmolean, *Pietro Palma / Young Collector*, Oxford, dated 1561, visibly modelled on his *Giulia de' Medici*. (Costamagna 2002, 210, identifies the *Collector* as Paolo Capranica.) It, too, com-

memorates a marriage and is replete with genealogical and political references. See Langdon 1989, 35, 44–5, fig. 10; my research on the Palma portrait continues.

45 They included the Pio da Carpi, Colocci, and Goritz gardens, venues for Pope Leo X's circle of *orti letterati*. See Langdon 1989, 38 n. 53 for related bibliography.

46 Bober 1977, 233. See especially Bober and Rubenstein 1986, a useful source book of antique statuary and their status and whereabouts in the Renaissance.

47 See Langdon 1989, 38 fig. 11.

48 For description of a similar composition by Rosso Fiorentino, see Langdon 1989, 38.

49 For the *Dying Cleopatra/Sleeping Ariadne* see Bober and Rubenstein 1986, cat. no. 79. For de Hollanda's 1540s drawing of its first location, see Cox-Rearick 1995, 354–5 figs. 385 and 386; for the reinstallation, see Caneday 1967. Further, see Langdon 1989, 38–40.

50 Ariadne, abandoned by Theseus on the island of Naxos, was saved by Bacchus.

51 See Langdon 1989, 39 nn. 58 and 59, on the new fountain and this installation.

52 Ibid., 40. On other associations with caverns and sleep, see Feinberg in Chicago and Detroit 2002, 64 n. 59, 'Kingdom of Sleep and Setting for Dreams.' Pilliod 2001, 180–5, connects Allori's slumbering figure to Endymion's eternal sleep. My Medici identification and interpretational sources apart (Langdon, 1989 and here), we concur that this is an allegory of the Counter-Reformation dogma of Redemption.

53 See Langdon 1989, 40–2, citing Graham Smith 1977[1], and Coffin 1955, 267–79. Also, see Brumble 1998, 123–6, and Carloni and Grasso 1994, who call attention to the existence of many variants on Ripa's versions of opposition between Vice and Virtue.

54 Her mirror is ubiquitous. On her sceptre and purse, see Tervarent 1958, 52.

55 See Alciati 1996, no. 133.

56 Kiefer 1979, 1–3, 5–13, 16 and 17, surveys variations on each: Alciati 1996, 133, dispensed with the figure of Fortuna, keeping only *Occasione* (Opportunity). Ripa 1988 2: 86 (first published in 1593), like Alciati, gives *Occasione* a razor to ward off assailants.

57 In her role of luminary, she may also hold a radiant sun. See Ripa 1988 2: 228.

58 On Medici yokes, see n. 72. For the decorously garbed *Matrimonio*'s yoke, see Ripa 1988, 2: 27–8, 81, and 102; see also *Servitù*, ibid., 168, and *Obedienza*, 102. See also text, 150, on the yoked figure of *Matrimonio* on the clasp of Isabella's *cintura*.

   Ripa, ibid., 182, gave wings to one version of *Fortuna*, but Allori's yoke cannot be mistaken for wings, always softly feathered in his works: see *Christ and the Adulteress* in Santo Spirito, and examples in Lecchini Giovannoni 1991, figs. 19, 101, and 139.

59 On Bronzino's London *Allegory*'s subtle *invenzione*, see text, 21 and 60.

60 Alciati 1996, no. 133. Kiefer 1979, 23–5, concludes with examples of the *Occasione-Fortuna* nexus with Time or an hourglass, and cites Jean Cousin's *Liber Fortunae*.

61 Cartari 1556, 463, text quoted in Langdon 1989, n. 73.

62 Uffizi. See G. Smith 1984, 394–6. At rest at *Felicitas publica*'s throne, she allegorizes Tuscany's good fortune under Francesco's assumption of rule. See also Borghini 1584, 3: 208–9, on Allori's Poggio a Caiano fresco, 1582, with 'nymphs, Hercules, and *buona Fortuna*.' See Lecchini Giovannoni 1991, cat. 71, pls. 198, 150.

63 See 'The Council of Trent: Original Sin and Justification,' in the *New Catholic Encyclopaedia*, 14: 272–3; see also G. Smith 1977[1], 104.

64 Alciati 1996, no. 133, *In Occasionem*, discussed above.

65 D.R. Wright 1976 2: 271. Quotations from *Aeneid* 4 embodied this claim. See also Cox-Rearick 1984, 256. This symbolism is suggested on Francesco's medal, where Mercury

rides above a landscape with a quadriga; a *Sol* is his companion. (Alciati 1996, 507–11, makes several references to the caduceus as a symbol of good governance.) For the medal's scene see Langedijk 1981, 2: cat. 42,92b, rev. Giambologna's *Mercury*, 1564, was a significant Medici commission.

66 See Langdon 1989, fig. 7, and Langedijk 1981, 2: cat. 42,12. Possibly the chosen verses, Psalm 85: 10–11, bear on Cosimo's dynastic claims. They reiterate the theme of righteousness and rule, as in Psalm 72: 1–5, praising Solomon's kingly powers: 'Give the king thy judgements, O God, and thy righteousness unto the king's son. / He shall judge thy people with righteousness, and thy poor with judgement. / The mountains shall bring peace to the people, and the little hills, by righteousness. / He shall judge the poor of the people, he shall save the children of the needy, and shall break in pieces the oppressor. / They shall fear Thee as long as the sun and the moon endure, throughout all the generations.' Discussion of the use of the Sun and Moon as metaphors for an eternal Medici dynasty concludes chap. 2.

67 Alciati 1996, emblem no. 15. Brumble 1998, 213–16, cites Jupiter as Mercury's father. Perhaps Cosimo-Jupiter is implicitly recalled, too. (For this, see text, 67, 78, 87, 185–8.)

68 M. Hall 1979, 8; also G. Smith 1977[1], 28, 32, and 67; Langdon 1989, 42–3; Young 1910, 579; and, on the new papal nuncio, Fenlon 1983, 2: 464.

69 Winspeare 1961, 111.

70 For the precedence row, see text, 140–2. In a Machiavellian bid to secure the grand-ducal crown, he delivered a Protestant convert, his faithful adviser Carnesecchi, to Pius; Carnesecchi – in his sixties – was burned alive in October 1567. See Cleugh 1975, 289–90. On Cosimo's awareness of the political ramifications of Trent before 1560, see Fenlon 1983, 2: 464–5.

71 Queen Caterina de' Medici of France, is also eulogized in the verse. Vincenzo de' Rossi sculpted a *Pius IV*; Lambert Sustris painted *Pius IV Receiving the Decrees of the Council of Trent*. For Vincenzo Borghini's preparatory drawings (BNF 2.10.100), see Starn and Partridge 1992, 286.

72 Gelli 1928, nos. 1658 (Leo X) and 1555 (Leo and Clement). Leo's astrological sign at birth, when his papacy was predicted, was Libra, the Yoke. Rousseau 1989, 120, and passim.

73 See Rousseau 1989, fig. 1 and 123–4, n. 7, on Giovio's version of the emblem, which was meant to show its close identity with Leo in the 1550s. Giovio's first edition, 1555, was dedicated to Cosimo.

74 Clement's link to *Fortuna* is suggested by Ripa (1603) 'Fortuna Pacifica Overo Clemente.' See Okayama 1992, 97. For Giovanni's investiture, see text, 132.

75 Hale ed. 1981, 182–3; for exhaustive accounts of Leo, see Pastor 1928, vols. 7 and 8.

76 Gaye 1840, 3: 23. No such portrait is known, and neither Vasari nor Raffaello Borghini refer to Allori as a papal portraitist; Borghini does refer to a portrait of Pius IV by Santi di Tito between 1560 and 1564. Pilliod 2001, 264 n. 39, suggests that Pius's inclusion in Bronzino's *Martyrdom of St Lawrence* of 1565 may derive from Santi's portrait.

77 See above, and especially Pastor 1928, 15: 13, 60–2. On Counter-Reformation fervour inculcated into the Florentine community in Rome, see Prodi 1995, 335 and passim.

78 See Kelso 1977, 132. St Jerome saw virginity as woman's preferred state, holding that if widowed, she must remain forever chaste. Valone 1992, 52–3 and 61. On widowhood and its attendant decorum, see chap. 1, 31–2.

79 See 1923 Frey 2: 868 for Vasari's *Bernardetto* entry; see also Costamagna 1988, 26 and n. 17, identifying the *Bernardetto* portrait from Vasari's *Ricordanze* reference. See Davis 1981, 201, on numerous discrepancies of dating, checked against Vasari's own letters, payments, and documents; he notes, too, that no accurate study of the *Ricordanze* has been carried out. Del Vita's (1927) edition, 58 and 78, calls attention to a '1538' instead of 1548, and '1528' for the Sala degli Elementi instead of 1558. (I thank Paola Tinagli for useful discussion on the topic.) These were busy decades for Vasari, whose expressed reluctance to portray (see my Introduction, n. 60) could explain a revised portrait or a 'modern' copy in 1559 of Vasari's 1549 *Bernadetto*. Costamagna 1988, 25–6, and 2002, 211, fig. 27; Corti 1989, 80 n. 59; and Lecchini Giovannoni 1991, 39, all attribute the *Bernardetto* to Vasari. See next note.

80 The *Bernardetto* panel appeared at auction in New York in 1931 as Bronzino's work. L. Corti 1989, 80, who has not queried the *Ricordanze* date that refers to it; see also Baccheschi 1973, cat. 127, as *Portrait of a Youth* by Bronzino. The *Giulia* was attributed to Bronzino until Costamagna's and Langdon's studies of 1988 and 1989 assigned it to Allori.

81 See Vasari 1878–85, 7: 655 for this. R. Borghini 1584, 3: 205, records a *Crucifixion* for Alessandro di Chiarissimo de' Medici painted by Allori at seventeen, for which Thieme and Becker 1903–50 (1: 319) records Ottaviano as patron; Lecchini Giovannoni 1991, 39 n. 16, proposes Ottaviano's son, Alessandro, not Chiarissimo's Alessandro, as patron.

82 Woodall ed. 1997, 2, notes that it was in the sixteenth century that the courtly console tables, chairs, curtains, columns, helmets, and handkerchiefs that appear in countless later works were introduced into the repertoire; also, dogs, dwarfs, servants, jesters, and black attendants were placed to demonstrate the sitter's elevated status and 'natural' authority. On the motif of the black slave child in portraiture, see Kaplan 1982 and 2005, on Isabella d'Este's slave women.

83 See Zanrè 2001, 189–204. See also Saltini in del Badia 1902, 2: 55–60.

84 Saltini, ibid., 56, citing *L'Apologia de' Cappucci*, in which Bernardetto is an interlocutor.

85 For Cellini's caustic comment on Bernardetto, see Bargellini and Guarnieri 1978, 4: 289.

86 Zanrè believes they had phallic connotations; burlesque poetry, too, used vegetables in ribald, homoerotic references. See Parker 2000 on Bronzino's *capitoli*.

87 Zanrè 2001, 193–4, 196, 198–202 and appendix; and del Badia 1902, 2: 54–9.

88 In 1717, Salvino Salvini recorded in his *Fasti consolare dell'Accademia Fiorentina* that Panciatichi's term had been 'one of the most magnificent and honoured that ever was.' He was appointed *Commissario* of Pisa in 1568. Zanrè 2001, 193 nn. 21 and 23. Bronzino's portrait of Bartolomeo ca. 1540, depicts him book in hand, his entire being seemingly infused with intense intellectual sensibility and courtly elegance. See Brock 2002, illus. p. 119.

89 See Gallucci in Eisenbichler ed. 2001, 37–46, on Cosimo's 'leniency,' which destroyed Cellini's career by mitigating a sentence for sodomy to house arrest. He could be genuinely lenient: the poet-courtesan Tullia d'Aragona was excluded from tighter sumptuary laws against prostitutes because of ties to Eleonora's circle, her links with the Accademia Fiorentina through Varchi, her lover, and her intellectual prowess. Basile ibid., 136.

90 Grassellini and A. Fracassini 1982, 81.

91 Richa 1972, 5: 217; Grassellini and Fracassini 1982, 81; and O. Medici 2000, 108, claiming title through Pius V's decree of continuity through the nearest surviving Medici branch. For this branch, see Litta 1899–1902, Serie G-0; and Anonymous, *Albo d'Oro*, vol. 10.

92 See ASF MDP 5925, f. 139, dated 23 February 1574.

93 For comparison of Bronzino's portraiture with Allori's, see Langdon 1989, 28–31.

94 De Hollanda 1868, 358. See also J. Bury 1977, 434.

95 For discussion of her portrayal there, see Langdon 1989, 33 and fig. 8.

96 Tridentine promulgations on religious art in 1564 merely codified an impact that was already felt. See M. Hall 1979, 1; and Blunt 1940, 111.

97 See Langdon 1992[1], ch. 1, on these; Woodall ed. 1997, 76–7, notes also that de Hollanda's demand for didacticism in portraiture was reiterated by Lomazzo, who said that only those of high rank, singular liberality, and virtue should be portrayed, 'and nobody else at all.' Armenini's lifespan (1533–1609) is concurrent with that of Alessandro Allori (1535–1607); each was strongly influenced by several years of training in Rome in the 1550s.

98 This is expressed, too, in interpretations of the Montauto chapel frescoes, 1560. See Costamagna 1988, 26–7; Langdon 1989, 45; and Pilliod 2001, 145–79.

99 See especially 'Eleonora and the Jesuits,' in Franceschini 2004, 181–206.

100 Hollingsworth 1996, 264. See n. 101.

101 ASF MDP 210, f. 33 (MARD 227), Cosimo to Alessandro Strozzi, 11 March 1559.

102 See text, 8, 72, 76 for ducal *entrate* in Siena, 1560, and 72, 83, 136 in Rome, 1560 and 1569.

103 Bronzino did not portray any of Cosimo's children in their maturity. Possibly he was not artistically in the vanguard in the new Tridentine climate. Cox-Rearick 1993, 87, documents his absence from Cosimo's payroll after 1563, proposing that in handing governance to Francesco, the duke no longer needed him. Perhaps Eleonora's death in 1562 had cut short the twenty-year patronage he had enjoyed. See Lloyd 1993, 4 n. 10.

Chapter 5

1 For this event, see Saltini 1883, 60–1.

2 Francesco warmly reported a meeting with Cardinal Carlo Borromeo in 1560, following his visit to Pius (ASF MDP 6377, *Viaggi dei Principi*, no. LXX), and an official reception for Federigo Borromeo was held in Florence early in 1560. ASF MDP 246, f. 332.

3 Saltini 1883, 70–1.

4 See 212n19, 277n70, on his delivery of Pietro Carnesecchi to the Inquisition in 1567.

5 See fig. 45, of before 1559, probably by Allori, and text below; see 287n94, on an *Isabella* copy of a lost original. Lloyd 1993, 2–4, proposed that a *Francesco* group (corresponding to Langedijk 1981, 2: series 42, 12–13) was begun as early as 1558. (For Allori's Florentine contacts in Rome and return visits to Florence, see Lecchini Giovannoni 1991, 36–8, and Pilliod 2001, 149.)

6 For the Montauto chapel, see Lecchini Giovannoni 1991, cat. 11, figs. 11–121; for the Santa Croce altarpiece, ibid., cat. 12, figs. 13–18. (Pilliod 2001, 10, 114–16, and 146–63, argues that Allori's inscribed date is spurious and dates its completion to 1571.) For the portraits, see Lecchini Giovannoni 1991, 179–80.

For Francesco, see Langedijk 1981, 1: 121–2, and 2: cat. series 42; see also Lloyd 1993, 2–5. For Lucrezia, see Langedijk 2: cat. series 76, all painted by February 1560.

7   See Saltini 1898, 89ff., and Balis-Crema de' Medici 1946.

8   Langedijk 1981, 2: 42,13. Francesco, dressed in red, is clearly not mourning her death (1561). For Ercole II's letters to Cosimo on Francesco and Lucrezia's arrival in Ferrara, see ASF 2912 II, ff. 56–9v.

9   North Carolina Museum of Art, no. G64.35.4. Oil on panel, 75.5 × 62.5 cm. Christie's sale cat., London, 9 March 1923, no. 5, *Portrait of a Lady*; and Ball and Graupe sale cat., Berlin, 28–29 Nov. 1930, no. 12, as Bronzino, *Portrait of a Medici Princess*. (The miniature measures 24 × 18 cm.) See Langedijk 1981, 2: cats. 76,5 and 76,3.

10   See Langedijk 1981, 2: cats. 76,3, 76,4; and ibid., cats. 42, 13 (Francesco with miniature in hand).

11   Ibid., cat. 76,4. See pl. 8 here, lowest series, third from left.

12   See ibid., cat. 76,1, measuring 58 × 44.5 cm; and Ambras: cat. 76,2, 13.5 × 10.5 cm.

13   See n. 1 on Allori's visits. Langedijk 1981, 2: cat. 109,6, records one uncertain identification for Lucrezia, the Lugano miniature, but it is identified here from an inscribed Ambras panel as Eleonora ('Dianora') di Pietro de' Medici. See 174–5. For a lost *Isabella*, known only from a copy, dressed in similar style to the North Carolina *Lucrezia*, see n. 5.

14   Ovid, *Met.*, 4: 285–388. Langedijk 1981, 2: 75,7a; 75,7b; and 76,7c. The armillary sphere's circular rings represented the celestial spheres.

15   Ovid., *Met.*, 2: 1ff.; Pliny, *Natural History*, 2: 91; Plato, *Timaeus*, 22–3c; Dante, *Inferno*, 17: 107, and *Purgatorio*, 4: 72 and 29: 118. I thank Maria Ausilia Pisano for translations of Latin inscriptions and for their sixteenth-century sources. See Langedijk 1981, 2: cats. 76,8, 76,8a, and 76,8a rev.

16   It follows the Berlin panel, but her hand is not posed to touch the pendant jewel.

17   Langedijk 1981, 2: cat. 76,5a.

18   Ibid., cat. 76,9 rev.

19   See Schaffers-Bodenhausen and Tiethoff-Spliethoff 1993, 13–14, fig. 3, cat. no. 635.

20   See ASF, MDP fil. 4072, 12–23 October 1550.

21   On Ercole's pro-French, anti-Medicean politics – notably during the Sienese War – see Eisenbichler 2003, 93. For Este history, see L. Chiappini, *Gli Estensi* (Milan, 1967), and R. Iotti 1998. For Cosimo's shrewd moves to overcome his parvenu status, see Fantoni 1999.

22   Ercole d'Este to Cosimo, 25 March 1558, quoted in full in Saltini 1898, 345–7.

23   See Saltini 1898, 67 and 74, on disdainful comments, and his opinion on the portrait.

24   For the dowry ('scudi dugentomila d'oro'), see ibid., 69. (For equivalents, see 226n70.) Correspondence between Duke Ercole and Alfonso, 19 July 1558, suggests that he has already expressed satisfaction with his young wife to Ercole (ibid., 70–3).

25   Litta 1899–1902, 2: 'Este,' pl. I; and Iotti (1998), 'L'arme ... d'Este'; for Orsini colours, see chap. 6, 150.

26   See Ghisi 1969, xxv and xliv.

27   Saltini 1898, 72–5.

28   From the early 1550s, Eleonora's decline was predicted by retainers. In 1561, the Venetian ambassador, Vincenzo Fedeli, reported that the duchess was sick each morning. To judge by a later portrait of Eleonora, her decline had been progressive. For this period in her life, see Cox-Rearick 2004, 225–7, and fig. 10.1. For Lucrezia's decline, see Saltini 1898, 100–7; Booth 1921, 139; Pieraccini 1986, 2: 93–103. Balis-Crema de' Medici 1946, 41,

and Saltini 1898, 96–7 and 100–1 describe Alfonso's gifted, personable sisters' growing affection for Lucrezia, but not his mother's (who was unsympathetic to Lucrezia's deep piety), and the young duchess's discomfort at being intellectually out of her depth. Francesco visited her in March 1561, a few weeks before her death, by which time her Este family, Alfonso included, were dedicated to the dying girl.

29 See appendix B.

30 See below; Balis-Crema de' Medici 1946, 42; Williams 1998; and see Tinagli 2001, 72, on Cosimo's compulsion to emphasize his power when still only Duke of Florence and Siena, as expressed in Vasari's *Ragionamenti*.

31 Richelson 1978, 25–78, and 40. Poggini's 1559 *Apollo* medal for Cosimo in the Bargello (ibid., fig. 9), and Poggini's eulogy to Cosimo (ibid., 37) also express the duke's attachment to Apollonian symbolism; see also M. Campbell 1985[2], 386.

32 Richelson 1978, 26–7, fig. 11.

33 Cosimo's determination to rank above other Italian houses is evident from the early years of his reign. See ASF 3, f. 29 (MAPD 82), from an unnamed Medici functionary to Averado Serristori in Rome, regarding precedence over Ferrara. The 1559 papal election was crucial. His confidence in the conclave's outcome is evident. See ASF MDP 2913, c. 70, of 18 December 1559 (eight days before its conclusion), where a list of Italian dukes has been prepared for Cosimo by Luca Scilli; and further, c. 65, 65v., and several unpaginated before the latter; ASF MDP 2914, f. 6–17 and 33, details the proposed order of ranks and attendant protocol. See chap. 4, on Cosimo's undermining of the Este cardinal at the conclave. Cardinals Ferdinando de' Medici, later grand duke, and Luigi d'Este later brought about amicable relationships. Coffin 1955, 173. See also Saltini 1883, 62; Quint 1990, 17–19; and especially Williams 1998.

34 See Allori's letter to Cosimo dated 29 December 1559, text 132 and 277n76. (Lloyd 1993, 5 n. 17, has narrowed the date of the portrait to between 1558 and 1560.)

35 For bibliography, see Langedijk 1981, 2: cat. 76,5; Baccheschi 1973, nos. 154 (the Medici miniatures on tin, pl. 8 here) and 161 (the longer version on tin in the Palazzo Pitti), believed their source – evidently the North Carolina panel – was by Bronzino. All are in Allori's style; also, Brock (2002) omits *Lucrezia* panels in Bronzino's *oeuvre*. See also Lloyd 1993, 4.

36 See Saltini 1898, 74, who quotes, Alfonso Rossetti's letter to Ercole, 19 June 1558.

37 Lapini 1906, 126. Mourning could be in any drab tone. Dark clothing (*'bruno'*) was adopted by the whole court during Eleonora di Toledo's 20 December 1562 obsequies. See Baia 1907, 90; see also Cox-Rearick 2004, 232 on black mourning for Duchess Eleonora; Cosimo ordered a black outfit and had his bedroom decorated in black following Eleonora's death. On various drab mourning colours for women, see Sangiorgi 1973.

38 See Saltini 1898, 7. On Medici state jewels, see Florence, Palazzo Pitti 2003.

39 Ercole II to Alfonso d'Este in Florence, 1 July 1558, Archivio di Stato, Modena (Lettere d'Ercole II), quoted in Saltini 1898, 76–7. (For *onestà*, see Battaglia 1981–.)

40 Ercole adamantly refused, however, to release an heirloom collar of pearls from Ferrara. Saltini, 1898, 77.

41 Ibid., 40–1, and passim.

42 Quoted from Pieraccini 1968, 2: 94–5; and see Saltini 1898, 82–4 and passim.

43 For the *entrata*, see Saltini 1898, 89–95, and Balis-Crema de' Medici 1946, 40–1. For her illness, see Pieraccini 1986, 2: 97–103.

44 Saltini 1898, 101, who notes his salary, 500 *scudi* per annum – about $175,000 U.S. in equivalent value today. His sojourn in Ferrara earned him 100 *scudi* – about U.S. $35,000 – suggesting that it was seen as critical for Lucrezia. (See 227n70 equivalents.)

45 Saltini 1898, 95–111. Cosimo's exchanges with Alfonso, his descriptions of Eleonora's deep sorrow, and his responses to condolences from the royal house of France and the Mantuan court express great empathy and are indicative also of his stature in the European sphere. See ASF 213, ff. 36–55, and 89.

46 See M. Hall 1979, passim. This may have contributed to Bronzino's temporary suspension from Medici patronage from 1564 to 1566. For his effusive, desperate letter to Cosimo, who by then had made Francesco his regent, see Simon 1982, 5–6.

47 See M. Hall 1979, 53ff.

Chapter 6

1 Pieraccini 1986, 2: 166.

2 Cardamone 2002, n. 12, from the seventeenth-century *Origine e discendenza de' Medici*. During mutual exchanges concerning Isabella, Donna Cardamone's musicological expertise was especially helpful, as was her critical reading of an earlier draft of this chapter.

3 On her early education, see Winspeare 1961, 19–21; and Saltini 1901, 1: 566, her most reliable biographer, and on whom Pieraccini, Winspeare, Celletti, and Micheletti ultimately depend.

4 See Saltini 1901, 1: 565; Hale ed. 1981, 228; and Young 1910, 607.

5 Saltini 1901, 1: 565. For equivalent monetary values, see 226n70.

6 Saltini 1901, 1: 567–8, cites Lapini, Settimani's *Memorie*, and Alfonso Contrari's dispatches to Ferrara. See also Winspeare 1961, 40.

7 Orsini's *magnificenza* is evident in Cosimo's letter of 12 February 1558, notifying Francesco Babbi that he will require 'qualche spasso di giardini' ('gardens where he can amuse himself') during his visit; the duke requested that the Bartolini gardens be made available. ASF MDP 28, f. 21 (MAPD 213).

8 Saltini 1901, 1: 567–8.

9 Ibid.

10 See Saltini 1901, 2: 607, 624, and 625; and 1902, 3: 627–30.

11 'Her innate vivacity never forsakes her.' Ibid., 2: 600–1.

12 The debts, thirty thousand *scudi* – were equivalent to about $10 million today. Ibid., 2: 602–3. See also Celletti 1963, 91.

13 In a letter to Cardinal Ferdinando in Rome, Isabella reports in detail on the effects of this bereavement on Francesco and Pietro. ASF MDP 6366, f. 234, dated 13 January 1563. Particularly poignant are her descriptions of ten-year-old Pietro's intractability and emotional distress. (See chap. 7, passim, for Pietro and Dianora's tragic marriage.)

14 Winspeare 1961, 59 and 60.

15 See n. 13 above.

16 Winspeare 1961, 83. On other possible children, see note 17 below. Leonora was probably Isabella's first daughter: Maria di Cosimo was given Maria Salviati's name; Eleonora's was given to her firstborn granddaughters of Francesco and Ferdinando.

17 Saltini 1901, 2: 605. A letter from Paolo Giordano to his cousin, Troilo, dated August 1564 mentions a newborn daughter. See ASF MDP 6373, f. 1. Unidentified, she may be a girl of about two in a panel rejected as Isabella. See Langedijk 1981, 2: cat. 63,19. In the full-length portrait, probably Allori's, the bejewelled little girl is dressed in 1560s style. It is probably posthumous.

18 Celletti held that Leonora was also known as Francesca or Virginia, born in 1568; other Orsini daughters may be unaccounted for – Orsini's letter to Isabella of June 1576, only weeks before he murdered her, expresses pleasure at the 'pupa's' (baby girl's) good health. Celletti 1963, 99 and 104.

19 Saltini 1902, 3: 625, and 1901, 2: 607–8.

20 Virginio (1572–1615), Settimani nothwithstanding, is accepted by biographers as legitimate heir in spite of her liaison with Troilo. A group of young children painted by Pulzone (1550–88), reputedly Paolo's, costumed in the 1580s – well after Isabella's death – cannot be hers. See Gustavo Colonna, *Gli Orsini* (Ceschina, 1955), pl. XL. For Virginio, see Winspeare 1961, 107, 193–6; Celletti 1963, 124; and my Epilogue.

21 See text, 66.

22 He willed her the Villa Baroncelli, with a living of 7000 *scudi* to offset her taxes in Siena, 30,000 *scudi* in trust for her daughter, Francesca Orsini, and 124,000 *scudi* to Paolo to redeem pledged benefices in favour of Orsini children. Celletti 1963, 99.

23 Booth 1921, 259, and Winspeare 1961, 119–24, who quotes her pacific letter to Cardinal Ferdinando in which she emphasizes that Camilla will not be titled grand duchess, and urges filial affection for Cosimo and calm in the face of what cannot be undone.

24 Celletti 1963, 101, quoting Settimani, and see Fantoni 1994, 27. Bianca was ignored by Francesco's family and vilified by Ferdinando. See Young 1910, 622–3.

25 Booth 1921, 260–2. On Cosimo's death, see Winspeare 1961, 142 and 146ff.

26 Alidori 1995, 88.

27 Saltini 1902, 3: 619–20, quoting the *Diario Fiorentino Anonimo*. Winspeare 1961, 60, 62–3, 93, and 155, details and dispels many other scandals. See also Mignani 1993, 109.

28 See Alidori 1995, 87–90 and Mignani 1993, 108–11; see also ASF MDP 220, f. 81, (MAPD 707), dated 24 February 1564, on funding for its builders.

29 ASF, Miscellanea medicea, fil. 844 (Lettere degli Orsini agli Orsini). Winspeare 1961, 95–108 quotes several. For an official version of Isabella's end ('illness') see de' Ricci, *Cronaca (1532–1606)* (1972), 197–8, with his editor-biographer Sapori's scholarly rebuttal of it, 197n1.

30 Winspeare 1961, 175–83. On Catherine's antagonism towards the Florentine duchy and Francesco, see Eisenbichler 2003, 92–3. Troilo is principal actor in one of the ten histories painted from 1625 to 1626 for Maria de' Medici for the Luxembourg Palace: *Caterina and Charles IX Receiving Troilo Orsini, Who Brings Military Assistance from Florence*. He is in full armour. See Florence, Palazzo Pitti and Museo degli Argenti 2005, cat. no. III, 34, with colour plate and bibliography. This panel was painted by Anastasio Fuontebuoni, and is now in the Mari-Cha Collection. (Events related to Troilo – and Isabella – were to prove tragic for others. A twenty-year-old page, Torello de' Nobile in Pietro's entourage was murdered by Troilo because he was attracted to Isabella. Ricci 1972, 136–7. After Isabella's murder in 1574, Francesco directed the arrests and imprisonment of several of her retainers. Ibid., 200.)

31 Orsini, a denizen of Rome's tenderloin district early in his marriage, is mentioned in

court records. When Camilla 'the Skinny' of Siena found Orsini with Pasqua the Paduan in his friend Giuliano's bedroom, an altercation ensued; Orsini urged the women to fist-fights and hair-pulling. Subsequently, Pasqua's door was burned down in May 1559 by Camilla. Orsini was called as a witness. See Cohen and Cohen 1993, 49–64. Orsini's greater notoriety revolved around internicine slaughter and papal fury over his infatuation with Vittoria Accoramboni in the 1580s. See next note.

32 See Saltini 1902, 3: 622–3 on her death. Balis-Crema de' Medici 1946, 42, and Pieraccini 1947, 2: 174–6 accept her murder, proven in Saltini 1901, 1: 553, and 2–5: passim. See also Micheletti 1983, 126–34. See Young 1910, 606–9, and Cleugh 1975 310–12 on the Orsini-Accoramboni tragedy, and the Epilogue here for later legends and myths.

33 See Langedijk 1981, 1: 128. The term *damnatio memoriae* dates from Roman times, and was current throughout the medieval period and in sixteenth-century Italy. I thank Dr Maria Ausilia Pisano for this information.

34 Ibid., 2: cat. 63,2 (Ambras).

35 Ella Gallup Sumner and Mary Catlin Sumner Collection, 1988, inv. no. TL.41.1988, oil on panel, 110.5 × 87 cm. See University Park, PA 1987, no. 18, and cover for colour pl. I thank Drs. Jean Cadogan and Eric Zafran for useful discussion on the panel.

36 Wadsworth Atheneum Gallery, Hartford, CT, 110 × 87 cm. See New York, Piero Corsini Gallery 1986, sale cat. no. 6 and p. 28, where it is attributed to Allori by C. Volpe, as *Portrait of a Noblewoman with Her Son*, in a private European collection until 1986.

37 See New York, ibid., no. 7. Oil on panel, 46.8 × 37.8 cm. For colour pl., see University Park, PA 1987, no. 19: it came from the Goldschmidt Collection Frankfurt sale, Lepke Galerie, Berlin, 27 April 1909; Horowitz Collection, London ('Bronzino'); and Christie's, London, 29 May 1981, lot 139 ('Bronzino'). I thank Patricia Simons for alerting me to this exhibition in 1986. See Langdon 1992[1], 348–59, for my original *Isabella* identification.

38 I thank Samuel Watters of the (now defunct) Corsini Gallery for discussion on slight but discernible differences between the two; he also judged the bust-length version to be superior. Both are illustrated in colour in University Park, PA 1987, cat. cover and cat. 19.

39 See ibid., 53; Berti 1955, no. 15, pl. VIII; and Kunsthistorisches Institut, Florence, photograph no. 151634.

40 On *passementerie*, see University Park, PA 1987, 50.

41 New York, Piero Corsini Gallery 1986, 28, no. 6, citing S. Meloni Trkulja; for other examples of the carnation used in this way, see Langedijk 1981, 2: cats. 86,11 (Maria di Francesco), 110,2 (Vittoria della Rovere), and 12,14 (Bianca Cappello).

42 For the Medici arms in colour, see Litta 1899–1902, vol. 3, or title page for Conti 1893.

43 Examples are found on 67, 112, 113, 123, 154, 174. See G. Smith, 1977[2], and 1982[2], 24 for more sixteenth-century Florentine examples of the use of armorial colours in portraits.

44 Okayama 1992, 167, 200, 210; and Ripa 1988, 2: 27–8, 81, 102, and 168 (*Servitù*).

45 Goffen 1992, 124 n. 50, citing Statius, *Silvae*, I, 2: 162–9. (Christian imagery suggested that it should be shared.)

46 Rousseau 1989, 121 and 125 n. 13, citing Valeriano's *Ieroglifici* (Venice, 1602), 746.

47 Winspeare 1961, 133–4, calculated Virginio's conception.

48 See Eiche 1995, 61, pls. 1 and 3, a drawing by Jacopo Zucchi; and for more on Medici yokes, see Chap. 4 here, and notes 36, 37, 58, and 72.

49 For court mourning costume of the period, see text, 138, 142, and 281n37.

50 Overt reference to age is rare in Italy, but common in Northern portraits. See Campbell 1990, figs. 26, 33, 40, 152, 213, 214, and 235. On earlier Italian busts, where it did occur, see Schuyler 1972, 240.

51 See University Park, PA 1987, no. 18, for analysis of compositional rhythms and their expressive effect; the panel is indentified there as a Florentine noblewoman and her son.

52 See McComb 1928, 138; McCorquodale 1981, 155; and Cecchi 1996[1], 78.

53 On this, see University Park, PA 1987, cat. 50.

54 See chap. 2: for other mother-child compositions, see University Park, PA 1987, 48–9, and Baccheschi 1973, cat. 176.

55 Filipczak 1997, 128–9. See Orso Landini and Westerman Bulgarella 2001, 91, on the preciousness of kerchiefs: Nannina de' Medici received a linen kerchief elaborated with gold, and another with pearls and silver, among her wedding gifts.

56 As noted in University Park, PA 1987, 49.

57 The naturalistic illumination was noted by Wollesen-Wisch, ibid., 49.

58 A. Maggi 1995, 51–2. (Tasso's great love was Virginia Bianchi.)

59 Farago 1991, 81–2.

60 Blunt 1940, 110–11 and 121–3.

61 For Borghini's dedication to clarity and historical truth, see Scorza 1998. I thank him for sharing his manuscript before its publication.

62 On his Roman immersion, see Costamagna 1988; Langdon 1989; Lecchini Giovannoni 1991, 32–40; and Pilliod 2001, 49 and passim. Spalding 1999, 311–14, attributes Allori's abandonment of Bronzino's style to Tridentine decrees on religious art.

63 Paleotti 1971, 2: 344.

64 'non poca debolezza di mente, la quale tanto più apparisce considerandosi che quel tale non ha potuto stare meno di due o tre ore oziosamente in lasciarsi rimirare dal pittore, per fare ritrarre quella figura di corpo, che in poco spazio di tempo s'ha da risolvere in polvere per la morte.' Ibid., 334.

65 Prodi 1984, 42 n. 68, citing Palmio's letter, 30 June 1581, and Paleotti's response.

66 On the Tridentine impact on moralizing forces in society, I thank John O'Malley, SJ, who discussed with me recent interpretational shifts after his presentation 'Trent and All That' to the Reformation and Renaissance Society Colloquium, University of Toronto, 17 October 1997.

67 Zapperi 1990, 85–6, commenting on private conclusions made by the Spanish Dominican Alfonso Chacon in letters to Lavinia Fontana, 1578–9.

68 See Zapperi, ibid.

69 See Gaston 1983, and Brock 2002, 292–4, for responses by Raffaello Borghini (1584) to the nude female portraits in Bronzino's *Christ in Limbo*, Santa Croce, of 1552. See Hauser 1951, 122–3, on Andrea Gilio's *Dialogo degli errori dei pittori* (1564) concerning Michelangelo's *Last Judgment*, on decorum and nudity in biblical contexts, and on responses to these in the aftermath of the Council of Trent, 'the birthday of prudery.'

70 See 213n44; on Armenini and Leonardo, see Williams 1997, 97 and passim.

71 Sotheby's cat., London, 28 October 1987, lot no. 121 (88 × 71 cm). I thank Julien Stock of Sotheby's, London and Rome, for his comments. On another *Isabella*, see n. 94.

72 Altered settings arose because of Cosimo's acquisition of precious stones, recorded with great frequency in his letters. One dated 23 June 1561 records a ruby purchased for

16,000 *scudi* (about $480,000 U.S. today) and a pendant with an oriental emerald. ASF MDP 211, f. 136 (MAPD 1305) see also Florence, Palazzo Pitti 2003, 24–35 and passim.

73 See Saslow 1996[2], 62–3, on *velluto verde*'s exclusiveness and costliness.

74 See n. 43 for other examples or armorial colours in Medici women's portraits.

75 'Di più, nei ritratti di persone di grado e dignità dovriano i patroni procurare che fossero espressi con la gravità e decoro che conviene alla conditione loro, e non con cagnuoli o fiori o ventarole in mano, non con uceletti o pappagalli o bertuccie appresso ...' Paleotti 1971, 2: 340. In sixteenth-century portraits, exotic pets could signal the sitter's identity as a courtesan. See Rogers ed. 2000, 92 and n. 7. Carpaccio's courtesans appear with lapdogs and a parrot in attendance, and 'pappagallo' (parrot), argot for 'lascivious one,' was used to describe Alessandro de' Medici. See D.R. Wright 1976, 2: 248–9.

76 The panel is signed and dated. Lecchini Giovannoni 1991, cat. no. 32, refers to other Allori examples of 1574 and 1576. Its iconography suggests a marriage, possibly that of Pietro to Dianora de' Toledo in April 1571. (See chap. 7).

77 For the parrot and *Eloquenza*, see Ripa in Okayama 1992, 320–9. For Vasari's *Eloquenza*, see Rubin 1995, fig. 20. For Clouet, see Paris 1996, 92–3, pl. 5 (*Marguerite*) and fig. 62 (*Francis as John the Baptist*).

78 In San Fortunato, Rimini; see Rubin 1995, fig. 47; Vasari mentions it in his own *Vita*.

79 On Veronese's brush with the Inquisition and his response, see Hauser 1951, 2: 122.

80 Ovid, *Met.*, 14; *Odyssey* 10; Ripa 1970, 2: 378; Ripa 1988, 2: 101.

81 The breed *cani bolognesi* were sought by Cosimo III to be given to Flemish female dignitaries. See C. Murphy 1997, 119 and 274. (Pepys, witnessing Charles II's repatriation in 1660 saw him as foppish because his familiars were small, yapping, King Charles terriers.)

82 Among others, Titian's *Federico II Gonzaga*, 1525, appears to warmly greet a lapdog.

83 On fidelity, carnality, and fertility in Van Eyck's *Arnolfini Marriage*, see Harbison 1990, 264.

84 A lapdog was also Potiphar's lustful wife's familiar. It lurks beneath her leg and underneath the bed in Bronzino's tapestry scene; see Cecchi 1996[1], colour pl. 53. It is her alter ego in Dirk Volckertsz Coornhert's engraving after Heemskerck (1549), where it straddles her thigh, echoing her fury and snarling at the fleeing Joseph. See Aston 1993, fig. 69.

85 Stevens 1995, 655 and fig. 5. Borromeo wrote the *Instructiones Fabricae et Supellectilis Ecclesiasticae* 1573. (See Barocchi ed. 1960–2, 3: 7–113.) See text, 18, 137, and 279n2, on his familiarity with the Medici.

86 Saslow 1996[2], nos. 85 and 86, 228–9, and see Okayama 1992, 210; and Ripa 1988, 2: 101. In Isaac Oliver's 1590s Arcadian scene, a 'respectable' couple happen on revellers only to have their dog set upon by a bare-breasted wanton's tiny lapdog. See Strong 2000, colour pl. 188–9.

87 In less elevated contexts, the joys of physical love and fertility could be made more explicit. In Allori's *Young Man with a Statue of Ceres* of 1561, a youth smiles and points to a flower-decked altar to Ceres, where *ignudi* make offerings. (See Costamagna 1988 [as Zucchi's], no. 34.) Baring her breasts, she pats a besotted, wreathed billy goat – *Libidine*'s familiar – who nestles against her. A 'chiselled' date and proferring of a ring to Ceres probably commemorates a marriage. For Ripa's *Libidine*, see Okayama 1992, 160.

88 For the Dijon panel and *Hercules and the Muses* (Uffizi, 40 × 29.5 cm), see Lecchini Giov-

annoni 1991, nos. 18 and 23. For the *Allegory of Human Life* (Uffizi, 37 × 27 cm) see ibid., no. 191, which agrees with Langedijk's dating of this piece as about 1564.

89 See Pieraccini 1986, 2: 101, and Lapini 1906, 133–4.

90 Medici patronage of the image was long-standing – an altar to it was commissioned from Michelozzo in 1448. Monopoly of the shrine in Cosimo's reign expressed the *magico-sacrale* of Medici sovereignty, and devotion to it was raised to a national cult on his elevation to grand duke in 1569. See Winspeare 1961, 84; Ważbiński 1985; Fantoni 1989, 771–5, and 1999, 269; see text, 106. Francesco had Allori paint replicas for Carlo Borromeo and for Philip II. See Mulcahy 2004, 76, and fig. 2.15, a version by Allori commissioned in 1584. The image also served to promote the doctrine of the Immaculate Conception, emphasizing Mary's purity in the context of the Tridentine decree on original sin. Ważbiński 1985, 546 n. 26.

The Medici co-opted the aura surrounding the cult by reorganizing processional routes through Via dei Servi to the church. Its miraculous efficacy was famous: when more replicas were sent to the Spanish court in 1589, Giulio Battaglio reported that everyone at the Escorial was 'in an emotional state' over them. See Goldberg 1996, 111 and fig. 5; and Mulcahy 2004, fig. 2.16.

91 Langedijk 1981, 2: cat. 76,13. Family likeness may account for these mis-identifications; also, the Ambras miniatures are on card and are hardly masterpiece works.

92 Florence, Poggio Imperiale. Ibid., 2: cat. 63,1: Raffaello Borghini 1584, 622, listed an *Isabella* by Santi di Tito – probably the oval Poggio Imperiale panel (fig. 51 here), as a bust-length portrait in oval of Isabella is recorded in the 1621 inventory. (Langedijk 1981, 1: 128.) Langedijk 1981, 2: cat. 63,1, links it to Butteri's altarpiece, *St Catherine with Members of the Medici Family* (ibid., cats. 27,39 and 63,6).

93 See Langedijk 1981, 2: cats. 63,2 (Ambras) and 63,3 (Uffizi, Tribuna, a fresco fragment removed in 1871). Heikamp 1953–6, 133, noted confusion of Bianca Cappello with Medici women.

94 One in a private collection, inscribed 'ISABELLA DE MEDICI,' oil on oak, 29 × 22.3 cm, is typical of those in Medici family sets. She is dressed in a dark green *zimarra* over a bright red, gold-embroidered dress close to the style of the *Lucrezia*, ca. 1559–60 (pl. 10). The owner's conservation reports confirm that the 'prettified' face and long ringlets were added; they are in canons typical of the eighteenth century. Unaltered areas suggest Allori's hand. Possibly its prototype *Isabella* recorded her wedding, or was painted as a keepsake in anticipation of her expected departure after her marriage to Orsini's seat at Bracciano – as proposed for the 1558–9 *Lucrezia* (fig. 45).

95 Poggio a Caiano, Inv. no. 63, 96 × 70 cm; Langedijk 1981, 2: no. 63,4a. For a fundamental study of its musicological status and its musical notation, and for female musicians in Italian sixteenth-century cultural contexts, see Cardamone 2002.

96 Langedijk 1981, 2: cat. 63,4d, then in the Villa d'Este, Tivoli. McComb 1928, 122, cited the Pitti panel (fig. 54 here) as its source; another evident derivative is the *Isabella with Music* at Poggio a Caiano (fig. 52 here).

97 See 244n55 on the Prague *Eleonora* and return of Duchess Bianca Cappello's robes of state and jewellery from Allori's workshop. Also, Maria Salviati's head was 'worked-up' from the death cast in Medici holdings. (See figs. 5, 9, and 14.)

98 See Rubin 1995, 394, on his sense of inadequacy in portraiture.

99 Langedijk 1981, 2: cat. 63,4.

100 For Eleonora's patronage of Bronzino's portraiture, see Edelstein 2001 and Cox-Rearick and Westerman Bulgarella 2004.

101 Payments made by Cosimo to Allori on her behalf in 1567 suggest that she personally
directed commissions. See ASF MDP 221, f. 33 (MAPD 1143).

102 See text and n. 106 below.

103 See Saltini 1902, 4: 209–11, and Winspeare 1961, 85–8. (Cosimo patronized archaeology, an endeavour intended to demonstrate Tuscany's historical superiority. See
Young 1910, 567.)

104 Saltini, ibid., 209–11.

105 Ibid., 209. Further, especially on Isabella's musical career and patronage of composers,
see Cardamone 2002.

106 Saltini, ibid., 209–13.

107 Ibid., 209; see also Winspeare 1961, 91–2. Tasso, an Estense retainer, was frequently
stricken with mental illness and privately circulated his unpublished poetry among
friends.

108 See de Logu and Marinelli 1975, 2: fig. 18, evidently by Allori.

109 On Tasso's Counter-Reformation ideology, see Quint 1990, 1–29.

110 Saltini 1902, 4: 213. The Crusca's emblem was a sieve. Fantoni 1999, 256, sees its founding as the crowning Medici contribution to the arts, extending into the fields of science, historiography, music, linguistic study, theatre, and the staging of public
spectacle.

111 Domenico Maria Manni's *Lezione di lingua toscana* (Florence: 1767 and Venice: 1768)
quotes it in full; also Saltini 1902, 4: 209–11.

112 Weinberg 1961, 1: 553. Her role in the Alterati is discussed in chap. 7, 177–8.

113 See Woodall 1997, 24, on its importance in literary theory and criticism.

114 Eleonora moved the Order to Pisa (1548–9) and Florence (1551). See chap. 4, 136.

115 'Un *Aristotele* corretto,' recorded 13 August. ASF MDP 188, f. 85 (MAPD 892).

116 His *Annotazione* of 1575 notes Vincenzo Maggi's *In partem poetices Aristotelis*, 1546, and
In De Poetica Communes Explanationes, 1560; Robortello's *Explicationes*, 1548, dedicated
to Charles V, Henry II, and Cosimo, printed by Torrentino, the ducal press; and Pier
Vettori's *Commentarii* of 1560, to Cosimo and Alfonso d'Este, printed by Giunti. See
Weinberg 1961, 1: 543. See Nencioni 1983, 693–4 on the enormous output of works in
the Tuscan vernacular from the ducal presses, and Ricci 2001, 103–19, on Torrentino
and the duke's cultural program.

117 Weinberg 1961, 2: 847–52, who notes the moral and theological bent of Vincenzo
Borghini's writings. On Vasari's dependence on Borghini, see Rubin 1995, 197.
     Decorum is discussed in other contemporary literary treatises. Carlo Sigonio's *De
Dialogo Liber* (Venice 1562) insisted that all matters relative to the dialogue must 'obey
above all else the laws of decorum and of verisimilitude.' His whole theory for the
genre is framed as a theory of decorum, which 'is based at once in observation of persons, times, places, and causes, and in keeping one's attention on them.' The ends
again are reduced to one, to convince the reader of the truth of what is being said.
Weinberg 1961, 1: 485.

118 Woodall 1997, 24 and n. 15.

119 In the *Trattato della poetica* Platonism is avoided. Weinberg 1961, 1: 494. For Aristotle in
Varchi's *paragone* discourse, see Barzman 1991, 38–40.

120 Haar 1986, 111.

121 Goldstein 1988, 82–5. For the intense interest in anatomy, and annual dissections at the hospital of Santa Maria Nuova, see Goldstein 1975, 146; Dempsey 1981, 552–69; Barzman 1989, 14–15, 20; and Rubin 1996, 212–15. On Allori's role from its founding, see Lecchini Giovannoni 1991, 51–61 and 65–81; Pilliod 2001; and Barzman 2001, 177–88.

122 See text, 8, 37, 45, 58, and 228n94 for Cosimo's admiration of Giovio. Cristoforo degli Altissimi was employed as copyist in Giovio's collection, in the early 1550s at a princely rate of five ducats per portrait. (ASF MDP 201, f. 16 MAPD 1699. Giovio also influenced Vasari's inclusion of portraits in his *Vite*.) For Cosimo's patronage of portraiture, see Hollingsworth 1996, 72 and 238–72.

123 See text, 36, where Vasari 'tutors' Francesco in his *Ragionamenti* on them.

124 The printing of engraved portraits effected a further expansion of portraiture in the 1600s.

125 Eleonora's nostalgia for performances *alla napolitana* confirms her love of music of a lighter vein. See Butchart 1985, 363–4: Francesco Susena, the Este retainer who remained in Florence after Lucrezia's 1558 marriage, reported in January 1559 that Orsini's musicians amused Lucrezia and Isabella by singing *napolitane* to the lute; eight days later, they entertained Eleonora nightly at Pisa during her recovery from illness.

126 I thank Donna Cardamone who, on being alerted to the portrait, investigated its musical notation. See Cardamone 2002.

127 See Minor and Mitchell 1968, 39–40; Haar 1986, 53, 66–7, and 105; and Winn 1981, 136–49, who credits the impact of Pietro Bembo (1470–1547) and Italian poets with its largely secular, Neopetrarchan development. *Canzoni* exhibit deeply affective musical structures such as 'word-painting' through contrasts of pitch, expressive intervals, musical punning, evocative rhythm, and high-low harmony to express irony, paradox, antitheses, or emotional conflict. Winn sees this development in music as comparable to rhetorical structures in poetry and literature.

128 Kaufmann 1972, 161–88. See Cardamone 2002, 5, on Cosimo's early court musicians.

129 See Cardamone 1996, 110, and 2002.

130 Leonora Orsini helped establish a *concerto di donne* in Rome in 1588, and Virginio became a notable patron of music later. Einstein 1971, 2: 661 and 667; and Kirkendale 1993. For a portrait and brief biography of Virgina in maturity, ca. 1610–15, see Florence, Palazzo Pitti and Museo degli Argenti 2005, cat. no. II, 14, artist unknown.

131 Kirkendale 1993, 70–5 and passim. When Cosimo died in 1574, Francesco became a generous patron to Striggio – who eventually introduced the madrigal to the English court.

132 See Butchart 1985, 366 n. 28. Madrigal books by Stefano Rossetti and Maddalena Casulana were dedicated to Isabella, and Giovampier Manenti and Antonio Pace eulogized her in individual madrigals. See Pescerelli 1979, 7–8 and passim, on Casulana's dedication and on the female 'voice' in madrigal texts. See Pirrotta 1983, 48, on Rossetti's dedications.

133 Simone Fortuna, undated letter ca. 1573. See Saltini 1902, 4: 209–11 and 218.

134 Bacharach and Pearce eds. 1977, 446–7, and see note above. The late-sixteenth-century madrigal could be unabashedly extrovert or even flagrantly sensuous. Towne 1996, 270–1.

135 Haar 1986, 111.

136 Ibid., 67 and 120–1. Musicians linked to the court were Philippe Verdelot, Jacques Arcadelt, and Costanzo Festa. Cardamone 2004, 6, names several others.

137 Rore's secular *canzoni* are infused with rhetorical, declamatory elements. Haar 1986, 120. (Rore, Lasso, Wert, and Monte were published from the 1550s. Butchart 1985, 366 n. 36.)

138 Butchart 1985, 364, also referring to Willaert (1490–1562); and see Einstein 1971, 2: 761ff.

139 See n. 125. Striggio juxtaposed *villanesche* with serious madrigal elements in a *serenata* in his *Primo libro de madrigali a sei voci*, published 1560. Einstein 1971, 2: 767.

140 Saltini 1902, 4: 219, found this at odds with her scholarly nature. They included frankly hedonistic, vividly emotive, and titillating burlesque forms. Haar 1986, 124.

141 His comment was made in 1587. See Haar 1986, 125.

142 See n. 75. See Mortari 1992, pl. 127: Salviati's youth grasps a tiny struggling nude.

143 Flora signifies Florence, and may play on Isabella's *impresa*, a cornucopia. Einstein 1971, 2: 498–9, from Filippo di Monte, *Il primo libro de' madrigali a sei voci di M. Filippo di Monte* (Venice, 1569), which Einstein believes was dedicated to Paolo Orsini.

144 Dedicated to Ferdinando Medici. See Einstein, ibid., 499–500 and 502–9.

145 My trans. Einstein 1971, 2: 509, from di Monte, *Il secondo libro de' madrigali a cinque voci* (Venice, 1567).

146 See Langedijk 1981, 2: cat. nos. 63,8, 9, and 11.

147 Reference to Isabella as a deity of fruitfulness in the river valley of her chosen city was used also to personify Margaret of Austria, ca. 1539, by the Sienese warrior-poetess Laudomia Forteguerri (1515–55), when Margaret, Duke Alessandro's young widow, departed for Rome to marry Ottavio Farnese. See Eisenbichler 2001, 285. I thank him for sharing the unpublished poem.

148 Einstein 1971, 2: 645: *Il primo libro de' madrigali a sei voci ... Ded. Donna Isabella de Medici Orsina. Firenze, 22. V. 1566* (Venice, 1566).

149 *Lamento di Olimpia di Stefano Rossetto ... All' illustrissima et eccellentiss. Signora, la Donna Isabella de' Medici Orsina Duchessa di Bracciano* (1567). For the *Lamento*'s stanzas, drawn from Ariosto, *Orlando Furioso* (10: 19–34), see Einstein 1971; see esp. Cardamone 2002, 16.

150 See the 'Villanella in Praise of Isabella' in Pompilio Venturi, *Il secondo libro delle villanelle a tre voci ...* (Venice, 1571), which praises her as an immortal goddess. See Cardamone 2002, 16.

151 The column format preserves the original metrical form. Cardamone 2002, 9–12, who analyses the composition's *arioso*-style lute intabulation, where rhythmically affective gestures mounting in range and intensity evoke love's power to alter one's state of mind. In the Medici courtier Francesco Bottegari's madrigal arrangements, it is listed as 'di Autore incerto,' but is amended to 'Id est S[ignor]a Isab[ell]a Medici'. Ibid., supporting her authorship, and see Raney 1971, 307.

152 Luca Marenzio's sensuous madrigals for Grand Duchess Bianca in 1585 include his 'Stringeami Galatea'; see Einstein 1971, 2: 646, who gives it historical primacy for its obscenity.

153 Louise Labé's twenty-four sonnets, e.g., introduced by one written in Italian, reworked the Petrarchan tradition into a wider range of speaking postures. See Roussel 1997, 997–8.

154 See Haar 1986, 111.

155 See Cardamone 1996, 110–11, and 2002, 3–4.

156 Saltini 1902, 4: 209.

157 Cardamone 2002, n. 53: Medici historians credit her with a 'raccoltina' of madrigals.

158 Oil on panel, 95 × 77.5 cm. Private coll., England. Slim 2002[1]; Berti 1993, 136–7; Rogers ed., 2000, 91–105; and Florence, Palazzo Pitti 2002, no. 122.

159 Vasari 1878–85, 4: 465. See Haar 1986, 104, on Barbara's performances.

160 Slim 2001[1], 459–63, analyses the inscriptions from Ovid and Petrarch, and notes that Machiavelli referred to his love for Barbara in a letter to Guicciardini of 3 January 1526. Its Latin inscriptions are from the Song of Songs, the 9th book of the *Aeneid*, and the *Metamorphoses*. See also Rogers ed., 2000, 94 and 101.

161 Slim 2002[1] 462–7.

162 Ibid., 465–6: Machiavelli refers to other lovers before he conquered her heart.

163 See Cardamone 1996, 112, citing also Austern 1989, 420–8; and Cardamone 2002, 12–13. Ann McNeil alerted me to the lute as *Carne*/Sensuality's attribute in *La Centaura*, Giovan Battista Andreini's play dedicated to Maria de' Medici (1622), and to its many instances as symbol of lasciviousness in carnival music. These associations endured: Rosenthal 1998, expounds on Gainsborough's *Ann Ford* (1760), whose father had her arrested and confined to prevent her performing music in public.

164 Vasari 1878–85, 4: 467.

165 'Psyche's Lament,' for example, in an *intermezzo* to Francesco d'Ambra's comedy *La Cofanaria*, for Francesco and Giovanna's wedding (1565), brought the audience close to tears. M. Brown 1972, 13. For novelty-seeking elements in madrigal development, see Haar 1986, 107.

166 As interlocutor in Allori's *Ragionamenti*, Bronzino rules on proportion, life drawing, and anatomical structures, reflecting Juan Valverde's *Historia de la composición del corpo humano* of 1556, published in Italian in 1560. Barzman 1989, 22. Allori's drawing *Anatomical Man*, showing muscular systems, is quoted from Vesalius's *De Humani corporis fabrica*, 1543. See Goldstein 1988, 62, and figs. 29 and 33. For his drawings, see Uffizi, GDSU 10263F and 10306F; Lecchini Giovannoni 1988, figs. 18 and 19, and 1991, 309–11 on figs. 432–40.

167 Vasari 1878–85, 7: 607. Allori's teacher was Varchi's nephew, the physician Alessandro Menchi. Michelangelo's admirer Vincenzo Danti's *Primo Libro del trattato delle perfette proporzioni* (1567) drew on Galen and Valverde. Cadavers were made available to Allori for dissection. See Barzman 1989, 21–2, and esp. 30 n. 58, on Allori's valiant endurance of the stench and loathsomeness of his environment, a room off the cloister of San Lorenzo where he worked on cadavers.

168 See Rubin 1995, 214.

169 ASF MDP 4906, f. 82r., 83v. and 84r., dated 7 August 1576, from Ambassador Baccio Orlandini in Madrid, expressing his affection for Isabella and horror at her death. I am indebted to Edward Goldberg for alerting me to this exchange on the deaths of Isabella and, five days before, of Dianora de' Medici (see 298–9n58). (Isabella's death was given officially as the result of an epileptic seizure. Winspeare 1961, 159.)

170 See Arditi 1970, 69, 109–10, and 164. See Winspeare 1961, 60ff., on her affair and possible children left in the orphanage of the Innocenti. (Records often coded parental names, with donations of lands made to offset expenses. Philip Gavitt to Gabrielle

Langdon, 13–15 February 2002.) See Mortadini 1965 for Troilo's diplomatic briefs to the court in 1574, and nn. 27–30 above for the affair.

171 Saltini 1902, 6: 188–9, from the Archivio di Stato, Modena, Cancelleria Ducale, dispacci da Firenze.

172 Cantagalli (ed.) in Arditi 1970, 110–11. Elicona was the nickname for the poet-improviser and antiquarian Giovan Battista Tedaldi, translator of *The Iliad* and valued member of Isabella's household. Morgante was Cosimo's dwarf court jester from the early years, a family retainer who was held in great affection and respect. (See text, 98.)

173 See Fraser 1992, 229; for Alessandro, see 42, and 231–2n140. Across the courts of Europe, Isabella's death was not accepted as accidental, as Francesco was advised by Filippo Cavriano, one of his ambassadors at the French court. See Winspeare 1961, 171–3.

The harrowing description of her death and postmortem appearance suggest that she died of asphyxiation by manual strangulation. For forensic information, see Simpson 1979, 91–104. Death can occur within five minutes. The outstanding postmortem appearance is venous congestion and cyanosis with pronounced lividity, i.e., bluish-grey colour of the face. If this did extend to Isabella's waist, she was bruised by further injuries inflicted on her by Orsini. (Pieraccini found no evidence of rumoured epilepsy, but convulsions do occur before death in asphyxiation. See Simpson, ibid.) Pieraccini 1986, 2: 178–9, concludes that she was probably murdered but had not seen the Ferrarese ambassador's account. (Cerreto Guidi is open to the public. The legend that Orsini hanged his wife with a noose dropped through the dining-room ceiling by an accomplice is abetted by a noose there now. The momentous account here, however, makes no mention of the ligature marks typical of hanging.)

174 For a graphic view of *Mastro Pasquino*, see Misson 1695, 1: opp. p. 54, and for useful references to *statue parlanti*, see Shearman 1992, 46n56. Ferdinando had to contain more than one Medici scandal. He was exasperated by scurrilous lampoons expressed in an epigram current in Rome, 'Il medico cavalca la mula del Farnese' ('The *medico* [Ferdinando] rides the Farnese mule,' i.e., bastard, referring to Clelia Farnese, Cardinal Farnese's daughter). Winspeare 1961, 159 and 162, citing ASF Carte Strozziane, serie I, f. 28.

175 Orsini did not murder Isabella to free him to marry Vittoria Accoramboni – they met a few years after her death. See Winspeare 1961, 184–96; and see the Epilogue, 194–5.

176 Reference to a portrait of Isabella by Bronzino in the inventories of 1560 is almost certainly to the original (dated around 1553–4) for the Stockholm copy, probably too late for inclusion in the 1553 inventory. For the 1560 entry, see Beck 1974^1, 66; Beck 1974^2, 62, and see Beck 1972, 10; and Florence, Palazzo Pitti 2003, cat. 13, for the 1595 entry.

177 Langedijk 1981, 2: 128.

178 On Francesco's duplicity in Isabella's death, see Winspeare 1961, 16.

179 Young 1910, 618–23. Francesco was buried with Giovanna of Austria. Confusion of Isabella and Bianca's identities discussed in the text may be due to a common *damnatio*.

180 On Queen Katherine Howard, see Fraser 1992, opposite p. 338; and, on Anne, 424.

181 See Zapperi 1990, 85–6.

182 Langedijk 1981, 2: cat. nos. 85,5a (based on fig. 37 here) and 76,5a (based on fig. 41. here).

183 Langedijk 1981, 2: cats. 63,4 (Palazzo Pitti) and 63,4a (Poggio a Caiano). Her 63,4d (Tivoli, fig. 67 here) was identified from the latter.

184 Ibid., 1: 137–8.

185 See Langedijk 1981, passim, for Ambras portraits of Cosimo's family.

186 Vasari 1878–85, 7: 603. The set appears in the 1553 inventory. See Baccheschi 1973, nos. 134–57.

187 Borghini 1584, 622; see Langedijk 1981, 2: 63,7, on this lost portrait by Santi. Isabella is believed to be included in Butteri's Medici–*Sacra conversazione* altarpiece, 1575, lower left; see Langedijk 1981, 1: cat. 27,39 and 2: 63,6); see also Cox-Rearick 1992, 261 and fig. 163.

188 See the Epilogue for some authors of this mythology.

189 The miniature of Pietro de' Medici, whose sorry life is discussed in chap. 7, remains in place in the Medici set with the other six ducal children. See pl. 8, end of series.

190 The Latin inscription on the cushion is from Catullus, *Carmina* 22: 20. I thank Dr Maria Ausilia Pisano for her translation. I thank Prof. Christopher Brown for useful discussion on his translation from the Greek inscription 'Record of my friend Alessandro Allori in the year 1580,' and its possible import with regard to the identity of the painter. Christie's 1971, lot. 18, describes the portrait as Allori, *Portrait of a Scholar*. Lecchini Giovannoni 1991, cat. 197, rejects Allori as the artist, but proposes that he is the subject. If a comparison is made of the inscription on the cushion with the inscription on Isabella's kerchief (fig. 47) painted by Allori in 1574, a strong case is made for accepting his hand in each painting. The subject is certainly Allori. His high forehead, long nose, large eyes, and his moustache resemble the marred, frescoed face of Allori in the *Martyrdom of San Lorenzo* (see Cox-Rearick 1993, fig. 143), but here he is balder. If we have here a self-portrait, which seems likely, the only explanation for the inscription 'Record of my friend Alessandro Allori' would be that this was intended – perhaps even requested – as an autographed endorsement on the panel on the occasion of being the artist's gift to another.

191 Bronzino, who supported his extended family and Alessandro's, lived in a tiny room on present-day Via Calzaiuoli, distracted by an intolerable and ceaseless din of artisan activity through all hours of the day and night, as expressed in his poem 'I romori.' See Parker 2000, 10, 17, 35, 69 and passim, and Pilliod 2001, 103. Allori's retirement to his villa was implicitly viewed as well deserved, after his recorded four years of diligent study of cadavers, in horrific surroundings. See Barzman 1989, 30 n. 58.

Chapter 7

An earlier version of this chapter, 'A Medici Miniature: Juno, and a Woman with "Eyes in Her Head Like Two Stars in Their Beauty,"' appeared in 2001. Thomas Jefferson University Press kindly allowed me to draw on that material. I am grateful to my former editors, Sheryl Reiss and David Wilkins, for refinements to it that may be reflected here. For examination of the miniature, see n. 67.

1 'era di età di anni ventuno, bella, graziosa, gentile, garbata, leggiadra, alla mano, e sopra tutto aveva due occhi in testa, che di belezza paraggiavono due stelle.' The diarist Lapini, 1906, 191, following her death during the night of 10–11 July 1576. (On her death, Dianora (1553–76) was actually twenty-three.)

2 She is the second of Saltini's 'Due Principesse,' incomplete on his death, but see Piccracini 1986, 2: 185–214 (Pietro); Winspeare 1961 (Isabella); and Guerrazzi 1845 (Isabella).

3 See Langedijk 1981, 1: cat. series 36.

4 Madrid, Colección Thyssen-Bornemisza, Inv. DEC0620 (formerly K112), oil on silver, in silver-gilt frame, enamelled in black and white, and set with blue stones and green glass doublets, 5.5 × 4 cm, frame 8 × 6.3 cm, formerly in the collection of Peter Bodmer, Zürich, acquired from Julius Böhler of Munich in 1975. (See Anonymous 1975, and Böhler sale cat., October–November 1975, no. 7.) See also Florence, Palazzo Pitti 2003, no. 15.

5 On Medici propaganda, see studies by Barocchi 1998; Cecchi 1991 and 1998; Cox-Rearick 1984, 1987, 1993, and 2002; Crum 2001[1]; Eisenbichler ed. 2001; Fantoni 1994 and 1999; Feinberg 1991 and 2002; Goldberg 1983, 1988, and 1996; Jacks ed. 1998; Starn and Partridge 1992; Rousseau 1983 and 1990; Rubin 1995; Scorza 1981 and 1988; Van Veen 1986 and 1998; and Williams 1988 and 1998. The list is not exhaustive.

6 Schaffers-Bodenhausen and Tiethoff-Spliethoff 1993, 37. See text below.

7 See Pointon 2001, 48.

8 Bury 1989, 87–8, citing de Hollanda, *Do tirar polo naturel* (1549), dialogue XI.

9 Vasari 1878–95, 7: 568–9. Miniaturists were in demand by royalty. Riding 1996, 43. Nicholas Hilliard opined that *miniatura* 'tendeth not to comon mens use ... none should medle with limning but gentlemen.' On the genre's private nature, see Ledes 1989, 1244, and below.

10 Sofonisba Anguissola's life-size *Elizabeth of Valois, Queen of Spain*, Prado, Madrid, ca. 1570, holds a miniature of her husband Philip II in her right hand.
     Intimate viewing is expressed in Isaac Oliver's miniature *Youth Surrounded by Flames* – signifying ardour – ca. 1585, who extends a pendant miniature of a woman in his hand; his *déshabillé* is telling. See Cuadrado 1991, 42, 46, and 54; and Pointon 2001, figs. 26 and 27. On Bronzino's *Ludovico Capponi* (fig. 56) see text. Cosimo kept 'little modern pictures, the rarest miniatures' with precious objects in his study, and Vasari praised a Bronzino *Francesco* worked 'with such diligence that it appears as a miniature.' Vasari 1878–85, 7: 603.

11 Schaffers-Bodenhausen and Tiethoff-Spliethoff 1993, 37. The decorative portrait miniature – as opposed to the larger-format 'cabinet' miniature – was not exhibited. Finsten 1979, 1: 1–2; Williamson and Buckman 1926, 3–9; and London 1982–3, exh. cat., no. 61, a watercolour-on-ivory oval of Queen Charlotte in a gold frame, surrounded by pearls. In Italy oil was used on metal; watercolour on an ivory or vellum support was common in the North.

12 On a husband or lover's response to a portrait, see Shearman 1992, chap. 3; Land 1994, 85; and Goffen 1992, 111 and 117. A talismanic association with miniatures endured: Lord Nelson died wearing a miniature of Lady Hamilton around his neck. Riding 1996, 43.

13 New York, Frick Collection, oil on panel, 116.5 × 86 cm. Its miniature is inscribed 'SORTE' (Fate/Destiny). See Brock 2002, 141 and 143. Ludovico, secretly betrothed to Maddalena, married her in 1559. See 270n126.

14 Shearman 1992, 118. See Land 1994, 81–97, for talismanic properties for portraits in Bembo's, della Casa's, and Aretino's poetry. See also Tinagli 1997, 85, and n. 42 below.

15 De Hollanda 1868, 340. Vasari asserted that Pontormo's half-folio study for his *Alessandro de' Medici* was so exceptional that 'the works of miniaturists cannot compare with it, since beyond being a good likeness, there is in this head everything that could be desired in the rarest painting.' Vasari 1878–85, 6: 278. For this, see Strehlke 2004, cat. 25.

16 Medals are not comparable. Made in multiples and being durable, they passed from
   hand to hand. (See Jones 1979, 7–8 and 29; and Hill 1978, 13–14.) See n. 10 on intimate
   decorum and the viewing of miniatures, and especially Finsten 1979, passim and fig.
   95; and London 1982–3 exh. cat., no. 63, for example, a watercolour on ivory of Queen
   Charlotte, which is fragile and tiny; see Pointon 2001, 48, on 'container' forms. Langedijk 1981, 1: cat. 12,35 records 'Uno scatolino col ritratto della Granduchessa Bianca'
   painted in the 1580s, in Don Antonio's estate, 1621. Uniqueness is typical – copies are
   very rare. A detailed history of the genre in Italy has yet to appear, but see Meloni 1994,
   625–8. For Clovio's *Eleonora of Toledo* of 1551, see Simon 1989, 481–5; Langdon 1992[1] 1:
   207, 223, 234, and 243–5; Costamagna 1992, 168–75 (including a Clovio *Francesco*); and
   Cox-Rearick 1993, 264 fig. 165.
17 Cuadrado 1991, 54. Hilliard prescribed the length and number of sittings, six hours in
   total. Edward Norgate's *Miniatura*, 1620, advises: '[B]e ready and sudden to catch at
   and steal your observations and to express them with a quick and constant hand.'
   Money 1984, 108–9.
18 Heikamp 1975, cat. no. 7, proposed Lucrezia, who married Alfonso d'Este in 1558, and
   linked the miniature to the Vienna, Kunsthistorisches Museum, Inv. no. 2583, 114.5 ×
   89.5 cm, 1973 cat. no. 5 (pl. 16 here), once identified as Anna di Francesco, who died
   unmarried in 1584 at the age of fifteen. As the obverse Juno allegory implies marriage,
   Anna is not the miniature's subject. Baccheschi 1973, cat. 174, describes the Vienna
   panel as a Medici princess. Langedijk 1981, 2: cat. 85.6 (and see Florence, Palazzo Pitti
   2003, 46–7), proposed Maria di Cosimo, but she had grey-blue eyes; Lucrezia had very
   dark eyes and hair (pls. 7 and 10). Maria died in 1557, Lucrezia in 1561, but this woman
   is dressed in early 1570s style, as noted by Somers Cocks and Truman in Sotheby's
   1984, 76–7. Virginia di Cosimo (1568–1615) has been tentatively proposed by Langedijk
   1981, 2: cat. 109,6; and see Florence, Palazzo Pitti 2003, cat. 15, p. 76, following Hackenbroch 1975, 31–4, and 1979, 35–6, who tied the Juno allegory to Buontalenti's set design
   for the fifth intermezzo of Giovanni Bardi's *L'Amico fido*, performed to celebrate Virginia's wedding in 1589. But Somers Cocks and Truman, ibid., 76, found that three of
   Juno's attendants, Comet, Rain, and Dew, did not coincide with any in *Day, Night,* and
   the *Seasons* in Bardi's intermezzo; also, as the subject's 1570s costume style was popular
   when Virginia (b. 1568) was a young child, this is not her. (It may be compared to that
   in Allori's *Isabella with Virginio*, dated 1574, pl. 11).
19 Anon., panel on paper, 13.5 × 10.5 cm, Vienna, Kunsthistorisches Museum, inscribed:
   'LEONORA / VXOR DI PIERO / MEDIC/CE' [*sic*]; and, reverse: '(E)leonora di
   toled(o) (mo)glie di s do Pie(tre) (M)edicci' [*sic*]; see Langedijk 1981, 1: cat. 36,4; a
   three-quarter version, cat. 36,6, by Francesco Brina, Museo Stibbert, Florence; and
   ibid., cat. 36,6b, where she is pregnant, perhaps late 1572 (fig. 58 here). For her only
   child, Cosimino's birth, 10 February 1573, see ASF MDP 5088, c. 14 and Saltini 1898,
   183–4. Florence, Palazzo Pitti 2003, no. 15, challenges my identification of the miniature with the inscribed '*Dianora*' in the Ambras Collection on which Langedijk bases
   her identifications of other Dianora portraits (Langedijk 1981, 1: 36,4), and the drawings and iconographical links set out in Langdon 2001. Identification with Virginia
   d'Este by Hackenbroch in 1975 and the *apparato* personifications for her wedding were
   proposed to lend support to the identification in spite of Somers Cocks and Truman's
   analysis that disproved this. (See n. 18 above.) Giovanna of Austria is not a likely

identification, either: she was blue-eyed. See Langedijk 1981, 2: cats. 52,1–36 for her portraits. (Its status as 'jewellery' may explain these anomalies.) Attribution was also left open.

20 See 245n67 for versions of the Toledo *stemma*.

21 Pieracinni 1986, 1: 186. See also n. 1.

22 See n. 2 above.

23 Bronzino's *Ludovico Capponi* wears family colours and his *Stefano Colonna* stands before a column, the Colonna *impresa*, and an armorial wine-red curtain. See G. Smith 1977[2], 266, and 1982[2], 21–5; and Freedman 1995, 75, on armorial codification. See also 284n43 above.

24 The motif is worked into Maria Salviati's collar (pl. 1), Maria de' Medici's earrings (fig. 38), young Francesco's costume (Langedijk 1981, 2: cat. 42,1) and the infant Garcia's (Brock 2002, 160), Cosimo's armour (ibid., 156–67), and Eleonora's burial gown, and appears on tondi around Allori's Studiolo portraits of Cosimo and Eleonora. See Feinberg 2002, fig. 25.

25 *Diamante* appear on the bodice of a posthumous *Dianora* in Baltimore. Langedijk 1981 1: 36,1.

26 Baia 1907, 21–3, and Cox-Rearick 1993, 42–5 and 51–3.

27 See Langdon 1992[1], 1: 237–8, and chap. 2, 85–6 for discussion of their import.

28 See Rodríguez-Salgado 1991, 233–9. Toledo was the wealthiest benefice in Christendom. The Alba were headed by the intensely assertive Fernando Alvarez de Toledo, third Duke (1507–82), the most formidable grandee in Philip II's court in the 1550s and 1560s. Her grandfather, Eleonora's father, Don Pietro di Toledo, was Spanish viceroy in Naples, part of a network of control and family alliances in Italy. See Sanchez 1999, 5; and Maltby 1983.

29 'Tu sé proprio nata in Fiorenza.' Saltini 1901, 1: 562; on her attachment to Lucrezia, see Saltini 1898, 82, citing Susena's letter to Alfonso d'Este from Poggio a Caiano, 31 August 1558.

30 See Langedijk 1981, 1: cat. series 36. A prenuptial *Dianora* was clearly not needed.

31 See chap. 6 for Isabella. For the close bond between Isabella and Dianora, see Winspeare 1961, 41, 135–58; and especially Saltini 1901–2.

32 See ASF MDP 5028, f. 413, 19 June 1568, registering the approval of Philip II, and congratulatory letters from Spain: f. 415, 22 July 1568; f. 360, 22 September 1568 from her uncle, Don Antonio; and ff. 493 and 494, 12 October 1571, from her relative, the Duke of Alba. I am indebted to Dr Edward Goldberg, director of the Medici Archive Project, Florence, for tracing these, and for other invaluable leads on Dianora.

   Prior Hapsburg approval for Medici sons' marriages was agreed to by Cosimo in 1557. Goldberg 1996, 105, citing ASF MDP 4919, f. 361, 4 July 1557. Saltini 1898, 182–3, records a papal dispensation to allow this marriage between cousins, granted 26 May 1568. On intentional encouragement of marriages between Spanish and Italian nobility to preserve political equilibrium in Italy, see Spagnoletti 1999, 3–4; and Guarini 1999, 8.

33 Saltini 1901, 1: 566, quotes ASF Atti internazionali without the folio. (I thank Bruce Edelstein for his exhaustive search for the still-missing document.) In 1565, for Francesco and Giovanna's wedding, Garzia joined Hapsburg rulers depicted on the Arch of Austria. Starn and Partridge 1992, 172–3. On Garzia, 2nd Marquis of Villafranca and Viceroy of Naples, see Maltby 1983, 34, 71, 101, and 275.

34 See ASF MDP 242 5127, ff. 216–73, dated 1605, which lists his Florentine creditors' appeals for indemnity one year after his death.

35 Saltini 1901, 1: 570–1, quoting ASF MDP 514, f. 11, Simone Fortuna to the Duke of Urbino, caustically refers to earlier proposals to wed Pietro to the duke's sister, Lavinia, to secure Medici succession on Giovanna of Austria's death in 1578. Pieraccini 1986, 2: 187, quotes Pietro's letter to Francesco on his initial failure to consummate the marriage. Bianca Cappello denounced his great maltreatment and murder of Dianora, but Pietro's youth, upbringing, and an enforced marriage were proposed as excuses. Saltini, ibid. She recorded his cruelty in letters to her family, which her brother, Pedro Toledo, disdainfully presented to the Medici envoy following Francesco's 'justification' for her murder. Pieraccini, ibid., 190.

Pietro's problems were long-standing, perhaps rooted in the enormous loss to him of his mother and two brothers in November and December 1562. Within weeks, Isabella reported the eight year old's intractability to Francesco during her father's and brothers' mourning. ASF MDP 6366, f. 234, 31 January 1563. His probable homosexuality (see Pieraccini 1986, 2: 198 and passim, and Winspeare 1961, 136–7) and perhaps Cosimo's hope that the marriage would correct this 'problem,' may have been extremely stressful for this troubled youth.

On a range of contemporary meanings of 'fatto per forza torre' see Darnton 1994, 69. See also Carroll 1989, 3–30. (I thank Sheryl Reiss for this reference.)

36 There was extreme concern over Francesco and Giovanna's lack of heirs. Their son, Filippo, was not born until 1577, after twelve years of marriage. (He died in 1582.) On this, see n. 169 below.

37 See Pieraccini 1986, 2: 185; and especially Saltini 1902, 6: 170–89.

38 For a conflicting reference to an unceremonious interment, see the courtier Ercole Cortile's description below. Arditi's *Diario* (1574–79) records that she was buried without rites. Her body was eventually placed in the Cappella dei Principi. Young 1910, 605.

Dianora was singled out from other young Medici women as especially beautiful by contemporary writers. See text n. 49 and below. Settimanni, ferociously anti-Medicean, recorded that she was 'the most beautiful young woman to be found in Florence.' Pieraccini 1986, 2: 186.

39 See Saltini 1902, 5: 228f., and 6: 167–87, for Antinori's military career at Lepanto, his escapades, Dianora's infatuation, and her distress at his trial and exile to prison in Elba in 1574 for killing Ceccino Ginori during a brawl, his letters to her, his forced return for treason, and his summary murder in the Bargello on Francesco's order. See also Winspeare 1961, 156, and Arditi 1970, 105–7.

40 The original, from Saltini 1902, 6: 173–5, is quoted in full in Langdon 2001, 279–83.

41 See Petrarch 1976, *canzone* CLIX. For Petrarchan saturation in all areas of cultural life and discussion of *ut pictura poesis*, see Lee 1940; Cropper 1976, 1986, 1995, and 1998, 1–10; Rogers 1986, 1988, and 1992 and Rogers ed. 2000; and Shearman 1992, chap. 3: 'Portraits and Poets,' 108–48. On Petrarch's influence on Bronzino's poetry and painting, see Parker 2000. See also Tinagli 1997, 85.

42 Castiglione's poem, which conjures up his wife Ippolita's reveries as she gazes on Raphael's portrait of him, testifies to this deeply emotive response, one that would be intensified by intimate viewing of a miniature portrait. See Goffen 1992, 111 and 117, on the reciprocity of the male-female gaze in viewing a portrait. Pointon 2001, 48, 63, and 67, posits an eroticism implicit in viewing a lover's miniature, the holding

and wearing of which carried the talismanic aura of a relic. See also nn. 10 and 12.

43 See Selvi's medal and Pazzi's engraving, Langedijk 1981, 1: cats. 36,11 and 36,8.

44 See Freedman 1995, 75–87, on the ekphrastic tradition, Petrarchism, and the literary aura infused into portraiture as a result of it. On this 'formidable machine' as a medium of communication and 'hyperconnotation,' see Quondam 1989, 9–44; see also Pinelli 1993, 129–30.

45 Sofonisba Anguissola's miniatures are typical. See Gregori et al. 1994, for examples. Possibly the Medici *ritrattini* were painted on tin to maintain a 'cooler' glow. See pl. 8.

46 Saltini 1902, 6: 173–87, upholds Antinori's loyalty to the Medici. On Cosimo's ambition, the importance of the Knights of San Stefano for his image, his touchy power relations, and the Medici-d'Este precedence row, see Williams 1998, 164–5; and 140–2, 269n108, 277n70 here.

47 Fantoni 1994, 32–3 and 43. Cosimo could now capitalize on a booming market in titles and sweep the Mediterranean of Corsair pirates in the process. See Terpstra 2000, 1331, and G. Ricci 1972, 131, 143, 175, 236, 253, and elsewhere, on the activities of the Tuscan navy in fighting piracy in this period.

48 See Worcester 1998, 1198–9.

49 Carnesecchi 1909, 51–61, who paraphrased Faciuta's Latin. (See also n. 38 above on Settimanni's reference to Dianora's beauty.) Giovanna's pilgrimage is recorded in ASF MDP 5094, f. 154, ins. 1, by Paolo Odescalchi, papal nuncio at the court of Naples. See also n. 175 below.

50 For the *Alterati*, see Weinberg 1954, 182–3, who refers to MS Ashburnham 558, Biblioteca Laurenziana, Florence, for Dianora's request for a judgment on Alessandro Piccolomini's Tuscan *Annotazione ... della Poetica d'Aristotele*, first published that year.

51 Fahy 2000, 444 and 447.

52 Weinberg 1961, 1: 553; and Weinberg 1954. Intellectuals, writers, and artists operated under the control of the ducal family. Fantoni 1994, 41–2. See Eisenbichler ed. 2001 for Cosimo's close monitoring of cultural institutions, artisans, printers, and officials.

53 See 166, and 292n174, on pasquinades vilifying Isabella and Dianora, and scurrilous lampoons proclaiming Ferdinando's own affair with Clelia Farnese, which provoked his fury.

54 Pieraccini 1986, 2: 187. For the killing of Luisa Strozzi to prevent any stain on her honour when Alessandro was rumoured to be about to turn his attention to her, see Cropper 2004, 32 nn. 76–8.

55 Saltini 1902, 6: 188–9, quoting Archivio di Stato, Modena, Cancelleria Ducale, dispacci da Firenze, 29 July 1576, and see Langdon 2001, 289n34. 'Due hore' and 'sei ore' refer to hours after sunset, i.e., about 11 pm in July. On timekeeping then in Italy, see Battaglia 1981–, 11: 1090. I also thank Edward Goldberg for useful discussion on this topic.

56 Pieraccini 1986, 2: 185, fig. 36, quoting ASF MDP 5154, f. 86. Pietro's handwriting shows extreme distortion, perhaps due to the injuries he sustained. Conflicting times given for Dianora's death suggest confusion by Cortile or dissembling by Pietro.

57 Pieraccini 1986, 2: 185.

58 ASF MDP 4906, f. 83v., 15 August 1576, from Madrid. Orlandini had to await official confirmation of her murder for fully four weeks. (I am indebted to Edward Goldberg for alerting me to exchanges, ff. 82r., 83v., and 84r., and others in this series). In f. 82 of 11 August, possibly a draft for a coded insert, Antinori's murder remained uncon-

firmed and amazement was expressed that two murders could be concealed. As Dianora's Alba kinsmen held immense power, Orlandini was severely compromised by the protracted delay in confirmation. See nn. 28 and 60; Perlingieri 1992, 106–7; and Maltby 1983.

59 See Stern 1994, 237–9. Even for males of less than noble rank, uxoricide was not punishable by death if a wife had been unfaithful; the musician Bartolomeo Tromboncino's murder of his wife went unpunished. Einstein 1971, 1: 42.

60 See n. 28. Alba power had further increased from the 1550s. The most powerful Alba, Fernando Alvarez de Toledo, Great Master of the King's Household, commander-in-chief of Spanish forces in Italy and Philip II's closest adviser, was an assertive, controlling influence on him. In 1559 Philip restructured the council of state. Alba and Prior Antonio de Toledo were included. See Maltby 1983 and Rodríguez-Salgado 1991, 209–23 and 234–5.

Spanish power in Italy later waned. The Armada's defeat in 1588 was followed by Ferdinando's marriage to the French Christine of Lorraine in 1589. See Saslow 1996[1], 145; Rodríguez 1999; Sánchez 1999; Guarini 1999; Spagnoletti 1999; and Gelabert 1999.

61 Galluzzi 1781, vol. 4, chap. 2.

62 Saltini 1902, 6: 191.

63 Saltini, ibid., 1902, quotes ASF MDP 4906, f. 269r.–70r., Antonio Serguidi to Francesco I. I thank Edward Goldberg for his transcript.

Philip's wrath over the murder was also appeased by Francesco's gift of a copy of the miraculous *Annunciation* at Santissima Annunziata, and Cellini's life-size marble crucifix. Mulcahy 2004, 74–6, figs 21.15 and 2.16. (On the *Annunciation*, see chap. 6, n. 90 here.) Francesco also needed Hapsburg confirmation of the grand-ducal title. Pietro, semi-exiled as a Spanish grandee, continued as admiral of the Tuscan fleet and, as Grand Duke Ferdinando's only brother, stood proxy for him in welcoming Christine of Lorraine at Livorno in 1589. Saslow 1996[2], 140.

64 Formerly Rose Museum of Art, Brandeis University, deaccessioned (Langedijk 1981, 2: cat. 100,5); sold by Sotheby-Parke-Bernet, New York, 7 June 1978, lot 8, describing Pietro as dressed in gold-embroidered red clothing. I thank John Rexine, former registrar of the Rose Museum, who gave all possible assistance to recall the miniature's details and to decipher photographs, available only in black and white. The side visible to the spectator has a dark upper band with a lighter area beneath – matching the dense band of figures over a bright sky in the Dianora *Allegory*; Rexine thought he recalled a landscape, but was unsure about its details because of the intervening years since he had seen it.

65 Spanierman Collection, New York, 98.1 × 79 cm, 1517–18. Lorenzo holds a small gold box, believed to hold the miniature of Madeleine de la Tour d'Auvergne, received by him in January that year. Scailliérez 1992, 68. See also Langedijk 1981, 2: cat. 75,7.

66 Hackenbroch 1975, 33; and Schaffers-Bodenhausen and Tiethoff-Spliethoff 1993, 11.

67 I thank Drs Carole Haensler and Mar Borobia of the Thyssen-Bornemisza Foundation for facilitating my detailed examination of the miniature and its frame.

68 As described by Hackenbroch 1975, 33, and confirmed by my study of it.

69 Hackenbroch 1975, 31–3; Somers Cocks and Truman in Sotheby's 1984, 76.

70 Medici standards were upheld after Cellini (d. 1571). For other masters, see Fock 1983,

831–45, noting Hans Dômes, Jaques Bylivelt, Eduard Vallet, Jonas Falchi, and Léonard Zaerles. For Spain's retarded development in the field, see Muller 1972, 3–4.

71 See ibid., 62, fig. 71, a cross by Joan Llado with table-cut gems in box-like settings, similar to one worn by the Infanta Isabella of Spain in a portrait by Frans Pourbus, ca. 1600: see Johnnson 1987, fig. on p. 77. See also Chicago 1975, no. 19, a pendant cross with typically Spanish, enamelled scrollwork surrounding table-cut emeralds.

72 Pieraccini 1986, 2: 189–90, citing ASF Strozziane, serie I, fol. 41, c. 261. On his exile, Pietro virtually became hostage to the Spanish crown. See Goldberg 1996, 105–14.

73 Pieraccini, ibid., 189–90, citing ASF MDP 1181, f. 481, ins. 12.

74 Ibid., 190, citing ASF MDP, ibid., f. 620.

75 Ibid., 194–6.

76 Pressure was exerted on Pietro by Francesco to sell off jewellery to offset his debts, which he was unwilling to do. Arditi 1970, 29. In 1595 Pietro willed his possessions to the Spanish crown. Mulcahy 2004, 319 n. 41. Pietro's estate is itemized in ASF MDP 5127. (See Saslow 1996², 18 and 270, for values in 1589.) On dispersal of the Duke of Lerma's effects, see Goldberg 1996, 111.

77 See Florence, Uffizi, GDSU, 1976, 2: 7. In 1664, Paolo del Sera began a search for miniatures for Leopoldo, who then had twenty-one; by 1675 he owned almost six hundred.

78 Anonymous 1975 (sale suppl.), pls. XI and XII; Hackenbroch 1975, 31–4, and 1979, 36, figs. 64a, 64b, and pl. II; and Sotheby's (sale cat.) 1984, 78–9. See also Heikamp 1978, fig. 63 here: his Juno fountain reconstruction shows her flanked by peacocks.

79 See above and nn. 32 and 33 for her betrothal.

80 Minor and Mitchell 1968, 135–9; Cox-Rearick 1984, 290; on the astrological import of Eleonora-Juno, and Juno as patron of brides in frescoes of 1555–6 for Eleonora's *Juno* terrace, as described in Vasari's *Ragionamenti*, see Mandel 1988, 86, 95–7, and figs. 8 and 12. Ammannati's ill-starred *Juno* fountain eulogized Eleonora; see n. 78 above, and M. Campbell 1983, 819–30. For Eleonora as Juno in her state portrait (pl. 4) see Langdon 1992¹, 1: 228–9; Cox-Rearick 1993, 42–5 and 51–3; and chap. 2 here.

81 Nagler 1964, 27.

82 Ibid., 59. See n. 106 for the Intermezzo of 1589, where Juno instructs her nymphs.

83 Nagler 1964, 65–7.

84 Somers Cocks and Truman in Sotheby's 1984, 76. For Eleonora's *entrata*, Muses signalled celestial harmony. Rousseau 1990, 417–23. For the 1589 wedding, see Saslow 1996¹ and 1996²; and see n. 106.

85 Mellini 1566; Baldini 1566; and Cini in Vasari 1878–85, 8: 516–617. (For Cini's authorship, see Scorza 1981, 57.) On the 1565 wedding *apparato*, see Rousseau 1990; Feinberg 1991, 32 n. 14; and Starn and Partridge 1992, 344 n. 64.

86 Nagler 1964, 1–2, records that 392 costumed 'actors' created the tableaux for the floats.

87 Cini, in Vasari 1878–85, 8: 605–6; for iconographical sources, see Baldini 1566, 78–84. The Juno *carro* recalls one with figured panels in Salviati's *Triumph of Furio Camillus* in the Sala delle Udienze of the Palazzo Vecchio, where Juno-Eleonora is borne aloft. See Mortari 1992, cat. 12.

88 For the 'cestus,' see Brumble 1998, 345. The broken stump held aloft by Ammannati's Juno was probably a clutch of Jupiter's thunderbolts, as in the miniature allegory, two *mascherata* drawings for Juno on her cart (see text below), and Baldini's description of the *mascherata* Juno. Florence, Uffizi 1966, no. 17, fig. 16. On Ammannati's Juno thun-

derbolts, see M. Campbell 1983, 824; Heikamp 1978, fig. 1; and Allegri and Cecchi 1980, 223–6.

89 Somers Cocks and Truman in Sotheby's 1984, 76, citing Ripa, *Iconologia* (1611): 80, 378–9 and 380–1. Scorza 1981, 58, commented that Borghini, the foremost classical scholar of his generation, did not need to refer to Cartari. Possibly Ripa's source for his Nymphs of the Air was inspired solely by Borghini's disciple Cini's *mascherata* description in Vasari's *Vite* in 1568, above. Also, during his Siena sojourns, Ripa would have almost certainly have known Cini.

90 Somers Cocks and Truman, ibid., citing Ripa, ibid.

91 Ibid., citing Ripa. The seventeen stars on her breast appear under magnification.

92 For Dew, citing Ripa, ibid., see Somers Cocks and Truman, ibid., 76.

93 Van Veen 1998, who prefers the title *Florence Crowns Cosimo I with Oakleaves. Amor della Patria* is an armed young man crowned with oak leaves with weapons under his feet (see Ripa in Okayama 1992, 13 and 620), but a *putto* hovers with a radiating crown – the model for Cosimo's 1569 grand-ducal one – to forecast his sovereignty. Van Veen 1998, 213. I thank the author for sharing his unpublished manuscript. See also nn. 135–6 below; and Williams 1998, who links the tondo themes to the 1565 *apparato*; and Scorza 1998.

94 See Testaverde 2002, 125–6, on the ceremonial marking the alliance. For its historic import for the Medici in the seventeenth century, see Harper 2001, 236–8.

95 Starn and Partridge 1992, 199.

96 Biblioteca Nazionale, Florence (hereafter BNF), II,I,143, no. 117. Her attributes, a honeybee and an altar, are in St Augustine's *City of God*, bk. 4; Horus's *Hieroglyphics*; and Pliny's *Natural History*. Baldini explains that the honeybee offers the gather of honey to the sovereign; the ancients also made sacrifices to Populonia. Her other attributes, a pomegranate and bee-balm, signify concord. Baldini 1566, 87; and Florence, Uffizi 1966, 51.

97 Somers Cocks and Truman in Sotheby's 1984, 76, citing Ripa 1611, 380–1, mused that she may be Pudicitia, but noted the absence of her tortoise. Pudicitia did appear, not in the twelfth (Juno) float but in the third (Saturn's). See Cini in Vasari 1878–85, 8: 594, or Baldini 1566, 24–5. Her attribute is the coot, emblem of wifely chastity; her tortoise symbolizes modesty (*Mulieris famam, non formam, vulgatam esse oportere*, i.e., 'a woman's reputation, not her beauty, should be known to the world'). Alciati 1996, nos. 55 and 219.

98 BNF, CB.III.53, vols. I and II. Vol. II includes Juno's *carro* (no. 123), *Iride* (no. 114), *Cometa* (no. 115), *Serenità* (no. 116), *Neve* (no. 118), *Nebbia* (no. 119), *Rugiada* (no. 126), *Pioggia* (no. 121), *Tre fanciulle* (no. 122 – one drawing for three identical virgins), and *Populonia* (no. 117). For the Uffizi Gabinetto dei Disegni e delle Stampe group, see *Vasariana*, vol. II: *Carro di Giunone* (no. 2830F), *Iride* (no. 2831F), *Cometa* (no. 2832F), *Serenità* (no. 2833F), *Neve* (no. 2834F), *Nebbia* (no. 2835F), *Rugiada* (no. 2836F), *Pioggia* (no. 2837F), *Tre fanciulle* (no. 2838F – for three virgins), and *Populonia* (no. 2839F).

I concur with Lecchini Giovannoni 1991, cat. 22, who attributes the entire BNF group of 132 annotated costume designs to Allori. Some of the 16 detailed *carro* designs must, however, be Allori's. ASF MDP 225, f. 118, (MAPD 1253) November 7 1567, records payment to 'Alessandro Allori pittore ... d'haver fatto, e disegno de carri, e le figure de trionfi.' (Lecchini Giovannoni believes the Uffizi group to be close workshop copies.)

99 Costuming was extravagantly expensive for wedding pageantry. See Saslow 1996[2], 58–74.

100 See n. 98 for the drawings. See also Florence, Uffizi 1966, 10–11.

101 Baldini 1566, 80, citing Hesiod's *Teogonia*. See Florence, Uffizi 1966, fig. 17, and Lecchini Giovannoni 1991, colour pl. 15. On Iris, Juno's messenger, see Brumble 1998, 181.

102 For concordance of Ripa's *Pioggia* in editions from 1603, see Okayama 1992, 196.

103 Uffizi no. 2834F, *La Neve* (Florence, Uffizi 1996, exh. cat., fig. 19), and no. 2835F, *La Nebbia*, are massed in with a *bistre* wash to express this indistinct effect. *La Rugiada* is Uffizi no. 2836F. (Baldini's commentaries for each are included by Petrioli, in Florence, Uffizi 1966, ibid.)

104 Petrioli in Florence, Uffizi 1966, 10–11; Nagler 1964, 24; and Scorza 1981, 58. On Borghini's fertile *invenzione* for Medici extravaganzas and private art, see Corrias 1993, 169–81; Scorza 1998; Van Veen 1998; and Williams 1988.

105 Nagler 1964, 25. *Carro* drawings bear this out; supporting figures are not included.

106 It is not clear if the 1565 nymphs enacted any dramatic role. Elaboration did increase for Medici wedding theatricals; the fifth intermezzo of *L'Amico fido* for Virginia de' Medici-d'Este's wedding in 1586 was staged with a complex deus ex machina apparatus for the airborne Juno and her train. Bastiano de' Rossi's *Descrizione* of 1586 casts light on the general theme of the *Dianora* miniature's allegory, even if supporting players have changed: 'Presently, when act four came to a close, the fifth intermezzo began … [L]ittle by little … the sky darkened, and was seemingly filled with clouds … and with great fury began to flash with lightning, and to thunder … and in a brief space of time, in the middle of these storms a serene cloud appeared, in which there was a chariot drawn by two large, beautiful peacocks as though real … and in it Juno with Iris, and with their fourteen Nymphs, two of which were Sirens of the Day and of the Night, and twelve had the signs of the zodiac on their heads, [signifying] the four seasons. Juno was seated regnant in the chariot, and beneath her, rank by rank, were all the Nymphs … She began to sing … [and] the sky was restored, became clear, and shone brightly.' de' Rossi 1585, 20–1. The score, set to Striggio's music, concludes with the nymphs ordering darkness to be dispelled from the sky. For this, see Ghisi 1969, xxv and xliv. (For the extravagant stage sets and machinery for Ferdinando and Christine of Lorraine's wedding in 1589, see Saslow 1996[2].)

107 For the annotated costume designs for Iris, see text and n. 98 above.

108 Medici wedding *apparati* were a source of pride. Grand Duke Ferdinando offered Buontalenti's complete *commedia*, *intermedii*, and *machine* of 1589 to the Spanish court in 1598 for the Crown Prince's marriage to Margarita of Austria. Goldberg 1996, 108.

109 On the eyes as the instrument through which love is communicated, see Tinagli 1997, 88–93: in Leonardo's *Cecilia Gallerani* and *Mona Lisa*, the three-quarters-view enhanced this effect, and oil pigments gave lustre and 'personality' to them. The enhanced *animus* in the portrait implicitly furthered engagement by the viewer with the sitter's gaze. See the Introduction, 22 and chap. 2, 82–4.

110 Langedijk 1981, 1: 99, quoting Vasari 1878–85, 8: 73; Heikamp 1978, 122; and see Mandel 1990, 81, 97 and fig. 8, Christofano Gherardi after Vasari's drawing, *Juno in Her Chariot* (1555–6), for the terrace ceiling.

111 Pointon 2001, 48 and 64; see nn. 12–14. Alois Riegl's theory of exchange between image and spectator involves a contest between ego and feeling – a striving for unification

with the universe – leading to transcendence of ego. See Brush 1994, 355–7; Iversen 1993, 9, 94, and 128; Olin 1989; and Shearman 1992, 6 and 36, with useful references on related theories.

112 See Cropper 1995, 194–9 and 205, on implicit physical beauty and its allure; and 1998, 5, on Charles Dempsey's proposal that a painting about love may be read as an extended series of Petrarchan metaphors of loss and remembrance, which is surely implied in Juno-Eleonora's presence here. On Petrarchan tropes, see also Parker 2000, 43, and Langdon 2004.

113 Olin 1992, 168, notes Riegl's defence of theatricality, apt in the context of the miniature allegory's scheme, which is drawn directly from the street theatre of the 1566 *Mascherata*.

114 See Vitzthum 1965; Schaefer 1976, passim, and figs. 5a–b; and Cox-Rearick 1984, 288–90.

115 See Schaefer 1976, 457–8, pls. 12e, and 17–21; and Feinberg 2002, figs. 27a and b: Juno holds a Medici *diamante*. Coscia's painting, *Juno Borrowing the Girdle of Venus*, covers one of the cupboards in the Studiolo. See Feinberg 2002, 55.

116 Uffizi, slate, 112 cm dia. See Lecchini Giovannoni 1991, cat. no. 190. On the posthumous Eleonora, see Cox-Rearick 2004. On ancestral values in self-fashioning of descendants and on patronage, see n. 129.

117 On Borghini's rigorous editing of Vasari's new *Vite*, 1568, see Rubin 1995, 218–30.

118 On their collaboration, see Scorza 1981, 58, and text here.

119 Schaefer 1976, 1: 460–1, and fig. 12b; Borghini corrects instructions to Vasari of 5 October. See Feinberg 2002, 60, on a crystal to be grasped by Elia Candido's *Boreas* and for crystals as formed from Boreas's breath. For Ripa's Boreas as snowy, see Okayama 1992, 280; and for Zephyr as the West Wind, ibid., 628.

120 Allori's drawings for Boreas and Zephyr are Uffizi 2835F and 2846F, respectively.

121 See Brumble 1998, 56–7 (Boreas) and 356 (Zephyr). Carloni and Grasso 1994, 426–7, emphasize such recurring oppositions of virtues and vices in Ripa. See also chap. 4, 129–30.

122 Their palace was on the Lungarno Mediceo, near Cosimo's, where he held court in his retirement. Saltini 1901, 2: 607; and 1902, 3: 627–60. For Pietro's rank and their domicile, see idem, and Winspeare 1961, 45 and 91; and on Pisa as regional capital at this time, including its dependencies, see Tolaini 1992, esp. 155ff.

123 The town of Collesalvetti incorporates the former holding. See Alidori 1995, 80. Livorno had very recently been fortified by Cosimo. On ducal villas as a strategic network in maintaining rural control, see Saslow 1996[2], 12–13, 122, and 134; and Fantoni 1999, 261.

124 For Utens's Villa Artimino lunettes, 1599, Florence, Museo Topografico – 'Firenze com'era,' see Mignani 1993, 17, 98, 99, and colour pl. 69; and Alidori 1995, 79–81. Eleonora di Toledo had received the living of the Collesalvetti Badia in 1553. Utens's prospect is directly north, just revealing the westerly path, enclosure, and side of the Badia; low hills, the Arno, and Appeninnes are visible to the north. The Badia is marked on Mascagni's 1756 Collesalvetti irrigation project (fig. 62) (ASF *Regio Possessioni* 1350, ins. 17), as is its footpath (west, towards the sea), the Medici *fattoria* (farm holdings) to the east, and surrounding woods and hills. Further, see Mineccia 1982, 62–5. I thank Prof. Mineccia, University of Lecce, for helpful correspondence; Prof.

Franco Angiolini, University of Pisa, provided useful bibliography concerning Medici holdings in the region.

I am most grateful to Signora Rondine Sciarrino, present owner of the Villa Medici at Collesalvetti – much rebuilt since the sixteenth century – who kindly toured the estate and pointed out landmarks and prospects recorded on Utens's lunette. The Badia is now ruined.

125 Saslow 1996[2], 12–13, 122, and 134.

126 See Scorza 1998; van Veen 1998; Williams 1998, 169; and Cox-Rearick 2002, 41, on Vasari's need to accommodate Cosimo's whims. See also Tinagli 2004, 120, and Benson 2004, 137–9 on his input.

127 See Fantoni 1994, 27–8. Cosimo, not given to sumptuousness, gave the Pitti to Francesco in 1568. (It functioned as an official residence for visiting dignitaries. Francesco preferred Bianca Cappello's palazzo on the Via Maggio and the Medici villas at Poggio a Caiano and Pratolino.)

128 See Rousseau 1990, 419–57, and Cox-Rearick 1993, 42, 52. Intended for this location, its installation was abandoned after Cosimo's death. M. Campbell 1985[1], 822–3 and 828.

129 In Spanish court portraiture, this is exquisitely conveyed in Anguissola's *Infanta Isabella Clara Eugenia*, 1578, the blueprint for which was Anguissola's portrait of her mother, 1563–5. The orphaned Clara Eugenia adopts precisely the same pose and wears jewellery similar to the beautiful, late Elizabeth's. See Perlingieri 1992, 164–6, pls. 74 and 98. On this topic, see Langdon 1992[1], 1: 176–8; Cropper 1997, 5 and 19–21; and Woodall ed. 1997, 3, noting that portraiture located a subject within chains or hierarchies of resemblance.

130 Oil on panel, 114.5 × 89.5 cm. See text and n. 18. Lecchini Giovannoni 1991, 301, preferred Santi di Tito, but the portrait exhibits the long, heavy forearms and recurring hand pose as Allori's signed *Isabella de' Medici* (pl. 11) and plate 12.

131 If the Vienna woman holds gloves made popular by Eleonora, this advances the link. See Lurie 1974, 8; see also a portrait after Bronzino, Florence, Museo Bandini, Lazzi 1993, 29, fig. 11. Miniatures, taken from life (n. 17), could logically precede a matching portrait.

132 Dianora was promised in both Cosimo's and her father, Garzia's names. See Saltini 1901, 1: 566. Pietro was severely admonished by Cosimo for adultery and mistreatment of her within months of the wedding, to no avail. Ibid., 2: 608, and 1902, 6: 190. See n. 35 above on her letters of complaint to her family.

133 On Cosimo's associations with Jupiter, see Richelson 1978, 77 n. 79; and 91–2 nn. 40 and 41 (citing Utz and Heikamp). The Jupiter-Cosimo conflation was well rooted: Paolo Giovio, Bronzino, and Vasari referred to a merging of mortal and divine for the two deities with the ducal couple. See M. Campbell 1983, 822. See also nn. 80 and 87 here.

134 Ficino 1989, chap. 19: ll. 53–8, 346–7.

135 Winspeare 1961, 115. See Ashengreen Piacenti 2002, 27, figs. 15–17, on the coronation, the crown, and Francesco's 1583 replacement – Cosimo was denied a royal one. See also Sframeli and Contu in Florence, Palazzo Pitti 2003, 28–30, with illustrations on those pages. Lazzi 1989, 99, lists regalia, livery, luxury fabrics, furs, artisans' pay, and expenses for the entourage to and from Rome.

136 Van Veen 1998, 213–17, and fig. 91, from a miniature appended to Pius V's bull, 9 September 1569. See Young 1910, 595–6, and Lazzi 1989, passim and fig. 2: Pius V lowers the *corona radiata* on to Cosimo's head in Philippe Galle's copy of Jan van Straet's record of the scene (Amsterdam, Rijksprenthenkabinet), Lazzi, ibid. Made by Jacques Bylivert, it was received on 15 March 1570 from Pius. See Fock 1970, 199, fig. 8; Ashengreen Piacenti 2002, 25–9, for the entire regalia; for portraits of Cosimo in the regalia, see Langedijk 1978; also Langedijk 1981, 1: cats. 27, 7–9, and 27, group 40, 41, 43, 43a, and 48 (posthumous). For the 1565 *carro* drawing of Juno's radiant crown, see Barocchi and Bertelà 1993, pl. 14; on Cosimo's Sala Grande tondo, see n. 93 above.

137 Widespread unease in European courts about Cosimo's 'regal' aspirations and Hapsburg fears of threats to Spanish control were checkmated by Pius's unilateral decision. Van Veen 1998, 214–15. See also Rodríguez 1999, 2–3, and Spagnoletti 1999, 3–4, on these conflicts.

138 The Alba advanced the imperial edict giving Medici precedence in 1547. On the long-standing conflict, see 141. Lucrezia's marriage in 1558 temporarily sealed a Medici-Este reconciliation effected by Philip II, but Francisco and Giovanna's wedding *apparato* flaunted Medici superiority. Williams 1998, 163–9.

139 A letter from Maximilian II, Giovanna of Austria's brother to her, Prague, 28 May 1570, expresses displeasure on Cosimo's independent acceptance of the crown and disdain for his recent marriage to Camilla Martelli, a commoner, on which the pope insisted if Cosimo was to be crowned grand duke. Giovanna passed the letter to Cosimo, who had it translated. His dignified reply of 16 July from Castello prompted her response to Maximilian that Camilla deserves respect, also hoping that he will continue his goodwill towards the grand duke and allow her to assume a pacific role with her Medici family. Saltini 1898, 356–60, believed this was penned under Cosimo and Francesco's supervision.

140 For Eleonora's periods of regency, see 9, 20, 59; Langdon 1992[1], 2: chap. 5; and paper delivered at the Renaissance Society Conference, Bloomington, Indiana, 1996, 'Bronzino's *Eleonora di Toledo with Giovanni*: A Declaration of Regency, "*Religio Regis*" and Ducal Patronage.' See also Cox-Rearick 1993, 34–5; and Edelstein 2001, 225.

141 Langedijk 1981, 1: cat. 35,42; and Cox-Rearick 2004, 258 and figs. 10–11. Eleonora is portrayed with Francesco on textile, designed by Jacopo Ligozzi, 1613–21; the crown is displayed on a plinth, to the left.

142 Illustrated in Thomas Cren, *Renaissance Painting and Manuscripts* (London, 1983), pl. 15. By 1516, Margaret of Austria had her own miniature and one of Countess Hoorn. L. Campbell 1990, 64.

143 Cox-Rearick 1995, figs. 9 (*Commentaires)* and 14 (treaty); see Scailliérez et al. 1992, 45, ill. 26 (manuscript); and cat. 3 (*atelier*, ca. 1525, 4.2 cm dia., framed). On miniatures, collected by the Medici, and another *François I* miniature, see Meloni 1994, 626. See Jollet 1997, 202–3, on Jean Clouet (d. 1540) and François Clouet (d. 1572); a miniature sent by Madame d'Alençon to Henry VIII in 1526; and see ibid., 202, for Jean's tiny *Charles de Cossé, Comte de Brissac*, ca. 1535, Metropolitan Museum of Art, New York. See also n. 65. See Strong 1995 for English forms, popularized by Hornebolte from the mid-1520s.

144 On Bronzino's *Nativity*, see Warnke 1993, 241. See Meloni 1994, 626–7, on Italian miniature developments, noting Clovio, Froeschl, Northerners, and monks in Florence. Experimentation, not specialization, by Italian artists was typical.

145 See also Langedijk 1981, 1: cats. 42, 12a, 12b, and 13 for copies; see also Lecchini Giovannoni 1991, cat. 180; Lloyd 1993, 3–5, figs. 1, 2, and p. 3, Francesco with a cameo (Chicago).

146 For the Italian preference for oils-on-metal miniatures, see Schaffers-Bodenhausen and Tiethoff-Spliethoff 1993, 29–31. This preference seems to have been adhered to by Maria de' Medici, Queen of France, for miniature portraits of her children and family members. See Florence, Palazzo Pitti and Museo degli Argenti 2005, cat. nos. III, 4–11, and III, 12, all early seventeenth century, and all by French artists. (Italian developments were central to the topic 'Up Close and Personal: The Italian Renaissance Miniature Portrait,' delivered by the author at the Universities Art Association of Canada Conference, London, Ontario, November 1998.)

147 He recorded this as a recent work, 'a little painting like a miniature, with forty figures, according to a beautiful invention of [Francesco's] own'. Vasari 1878–85, 7: 709.

148 Vasari, ibid., 606–8. As Allori had been court portraitist for some years for Lucrezia, Francesco, and Isabella, his need to 'practise' surely refers to miniaturization.

149 Schaffers-Bodenhausen and Tiethoff-Spliethoff 1993, 29–31. See n. 155.

150 On their rarity, see ibid.

151 Lecchini Giovannoni 1991, cat. 191; it measures 37 × 27 cm. On dating, see n. 159.

152 See Coniglielli in Phoenix 1997–8, 128, cat. no. 91, for Jacopo Ligozzi's (1547–1626) *memento mori* for Francesco, silver on copper, and Bowron 1997–8, 14 and 223. Guido Reni's *Coronation of the Virgin*, 1607, National Gallery, London, is another rare example.

153 His workshop's Medici *ritrattini* set is most often reported as painted on tin or pewter.

154 For the attribution to Allori, see Anonymous 1975, citing Heikamp; Hackenbroch 1975, 33; and Hackenbroch 1979, 36. Somers-Cocks and Truman in Sotheby's 1984, 77, left this open. Also see Langedijk 1981, 2: cat. 109,6 as Virginia de' Medici d'Este (?) by Allori, but she was a mere child in 1571. (For identifications, see n. 18 above.)

155 See Scorza 1995, 175, on his 'highly wrought miniaturist detail' on the *Pearl Fishers* for Francesco's Studiolo, 1571–3 and Lecchini Giovannoni 1991, cats. 28 and 29.

156 Lecchini Giovannoni 1991, fig. 50, cat. 23. Allori was paid for a small work on copper in October 1568, it seems for his *Hercules Crowned by the Muses*.

157 On his repetitiveness, see M. Campbell[2], 1985, 388. His *Susannah and the Elders*, Dijon, dated 1561, shows these traits in his early nudes. For this see Lecchini Giovannoni 1991, fig. 23, cat. 18; see also Allori's study for a *Venus and Cupid*, Hackenbroch 1975, 34.

158 Lecchini Giovannoni 1991, 67, 78: an Angel and Virgin from the miraculous *Annunciation* for reliquary covers are recorded, 1579–80, and a *ritrattino* for Giovanni de' Ricci in 1583.

159 Ibid., figs. 426 and 427, cat. no. 191; Langedijk 1981, 1: cat. 12,8. This is the youngest extant portrait of Bianca, who was later very corpulent. Her liaison with Francesco began in 1564; its costume details compare with Isabella's mid-1560s portraits (figs. 52 and 54).

160 Hackenbroch 1975, 34.

161 Museo Nazionale del Bargello, Florence, 139 × 232 cm. It is inscribed 'A.D.M./ DLXXII/AL.AL.FA.' Lecchini Giovannoni 1991, cat. 32, figs. 67 and 68. See 155 here. Emblems of dalliance, seduction, and fertility were a stock repertoire in wedding pageantry, and on bedroom furniture such as *spalliere* and *cassoni*. See Holmes 1997, 184–7, on the status and familial regard of the nuptial bed, expressed in Margherita

Borgherini's tirade against henchmen who sought it for Francis I during the siege of 1529: '[She] berated Giovan Battista with the greatest abuse that was ever spoken to anyone. "... you vile slop dealer, you little two-penny pedlar ... base plebian and enemy of your country ... This bed, which you would seize for your own private interest and for greed of gain ... is the bed of my nuptials, in honour of which my husband's father Salvi made these magnificent and regal decorations, which I revere in memory of him and from love of my husband, and mean to defend with my very blood and with life itself."' Vasari 1878–85, 6: 262–63. Lighthearted iconography in marriage portraiture and its reflections in the Bargello *spalliera* were topics in my 'Decorum for a Bridegroom,' for the Sixteenth Century Studies Conference, St Louis, October 1996. My research continues.

162 See n. 2.

163 See Langdon 2001, 279 n. 123. I am indebted to Lorne Campbell for useful exchanges. On implicit womens' patronage, see Crum 2001[2], 37 and 47, and McIver 2001, 164.

164 For Cosimo as artificer of the centralized, absolute state, see Fantoni, 1989, 24–9, and Testaverde 2002, 125, with bibliography. In the next century, codification of this absolutist ethos was effected through control of civic space, ceremonial order, and social hierarchy – a physical expression of the earlier rippling effect of patronage with the 'Big Man,' Cosimo, at the epicentre. Ceremonial boundaries, 'like so many concentric circles, started at the confines of the realm, closing in through the city walls and the palace gates to centre on the throne-room' of the Palazzo Pitti. See Fantoni 1999, 268; see also Testaverde 2002, 125, on spectacle and organization. On works of art as instrumental in exposing the court's propagandistic rhetoric, see Starn and Partridge 1992, 5, and Saslow 1994, 1006–7.

165 Gundersheimer 1981, 19–20. Saslow 1996[2], 35, has succinctly expressed the notion that human history, in princely iconography, is a series of oscillations toward and away from that venerable fixed centre, with the present always declared to be the perigee, or closest point. See also Crum 2001[1], 47–51. See Harper 2001, 223–41, on Ferdinand II's bid to acquire his ancestor Cosimo's aura: 'half biography, half allegory, Cosimo's life had become a protean model of Good Rulership.' Cox-Rearick 2002, 41, comments on Vasari's 'il senso nostro' as expressing implicit awareness of Medicean intentions in art.

166 On the momentum of family patronage, see Goldberg 1983, ix; and Hollingsworth 1994, 1–2.

167 See Testaverde 2002, 125, also asserting Borghini's role.

168 Gundersheimer 1981, 19, believed that the most important of the 'Big Man's' links are with his family. Assessment of Pietro is hampered by Pieraccini's fulminations on his homosexuality; however, his reputation as a psychopath and murderer, and as an insolvent and incorrigible, may explain his exclusion from the Medici succession. (See n. 35.) He had fathered children and could potentially found a legitimate dynasty, but on Francesco's death in 1587 Ferdinando abandoned his role as a prospective Medici pope to become grand duke.

169 Cosimo, concerned for the succession, was avidly interested in Giovanna's pregnancies. In 1569 he bet a ruby valued at 1500 *scudi* on the gender of the unborn Anna and had to pay up. ASF MDP 232, f. 102ff. (MAPD 149), 19 December 1569; f. 117, 7 February 1570; and f. 129, 13 May 1570.

Pietro and Dianora's son, Cosimino, born in 1573 (see n. 19), was sole ducal heir until his death in 1576, soon after his mother's. (He rests near her in the Cappella dei Principi mausoleum in San Lorenzo.) Francesco's heir, Filippo, born in 1577, died in 1582. Langedijk 1981, 1: 118–19, cat. 27,39 refutes Levey's (1971) identification of Dianora as Butteri's *Madonna* in his 1575 altarpiece with Medici portraits for its saints, but Cosimino's importance as heir to the grand duchy at this time deserves consideration. Ferdinando, released from his vows in 1587 by Sixtus V to succeed Francesco, produced numerous progeny by Christine of Lorraine, thus ensuring Medici continuity.

170 See Gundersheimer 1981, 13 and 19–20, on how networks of mental attitudes and social connections create a saturated ambiance that supports a puissant ruler's taste.

171 Evans 1998, 486.

172 See Saslow 1996[2], 8–10, and Crum 2001[1], on princely patronage as 'energy from a vortex.'

173 See Evans 1998, 490–1, on the criteria for a streamlined court establishment.

174 See Schalk 1991, 245, discussing Henri de Boulainvilliers, *Essais sur la nobless de France* (1732), and tracing a degeneration of high standards established by Francis I of France.

175 See Evans 1998, 481–2, and n. 49 above on the enormous retinue of the devout grand duchess, Giovanna of Austria, on pilgrimage to Loreto, entrained by 430 horses, eighty carriages, thirty lancers liveried in green and white, twelve pages dressed in velvet *alla Turca* with silver embroidery, and twelve of her Flemish ladies in black. Her litter was similar to Eleonora's (see chap. 2). The two-week-long solemn procession moved through Passignano, Cortona, Foligno, Camerino, Tolentino, and Macerata, and on to Loreto. Giovanna attracted great interest and obeisance. Her pilgrimage was in effect a perambulation of majesty similar to the progresses of Elizabeth I through her realm.

176 See 283–4n31.

177 Fantoni 1994, 24–6, and 30–1, views Francesco's reign as a hiatus between the confident reigns of Cosimo and Ferdinando.
For an historical-anthropological approach to codes of female chastity as indicators of a construct of shared beliefs and values within the historical emergence of the state, especially its rigidity relative to the upward-stratification of social hierarchies, see Giovannini 1987, 61–74.

178 See ibid., 65, on differential laws and punishments for female and male adultery. On *delitto d'onore* enacted for the good of the state see Caneva, Orsi Landini, and Sframeli 1999, 24.

Epilogue

1 The events in the Epilogue are referenced in foregoing chapters.
However unconsciously, moderns have absorbed the decorum of royalty that Eleonora so famously adopted in her portrait. Shocked disbelief has greeted portrayals of Elizabeth II whenever there have been attempts to show her as other than she appears in state portraits such as Pietro Annigoni's youthful, official version of 1954. She, too, gazes beyond the viewer into a remote landscape, clothed, as Eleonora was, in lavish robes of state that proclaim her office. Strongly lit, honestly rendered versions of her such as Anthony Williams's or Lucien Freud's showing her in late middle age have been greeted with some dismay. She resumes her 'proper' decorum as Queen only in

the recent Sergei Pavlenko version. There, at proper distance from the spectator and mounted on a titanic staircase of indeterminate distance to suggest her remoteness, her proportions are stretched to majestic heights to allow for the traditional display of jewelled accoutrements and the trappings of power. For all of these portraits, see Milroy 2002.

2 On Christine's dowry, see Saslow 1996², 270n32.

Bibliography

Documents

Archivio di Stato, Florence
- *Carte Dei*: 'Montauto': filza 33, ins. 11
- *Carteggio Universale*: filza 567, f. 187
- *Medici Avanti il Principato*: filza 140, f. 7, ins. 1
- *Mediceo del Principato*: filza 3, I, f. 70 and 70v.; filza 7 passim; filza 28, f. 21 (MAPD 213); filza 59 (MAPD 7159); filza 210, f. 33 (MAPD 227); filza 211, f. 136 (MAPD 1305); filza 213, ff. 21, 28; filza 225, f. 118 (MAPD 1523); filza 227, f. 210; filza 232, f. 102ff. (MDAP 149); filza 246, f. 232; filza 345, ff. 364, 380, 429, and 435; filza 514, f. 11; filza 523, f. 43, ins. 4 (MAPD 1175) ; filza 600, f. 23; filza 707, ff. 81 and 220; filza 892, ff. 85 and 188; filza 1212, f. 74 (MAPD 4202); filza 1305, II, f. 1356; filza 1171, f. 62, ins. 2 (MAPD 6488); —, f. 147, ins. 3 (MAPD 6020), and f. 150; —, f. 174, ins. 4 (MAPD 2419); —, f. 260, ins. 6 (MAPD 2445); filza 1176, f. 44, ins. 5 (MAPD 3117) and ins. 12 (MAPD 3177); —, f. 24 and f. 30, ins. 6 (MAPD 3122), f. 30 (MAPD 3126); —, f. 43, ins. 9 (MAPD 3216) ; filza 1181, f. 14, ins. 12, and ff. 82r–84r, 269–70, 481, and 620; filza 1182, f. 14; filza 1542, f.7; filza 1699, ff. 16 and 201; filza 2912, I, ff. 39–46v., and II, 56–9v.; filza 2913, ff. 65, 65v., and 70; filza 2914, ff. 6–17 and 33; filza 4068, f.210; filza 4072, passim; filza 4906, ff. 82r., 83v., 84r., and 269r.– 70r.; filza 5028, ff. 360, 413, 415, and 493–5; filza 5088, ff. 14 and 34; filza 5094, f. 154, ins. 1; filza 5127, ff. 216–73; filza 5154, f. 86; filza 5925, f. 139; filza 5926, f. 8; filza 6106 (MAPD 7159); filza 6366, f. 234; filza 6357, f. 8; filza 6373, ff. 28v., 36, and 36v.
- *Miscellanea medicea*: filza 844 (Lettere degli Orsini agli Orsini)
- *Regio Possessioni*: filza 1350, ins. 17
- *Viaggi dei Principi*: filza 6377, no. LXX

Biblioteca Nazionale Centrale, Florence: MS Palat. C.B.III.53, I, filza 115

Gabinetto Disegni e Stampe degli Uffizi, Florence: drawings 2667F–2829F, vol. I; drawings 2830F–2945F, vol. II; drawing 6503F; drawing 6680F

Primary Sources

Adriani, Giovambatista. 1583. *Istoria de' suoi tempi di Giovambatista Adriani*. Vols. 1 and 2. Florence. Reprint Prato, 1872.

Albèri, Eugenio, ed. 1839–63. *Relazioni degli ambasciatori veneti al Senato*. 15 vols. *Serie* II, *Relazioni d'Italia*. Florence.

Alberti, Leon Battista. 1956. *On Painting* (1435). Trans. John R. Spencer. New Haven, CT.

– 1969. *I libri della famiglia* (1437–41). *The Family in Renaissance Florence*. Trans. Renée Neu Watkins. Columbia, SC.

Alciati, Andrea. 1621. *Emblemata cum commentariis* (1531). Reprint, Padua.

– 1996. *Emblemata: Lyons, 1550*. Trans. Betty I. Knott; intro. John Manning. Aldershot, UK, and Brookfield, VT.

Allori, Alessandro. 1971. *Il primo libro de' ragionamenti delle regole del disegno d'Alessandro Allori con M. Agnolo Bronzino* (1565). In Barocchi ed. 1971–3, 2: 1941–81. Milan and Naples.

Arditi, Bastiano. 1970. *Diario di Firenze e di Altre Parti della Cristianità (1574–1579)*. Ed. R. Cantagalli. Florence.

Aretino, Pietro. 1957–60. *Lettere sull'arte*. Ed. Ettore Camesasca and Fidenzio Pertile. 4 vols. Milan.

Aristotle. 1978. *Poetics*. Trans. Gerald F. Else. 5th ed. Ann Arbor.

Armenini, Giovanni Battista. 1977. *On the True Precepts of the Art of Painting*. (Ravenna, 1586.) Trans. Edward J. Olszewski. New York.

Baldini, Baccio. 1566. *Discorso sopra la Mascherata della Genealogia degl' Iddei de' Gentili. Mandata fuori dall'Illustrissimo e Eccellentiss. S. Duca di Firenze, e Siena, il giorno 21 di Febbraio MDLXV*. Florence.

– 1578. *Vita di Cosimo de' Medici, primo Gran Duca di Toscana*. Florence.

Barocchi, Paola, ed. 1960–2. *Trattati d'arte del cinquecento fra manierismo e controriforma*. 3 vols. Bari.

– 1971–73. *Scritti d'arte del cinquecento*. 2 vols. Milan and Naples.

Barocchi, Paola, and Giovanna Gaeta Bertelà, eds. 1993. *Collezionismo mediceo Cosimo I, Francesco I e il Cardinale Ferdinando, documenti 1540–1587*. Modena.

Biondo, Michelangelo. 1982. *Della nobilissima pittura* (Venice, 1549). In Janet Seiz, 'Michelangelo Biondo's *On the Noble Art of Painting*, a Sixteenth Century Venetian Physician's Handbook for Young Painters.' MA diss., Case Western Reserve University.

Boccaccio, Giovanni. 1545. *Libro di M. Giovanni Boccaccio delle donne illustre*. Venice.

Borghini, Raffaello. 1584. *Il Riposo*. 3 vols. Florence; reprint, Milan, 1807.

Bronzino, Agnolo 1823. *Sonnetti di Angiolo Allori detto il Bronzino ed altre rime inedite di più insigni poeti*. Ed. Domenico Moreni. Florence.

– 1988. *Rime in burla*. Ed. Franca Petrucci Nardelli. Rome.

Cartari, Vincenzo. 1556. *Le Imagine degli dei degli antichi*. Venice; repr. New York, 1976.

Castiglione, Baldassare. 1959. *The Book of the Courtier* (Venice, 1528). Trans. Charles S. Singleton. New York.

Cattani di Diacceto, Francesco. 1561. *I tre libri d'amore di M. Francesco Cattani di Diacceto. Con un panegirico all'amore; e con la vita del detto autore, fatta da M. Benedetto Varchi*. Venice.

Cennini, Cennino. 1932. *Il libro dell'arte*. Trans. Daniel V. Thompson, Jr. New Haven, CT.

Cini, Giambattista. 1565. *Descrizione dell'apparato fatto in Firenze per le nozze dell'illustrissimo ed eccellentissimo Don Francesco de' Medici Principe di Firenze e di Siena e dala Serenissima Regina Giovanna d'Austria*. In Vasari 1878–85, 8: 516–617.

Cirni, Anton Francesco Corso. 1560. *La Reale entrata dell Ecc.mo Sig.nor Duca e Duchessa di Fiorenza in Siena con la significatione delle latine inscrittione e con alcuni sonnetti*. Rome.

de Hollanda, Francisco. 1868. *Do tirar polo natural* (1549). In 'Die Manuscripte des Francesco d'Ollanda,' ed. and trans. Th. von Fournier. *Jahrbucher für Kunstwissenschaft* 1: 334–58.

– 1979. *Four Dialogues on Painting* (Lisbon, 1548). Trans. Aubrey G. Bell. Westport, CT.

– 1984. *Do tirar polo natural*. Ed. and trans. José da Felicidade Alves. Lisbon.

– 1998. *Diálogos em Roma (1538): Conversations on Art with Michelangelo Buonarroti*, ed. Grazia Dolores Folliero-Metz. Heidelberg.

Della Casa, Giovanni. 1994. *Galateo: A Renaissance Treatise on Manners* (1552–5). 3rd rev. ed. Ed. and trans. Konrad Eisenbichler and Kenneth R. Bartlett. Toronto.

de' Medici, Lorenzo. 1992. *Opere*. Ed. T. Zanato. Turin.

de' Rossi, Bastiano. 1585. *Descrizione/del magnificentiss./apparato/ E de'maravigliosi intermedi/ fatti per la commedia/rappresentata in Firenze/nelle felicissime Nozze degl'Illustrissimi,/ed Eccellentissimi Signori/il Signor Don Cesare D'Este,/e la Signora Donna/Virginia Medici./ In Firenze, Apresso Giorgio Marescotti./l' Anno MDLXXXV*. Florence.

de' Rossi, Giovangirolamo. 1997. *Vita di Giovanni de' Medici detto delle Bande Nere* [ca. 1530–60]. Ed. Vanni Bramanti. Rome.

de Valdés, Juan. 1990. *Diálogo de la lengua* (1532–5). Ed. Cristina Barbolani. Madrid.

Dolce, Lodovico. 1968. *Dolce's 'Aretino' and Venetian Art Theory of the Cinquecento*. Trans. Mark W. Roskill. New York.

Domenichi, Lodovico. 1564. *La donna di corte, discorso di Lodovico Domenichi nel quale so ragiona dell'affabilità & honestà creanza da doversi usare per gentildonna d'honore*. Lucca.

Ficino, Marsilio. 1989. *Three Books on Life* (1489). Ed. and trans. Carol V. Kaske and John R. Clark. Binghampton, NY.

Firenzuola, Agnolo. 1848. *Dialogo della bellezza delle donne* (Florence, 1548). In *Le opere di Agnolo Firenzuola*, ed. B. Bianchi. Florence.

– 1892. *On the Beauty of Women*. Trans. Clara Bell. London, 1892.

– 1992. *On the Beauty of Women*. Ed. and trans. Konrad Eisenbichler and Jacqueline Murray. Toronto.

Fusco, Horatio. 1570. *La vedova del Fusco: Alla illustriss. s. Clelia Salamona Oliva Contessa di Pian di Mileto, e Piagnano*. Rome.

Galluzzi, Jacopo Riguccio. 1781. *Istoria del Granducato di Toscano sotto il Governo della Casa Medici*. Florence.

Gaye, Johann Wilhelm. 1840. *Carteggio inedito d'artisti dei secolo XIV, XV, XVI pubblicato ed illustrato con documenti pure inedito*. 3 vols. Florence.

Gelli, Jacopo. 1928. *Divise, Motti e Imprese di Famiglie e Personaggi italian*. 2nd rev. ed.Milan.

Gilio, G.A. 1971. *Dialogo nel quale si ragiona degli errori e degli abusi de'pittori circa l'istorie* (1564). In Barocchi 1971, 1: 1–115.

Giovio, Paolo. 1556. *Ragionamenti sopra i motti, e disegni d'arme, e d'amore, che comunemente chiamono imprese*. Venice.

– 1559. *Gli Elogi: vite brevemente scritte d'huomini illustri di guerra antichi et moderni*. Trans. L. Domenichi. Venice.

Hermes Trismegistus. 1992. *Hermetica: The Ancient Greek and Latin Writings Which Contain Religious or Philosophic Teachings Ascribed to Hermes Trismegistus*. Trans. Sir Walter Scott, foreword A.G. Gilbert. Bath.

Horace. 1859. *The Works of Horace, translated literally into English prose*. Rev. ed. Theodore Alois Buckley. London.

– 1963. *Horace on the Art of Poetry*. Ed., and trans. Charles Oscar Brink. Cambridge.

Kemp, Martin, ed. 1989. *Leonardo on Painting*. Trans. Martin Kemp and Margaret Walker. New Haven, CT, and London.

Lapini, Agostino. 1906. *Diario fiorentino di Agostino Lapini dal 252 al 1596*. Florence.

Leonardo da Vinci. 1890. *Trattato della pittura*. Ed. Marco Tabarrini. Rome.

– 1956. *Treatise on Painting*. Trans. A. Philip McMahon. 2 vols. Princeton.

Lomazzo, Giovanni Paolo. 1844. *Trattato dell'Arte della Pittura, Scultura, ed Architettura di Gio. Paolo Lomazzo (1584)*. 3 vols. Rome.

Luigini, Federigo. 1907. *The Book of Fair Women* (Venice, 1554). Trans. Elsie M. Lang, J. Pott, et al. London and New York.

– 1913. *Il libro della bella donna*. In *Trattati del cinquecento*, ed. Giuseppe Zonta, 276ff. Bari.

Maggi, Vincenzo. 1546. *In partem poetices Aristotelis*. Florence.

Mannucci, Aldo. 1586. *Vita di Cosimo de' Medici Gran Primo Gran Duca di Toscano descritta da Aldo Manucc*i. Bologna.

Matasilani, Mario. 1572. *La felicita del Serenissimo Cosimo Medici Granduca di Toscana*. Florence.

Medici, Lorenzino de'. 2004. *Apology for a Murder* (1539). Foreword by Tim Parks. Trans. Andrew Brown. London.

Mellini, Domenico. 1566. *Descrizione dell'entrata della serenissima regna Giovanna d'Austria, et dell'apparato, fatto in Firenze nella venuta, & per le felicissime nozze di Sua Altezza Et dell'illustrissimo & eccellentissimo S. Don Francesco de Medici, principe di Firenze, & di Siena*. Florence.

Misson, Maximilien. 1695. *A New Voyage to Italy: with a description of the chief towns, churches, tombs, libraries, palaces, statues, and antiquities of that country; together with useful Instructions for those who shall travel there*. 2 vols. London.

Ovid. 1960. *Metamorphoses*. Trans. Frank Justus Miller. 1st ed., London, 1916; 2 vols., London and Cambridge, MA.

– 1998. *Metamorphoses*. Trans. Ted Hughes. London.

Perondini, Pietro. 1563. *Oratio Petri Perondini habita ad populum pratensem in funere illust. D. Eleonorae Cosmi Medicis Florentiae, & Senarum Duicis coniugis. Tertio kalend. Ianuarii. MDLXII*. Florence.

Pescerelli, Beatrice. 1979. *I Madrigali di Maddalena Casulana*. Florence.

Pino, Paolo. 1946. *Dialogo di Pittura* (Venice, 1548). Eds. Rudolfo and Anna Pallucchini. Venice.

– 1983. In Mary Pardo, ed., 'Paolo Pino's *Dialogo della Pittura:* A Translation with Commentary.' PhD diss., University of Pittsburgh.

Ricci, Giuliano de'. 1972. *Cronaca di Giuliano de' Ricci (1532–1606)*. Ed. Giuliana Sapori. Milan.

Ripa, Cesare. 1611. *Iconologia*. Padua.

– 1970. *Iconologia overo descrittione di diverse immagini cavate dall' antichità, e di propria invenzione* (Rome, 1603). Reprint ed., intro. by Erna Mandowsky. New York.

– 1988. *Nova Iconologia di Cesare Ripa Perugino* (Padua, 1618). 2 vols. Repr., ed. Piero Buscaroli, preface Mario Praz. Turin.

Segni, Bernardo. 1805. *Storie fiorentine di messer Bernardo Segni gentiluomo fiorentino dall'Anno MDXXVII al MDLV: Colla vita di Niccolò Capponi ... descritta dal Medesimo Segni, suo nipote*. 3 vols. Milan.

Settimani, Francesco. Circa 1720. *Memorie fiorentine*. Archivio di Stato di Firenze, Archivio dei manoscritti, Mss. 125–47.

Spini, G., ed. 1940. *Lettere di Cosimo I de' Medici*. Florence.

Supino, I.B. 1908. *I ricordi di Alessandro Allori, 1579–84*. Florence.

Thomas, William. 1963. *The History of Italy* (1549). Reprint. Ed. George B. Parks. New York.

Trissino, Giovangiorgio. 1524. *I ritratti di M. Giovangiorgio Trissino*. Rome.

Varchi, Benedetto, and Vincenzo Borghini. 1998. *Pittura e Scultura nel Cinquecento*. Ed. Paola Barocchi. Livorno.

Vasari, Giorgio. 1878–85. *Le vite de' più eccellenti pittori scultori ed architettori scritte da Giorgio Vasari pittore aretino con nuove annotazioni e commenti di Gaetano Milanesi*. 9 vols. Florence.

– 1938. *Il libro delle ricordanze di Giorgio Vasari, 1527–72*. Ed. Alessandro del Vita. Arezzo.

– 1996. *Lives of the Painters, Sculptors and Architects*. Trans. Gaston C. de Vere, intro. David Ekserdjian. 2 vols. New York and Toronto.

Vives, Juan Luis. 1912. *Joannis Lodovici Vivis Valentini. De institutione feminae Christianae, ad inclytam d. Catharinam Hispanam, Angliae reginam, libri tres* (Basle, 1523). Trans. Richard Hyrde (ca. 1540) in Foster Watson, ed., *Vives and the Renascence Education of Women*. London.

Secondary Sources

Acidini Luchinat, Cristina. 1993. 'Medici e cittadini nei cortei dei Re Magi: Ritratto di una società.' In Acidini Luchinat ed. 1993: 363–70.

Acidini Luchinat, Christina, ed. 1993. *Benozzo Gozzoli. La Capella dei Magi*. Milan.

– Acidini Luchinat, Cristina, ed. 1997. *Treasures of Florence: The Medici Collection 1400–1700*. Trans. Eve Leckey. Munich and New York.

Adamson, John, ed. 1999. *The Princely Courts of Europe: Ritual, Politics and Culture Under the Ancien Régime, 1500–1750*. London.

Adelson, Candace. 1983. 'Cosimo I de' Medici and the Foundation of Tapestry Production in Florence.' In Diaz ed. 1983, 3: 899–924. Florence

– 1985. 'The Decoration of Palazzo Vecchio in Tapestry: The "Joseph" Cycle and Other Precedents for Vasari's Decorative Campaigns.' In Garfagnini ed. 1985: 145–78.

Ademollo, Agostino. 1845. *Note Marietta de' Ricci, ovvero Firenze al Tempo dell' Assedio: Racconto Storico*. 2nd ed. Ed. Luigi Passerini. 6 vols. Florence.

Agoston, Laura. 2000. Review of *Concepts of Beauty in Renaissance Art*, ed. Francis Ames-Lewis and Mary Rogers. *Art Bulletin* 82: 768–70.

Ainsworth, Maryan. 1990. '"Paternes for phiosioneamyes": Holbein's Portraiture Reconsidered.' *Burlington Magazine* 132, 1044: 173–86.

Alazard, Jean. 1951. *Le Portrait florentin de Botticelli à Bronzino*. 3rd ed. Paris.

– 1968. *The Florentine Portrait*. Trans. Barbara Whelpton. New York.

Alidori, Laura. 1995. *Le Dimore dei Medici in Toscana*. Florence.

Allegri, Ettore, and Alessandro Cecchi. 1980. *Palazzo Vecchio e i Medici: Guida storica*. Florence.

Allegrini, Giuseppe. 1761. *Chronologica Series simulacrorum regiae familae Mediceae*. Florence.

Alpers, Svetlana. 1960. 'Ekphrasis and Aesthetic Attitudes in Vasari's Lives.' *Journal of the Warburg and Courtauld Institutes* 23: 190–215.

– 1983. *The Art of Describing: Dutch Art of the Seventeenth Century*. Chicago and London.

Ames-Lewis, Francis. 1979. 'Early Medici Devices.' *Journal of the Warburg and Courtauld Institutes* 42: 122–41.

– 1992. Introduction. In Ames-Lewis and Bednarek eds. 1992: 7–14.

Ames-Lewis, Francis, and Anka Bednarek, eds. 1992. *Decorum and Renaissance Narrative Art.* London.

Ames-Lewis, Francis, and Mary Rogers, eds. 1998. *Concepts of Beauty in Renaissance Art.* Aldershot, UK, and Brookfield, VT.

Ancel, D.R. 1908. 'Le Vatican sous Paul IV: Contribution à l'histoire du Palais Pontifical.' *Revue bénédictine* 25: 63–5.

Anglo, Sydney. 1977. 'The Courtier: The Renaissance and Changing Ideals.' In Dickens ed. 1977: 33–8.

Ann Arbor. 2002. *Women Who Ruled: Queens, Goddesses, Amazons in Renaissance and Baroque Art.* Exh. cat., ed. Annette Dixon. University of Michigan Museum of Art. London and Ann Arbor.

Anonymous. 1889. 'Andata di Donna Lucrezia de' Medici a Ferrara.' In *Zibaldone, notizie, anedotti, curiosità e documenti inediti o rari*, ed. Giuseppe Baccini, 137–8. Florence.

– 1973. *Albo d'oro delle famiglie nobile e notabile italiane.* 12 vols. Florence.

– 1975. 'Notable Works of Art Now on the Market.' *Burlington Magazine* 207 (sale supplement).

Arezzo and Florence. 1981. *Giorgio Vasari: Principi, letterati e artisti nelle carte di Giorgio Vasari, Casa Vasari. Pittura vasariana dal 1532 al 1554, Sottochiesa di S. Francesco.* Exh. cat. Florence.

Arnold, Janet. 1985. *Patterns of Fashion: The Cut and Construction of Clothes for Men and Women c. 1560–1620.* London.

– 1988. 'Preliminary Investigation into the Medici Grave Clothes.' In Bemporad ed. 1988: 149–57.

– 1993. 'Cut and Construction.' In Florence, Palazzo Pitti 1993: 49–74.

Asch, Ronald G. 1991. 'Court and Household from the Fifteenth to the Seventeenth Centuries.' In Asch and Birke eds. 1991: 1–40.

Asch, Ronald G., and Adolf M. Birke, eds. 1991. *Princes, Patronage, and the Nobility.* London. 1991.

Ashengreen Piacenti, Kirsten. 2002. 'The Medici Grand-Ducal Family and the Symbols of Power.' In Chicago and Detroit 2002, 25–9.

Aston, Margaret. 1993. *The King's Bedpost: Reformation and Iconography in a Tudor Group Portrait.* Cambridge, Mass.

Austern, Linda. 1989. 'Sing Again Syren: The Female Musician and Sexual Enchantment in Elizabethan Life and Literature.' *Renaissance Quarterly* 42: 420–48.

Baccheschi, Edi. 1973. *L'Opera completa del Bronzino.* Milan.

Bacharach, A.L. and J.R. Pearce, eds. 1977. *The Musical Companion.* Rev. ed. New York, London, and Santiago.

Baia, Anna. 1907. *Leonora di Toledo, Duchessa di Firenza e di Siena.* Todi.

Baldass, Ludwig. 1935. 'The Portraiture of Master Michiel.' *Burlington Magazine* 67: 76–82.

Balis-Crema de' Medici, Giulio. 1946. 'Lucrezia de' Medici, Duchessa di Ferrara.' *Rivista araldica* 44: 39–42.

Baltimore. 1981. *Italian Paintings XIV–XVIII Centuries.* Exh. cat. by Gertrude Rosenthal. Baltimore Museum of Art.

Bargellini, Piero. 1968. 'Le Donne di Lorenzo de' Medici.' In *Donne di Casa Medici*, ed. Niccolò Rodolico, 11–32. Florence.

Bargellini, Piero, and Guarnieri, Ennio. 1977–8. *Le Strade di Firenze.* Vol. 4. Florence, 1978.

Barocchi, Paola, ed. 1998. *Pittura e scultura nel Cinquecento. Benedetto Varchi, Vincenzo Borghini*. Livorno.

Barolsky, Paul. 1990. 'Imaginative Literature and the Writing of Art History.' Review of *Poets on Painters*, ed. J.D. McClatchy, and *Writers on Artists*, ed. Daniel Halpern. *Source 9*, 4: 35–9.

– 1992–3. 'La Galerani's Galee.' *Source* 12: 13–14.

– 1998. 'As in Ovid, So in Renaissance Art.' *Renaissance Quarterly* 51, 2: 451–74.

Barolsky, Paul, and Andrew Ladis. 1991. 'The "Pleasurable Deceits" of Bronzino's So-called London *Allegory*.' *Source* 10: 32–6.

Barzman, Karen-edis. 1989. 'The Florentine Accademia del Disegno: Liberal Education and the Renaissance Artist.' In Boschloo et al. eds. 1989: 15–31.

– 1991. 'Perception, Knowledge, and the Theory of *Disegno* in Sixteenth-Century Florence.' In Feinberg 1991: 37–48.

– 2001. 'The Florentine Accademia del Disegno and Fellowships of Discourse at the Court of Cosimo I de' Medici.' In Eisenbichler ed. 2001: 177–88.

Basile, Deana. 2001. '*Fasseli gratia per poetessa*: Duke Cosimo I de' Medici's Role in the Florentine Circle of Tullia d'Aragona.' In Eisenbichler ed. 2001: 135–48.

Battaglia, Salvatore. 1981–. *Grande Dizionario della Lingua Italiana*. Turin.

Baumgärtel, Bettina. 2002. 'Is the King Genderless? The Staging of the Female Regent as *Minerva Pacifera*.' In Ann Arbor 2002: 97–118.

Baxandall, Michael. 1988. *Painting and Experience in Fifteenth-Century Italy: A Primer in the Social History of Pictorial Style*. 2nd ed. Oxford.

Becherucci, Luisa. 1964. *Manieristi toscani*. Bergamo.

Beck, James. 1972. 'Bronzino nell' inventario medéceo del 1560.' *Antichità viva* 11, 3: 10–12.

– 1974[1], 1974[2]. 'The Medici Inventory of 1560.' *Antichità viva* 13, 3: 64–6; and 13, 5: 61–3.

– 1975. 'Raphael and Medici "State Portraits."' *Zeitschrift für Kunstgeschichte* 38: 127–45.

– 1994. *Raphael*. New York.

Belozerskaya, Marina. 2002. *Rethinking the Renaissance: Burgundian Arts Across Europe*. Cambridge, MA.

Bemporad, Dora L. 1988. 'Il rapporto gioiello/abito nel costume del Rinascimento.' In *Il costume nell'età del Rinascimento*, ed. Dora L. Bemporad et al., 59–66. Florence.

Benson, Pamela J. 2004. 'Eleonora di Toledo among the Famous Women: Iconographic Innovation after the Conquest of Siena.' In Eisenbichler ed. 2004: 136–56.

Berenson, Bernard. 1963. *Italian Painters of the Renaissance, Florentine School*. London.

Bergdolt, Klaus, and Giorgio Bonsanti, eds. 2001. *Opere e giorni: Studi su mille anni di arte europea dedicati a Max Seidel*. Venice.

Berger, Harry Jr. 2000. *The Absence of Grace: Sprezzatura and Suspicion in Two Renaissance Courtesy Books*. Stanford.

Bergstein, Mary. 2001. Review of *Revaluing Renaissance Art*, ed. Gabriele Neher and Rupert Shepherd. *Renaissance Quarterly* 54: 1598–9.

Berman, Laurence, ed. 1972. *Words and Music: The Scholar's View. A Medley of Problems and Solutions Compiled in Honor of A. Tillman Merritt by Sundry Hands*. Cambridge, MA.

Bertelà, Giovanna Gaeta. 1997. *La Tribuna di Ferdinando I de' Medici. Inventari 1589–1631*. Modena.

Bertelli, Sergio, ed. 1985. *Le Corti italiane del Rinascimeno*. Milan.

Bertelli, Sergio, and G. Crifò, eds. 1985. *Rituale, ceremoniale, etichetta*. Milan.

Bertelli, Sergio, and Gloria Ramakus, eds. 1978. *Essays Presented to Myron T. Gilmore.* 2 vols. Florence.

Berti, Luciano. 1955. *La Casa del Vasari in Arezzo e il suo museo.* Florence.

– 1964. *Pontormo.* Florence.

– 1973. *Opera completa del Pontormo.* Milan.

– 1990. 'L'*Albardiere* del Pontormo.' *Critica d'Arte* 55: 39–49.

– 1993. *Pontormo e il suo tempo.* 1993.

– 2003. 'Michelangelo and Florentine Painting of the Sixteenth Century.' In Florence, Galleria dell' Accademia 2003: 29–73.

Blunt, Anthony. 1940. *Artistic Theory in Italy, 1450–1600.* Oxford.

– 1967. 'A Series of Paintings illustrating the History of the Medici Family Executed for Marie de Médicis – I.' *Burlington Magazine* 109: 492–8; 562–6.

Bober, Phyllis Pray. 1977. 'The Coryciana and the Nymph Corycia.' *Journal of the Warburg and Courtauld Institutes* 40: 223–39.

Bober, Phyllis Pray, and Ruth O. Rubenstein. 1986. *Renaissance Artists and Antique Sculpture. A Handbook of Sources.* London.

Bocci, M., and R. Bencini. 1971. *Palazzi di Firenze.* 4 vols. Florence.

Böhler, Julius. 1975. *Sale catalogue* (October–November). Munich.

Bonniwell, William R., O.P. 1944. *A History of the Dominican Liturgy.* New York.

Booth, Cecily. 1921. *Cosimo I, Duke of Florence.* Cambridge.

Borsook, Eve. 1979. *The Companion Guide to Florence.* 3rd ed. Englewood Cliffs, NJ, and London.

Bosch, Lynette M.F. 1983. 'Time, Truth and Destiny: Some Iconographical Themes in Bronzino's *Primavera* and *Giustizia.*' *Mitteilungen des Kunsthistorischen Institutes in Florenz* 27, 1: 73–82.

Boschloo, W.A., E.J. Hendrikse, L.C. Smit, and G.J. van der Sman, eds. 1989. *Academies of Art between Renaissance and Romantic.* Gravenhage.

Boskovits, Miklós. 1985. *The Martello Collection. Paintings, Drawings amd Miniatures from the XIVth to the XVIIIth Centuries.* Florence.

Bowen, William. 2003. 'The Contribution of French Musicians to the Genesis of the Italian Madrigal.' *Renaissance and Reformation / Renaissance et Réforme* 27, 2: 101–14.

Bowron, Edgar P. 1999. 'A Brief History of European Painting on Copper.' In Phoenix 1999: 9–30.

Brackett, John K. 1992. *Criminal Justice and Crime in Late Renaissance Florence.* Cambridge.

– 2005. 'Race and Rulership: Alessandro de' Medici, First Medici Duke of Florence.' In Earle and Lowe eds. 2005: 303–25.

Bremmer, J., and H. Roodenburg, eds. 1992. *A Cultural History of Gesture.* Ithaca, NY.

Bridgeman, Jane. 1998. '"*Condecenti et netti* ...": Beauty, Dress and Gender in Italian Renaissance Art.' In Ames-Lewis and Rogers 1998: 44–51.

Brilliant, Richard. 1971. 'On Portraits.' *Zeitschrift für Aesthetik und allgemeine Kunstwissenschaft* 16, 1: 11–16.

– 1987. 'Editor's Statement. Portraits: The Limitations of Likeness.' *Art Journal* 46: 171–2.

Brock, Maurice. 2002. *Bronzino.* Trans. David Poole Radzinowicz and Christine Schultz-Touge. Paris.

Brogi, Renato. 1921. *Isabella Orsini: Tragedia lirica in 4 atti. Riduzione scenica di Valentino Soldani da F.D. Guerrazzi. Versi di Eugenio Coleschi.* Florence.

Broude, Norma, and Mary D. Garrard, eds. 1992. *The Expanding Discourse: Feminism and Art History.* New York.

Brown, Alison, ed. 1995. *Language and Images in Renaissance Italy.* Oxford.

Brown, David Alan. 1983. 'Leonardo and the Idealized Portrait in Milan.' *Arte Lombardia* 67: 108–11.

– 1988. *Leonardo da Vinci: Origins of a Genius.* New Haven, CT, and London.

– ed. 2001. *Virtue and Beauty: Leonardo's 'Ginevra de' Benci' and Renaissance Portraits of Women.* Exh. cat. with contributions by Elizabeth Cropper, Eleanor Luciano, Dale Kent, Victoria Kirkham, Joanna Woods-Marsden, Roberta Orsi Landini, and Mary Westerman Bulgarella. National Gallery of Art, Washington.

Brown, Mayer Howard. 1972. 'Psyche's Lament: Some Music for the Medici Wedding in 1565.' In Berman, ed. 1972: 1–27.

Brumble, H. David. 1998. *Classical Myths and Legends in the Middle Ages and the Renaissance.* Westport, CT.

Brush, Kathryn. 1994. Review of Mararet Iversen, *Alois Riegl: Art History and Theory* and of Margaret Olin, *Forms of Representation in Alois Riegl's Theory of Art. Art Bulletin* 76, 2: 355–8.

Bryson, Norman. 1989. Review of Mark Roskill, *The Interpretation of Pictures. Art Bulletin* 71, 4: 704–7.

Burke, Peter. 1987. 'The Presentation of self in the Renaissance Portrait.' In *The Historical Anthropology of Early Modern Italy*, 150–67. Cambridge.

– 1989. 'The Renaissance Dialogue.' *Renaissance Studies* 3, 1: 1–12.

– 1992. 'The Language of Gesture in Early Modern Italy.' In Bremmer and Roodenberg eds. 1992: 59–83.

Bury, John Bernard. 1977. 'The Use of Candle-Light for Portrait Painting in Sixteenth-Century Italy.' *Burlington Magazine* 119, 891 (June): 434–7.

– 1989. 'Francisco de Holanda's Treatise on Portraiture.' In *IV Simpòsio Luso-Espanhol de Historòia da Arte Portugal e Espanha entre a Europa e Além-mar Coimbra, 13 a 17 de Abril de 1987*, 87–103. Coimbra.

Bury, Michael. 1994. Review of F. Haskell, *History and its Images: Art and the Interpretation of the Past. History* 79, 258: 89–90.

Butchart, David S. 1985. '"La Pecorina" at Mantua, *Musica Nova* at Florence.' *Early Music* 13, 3: 358–66.

Campbell, Lorne. 1985. *The Early Flemish Pictures in the Collection of Her Majesty the Queen.* Cambridge.

– 1990. *Renaissance Portraits.* New Haven, CT, and London.

Campbell, Malcolm. 1983. 'Observations on the Salone dei 500.' In Diaz ed. 1983, 3: 819–30.

– 1985[1]. 'Il ritratto del duca Alessandro de' Medici di Giorgio Vasari: Contesto e significato.' In Garfagnini ed. 1985: 339–62.

– 1985[2]. Review of Karla Langedijk, *The Portraits of the Medici. Burlington Magazine* 127, 988: 386–8.

Campbell, Stephen, and Stephen Milner, eds. 2004. *Artistic Exchange and Cultural Translation in the Italian Renaissance City.* New York.

Caneday, Norman. 1967. 'The Decoration of the Stanza della Cleopatra.' In *Essays in the History of Art Presented to Rudolf Wittkower.* 2 vols. London.

Caneva, Caterina, Roberta Orsi Landini, and Maria Sframeli. 1999. 'The Medici Portraits,'
    in Providence, RI 1999: 23–43.

Cantagelli, Roberto. 1985. *Cosimo de' Medici, Granduca di Toscana*. Milan.

Capretti, Elena. 2002. In Florence, Palazzo Pitti 2002: 122–3.

Cardamone, Donna. 1996. 'Lifting the Protective Veil of Anonymity: Women as Com-
    poser-Performers, ca. 1300–1566.' In *Music Through the Ages: Women Composers. Compos-
    ers Born before 1599*, vol. 1, ed. Martha Furman Schleifer and Sylvia Glickman, 110–17.
    New York.

– 2002. 'Isabella Medici-Orsini: A Portrait of Self-Affirmation.' In *Gender, Sexuality, and
    Early Music*, ed. Todd Borgerding, 1–27. New York.

Carloni, Paolo, and Monica Grasso. 1994. 'L'eloquenza della virtù: Giorgio Vasari, Anton
    Francesco Doni e il linguaggio allegorico nel Cinquecento. Riflessioni attorno a una
    ricerca compiuta.' *Storia dell'arte* 82: 425–43.

Carnesecchi, C. 1909. 'Giovanna d'Austria in pellegrinaggio.' *L'Illustratore fiorentino*: 51–61.

Caroli, Flavio. 1987. *Sofonisba Anguissola e le sue sorelle*. Exh. cat. Tel Aviv Museum, Milan.

Carroll, Margaret. 1989. 'The Erotics of Absolutism: Rubens and the Mystification of Sexual
    Violence.' *Representations* 25: 3–30.

Cecchi, Alessandro. 1991. 'Il Bronzino, Benedetto Varchi e l'Accademia Fiorentina:
    Ritratti di poeti, letterati e personaggi illustri della corte medicea.' *Antichità viva* 30,
    1–2: 17–28.

– 1996[1]. *Bronzino*. Florence, 1996.

– 1996[2]. 'L'Ultima Repubblica, 1527–1530. L'Assedio, la Libertà Perduta, e la Nascita del
    Regime.' In Florence, Uffizi 1996: 370–2.

– 1998. 'Il Maggiordomo ducale Pierfrancesco Riccio e gli artisti della corte medicea.' *Mit-
    teilungen des Kunsthistorischen Institut in Florenz* 42, 1: 115–43.

Celletti, Vincenzo. 1963. *Gli Orsini di Bracciano*. Rome.

Cesati, Franco. 1999. *The Medici: Story of a European Dynasty*. Prato.

Chabot, Isabelle. 1994. '"La sposa in nero": La ritualizzazione del lutto delle vedove fioren-
    tine (secoli XIV–XVI).' *Quaderni Storici* 86: 421–62.

Chater, James. 1985. 'Bianca Cappello and Music.' In Morrogh et al. eds. 1985: 569–79.

Cheetham, Nicholas. 1982. *A History of the Popes*. New York.

Cheney, Liana De Girolami. 1998. 'Vasari's Interpretation of Female Beauty.' In Ames-
    Lewis and Rogers, eds. 1998: 179–90.

Chicago. 1975. *The Art of Jewelry, 1450–1650*. Exh. cat. Martin d'Arcy Gallery of Art, Loyola
    University of Chicago.

Chicago and Detroit. 2002. *The Medici, Michelangelo, and the Art of Late Renaissance Florence*.
    Exh. cat. by Cristina Acidini Luchinat *et al*. New Haven and London.

Christie's. 1971. *Fine Pictures by Old Masters*. Sale catalogue, 14 May.

– 1989. *Pontormo*. Sale cat. New York, 31 May.

Ciabani, Roberto, ed. 1992. *Le famiglie di Firenze*. Vol. 1. Florence.

Ciardi, Roberto P., and Antonio Natali, eds. 1996. *Pontormo e Rosso*. Venice.

Cionini-Visani, Maria, and Grgo Ganulin. 1980. *Giulio Clovio, Miniaturist of the Renaissance*.
    New York.

Clapp, Frederick M. 1916. *Jacopo Carucci da Pontormo: His Life and Work*. New Haven, CT,
    and London.

Clark, Kenneth. 1967. *Leonardo da Vinci*. Rev., 2nd ed. Harmondsworth.

Clements, Robert. 1969. 'The Authenticity of De Hollanda's Dialogos em Roma.' In Robert Clements, *The Peregrine Muse: Studies in Comparative Renaissance Literature*, 110–24. Chapel Hill, NC.

Cleugh, James. 1975. *The Medici*. New York.

Clough, C.H. 1967. 'Federigo da Montefeltro's Private Study in His Ducal Palace of Gubbio.' *Apollo* 71: 279–89.

Cochrane, Eric. 1973. *Florence in the Forgotten Centuries, 1527–1800*. Chicago.

Coffin, David R. 1955. 'Pirro Ligorio and the Decoration of the Late Sixteenth Century at Ferrara.' *Art Bulletin* 37, 2: 167–85.

Cohen, Charles E. 1981. Review of David Rosand, *Titian*. *Art Bulletin* 63, 1: 160–2.

Cohen, Sarah. 2003. 'Rubens's France: Gender and Personification in the Marie de Médicis Cycle.' *Art Bulletin* 83, 3: 490–522.

Cohen, Thomas V., and Elizabeth S. Cohen. 1993. *Words and Deeds in Renaissance Rome: Trials before the Papal Magistrates*. Toronto.

Cole, Alison. 1995. *Virtue and Magnificence: Art of the Italian Renaissance Courts*. New York.

– 1998. 'The Perception of Beauty in Landscape in the Quattrocentro.' In Ames-Lewis and Rogers eds. 1998: 28–43.

Cole Ahl, Diane. 1997. *Benozzo Gozzoli*. Trans. Diane Cole Ahl. New Haven, CT.

Conti, Cosimo. 1893. *La Prima Reggia di Cosimo de' Medici nel Palazzo gia della Signoria di Firenze coll'appoggio di un inventario inedito del 1553*. Florence.

Corradini, Elena. 1998. 'Medallic Portraits of the d' Este: *Effigies ad vivum expressae*.' In Mann and Syson eds. 1998: 22–39.

Corrias, Paola. 1993. 'Don Vincenzo Borghini e l'iconologia del potere alla corte di Cosimo I e di Francesco I de' Medici.' *Storia dell'arte* 81: 169–81.

Corti, Laura. 1989. *Vasari: Catalogo Completo dei dipinti*. Florence.

Costamagna, Philippe. 1988. 'Seconde parte: Les portraits.' *Antichità viva* 27, 1: 23–31.

– 1992. 'A propos du séjour Florentin de Giulio Clovio (1498–1578).' In *Kunst des Cinquecento in der Toskana*, ed. Monika Cämmerer, 168–75. Munich.

– 1994. *Pontormo*. Milan.

– 2002. 'De l'idéal de beauté aux problèmes d'attribution: Vingt ans de recherche sur le portrait florentin au XVIᵉ siècle.' *Studiolo* 1: 193–213.

Cox-Rearick, Janet. 1964. *The Drawings of Pontormo*. Cambridge, MA.

– 1981. *The Drawings of Pontormo*. Rev. ed., 2 vols. New York.

– 1982. 'Bronzino's *Young Woman with Her Little Boy*.' *Studies in the History of Art* 12: 67–79.

– 1984. *Dynasty and Destiny in Medici Art: Pontormo, Leo X, and the Two Cosimos*. Princeton, NJ.

– 1987. 'Bronzino's *Crossing of the Red Sea and Moses Appointing Joshua*: Prolegomena to the Chapel of Eleonora di Toledo.' *Art Bulletin* 69, 1: 45–67.

– 1989. 'From Bandinelli to Bronzino: The Genesis of the *Lamentation* for the Chapel of Eleonora di Toledo.' *Mitteilungen des Kunsthistorischen Institutes in Florenz* 33, 1: 70–83.

– 1991. 'Deux Dessins de Bronzino découverts au Louvre.' *Revue du Louvre* 5, 6: 35–47.

– 1993. *Bronzino's Chapel of Eleonora in the Palazzo Vecchio*. Berkeley, Los Angeles, and Oxford.

– 1995. *The Collection of Francis I: Royal Treasures*. New York, 1995.

– 1997. Review of Philippe Costamagna, *Pontormo*. *Burlington Magazine* 39, 1127: 127–8.

– 2002. 'Art at the Court of Duke Cosimo de' Medici (1537–1574).' In Chicago and Detroit 2002: 35–45.

– 2004. *'La Ill.ma Sig.ra Duchessa felice memoria:* The Posthumous Eleonora di Toledo.' In Eisenbichler ed. 2004: 225–66.

– 2005. 'Pontormo and Bronzino' Review of Carl Brandon Strehlke, *Pontormo, Bronzino and the Medici: The Transformation of the Renaissance Portrait in Florence.* Exh. cat., Philadelphia Museum of Art, 2004. *Burlington Magazine* 147: 211–13.

Cox-Rearick, Janet, and Mary Westerman Bulgarella. 2004. 'Public and Private Portraits of Cosimo I de' Medici and Eleonora di Toledo: Bronzino's Paintings of His Ducal Patrons in Ottawa and Turin.' *Artibus et Historiae* 49: 101–59.

Cranston, Jodi. 2000. *The Poetics of Portraiture in the Italian Renaissance.* Cambridge.

Cren, Thomas. 1983. *Renaissance Painting and Manuscripts.* London.

Cropper, Elizabeth. 1976. 'On Beautiful Women: Parmigianino, Petrarchismo and the Vernacular Style.' *Art Bulletin* 58, 4: 374–94.

– 1986. 'The Beauty of Women: Problems in the Rhetoric of Renaissance Portraiture.' In Fergusen et al. 1986: 175–90.

– 1995. 'The Place of Beauty in the High Renaissance and Its Displacement in the History of Art.' In Vos ed. 1995: 159–206.

– 1997. *Pontormo: Portrait of a Halberdier.* Los Angeles.

– 1998. Introduction. In Ames-Lewis and Rogers eds. 1998: 1–11.

– 2000. 'L'arte cortigiana a Firenze: Dalla Repubblica dissimulata allo Stato paterno.' In *Storia delle arti in Toscana: Il Cinquecento*, Robert P. Ciardi and Antonio Natali, eds. 85–116. Florence.

– 2001[1]. 'Afterface.' In Catherine Monbeig Goguel, Philippe Costamagna, and Michel Hochmann, *Francesco Salviati et la Bella Maniera. Actes des colloques de Rome et de Paris (1998)*, 691–8. Rome.

– 2001[2]. 'Preparing to Finish: Portraits by Pontormo and Bronzino around 1530.' In Bergdolt and Bonsanti eds. 2001: 499–504.

– 2001[3]. In Washington 2001 (exh. cat.)

– 2004. 'Pontormo and Bronzino in Philadelphia: A Double Portrait.' In Strehlke 2004: 1–33.

Crum, Roger. 2001[1]. 'Lessons from the Past: The Palazzo Medici as Political "Mentor" in Sixteenth-Century Florence.' In Eisenbichler ed. 2001: 47–51.

– 2001[2]. 'Controlling Women or Women Controlled? Suggestions for Gender Roles and Visual Culture in the Italian Renaissance Palace.' In Reiss and Wilkins eds. 2001: 37–50.

Cuadrado, John A. 1991. 'Portrait Miniatures – Captivating Glimpses into History.' *Architectural Digest* 48, 4: 40–54.

D'Addario, Arnaldo. 1968. 'Eleonora di Toledo, duchessa di Firenze e Siena.' In Rodolico ed. 1968: 33–62.

– 1972. *Aspetti della Controriforma a Firenze.* Rome.

Daly Davis, M. 1982. 'Vincenzo Danti's *Trattato delle perfette proporzioni*.' *Mitteilungen des Kunsthistorischen Institutes in Florenz* 26, 1: 63–84.

Darnton, Robert. 1994. 'Sex for Thought.' Review of ed. Raymond Trousson, *L'Enfer de la Bibliotheque Nationale: Romans libertins du XVIIIe siècle*, and Jean Marie Goulemot, *Ces Livres qu'on ne lit que d'une main: Lecture et lecteurs de livres pornographiques au XVIIIe siècle. New York Review of Books* 41, 21 (1994): 65–74.

Darr, Alan P. 2002. 'The Medici and the Legacy of Michelangelo in Late Renaissance Florence: An Introduction.' In Detroit and Chicago 2002: 1–7.

Davis, Charles. 1978. 'Aspects of Imitation in Cavino's Medals.' *Journal of the Warburg and Courtauld Institutes* 41: 331–5.

– 1981. In Arezzo 1981, sect. 7, no. 14: 300–11.

de Amezua y Mayo, A.G. 1949. *Isabel de Valois, reina de Espagña (1546–1568)*. Madrid.

Del Badia, Iodocco. 1902. *Miscellanea fiorentina di erudizione e storia*. 2 vols. Florence.

De Lellis, C. 1654. *Famiglie nobili del Regno di Napoli*. Vol. 1. Naples.

Del Lungo, Isodoro. 1906. *La donna fiorentina del buon tempo antico*. Florence.

de Logu, Giuseppe, and Guido Marinelli. 1975. *Il ritratto nella pittura Italiana*. 2 vols. Bergamo.

Dempsey, Charles. 1981. 'Some Observations on the Education of Artists in Florence and Bologna during the Later Sixteenth Century.' *Art Bulletin* 63, 4: 553–69.

Deswarte-Rosa, Sylvie. 1991. '*Idea* et le Temple de la Peinture: I, Michelangelo Buonarroti et Francisco de Hollanda.' *Revue de l'Art* 92: 20–41.

Detroit Institute of Arts. 1988. *Sixteenth-Century Tuscan Drawings from the Uffizi*. Exh. cat. by Anna-Maria Petrioli Tofani and Graham Smith. Detroit.

De Vecchi, Pierluigi. 1979. *L'Opera completa di Raffaello*. Milan.

Diaz, Furio. 1978. 'Cosimo I e il consolidarsi dello Stato assoluto.' In Guarini ed. 1978: 75–97.

Diaz, Furio, ed. 1983. *Firenze e la Toscana dei Medici nell'Europa dell' 500*. 3 vols. Vol. 1: *Strumenti e veicoli della cultura. Relazione politiche ed economiche*; vol. 2: *Musica e spettacolo. Scienze dell' uomo e della natura*; vol. 3: *Relazione artistiche. Il linguaggio architettonico*. Florence.

Dickens, A.G., ed. 1977. *The Courts of Europe: Politics, Patronage and Royalty, 1400–1800*. London.

Di Domenico, Cristina, and Donatella Lippi. 2005. *I Medici: Una dinastia ai raggi X*. Siena.

Dixon, Annette. 2002. 'Women Who Ruled: Queens, Goddesses, Amazons 1500–1650. A Thematic Overview.' In Ann Arbor 2002: 119–78.

Duby, Georges, Michelle Perrot, et al. 1992. *Power and Beauty: Images of Women in Art*. London.

Earle, T.F., and K.J.P. Lowe, eds. 2005. *Black Africans in Renaissance Europe*. New York.

Edelstein, Bruce. 1995. 'The Early Patronage of Eleanora di Toledo. The *Camera Verde* and Its Dependencies in the Palazzo Vecchio.' PhD diss., Harvard University.

– 2000. 'Nobildonne napoletane e committenza: Eleonora d'Aragona ed Eleonora di Toledo a confronto.' *Quaderno Storici* 104, 2: 295–329.

– 2001. 'Bronzino in the Service of Eleonora di Toledo and Cosimo I de' Medici: Conjugal Patronage and the Painter-Courtier.' In Reiss and Wilkins eds. 2001: 225–62.

– 2004[1]. '"*Aqua viva e corrente*": Private Display and Public Distribution of Fresh Water in the Neapolitan Villa of Poggioreale as a Hydraulic Model for Sixteenth-Century Medici Gardens.' In S. Campbell and Milner eds. 2004: 187–200.

– 2004[2]. '*La fecundissima Signora Duchessa*: The Courtly Persona of Eleonora di Toledo and the Iconography of Abundance.' In Eisenbichler ed. 2004: 71–97.

Edgerton, Samuel Y., Jr. 1985. *Pictures and Punishment. Art and Criminal Prosecution during the Florentine Renaissance*. Ithaca and London.

Eiche, Sabina. 1995. 'Un dessin inconnu de Jacopo Zucchi pour la villa Médicis.' *Revue de l'Art* 108: 61–4.

Einstein, Alfred. 1971. *The Italian Madrigal*. 2 vols. Princeton, NJ., 1949. Repr., 1971.

Eisenbichler, Konrad. 1988. 'Bronzino's Portrait of Guidobaldo II della Rovere.' *Renaissance and Reformation* 24 (1988): 21–33.

– 1998. Review of James M. Saslow, *The Medici Wedding of 1589: Florentine Festival as Theatrum Mundi*. *Renaissance Quarterly* 51, 1: 204–5.

– 2001. 'Laudomia Forteguerri Loves Margaret of Austria.' In *Same-Sex Love and Desire among Women in the Middle Ages*, ed. Francesca Canadé Sautman and Pamela Sheingorn, 277–304. New York.

– 2003. '"*Un chant à l'honneur de la France*": Women's Voices at the end of the Republic of Siena.' *Renaissance and Reformation* 27, 2 (2003): 87–99.

Eisenbichler, Konrad, ed. 2001. *The Cultural Politics of Duke Cosimo I de' Medici*. Aldershot, UK, and Burlington, VT.

– ed. 2004. *The Cultural World of Eleonora di Toledo, Duchess of Florence and Siena*. Aldershot, UK, and Burlington, VT.

Eisler, Colin. 1989. *The Thyssen-Bornemisza Collection. Early Netherlandish Painting*. London.

Elam, Caroline. 1988. 'The Position of Women in Renaissance Florence: neither Autonomy nor Subjection.' In *Florence and Italy: Renaissance Studies in Honour of Nicolai Rubenstein*, P. Denley and C. Elam, ed. 369–81. London.

Elsen, Albert. 1988. 'The Artist's Oldest Right?' *Art History* 2, 2: 218–29.

Emiliani, Andrea. 1960. *Il Bronzino*. Milan.

Emison, Patricia. 1991. 'Grazia.' *Renaissance Studies* 5, 4: 427–54.

Ettlinger, Helen S. 1994. '*Visibilis et Invisibilis*: The Mistress in Italian Renaissance Court Society.' *Renaissance Quarterly* 47, 4: 770–90.

Evans, Mark. 1991. 'The Court: A Protean Institution and an Elusive Subject.' In Asch and Birke eds. 1991: 481–91. London.

– 1998. *Princes as Patrons: The Art Collections of the Princes of Wales from the Renaissance to the Present Day. An Exhibition from the Royal Collection*. With an introduction by Charles, Prince of Wales. Exh. cat. National Museum and Gallery of Wales, Cardiff, 25 July–8 November.

Fahy, Conor. 2000. 'Women in Italian Cinquecento Academies.' In Panizza ed. 2000: 438–52.

Falciani, Carlo. 1995. 'Maria Salviati ritratta dal Pontormo.' In Natali ed. 1995: 119–34.

– 1996. *Pontormo: Disegni degli Uffizi*. Gabinetto Disegni e Stampe degli Uffizi. Florence.

Fantoni, Marcello. 1989. 'Il culto dell'Annunziata e la sacralità del potere mediceo.' *Archivio Storico Italiano* 4: 771–93.

– 1994. *La Corte del Granduca: Forma e simboli del potere mediceo fra Cinque e Seicento*. Rome.

– 1999. 'The Grand Duchy of Tuscany: The Courts of the Medici 1532–1737.' In Adamson ed. 1999: 255–73.

Farago, Claire. 1991. 'Leonardo's Color and Chiaroscuro Reconsidered: The Visual Force of Painted Images.' *Art Bulletin* 73, 1: 63–88.

– 1994. 'Leonardo's *Battle of Anghiari*: A Study in the Exchange between Theory and Practice.' *Art Bulletin* 76, 2: 301–30.

Feinberg, Larry J. 1991. *From Studio to Studiolo: Florentine Draftsmanship under the First Medici Grand Dukes*. Seattle and London.

– 2002. 'The Studiolo of Francesco I Reconsidered.' In Chicago and Detroit 2002: 47–65.

Felice, B. 1905. 'Maria Salviati, moglie di Giovanni delle Bande Nere.' *Rassegna nazionale* 152: 620–5.

Fenlon, Iain. 1983. 'Music, Piety and Politics under Cosimo I: The Case of Costanzo Porta.'
     In Diaz 1983, 2: 457–68.
– 1995. *Music, Print and Culture in Early Sixteenth-Century Italy*. London.
Fenlon, Iain, and James Haar. 1988. *The Italian Madrigal in the Early Sixteenth Century*. Cam-
     bridge and New York.
Fergusen, Margaret W., et al. 1986. *Rewriting the Renaissance: The Discourse of Sexual Differ-
     ence in Early Modern Europe*. Chicago.
Fermor, Sharon. 1991. 'In a Glass Darkly: Three Views of Renaissance Portraiture.' *Art His-
     tory* 5, 14: 431–4.
– 1993. 'Movement and Gender in Sixteenth-Century Italian Painting.' In *Body Imaged: The
     Human Form and Visual Culture Since the Renaissance*, ed. Kathleen Adler and Marcia
     Pointon, 129–45. Cambridge, 1993.
– 1998. 'Poetry in Motion: Beauty in Movement and the Renaissance Conception of
     leggiadria.' In Ames-Lewis and Rogers eds. 1998: 124–33.
Fernie, Eric. 1995. *Art History and Its Methods: A Critical Anthology*. London.
Ferrai, Luigi Alberto. 1882. *Cosimo I de' Medici, Duca di Firenze*. Bologna.
– 1891. *Lorenzino de' Medici e la società cortegiana del Cinquecento*. Milan.
ffolliott, Sheila. 1989. 'Casting a Rival into the Shade: Catherine de' Medici and Diane de
     Poitiers.' *Art Journal* 48, 2: 138–43.
Filipczak, Zirka A. 1997. *Hot Dry Men and Cold Wet Women: The Theory of Humors in Western
     European Art 1575–1700*. Exh. cat. Williams College Museum of Art, New York.
Finsten, Jill. 1979. 'Isaac Oliver: Art at the Courts of Elizabeth I and James I.' PhD diss.,
     2 vols., Harvard University.
Fischlin, Daniel. 1997. 'Political Allegory, Absolutist Ideology, and the "Rainbow Portrait"
     of Queen Elizabeth I.' *Renaissance Quarterly* 50, 1: 175–206.
Florence, Galleria dell' Accademia. 2003. *Around the David: The Great Art of Michelangelo's
     Century*. Exh. cat. by Franca Faletti and Magnolia Scudieri. Florence.
Florence, Palazzo Pitti. 1985. *I Principe Bambini*. Exh. cat. by Kirsten Ashengreen Piacenti
     and Roberta Orsi Landini. Florence.
– 1993. *Moda alla corte dei Medici: Gli abiti di Cosimo, Eleonora e don Garzia*. Exh. cat. by Janet
     Arnold, Mary Westerman Bulgarella, Roberta Orsi Landini, Giovanna Lazzi, Kirsten
     Aschengreen Piacenti, and Stefania Ricci. Florence.
– 2002. *Domenico Puligo (1492–1527). Un potagonista dimenticato della pittura fiorentina*. Exh.
     cat. by Elena Capretti, Serena Padovani, and Stefano Casciu, with essay by Anna Forlani
     Tempesti. Florence.
– 2003. *I gioielli dei Medici dal vero e in ritratto*. Exh. cat. Ed. Maria Sframeli and Costanza
     Contu. Florence.
Florence, Palazzo Pitti, and Museo degli Argenti. 1997–8. *Magnificenza alla Corte dei Medici:
     Arte a Firenze alla fine del Cinquecento*. Ed. C. Acidini Luchinat, M. Gregori, D. Heikamp,
     and A. Paolucci. Florence.
– 2005. *Maria de' Medici: Una Principessa Fiorentina sul Trono di Francia*. Exh. cat. Ed. by
     Caterina Caneva and Francesco Solinas. Livorno.
Florence, Palazzo Strozzi. 1956. *Mostra del Pontormo e del primo manierismo fiorentino*. Exh.
     cat. by Luciano Berti, Umberto Baldini, and Luisa Marucci. Florence.
– 1980. *Il Primato del disegno: Firenze e la Toscana dei Medici nell'Europa del Cinquecento*. Exh.
     cat. by Luciano Berti. Florence.

– 2002. *L'Ombra del genio: Michelangelo e l'arte a Firenze, 1537–1631*. Exh. cat.

Florence, Palazzo Vecchio. 1980. *Palazzo Vecchio: Committenza e collezionismo medicei (Firenze e la Toscana dei Medici nell'Europa del Cinquecento)*. Exh. cat. by various authors. Florence.

Florence, Uffizi. 1966. *Mostra di disegni vasariani: Carri trionfali e costumi per la genealogia degli dei (1565)*. Exh. cat. by Anna Maria Petrioli. Florence.

– 1970. *Mostra di disegni di Alessandro Allori (Firenze 1535–1607)*. Exh. cat. by Simona Lecchini Giovannoni. Florence.

– 1980. *Gli Uffizi: Catalogo Generale*. 2nd ed. Florence.

– 1996[1]. *L'Officina della Maniera: Varietà e fierezza nell' arte fiorentina del Cinquecento fra le due Repubbliche, 1494–1530*. Exh. cat. by Alessandro Cecchi and Antonio Natali. Florence.

– 1996[2]. *Pontormo: Desegni degli Uffizi*. Exh. cat. by Carlo Falciani. Florence.

Florence, Uffizi, Gabinetto dei Disegni e delle Stampe 1976. *Omaggio a Leopoldo de' Medici 2: Ritrattini*. Exh. cat. by Silvia Meloni Trkulja. Florence.

Fock, C. Willemijn. 1970. 'The Medici Crown: Work of the Delft Goldsmith Jacques Bylivert.' *Oud Holland* 85: 197–209.

– 1983. 'Les orfèvres-joailliers étrangers à la cour des Médicis.' In Diaz ed. 1983, 3: 831–45.

Foister, Susan. 1995. 'The Production and Reproduction of Holbein's Paintings.' In Hearn ed. 1995: 21–6.

Follain, John. 2004. 'Medici Bones Reveal Truth of "Murders."' *Sunday Times*, 'World' section, 15 August.

Forlani Tempesti, Anna, and Alessandro Giovannetti. 1994. *Pontormo*. Florence.

Forster, Kurt W. 1964, 1965, 1967. 'Probleme um Pontormos Porträtmalerei.' *Pantheon* 22 (1964): 376–84; 23 (1965): 217–31; 25 (1967): 27–34.

– 1966. *Pontormo: Monographie mit kritischem Katalog*. Munich.

– 1971. 'Metaphors of Rule: Political Ideology and History in the Portraits of Cosimo I de' Medici.' *Mitteilungen des Kunsthistorischen Institutes in Florenz* 15: 65–104.

Forsyth, Ilene. 1972. *The Throne of Wisdom: Wood Sculptures of the Madonna in Romanesque France*. Princeton, NJ.

Foskett, Daphne. 1987. *Miniatures: Dictionary and Guide*. Woodbridge, UK.

Fowden, Garth. 1993. *The Egyptian Hermes: A Historical Approach to the Late Pagan Mind*. 2nd ed. Princeton, NJ.

Francastel, Galienne, and Pierre Francastel. 1969. *Le portrait: 50 siècles d'humanisme en peinture*. Paris.

Franceschini, Chiara. 2004. '*Los scholares son cosa de su excelentia, como lo es toda la Compañia*: Eleonora di Toledo and the Jesuits.' In Eisenbichler ed. 2004: 181–206.

Fraser, Antonia. 1992. *The Wives of Henry VIII*. New York.

Freedberg, David. 1969. *The Power of Images: Studies in the History and Theory of Reponse*. Chicago.

Freedberg, Sydney. 1950. *Parmigianino: His Works in Painting*. Cambridge, MA.

– 1961. *Painting of the High Renaissance in Rome and Florence*. Cambridge, MA.

– 1966. 'Observations on the Painting of the Maniera.' *Art Bulletin* 47, 3–4: 187–97.

– 1971. *Painting in Italy: 1500–1600*. New Haven, CT, and Harmondsworth.

– 1993. *Painting in Italy: 1500–1600*. 3rd ed. New Haven, CT, and Harmondsworth.

Freedman, Luba. 1989. 'Raphael's Perception of the Mona Lisa.' *Gazette des Beaux-Arts* 114, 1450: 168–83.

– 1993. 'The Counter-Portrait: The Quest for the Ideal in Italian Renaissance Portraiture.' In Gentile et al. eds. 1993: 63–81.

– 1995. *Titian's Portraits through Aretino's Lens*. University Park, PA.

Frey, K. 1923. *Der literarische Nachlass Giorgio Vasaris*. 2 vols. Munich.

Furno, Albertina. 1902. *La vita e le rime di Angiolo Bronzino*. Pistoia.

Gallucci, Margaret. 2001. 'Cellini's Trial for Sodomy: Power and Patronage at the Court of Cosimo I.' In Eisenbichler ed. 2001: 37–46.

Gamba, Carlo. 1910. 'Un Ritratto di Cosimo I del Pontormo.' *Rivista d'arte* 7: 125–7.

– 1929. 'A Proposito di Alessandro Allori e di un suo ritratto.' *Rivista del R. Instituto d'Archeologia e Storia dell'arte* 5: 265–77.

– 1956. *Contributo alla conoscenza del Pontormo*. Florence.

Garciá, Eladi Romero. 1986. *El Imperialismo Hispanico en la Toscana durante el Siglo XVI*. Lleida.

Garfagnini, Gian Carlo, ed. 1985. *Giorgio Vasari: Tra decorazione ambientale e storiografia artistica. Convegno di studi (Arezzo, 8–10 ottobre 1981)*. Florence.

Garrard, Mary. 1992. 'Leonardo da Vinci: Female Portraits, Female Nature.' In Broude and Garrard eds. 1992: 58–85.

Gaston, Robert W. 1983. 'Iconography and Portraiture in Bronzino's "Christ in Limbo."' *Mitteilungen des Kunsthistorischen Institutes in Florenz* 27: 41–72.

– 1991. 'Love's Sweet Poison: A New Reading of Bronzino's London *Allegory*.' *I Tatti Studies* 4: 249–88.

– 1997. Review of Elizabeth Cropper and Charles Dempsey, *Nicholas Poussin: Friendship and the Love of Painting. Sixteenth Century Journal* 28, 3: 993–5.

– 2004. 'Eleonora di Toledo's Chapel: Lineage, Salvation and the War against the Turks. In Eisenbichler ed. 2004: 157–81.

Gaunt, William. 1980. *Court Painters in England*. London.

Gauthiez, Pierre. 1901. *Jean des Bandes Noires*. 2nd ed. Paris.

Gelabert, Juan E. 1999. 'I banchieri genovesi nel sistema finanziario spagnolo.' In Report of *Italia non Spagnola e Monarchia Spagnola tra '500 e '600. Convegno Internazionale di Studi Promosso dal Dipartmento di Storia moderna e contemporanea e dal Dipartmento di Lingue e Letterature romanze dell' Università, dalla Scuola Normale Superiore di Pisa, dalla Provincia di Pisa e dalla Sociedad Estatal para la commemoración de los centenarios de Felipe II y Carlos V*. Pisa, 11–12 December 1998: 8. Accessed at listserve h-italy@h-net.msu/edu, 28 January 1999.

Gentile, Augusto, Philippe Morel, and Claudia Cieri Via, eds. *Il ritratto e la memoria. Materiale I: Europa delle Corte*. Rome, 1981.

Ghisalberti, Alberto M., General ed. 1960– *Dizionario Biografico degli Italiani*. Rome.

Ghisi, Federico. 1969. *Feste musicali della Firenza Medicea*. Bologna.

Gilbert, Creighton. 1943–44. 'Antique Frameworks for Renaissance Art Theory: Alberti and Pino.' *Marsyas* 3: 88–109.

Gilmore, David, ed. 1987. *Honor and Shame and the Unity of the Mediterranean*. Special publication of the American Anthropological Association 22: 61–74.

Ginori Conti, Piero, ed. 1936–44. *L'apparato per le nozze di Francesco de' Medici e di Giovanna d'Austria nelle narrazioni del tempo e de lettere inedite di Vincenzio Borghini e di Giorgio Vasari*. Florence.

Ginori-Lisci, Leonardo. 1985. *The Palazzi of Florence, Their History and Their Art*. Trans. Jennifer Grillo. Florence.

Giovannini, Maureen J. 1987. 'Female Chastity Codes in the Circum-Mediterranean: Comparative Perspectives.' In David Gilmore ed., 1987: 61–74.

Goffen, Rona. 1992. 'Titian's *Sacred and Profane Love* and Marriage.' In Broude and Garrard 1992: 111–26.

– 1995. Review of John Shearman, *Only Connect ... Art and the Spectator in the Italian Renaissance. Renaissance Quarterly* 48, 1: 192–4.

Goffen, Rona, ed. 1997. *Titian's 'Venus of Urbino.'* Cambridge and New York.

Goldberg, Edward L. 1983. *Patterns in Late Medici Art Patronage.* Princeton, NJ.

– 1988. *After Vasari: History, Art and Patronage in Late Medici Florence.* Princeton, NJ.

– 1996. 'Artistic Relations between the Medici and the Spanish Courts, 1587–1621: Part I.' *Burlington Magazine* 137, 1115: 105–14.

Goldstein, Carl. 1975. 'Vasari and the Florentine Accademia del Disegno.' *Zeitschrift für Kunstgeschichte* 38, 2: 145–52.

– 1988. *Visual Fact over Verbal Fiction.* Greensboro, NC.

– 1997. *Teaching Art: Academies and Schools from Vasari to Albers.* Cambridge.

Goodman-Soellner, Elise. 1983. 'Poetic Interpretations of the "Lady at Her Toilette" Theme in Sixteenth-Century Painting.' *Sixteenth Century Journal* 14, 1: 426–42.

Gopnik, Blake. 1997. 'Whose Work Is It Anyway?' *Globe and Mail*, Toronto, 19 November: C1 and C19.

– 1999. 'Portraits Make Princes Out of Frogs.' *Globe and Mail*, Toronto, 7 October: C1.

Grassellini, E., and A. Fracassini. 1982. *Profili medicei.* Florence.

Greenblatt, S. 1980. *Renaissance Self-Fashioning.* Chicago.

Gregori, Mina. 1994. *Paintings in the Uffizi and Pitti Galleries.* Intros. by Antonio Paolucci and Marco Chiarini. London.

Gregori, Mina, Valerio Guazzoni, Maria Kusche, and Rossana Sacchi, eds. 1994. *Sofonisba Anguissola and Her Sisters.* Exh. cat. Cremona, Vienna, and Washington.

Grohn, H.W. 1982. 'Ein unveroffentlichtes werk des Bronzino.' *Niederdeutsche Beitrage zur Kunstgeschichte* 21: 59–68.

Gronau, Charles. 1903. 'Titian's Portrait of the Empress Isabella.' *Burlington Magazine* 2: 281–5.

Guarini, Elena Fasano. 1999. 'Toscana e Mediterraneo: Ferdinando I tra Francia e Spagna.' In Report of *Italia non Spagnola e Monarchia Spagnola tra '500 e '600. Convegno Internazionale di Studi Promosso dal Dipartmento di Storia moderna e contemporanea e dal Dipartmento di Lingue e Letterature romanze dell' Università, dalla Scuola Normale Superiore di Pisa, dalla Provincia di Pisa e dalla Sociedad Estatal para la commemoración de los centenarios de Felipe II y Carlos V.* Pisa, 11–12 December 1998: 8. Accessed at listserve h-italy@h-net.msu/edu, 28 January 1999.

Guarini, Elena Fasano, ed. 1978. *Potere e società negli stati regionali italiani del '500 e '600.* Bologna.

Guerrazzi, F.D. 1845. *Isabella Orsini, Duchessa di Bracciano.* Paris.

Gundersheimer, Werner. 1981. 'Patronage in the Renaissance: An Exploratory Approach.' In *Patronage in the Renaissance*, ed. G.F. Lytle and S. Orgel, 1–44. Princeton.

– 1994. 'Renaissance Concepts of Shame and Pocaterra's *Dialoghi della Vergogna.' Renaissance Quarterly* 57: 34–56.

Haar, James. 1986. *Essays on Italian Poetry and Music in the Renaissance, 1350–1600.* Berkeley, Los Angeles, and London.

Haboldt & Co. 1990–1. *Tableaux Anciennes des Écoles du Nord Française et Italienne*. Sale cat. Paris.

Hackenbroch, Yvonne. 1975. 'Un gioiello Mediceo inedito.' *Antichità viva* 14, 6: 31–4.

– 1979. *Renaissance Jewellery*. London.

Hale, John R. 1994. *The Civilisation of the Renaissance in Europe*. New York.

Hale, John R., ed. 1981. *Encyclopaedia of the Italian Renaissance*. London.

Hall, James. 1979. *Dictionary of Subjects and Symbols in Art*. Rev. ed. New York.

Hall, Marcia B. 1979. *Renovation and Counter Reformation: Vasari and Duke Cosimo in Sta. Maria Novella and Sta. Croce 1565–1577*. Oxford.

Hall, R.J., Jr. 1942. *The Italian Questione della Lingua: An Interpretative Essay*, chaps. 3 and 4. Chapel Hill, NC.

Hallman, Barbara McClung. 1985. *Italian Cardinals, Reform, and the Church as Property*. Los Angeles.

Harbison, Craig. 1990. 'Sexuality and Social Standing in Jan van Eyk's Arnolfini Double Portrait.' *Renaissance Quarterly* 43, 2: 249–91.

Harper, James. 2001. 'The High Baroque Tapestries of the *Life of Cosimo I*: The Man and His Myth in the Service of Ferdinando II.' In Eisenbichler ed. 2001: 223–52.

Hart, Jonathon, ed. 1996. *Reading the Renaissance: Culture, Poetics, and Drama*. New York.

Hartt, Frederick. 1994. *History of Italian Renaissance Art*, 4th ed. rev. David G. Wilkins. Englewood Cliffs, NJ.

Haskell, Francis. 1986. 'What's in a Portrait?' *New York Review of Books* 32, 5, 27 March: 7.

Haskell, Francis, and Nicholas Penny. 1981. *Taste and the Antique: The Lure of Classical Sculpture, 1500–1900*. New Haven, CT.

Hatfield, Rab. 1965. 'Five Early Renaissance Portraits.' *Art Bulletin* 47: 315–34.

– 1984. Review of Karla Langedijk, *Portraits of the Medici*. *Renaissance Quarterly* 34: 471–5.

Hauser, Arnold. 1951. *The Social History of Art*. Vol. 2. New York.

Hearn, Karen. 1995. 'Edward VI, Mary I and Continental Art.' In Hearn ed. 1995: 45–62.

Hearn, Karen, ed. 1995. *Dynasties: Painting in Tudor and Jacobean England 1530–1630*. Exh. cat., Tate Gallery, London.

Heckscher, William S. 1989. *The Princeton Alciati Companion*. New York.

Heikamp, Detlef. 1953–6. 'Angelo Bronzinos Kinderbildnisse aus dem Jahre 1551.' *Mitteilungen des Kunsthistorischen Institutes in Florenz* 7: 133–8.

– 1968. 'La manufacture de tapisserie des Medicis.' *L'Oeil* 164–5: 22–9.

– 1975. In Munich, Böhler Sale Catalogue, no. 7. October–November.

– 1978. 'Ammannati's Fountain for the "Sala Grande" of the Palazzo Vecchio in Florence.' In *Fons Sapientiae: Renaissance Garden Fountains*, 115–73. Dumbarton Oaks, Washington, DC.

Held, Julius. 1980. *The Oil Sketches of Peter Paul Rubens. A Critical Catalogue*. 2 vols. Princeton, NJ.

Heydenreich, Ludwig H. 1956. Introduction. In Leonardo da Vinci 1956: i–xiv.

– 1974. *Leonardo da Vinci*. New York.

Hibbert, Christopher. 1980. *The Rise and Fall of the House of Medici*. New York.

Hill, George. 1978. *Medals of the Renaissance*. Rev. and ed. Graham Pollard. London.

Hiller von Gaertringen, Rudolf. 2004. *Italienische Gemälde im Städel 1300–1550: Toscana und Umbrien. Kataloge der Gemälde im Städelschen Kunstinstitut Frankfurt am Main, no. 6*. Ed. Herbert Beck and Jochen Sander. Mainz.

Hills, Paul. 1988. *The Light of Early Italian Painting*. New Haven and London.

– 1990. 'Ray, Line, Vision and Trace in Renaissance Art.' *Word and Image* 6, 3: 217–25.

Hollingsworth, Mary. 1994. *Patronage in Renaissance Italy from 1400 to the Early Sixteenth Century*. London.

– 1996. *Patronage in Sixteenth-Century Italy*. London.

Holly, Michael Ann. 1998. 'Pattern in the Shadows: Attention in/to the Writings of Michael Baxandall. *Art History* 21, 4: 467–78.

Holmes, Megan. 1997. 'Disrobing the Virgin: The Madonna Lactans in Fifteenth-Century Florentine Art.' In *Picturing Women in Renaissance and Baroque Italy*, ed. Geraldine A. Johnson and Sara Matthews Grieco, 167–95. Cambridge.

Hope, Charles. 1980. *Titian*. London.

– 1982. 'Bronzino's *Allegory* in the National Gallery.' *Journal of the Warburg and Courtauld Institutes* 45: 239–43.

– 1995. 'Can You Trust Vasari?' *New York Review of Books* 5: 11–13.

Hoppe, Ilaria. 2004. 'A Duchess' Place at Court: The Quartiere di Eleonora in the Palazzo della Signoria in Florence.' In Eisenbichler ed. 2004: 67–80.

Howarth, David. 1993. *Images of Rule. Art and Politics in the English Renaissance, 1485–1649*. London.

Iotti, R. 1998. *Gli Estensi*. Modena.

Iversen, Margaret. 1993. *Alois Riegl: Art History and Theory*. Cambridge, MA. and London.

Jacks, Philip, ed. 1998. *Vasari's Florence: Artists and Literati at the Medicean Court*. Cambridge.

James, Susan E. 1996. 'Lady Jane Grey or Queen Kathyrn Parr?' *Burlington Magazine* 138, 1114: 20–4.

Jenkins, Marianna. 1947. *The State Portrait: Its Origins and Evolution*. New York.

Joannides, Paul. 1983. *The Drawings of Raphael*. Los Angeles.

Johnson, Geraldine A. 1997. 'Idol or Ideal? The Power and the Potency of Female Public Sculpture.' In Johnson and Matthews Grieco eds. 1997: 222–45.

Johnson, Geraldine, and Sara Matthews Grieco, eds. 1997. *Picturing Women in Renaissance and Baroque Italy*. Cambridge.

Johnsson, Ulf G. 1987. *Porträtt, Porträtt: Studier I, Statens Porträttsamling på Gripsholm*, exh. cat., National Gallery, Stockholm. Stockholm.

Jollet, Étienne. 1997. *Jean and François Clouet*. Paris.

Jones, Mark. 1979. *The Art of the Medal*. London.

Junkerman, A. Christine. 1990. 'Giorgione's *Laura* Re-examined.' Unpublished paper, delivered at Annual Conference of the College Art Association, New York, 15 February.

Kaplan, Paul. 1982. 'Titian's *Laura Dianti* and the Origins of the Motif of the Black Page in Portraiture,' parts 1 and 2. *Antichità viva* 21, 1: 11–18, and 21, 4: 10–18.

– 2005. 'Isabella d'Este and Black African Women.' In Earle and Lowe eds. 2005: 124–54.

Kaufmann, Henry W. 1972. 'Music for a Noble Wedding.' In *Words and Music: The Scholar's View. A Medley of Problems and Solutions Compiled in Honor of A. Tillman Merritt by Sundry Hands*, ed. Laurence Berman, 161–88. Cambridge, MA.

– 1977. 'Art for the Wedding of Cosimo de' Medici and Eleonora of Toledo (1539).' *Paragone* 22, 243: 52–67.

Kaufmann, Thomas DaCosta. 1989. 'Images of Rule: Issues of Interpretation.' *Art Journal* 48, 2: 119–22.

Kelso, Ruth. 1977. *Doctrine for the Lady of the Renaissance*. 2nd ed. New York.

Kemp, Martin 1992. 'Virtuous Artists and Virtuous Art.' In Ames-Lewis and Bednarek eds. 1992: 15–23.

Kempers, Bram. 1992. *Painting, Power and Patronage: The Rise of the Professional Artist in the Renaissance*. Trans. Beverley Jackson. London.

Kennedy, William. 2001. Review of Harry Berger, Jr, *The Absence of Grace: Sprezzatura and Suspicion in Two Renaissance Courtesy Books. Renaissance Quarterly* 54: 1595–6.

Kent, Dale. 2001. 'Women in Renaissance Florence.' In D.A. Brown ed. 2001: 25–48.

Kent, F.W., and Simons, Patricia. 1987. 'Renaissance Patronage: An Introductory Essay.' In *Patronage, Art, and Society in Renaissance Italy*, ed. F.W. Kent, P. Simons, and J. Eade. Canberra and Oxford.

Keutner, H. 1959. 'Zu einegen Bildnissen des frühen Florentiner Manierismus.' *Mitteilungen des Kunsthistorischen Institutes in Florenz* 8: 139–54.

Kiefer, Frederick. 1979. 'The Conflation of Fortuna and Occasione in Renaissance Thought and Iconography.' *Journal of Medieval and Renaissance Studies* 9, 1: 1–28.

King, Edward S. 1940. 'An Addition to Medici Iconography.' *Walters Journal* 3: 74–84.

King, Margaret L. 1991. *Women of the Renaissance*. Chicago and London.

Kirkendale, Warren. 1993. *The Court Musicians in Florence during the Principate of the Medici*. Florence.

Kirkham, Victoria. 2001. 'Poetic Ideals of Love and Beauty.' In Washington 2001: 49–61.

Klinger Aleci, Linda. 1998. 'Images of Identity: Italian Portrait Collections of the Fifteenth and Sixteenth Centuries.' In Mann and Syson eds. 1998: 67–80.

Knecht, R.J. 1977. 'Francis I: Prince and Patron of the Northern Renaissance.' In Dickens ed. 1977: 99–120.

Knoppers, Laura Lunger. 1988. 'The Politics of Portraiture: Oliver Cromwell and the Plain Style.' *Renaissance Quarterly* 51, 4: 1283–1319.

Kristeller, Paul Oskar. 1961. *Renaissance Thought*. New York.

– 1964. *Eight Philosophers of the Italian Renaissance*. Stanford, CA.

Krystof, Doris. 1998. *Jacopo Carucci, Known as Pontormo, 1494–1557*. Cologne.

Kuehn, Thomas J. 2002. *Illegitimacy in Renaissance Florence*. Ann Arbor.

Lacan, Jacques. 1977. 'The Mirror Stage as Formative of the Function of the "I."' In *Ecrits: A Selection*, ed. and trans. A. Sheridan. London and Tavistock.

Land, Norman. 1986. '*Ekphrasis* and Imagination: Some Observations on Pietro Aretino's Art Criticism.' *Art Bulletin* 67, 2: 207–15.

– 1994. *The Viewer as Poet: The Renaissance Response to Art*. University Park, PA.

Langdale, Allan. 1998. 'Aspects of the Critical Reception and Intellectual History of Baxandall's Concept of the Period Eye.' *Art History* 21, 4: 479–97.

Langdon, Gabrielle. 1989. 'A Reattribution: Alessandro Allori's *Portrait of a Lady with a Cameo*.' *Zeitschrift für Kunstgeschichte* 52, 1: 25–45.

– 1992[1]. 'Decorum in Portraits of Medici Women at the Court of Cosimo I, 1537–1574.' PhD diss., 2 vols., University of Michigan.

– 1992[2]. 'Pontormo and Medici Lineages: Maria Salviati, Alessandro, Guilia and Giulio de' Medici.' *Revue d'art canadienne / Canadian Art Review (RACAR)* 19, 1–2: 20–40.

– 2000. Review of *The Cultural Politics of Duke Cosimo I de' Medici*, ed Konrad Eisenbichler. *Quaderni d'Italianista* 21, 2.

– 2001. 'A Medici Miniature: Juno, and a Woman "With Eyes in Her Head Like Two Stars in Their Beauty."' In Reiss and Wilkins eds. 2001: 263–300.

– 2004. 'A "Laura" for Cosimo: Bronzino's Portrait of Eleonora di Toledo.' In Eisenbichler ed. 2004: 40–70.

– 2005. Review of *Pontormo, Bronzino, and the Medici. The Transformation of the Renaissance Portrait in Florence*. Philadelphia Museum of Art, Nov. 2004–Feb. 2005. Catalogue by Carl Brandon Strehlke, with essays by Elizabeth Cropper, Mark Tucker, Irma Passeri, Ken Sutherland, and Beth A. Price. In College Art Association, Exhibition Reviews Online, at www.collegeart.org.

Langedijk, Karla. 1978. 'Ritratti granducali a Firenze, una volta all'Ospedale di Santa Maria Nuova, e al Palazzo Pitti.' *Prospettiva* 13: 64–7.

– 1980. *Index iconologicus*. Sanford, NC.

– 1981–7. *Portraits of the Medici*. 3 vols. Florence.

– 1990/1. Review of Janet Cox-Rearick, *Dynasty and Destiny in Medici Art: Pontormo, Leo X and the Two Cosimos. Simiolus* 20, 4: 288–90.

– 1991. Review of Lorne Campbell, *Renaissance Portraits: European Portrait-Painting in the Fourteenth, Fifteenth and Sixteenth Centuries. Apollo* 133, 351: 363–4.

Lanyi, Jeno. 1933. 'Pontormo's Bildnis der Maria Salviati de' Medici.' *Mitteilungen des Kunsthistorischen Institutes in Florenz* 4, 2–3: 88–102.

Lari, Rossella. 1995. 'Nota sul restauro del *Ritratto di Maria Salviati* del Pontormo.' In Natali ed. 1995: 135–9.

Lavin, Irving. 1970. 'On the Sources and Meaning of the Renaissance Portrait Bust.' *Art Quarterly* 33: 207–26.

Lawrence, Cynthia, ed. 1997. *Women and Art in Early Modern Europe: Patrons, Collectors, and Connoisseurs*. University Park, PA.

Lazzi, Giovanna. 1988. 'Gli abiti di Eleonora da Toledo e di Cosimo I attraverso i documenti di archivio.' In Bemporad et al. eds. 1988: 161–73.

– 1989. 'Un'eccezionale occasione di lusso: L'incoronazione di Cosimo de' Medici (1569).' *Archivio Storico Italiana* 1: 99–119.

– 1993. 'La moda alla corte di Cosimo I de' Medici.' In Florence, Palazzo Pitti 1993: 27–34.

Le Mollé, Roland. 1988. *Georges Vasari et le vocabulaire de la critique d'art dans les 'Vite.'* Grenoble.

– 1995. *Giorgio Vasari. L'Homme des Médicis*. Paris.

Lecchini Giovannoni, Simona. 1968. 'Alcune proposte per l'attività ritrattistica di Alessandro Allori.' *Antichità viva* 7, 1: 48–57.

– 1988. 'Osservazioni sull'attività giovanile di Alessandro Allori.' (Part I.) *Antichità viva* 27, 1: 9–22.

– 1991. *Alessandro Allori*. Turin.

Ledes, Alison Eckhardt. 1989. 'Portraits in Miniature.' *The Magazine Antiques* 136, 6: 1242–50.

Lee, Rensselaer W. 1940. '*Ut pictura poesis*: The Humanistic Theory of Painting.' *Art Bulletin* 22: 196–269.

– 1951. Review of Dennis Mahon, *Studies in Seicento Art and Theory. Art Bulletin* 30: 204–12.

Lensi-Orlandi, G. 1977. *Il Palazzo Vecchio di Firenze*. Florence.

Levey, Michael. 1962. 'A Prince of Court Painters: Bronzino.' *Apollo* 76: 165–73.

– 1971. *Painting at Court*. New York.

Lincoln, Evelyn. 1999. In Providence, RI 1999: 15–22.

Litta, Pompeo. 1899–1902. *Famiglie celebri in Italia*. 13 vols. Vol. 3: Medici. Milan.

Lloyd, Christopher. 1993. *Italian Paintings before 1600 in The Art Institute of Chicago. A Catalogue of the Collection.* Chicago.

London, Queen's Gallery, Buckingham Palace. 1982–3. *Kings and Queens.* Exh. cat. London.

Lunenfeld, Marvin. 1981. 'The Royal Image: Symbol and Paradigm in Portraits of Early Modern Female Sovereigns and Regents.' *Gazette des Beaux-Arts* 97: 157–62.

Lupo Gentile, M. 1905. 'Studi sulla storiografia fiorentina alla Corte di Cosimo I de' Medici.' *Annali della Scuola Normale Superiore di Pisa* 19, 2: 1–164.

Lurie, Alison. 1974. 'Agnolo Bronzino: Portrait of a Young Lady.' *Bulletin of the Cleveland Museum of Art* 61, 50: 2–13.

Lytle, G.F., and S. Orgel. 1981. *Patronage in the Renaissance.* Princeton.

Maczak, Antoni. 1991. 'From Aristocratic Household to Princely Court: Restructuring Patronage in the Sixteenth and Seventeenth Centuries.' In Asch and Birke, eds., 1991: 315–28.

Madrid, Thyssen-Bornemisza. 2000. *Obras Maestras.* Exh. cat. by Tomàs Llorens, Mar Borobia, and Paloma Alarcó. Madrid.

Maggi, Armando. 1995. 'Depicting One's Self: Imprese and Sonnets in "La Virginia Ovvero la Dea de' Nostri Tempi" by Ercole Tasso.' *Quaderni d'Italianistica* 16, 1: 51–60.

Maguire, Yvonne. 1927. *The Women of the Medici.* London.

Maltby, William. 1983. *Alba: A Biography of Fernando Alvarez de Toledo.* Berkeley.

Mandel, Corinne. 1990. 'Verrocchio's *Putto with a Dolphin*: The Metamorphosis of a Medicean Symbol.' In *Italian Echoes in the Rocky Mountains: Papers from the 1988 Annual Conference of the American Association for Italian Studies*, 86–97. Provo, Utah.

– 1995. 'Traballesi's *Rain of Gold* and the Poetics of Power in Francesco I's Scrittoio.' *Revue d'art canadienne / Canadian Art Review (RACAR)* 22, 1–2: 53–79.

– 1998. Review of Paola Tinagli, *Women in Italian Renaissance Art: Gender, Representation, Identity.* *Sixteenth Century Journal* 29, 2: 594–7.

Mann, Nicholas. 1998. 'Petrarch and Portraits.' In Mann and Syson eds. 1998: 15–20.

Mann, Nicholas, and Luke Syson, eds. 1998. *The Image of the Individual: Portraits in the Renaissance.* London.

Manni, Domenio Maria. 1767, 1768. *Lezione di lingua toscana.* Florence, Venice.

Mantini, Silvia. 1995. *Lo spazio sacro della Firenze medicea. Transformazione urbane e cerimoniali pubblici tra Quattrocento e Cinquecento.* Florence.

Martines, Lauro. 1974. 'A Way of Looking at Women in Renaissance Florence.' *Journal of Medieval and Renaissance Studies* 4, 1: 15–28.

Mateer, David, ed. 2000. *Courts, Patrons and Poets.* New Haven and London.

Matthews Grieco, Sara F. 1994. 'Georgette de Montenay: A Different Voice in Sixteenth-Century Emblematics.' *Renaissance Quarterly* 42, 4: 793–871.

– 1997. 'Pedagogical Prints: Moralizing Broadsheets and Wayward Women in Counter Reformation Italy.' In *Picturing Women in Renaissance and Baroque Italy*, ed. Geraldine A. Johnson and Sara Matthews Grieco, 61–87. Cambridge.

May, Florence L. 1965. 'Spanish Brocade for Royal Ladies.' *Pantheon* 23: 8–17.

Mayer, Rosemary, Julia Ballerini, and Richard Milazzo. 1982. *Pontormo's Diary.* New York.

McComb, Arthur. 1928. *Agnolo Bronzino, His Life and Works.* Cambridge, MA.

McCorquodale, Charles. 1981. *Bronzino.* London.

McCrory, Martha. 1998. 'Immutable Images: Glyptic Portraits at the Medici Court in Sixteenth-Century Florence.' In Mann and Syson eds. 1998: 40–54.

McGrath, Elizabeth. 1985. '"Il senso nostro": The Medici Allegory Applied to Vasari's Mythological Frescoes in the Palazzo Vecchio.' In Garfagnini ed. 1985: 117–34.

McIver, Katherine A. 2001. 'Two Emilian Noblewomen and Patronage Networks in the Cinquecento.' In Reiss and Wilkins eds. 2001: 159–76.

McManamon, John. 1989. *Funeral Oratory and the Cultural Ideals of Italian Humanism*. Chapel Hill, NC.

Medici, Ottaviano di Toscana di Ottajano. 2000. *Storia del Mia Dinastia*. Florence.

Mellen, Peter. 1963. 'Physiognomical Theory in Renaissance Heroic Portraits.' In *The Renaissance and Mannerism: Acts of the International Congress of the History of Art*, vol. 1: 53–69. Princeton.

– 1971. *Jean Clouet*. London.

Meloni, Silvia. 1994. 'The Collection of Miniatures and Small Portraits.' In Gregori ed. 1994: 626–8.

Meloni-Trkulja, Silvia. 1983. 'Giulio Clovio e i Medici.' *Peristil* 24, 26: 91–100.

Mendelsohn, Leatrice. 1982. *Paragone: Benedetto Varchi's 'Due Lezzioni' and Cinquecento Art Theory*. Ann Arbor, MI.

Micheletti, Emma. 1983. *Le Donne dei Medici*. Florence.

Mignani, Daniela. 1993. *Le Ville Medicee di Giusto Utens*. Florence.

Millen, Ronald Forsyth, and Robert Erich Wolf. 1989. *Heroic Deeds and Mystic Figures: A New Reading of Rubens' 'Life of Maria de' Medici.'* Princeton, NJ.

Milroy, Sarah. 2002. 'Pictures of Liz.' *Globe and Mail*, Toronto, 9 February: R1.

Mineccia, Francesco. 1982. *Da fattoria granducale a comunità: Collesalvetti 1737–1861*. Naples.

Minnich, Nelson. 2003. 'Raphael's *Portrait of Leo X with Cardinals Giulio de' Medici and Luigi de' Rossi*: A Religious Interpretation.' *Renaissance Quarterly* 56: 1005–52.

Minor, A.C., and B. Mitchell. 1968. *A Renaissance Entertainment: Festivities for the Marriage of Cosimo I, Duke of Florence, in 1539*. Columbia, MO.

Mitchell, Bonner. 1986. *The Majesty of the State: Triumphal Progresses of Foreign Sovereigns in Renaissance Italy (1494–1600)*. Florence.

Mitchell, W.J.T. 1994. *Picture Theory: Essays on Verbal and Visual Representation*. Chicago.

Moffitt, John F. 1993. 'A Hidden Sphinx by Agnolo Bronzino, *ex tabula Cebetis Thebani*.' *Renaissance Quarterly* 46: 277–307.

Monari-Lipira, F. 1984. 'Alberti and Leonardo: Theory and Practice in the Italian Renaissance.' PhD diss., State University of New York at Stoneybrook.

Money, Ernle. 1984. 'The Art of the Limners.' Review of Sir Roy Strong, *The English Renaissance Miniature*. *Contemporary Review* 244, 1417: 108–9.

Monnas, Lisa. 1990. 'Silk Textiles in the Paintings of Bernardo Daddi, Andrea di Cione and Their Followers.' *Zeitschrift für Kunstwissenschaft* 53, 1: 39–58.

Morrogh, A., F.S. Gioffredi, P. Morselli, and E. Borsook, eds. 1985. *Renaissance Studies in Honor of Craig Hugh Smyth*. Florence.

Mortadini, Antonietta. 1965. 'Una missione di Troilo Orsini in Polonia per il Granduca di Toscana (maggio–luglio 1574).' *Archivio Storico Italiano* 1: 94–112.

Mortari, Luisa. 1992. *Francesco Salviati*. Rome.

Mulcahy, Rosemarie. 2004. *Philip II of Spain: Patron of the Arts*. Dublin.

Muller, P.E. 1972. *Jewels in Spain, 1500–1800*. New York.

Munich. 1975. Julius Böhler Sale Catalogue. October–November. Munich.

Müntz, E. 1895. 'Les Collections de Cosime Ier de Médicis.' *Revue archéologique* 1: 87–167.

Murphy, Caroline P. 1997. 'Lavinia Fontana and Female Life Cycle Experience in Late Sixteenth-Century Bologna.' In Johnson and Matthews Grieco eds. 1997: 111–38, 272–7.

Murphy, Marèse. 2000. 'A Proper Charlie.' *The Irish Times*, 10 August: 16.

Murray, Alex M. 1994. *Who's Who in Mythology*. London.

Nagler, A.M. 1964. *Theatre Festivals of the Medici 1539–1637*. New Haven, CT.

Natali, Antonio. 1995. 'Ritratto di Maria Salviati.' In *Gli Uffizi. Studi e richerche. I pieghevoli 2 Quattro restauri agli Uffizi*. Florence.

Natali, Antonio, ed. 1995. *Rosso e Pontormo. Fierezza e Solitudine. Esercizi di lettura e rendiconti di restauro per tre dipinti degli Uffizi*. Florence.

Nelson, Jonathan. 1995. 'Creative Patronage: Luca Martini and the Renaissance Portrait.' *Mitteilungen des Kunsthistorischen Institutes in Florenz* 39, 2–3: 282–305.

Nencioni, Giovanni. 1983. 'Il Volgare nell'Avvio del Principato.' In Diaz ed. 1983, 2: 683–703.

New York, Piero Corsini Gallery. 1986. *Important Old Master Paintings and Discoveries of the Past Year*. Exh. cat. 1–29 November. New York.

Nicco-Fasola, G. 1947. *Pontormo o del Cinquecento*. Florence.

Nigro, Salvatore. 1994. *Pontormo: Paintings and Frescoes*. Munich.

Novotny, V. 1959. *Treasures of the Prague National Gallery*. London, n.d.; German ed., Prague.

Okayama, Yassu. 1992. *The Ripa Index: Personifications and Their Attributes in Five Editions of the Iconologia*. Doornspick, Netherlands.

Olin, Margaret. 1989. 'Forms of Respect: Alois Riegl's Concept of Attentiveness.' *Art Bulletin*, 71: 283–99.

– 1992. *Forms of Representation in Alois Riegl's Theory of Art*. University Park, PA.

Olson, Roberta. 1992. *Italian Renaissance Sculpture*. New York.

Olszewski, Edward J. 1981. *The Draftsman's Eye: Late Italian Renaissance Schools and Styles*. Bloomington, IN.

O'Meara, Carra Ferguson. 1981. 'Isabelle de Portugal as the Virgin in Jean Van Eyck's Washington *Annunciation*.' *Gazette des Beaux-Arts* 97: 99–103.

Orsi Landini, Roberta. 1993. 'L'amore del lusso e la necessità della modestia: Eleonora fra sete e oro.' In Florence, Palazzo Pitti 1993: 35–45.

Orsi Landini, Roberta, and Mary Westerman Bulgarella. 2001. 'Costume in Fifteenth-Century Florentine Portraits of Women.' In D.A. Brown 2001: 89–98.

O'Rourke Boyle, Marjorie. 1999. 'Gracious Laughter: Marsilio Ficino's Anthropology.' *Renaissance Quarterly* 51, 3: 712–41.

Orth, Myra D. 1997. Review of Cécile Scailliérez, *François I par Clouet*, exh. cat. *Sixteenth Century Journal* 28, 3: 1001–2.

Ottawa, National Gallery of Canada. 2005. *Leonardo da Vinci, Michelangelo, and the Renaissance in Florence*. Exh. cat. General editor, David Franklin, with essays by David Franklin, Louis A. Waldman, and Andrew Butterfield. Ottawa, New Haven, and London.

Paatz, Walter and Elisabeth. 1940–54. *Die Kirchen von Florenz*. 6 vols. Frankfurt am Main.

Paleotti, Gabriele. 1971. *Discorso intorno alle imagini sacre e profane* (Bologna, 1582). In *Scritti d'arte del cinquecento*, ed. Paola Barocchi, vol. 1: 117–517. Milan and Naples.

Palladino, Lora A. 1981. 'Pietro Aretino: Orator and Art Theorist.' PhD diss., Yale University.

Palluccini, Rodolfo, ed. 1981. *Giorgione e l'umanesimo veneziano*. 2 vols. Florence.

Pane, Giulio. 1975. 'Pietro di Toledo Vinceré urbanista,' part 2. *Napoli nobilissima* 14, 3: 189–96.

Panizza, Letizia, ed. 2000. *Women in Italian Renaissance Culture and Society.* Oxford.

Panofsky, Erwin. 1962. *Studies in Iconology: Humanistic Themes in the Art of the Renaissance.* New York.

– 1968. *Idea, A Concept in Art Theory.* Trans. J. Peake. Columbia, SC.

Pardo, Mary. 1983. 'Paolo Pino's *Dialogo di Pittura*: A Translation with Commentary.' PhD diss., University of Pittsburgh.

Paris. 1914. Hôtel Drouot. Sales catalogue. 13 March.

– 1996. *François I par Clouet.* Exh. cat. by Cécile Scailliérez.

Parker, Deborah. 1995. 'Towards a Reading of Bronzino's Poetry.' *Renaissance Society of America Annual Meeting, New York City, March 30–April 2, 1995: Abstracts,* 99. New York.

– 1997. 'Towards a Reading of Bronzino's Poetry.' *Renaissance Quarterly* 50: 1011–44.

– 2000. *Bronzino. Renaissance Painter as Poet.* Cambridge.

– 2003. 'The Poetry of Patronage: Bronzino and the Medici.' *Renaissance Studies* 17, 2: 230–45.

– 2004. 'Bronzino and the Diligence of Art.' *Artibus et Historiae* 49: 161–74.

Pastor, Ludwig. 1928. *The History of the Popes from the Close of the Middle Ages.* 16 vols. Trans. and ed. Ralph F. Kerr. London.

Pepys, Samuel. 1871. *Diary and Correspondence of Samuel Pepys, F.R.S.* 4 vols. Ed. J. Smith. London.

Perlingieri, Ilya Sandra. 1992. *Sofonisba Anguissola.* New York.

Petrarch. 1976. *Petrarch's Lyric Poems.* Ed., and trans. Robert M. Durling. Cambridge, MA.

Pevsner, Nicholas. 1973. *Academies of Art Past and Present.* New York.

Philadelphia. 2004. *Pontormo, Bronzino, and the Medici.* Exh. cat. by Carl Brandon Strehlke, with essays by Elizabeth Cropper, Mark S. Tucker, Irma Passeri, Ken Sutherland, and Beth A. Price. Philadelphia Museum of Art.

Phoenix, Phoenix Museum of Art. 1999. *Copper as Canvas. Two Centuries of Masterpiece Paintings on Copper, 1575–1775.* Exh. cat. Ed. Michael K. Komanecky, with contributions by Laura Conigliello et al. Oxford.

Piccinini, Anna Maria. 'La saggia Ortensia.' *Il Giornale degli Uffizi. Associazione Amici degli Uffizi* 32 (April 2005): 3–4.

Picenardi, G.S. 1888. 'Esumazione e ricognizione delle ceneri dei principi Medici fatto nell'anno 1857.' *Archivio storico italiano* 1888: 333–60.

Pieraccini, Gaetano. 1986 (1947). *La stirpe de' Medici di Cafaggiolo: Saggio di richerche sulla trasmissione ereditaria dei caratteri biologici.* 2nd, facsimile ed. 3 vols. Florence.

Pietrosanti, Susanna. 1991. *Sacralità Medicee.* Florence.

Pilliod, Elizabeth. 1998. 'Representation, Misrepresentation, and Non Representation: Vasari and His Competitors.' In Jacks ed. 1998: 30–54.

– 2001. *Pontormo, Bronzino, and Allori: A Genealogy of Florentine Art.* New Haven and London.

Pinelli, Antonio. 1993. *La Bella Maniera: Artisti del Cinquecento tra regola e licenza.* Turin.

Piper, David. 1957. *The English Face.* London.

Pirrotta, Nino. 1983. 'Instituzioni Musicali nella Firenze dei Medici.' In Diaz ed. 1983, 1: 37–54.

Pisetzky, R.L. 1965. *Storia del costume in Italia,* vols. 1–3. Milan.

Plaisance, M. 1973. 'Une première affirmation de la politique culturelle de Come Ier: La transformation de l'Academie des "Humidi" en Academie Florentine (1540–1542).' In *Les écrivains et la pouvoir en Italie à l'époque de la Renaissance*, I, ed. A. Rochon, 361–438. Paris.

– 1975. 'La politique culturelle de Cosme 1er et les fetes annuelles à Florence, 1541–1550.' In *Les fêtes de la Renaissance. Actes du quinzième colloque international d'études humanistes (Tours 1972)*. Ed. J. Jacquot and R. Konigson, vol. 3: 133–52. Paris.

Plazzotta, Carol. 1988. '"Il pennel Dotto": The Presentation of Women in Three Portraits by Bronzino.' MA diss., Courtauld Institute of Art, University of London.

– 1998. 'Bronzino's *Laura*.' *Burlington Magazine* 140, 1141: 251–63.

Plazzotta, Carol, and Larry Keith. 1999. 'Bronzino's "Allegory": New Evidence of the Artist's Revisions.' *Burlington Magazine* 141, 1151: 89–99.

Pochat, Gotz. 1973–4. 'The Ermine – A Metaphor in Renaissance Poetry.' *Tidschrift für Litteraturvetenskap* 3: 140.

Pointon, Marcia. 2001. 'Surrounded with Brilliants: Miniature Portraits in Eighteenth-Century England.' *Art Bulletin* 83, 1: 48–71.

Pommier, Édouard. 1998. *Théories du Portrait de la Renaissance aux Lumières*. Paris.

Pope-Hennessy, John. 1943. 'Nicholas Hilliard and Mannerist Art Theory.' *Journal of the Warburg and Courtauld Institutes* 6: 89–100.

– 1966. *The Portrait in the Renaissance*. London.

– 1970. *Raphael*. London.

– 1981. *Angelico*. Florence.

Posner, Michael. 2001. 'Solved: A Medici Mystery.' *Globe and Mail*, Toronto, 8 December: R3.

Pozzi, Giovanni. 1979. 'Il ritratto della donna nel la poesia d'inizio Cinquecinto e la pittura di Giorgione.' *Lettere italiane* 31: 3–30.

Pratesi, Luigi. 1909. 'Maria Salviati.' *Rivista fiorentina* 1: 9–17.

Prodi, Paolo. 1984. *Ricerca sulla teoreticale delle arti figurative nella riforma cattolica*. Bologna.

– 1995. 'San Filippo Neri: Un' anomalia nella Roma della Controriforma?' *Storia del Arte* 85: 333–9.

Providence, RI. 1999. *Crafting the Medici: Patrons and Artisans in Florence, 1537–1737*. Exh. cat. edited by Jo-Ann Conklin. Curated by Caterina Caneva, Evelyn Lincoln, and Catherine W. Zerner, with contributions by Roberta Orsi Landini, Maria Sframeli. David Winton Bell Gallery, Brown University. Providence, RI.

Quint, David. 1990. 'Political Allegory in the *Gerusalemme Liberata*.' *Renaissance Quarterly* 43, 1: 1–29.

Quiviger, F. 1987. 'Benedetto Varchi and the Visual Arts.' *Journal of the Warburg and Courtauld Institutes* 1: 219–24.

Quondam, Amedeo. 1989. 'Il naso di Laura.' In *Il Ritratto e la Memoria: Europa delle Corti*, ed. Augusto Gentili et al., 9–44. Rome.

Rabb, Theodore K., and Jonathan Brown. 1986. Introduction. *Journal of Interdisciplinary History* 18, 1: 1–6.

Raffini, Christine. 1998. *Marsilio Ficino, Pietro Bembo, Baldassare Castiglione: Philosophical, Aesthetic, and Political Approaches to Renaissance Platonism*. New York.

Ragghianti, Licia. 1971. 'Il *Libro de' disegni* ed i ritratti per le *Vite* del Vasari.' *Critica d'arte* 149: 37–65.

Raney, C. 1971. 'A Solution to the Lute Entablature of Isabella de' Medici.' *Quadrivium* 12, 1: 299–305.

Reilly, Patricia. 1989. 'The Taming of the Blue: Writing Out Color in Renaissance Theory.' Unpub. paper delivered at the College Art Association Conference, New York.
– 1992. 'The Taming of the Blue.' In *The Expanding Discourse*, ed. Norma Broude and Mary D. Garrard, 87–100. New York.
Reinhard, Wolfgang. 1991. 'Papal Power and Family Strategy in the Sixteenth and Seventeenth Centuries.' In Asch and Birke eds. 1991: 329–56.
Reiss, Sheryl E. 1992. 'Cardinal Giulio de' Medici as a Patron of Art, 1513–1523.' PhD diss., 3 vols., Princeton University.
– 2001. 'Widow, Mother, Patron of Art: Alfonsina Orsini de' Medici.' In Reiss and Wilkins eds. 2001: 125–58.
– Reiss, Sheryl E., and David Wilkins, eds. 2001. *Beyond Isabella: Secular Women Patrons of Art in Renaissance Italy*. Kirksville, MO.
Ricci, Antonio. 2001. 'Lorenzo Torrentino and the Cultural Programme of Cosimo I de' Medici.' In Eisenbichler ed. 2001: 103–20.
Ricci, Stefania. 1993. 'Tra storia e leggenda: cronaca di vita medicea.' In Florence, Palazzo Pitti 1993: 11–26.
Richa, Giuseppe. 1972. *Notizie Istorische delle Chiese fiorentine divise ne' suoi quartieri* (1752). 10 vols. Reprint, Rome.
Richelson, William Paul. 1978. *Studies in the Personal Imagery of Cosimo I de' Medici, Duke of Florence*. New York and London.
Riding, Alan. 1996. 'Henry, Georges and Victorias, Writ Small.' *New York Times*, Sunday, 3 November: H43.
Roberts, Jane. 1988. *Drawings by Holbein from the Court of Henry VIII*. Exh. cat. Art Gallery of Ontario, October 1988–January 1989. Toronto.
Rodocanachi, Emmanuel P. 1907. *La Femme italienne à l'Epoque de la Renaissance*. Paris.
– 1922. *La Femme italienne: Avant, pendant et après la Renaissance, sa vie privée et mondaine, son influence sociale*. Paris.
Rodolico, Niccolò, ed. 1968. *Donne di Casa Medici*. Florence.
Rodríguez, Manuel Rivero. 1999. 'Rey católico o monarca hispano? Italia en la construcción de la Monarquía de Felipe II (1559–1565).' In Report of *Italia non Spagnola e Monarchia Spagnola tra '500 e '600. Convegno Internazionale di Studi Promosso dal Dipartmento di Storia moderna e contemporanea e dal Dipartmento di Lingue e Letterature romanze dell' Università, dalla Scuola Normale Superiore di Pisa, dalla Provincia di Pisa e dalla Sociedad Estatal para la commemoración de los centenarios de Felipe II y Carlos V*. Pisa, 11–12 December 1998: 2–3. Accessed at listserve h-italy@h-net.Msu/edu, 28 January 1999.
Rodríguez-Salgado, M.J. 1991. 'The Court of Philip II of Spain.' In Asch and Birke eds. 1991: 205–44.
Rogers, Mary. 1986. 'Sonnets on Female Portraits from Renaissance North Italy.' *Word & Image* 2, 4: 291–305.
– 1988. 'The Decorum of Women's Beauty: Trissino, Firenzuola, Luigini and the Representation of Women in Sixteenth Century Painting.' *Renaissance Studies* 2, 1: 47–88.
– 1991. 'Decorum in Lodovico Dolce and Titian's *poesie*.' In Ames-Lewis and Bednarek eds. 1991: 111–20.
– 1998. 'The Artist as Beauty.' In Ames-Lewis and Rogers eds. 1998: 93–106.
– 2000[1]. Review of Joanna Woods-Marsden, *Renaissance Self-Portraiture: The Visual Construction of Identity and the Social Status of the Artist* (1998). *Renaissance Studies* 14, 3: 375–8.

– 2000[2]. Review of *The Image of the Individual. Portraits in the Renaissance*, ed. Nicholas Mann and Luke Syson (1998). *Renaissance Studies* 14, 3: 375–8.

Rogers, Mary, ed. 2000. *Fashioning Identities in Renaissance Art*. Aldershot, UK, and Burlington, VT.

Rogers, Mary, and Paola Tinagli. 2005. *Women in Italy, 1350–1650. Ideals and Realities*. Manchester.

Rosand, David. 1981. 'Alcuni pensieri sul ritratto e la morte.' In Pallucchini ed. 1981, 1: 293–308. 2 vols. Florence.

Rosci, Marco. 1978. *The Hidden Leonardo*. Trans. Arnoldo Mondadori. Oxford.

Rosenberg, Charles. 1986. 'The Double Portrait of Federico da Montefeltro and Guidobaldo: Power, Wisdom and Dynasty.' In *Federico di Montefeltro: Lo stato, le arti, la cultura*, ed. Giorgio Cerboni Baiardi, Giorgio Chittolini, and Piero Floriani, 213–22. Urbino.

Rosenthal, Michael. 1998. 'Thomas Gainsborough's *Ann Ford*.' *Art Bulletin* 80, 4: 649–65.

Roskill, Mark W. 1968. *Dolce's Aretino and Venetian Art Theory of the Cinquecento*. New York.

– 1989. *The Interpretation of Pictures*. Amherst, MA.

Rossi, Sergio. 1977. 'Il *Trattato delle perfette proporzioni* di V. Danti e l'incidenza della *Poetica* sulle teorie artistiche del secondo Cinquecento.' *Storia dell'arte* 14: 127–47.

Rotondo, A. 1977. *Dizionario Biografica degli Italiani*. Rome.

Rousseau, Claudia. 1983. 'Cosimo I de' Medici and Astrology: The Symbolism of Prophesy.' PhD diss., Columbia University.

– 1989. 'The Yoke *Impresa* of Leo X.' *Mitteilungen des Kunsthistorischen Institut in Florenz* 33: 113–26.

– 1990. 'The Pageant of the Muses at the Medici Wedding of 1539 and the Decoration of the Salone dei Cinquecento.' In Wisch and Scott Munshower eds. 1990.

Roussel, Isabella Brigitte. 1997. Review of Deborah Lesko Baker, *The Subject of Desire: Petrarchan Poetics and the Female Voice in Louise Labé. Sixteenth Century Journal* 28, 3: 997–9.

Rowe, D.F. 1975. *The Art of Jewelry, 1450–1650*. Exh. cat. Martin d'Arcy Gallery of Art, Loyola University of Chicago.

Rubenstein, Nicolai. 1995. *The Palazzo Vecchio 1298–1352*. Oxford.

– 1996[1]. 'Firenze tra repubblica e principato e i ritratti dei Medici del Pontormo.' In Ciardi and Natali eds. 1996: 18–25.

Rubin, Patricia. 1990. 'What Men Saw: Vasari's Life of Leonardo da Vinci and the Image of the Renaissance Artist.' *Art History* 13, 1: 34–46.

– 1991. 'The Art of Color in Florentine Painting of the Early Sixteenth Century: Rosso Fiorentino and Jacopo Pontormo.' *Art History* 14, 2: 175–93.

– 1995. *Giorgio Vasari: Art and History*. New Haven and London.

– 1996[2]. *Pontormo e Rosso*. Exh. cat. Florence, Uffizi.

Rufini, Emilio. 1957. *S. Giovanni de' Fiorentini. Le Chiese di Roma illustrate, no. 39*. Rome.

Saisselin, Remy. 1963. *Style, Truth and the Portrait*. Cleveland.

Saltini, Guglielmo Enrico. 1883. 'L'educazione del Principe don Francesco de' Medici.' *Archivio storico italiano* 11, 47: 49–84.

– 1898. *Tragedie medicee domestiche, 1557–87*. Florence.

– 1901–2. 'Due principesse medicee del secolo XVI.' *Rassegna nazionale* 121, part 1 (Sept.–Oct. 1901): 553–71; 122, part 2 (Dec. 1901): 599–613; 123, part 3, (Feb. 1902): 618–30; 125, part 4 (May 1902): 207–20; 127, part 5 (Sept. 1902): 227–41; 128, part 6 (Nov. 1902): 169–91.

Sanchez, Carlos Hernando. 1999. 'Potere spagnolo e clientele: La rete dei Toledo in Italia.' In Report of *Italia non Spagnola e Monarchia Spagnola tra '500 e '600. Convegno Internazionale di Studi Promosso dal Dipartmento di Storia moderna e contemporanea e dal Dipartmento di Lingue e Letterature romanze dell' Università, dalla Scuola Normale Superiore di Pisa, dalla Provincia di Pisa e dalla Sociedad Estatal para la commemoración de los centenarios de Felipe II y Carlos V.* Pisa, 1998: 5. Accessed at listserve h-italy@h-net.msu/edu, 28 January 1999.

Sangiorgi, Fert. 1973. 'La Muta di Rafaello: Considerazioni istorico-iconografiche.' *Commentari: Rivista di critica e storia dell'arte* 24, 1–2: 90–7.

Sansovino, Francesco. 1670. *Origine e Fatti delle Famiglie Illustre d' Italia di M. Francesco Sansovino (1582).* Venice.

Santi, Bruno. 1981. *Leonardo da Vinci.* London.

Saslow, James. 1991. *The Poetry of Michelangelo.* New Haven, CT.

– 1994. Review of Randolf Starn and Loren Partridge, *Arts of Power: Three Halls of State in Italy, 1300–1600. Renaissance Quarterly* 47, 4: 1006–7.

– 1996[1]. *The Marriage Festivities of Ferdinando de' Medici and Christine of Lorraine.* Cambridge.

– 1996[2]. *The Medici Wedding of 1589: Florentine Festival as Theatrum Mundi.* New Haven, CT, and London.

Sautman, Francesca, and Pamela Sheingorn, eds. 2001. *Same-sex Love and Desire among Women in the Middle Ages.* New York.

Saward, Gillian. 1982. *The Golden Age of Marie de' Medici.* Ann Arbor.

Scailliérez, Cécile, et al. 1992. *François Ier e ses artistes dans les collections du Louvre.* Paris.

Scalini, Mario, ed. 2001. *Giovanni delle Bande Nere.* Florence.

Schaefer, Scott. 1976. 'The *Studiolo* of Francesco I de' Medici in the Palazzo Vecchio in Florence.' PhD diss., Bryn Mawr University.

Schaffers-Bodenhausen, K., and Marieke Tiethoff-Spliethoff. 1993. *The Portrait Miniatures in the Collection of the House of Orange-Nassau.* Zwolle, Netherlands.

Schalk, Ellery. 1991. 'The Court as "Civilizer" of the Nobility: Noble Attitudes and the Court in France in the Late Sixteenth and Early Seventeenth Centuries.' In Asch and Birke eds. 1991: 245–64.

Schmitt, Charles B., Quentin Skinner, Eckhard Kessler, and Jill Kraye, eds. 1988. *The Cambridge History of Renaissance Philosophy.* Cambridge.

Schneider, Norbert. 1994. *The Art of the Portrait.* Trans. Iain Galbraith. Weisbaden.

Schuyler, Jane. 1972. 'Florentine Busts: Sculpted Portraiture in the Fifteenth Century.' PhD diss., Columbia University.

Schwartz, Michael. 1997. 'Raphael's Authorship in the *Expulsion of Heliodorus.' Art Bulletin* 79, 3: 467–92.

Scorza, Richard. 1981. 'Vincenzo Borghini and *Invenzione*: The Florentine *Apparato* of 1565.' *Journal of the Warburg and Courtauld Institutes* 44: 57–75.

– 1988. '*Imprese* and Medals: *Invenzione all'Antica* by Vincenzo Borghini.' *The Medal* 13: 13–32.

– 1989. 'Vincenzo Borghini and the *Impresa.' Journal of the Warburg and Courtauld Institutes* 52: 85–111.

– 1995. 'Borghini, Butteri and Allori: A Further Drawing for the 1565 *Apparato.' Burlington Magazine* 137, 1104: 173–6.

– 1998. 'Vasari's Painting of the *Terzio Cerchio* in the Palazzo Vecchio: A Reconstruction of Medieval Florence.' In Jacks ed. 1998: 182–205.

Sebregondi, Carlo. 1940. *Famiglie Patrizie Fiorentine*. Florence.

Seidel, Linda. 1993. *Jan Van Eyck's Arnolfini Portrait: Stories of an Icon*. Cambridge, MA.

Seiz, Janet. 1982. 'Michelangelo Biondo's *On the Noble Art of Painting*, a Sixteenth-Century Venetian Physician's Handbook for Young Painters.' MA thesis, University of Cleveland.

Sframeli, Maria, and Costanza Contu. 'I Gioielli nel tempo del Principato.' In Florence, Palazzo Pitti 2003: 24–45.

Shapiro, Meyer. 1994. *Theory and Philosophy of Art*. New York.

Shapley, Fern Rusk. 1979. *Catalog of the Italian Paintings*. National Gallery of Art, Washington.

Shearman, John K.G. 1963. *The Renaissance and Mannerism: Studies in Western Art. Acts of the Twentieth International Congress of the History of Art*. 2 vols. Princeton, NJ.

– 1967. *Mannerism*. Harmondsworth, UK.

– 1970. 'Raphael at the Court of Urbino.' *Burlington Magazine* 112: 72–8.

– 1983. *The Early Italian Pictures in the Collection of Her Majesty the Queen*. Cambridge.

– 1992. *Only Connect ... Art and the Spectator in the Italian Renaissance*. The A.W. Mellon Lectures in the Fine Arts, 1988. Bollinger Series 35, 37. Princeton, NJ.

– 1998. 'Giorgio Vasari and the Paragons of Art.' In Jacks ed. 1998: 13–22.

– 2003. *Raphael in Early Modern Sources*. 2 vols. New Haven, CT and Rome.

Sherberg, Michael. 2003. 'The Accademia Fiorentina and the Question of Language: The Politics of Theory in Ducal Florence.' *Renaissance Quarterly* 56: 26–55.

Simon, Robert B. 1982. 'Bronzino's Portraits of Cosimo I de' Medici.' PhD diss., Columbia University.

– 1983. 'Bronzino's Portrait of Cosimo I in Armour.' *Burlington Magazine* 125, 966: 527–39.

– 1985. 'Bronzino's *Cosimo I de' Medici as Orpheus*.' *Bulletin of the Philadelphia Museum of Art* 81, 346: 15–27.

– 1987. 'Blessed Be the Hand of Bronzino: The Portrait of Cosimo I in Armour.' *Burlington Magazine* 129, 1011: 387–8.

– 1989. 'Giulio Clovio's Portrait of Eleonora di Toledo.' *Burlington Magazine* 131, 1036: 481–5.

Simons, Patricia. 1987. 'A Profile Portrait of a Renaissance Woman in the National Gallery of Victoria.' *Art Bulletin of Victoria* 28: 34–52.

– 1988. 'Women in Frames: The Gaze, the Eye, the Profile in Renaissance Portraiture.' *History Workshop Journal* 25: 4–30.

– 1994. 'Alert and Erect: Masculinity in Some Italian Renaissance Portraits of Fathers and Sons.' In *Gender Rhetorics: Postures of Dominance and Submission in History*, ed. R.C. Trexler, 163–86. Binghamton, NY.

– 1995. 'Portraiture, Portrayal and Idealization: Ambiguous Individualism in Representations of Renaissance Women.' In A. Brown, ed. 1995: 263–311.

Simpson, Keith. 1979. *Forensic Medicine*. 8th ed. London.

Slim, H. Colin. 2002[1]. 'A Motet for Machiavelli's Mistress and a Chanson for a Courtesan. In Slim 2002[2]: 457–72.

– 2002[2]. *Painting Music in the Sixteenth-Century: Essays in Iconography*. London.

Smith, Graham. 1977[1]. *The Casino of Pius IV*. Princeton.

– 1977[2]. 'Bronzino's Portrait of Stefano Colonna: A Note on Its Florentine Provenance.' *Zeitschrift für Kunstgeschichte* 40: 265–9.

– 1981. 'Jealousy, Pleasure and Pain in Agnolo Bronzino's *Allegory of Venus and Cupid*.' *Pantheon* 29: 250–8.

– 1982[1]. 'Cosimo I and the Joseph Tapestries for the Palazzo Vecchio.' *Renaissance and Reformation* 6: 183–96.

– 1982[2]. 'Bronzino's *Holy Family* in Vienna: A Note on the Identity of Its Patron.' *Source* 2, 1: 21–5.

– 1984. 'Bronzino's *Allegory of Happiness*.' *Art Bulletin* 64, 2: 390–8.

– 1987. Review of Janet Cox-Rearick, *Dynasty and Destiny in Medici Art; Pontormo, Leo X and the Two Cosimos*. *Art Bulletin* 69, 2: 304–7.

– 1996. 'Bronzino's *Portrait of Laura Battiferri*.' *Source* 15: 30–8.

Smith, Graham, and Anna Maria Petrioli Tofani. 1988. *Sixteenth-Century Tuscan Drawings from the Uffizi*. Exh. cat. Detroit and New York.

Smyth, Carolyn. 1997. 'An Instance of Feminine Patronage: The Chapel of Eleonora da Toledo in the Palazzo Vecchio.' In Lawrence ed. 1997: 72–98.

Smyth, Craig Hugh. 1949[1]. *Bronzino as Draughtsman*. New York.

– 1949[2]. 'The Earliest Works of Bronzino.' *Art Bulletin* 31, 2: 184–210.

– 1955. 'Bronzino Studies.' PhD diss., Princeton University.

– 1963. *Mannerism and Maniera*. Princeton, NJ.

– 1971. *Bronzino as Draughtsman: An Introduction with Notes on His Portraiture*. Locust Valley, NY.

– 1992. *Mannerism and Maniera*. Intro. Elizabeth Cropper. Vienna.

Sohm, Philip. 1994. 'Gendered Style in Italian Art Criticism from Michelangelo to Malvasia.' *Renaissance Quarterly* 47, 4: 759–808.

Somers Cocks, Anna, and Charles Truman. 1984. In Sotheby's 1984: 71–9.

Sotheby's. 1984. *Renaissance Jewels, Gold Boxes and Objets de Vertu*. The Thyssen-Bornemisza Collection. Sales cat. by Anna Somers Cocks and Charles Truman. Ed. Simon de Pury. London.

– 1987. *Old Master Paintings and British Paintings 1500–1850*. London, 28 October.

Soussloff, Charles. 1989. Review of Edward L. Goldberg, *Patterns in Late Medici Art Patronage*. *Art Bulletin* 71, 4: 697–8.

Spagnoletti, Angelantonio. 1999. 'Potere spagnolo e clientele: La rete dei Toledo in Italia.' In Report of *Italia non Spagnola e Monarchia Spagnola tra '500 e '600. Convegno Internazionale di Studi Promosso dal Dipartmento di Storia moderna e contemporanea e dal Dipartmento di Lingue e Letterature romanze dell' Università, dalla Scuola Normale Superiore di Pisa, dalla Provincia di Pisa e dalla Sociedad Estatal para la commemoración de los centenarios de Felipe II y Carlos V*. Pisa, 1998: 3–4. Accessed at listserve h-italy@h-net.msu/edu, 28 January 1999.

Spalding, Jack. 1999. 'Alessandro Allori's Altarpieces in Santa Maria Novella.' *Storia dell'arte* 97: 311–16.

Spallanzani, Marco. 1994. *Ceramiche alla Corte dei Medici nel Cinquecento*. Pisa.

Sparrow, John. 1967. 'Pontormo's *Cosimo il Vecchio*, a New Dating.' *Journal of the Warburg and Courtauld Institutes* 30: 163–75.

Spicer, Joaneath. 2001. 'Pontormo's *Maria Salviati with Giulia de' Medici*.' *The Walters*: 4–6.

Spreti, Vittorio. 1928–36. *Enciclopedia Storico Nobiliare Italiana*. Milan.

Spini, Giorgio, ed. 1976. *Architettura e Politica da Cosimo I a Ferdinando I*. Florence.

Starn, Randolf, and Loren Partridge. 1992. *Arts of Power: Three Halls of State in Italy, 1300–1600*. Berkeley, Los Angeles, and Oxford.

Steiner, Wendy. 1987. 'Postmodern Portraits.' *Art Journal* 46, 3: 173–7.

Steinitz, K. 1958. *Leonardo da Vinci's 'Trattato della Pittura' ... a Bibliography of the Printed Editions*. Copenhagen.

Steppe, J.K. 1969. 'Mencía di Mendoza et ses relations avec Erasme, Gilles de Busleyden et Jean-Louis Vivès.' In *Scrinium Erasmianum*, ed. J. Coppens, 2 vols., 2: 447–506. Leyden.

Stern, Laura Ilkins. 1994. *The Criminal Law System of Medieval and Renaissance Florence*. Baltimore and London.

Stevens, Kevin M. 1995. 'Vincenzo Girardone and the Popular Press in Counter-Reformation Milan: A Case Study (1570).' *Sixteenth Century Journal* 26, 3: 639–59.

Strehlke, Carl Brandon. 1985. 'Pontormo, Alessandro de' Medici and the Palazzo Pitti.' *Bulletin of the Philadelphia Museum of Art* 85, 348: 3–15.

– 2004. *Pontormo, Bronzino, and the Medici: The Transformation of the Renaissance Portrait in Florence*. Exh. cat. With essays by Elizabeth Croper, Mark Tucker, Irma Passeri, Ken Sutherland, and Betti A. Price. Philadelphia Museum of Art.

Strong, Sir Roy. 1995. *The Tudor and Stuart Monarchy: Pageantry, Painting, Iconography*. Vol. 2: *Elizabethan*. Rochester, NY.

– 2000. *The Spirit of Britain: A Narrative History of the Arts*. London.

Summers, David. 1979. *The Sculpture of Vincenzo Danti: A Study in the Influence of Michelangelo and the Ideals of the Maniera*. New York.

– 1981. *Michelangelo and the Language of Art*. Princeton.

– 1987. 'This Is Not a Sign: Some Remarks on Art and Semiotics.' *Art Criticism* 3, 1: 30–45.

– 1993. 'Form and Gender.' *New Literary History* 24: 243–71.

Syson, Luke. 1998. Introduction. In Mann and Syson eds. 1998: 9–14.

Tanner, Marie. 1993. *The Last Descendant of Aeneas: The Hapsburgs and the Mythic Image of the Emperor*. New Haven and London.

Tazartes, Maurizio. 2003. *Bronzino*. Milan.

Tel Aviv. 1987. *Sofonisba Anguissola e le sue sorelle*. Exh. cat. by Flavio Carioli. Tel Aviv Museum. Milan.

Tenhove, Nicholas. 1747. *Memoirs of the House of Medici from its Origin to the Death of Francesco, the Second Grand Duke of Tuscany and of the Great Men Who Flourished in that Period*. Trans. Sir Richard Clayton. 2 vols. Bath.

Terpstra, Nicholas. 2000. 'Competing Visions of the State and Social Welfare: The Medici Dukes, the Bigallo Magistrates, and Local Hospitals in Sixteenth-Century Tuscany.' *Renaissance Quarterly* 54: 1319–55.

Tervarent, Guy de. 1958. *Attributs et symboles dans l'art profane, 1450–1600*. Geneva.

Testaverde Matteini, Anna Maria. 1983. 'La biblioteca di don V. Borghini.' In Florence, Palazzo Vecchio 1983, 2: 611–43.

– 2002. 'Spectacle, Theater, and Propaganda at the Court of the Medici.' In Chicago and Detroit 2002: 123–31.

Thieme, U., and F. Becker. 1903–50. *Allgemeines Lexikon der Bildenden Künstler von der Antike bis zur Gegenwart*. 37 vols. Leipzig.

Thomas, Anabel. 2000. 'Fifteenth-Century Florence and Court Culture under the Medici.' In Mateer ed. 2000: 159–222.

Thomas, Joe A. 1994. 'Fabric and Dress in Bronzino's *Portrait of Eleonora of Toledo and Her Son Giovanni*.' *Zeitschrift für Kunstgeschichte* 57, 2: 262–7.

Tinagli, Paola. 1985. 'Rileggendo i "Ragionamenti."' In Garfagnini ed. 1985: 83–94.

– 1997. *Women in Italian Renaissance Art: Gender, Representation, Identity*. New York and Manchester.

– 2000. 'Womanly virtues in Quattrocento Florentine Marriage Furnishings.' In Panizza ed. 2000: 265–84.

– 2001. 'Claiming a Place in History: Giorgio Vasari's *Ragionamenti* and the Primacy of the Medici.' In Eisenbichler ed. 2001: 63–76.

– 2004. 'Eleonora and Her "Famous Sisters." The Tradition of "Illustrious Women" in Paintings for the Domestic Interior.' In Eisenbichler ed. 2004: 119–35.

Tolaini, Emilio. 1992. *Forma Pisarum: Storia urbanistica della città di Pisa*. Pisa.

Tomas, Natalie. 2000. 'Alfonsina Orsini de' Medici and the "problem" of a Female Ruler in Early Sixteenth-Century Florence.' *Renaissance Studies* 14, 1: 70–90.

– 2003. *The Medici Women: Gender and Power in Florence*. Aldershot, UK, and Brookfield, VT.

Tonelli, Luigi. 1933. *L'Amore nella poesia e nel pensiero del Rinascimento*. Florence.

Toronto. 1988. *Drawings by Holbein from the Court of Henry VIII*. Exh. cat. by Jane Roberts. Art Gallery of Ontario, Toronto.

Tosi, C.O. 1906. 'Una Lettera di M. Francesco Campana.' *Arte e storia* 25, 13–14: 106–7.

– 1908. 'Maria Salviati Medici.' *Arte e storia* 27, 9–10: 74–5.

– 1909[1]. 'Cosimo I gentiluomo privato.' *L'illustratore fiorentino*: 55–8.

– 1909[2]. 'Eleonora di Toledo reggente lo Stato.' *L'Illustratore fiorentino*: 162–5.

– 1910. 'A proposito di una inesattezza di Riguccio Galluzzi nella sua storia.' *Arte e storia* 29, 5: 152–3.

Towne, Gary. 1996. Review of Martha Feldman, *City Culture and the Madrigal at Venice*. *Sixteenth Century Journal* 26, 1: 270–1.

Travitsky, Betty S. 1997. 'Reprinting Tudor History: The Case of Catherine of Aragon.' *Renaissance Quarterly* 50, 1: 164–74.

Trexler, Richard. 1980. *Public Life in Renaissance Florence*. New York.

– 1993. *Power and Dependence in Renaissance Florence: The Women of Renaissance Florence*. 2 vols. Binghamton, NY.

– 1994. 'Florentine Prostitution in the Fifteenth Century: Patrons and Clients.' In Trexler ed. 1994: 373–8.

Trexler, Richard, ed. 1994. *Gender Rhetorics: Postures of Dominance and Submission in History*. Binghamton, NY.

Tucker, Mark S., Irma Passeri, Ken Sutherland, and Beth A. Price. 2004. 'Technique and Pontormo's Portrait of Alessandro de' Medici.' In Strehlke ed. 2004: 34–54.

Turner, Nicholas. 1986. *Florentine Drawings of the Sixteenth Century*. London.

Turrill, Catherine. 1990. 'Girolamo da Carpi's Muzzarelli Altarpiece.' *Studies in the History of Art* 24: 75–86.

University Park, PA. 1987. *Italian Renaissance Art. Selections from the Piero Corsini Gallery*. Exh. cat. by Barbara Wollesen-Wisch. Museum of Art, Pennsylvania State University. University Park, PA.

Urry, Selena. 1998. 'Evidence of Replication in a Portrait of Eleonora da Toledo by Agnolo Bronzino and Workshop.' *Journal of the American Institute of Conservation* 37, 2: 211–21.

Vaccari, Maria Grazia. 1997. *La Guardaroba medicea dell'Archivio di Stato di Firenze: Inventaria*. Collana 'Toscana Beni librari' 8. Florence.

Vaccaro, Mary. 2001. 'Dutiful Widows: Female Patronage and Two Marian Altarpieces by Parmigianino.' In Reiss and Wilkins eds. 2001: 177–92.

Valone, Carolyn. 1992. 'Roman Matrons as Patrons: Various Views of the Cloister Wall.' In *The Crannied Wall: Women, Religion, and the Arts in Early Modern Europe*, ed. Craig A. Monson, 49–72. Ann Arbor.

Van Veen, Henk Th. 1986. 'Vasari e l'analisi logica della pittura.' In *Letteratura artistica e arte di corte nella Firenze granducale*, ed. Henk Th. van Veen, 21–42. Florence.

– 1998. 'Circles of Sovereignty: The Tondi of the Sala Grande in the Palazzo Vecchio and the Medici Crown.' In Jacks ed. 1998: 206–19.

Van der Velden, Hugo. 1998. 'Medici Votive Images and the Scope and Limits of Likeness.' In Mann and Syson eds. 1998: 126–37.

Venice, Palazzo Ducale. 1955. *Giorgione e i Giorgioneschi*. Exh. cat. Ed. Pietro Zampetti. Venice.

Vitzthum, Walter. 1965. *Lo studiolo di Francesco I a Firenze*. Milan.

Vogel, Emil, Alfred Einstein, François Lesure, and Claudio Sartori. 1977. *Il Nuovo Vogel: Bibliografia della musica italiana vocale profana pubblicata dal 1500 al 1700*. 3 vols. Pomezia.

Vos, A., ed. 1995. *Place and Displacement in the Renaissance*. Binghamton, NY.

Waage, Frederick O. 1984. *The White Devil Discover'd: Backgrounds and Foregrounds to Webster's Tragedy*. New York.

Wackernagel, Martin. 1980. *The World of the Florentine Renaissance Artist*. Trans. Alison Luchs. Princeton, NJ.

Walker, John. 1968. '*Ginevra de' Benci* by Leonardo da Vinci.' *National Gallery of Art: Report and Studies in the History of Art*. Washington, DC.

Warnke, Martin. 1993. *The Court Artist*. Trans. David McLintock. Cambridge, MA.

– 1998. 'Individuality as Argument: Piero della Francesco's Portrait of the Duke and Duchess of Urbino.' In Mann and Syson eds. 1998: 81–90.

Warsaw. 1969. *Catalog*. National Museum. Warsaw.

Washington. 2001. *Virtue and Beauty: Leonardo's 'Ginevra de' Benci and Renaissance Portraits of Women*. Exh. cat. Ed. David Alan Brown, with contributions by Elizabeth Cropper, Eleanor Luciano, Dale Kent, Victoria Kirkham, Joanna Woods-Marsden, Roberta Orsi Landini, and Mary Westerman Bulgarella. National Gallery of Art. Washington, DC.

Watt, Mary A. 2004. '*Veni, sponsa*: Love and Politics at the Wedding of Eleonora di Toledo.' In Eisenbichler ed., 2004: 18–39.

Ważbiński, Zygmunt. 1985. '*L'Annunziazione della Vergine* nella chiesa della SS. Annunziata a Firenze: Un contributo al moderno culto dei quadri.' In Morrogh et al. eds. 1985: 533–54.

Webster, John. 1995[1]. 'The Duchess of Malfi' (1612–13). In *The Works of John Webster*, vol. 1. Ed. David Grunby, David Carnegie, and Anthony Hammond. Cambridge, MA.

– 1995[2]. 'The White Devil' (1609–12). In *The Works of John Webster*, vol. 1. Ed. David Grunby, David Carnegie, and Anthony Hammond. Cambridge, MA.

Weil-Garris Posner, Kathleen. 1974. *Leonardo and Central Italian Art: 1515–1550*. New York.

Weinberg, Bernard. 1954. 'Argomenti di Discussione letteraria nell' Accademia degli Alterati (1570–1600).' *Giornale storico della letteratura italiana* 131: 178–94.

– 1961. *A History of Literary Criticism in the Italian Renaissance*. 2 vols. Chicago.

Weinberger, M. 1948. 'Notes on Maître Michiel.' *Burlington Magazine* 90: 247–53.

Weisner, Merry. 1993. *Women and Gender in Early Modern Europe*. Oxford.

Weitzel Gibbons, Mary. 2001. 'Cosimo's *Cavallo*: A Study in Imperial Imagery.' In Eisenbichler ed. 2001: 77–102.

Welch, Evelyn. 1997. *Art and Society in Italy 1350–1500*. Oxford and New York.

Westerman Bulgarella, Mary. 1993. 'Recupero e restauro.' In Florence, Palazzo Pitti 1993: 75–103.

– 2004. 'The Burial Attire of Eleonora di Toledo.' In Eisenbichler ed. 2004: 207–24.

Wethey, Harold E. 1971. *The Paintings of Titian*. Vol. 2: *The Portraits*. London.

White, Christopher. 1987. *Peter Paul Rubens: Man and Artist*. New Haven and London.

Williams, Robert. 1988. 'Borghini and Vasari's *Lives*.' PhD diss., Princeton University.

– 1997. *Art, Theory, and Culture in Sixteenth-Century Italy: From Techne to Metatechne*. Cambridge, MA.

– 1998. 'The Sala Grande in the Palazzo Vecchio and the Precedence Controversy between Florence and Ferrara.' In Jacks ed. 1998: 163–81.

– 2000. Review of Patricia Emison, *Low and High Style in Italian Renaissance Art*. *Art Bulletin* 82, 2: 356–7.

Williamson, George C., and Percy Buckman. 1926. *The Art of the Miniature Painter*. London.

Winn, James Anderson. 1981. *Unsuspected Eloquence: A History of the Relations between Poetry and Music*. New Haven and London.

Winspeare, Fabrizio. 1961. *Isabella Orsini e la corte medicea del suo tempo*. Florence.

Wisch, Barbara, and Susan Scott Munshower, eds. 1990. '"All the world's a stage ..." Art and Pageantry in the Renaissance and Baroque*. Papers in Art History from Pennsylvania State University, vol. 6. Part 1: 'Triumphal Celebrations and the Rituals of Statecraft.' Part 2: 'Theatrical Spectacle and Spectacular Theatre.' Philadelphia, PA.

Woerman, Karl. 1906. *Die Italienische Bildnismalerei der Renaissance*. Esslingen.

Wohl, Helmut. 1986. 'The Eye of Vasari.' *Mitteilungen des Kunsthistorischen Institutes in Florenz* 30, 3: 537–68.

Woodall, Joanna. 1989. 'Honor and Profit: Antonis Mor and the Status of Portraiture.' *Leids Kunsthistorisch Jaarboek (Nederlandse Portretten: Bijdragen over de Portretkunst in de Nederlanden uit de Zestiende, Zeventiende en Achtiende Eeuw)* 8: 69–89.

– 1991. 'An Exemplary Consort: Antonis Mor's Portrait of Mary Tudor.' *Art History* 14, 2: 192–224.

Woodall, Joanna, ed. 1997. *Portraiture: Facing the Subject*. Manchester and New York.

Woods-Marsden, Joanna. 1987. '"Ritratto al Naturale": Questions of Realism and Idealism in Early Renaissance Portraits.' *Art Journal* 46: 209–16.

– 1998. *Renaissance Self-Portraiture: The Visual Construction of Identity and the Social Status of the Artist*. New Haven and London.

– 2000. 'Introduction: Collective Identity / Individual Identity.' In Rogers ed. 2000: 1–14.

– 2001. 'Portrait of the Lady, 1430–1520.' In D.A. Brown 2001: 63–88.

Worcester, T. 1998. Review of *Il Concilio di Trento e il moderno*, ed. Paolo Prodi and Wolfgang Reinhard. *Sixteenth Century Journal* 29, 4: 1198–9.

Wright, Alison. 2001. 'Washington. Renaissance Portraits of Women.' Review of D.A. Brown, *Virtue and Beauty: Leonardo's 'Ginevra de' Benci' and Renaissance Portraits of Women*, exh. cat., National Gallery, Washington, 2001. *Burlington Magazine* 144, 1185: 786–7.

Wright, D.R. Edward. 1976. 'The Medici Villa at Olmo a Castello: Its History and Iconography.' 2 vols. PhD diss., Princeton.

– 1986. 'Benedetto Pagni's "Medici Madonna" in Saratoga: A Study in Medici Patronage and Iconography.' *Burlington Magazine* 128, 995: 90–9.

Würtenberger, Franzsepp. 1963. *Mannerism: The European Style of the Sixteenth Century.* Trans. Michael Heron. New York.

Young, George F. 1910. *The Medici.* New York.

Zampetti, Pietro. 1955. *Giorgione e i Giorgioneschi.* Exh. cat. Palazzo Ducale, Venice.

Zanrè, Domenico. 2001. 'Ritual and Parody in Mid-Cinquecento Florence: Cosimo de' Medici and the Accademia del Piano.' In Eisenbichler ed. 2001: 189–204.

Zapperi, Roberto. 1990. 'Il ritratto e la maschera: Richerche su Annibale Carracci ritrattista.' *Bollettino d'arte* 75, 60: 85–94.

Zeri, Federico. 1976. *Italian Paintings in the Walters Art Gallery.* 2 vols. Baltimore, MD.

Zerner, Catherine W. 1999. In Providence, RI 1999: 9–14.

Zollner, Frank. 1993. 'Leonardo's Portrait of Mona Lisa del Giocondo.' *Gazette des Beaux Arts* 121, 6: 115–38.

Zonta, Giuseppe, ed. 1913. *Trattati del cinquecento sulla donna.* Bari.

Zupnick, I.L. 1953. 'The Aesthetics of the Early Mannerists.' *Art Bulletin* 35: 302–5.

– 1965. 'Pontormo's Early Style.' *Art Bulletin* 47: 345–53.

Photograph Credits

Photographs were supplied by their owners and/or the following:

© Alinari/Art Resource, New York: figs. 4, 12, 15, 16, 25, 27, 49, 52, 53, 54, 61, 64
© Archivio Storico Diocesano di Mantova: fig. 30.
© Art Resource, New York: Photograph by Erich Lessing, fig. 1.
© The Bridgeman Art Library: pls. 3, 4, 7, 9; fig. 14.
© Christie's Images Inc. 2005: figs. 43, 48, 65.
© 2001 The Detroit Institute of Arts: fig. 17.
© Fine Arts Museum of San Francisco: fig. 3.
© The Frick Art Reference Library, New York: fig. 23.
© The Frick Collection, New York: fig. 56.
© Photograph courtesy of Deborah Gage: pl. 12.
© Photograph courtesy of Detlef Heikamp: fig. 63.
© Kunsthistorisches Institüt, Florence: fig. 42.
© Kunsthistorisches Museum, Wein oder KHM, Wien: pl. 16; figs. 7, 36, 46, 50, 57
© Museo Nacional del Prado: fig. 24.
© Museo Thyssen-Bornemisza, Madrid: figs. 34, 39.
© The National Gallery, London: fig. 29.
© The National Gallery in Prague 2004: pl. 5; figs. 19, 20.
© The National Museum of Fine Arts, Stockholm: fig. 32.
© North Carolina Museum of Art, Raleigh, Gift of Mrs. George Khuner: pl. 10.
© Philadelphia Museum of Art: John G. Johnson Collection, 1917: fig. 11.
© Private collections: pl. 12; figs. 58, 62.
© The Royal Collection © 2004, Her Majesty Queen Elizabeth II: fig. 35.
© Scala/Art Resource, New York: pls. 4, 6.
© Scottish National Portrait Gallery: fig. 26.
© Photograph courtesy of Robert B. Simon Fine Art: figs. 21, 22.
© Soprintendenza speciale per il Polo Museale fiorentino: pl. 8; figs. 5, 6, 9, 10, 18, 37, 38, 40, 45, 51, 60.
© Sotheby's Picture Library: pl. 12; fig. 60.
© Städelsches Kunstinstitut, Frankfurt am Main: pl. 1; fig. 2.
© Staatliche Museen, Berlin. Photo: Jörg P. Anders: fig. 41.
© Thomas Fisher Rare Book Library, University of Toronto: fig. 28.

© Thyssen-Bornemisza Collections: pls. 14, 15.
© Wadsworth Atheneum Museum of Art, Hartford, CT: pl. 11; fig. 47.
© The Walters Art Museum, Baltimore: pl. 2; fig. 13.
© The Warburg Institute: figs. 8, 31, 44, 55.

Index

drawings: *Maria Salviati* (Florence, 6680F) **fig. 6**, 25, 27, 28, 221n33; learning 65, 93; —, Dante and Petrarch 15, 81, 94, 251n155, 255n219; letters 110, 282n146; and Ovid, *Metamorphoses* 89, 114, 260n296; *paragone* debate between painting and sculpture, *see* Varchi; at Pesaro court 27, 28, 31, 59, 78, 94, 95; Petrarchan inspiration 81, 84–5, 103, 152, 257n247; poetry 15, 87, 94, 103, 104; —, on death of Lucrezia de' Medici d'Este, 204–5; —, *rime in burla* (parodic) 94, 104; style 25, 26, 27, 32, 94, 151, 160, 219nn11 and 18, 221nn28 and 31; technique 15, 20, 89, 94, 104, 262n339; and Varchi 8, 80, 94, 97
– and artists
  Leonardo da Vinci 94–5, 116–17, 271n136
  Parmiginiano 219n16
  Pontormo 65, 94, 95
  Raphael 29–30, 100
  Raffaellino del Garbo 221n31, 266n37
  Titian 68, 87, 88
  Tribolo 127
  See also Vasari, on Bronzino
– Chapel of Eleonora di Toledo 9, 59, 87, 241n5
  Crossing of the Red Sea and Moses Appointing Joshua 59, 87
  Lamentation (Besançon) 62; copy (Chapel of Eleonora, Palazzo Vecchio)
  Trinity (vault)
– paintings
  Allegory of Happiness 130
  Allegory of Venus and Cupid (London) **fig. 29** (Fraude), 21, 60, 104, 276n59
  Evangelist tondi (Capponi Chapel, Santa Felicita) 25, 26, 28
  Holy Family (Washington) 25
  Pietà (Uffizi) 25
  Pygmalion and Galatea 89
– paintings (lost)
  apparato work for the wedding of Cosimo I and Eleonora di Toledo 65
  Madonna and Child (after Leonardo) 94
– portraits 4, 24, 25, 26, 61–4, 87; beauty and virtue in women's portraiture 87

Bia de' Medici (Uffizi) **pl. 6**, 26, 99–107
Bartolommeo Panciatichi (Uffizi) 278n88
Duke Cosimo I de' Medici in Armour (Uffizi) **pl. 3**, 59, 61, 64, 67–8, 77, 82, 83, 92, 228n94, 240n246, 271n136; copy (Kassel) 68, 70; Giovio's praise of 61, 228n94; as official state portrait 61, 77, 82; resemblance to Giovanni delle Bande Nere 228n94
Duke Cosimo I and Eleonora di Toledo with Maps (after Bronzino) (Private coll.) **fig. 21**, 64, 78–9, 88
Elderly Lady (San Francisco) **fig. 3**, 25
Eleonora di Toledo (Prague) **pl. 5 and figs. 19, 20**, 64–5, 78, 83, 88, 90, 102, 110, 158; dress in 112; pigment used for dress 32
Eleonora di Toledo with Her Son Giovanni (Uffizi) **pl. 4**, detail **fig. 15**, 20, 60–97, 89, 90, 91–3, 99, 104, 116, 142, 151, 186, 187; copies of 93; —, Bronzino and workshop (Detroit) **fig. 17**, 71, 260n315; —, Lorenzo della Sciorina (Uffizi, Serie Aulica) **fig. 18**, 71; colour in 90; dress in 83; iconography in, *see below*; and Leonardo 78; pigments 89, 224n51; propaganda in 60, 79–80, 82–4, 86, 87, 91–3; viewer/beholder's approach to 82–4, 91–3
Eleonora di Toledo ... (Uffizi), iconography in: of absolutism 83, 92, 264n371; biblical *personae* 72–7, as Madonna 7, 92, 214n59; classical deification 86, as Diana 75, 80, 86, as Juno 67, 77, 174, as Venus 7, 85, 86; as dynastic *genetrix* 86, 93, 258n269; eternal (Sol and Luna) 93; as fecund 86–7; in landscape 77–80, 87; as 'Madre della repubblica fiorentina' 93; as 'Nature' 78, 81–2; as Petrarchan ideal of Love 80, 81–2; as Petrarch's 'Laura' 7, 81, 84, 86, 92, 214n59, 257n247; as regent 60, 67–97, 68–70, 75, 79–80, 84, 91–3; as Wisdom 74–5
Francesco de' Medici (Uffizi) 110
Giovanni de' Medici (Oxford)

8; 'Dianora' di Toledo 173–4; identities confirmed by computer (photogammetry) 221–2n34

– and the spectator 11, 16, 19, 20, 21–2, 70, 82, 94, 104–6, 118–19, 142, 152; reciprocity of the gaze 116, 119, 171, 176, 184, 213n43; transference between subject and spectator 108, 172; the twenty-first-century spectator 21–2

See also Allori portraits; Bronzino portraits; *damnatio memoriae*; Medici family; miniatures; Pontormo portraits; Vasari on artists, on portraiture

Pourbus, Frans 118

precedence controversy 3, 6, 113, 131, 140–2, 269n108, 281n33

presses, printers, and printing 7, 53, 156, 160, 189, 259n279, 288n116

Puligo, Domenico: portraits, *Barbara Salutati* (Private coll.) **pl. 13**, 164, 220n20, *Portrait of a Woman as the Magdalen* (Ottawa) 220n20

questione della lingua (codification of Italian) 8, 15, 79, 147, 159–60, 252n171, 253n200; and Boccaccio 78, 159–60; and Dante 159; and Petrarch 159; translations of classical texts, *see* Accademia della Crusca, Cerratani, literary patronage

Quinta, Claudia 112

Raffaellino del Garbo 221n31, 266n37

Raphael portraits: *Alessandro de' Medici as a Boy* (or by Giulio Romano) (Madrid) **fig. 39**, 123, 231n139; *Baldassare Castiglione* (Paris) 213n43; *Julius II* (London) 266–7n50; *Leo X with Cardinals Giulio de' Medici and Luigi de' Rossi* (Uffizi) 29–30; —, compositional influence on Bronzino's portraits 29–30, 100–1; —, as esteemed 30, and exhibited at Medici wedding celebrations 223n40; —, Vasari's description 13–14; *Lorenzo de' Medici* (New York, Spanierman coll.) 179

Renée of France, Duchess of Ferrara. *See* Este, Alfonso II

Riccardi family 33, 35, 40, 47, 224n53

Riccio, Pierfrancesco 41, 59, 108, 110, 212n21, 241n261, 241n2

Ridolfi, Pierino 177

rime in burla. See Bronzino, poetry; poetry

Ripa, Cesare 183; *Iconologia* 300n89: Cometa (Comet) 182, Eloquenza (Eloquence) 286n77, Innocenza (Innocence) 103, Juno-Aria (Juno) 182, 252n179, Libidine (Libidine) 286n87, Matrimonio (Matrimony) 150, Obedienza (Obedience) 150, Occasione (Chance) 129, Passione d'Amore (Passions of Love) 155, Patienza (Patience) 150, Pioggia (Rain) 182, Rugiada (Dew) 182

Robortello, Francesco 96; *In librum Aristotelis de arte poetica explicationes* 263–4n366, 288n116

Romano, Giulio: death mask of Giovanni delle Bande Nere 225n63; *Isabella d'Este* (Hampton Court) 220n20

Rome. *See also* Michelangelo; 'Pasquino'; popes; Sack of Rome

Rosello, Lucio Paolo: *Il Ritratto del vero governo del Principe* 256n230

Rossi, Vincenzo 277n71

Rosso Fiorentino 275n48

Rouillé, G. 14

delle Rovere family: Guidobaldo 38–9 (*see also* Bronzino, portraits); Pesaro court 27, 28, 31, 32, 59, 78, 94, 95; Urbino court 12, 38

Rubens, Peter Paul: *Birth of Maria de' Medici* (Louvre) 257n252; *Presentation of the Portrait of Maria de' Medici to Henry IV* (Paris) **fig. 1**, 3

Rucellai family 112

Sack of Rome 5, 28

Salutati, Barbara Raffacani 164. *See also* Machiavelli

Salviati, Francesca 124, 219n16, 222–3n39, 223–4n44; children of 40–1, 133, 218n4, 274n27

Salviati, Francesco. *Lute Player* (Paris) 257n242; *Triumph of Camillus* (Palazzo